A
WORLD OF
IDEAS

ESSENTIAL READINGS
FOR
COLLEGE WRITERS

FIFTH EDITION

A WORLD OF IDEAS

ESSENTIAL READINGS FOR COLLEGE WRITERS

LEE A. JACOBUS

University of Connecticut

BEDFORD/ST. MARTIN'S

Boston ◆ *New York*

For Bedford/St. Martin's

President and Publisher: Charles H. Christensen
General Manager and Associate Publisher: Joan E. Feinberg
Managing Editor: Elizabeth M. Schaaf
Developmental Editor: Sarah E. Cornog
Editorial Assistant: Michelle M. Clark
Production Editor: Bridget Leahy
Copyeditor: Rosemary Winfield
Text Design: Anna Post George
Cover Design: Night & Day Design
Cover Art: Johannes Vermeer, *The Geographer,* c. 1668–69,
Städelsches Kunstinstitut, Frankfurt. Photograph Artothek.
Composition: Pine Tree Composition, Inc.
Printing and Binding: Haddon Craftsmen, Inc.

Library of Congress Catalog Card Number: 97–72372

Manufactured in the United States of America.

5   4   3   2   1   0
l   k   j   i   h   g

For information, write: Bedford/St. Martin's, 75 Arlington Street, Boston, MA 02116
(617-426-7440)

ISBN: 0–312–14863–1

Acknowledgments

Hannah Arendt, "Ideology and Terror: A Novel Form of Government." Excerpt from "Ideology and
    Terror: A Novel Form of Government" in *The Origins of Totalitarianism* by Hannah Arendt, copy-
    right 1951 and renewed 1979 by Mary McCarthy West, reprinted by permission of Harcourt
    Brace & Company.
Aristotle, "Tragedy and the Emotions of Pity and Fear." From *Poetics,* translated by Gerald F. Else.
    Copyright © 1967 by the University of Michigan. Used by permission of the University of
    Michigan Press.
Simone de Beauvoir, from *The Second Sex* by Simone de Beauvoir, translated by H. M. Parshley. Copy-
    right 1952 and renewed 1980 by Alfred A. Knopf, Inc. Reprinted by permission of the pub-
    lisher.
Ruth Benedict, "The Pueblos of New Mexico." Excerpt from *Patterns of Culture* by Ruth Benedict.
    Copyright 1934 by Ruth Benedict, © renewed 1961 by Ruth Valentine. Reprinted by permission
    of Houghton Mifflin Co. All rights reserved.

PREFACE

Since its first edition, *A World of Ideas* has attracted an audience of teachers and students who value the ideas that affect the way we see the world. The very first person who read the book was a recent graduate of a prestigious university. She wrote to tell me that she had heard about many of the figures in the book but had never read them, and was delighted to meet them together in this book. Indeed, the number of those who value the approach to writing and reading represented by *A World of Ideas* has grown with each edition.

In preparing the fifth edition of *A World of Ideas,* I have, as usual, benefited from the suggestions of hundreds of users of earlier editions. The primary concern of both students and teachers is that the book remain centered on the tradition of important ideas and on the writers whose work has had a lasting impact on society. To that end, I have chosen writers whose ideas seem central to our most important concerns. A new edition offers the opportunity for revaluations and new choices, but the fundamental purpose of the book remains what it always has been — to present college students with a representative sampling of important ideas examined by men and women who have shaped the way we think today.

The selections in this volume are of the highest quality. Each was chosen because it clarifies important ideas and can sustain discussion and stimulate good writing. Unlike most composition readers, *A World of Ideas* presents substantial excerpts from each of its authors. The selections are presented as they originally appeared and only rarely are edited and marked by ellipses. They average fifteen pages in length, and their arguments are presented completely as the authors wrote them. Developing a serious idea takes time and a willingness to experiment, and most students are willing to read deeply in the work of important thinkers to better grasp their ideas.

New in This Edition

The fifth edition offers a new structure for the essays. Its eight sections — Government, Justice, Wealth, Mind, Nature, Culture, Faith, and Poetics — represent a wide range of thought. Of the forty-one selections (six more than in the fourth edition), twenty-three are new to the fifth edition. Those writers with selections that remain from the fourth edition are Niccolò Machiavelli, Thomas Jefferson, Frederick Douglass, Henry David Thoreau, Martin Luther King, Jr., Karl Marx, John Kenneth Galbraith, Robert B. Reich, Plato, Karen Horney, Francis Bacon, Charles Darwin, Stephen Jay Gould, Ruth Benedict, Margaret Mead, Clifford Geertz, Siddhārtha Gautama, the Buddha, and Friedrich Nietzsche. Some of the authors in the fourth edition appear now with different selections or translations: Lao-tzu, Sigmund Freud, Carl Jung, and Aristotle. Those new to the fifth edition are Jean-Jacques Rousseau, Hannah Arendt, Simone de Beauvoir, Adam Smith, Moses Maimonides, Howard Gardner, Richard Dawkins, Michio Kaku, Herodotus, Álvar Núñez Cabeza de Vaca, St. Matthew, the *Bhagavad Gītā*, the Prophet Muhammad, St. Teresa of Avila, Martin Buber, Alexander Pope, William Wordsworth, Virginia Woolf, and Susan Sontag.

Perhaps the most notable addition is a section on Faith, which offers important texts from a range of religions and religious texts. Buddhism, Christianity, Hinduism, Islam, and Judaism are represented by key texts exploring the relationship between the individual and a supreme being. The focus on particular disciplines in earlier editions would have made it difficult to include these selections. The same is true for the section on Poetics, which examines the cultural importance of poetry from a wide range of viewpoints, centering ultimately on matters of form and interpretation.

A Text for Readers and Writers

Emphasis on Critical Thinking. A *World of Ideas* has always been predicated on interactions between student and teacher, student and student, and student and author. To strengthen the emphasis of previous editions on critical thinking, the fifth edition offers a number of features designed to help students benefit from these interactions as they learn to analyze ideas and develop ideas of their own. The book begins with an introduction, "Evaluating Ideas: An Introduction to Critical Reading," that demonstrates a range of methods students can adopt to participate in an active dialogue with each selection. This dialogue — an active, questioning approach to texts and ideas — is one of the keys to critical reading.

Because this book has always been a reader for writers, I try to emphasize ways in which the text can be read to develop ideas for writing. The best method for developing such ideas is annotating carefully: this establishes both a dialogue with the text and a system for retrieving ideas formulated during that dialogue. In the introduction, a portion of Machiavelli's essay on "The Qualities of the Prince" is presented in annotated form, and the annotations are discussed for their usefulness in understanding this essay and in developing other annotations while reading the essays in the book.

The emphasis on critical reading is developed further in the appendix, "Writing about Ideas: An Introduction to Rhetoric." This section explains how a reader can make annotations while reading critically and then use those annotations to write effectively in response to the ideas in any selection in the book. The appendix relies on the annotations of the Machiavelli selection expounded in "Evaluating Ideas: An Introduction to Critical Reading." A sample essay on Machiavelli, using all the techniques taught in the context of reading and writing, gives students a model for writing their own material. In addition, this section helps students understand how they can apply some of the basic rhetorical principles discussed throughout the book.

Introductions for Each Selection. Each selection is preceded by a detailed introduction to the life and work of the author and by comments about the selection's primary ideas. The most interesting rhetorical achievements of the selection are identified and discussed to help students discover how rhetorical techniques can achieve specific effects. These essays all offer useful models for writing: Douglass representing narrative; Darwin and Gould, example; Bacon and Geertz, enumeration; Kaku, cause and effect; Machiavelli, analysis of circumstance; Woolf, analysis of quotations. These kinds of models of thought and structure are the materials of invention and arrangement that beginning writers find useful.

"Questions for Critical Reading" and "Suggestions for Writing," Including "Connections Questions." At the end of each essay is a group of discussion questions designed for use inside or outside the classroom. Although the "Questions for Critical Reading" focus on key issues and ideas, they also can be used to stimulate general discussion and

critical thinking. The "Suggestions for Writing" that follow selections help students practice some of the rhetorical strategies employed by the selection author. These suggestions ask for personal responses as well as complete essays that involve research. A number of these assignments, labeled "Connections," promote critical reading by asking the reader to connect particular passages in a selection with a selection by another writer, either in the same section or in another section. The variety of possible connections is intriguing — Arendt with Darwin, Benedict with Nietzsche, Jefferson with Douglass and Rousseau, Beauvoir with Mead, and many more.

Instructor's Manual.   I have prepared an extensive manual, *Resources for Teaching A WORLD OF IDEAS,* that contains further background on the selections, examples from my own classroom responses to the selections, and more suggestions for classroom discussion as well as student writing assignments. Sentence outlines for the selections have been carefully prepared by Carol Verburg, Ellen Troutman, Ellen Darion, and Michael Hennessey and can be photocopied and given to students. The idea for these sentence outlines came from the phrase outlines that Darwin created to precede each chapter of *On the Origin of Species.* These outlines may be used to discuss the more difficult selections and to provide guidance for cautious students. At the end of the manual, brief bibliographies have been provided for all forty-one authors. These bibliographies may be photocopied and distributed to students who wish to explore the primary selections in greater depth.

Acknowledgments

I am grateful to a number of people who made important suggestions for the fifth edition. I am especially grateful to Shoshana Milgram Knapp of Virginia Polytechnic Institute and State University for a conversation at a Modern Language Association conference in which she recommended including Maimonides, who is represented by a selection that she has taught. She made a number of other suggestions that I am still mulling over. For this edition, the encouragement and suggestions of Michael Hennessey of Southwest Texas State University were invaluable. Among his suggestions for inclusion were the passages from Álvar Núñez Cabeza de Vaca and the Koran. I remain grateful to Michael Bybee at the University of Oregon for his suggestions of pieces to include in the fourth edition. He sent me many fascinating pieces by Asian thinkers, all of which he has taught to his own students. Thanks to him, this edition includes Lao-tzu and Siddhārtha Gautama, the Buddha, as interpreted by Buddhist monks.

Like its predecessors, this edition is indebted to a great many creative people at Bedford Books, whose support is invaluable. I want to thank Charles H. Christensen, whose concern for the continued excellence of this book and whose close attention to detail is truly admirable. I appreciate as always the advice of Joan E. Feinberg. My editor, Sarah Cornog, was supportive at every step of the process of developing the table of contents. She was perceptive, informed, and a good critic. Karen Henry, editor and friend, helped in the final stages of development and was a sounding board for ideas at every step of the way. Bridget Leahy, production editor, also helped with innumerable important details and suggestions. Rosemary Winfield, my copyeditor, found ways to shorten and sharpen the prose. Thanks also to some important staff members and researchers: Michelle Clark kept the manuscript moving and cleared permissions; Professor Mary W. Cornog was scrupulous in fact checking; Donna Dennison designed and secured the art for the cover. In earlier editions I had help from Ellen Kuhl, Mark Reimold, Andrea Goldman, Beth Castrodale, Jonathan Burns, Mary Beth McNulty, and Beth Chapman; I felt I had a personal relationship with each of them. I want to thank Anatoly Dverin, Lyrl Ahern, and Bill Ogden of PC&F, Incorporated, for their wonderful portraits, which have added a special human touch to the book. I also want to thank the students — quite a few of them — who wrote me directly about their experiences in reading the first four editions. I have attended to all that they said, and I am warmed by their high regard for the materials in this book.

Earlier editions have named the hundreds of users of this book who sent their comments and encouragement. I would like to thank them again (you know who you are). In addition, the following professors were generous with criticism, praise, and detailed recommendations for this fifth edition:

Sandra Adicues, Winona State University; Belinda C. Anderson, Norfolk State University; Kathryn Murphy Anderson, Boston University; Kit Andrews, Western Oregon State College; Liza Bachman, The Alexander School; John Batty-Sylvan, City College of San Francisco; Chester Benson, Clark College; Kevin Binfield, Gardiner-Webb University; Ellen Bonds, Villanova University; Tracy Bragen, Baruch College; David Cope, Grand Rapids Community College; Roberta M. Costa, Gwynedd-Mercy College; Helen Cothran, San Diego Mesa College; Robert Daley, State University of New York at Buffalo; Sauny Dills, University of California Polytechnic Institute; Russ Doyle, McKendree College; Rosemary Fisk, Samford University; Sallyanne Fitzgerald, Chabot College; Elizabeth A. Flyn, Chabot College; Michael Friedlander, Sacramento City College; Craig A. Gannon, Sterling College; Sydney Morgan Harrison, Manatee College; William Hathaway, State University of New York College at Cortland; Lilith M. Haynes, Harvard University Division of Continuing Education; Donald Heidt, College of the Canyon; James Heldman, Western Kentucky University; Rick Joines, University of Florida; Mary Kochlefl, Indiana University; Janice Kollitz, Riverside Community College; Craig Kramer, La Pierce College; Melissa Lang, Paul Smith's College of Arts and Sciences; Pamela Lundin, Lakeland College; Jane Melbourne, Lynchburg College; Paul Miller, College of Marin; Nancy Alpert Mower, University of Hawaii at Manoa; Thomas F. O'Conner, Cape Cod Community College; Scott Orme, Spokane Community College; Randi Pahlau, Malone College; Gary Pak, University of Hawaii at Manoa; P. E. Phillips, Vanderbilt University; Cecilia Di A. Ready, Villanova University; Richard Reid, Grand Rapids Community College; Margaret Scarborough, Edmonds Community College; Robert Schuler, University of Wisconsin-Stout; Annabel Serval, Southeastern Louisiana University; Arnold A. Sherman, Champlain College; Nicole Skinner, California State University at Sacramento; Yvonne Souliere, University of Southern Maine; Bob Stanton, Jacksonville University; Steven Strang, Massachusetts Institute of Technology; Paula Sullivan, Tulsa Junior College; Sandia Tuttle, Grossmont College; Sharon K. Walsh, Loyola University of Chicago; Joel Westerholm, Northwestern College.

CONTENTS

PART ONE

GOVERNMENT

– 11 –

PART TWO

JUSTICE

– 103 –

PART THREE

WEALTH

– 187 –

linguistic, logical-mathematical, spatial, musical, bodily-kinesthetic, interpersonal, and intrapersonal.

PART FIVE

NATURE

– 373 –

PART SIX

CULTURE

– 471 –

PART SEVEN

FAITH

– 563 –

PART EIGHT

POETICS

– 675 –

EVALUATING IDEAS

An Introduction to Critical Reading

The selections in this book demand a careful and attentive reading. The authors, whose works have changed the way we view our world, our institutions, and ourselves, make every effort to communicate their views with clarity and style. But their views are complex and subtle, and we must train ourselves to read them sensitively, responsively, and critically. Critical reading is basic for approaching the essays in this book. Indeed, it is basic for approaching any reading material that deserves serious attention.

Reading critically means reading actively: questioning the premises of the argument, speculating on the ways in which evidence is used, comparing the statements of one writer with those of another, and holding an inner dialogue with the author. These skills differ from the passive reception we employ when we watch television or read lightweight materials. Being an active, participating reader makes it possible for us to derive the most from good books.

Critical reading involves most of the following processes:

- *Prereading* Developing a sense of what the piece is about and what its general purposes seem to be.

- *Annotating* Using a pencil or a pen to mark those passages that seem important enough to return to later. Annotations establish a dialogue between you and the author.

- *Questioning* Raising issues that you feel need to be taken into consideration. These may be issues that you believe the author has treated either well or badly and that you feel are important. Questioning can be part of the annotation process.

1

- *Reviewing* Rereading your annotations and underlinings in order to grasp the entire "picture" of what you've just read. Sometimes writing a summary of the piece as you review makes the meaning even clearer.

- *Forming your own ideas* Reviewing what you have read, developing your own views on the issues, and evaluating the way that the writer presents the issues. This is the final step.

THE PROCESS OF CRITICAL READING

Prereading

Before you read a particular selection, you may find it useful to turn to the beginning of the part in which it appears. There you will find an introduction discussing the broader issues and questions central to all the selections in the part that may help you to focus your thoughts and formulate your opinions as you read the essays themselves.

Begin any selection in this book by reading its headnote. Each headnote supplies historical background on the writer, sets the intellectual stage for the ideas discussed in the essay, and comments on the writer's main points. The second part of each headnote also introduces the main rhetorical or stylistic methods that the writers use to communicate their thoughts. In the process of reading the headnote, you will develop an overview that helps prepare you for reading the essay.

This kind of preparation is typical of critical reading. It makes the task of reading more delightful, more useful, and much easier. A review of the headnote to Niccolò Machiavelli and part of his essay "The Qualities of the Prince" will illustrate the usefulness of such preparation. This essay appears in Part One — Government — so the content can already be expected to be concerned with styles of government. The introduction to Machiavelli provides the following points, each followed here by the number of the paragraph in which it appears:

Machiavelli was an Italian aristocrat in Renaissance Italy. (1)

Machiavelli describes the qualities necessary for a prince — that is, any ruler — to maintain power. (2)

A weak Italy was prey to the much stronger France and Spain at this time. (2)

Machiavelli recommends securing power by whatever means necessary and maintaining it. (3)

His concern for moralizing or acting out of high moral principle is not great. (3)

He supports questionable means of becoming and remaining prince. (3)

Machiavelli does not fret over the means used to achieve his ends and sometimes advocates repression, imprisonment, and torture. (3)

Machiavelli has been said to have a cynical view of human nature. (4)

His rhetorical method is to discuss both sides of an issue: cruelty and mercy, liberality and stinginess. (8)

He uses aphorisms to persuade the reader that he is saying something wise and true. (9)

With these observations in mind, the reader knows that the selection following will be concerned with governance in Renaissance Italy. The question of ends versus means is central to Machiavelli's discussion, and he does not idealize people and their general goodness. Yet because of Machiavelli's rhetorical methods, particularly his use of aphorism, the reader can expect that Machiavelli's argument will be exceptionally persuasive.

Thus, as a critical reader, you will be well advised to keep track of these basic statements from the headnote. You need not accept all of them, but you should certainly be alert to the issues that will probably be central to your experience of the essay. Remember: it is just as reasonable to question the headnote as it is to question the essay itself.

Before reading the essay in detail, you might develop an overview of its meaning by scanning it quickly. In the case of "The Qualities of the Prince," note the subheadings, such as "On Those Things for Which Men, and Particularly Princes, Are Praised or Blamed." Checking each of the subheadings before you read the entire piece might provide you with a map or guide to the essay.

Annotating and Questioning

As you read a text, your annotations establish a dialogue between you and the author. You can underline or highlight important statements that you feel help clarify the author's position. They may be statements to which you will want to refer later. Think of them as serving one overriding purpose: to make it possible for you to review the piece and understand its key points without having to reread it entirely.

Your dialogue with the author will be most visible in the margins of the essay, which is one reason the margins in this book are so generous. Take issue with key points or note your assent — the more you annotate, the more you free your imagination to develop your own ideas. My own methods involve notating both agreement and disagreement. I annotate thoroughly, so that after a quick second glance I know what the author is saying as well as what I thought of the essay when I read it closely. My annotations help me keep the major points fresh in my mind.

Annotation keeps track both of what the author says and of what our responses are. No one can reduce annotation to a formula — we all do it differently — but it is not a passive act. Reading with a pencil or a pen in hand should become second nature. Without annotations, you often have to reread entire sections of an essay to remember an argument that once was clear and understandable but after time has become part of the fabric of the prose and thus "invisible." Annotation is the conquest of the invisible; it provides a quick view of the main points.

When you annotate,

- Read with a pen or a pencil.
- Underline key sentences — for example, definitions and statements of purpose.
- Underline key words that appear often.
- Note the topic of paragraphs in the margins.
- Ask questions in the margins.
- Make notes in the margins to remind yourself to develop ideas later.
- Mark passages you might want to quote in your essay.
- Keep track of points with which you disagree.

Some sample annotations follow, again from the second essay in the book, Niccolò Machiavelli's "The Qualities of the Prince." A sixteenth-century text in translation, *The Prince* is challenging to work with. My annotations appear in the form of underlinings and marginal comments and questions. Only the first few paragraphs appear here, but the entire essay is annotated in my copy of the book.

A Prince's Duty Concerning Military Matters

The prince's profession should be war.

A prince, therefore, must not have any other object nor any other thought, nor must he take anything as <u>his profession but war</u>, its institutions, and its discipline; because that is the only profession which befits one who commands; and it is of such importance that not only does it maintain those who were born princes, but many times it enables men of private station to rise to that position; and, on the other hand, it is evident that <u>when princes have given more thought to personal luxuries than to arms, they have lost their state</u>. And the first way to lose it is to neglect this art; and the way to acquire it is to be well versed in this art.

Examples

Francesco Sforza became Duke of Milan from being a private citizen because he was armed; his sons, since they avoided the inconveniences of arms, became private citizens after having been dukes. For, among the other bad effects it causes,

Being disarmed makes you despised. Is this true?

being disarmed makes you despised; this is one of those infamies a prince should guard himself against, as will be treated below: for between an armed and an unarmed man there is no comparison whatsoever, and it is not reasonable for an armed man to obey an unarmed man willingly, nor that an unarmed man should be safe among armed servants; since, when the former is suspicious and the latter are contemptuous, it is impossible for them to work well together. And therefore, a prince who does not understand military matters, besides the other misfortunes already noted, cannot be esteemed by his own soldiers, nor can he trust them.

Training action/mind

He must, therefore, never raise his thought from this exercise of war, and in peacetime he must train himself more than in time of war; this can be done in two ways: one by <u>action, the other by the mind.</u> And as far as actions are concerned, besides <u>keeping his soldiers well disciplined and trained,</u> he must always be out hunting, and must <u>accustom his body to hardships</u> in this manner; and he must

Knowledge of terrain

also learn the nature of the terrain, and know how mountains slope, how valleys open, how plains lie, and understand the nature of rivers and swamps; and he should devote much attention to such activities. *Two benefits* ities. Such knowledge is useful in two ways: first, one learns to know one's own country and can better understand how to defend it; second, with the knowledge and experience of the terrain, one can easily comprehend the characteristics of any other terrain that it is necessary to explore for the first time; for the hills, valleys, plains, rivers, and swamps of Tuscany, for instance, have certain similarities to those of other provinces; so that by knowing the lay of the land in one province one can easily understand it in others. And a prince who lacks this ability lacks the most important quality in a leader; because this skill teaches you to find the enemy, choose a campsite, lead troops, organize them for battle, and besiege towns to your own advantage.

[There follow the examples of Philopoemon, who was always observing terrain for its military usefulness, and a recommendation that princes read histories and learn from them. Three paragraphs are omitted.]

On Those Things for Which Men, and Particularly Princes, Are Praised or Blamed

Now there remains to be examined what should be the methods and procedures of a prince in dealing with his subjects and friends. And because I know that many have written about this, I am afraid that writing about it again I shall be thought of as presumptuous, since in discussing this material I depart radically from the procedures of others. But since my intention is to write something useful for anyone who understands it, it seemed more suitable to me to search after the effectual truth of the matter rather than its imagined one. And many writers have imagined for themselves republics and principalities that have never been seen nor known to exist in reality; for there is such a gap between how one lives and how one ought to live that anyone who abandons what is done for what ought to be done learns his ruin rather than his preservation: for a man who wishes

Two benefits

Those who are good at all times come to ruin among those who are not good.

Prince must learn how not to be good.

to make a vocation of being good at all times will come to ruin among so many who are not good. Hence it is necessary for a prince who wishes to maintain his position to learn how not to be good, and to use this knowledge or not to use it according to necessity.

Note the prince's reputation.

Leaving aside, therefore, the imagined things concerning a prince, and taking into account those that are true, I say that all men, when they are spoken of, and particularly princes, since they are placed on a higher level, are judged by some of these qualities which bring them either blame or praise. And this is why one is considered generous, another miserly (to use a Tuscan word, since "avaricious" in our language is still used to mean one who wishes to acquire by means of theft; we call "miserly" one who excessively avoids using what he has); one is considered a giver, the other rapacious; one cruel, another merciful; one treacherous, another faithful; one effeminate and cowardly, another bold and courageous; one humane, another haughty; one lascivious, another chaste; one trustworthy, another cunning; one harsh, another lenient; one serious, another frivolous; one religious, another unbelieving; and the like. And I know that everyone will admit that it would be a very praiseworthy thing to find in a prince, of the qualities mentioned above, those that are held to be good, but since it is neither possible to have them nor to observe them all completely, because human nature does not permit it, a prince must be prudent enough to know how to escape the bad reputation of those vices that would lose the state for him, and must protect himself from those that will not lose it for him, if this is possible; but if he cannot, he need not concern himself unduly if he ignores these less serious vices. And, moreover, he need not worry about incurring the bad reputation of those vices without which it would be difficult to hold his state; since, carefully taking everything into account, one will discover that something which appears to be a virtue, if pursued, will end in his destruction; while some other thing which seems to be a vice, if pursued, will result in his safety and his well-being.

Prince must avoid reputation for the worst vices.

Some vices may be needed to hold the state. True?

Some virtues may end in destruction.

Reviewing

The process of review, which takes place after a careful reading, is much more useful if you have annotated and underlined the text well. To a large extent, the review process can be devoted to accounting for the primary ideas that have been uncovered by your annotations and underlinings. For example, reviewing the Machiavelli annotations shows that the following ideas are crucial to Machiavelli's thinking:

The prince's profession should be war, so the most successful princes are probably experienced in the military.

If they do not pay attention to military matters, princes will lose their power.

Being disarmed makes the prince despised.

The prince should be in constant training.

The prince needs a sound knowledge of terrain.

Machiavelli says he tells us what is true, not what ought to be true.

Those who are always good will come to ruin among those who are not good.

To remain in power, the prince must learn how not to be good.

The prince should avoid the worst vices in order not to harm his reputation.

To maintain power, some vices may be necessary.

Some virtues may end in destruction.

Putting Machiavelli's ideas in this raw form does an injustice to his skill as a writer, but annotation is designed to result in such summary statements. We can see that there are some constant themes, such as the insistence that the prince be a military person. As the headnote tells us, in Machiavelli's day Italy was a group of rival city-states, and France, a larger, united nation, was invading these states one by one. Machiavelli dreamed that one powerful prince, such as his favorite, Cesare Borgia, could fight the French and save Italy. He emphasized the importance of the military be-cause he lived in an age in which war was a constant threat.

Machiavelli anticipates the complaints of pacifists — those who argue against war — by telling us that those who remain unarmed are despised. To demonstrate his point, he gives us examples of those who lost their positions as princes because they avoided being armed. He clearly expects these examples to be persuasive.

A second important theme pervading Machiavelli's essay is his view on moral behavior. For Machiavelli, being in power is much more important than being virtuous. He is quick to admit that vice is not desirable and that the worst vices will harm the prince's reputation. But he also says that the prince need not worry about the "less serious" vices. Moreover, he need not worry about incurring a bad reputation by practicing vices that are necessary if he wishes to hold his state. In the same spirit, he tells us that there are some virtues that might lead to the destruction of the prince.

Forming Your Own Ideas

One of the most important reasons for critically reading texts of the kind that appear in this book is to enable you to develop your own positions on issues that these writers raise. Identifying and clarifying the main ideas is only the first step; the next step in critical reading is evaluating those ideas.

For example, you might ask whether Machiavelli's ideas have any relevance for today. After all, he wrote four hundred years ago and times have changed. You might feel that Machiavelli was relevant strictly during the Italian Renaissance or, alternatively, that his principles are timeless and have something to teach every age. For most people, Machiavelli is a political philosopher whose views are useful anytime and anywhere.

If you agree with the majority, then you may want to examine Machiavelli's ideas to see whether you can accept them. Consider just two of those ideas and their implications:

Should rulers always be members of the military? Should they always be armed?

Should rulers ignore virtue and practice vice when it is convenient?

Should the ruler of a nation first demonstrate competence as a military leader? In his commentary on government, Lao-tzu offers different advice because his assumptions are that the ruler ought to respect the rights of individuals. For Lao-tzu the waging of war is an annoying, essentially wasteful activity. On the other hand, Machiavelli never once questions the usefulness of war: to him, it is basic to government. As a critical reader, you can take issue with such an assumption, and in doing so you will deepen your understanding of Machiavelli.

If we were to follow Machiavelli's advice, then we would choose presidents on the basis of whether or not they had been good military leaders. Among those we would not have chosen from American history might be Thomas Jefferson, Abraham Lincoln, and

Franklin Delano Roosevelt. Those who were high-ranking military men include George Washington, Ulysses S. Grant, and Dwight D. Eisenhower. If you followed Machiavelli's rhetorical technique of using examples to convince your audience, you could choose from either group to prove your case.

Of course, there are examples from other nations. It has been common since the 1930s to see certain leaders dressed in their military uniforms: Benito Mussolini (Italy), Adolf Hitler (Germany), Joseph Stalin (Russia), Idi Amin (Uganda), Muammar al-Qaddafi (Libya). These are all tyrants who have tormented their citizens and their neighbors. That gives us something to think about. Should a president dress in full military regalia all the time? Is that a good image for the ruler of a free nation?

Do you want a ruler, then, who is usually virtuous, but embraces vice when it is necessary? This is a very difficult question to answer. When Jimmy Carter swore to the American people that he would never lie to them, many Americans were skeptical. They thought that politics was essentially a game of careful and judicious lying — at least at times. In other words, these Americans were already committed to Machiavelli's position.

These are only a few of the questions that are raised by my annotations in the few pages from Machiavelli examined here. Many other issues could be uncovered by these annotations, and many more from subsequent pages of the essay. Critical reading can be a powerful means by which to open what you read to discovery and discussion.

Once you begin a line of questioning, the ways in which you think about a passage begin expanding. You find yourself with more ideas of your own that have grown in response to those you have been reading about. Reading critically, in other words, gives you an enormous return on your investment of time. If you have the chance to investigate your responses to the assumptions and underlying premises of passages such as Machiavelli's, you will be able to refine your thinking even further. For example, if you agree with Machiavelli that rulers should be successful military leaders for whom small vices may be useful at times, and you find yourself in a position to argue with someone who feels Machiavelli is mistaken in this view, then you will have a good opportunity to evaluate the soundness of your thinking. You will have a chance to see your own assumptions and arguments tested.

In many ways, this entire book is about such opportunities. The essays that follow offer you powerful ideas from great thinkers. They invite you to participate in their thoughts, exercise your own knowledge and assumptions, and arrive at your own conclusions. Basically, that is the meaning of education.

PART ONE

GOVERNMENT

Lao-tzu
Niccolò Machiavelli
Jean-Jacques Rousseau
Thomas Jefferson
Hannah Arendt

At the core of any idea of government is the belief that individuals need an organized allocation of authority to protect their well-being. However, throughout history the form of that allocation of authority has undergone profound shifts, and each successive type of government has inspired debates and defenses. The first civilizations in Mesopotamia and Egypt (4000 – 3000 B.C.) were theocracies ruled by a high priest. Gradually these political systems evolved into monarchies in which a king whose role was separate from that of the religious leaders held power. During the sixth century B.C. the Greek city-state Athens developed the first democratic system wherein male citizens (but not women or slaves) could elect a body of leaders. As these forms of government developed so too did the concept of government as the center of law and administration. However, governments and ideas of governments (actual or ideal) have not followed a straight path. History has witnessed constant oscillations between various forms and functions of government, from tyrannies to republics. In turn, these governments and their relation to the individual citizen have been the focus of many great thinkers.

In this section, the thinkers represented have concentrated on both the role and form of government. Lao-tzu reflects on the ruler who would, by careful management, maintain a happy citizenry. Machiavelli places the survival of the prince first before all other considerations of government and, unlike Lao-tzu, ignores the concerns and rights of the individual. For Machiavelli power is the issue, and maintaining it is the sign of good government. Rousseau's emphasis on the social contract focuses on the theory that citizens voluntarily submit to governance in the hopes of gaining greater personal freedom. Rousseau explores this idea in clear, original terms.

While governing well concerns most of these thinkers, the forms of government concern others. Thomas Jefferson struggled with the monarchical form of government, as did Rousseau before him, and envisioned a republic that would serve the people. Kings were a threatened species in eighteenth-century Europe, and with Jefferson's aid, they became extinct in the United States. Hannah Arendt was convinced that the totalitarian governments of the twentieth century were the product of new ideologies formed from misunderstanding Darwinian theories and misapplying Marxian concepts of class struggle.

Lao-tzu, whose writings provide the basis for Taoism, one of three major Chinese religions, was interested primarily in political systems. His work, the *Tao-te Ching,* has been translated loosely as

"The Way of Power." One thing that becomes clear from reading his work — especially the selections presented here — is his concern for the well-being of the people in any government. He does not recommend specific forms of government (monarchic, representative, democratic) or advocate election versus the hereditary transfer of power. But he does make it clear that the success of the existing forms of government (in his era, monarchic) depends on good relations between the leader and the people. He refers to the chief of state as Master or Sage, implying that one obligation of the governor is to be wise. One expression of that wisdom is the willingness to permit things to take their natural course. Lao-tzu's insistence on inactivity in government is complex. It does not imply sloth. It implies, instead, the ability to participate in the natural order of events and to resist the impulse to do things that do not need to be done. In other words, he condemns useless busyness. His view is that the less the Master needs to do — or perhaps the less government needs to intervene — the happier the people will be.

Niccolò Machiavelli was a pragmatic man of the Renaissance in Italy. As a theoretician and as a member of the political court, he understood government from the inside and carefully examined its philosophy. Because his writings stress the importance of gaining and holding power at any cost, Machiavelli's name has become synonymous with political cunning. However, a careful reading of his work as a reflection of the instability of his time shows that his advice to wield power ruthlessly derived largely from his fear that a weak prince would lose his city-state of Florence to France or to another powerful, plundering nation. His commitment to a powerful prince is based on his view that in the long run strength will guarantee the peace and happiness of the citizen for whom independence is otherwise irrelevant. Therefore, Machiavelli generally ignores questions concerning the comfort and rights of the individual.

In contrast, Jean-Jacques Rousseau is continually concerned with the basic questions of personal freedom and liberty. A fundamental principle in "The Origin of Civil Society" is that the individual's agreement with the state is designed to increase the individual's freedoms and not to diminish them. Rousseau says this while at the same time admitting that the individual forfeits certain rights to the body politic in order to guarantee overall freedom. Moreover, Rousseau describes civil society as a body politic that expects its rulers — including the monarch — to behave in a way designed to benefit the people. Such a view in late eighteenth-century France was revolutionary. The ruling classes at that time treated the people with great contempt, and the monarch rarely thought of the well-being of the common people. Rousseau's advocacy of a republican form of government in which the monarch served the people was a radical view at the time and would find its ultimate expression decades later in the French Revolution.

Thomas Jefferson's views were also radical. Armed with the philosophy of Rousseau and others, his Declaration of Independence advocates the eradication of the monarch entirely. Not everyone in the colonies agreed with this view. Indeed, his political opponents, such as Alexander Hamilton and Aaron Burr, were far from certain such a view was correct. In fact, some efforts were made to install George Washington as king (he refused). In the Declaration of Independence, Jefferson reflects Rousseau's philosophy by emphasizing the right of the individual to "life, liberty, and the pursuit of happiness" and the obligation of government to serve the people by protecting those rights.

The issues of freedom, justice, and individual rights were all virtually irrelevant in the totalitarian regimes that served as the focus of Hannah Arendt's work. Arendt argued that the fascist states, especially Nazi Germany, and the communist states, especially the Soviet Union, represented a novel form of government, one in which individual rights were sacrificed for the good of "the state." In her work *The Origins of Totalitarianism,* Arendt argues that the power of totalitarian states rises from the extreme distortion of logical premises coupled with the use of terror to enforce the ideology. The result is a form of government that eclipses the tyrannical extremes Rousseau and Jefferson sought to eradicate and exceeds even Machiavelli's imaginings of absolute power.

LAO-TZU
Thoughts from the *Tao-te Ching*

THE AUTHOR of the *Tao-te Ching* (in English often pronounced "dow deh ching") is unknown, although the earliest texts
ascribe the work to Lao-tzu (sixth century B.C.), whose name can
be translated as "Old Master." However, nothing can be said with
certainty about Lao-tzu as a historical figure. One tradition holds
that he was named Li Erh and born in the state of Ch'u at a time
that would have made him a slightly older contemporary of Confucius (551 – 479 B.C.). Lao-tzu was said to have worked in the court
of the Chou dynasty for most of his life. When he decided to leave
the court to pursue a life of contemplation, the keeper of the gate
urged him to write down his thoughts before he went into a self-
imposed exile. Legend has it that he wrote the *Tao-te Ching* and
then left the state of Ch'u, never to be seen again.

Taoism is a religion founded by Chang Tao-ling in about 150
A.D., but the *Tao-te Ching* is a philosophical document as much
about good government as it is about moral behavior. The term *Tao*
cannot be easily understood or easily translated. In one sense it
means "the way," but it also means "the method," as in "the way to
enlightenment" or "the way to live." Some of the chapters of the
Tao-te Ching imply that the Tao is the allness of the universe, the
ultimate reality of existence, and perhaps even a synonym for God.
The text is marked by such complex ambiguities and paradoxes. It
constantly urges us to look beyond ourselves, beyond our circumstances, and become one with the Tao — even though it cannot tell
us what the Tao is.

The *Tao-te Ching* has often been called a feminine treatise because it emphasizes the creative forces of the universe and frequently employs the imagery and metaphor of the womb — for ex-

From *Tao-te Ching*. Translated by Stephen Mitchell.

ample, "The Tao is called the Great Mother." The translator, Stephen Mitchell, translates some of the pronouns associated with the Master as "she," with the explanation that Chinese has no equivalent for the male- and female-gendered pronouns and that "of all the great world religions the teaching of Lao-tzu is by far the most female."

The teachings of Lao-tzu are the opposite of the materialist quest for power, dominance, authority, and wealth. Lao-tzu takes the view that possessions and wealth are leaden weights of the soul, that they are meaningless and trivial, and that the truly free and enlightened person will regard them as evil. Because of his antimaterialist view, his recommendations may seem ironic or unclear, especially when he urges politicians to adopt a practice of judicious inaction. Lao-tzu's advice to politicians is not to do nothing but to intercede only when it is a necessity and then only inconspicuously. Above all, Lao-tzu counsels avoiding useless activity: "the Master / acts without doing anything / and teaches without saying anything." Such a statement is difficult for modern westerners to comprehend, although it points to the concept of enlightenment, a state of spiritual peace and fulfillment that is central to the *Tao-te Ching*.

Lao-tzu's political philosophy minimizes the power of the state — especially the power of the state to oppress the people. Lao-tzu takes the question of the freedom of the individual into account by asserting that the wise leader will provide the people with what they need but not annoy them with promises of what they do not need. He argues that by keeping people unaware that they are being governed, the leader allows the people to achieve good things for themselves. As he writes, "If you want to be a great leader, / you must learn to follow the Tao. / Stop trying to control. / Let go of fixed plans and concepts, / and the world will govern itself" (Verse 57); or in contrast, "If a country is governed with repression, / the people are depressed and crafty" (Verse 58).

To our modern ears this advice may or may not sound sensible. For those who feel government can solve the problems of the people, it will seem strange and unwise. For those who believe that the less government the better, the advice will sound sane and powerful.

THE RHETORIC OF THE *TAO-TE CHING*

Traditionally, Lao-tzu is said to have written the *Tao-te Ching* as a guide for the ruling sage to follow. In other words, it is a handbook for politicians. The *Te* emphasizes the virtues that the ruler must possess, and in this sense the *Tao-te Ching* invites comparison with Machiavelli's efforts to instruct his ruler.

The visual form of the text is poetry, although the text is not metrical or image-laden. Instead of thoroughly developing his ideas, Lao-tzu uses a traditional Chinese form that resembles the aphorism, a compressed statement weighty with meaning. Virtually every statement requires thought and reflection. Thus, the act of reading becomes an act of cooperation with the text.

One way of reading the text is to explore the varieties of interpretation it will sustain. The act of analysis requires patience and willingness to examine a statement to see what lies beneath the surface. Take, for example, one of the opening statements:

> The Master leads
> by emptying people's minds
> and filling their cores,
> by weakening their ambition
> and toughening their resolve.
> He helps people lose everything
> they know, everything they desire,
> and creates confusion
> in those who think that they know.

This passage supports a number of readings. One centers on the question of the people's desire. "Emptying people's minds" implies eliminating desires that lead the people to steal or compete for power. "Weakening their ambition" implies helping people direct their powers toward the attainable and useful. Such a text is at odds with western views that support advertisements for expensive sneakers, color television sets, luxury cars, and other items that generate ambition and desire in the people.

In part because the text resembles poetry, it needs to be read with attention to innuendo, subtle interpretation, and possible hidden meanings. One of the rhetorical virtues of paradox is that it forces the reader to consider several sides of an issue. The resulting confusion yields a wider range of possibilities than would be possible with a self-evident statement. Through these complicated messages, Lao-tzu felt he was contributing to the spiritual enlightenment of the ruling sage, although he had no immediate hope that his message would be put into action. A modern state might have a difficult time following Lao-tzu's philosophy, but many individuals have tried to attain peace and contentment by leading lives by its principles.

Thoughts from the *Tao-te Ching*

3

If you overesteem great men,
people become powerless.
If you overvalue possessions,
people begin to steal.

The Master leads
by emptying people's minds
and filling their cores,
by weakening their ambition
and toughening their resolve.
He helps people lose everything
they know, everything they desire,
and creates confusion
in those who think that they know.

Practice not-doing,
and everything will fall into place.

17

When the Master governs, the people
are hardly aware that he exists.
Next best is a leader who is loved.
Next, one who is feared.
The worst is one who is despised.

If you don't trust the people,
you make them untrustworthy.

The Master doesn't talk, he acts.
When his work is done,
the people say, "Amazing:
we did it, all by ourselves!"

18

When the great Tao is forgotten,
goodness and piety appear.
When the body's intelligence declines,

cleverness and knowledge step forth.
When there is no peace in the family,
filial piety begins.
When the country falls into chaos,
patriotism is born.

19

Throw away holiness and wisdom,   8
and people will be a hundred times happier.
Throw away morality and justice,
and people will do the right thing.
Throw away industry and profit,
and there won't be any thieves.

If these three aren't enough,   9
just stay at the center of the circle
and let all things take their course.

26

The heavy is the root of the light.   10
The unmoved is the source of all movement.

Thus the Master travels all day   11
without leaving home.
However splendid the views,
she stays serenely in herself.

Why should the lord of the country   12
flit about like a fool?
If you let yourself be blown to and fro,
you lose touch with your root.
If you let restlessness move you,
you lose touch with who you are.

29

Do you want to improve the world?   13
I don't think it can be done.

The world is sacred.   14
It can't be improved.

If you tamper with it, you'll ruin it.
If you treat it like an object, you'll lose it.

There is a time for being ahead,   15
a time for being behind;
a time for being in motion,
a time for being at rest;
a time for being vigorous,
a time for being exhausted;
a time for being safe,
a time for being in danger.

The Master sees things as they are,   16
without trying to control them.
She lets them go their own way,
and resides at the center of the circle.

30

Whoever relies on the Tao in governing men   17
doesn't try to force issues
or defeat enemies by force of arms.
For every force there is a counterforce.
Violence, even well intentioned,
always rebounds upon oneself.

The Master does his job   18
and then stops.
He understands that the universe
is forever out of control,
and that trying to dominate events
goes against the current of the Tao.
Because he believes in himself,
he doesn't try to convince others.
Because he is content with himself,
he doesn't need others' approval.
Because he accepts himself,
the whole world accepts him.

31

Weapons are the tools of violence;   19
all decent men detest them.

Weapons are the tools of fear;   20
a decent man will avoid them
except in the direst necessity
and, if compelled, will use them
only with the utmost restraint.
Peace is his highest value.
If the peace has been shattered,
how can he be content?
His enemies are not demons,
but human beings like himself.
He doesn't wish them personal harm.
Nor does he rejoice in victory.
How could he rejoice in victory
and delight in the slaughter of men?

He enters a battle gravely,   21
with sorrow and with great compassion,
as if he were attending a funeral.

37

The Tao never does anything,   22
yet through it all things are done.

If powerful men and women   23
could center themselves in it,
the whole world would be transformed
by itself, in its natural rhythms.
People would be content
with their simple, everyday lives,
in harmony, and free of desire.

When there is no desire,   24
all things are at peace.

38

The Master doesn't try to be powerful;   25
thus he is truly powerful.
The ordinary man keeps reaching for power;
thus he never has enough.

The Master does nothing,   26
yet he leaves nothing undone.
The ordinary man is always doing things,
yet many more are left to be done.

The kind man does something,   27
yet something remains undone.
The just man does something,
and leaves many things to be done.
The moral man does something,
and when no one responds
he rolls up his sleeves and uses force.

When the Tao is lost, there is goodness.   28
When goodness is lost, there is morality.
When morality is lost, there is ritual.
Ritual is the husk of true faith,
the beginning of chaos.

Therefore the Master concerns himself   29
with the depths and not the surface,
with the fruit and not the flower.
He has no will of his own.
He dwells in reality,
and lets all illusions go.

46

When a country is in harmony with the Tao,   30
the factories make trucks and tractors.
When a country goes counter to the Tao,
warheads are stockpiled outside the cities.

There is no greater illusion than fear,   31
no greater wrong than preparing to defend yourself,
no greater misfortune than having an enemy.

Whoever can see through all fear   32
will always be safe.

53

The great Way is easy,   33
yet people prefer the side paths.

Be aware when things are out of balance.
Stay centered within the Tao.

When rich speculators prosper   34
while farmers lose their land;
when government officials spend money
on weapons instead of cures;
when the upper class is extravagant and irresponsible
while the poor have nowhere to turn —
all this is robbery and chaos.
It is not in keeping with the Tao.

57

If you want to be a great leader,   35
you must learn to follow the Tao.
Stop trying to control.
Let go of fixed plans and concepts,
and the world will govern itself.

The more prohibitions you have,   36
the less virtuous people will be.
The more weapons you have,
the less secure people will be.
The more subsidies you have,
the less self-reliant people will be.

Therefore the Master says: 37
I let go of the law,
and people become honest.
I let go of economics,
and people become prosperous.
I let go of religion,
and people become serene.
I let go of all desire for the common good,
and the good becomes common as grass.

58

If a country is governed with tolerance,   38
the people are comfortable and honest.
If a country is governed with repression,
the people are depressed and crafty.

When the will to power is in charge,   39
the higher the ideals, the lower the results.
Try to make people happy,
and you lay the groundwork for misery.
Try to make people moral,
and you lay the groundwork for vice.

Thus the Master is content   40
to serve as an example
and not to impose her will.
She is pointed, but doesn't pierce.
Straightforward, but supple.
Radiant, but easy on the eyes.

59

For governing a country well   41
there is nothing better than moderation.

The mark of a moderate man   42
is freedom from his own ideas.
Tolerant like the sky,
all-pervading like sunlight,
firm like a mountain,
supple like a tree in the wind,
he has no destination in view
and makes use of anything
life happens to bring his way.

Nothing is impossible for him.   43
Because he has let go,
he can care for the people's welfare
as a mother cares for her child.

60

Governing a large country   44
is like frying a small fish.
You spoil it with too much poking.

Center your country in the Tao   45
and evil will have no power.

Not that it isn't there,
but you'll be able to step out of its way.

Give evil nothing to oppose　　　　　　　　　46
and it will disappear by itself.

61

When a country obtains great power,　　　　47
it becomes like the sea:
all streams run downward into it.
The more powerful it grows,
the greater the need for humility.
Humility means trusting the Tao,
thus never needing to be defensive.

A great nation is like a great man:　　　　48
When he makes a mistake, he realizes it.
Having realized it, he admits it.
Having admitted it, he corrects it.
He considers those who point out his faults
as his most benevolent teachers.
He thinks of his enemy
as the shadow that he himself casts.

If a nation is centered in the Tao,　　　　49
if it nourishes its own people
and doesn't meddle in the affairs of others,
it will be a light to all nations in the world.

65

The ancient Masters　　　　　　　　　　50
didn't try to educate the people,
but kindly taught them to not-know.

When they think that they know the answers,　　51
people are difficult to guide.
When they know that they don't know,
people can find their own way.

If you want to learn how to govern,
avoid being clever or rich.
The simplest pattern is the clearest.
Content with an ordinary life,
you can show all people the way
back to their own true nature.

52

66

All streams flow to the sea
because it is lower than they are.
Humility gives it its power.

53

If you want to govern the people,
you must place yourself below them.
If you want to lead the people,
you must learn how to follow them.

54

The Master is above the people,
and no one feels oppressed.
She goes ahead of the people,
and no one feels manipulated.
The whole world is grateful to her.
Because she competes with no one,
no one can compete with her.

55

67

Some say that my teaching is nonsense.
Others call it lofty but impractical.
But to those who have looked inside themselves,
this nonsense makes perfect sense.
And to those who put it into practice,
this loftiness has roots that go deep.

56

I have just three things to teach:
simplicity, patience, compassion.
These three are your greatest treasures.
Simple in actions and in thoughts,
you return to the source of being.
Patient with both friends and enemies,
you accord with the way things are.

57

Compassionate toward yourself,
you reconcile all beings in the world.

75

When taxes are too high,   58
people go hungry.
When the government is too intrusive,
people lose their spirit.

Act for the people's benefit.   59
Trust them; leave them alone.

80

If a country is governed wisely,   60
its inhabitants will be content.
They enjoy the labor of their hands
and don't waste time inventing
labor-saving machines.
Since they dearly love their homes,
they aren't interested in travel.
There may be a few wagons and boats,
but these don't go anywhere.
There may be an arsenal of weapons,
but nobody ever uses them.
People enjoy their food,
take pleasure in being with their families,
spend weekends working in their gardens,
delight in the doings of the neighborhood.
And even though the next country is so close
that people can hear its roosters crowing and its dogs barking,
they are content to die of old age
without ever having gone to see it.

QUESTIONS FOR CRITICAL READING

1. According to Lao-tzu, what must the ruler provide the people with if
   they are to be happy? See especially Verse 66.

2. To what extent does Lao-tzu concern himself with individual happiness?
3. How would you describe Lao-tzu's attitude toward the people?
4. Why does Lao-tzu think the world cannot be improved? See Verse 29.
5. Which statements made in this selection do you feel support a materialist view of experience? Can they be resolved with Lao-tzu's overall thinking in the selection?
6. What are the limits and benefits of the expression: "Practice not-doing / and everything will fall into place"?
7. To what extent is Lao-tzu in favor of military action? What seem to be his views about the military? See Verse 31.
8. The term "Master" is used frequently in the selection. What can you tell about the character of the Master?

SUGGESTIONS FOR WRITING

1. The term "the Tao" is used often in this selection. Write a short essay that defines what Lao-tzu seems to mean by the term. If you were a politician and had the responsibility of governing a state, how would you follow the Tao as it is implied in Lao-tzu's statements? Is the Tao restrictive? Difficult? Open to interpretation? How well do you think it would work?
2. Write a brief essay that examines the following statements from the perspective of a young person today:

> The more prohibitions you have,
> the less virtuous people will be.
> The more weapons you have,
> the less secure people will be.
> The more subsidies you have,
> the less self-reliant people will be.

To what extent do you agree with these statements, and to what extent do you feel they are statements that have a political importance? Do people in the United States, as you interpret it, seem to agree with these views, or do they disagree? What are the most visible political consequences of our nation's position regarding these ideas?
3. Some people have asserted that the American political system benefits the people most when the following views of Lao-tzu are carefully followed:

> Therefore the Master says:
> I let go of the law,
> and people become honest.
> I let go of economics,
> and people become prosperous.
> I let go of religion,
> and people become serene.
> I let go of all desire for the common good,
> and the good becomes common as grass.

In a brief essay, decide to what extent American leaders follow these precepts. Whether you feel they do or not, do you think that they should follow these precepts? What are the likely results of their being put into practice?

4. Some of the statements Lao-tzu makes are so packed with meaning that it would take pages to explore them. One example is "When they think that they know the answers, / people are difficult to guide." Take this statement as the basis of a short essay and, in reference to a personal experience, explain the significance of this statement.

5. What does Lao-tzu imply about the obligation of the state to the individual it governs, and about the obligation of the individual to the state? Is one much more important than the other? Using the texts in this selection, establish what you feel is the optimum balance in the relationship between the two.

6. **CONNECTIONS** Compare Lao-tzu's view of government with that of Machiavelli in the next selection. Consider what seem to be the ultimate purposes of government, what seem to be the obligations of the leader to the people being led, and what seems to be the main work of the state. What comparisons can you make between Lao-tzu's Master and Machiavelli's Prince?

NICCOLÒ MACHIAVELLI
The Qualities of the Prince

NICCOLÒ MACHIAVELLI (1469–1527) was an aristocrat whose fortunes wavered according to the shifts in power in Florence. Renaissance Italy was a collection of powerful city-states, which were sometimes volatile and unstable. When Florence's famed Medici princes were returned to power in 1512 after eighteen years of banishment, Machiavelli did not fare well. He was suspected of crimes against the state and imprisoned. Even though he was not guilty, he had to learn to support himself as a writer instead of continuing his career in civil service.

His works often contrast two forces: luck (one's fortune) and character (one's virtues). His own character outlasted his bad luck in regard to the Medicis, and he was returned to a position of responsibility. *The Prince* (1513), his most celebrated work, was a general treatise on the qualities the prince (that is, ruler) must have to maintain his power. In a more particular way, it was directed at the Medicis to encourage them to save Italy from the predatory incursions of France and Spain, whose troops were nibbling at the crumbling Italian principalities and who would, in time, control much of Italy.

The chapters presented here contain the core of the philosophy for which Machiavelli became famous. His instructions to the prince are curiously devoid of any high-sounding moralizing or any encouragement to be good as a matter of principle. Instead, Machiavelli recommends a very practical course of action for the prince: secure power by direct and effective means. It may be that Machiavelli fully expects that the prince will use his power for good ends — certainly he does not recommend tyranny. But he also supports

From *The Prince*. Translated by Peter Bondanella and Mark Musa.

using questionable means to achieve the final end of becoming and remaining the prince. Although Machiavelli recognizes that there is often a conflict between the ends and the means used to achieve them, he does not fret over the possible problems that may accompany the use of "unpleasant" means, such as punishment of upstarts, or the use of repression, imprisonment, and torture.

Through the years Machiavelli's view of human nature has come under criticism for its cynicism. For instance, he suggests that a morally good person would not remain long in any high office because that person would have to compete with the mass of people, who, he says, are basically bad. Machiavelli constantly tells us that he is describing the world as it really is, not as it should be. Perhaps Machiavelli is correct, but people have long condemned the way he approves of cunning, deceit, and outright lying as means of staying in power.

The contrast between Machiavelli's writings and Lao-tzu's opinions in the *Tao-te Ching* is instructive. Lao-tzu's advice issues from a detached view of a universal ruler; Machiavelli's advice is very personal, embodying a set of directives for a specific prince. Machiavelli expounds upon a litany of actions that must be taken; Lao-tzu, on the other hand, advises that judicious inaction will produce the best results.

MACHIAVELLI'S RHETORIC

Machiavelli's approach is less poetic and more pragmatic than Lao-tzu's. While Lao-tzu's tone is almost biblical, Machiavelli's is that of a how-to book, relevant to a particular time and a particular place. Yet, like Lao-tzu, Machiavelli is brief and to the point. Each segment of the discussion is terse and economical. Nothing is wasted.

Machiavelli announces his primary point clearly, refers to a historical precedent (or several) to support his point, and then explains why his position is the best one by appealing to both common sense and historical experience. When he suspects the reader will not share his view wholeheartedly, he suggests an alternate argument and then explains why it is wrong. This is a very forceful way of presenting one's views. It gives the appearance of fairness and thoroughness — and, as we learn from reading Machiavelli, he is very much concerned with appearances. His method also gives his work fullness, a quality that makes us forget how brief it really is.

Another of his rhetorical methods is to discuss opposites, including both sides of an issue. From the first he explores a number of oppositions — the art of war and the art of life, liberality and stinginess, cruelty and clemency, the fox and the lion. The method may seem simple, but it is important because it employs two of the basic techniques of rhetoric — comparison and contrast.

The aphorism is another of Machiavelli's rhetorical weapons. An aphorism is a saying — or a sentence that sounds like a saying — that has been accepted as true. Familiar examples are "A penny saved is a penny earned" and "There is no fool like an old fool." Machiavelli tells us: "It is much safer to be feared than to be loved" and "A man who wishes to make a vocation of being good at all times will come to ruin among so many who are not good."

Such definite statements have several important qualities. One is that they are pithy: they seem to say a great deal in a few words. Another is that they appear to contain a great deal of wisdom, in part because they are delivered with such certainty, and in part because they have the ring of other aphorisms that we accept as true. Because they sound like aphorisms, they gain a claim to (unsubstantiated) truth, and we tend to accept them much more readily than perhaps we should. This may be why the speeches of contemporary politicians (modern versions of the prince) are often sprinkled with such expressions and illustrates why Machiavelli's rhetorical technique is still reliable, still effective, and still worth studying.

The Qualities of the Prince

A Prince's Duty Concerning Military Matters

A prince, therefore, must not have any other object nor any   1
other thought, nor must he take anything as his profession but war, its institutions, and its discipline; because that is the only profession which befits one who commands; and it is of such importance that not only does it maintain those who were born princes, but many times it enables men of private station to rise to that position; and, on the other hand, it is evident that when princes have given more thought to personal luxuries than to arms, they have lost their state. And the first way to lose it is to neglect this art; and the way to acquire it is to be well versed in this art.

Francesco Sforza[1] became Duke of Milan from being a private   2
citizen because he was armed; his sons, since they avoided the in-

---

[1] **Francesco Sforza (1401–1466)** Became duke of Milan in 1450. He was, like most of Machiavelli's examples, a skilled diplomat and soldier. His court was a model of Renaissance scholarship and achievement.

conveniences of arms, became private citizens after having been dukes. For, among the other bad effects it causes, being disarmed makes you despised; this is one of those infamies a prince should guard himself against, as will be treated below: for between an armed and an unarmed man there is no comparison whatsoever, and it is not reasonable for an armed man to obey an unarmed man willingly, nor that an unarmed man should be safe among armed servants; since, when the former is suspicious and the latter are contemptuous, it is impossible for them to work well together. And therefore, a prince who does not understand military matters, besides the other misfortunes already noted, cannot be esteemed by his own soldiers, nor can he trust them.

He must, therefore, never raise his thought from this exercise of war, and in peacetime he must train himself more than in time of war; this can be done in two ways: one by action, the other by the mind. And as far as actions are concerned, besides keeping his soldiers well disciplined and trained, he must always be out hunting, and must accustom his body to hardships in this manner; and he must also learn the nature of the terrain, and know how mountains slope, how valleys open, how plains lie, and understand the nature of rivers and swamps; and he should devote much attention to such activities. Such knowledge is useful in two ways: first, one learns to know one's own country and can better understand how to defend it; second, with the knowledge and experience of the terrain, one can easily comprehend the characteristics of any other terrain that it is necessary to explore for the first time; for the hills, valleys, plains, rivers, and swamps of Tuscany,[2] for instance, have certain similarities to those of other provinces; so that by knowing the lay of the land in one province one can easily understand it in others. And a prince who lacks this ability lacks the most important quality in a leader; because this skill teaches you to find the enemy, choose a campsite, lead troops, organize them for battle, and besiege towns to your own advantage. 3

Philopoemon, Prince of the Achaeans,[3] among the other praises given to him by writers, is praised because in peacetime he thought of nothing except the means of waging war; and when he was out in 4

---

[2] **Tuscany** Florence is in the region of Italy known as Tuscany.

[3] **Philopoemon (252? – 182 B.C.), Prince of the Achaeans** Philopoemon, from the city-state of Megalopolis, was a Greek general noted for skillful diplomacy. He led the Achaeans, a group of Greek states that formed the Achaean League, in several important expeditions, notably against Sparta. His cruelty in putting down a Spartan uprising caused him to be reprimanded by his superiors.

the country with his friends, he often stopped and reasoned with them: "If the enemy were on that hilltop and we were here with our army, which of the two of us would have the advantage? How could we attack them without breaking formation? If we wanted to retreat, how could we do this? If they were to retreat, how could we pursue them?" And he proposed to them, as they rode along, all the contingencies that can occur in an army; he heard their opinions, expressed his own, and backed it up with arguments; so that, because of these continuous deliberations, when leading his troops no unforeseen incident could arise for which he did not have the remedy.

But as for the exercise of the mind, the prince must read histories and in them study the deeds of great men; he must see how they conducted themselves in wars; he must examine the reasons for their victories and for their defeats in order to avoid the latter and to imitate the former; and above all else he must do as some distinguished man before him has done, who elected to imitate someone who had been praised and honored before him, and always keep in mind his deeds and actions; just as it is reported that Alexander the Great imitated Achilles; Caesar, Alexander; Scipio, Cyrus.[4] And anyone who reads the life of Cyrus written by Xenophon then realizes how important in the life of Scipio that imitation was to his glory and how much, in purity, goodness, humanity, and generosity, Scipio conformed to those characteristics of Cyrus that Xenophon had written about.

Such methods as these a wise prince must follow, and never in peaceful times must he be idle; but he must turn them diligently to his advantage in order to be able to profit from them in times of adversity, so that, when Fortune changes, she will find him prepared to withstand such times.

On Those Things for Which Men, and Particularly Princes, Are Praised or Blamed

Now there remains to be examined what should be the methods and procedures of a prince in dealing with his subjects and friends. And because I know that many have written about this, I am afraid

---

[4] **Cyrus (585? – 529? B.C.)** Cyrus II (the Great), Persian emperor. Cyrus and the other figures featured in this sentence — Alexander the Great (356 – 323 B.C.); Achilles, hero of Homer's *Iliad;* Julius Caesar (100? – 44 B.C.); and Scipio Africanus (236 – 184/3 B.C.), legendary Roman general — are all examples of politicians who were also great military geniuses. Xenophon (431 – 350? B.C.) was one of the earliest Greek historians; he chronicled the lives and military exploits of Cyrus and his son-in-law Darius.

that by writing about it again I shall be thought of as presumptuous, since in discussing this material I depart radically from the procedures of others. But since my intention is to write something useful for anyone who understands it, it seemed more suitable to me to search after the effectual truth of the matter rather than its imagined one. And many writers have imagined for themselves republics and principalities that have never been seen nor known to exist in reality; for there is such a gap between how one lives and how one ought to live that anyone who abandons what is done for what ought to be done learns his ruin rather than his preservation: for a man who wishes to make a vocation of being good at all times will come to ruin among so many who are not good. Hence it is necessary for a prince who wishes to maintain his position to learn how not to be good, and to use this knowledge or not to use it according to necessity.

Leaving aside, therefore, the imagined things concerning a 8 prince, and taking into account those that are true, I say that all men, when they are spoken of, and particularly princes, since they are placed on a higher level, are judged by some of these qualities which bring them either blame or praise. And this is why one is considered generous, another miserly (to use a Tuscan word, since "avaricious" in our language is still used to mean one who wishes to acquire by means of theft; we call "miserly" one who excessively avoids using what he has); one is considered a giver, the other rapacious; one cruel, another merciful; one treacherous, another faithful; one effeminate and cowardly, another bold and courageous; one humane, another haughty; one lascivious, another chaste; one trustworthy, another cunning; one harsh, another lenient; one serious, another frivolous; one religious, another unbelieving; and the like. And I know that everyone will admit that it would be a very praiseworthy thing to find in a prince, of the qualities mentioned above, those that are held to be good, but since it is neither possible to have them nor to observe them all completely, because human nature does not permit it, a prince must be prudent enough to know how to escape the bad reputation of those vices that would lose the state for him, and must protect himself from those that will not lose it for him, if this is possible; but if he cannot, he need not concern himself unduly if he ignores these less serious vices. And, moreover, he need not worry about incurring the bad reputation of those vices without which it would be difficult to hold his state; since, carefully taking everything into account, one will discover that something which appears to be a virtue, if pursued, will end in his destruction; while some other thing which seems to be a vice, if pursued, will result in his safety and his well-being.

On Generosity and Miserliness

Beginning, therefore, with the first of the above-mentioned qual- 9
ities, I say that it would be good to be considered generous; nevertheless, generosity used in such a manner as to give you a reputation for
it will harm you; because if it is employed virtuously and as one
should employ it, it will not be recognized and you will not avoid the
reproach of its opposite. And so, if a prince wants to maintain his
reputation for generosity among men, it is necessary for him not to
neglect any possible means of lavish display; in so doing such a
prince will always use up all his resources and he will be obliged,
eventually, if he wishes to maintain his reputation for generosity, to
burden the people with excessive taxes and to do everything possible
to raise funds. This will begin to make him hateful to his subjects,
and, becoming impoverished, he will not be much esteemed by anyone; so that, as a consequence of his generosity, having offended
many and rewarded few, he will feel the effects of any slight unrest
and will be ruined at the first sign of danger; recognizing this and
wishing to alter his policies, he immediately runs the risk of being reproached as a miser.

A prince, therefore, unable to use this virtue of generosity in a 10
manner which will not harm himself if he is known for it, should, if
he is wise, not worry about being called a miser; for with time he
will come to be considered more generous once it is evident that, as
a result of his parsimony, his income is sufficient, he can defend
himself from anyone who makes war against him, and he can undertake enterprises without overburdening his people, so that he comes
to be generous with all those from whom he takes nothing, who are
countless, and miserly with all those to whom he gives nothing, who
are few. In our times we have not seen great deeds accomplished except by those who were considered miserly; all others were done
away with. Pope Julius II,[5] although he made use of his reputation
for generosity in order to gain the papacy, then decided not to maintain it in order to be able to wage war; the present King of France[6]
has waged many wars without imposing extra taxes on his subjects,
only because his habitual parsimony has provided for the additional

---

[5] **Pope Julius II (1443–1513)** Giuliano della Rovere, pope from 1503 to
1513. Like many of the popes of the day, Julius II was also a diplomat and a general.

[6] **present King of France** Louis XII (1462–1515). He entered Italy on a successful military campaign in 1494.

expenditures; the present King of Spain,[7] if he had been considered generous, would not have engaged in nor won so many campaigns.

Therefore, in order not to have to rob his subjects, to be able   11 to defend himself, not to become poor and contemptible, and not to be forced to become rapacious, a prince must consider it of little importance if he incurs the name of miser, for this is one of those vices that permits him to rule. And if someone were to say: Caesar with his generosity came to rule the empire, and many others, because they were generous and known to be so, achieved very high positions; I reply: you are either already a prince or you are on the way to becoming one; in the first instance such generosity is damaging; in the second it is very necessary to be thought generous. And Caesar was one of those who wanted to gain the principality of Rome; but if, after obtaining this, he had lived and had not moderated his expenditures, he would have destroyed that empire. And if someone were to reply: there have existed many princes who have accomplished great deeds with their armies who have been reputed to be generous; I answer you: a prince either spends his own money and that of his subjects or that of others; in the first case he must be economical; in the second he must not restrain any part of his generosity. And for that prince who goes out with his soldiers and lives by looting, sacking, and ransoms, who controls the property of others, such generosity is necessary; otherwise he would not be followed by his troops. And with what does not belong to you or to your subjects you can be a more liberal giver, as were Cyrus, Caesar, and Alexander; for spending the wealth of others does not lessen your reputation but adds to it; only the spending of your own is what harms you. And there is nothing that uses itself up faster than generosity, for as you employ it you lose the means of employing it, and you become either poor or despised or, in order to escape poverty, rapacious and hated. And above all other things a prince must guard himself against being despised and hated; and generosity leads you to both one and the other. So it is wiser to live with the reputation of a miser, which produces reproach without hatred, than to be forced to incur the reputation of rapacity, which produces reproach along with hatred, because you want to be considered as generous.

----

[7] **present King of Spain** Ferdinand V (1452 – 1516). A studied politician; he and Queen Isabella (1451 – 1504) financed Christopher Columbus's voyage to the New World in 1492.

On Cruelty and Mercy and Whether It Is Better to Be Loved Than to Be Feared or the Contrary

Proceeding to the other qualities mentioned above, I say that 12 every prince must desire to be considered merciful and not cruel; nevertheless, he must take care not to misuse this mercy. Cesare Borgia[8] was considered cruel; nonetheless, his cruelty had brought order to Romagna,[9] united it, restored it to peace and obedience. If we examine this carefully, we shall see that he was more merciful than the Florentine people, who, in order to avoid being considered cruel, allowed the destruction of Pistoia.[10] Therefore, a prince must not worry about the reproach of cruelty when it is a matter of keeping his subjects united and loyal; for with a very few examples of cruelty he will be more compassionate than those who, out of excessive mercy, permit disorders to continue, from which arise murders and plundering; for these usually harm the community at large, while the executions that come from the prince harm one individual in particular. And the new prince, above all other princes, cannot escape the reputation of being called cruel, since new states are full of dangers. And Virgil, through Dido, states: "My difficult condition and the newness of my rule make me act in such a manner, and to set guards over my land on all sides."[11]

Nevertheless, a prince must be cautious in believing and in acting, nor should he be afraid of his own shadow; and he should proceed in such a manner, tempered by prudence and humanity, so that too much trust may not render him imprudent nor too much distrust render him intolerable.

From this arises an argument: whether it is better to be loved 14 than to be feared, or the contrary. I reply that one should like to be both one and the other; but since it is difficult to join them together, it is much safer to be feared than to be loved when one of the two must be lacking. For one can generally say this about men: that they

[8] **Cesare Borgia (1476–1507)** He was known for his brutality and lack of scruples, not to mention his exceptionally good luck. He was a firm ruler, son of Pope Alexander VI.

[9] **Romagna** Region northeast of Tuscany; includes the towns of Bologna, Ferrara, Ravenna, and Rimini. Borgia united it as his base of power in 1501.

[10] **Pistoia** (also known as Pistoria) A town near Florence, disturbed in 1501 by a civil war that could have been averted by strong repressive measures.

[11] The quotation is from the *Aeneid* (II. 563–564), the greatest Latin epic poem, written by Virgil (70–19 B.C.). Dido was a woman general who ruled Carthage.

are ungrateful, fickle, simulators and deceivers, avoiders of danger, greedy for gain; and while you work for their good they are completely yours, offering you their blood, their property, their lives, and their sons, as I said earlier, when danger is far away; but when it comes nearer to you they turn away. And that prince who bases his power entirely on their words, finding himself stripped of other preparations, comes to ruin; for friendships that are acquired by a price and not by greatness and nobility of character are purchased but are not owned, and at the proper moment they cannot be spent. And men are less hesitant about harming someone who makes himself loved than one who makes himself feared because love is held together by a chain of obligation which, since men are a sorry lot, is broken on every occasion in which their own self-interest is concerned; but fear is held together by a dread of punishment which will never abandon you.

A prince must nevertheless make himself feared in such a man- 15
ner that he will avoid hatred, even if he does not acquire love; since to be feared and not to be hated can very well be combined; and this will always be so when he keeps his hands off the property and the women of his citizens and his subjects. And if he must take someone's life, he should do so when there is proper justification and manifest cause; but, above all, he should avoid the property of others; for men forget more quickly the death of their father than the loss of their patrimony. Moreover, the reasons for seizing their property are never lacking; and he who begins to live by stealing always finds a reason for taking what belongs to others; on the contrary, reasons for taking a life are rarer and disappear sooner.

But when the prince is with his armies and has under his com- 16
mand a multitude of troops, then it is absolutely necessary that he not worry about being considered cruel; for without that reputation he will never keep an army united or prepared for any combat. Among the praiseworthy deeds of Hannibal[12] is counted this: that, having a very large army, made up of all kinds of men, which he commanded in foreign lands, there never arose the slightest dissention, neither among themselves nor against their prince, both during his good and his bad fortune. This could not have arisen from anything other than his inhuman cruelty, which, along with his many other abilities, made him always respected and terrifying in the eyes of his soldiers; and without that, to attain the same effect,

---

[12] **Hannibal (247 – 183 B.C.)** An amazingly inventive military tactician who led the Carthaginian armies against Rome for more than fifteen years. He crossed the Alps from Gaul (France) in order to surprise Rome. He was noted for use of the ambush and for "inhuman cruelty."

his other abilities would not have sufficed. And the writers of history, having considered this matter very little, on the one hand admire these deeds of his and on the other condemn the main cause of them.

And that it be true that his other abilities would not have been 17
sufficient can be seen from the example of Scipio, a most extraordinary man not only in his time but in all recorded history, whose armies in Spain rebelled against him; this came about from nothing other than his excessive compassion, which gave to his soldiers more liberty than military discipline allowed. For this he was censured in the senate by Fabius Maximus,[13] who called him the corruptor of the Roman militia. The Locrians,[14] having been ruined by one of Scipio's officers, were not avenged by him, nor was the arrogance of that officer corrected, all because of his tolerant nature; so that someone in the senate who tried to apologize for him said that there were many men who knew how not to err better than they knew how to correct errors. Such a nature would have, in time, damaged Scipio's fame and glory if he had maintained it during the empire; but, living under the control of the senate, this harmful characteristic of his not only concealed itself but brought him fame.

I conclude, therefore, returning to the problem of being feared 18
and loved, that since men love at their own pleasure and fear at the pleasure of the prince, a wise prince should build his foundation upon that which belongs to him, not upon that which belongs to others: he must strive only to avoid hatred, as has been said.

How a Prince Should Keep His Word

How praiseworthy it is for a prince to keep his word and to live 19
by integrity and not by deceit everyone knows; nevertheless, one sees from the experience of our times that the princes who have accomplished great deeds are those who have cared little for keeping their promises and who have known how to manipulate the minds of men by shrewdness; and in the end they have surpassed those who laid their foundations upon honesty.

You must, therefore, know that there are two means of fighting: 20
one according to the laws, the other with force; the first way is proper to man, the second to beasts; but because the first, in many

---

[13] **Fabius Maximus (? – 203 B.C.)** Roman general who fought Hannibal. He was jealous of the younger Roman general Scipio.

[14] **Locrians** Inhabitants of Locri, an Italian town settled by the Greeks in c. 680 B.C.

cases, is not sufficient, it becomes necessary to have recourse to the second. Therefore, a prince must know how to use wisely the natures of the beast and the man. This policy was taught to princes allegorically by the ancient writers, who described how Achilles and many other ancient princes were given to Chiron[15] the Centaur to be raised and taught under his discipline. This can only mean that, having a half-beast and half-man as a teacher, a prince must know how to employ the nature of the one and the other; and the one without the other cannot endure.

Since, then, a prince must know how to make good use of the nature of the beast, he should choose from among the beasts the fox and the lion; for the lion cannot defend itself from traps and the fox cannot protect itself from wolves. It is therefore necessary to be a fox in order to recognize the traps and a lion in order to frighten the wolves. Those who play only the part of the lion do not understand matters. A wise ruler, therefore, cannot and should not keep his word when such an observance of faith would be to his disadvantage and when the reasons which made him promise are removed. And if men were all good, this rule would not be good; but since men are a sorry lot and will not keep their promises to you, you likewise need not keep yours to them. A prince never lacks legitimate reasons to break his promises. Of this one could cite an endless number of modern examples to show how many pacts, how many promises have been made null and void because of the infidelity of princes; and he who has known best how to use the fox has come to a better end. But it is necessary to know how to disguise this nature well and to be a great hypocrite and a liar: and men are so simpleminded and so controlled by their present necessities that one who deceives will always find another who will allow himself to be deceived.

I do not wish to remain silent about one of these recent instances. Alexander VI[16] did nothing else, he thought about nothing else, except to deceive men, and he always found the occasion to do this. And there never was a man who had more forcefulness in his oaths, who affirmed a thing with more promises, and who honored his word less; nevertheless, his tricks always succeeded perfectly since he was well acquainted with this aspect of the world.

---

[15] **Chiron** A mythical figure, a centaur (half man, half horse). Unlike most centaurs, he was wise and benevolent; he was also a legendary physician.

[16] **Alexander VI (1431 – 1503)** Roderigo Borgia, pope from 1492 to 1503. He was Cesare Borgia's father and a corrupt but immensely powerful pope.

Therefore, it is not necessary for a prince to have all of the 23
above-mentioned qualities, but it is very necessary for him to appear
to have them. Furthermore, I shall be so bold as to assert this: that
having them and practicing them at all times is harmful; and appearing to have them is useful; for instance, to seem merciful, faithful,
humane, forthright, religious, and to be so; but his mind should be
disposed in such a way that should it become necessary not to be so,
he will be able and know how to change to the contrary. And it is
essential to understand this: that a prince, and especially a new
prince, cannot observe all those things by which men are considered
good, for in order to maintain the state he is often obliged to act
against his promise, against charity, against humanity, and against
religion. And therefore, it is necessary that he have a mind ready to
turn itself according to the way the winds of Fortune and the
changeability of affairs require him; and, as I said above, as long as it
is possible, he should not stray from the good, but he should know
how to enter into evil when necessity commands.

A prince, therefore, must be very careful never to let anything 24
slip from his lips which is not full of the five qualities mentioned
above: he should appear, upon seeing and hearing him, to be all
mercy, all faithfulness, all integrity, all kindness, all religion. And
there is nothing more necessary than to seem to possess this last
quality. And men in general judge more by their eyes than their
hands; for everyone can see but few can feel. Everyone sees what
you seem to be, few perceive what you are, and those few do not
dare to contradict the opinion of the many who have the majesty of
the state to defend them; and in the actions of all men, and especially of princes, where there is no impartial arbiter, one must consider the final result.[17] Let a prince therefore act to seize and to
maintain the state; his methods will always be judged honorable and
will be praised by all; for ordinary people are always deceived by appearances and by the outcome of a thing; and in the world there is
nothing but ordinary people; and there is no room for the few, while
the many have a place to lean on. A certain prince[18] of the present
day, whom I shall refrain from naming, preaches nothing but peace
and faith, and to both one and the other he is entirely opposed; and
both, if he had put them into practice, would have cost him many
times over either his reputation or his state.

---

[17] The Italian original, *si guarda al fine,* has often been mistranslated as "the
ends justify the means," something Machiavelli never wrote. [Translators' note]

[18] **A certain prince** Probably King Ferdinand V of Spain (1452 – 1516).

On Avoiding Being Despised and Hated

But since, concerning the qualities mentioned above, I have 25
spoken about the most important, I should like to discuss the others
briefly in this general manner: that the prince, as was noted above,
should think about avoiding those things which make him hated
and despised; and when he has avoided this, he will have carried
out his duties and will find no danger whatsoever in other vices. As I
have said, what makes him hated above all else is being rapacious
and a usurper of the property and the women of his subjects; he
must refrain from this; and in most cases, so long as you do not deprive them of either their property or their honor, the majority of
men live happily; and you have only to deal with the ambition of a
few, who can be restrained without difficulty and by many means.
What makes him despised is being considered changeable, frivolous, effeminate, cowardly, irresolute; from these qualities a prince
must guard himself as if from a reef, and he must strive to make
everyone recognize in his actions greatness, spirit, dignity, and
strength; and concerning the private affairs of his subjects, he must
insist that his decision be irrevocable; and he should maintain himself in such a way that no man could imagine that he can deceive or
cheat him.

That prince who projects such an opinion of himself is greatly 26
esteemed; and it is difficult to conspire against a man with such a
reputation and difficult to attack him, provided that he is understood to be of great merit and revered by his subjects. For a prince
must have two fears: one, internal, concerning his subjects; the
other, external, concerning foreign powers. From the latter he can
defend himself by his good troops and friends; and he will always
have good friends if he has good troops; and internal affairs will always be stable when external affairs are stable, provided that they
are not already disturbed by a conspiracy; and even if external conditions change, if he is properly organized and lives as I have said
and does not lose control of himself, he will always be able to withstand every attack, just as I said that Nabis the Spartan[19] did. But
concerning his subjects, when external affairs do not change, he has
to fear that they may conspire secretly: the prince secures himself
from this by avoiding being hated or despised and by keeping the
people satisfied with him; this is a necessary matter, as was treated
above at length. And one of the most powerful remedies a prince has

---

[19] **Nabis the Spartan** Tyrant of Sparta from 207 to 192 B.C., routed by
Philopoemon and the Achaean League.

against conspiracies is not to be hated by the masses; for a man who plans a conspiracy always believes that he will satisfy the people by killing the prince; but when he thinks he might anger them, he cannot work up the courage to undertake such a deed; for the problems on the side of the conspirators are countless. And experience demonstrates that conspiracies have been many but few have been concluded successfully; for anyone who conspires cannot be alone, nor can he find companions except from amongst those whom he believes to be dissatisfied; and as soon as you have uncovered your intent to one dissatisfied man, you give him the means to make himself happy, since he can have everything he desires by uncovering the plot; so much is this so that, seeing a sure gain on the one hand and one doubtful and full of danger on the other, if he is to maintain faith with you he has to be either an unusually good friend or a completely determined enemy of the prince. And to treat the matter briefly, I say that on the part of the conspirator there is nothing but fear, jealousy, and the thought of punishment that terrifies him; but on the part of the prince there is the majesty of the principality, the laws, the defenses of friends and the state to protect him; so that, with the good will of the people added to all these things, it is impossible for anyone to be so rash as to plot against him. For, where usually a conspirator has to be afraid before he executes his evil deed, in this case he must be afraid, having the people as an enemy, even after the crime is performed, nor can he hope to find any refuge because of this.

One could cite countless examples on this subject; but I want to satisfy myself with only one which occurred during the time of our fathers. Messer Annibale Bentivoglio, prince of Bologna and grandfather of the present Messer Annibale, was murdered by the Canneschi[20] family, who conspired against him; he left behind no heir except Messer Giovanni,[21] then only a baby. As soon as this murder occurred, the people rose up and killed all the Canneschi. This came about because of the good will that the house of the Bentivoglio enjoyed in those days; this good will was so great that with Annibale dead, and there being no one of that family left in the city who could rule Bologna, the Bolognese people, having heard that in Florence there was one of the Bentivoglio blood who was believed until that time to be the son of a blacksmith, went to Florence to find him, and they gave him the control of that city; it was ruled by him until Messer Giovanni became of age to rule.

27

---

[20] **Canneschi** Prominent family in Bologna.

[21] **Giovanni Bentivoglio (1443–1508)** Former tyrant of Bologna. In sequence he was a conspirator against, then a conspirator with, Cesare Borgia.

I conclude, therefore, that a prince must be little concerned 28 with conspiracies when the people are well disposed toward him; but when the populace is hostile and regards him with hatred, he must fear everything and everyone. And well-organized states and wise princes have, with great diligence, taken care not to anger the nobles and to satisfy the common people and keep them contented; for this is one of the most important concerns that a prince has.

QUESTIONS FOR CRITICAL READING

1. The usual criticism of Machiavelli is that he advises his prince to be unscrupulous. Find examples for and against this claim.
2. Why do you agree or disagree with Machiavelli when he asserts that the great majority of people are not good? Does our government assume that to be true too?
3. Politicians — especially heads of state — are the contemporary counterparts of the prince. To what extent should successful heads of state show the skill in war that Machiavelli's prince must?
4. Clarify the advice Machiavelli gives concerning liberality and stinginess. Is this still good advice?
5. Are modern politicians likely to succeed by following all or most of Machiavelli's recommendations? Why or why not?

SUGGESTIONS FOR WRITING

1. In speaking of the prince's military duties Machiavelli says that "being disarmed makes you despised." Choose an example or instance to strengthen your argument for or against this position. Is it possible that in modern society being defenseless is an advantage?
2. Find evidence within this excerpt to demonstrate that Machiavelli's attitude toward human nature is accurate. Remember that the usual criticism of Machiavelli is that he is cynical — that he thinks the worst of people rather than the best. Find quotations from the excerpt that support either or both of these views; then use them as the basis for an essay analyzing Machiavelli's views on human nature.
3. By referring to current events and current leaders — either local, national, or international — decide whether Machiavelli's advice to the prince is useful to the modern politician. Consider whether the advice is completely useless or completely reliable or whether its value depends on specific conditions. First state the advice, then show how it applies (or does not apply) to specific politicians, and finally critique its general usefulness.
4. Probably the chief ethical issue raised by *The Prince* is the question of whether the desired ends justify the means used to achieve them.

Write an essay in which you take a stand on this question. Begin by defining the issue: What does the concept "the ends justify the means" actually mean? What difficulties may arise when unworthy means are used to achieve worthy ends? Analyze Machiavelli's references to circumstances in which questionable means were (or should have been) used to achieve worthy ends. Use historical or personal examples to give your argument substance.

5. **CONNECTIONS**   One of Machiavelli's most controversial statements is: "A man who wishes to make a vocation of being good at all times will come to ruin among so many who are not good." How would Lao-tzu respond to this statement? How does the American political environment in the current decade support this statement? Under what conditions would such a statement become irrelevant?

JEAN-JACQUES ROUSSEAU
The Origin of Civil Society

JEAN-JACQUES ROUSSEAU (1712 – 1778) was the son of
Suzanne Bernard and Isaac Rousseau, a watchmaker in Geneva,
Switzerland. Shortly after his birth, Rousseau's mother died, and a
rash duel forced his father from Geneva. Rousseau was then ap-
prenticed at age thirteen to an engraver, a master who treated him
badly. He soon ran away from his master and found a home with a
Catholic noblewoman who at first raised him as her son and then,
when he was twenty, took him as her lover. In the process
Rousseau converted from Calvinist Protestantism to Roman
Catholicism. Eventually, he left Switzerland for Paris, where he
won an important essay contest and became celebrated in society.

Over the course of his lifetime, Rousseau produced a wide variety of literary and musical works, including a novel, *Emile* (1762),
an opera, *The Village Soothsayer* (1752), and an autobiography, *The
Confessions* (published posthumously in 1789). *The Social Contract*
(1762) was part of a never-completed longer work on political systems. In many ways Rousseau wrote in reaction to political
thinkers such as Hugo Grotius and Thomas Hobbes, to whom he
responds in the following selection. He contended that the Dutch
philosopher and legal expert Grotius unquestioningly accepted the
power of the aristocracy. He felt Grotius paid too much attention to
what was rather than what ought to be. On the other hand, Hobbes,
the English political philosopher, asserted that people had a choice
of being free or being ruled. In other words, those who were members of civil society chose to give up their freedom and submit to

Translated by Gerald Hopkins. From *Social Contract: Essays by Locke, Hume, and
Rousseau*.

the monarch's rule. Either they relinquished their freedom, or they removed themselves from civil society to live a brutish existence.

Rousseau argued against Grotius by examining the way things ought to be. He argued against Hobbes by asserting that both the body politic and the monarch were sovereign and that when people created a civil society they surrendered their freedom to themselves as a group. If one person acted as sovereign or lawgiver, then that lawgiver had the responsibility of acting in accord with the will of the people. In a sense, this view parallels some of the views of Lao-tzu in the *Tao-te Ching*.

Popularly referred to as a defender of republicanism, Rousseau looked to the Republic of Geneva, his birthplace, as a model of government. He also idealized the generally democratic government of smaller Swiss cantons, such as Neuchatel, which used a form of town meeting where people gathered face to face to settle important issues. Ironically, Geneva put out a warrant for his arrest upon the publication of *The Social Contract* because, while it praised Geneva's republicanism, it also condemned societies that depended on rule by a limited aristocracy. Unfortunately for Rousseau, at that time Geneva was governed by a small number of aristocratic families. Rousseau was deprived of his citizenship and could not return to his native home.

As in Geneva, Rousseau's novel and controversial views were not easily received by those in power in France. After the publication of *Emile* offended the French Parliament, Rousseau was forced to abandon his comfortable rustic circumstances — living on country estates provided by patrons from the court — and spend the rest of his life in financial uncertainty. Ironically, in 1789, ten years after his death, Rousseau's philosophy would be adopted by supporters of the French Revolution in their bloody revolt against the aristocracy.

ROUSSEAU'S RHETORIC

Rousseau's method is in many ways antagonistic: he establishes the views of other thinkers, counters them, and then offers his own ideas. An early example appears in the opening of paragraph 8: "Grotius denies that political power is ever exercised in the interest of the governed, and quotes the institution of slavery in support of his contention. His invariable method of arguing is to derive Right from Fact." Among other things, Rousseau expects his readers to know who Grotius was and what he said. He also expects his readers to agree that Grotius derives "Right from Fact" by understanding that the fact of monarchy justifies it as being right. As Rousseau tells us, that kind of circular reasoning is especially kind to tyrants, since it justifies them by their existence.

Analysis and examination of detail are the main rhetorical approaches Rousseau uses. Whether he examines the ideas of others or presents ideas of his own, he is careful to examine the bases of the argument and to follow the arguments to their conclusion. He does this very thoroughly in his section "Of Slavery," in which he demonstrates that slavery is unjustifiable no matter which of the current arguments are used to support it, including the widely held view that it was justifiable to enslave captured soldiers on the grounds that they owed their lives to their captors.

Rousseau makes careful use of aphorism and analogy. His opening statement, "Man is born free, and everywhere he is in chains," is an aphorism that has been often quoted. It is a powerful and perplexing statement. How do people who are born free lose their freedom? Is it taken from them, or do they willingly surrender it? Rousseau spends considerable time examining this point.

The use of analogy is probably most striking in his comparison of government with the family. The force of the analogy reminds us that the members of a family are to be looked after by the family. As he tells us beginning in paragraph 5, the family is the only natural form of society. But instead of stopping there, he goes on to say that children are bound to the father only as long as they need him. Once they are able to be independent, they dissolve the natural bond and "return to a condition of equal independence." This analogy differs from the existing popular view that the monarch was like the father in a family and the people like his children and, in fact, works against the legitimacy of the traditional monarchy as it was known in eighteenth-century France.

Rousseau also refers to other writers, using a rhetorical device known as *testimony:* he paraphrases the views of other authorities and moves on to promote his own. But in referring to other writers, Rousseau is unusually clever. For example, in paragraph 10 he begins with the analogy of the shepherd as the ruler in this fashion: "Just as the shepherd is superior in kind to his sheep, so, too, the shepherds of men, or, in other words, their rulers, are superior in kind to their peoples. This, according to Philo, was the argument advanced by Caligula, the Emperor, who drew from the analogy the perfectly true conclusion that either Kings are Gods or their subjects brute beasts." Caligula was a madman and an emperor guilty of enormous cruelty; from his point of view it may have seemed true that kings were gods. But Rousseau, in citing this questionable authority, disputes the validity of the analogy.

He argues as well against the view that might makes right in
"Of the Right of the Strongest." The value of the social contract, he
explains as he develops his thoughts, is to produce a society that is
not governed by the mightiest and most ruthless and that permits
those who are not mighty to live peacefully and unmolested. Thus,
those who participate in the social contract give up certain freedoms but gain many more — among them the freedom not to be
dominated by physical brutality.

Rousseau concentrates on the question of man in nature, or
natural society. His view is that natural society is dominated by the
strongest individuals but that at some point natural society necessarily breaks down. Thus, in order to guarantee the rights of those
who are not the strongest, the political order must change. "Some
form of association" is developed "for the protection of the person
and property of each constituent member." By surrendering some
freedom to the group as a whole — to "the general will" — the individuals in the group can expect to prosper more widely and to live
more happily. According to Rousseau, the establishment of a social
contract ensures the stability of this form of civil society.

The Origin of Civil Society

Note

It is my wish to inquire whether it be possible, within the civil   1
order, to discover a legitimate and stable basis of Government. This I
shall do by considering human beings as they are and laws as they
might be. I shall attempt, throughout my investigations, to maintain a
constant connection between what right permits and interest demands, in order that no separation may be made between justice and
utility. I intend to begin without first proving the importance of my
subject. Am I, it will be asked, either prince or legislator that I take it
upon me to write of politics? My answer is — No; and it is for that
very reason that I have chosen politics as the matter of my book.
Were I either the one or the other I should not waste my time in laying down what has to be done. I should do it, or else hold my peace.

I was born into a free state and am a member of its sovereign   2
body. My influence on public affairs may be small, but because I have
a right to exercise my vote, it is my duty to learn their nature, and it
has been for me a matter of constant delight, while mediating on
problems of Government in general, to find ever fresh reasons for re-

garding with true affection the way in which these things are ordered in my native land.

The Subject of the First Book

Man is born free, and everywhere he is in chains. Many a man 3 believes himself to be the master of others who is, no less than they, a slave. How did this change take place? I do not know. What can make it legitimate? To this question I hope to be able to furnish an answer.

Were I considering only force and the effects of force, I should 4 say: "So long as a People is constrained to obey, and does, in fact, obey, it does well. So soon as it can shake off its yoke, and succeeds in doing so, it does better. The fact that it has recovered its liberty by virtue of that same right by which it was stolen, means either that it is entitled to resume it, or that its theft by others was, in the first place, without justification." But the social order is a sacred right which serves as a foundation for all other rights. This right, however, since it comes not by nature, must have been built upon conventions. To discover what these conventions are is the matter of our inquiry. But, before proceeding further, I must establish the truth of what I have so far advanced.

Of Primitive Societies

The oldest form of society — and the only natural one — is the 5 family. Children remain bound to their father for only just so long as they feel the need of him for their self-preservation. Once that need ceases the natural bond is dissolved. From then on, the children, freed from the obedience which they formerly owed, and the father, cleared of his debt of responsibility to them, return to a condition of equal independence. If the bond remain operative it is no longer something imposed by nature, but has become a matter of deliberate choice. The family is a family still, but by reason of convention only.

This shared liberty is a consequence of man's nature. Its first law 6 is that of self-preservation: its first concern is for what it owes itself. As soon as a man attains the age of reason he becomes his own master, because he alone can judge of what will best assure his continued existence.

We may, therefore, if we will, regard the family as the basic model 7 of all political associations. The ruler is the father writ large: the people are, by analogy, his children, and all, ruler and people alike, alienate their freedom only so far as it is to their advantage to do so. The only difference is that, whereas in the family the father's love for his children is sufficient reward to him for the care he has lavished on them, in the State, the pleasure of commanding others takes its place, since the ruler is not in a relation of love to his people.

Grotius[1] denies that political power is ever exercised in the in- 8 terests of the governed, and quotes the institution of slavery in support of his contention. His invariable method of arguing is to derive Right from Fact. It might be possible to adopt a more logical system of reasoning, but none which would be more favorable to tyrants.

According to Grotius, therefore, it is doubtful whether the term 9 "human race" belongs to only a few hundred men, or whether those few hundred men belong to the human race. From the evidence of his book it seems clear that he holds by the first of these alternatives, and on this point Hobbes[2] is in agreement with him. If this is so, then humanity is divided into herds of livestock, each with its "guardian" who watches over his changes only that he may ultimately devour them.

Just as the shepherd is superior in kind to his sheep, so, too, the 10 shepherds of men, or, in other words, their rulers, are superior in kind to their peoples. This, according to Philo,[3] was the argument advanced by Caligula,[4] the Emperor, who drew from the analogy the perfectly true conclusion that either Kings are Gods or their subjects brute beasts.

The reasoning of Caligula, of Hobbes, and of Grotius is funda- 11 mentally the same. Far earlier, Aristotle, too, had maintained that men are not by nature equal, but that some are born to be slaves, others to be masters.

Aristotle[5] was right: but he mistook the effect for the cause. 12 Nothing is more certain than that a man born into a condition of

---

[1] **Hugo Grotius (1583 – 1645)** A Dutch lawyer who spent some time in exile in Paris. His fame as a child prodigy was considerable; his book on the laws of war (*De jure belli ac Pacis*) was widely known in Europe.

[2] **Thomas Hobbes (1588 – 1679)** Known as a materialist philosopher who did not credit divine influence in politics. An Englishman, he became famous for *Leviathan*, a study of politics that treated the state as if it were a monster (leviathan) with a life of its own.

[3] **Philo (13? B.C. – 47? A.D.)** A Jew who had absorbed Greek culture and who wrote widely on many subjects. His studies on Mosaic Law were considered important.

[4] **Caligula (12 – 41 A.D.)** Roman emperor of uncertain sanity. He loved his sister Drusilla so much that he had her deified when she died. A military commander, he was assassinated by an officer.

[5] **Aristotle (384 – 322 B.C.)** A student of Plato; his philosophical method became the dominant intellectual force in Western thought.

slavery is a slave by nature. A slave in fetters loses everything — even the desire to be freed from them. He grows to love his slavery, as the companions of Ulysses grew to love their state of brutish transformation.[6]

If some men are by nature slaves, the reason is that they have been made slaves *against* nature. Force made the first slaves: cowardice has perpetuated the species.   13

I have made no mention of King Adam or of the Emperor Noah, the father of three great Monarchs[7] who divided up the universe between them, as did the children of Saturn,[8] whom some have been tempted to identify with them. I trust that I may be given credit for my moderation, since, being descended in a direct line from one of these Princes, and quite possibly belonging to the elder branch, I may, for all I know, were my claims supported in law, be even now the legitimate Sovereign of the Human Race.[9] However that may be, all will concur in the view that Adam was King of the World, as was Robinson Crusoe of his island, only so long as he was its only inhabitant, and the great advantage of empire held on such terms was that the Monarch, firmly seated on his throne, had no need to fear rebellions, conspiracy, or war.   14

Of the Right of the Strongest

However strong a man, he is never strong enough to remain master always, unless he transform his Might into Right, and Obedience into Duty. Hence we have come to speak of the Right of the Strongest, a right which, seemingly assumed in irony, has, in fact, become established in principle. But the meaning of the phrase has never been adequately explained. Strength is a physical attribute,   15

---

[6] **state of brutish transformation** This sentence refers to the Circe episode in Homer's *Odyssey* (X, XII). Circe was a sorceress who, by means of drugs, enchanted men and turned them into swine. Ulysses (Latin name of Odysseus), king of Ithaca, is the central figure of the *Odyssey*.

[7] **the father of three great Monarchs** Adam in the Bible (Genesis 4:1 – 25) fathered Cain, Abel, Enoch, and Seth. Noah's sons, Shem, Ham, and Japheth, repopulated the world after the Flood (Genesis 6:9 – 9:19).

[8] **children of Saturn** Saturn is a mythic god associated with the golden age of Rome and with the Greek god Cronus. It is probably the children of Cronus — Zeus, Poseidon, Hades, Demeter, and Hera — referred to here, since the Roman god, Saturn, had only one son, Picus.

[9] **Sovereign of the Human Race** Rousseau is being ironic, of course; like the rest of us, he is descended from Adam.

and I fail to see how any moral sanction can attach to its effects. To yield to the strong is an act of necessity, not of will. At most it is the result of a dictate of prudence. How, then, can it become a duty?

Let us assume for a moment that some such Right does really   16
exist. The only deduction from this premise is inexplicable gibberish. For to admit that Might makes Right is to reverse the process of effect and cause. The mighty man who defeats his rival becomes heir to his Right. So soon as we can disobey with impunity, disobedience becomes legitimate. And, since the Mightiest is always right, it merely remains for us to become possessed of Might. But what validity can there be in a Right which ceases to exist when Might changes hands? If a man be constrained by Might to obey, what need has he to obey by Duty? And if he is not constrained to obey, there is no further obligation on him to do so. It follows, therefore, that the word Right adds nothing to the idea of Might. It becomes, in this connection, completely meaningless.

Obey the Powers that be. If that means Yield to Force, the pre-   17
cept is admirable but redundant. My reply to those who advance it is that no case will ever be found of its violation. All power comes from God. Certainly, but so do all ailments. Are we to conclude from such an argument that we are never to call in the doctor? If I am waylaid by a footpad at the corner of a wood, I am constrained by force to give him my purse. But if I can manage to keep it from him, is it my duty to hand it over? His pistol is also a symbol of Power. It must, then, be admitted that Might does not create Right, and that no man is under an obligation to obey any but the legitimate powers of the State. And so I continually come back to the question I first asked.

Of Slavery

Since no man has natural authority over his fellows, and since   18
Might can produce no Right, the only foundation left for legitimate authority in human societies is Agreement.

If a private citizen, says Grotius, can alienate his liberty and   19
make himself another man's slave, why should not a whole people do the same, and subject themselves to the will of a King? The argument contains a number of ambiguous words which stand in need of explanation. But let us confine our attention to one only — *alienate*. To alienate means to give or to sell. Now a man who becomes the slave of another does not give himself. He sells himself in return for bare subsistence, if for nothing more. But why should a whole people sell themselves? So far from furnishing subsistence to his

subjects, a King draws his own from them, and from them alone. According to Rabelais,[10] it takes a lot to keep a King. Do we, then, maintain that a subject surrenders his person on condition that his property be taken too? It is difficult to see what he will have left.

It will be said that the despot guarantees civil peace to his sub-   20 jects. So be it. But how are they the gainers if the wars to which his ambition may expose them, his insatiable greed, and the vexatious demands of his Ministers cause them more loss than would any outbreak of internal dissension? How do they benefit if that very condition of civil peace be one of the causes of their wretchedness? One can live peacefully enough in a dungeon, but such peace will hardly, of itself, ensure one's happiness. The Greeks imprisoned in the cave of Cyclops[11] lived peacefully while awaiting their turn to be devoured.

To say that a man gives himself for nothing is to commit oneself   21 to an absurd and inconceivable statement. Such an act of surrender is illegitimate, null, and void by the mere fact that he who makes it is not in his right mind. To say the same thing of a whole People is tantamount to admitting that the People in question are a nation of imbeciles. Imbecility does not produce Right.

Even if a man can alienate himself, he cannot alienate his chil-   22 dren. They are born free, their liberty belongs to them, and no one but themselves has a right to dispose of it. Before they have attained the age of reason their father may make, on their behalf, certain rules with a view to ensuring their preservation and well-being. But any such limitation of their freedom of choice must be regarded as neither irrevocable nor unconditional, for to alienate another's liberty is contrary to the natural order, and is an abuse of the father's rights. It follows that an arbitrary government can be legitimate only on condition that each successive generation of subjects is free either to accept or to reject it, and if this is so, then the government will no longer be arbitrary.

When a man renounces his liberty he renounces his essential   23 manhood, his rights, and even his duty as a human being. There is no compensation possible for such complete renunciation. It is incompatible with man's nature, and to deprive him of his free will is to deprive his actions of all moral sanction. The convention, in short, which sets up on one side an absolute authority, and on the

---

[10] **François Rabelais (c. 1494 – 1553)** French writer, author of *Gargantua* and *Pantagruel*, satires on politics and religion.
[11] **cave of Cyclops** The cyclops is a one-eyed giant cannibal whose cave is the scene of one of Odysseus's triumphs in Homer's *Odyssey* (IX).

other an obligation to obey without question, is vain and meaningless. Is it not obvious that where we can demand everything we owe nothing? Where there is no mutual obligation, no interchange of duties, it must, surely, be clear that the actions of the commanded cease to have any moral value? For how can it be maintained that my slave has any "right" against me when everything that he has is my property? His right being *my* right, it is absurd to speak of it as ever operating to my disadvantage.

Grotius, and those who think like him, have found in the fact of 24 war another justification for the so-called "right" of slavery. They argue that since the victor has a *right* to kill his defeated enemy, the latter may, if he so wish, ransom his life at the expense of his liberty, and that this compact is the more legitimate in that it benefits both parties.

But it is evident that this alleged *right* of a man to kill his ene- 25 mies is not in any way a derivative of the state of war, if only because men, in their primitive condition of independence, are not bound to one another by any relationship sufficiently stable to produce a state either of war or of peace. They are not *naturally* enemies. It is the link between *things* rather than between *men* that constitutes war, and since a state of war cannot originate in simple personal relations, but only in relations between things, private hostility between man and man cannot obtain either in a state of nature where there is no generally accepted system of private property, or in a state of society where law is the supreme authority.

Single combats, duels, personal encounters are incidents which 26 do not constitute a "state" of anything. As to those private wars which were authorized by the Ordinances of King Louis IX[12] and suspended by the Peace of God, they were merely an abuse of Feudalism — that most absurd of all systems of government, so contrary was it to the principles of Natural Right and of all good polity.

War, therefore, is something that occurs not between man and 27 man, but between States. The individuals who become involved in it are enemies only by accident. They fight not as men or even as citizens, but as soldiers: not as members of this or that national group, but as its defenders. A State can have as its enemies only other States, not men at all, seeing that there can be no true relationship between things of a different nature.

---

[12] **King Louis IX (1214–1270)** King of France, also called St. Louis. He was looked upon as an ideal monarch.

This principle is in harmony with that of all periods, and with   28
the constant practice of every civilized society. A declaration of war
is a warning, not so much to Governments as to their subjects. The
foreigner — whether king, private person, or nation as a whole —
who steals, murders, or holds in durance the subjects of another
country without first declaring war on that country's Prince, acts not
as an enemy but as a brigand. Even when war has been joined, the
just Prince, though he may seize all public property in enemy territory, yet respects the property and possessions of individuals, and,
in so doing, shows his concern for those rights on which his own
laws are based. The object of war being the destruction of the enemy
State, a commander has a perfect right to kill its defenders so long as
their arms are in their hands: but once they have laid them down
and have submitted, they cease to be enemies, or instruments employed by an enemy, and revert to the condition of men, pure and
simple, over whose lives no one can any longer exercise a rightful
claim. Sometimes it is possible to destroy a State without killing any
of its subjects, and nothing in war can be claimed as a right save
what may be necessary for the accomplishment of the victor's end.
These principles are not those of Grotius, nor are they based on the
authority of poets, but derive from the Nature of Things, and are
founded upon Reason.

The Right of Conquest finds its sole sanction in the Law of the   29
Strongest. If war does not give to the victor the right to massacre his
defeated enemies, he cannot base upon a nonexistent right any claim
to the further one of enslaving them. We have the right to kill our
enemies only when we cannot enslave them. It follows, therefore,
that the right to enslave cannot be deduced from the right to kill,
and that we are guilty of enforcing an iniquitous exchange if we
make a vanquished foeman purchase with his liberty that life over
which we have no right. Is it not obvious that once we begin basing
the right of life and death on the right to enslave, and the right to
enslave on the right of life and death, we are caught in a vicious circle? Even if we assume the existence of this terrible right to kill all
and sundry, I still maintain that a man enslaved, or a People conquered, in war is under no obligation to obey beyond the point at
which force ceases to be operative. If the victor spares the life of his
defeated opponent in return for an equivalent, he cannot be said to
have shown him mercy. In either case he destroys him, but in the
latter case he derives value from his act, while in the former he gains
nothing. His authority, however, rests on no basis but that of force.
There is still a state of war between the two men, and it conditions
the whole relationship in which they stand to one another. The en-

joyment of the Rights of War presupposes that there has been no treaty of Peace. Conqueror and conquered have, to be sure, entered into a compact, but such a compact, far from liquidating the state of war, assumes its continuance.

Thus, in whatever way we look at the matter, the "Right" to en-   30
slave has no existence, not only because it is without legal validity, but because the very term is absurd and meaningless. The words *Slavery* and *Right* are contradictory and mutually exclusive. Whether we be considering the relation of one man to another man, or of an individual to a whole People, it is equally idiotic to say — "You and I have made a compact which represents nothing but loss to you and gain to me. I shall observe it so long as it pleases me to do so — and so shall you, until I cease to find it convenient."

That We Must Always Go Back to an Original Compact

Even were I to grant all that I have so far refuted, the champions   31
of despotism would not be one whit the better off. There will always be a vast difference between subduing a mob and governing a social group. No matter how many isolated individuals may submit to the enforced control of a single conqueror, the resulting relationship will ever be that of Master and Slave, never of People and Ruler. The body of men so controlled may be an agglomeration; it is not an association. It implies neither public welfare nor a body politic. An individual may conquer half the world, but he is still only an individual. His interests, wholly different from those of his subjects, are private to himself. When he dies his empire is left scattered and disintegrated. He is like an oak which crumbles and collapses in ashes so soon as the fire consumes it.

"A People," says Grotius, "may give themselves to a king." His ar-   32
gument implies that the said People were already a People before this act of surrender. The very act of gift was that of a political group and presupposed deliberation. Before, therefore, we consider the act by which a People chooses their king, it were well if we considered the act by which a People is constituted as such. For it necessarily precedes the other, and is the true foundation on which all Societies rest.

Had there been no original compact, why, unless the choice   33
were unanimous, should the minority ever have agreed to accept the decision of the majority? What right have the hundred who desire a master to vote for the ten who do not? The institution of the franchise is, in itself, a form of compact, and assumes that, at least once in its operation, complete unanimity existed.

Of the Social Pact

I assume, for the sake of argument, that a point was reached in   34
the history of mankind when the obstacles to continuing in a state of
Nature were stronger than the forces which each individual could
employ to the end of continuing in it. The original state of Nature,
therefore, could no longer endure, and the human race would have
perished had it not changed its manner of existence.

Now, since men can by no means engender new powers, but can   35
only unite and control those of which they are already possessed,
there is no way in which they can maintain themselves save by coming
together and pooling their strength in a way that will enable them to
withstand any resistance exerted upon them from without. They must
develop some sort of central direction and learn to act in concert.

Such a concentration of powers can be brought about only as   36
the consequence of an agreement reached between individuals. But
the self-preservation of each single man derives primarily from his
own strength and from his own freedom. How, then, can he limit
these without, at the same time, doing himself an injury and neglecting that care which it is his duty to devote to his own concerns?
This difficulty, in so far as it is relevant to my subject, can be expressed as follows:

"Some form of association must be found as a result of which   37
the whole strength of the community will be enlisted for the protection of the person and property of each constituent member, in such
a way that each, when united to his fellows, renders obedience to his
own will, and remains as free as he was before." That is the basic
problem of which the Social Contract provides the solution.

The clauses of this Contract are determined by the Act of Asso-   38
ciation in such a way that the least modification must render them
null and void. Even though they may never have been formally
enunciated, they must be everywhere the same, and everywhere tac-
itly admitted and recognized. So completely must this be the case
that, should the social compact be violated, each associated individual would at once resume all the rights which once were his, and re-
gain his natural liberty, by the mere fact of losing the agreed liberty
for which he renounced it.

It must be clearly understood that the clauses in question can be   39
reduced, in the last analysis, to one only, to wit, the complete alienation by each associate member to the community of *all his rights*.
For, in the first place, since each has made surrender of himself
without reservation, the resultant conditions are the same for all:
and, because they are the same for all, it is in the interest of none to
make them onerous to his fellows.

Furthermore, this alienation having been made unreservedly,   40
the union of individuals is as perfect as it well can be, none of the
associated members having any claim against the community. For
should there be any rights left to individuals, and no common authority be empowered to pronounce as between them and the public, then each, being in some things his own judge, would soon
claim to be so in all. Were that so, a state of Nature would still remain in being, the conditions of association becoming either
despotic or ineffective.

In short, whoso gives himself to all gives himself to none. And,   41
since there is no member of the social group over whom we do not
acquire precisely the same rights as those over ourselves which we
have surrendered to him, it follows that we gain the exact equivalent
of what we lose, as well as an added power to conserve what we already have.

If, then, we take from the social pact everything which is not es-   42
sential to it, we shall find it to be reduced to the following terms:
"each of us contributes to the group his person and the powers
which he wields as a person under the supreme direction of the general will, and we receive into the body politic each individual as
forming an indivisible part of the whole."

As soon as the act of association becomes a reality, it substitutes   43
for the person of each of the contracting parties a moral and collective body made up of as many members as the constituting assembly
has votes, which body receives from this very act of constitution its
unity, its dispersed *self,* and its will. The public person thus formed
by the union of individuals was known in the old days as a *City,* but
now as the *Republic* or *Body Politic.* This, when it fulfils a passive
role, is known by its members as *The State,* when an active one, as
The Sovereign People, and, in contrast to other similar bodies, as a
Power. In respect of the constituent associates, it enjoys the collective name of *The People,* the individuals who compose it being
known as *Citizens* in so far as they share in the sovereign authority,
as *Subjects* in so far as they owe obedience to the laws of the State.
But these different terms frequently overlap, and are used indiscriminately one for the other. It is enough that we should realize the difference between them when they are employed in a precise sense.

Of the Sovereign

It is clear from the above formula that the act of association im-   44
plies a mutual undertaking between the body politic and its constituent members. Each individual comprising the former contracts,

so to speak, with himself and has a twofold function. As a member of the sovereign people he owes a duty to each of his neighbors, and, as a Citizen, to the sovereign people as a whole. But we cannot here apply that maxim of Civil Law according to which no man can be held to an undertaking entered into with himself, because there is a great difference between a man's duty to himself and to a whole of which he forms a part.

Here it should be pointed out that a public decision which can   45
enjoin obedience on all subjects to their Sovereign, by reason of the double aspect under which each is seen, cannot, on the contrary, bind the sovereign in his dealings with himself. Consequently, it is against the nature of the body politic that the sovereign should impose upon himself a law which he cannot infringe. For, since he can regard himself under one aspect only, he is in the position of an individual entering into a contract with himself. Whence it follows that there is not, nor can be, any fundamental law which is obligatory for the whole body of the People, not even the social contract itself. This does not mean that the body politic is unable to enter into engagements with some other Power, provided always that such engagements do not derogate from the nature of the Contract; for the relation of the body politic to a foreign Power is that of a simple individual.

But the body politic, or Sovereign, in that it derives its being   46
simply and solely from the sanctity of the said Contract, can never bind itself, even in its relations with a foreign Power, by any decision which might derogate from the validity of the original act. It may not, for instance, alienate any portion of itself, nor make submission to any other sovereign. To violate the act by reason of which it exists would be tantamount to destroying itself, and that which is nothing can produce nothing.

As soon as a mob has become united into a body politic, any at-   47
tack upon one of its members is an attack upon itself. Still more important is the fact that, should any offense be committed against the body politic as a whole, the effect must be felt by each of its members. Both duty and interest, therefore, oblige the two contracting parties to render one another mutual assistance. The same individuals should seek to unite under this double aspect all the advantages which flow from it.

Now, the Sovereign People, having no existence, outside that of   48
the individuals who compose it, has, and can have, no interest at variance with theirs. Consequently, the sovereign power need give no guarantee to its subjects, since it is impossible that the body should wish to injure all its members, nor, as we shall see later, can it injure any single individual. The Sovereign, by merely existing, is always what it should be.

But the same does not hold true of the relation of subject to sov-   49
ereign. In spite of common interest, there can be no guarantee that
the subject will observe his duty to the sovereign unless means are
found to ensure his loyalty.

Each individual, indeed, may, as a man, exercise a will at vari-   50
ance with, or different from, that general will to which, as citizen, he
contributes. His personal interest may dictate a line of action quite
other than that demanded by the interest of all. The fact that his
own existence as an individual has an absolute value, and that he is,
by nature, an independent being, may lead him to conclude that
what he owes to the common cause is something that he renders of
his own free will; and he may decide that by leaving the debt unpaid
he does less harm to his fellows than he would to himself should he
make the necessary surrender. Regarding the moral entity constituting the State as a rational abstraction because it is not a man, he
might enjoy his rights as a citizen without, at the same time, fulfill-
ing his duties as a subject, and the resultant injustice might grow
until it brought ruin upon the whole body politic.

In order, then, that the social compact may not be but a vain   51
formula, it must contain, though unexpressed, the single undertaking which can alone give force to the whole, namely, that whoever
shall refuse to obey the general will must be constrained by the
whole body of his fellow citizens to do so: which is no more than to
say that it may be necessary to compel a man to be free — freedom
being that condition which, by giving each citizen to his country,
guarantees him from all personal dependence and is the foundation
upon which the whole political machine rests, and supplies the
power which works it. Only the recognition by the individual of the
rights of the community can give legal force to undertakings entered
into between citizens, which, otherwise, would become absurd,
tyrannical, and exposed to vast abuses.

Of the Civil State

The passage from the state of nature to the civil state produces a   52
truly remarkable change in the individual. It substitutes justice for
instinct in his behavior, and gives to his actions a moral basis which
formerly was lacking. Only when the voice of duty replaces physical
impulse and when right replaces the cravings of appetite does the
man who, till then, was concerned solely with himself, realize that
he is under compulsion to obey quite different principles, and that
he must now consult his reason and not merely respond to the

promptings of desire. Although he may find himself deprived of many advantages which were his in a state of nature, he will recognize that he has gained others which are of far greater value. By dint of being exercised, his faculties will develop, his ideas take on a wider scope, his sentiments become ennobled, and his whole soul be so elevated, that, but for the fact that misuse of the new conditions still, at times, degrades him to a point below that from which he has emerged, he would unceasingly bless the day which freed him for ever from his ancient state, and turned him from a limited and stupid animal into an intelligent being and a Man.

Let us reduce all this to terms which can be easily compared. 53 What a man loses as a result of the Social Contract is his natural liberty and his unqualified right to lay hands on all that tempts him, provided only that he can compass its possession. What he gains is civil liberty and the ownership of what belongs to him. That we may labor under no illusion concerning these compensations, it is well that we distinguish between natural liberty which the individual enjoys so long as he is strong enough to maintain it, and civil liberty which is curtailed by the general will. Between possessions which derive from physical strength and the right of the first-comer, and ownership which can be based only on a positive title.

To the benefits conferred by the status of citizenship might be 54 added that of Moral Freedom, which alone makes a man his own master. For to be subject to appetite is to be a slave, while to obey the laws laid down by society is to be free. But I have already said enough on this point, and am not concerned here with the philosophical meaning of the word *liberty*.

Of Real Property

Each individual member of the Community gives himself to it at 55 the moment of its formation. What he gives is the whole man as he then is, with all his qualities of strength and power, and everything of which he stands possessed. Not that, as a result of this act of gift, such possessions, by changing hands and becoming the property of the Sovereign, change their nature. Just as the resources of strength upon which the City can draw are incomparably greater than those at the disposition of any single individual, so, too, is public possession when backed by a greater power. It is made more irrevocable, though not, so far, at least, as regards foreigners, more legitimate. For the State, by reason of the Social Contract which, within it, is the basis of all Rights, is the master of all its members' goods, though, in its dealings with other Powers, it is so only by virtue of its rights as first occupier, which come to it from the individuals who make it up.

The Right of "first occupancy," though more real than the "Right 56 of the strongest," becomes a genuine right only after the right of property has been established. All men have a natural right to what is necessary to them. But the positive act which establishes a man's claim to any particular item of property limits him to that and excludes him from all others. His share having been determined, he must confine himself to that, and no longer has any claim on the property of the community. That is why the right of "first occupancy," however weak it be in a state of nature, is guaranteed to every man enjoying the status of citizen. In so far as he benefits from this right, he withholds his claim, not so much from what is another's, as from what is not specifically his.

In order that the right of "first occupancy" may be legalized, the 57 following conditions must be present. (1) There must be no one already living on the land in question. (2) A man must occupy only so much of it as is necessary for his subsistence. (3) He must take possession of it, not by empty ceremony, but by virtue of his intention to work and to cultivate it, for that, in the absence of legal title, alone constitutes a claim which will be respected by others.

In effect, by according the right of "first occupancy" to a man's 58 needs and to his will to work, are we not stretching it as far as it will go? Should not some limits be set to this right? Has a man only to set foot on land belonging to the community to justify his claim to be its master? Just because he is strong enough, at one particular moment, to keep others off, can he demand that they shall never return? How can a man or a People take possession of vast territories, thereby excluding the rest of the world from their enjoyment, save by an act of criminal usurpation, since, as the result of such an act, the rest of humanity is deprived of the amenities of dwelling and subsistence which nature has provided for their common enjoyment? When Nuñez Balboa,[13] landing upon a strip of coast, claimed the Southern Sea and the whole of South America as the property of the crown of Castille, was he thereby justified in dispossessing its former inhabitants, and in excluding from it all the other princes of the earth? Grant that, and there will be no end to such vain ceremonies. It would be open to His Catholic Majesty[14] to claim from

---

[13] **Nuñez Balboa (1475 – 1519)** Spanish explorer who discovered the Pacific Ocean.
[14] **His Catholic Majesty** A reference to the king of Spain, probably Ferdinand II of Aragon (1452 – 1516).

his Council Chamber possession of the whole Universe, only excepting those portions of it already in the ownership of other princes.

One can understand how the lands of individuals, separate but   59
contiguous, become public territory, and how the right of sovereignty, extending from men to the land they occupy, becomes at one real and personal — a fact which makes their owners more than ever dependent, and turns their very strength into a guarantee of their fidelity. This is an advantage which does not seem to have been considered by the monarchs of the ancient world, who, claiming to be no more than kings of the Persians, the Scythians, the Macedonians, seem to have regarded themselves rather as the rulers of men than as the masters of countries. Those of our day are cleverer, for they style themselves kings of France, of Spain, of England, and so forth. Thus, by controlling the land, they can be very sure of controlling its inhabitants.

The strange thing about this act of alienation is that, far from   60
depriving its members of their property by accepting its surrender, the Community actually establishes their claim to its legitimate ownership, and changes what was formerly mere usurpation into a right, by virtue of which they may enjoy possession. As owners they are Trustees for the Commonwealth. Their rights are respected by their fellow citizens and are maintained by the united strength of the community against any outside attack. From ceding their property to the State — and thus, to themselves — they derive nothing but advantage, since they have, so to speak, acquired all that they have surrendered. This paradox is easily explained once we realize the distinction between the rights exercised by the Sovereign and by the Owner over the same piece of property, as will be seen later.

It may so happen that a number of men begin to group them-   61
selves into a community before ever they own property at all, and that only later, when they have got possession of land sufficient to maintain them all, do they either enjoy it in common or parcel it between themselves in equal lots or in accordance with such scale of proportion as may be established by the sovereign. However this acquisition be made, the right exercised by each individual over his own particular share must always be subordinated to the overriding claim of the Community as such. Otherwise there would be no strength in the social bond, nor any real power in the exercise of sovereignty.

I will conclude this chapter, and the present Book, with a re-   62
mark which should serve as basis for every social system: that, so far from destroying natural equality, the primitive compact substitutes for it a moral and legal equality which compensates for all those physical inequalities from which men suffer. However unequal they

may be in bodily strength or in intellectual gifts, they become equal in the eyes of the law, and as a result of the compact into which they have entered.

QUESTIONS FOR CRITICAL READING

1. Examine Rousseau's analogy of the family as the oldest and only natural form of government. Do you agree that the analogy is useful and that its contentions are true? Which aspects of this natural form of government do not work to help us understand the basis of government?
2. Rousseau seems to accept the family as a patriarchal structure. How would his views change if he accepted it as a matriarchal structure? How would they change if he regarded each member of the family as absolutely equal in authority from birth?
3. What does it mean to reason from what is fact instead of from what is morally right?
4. What features of Rousseau's social contract are like those of a legal contract? How does one contract to be part of society?
5. What distinctions can be made between natural, moral, and legal equality? Which kind of equality is most important to a social system?

SUGGESTIONS FOR WRITING

1. When Rousseau wrote "Man is born free, and everywhere he is in chains," the institution of slavery was widely practiced and justified by many authorities. Today slavery has been generally abolished. How is this statement relevant to people's condition in society now? What are some ways in which people relinquish their independence or freedom?
2. Clarify the difference between your duty to yourself and your duty to society (your social structure — personal, local, national). Establish your duties in relation to each structure. How can these duties conflict with one another? How does the individual resolve the conflicts?
3. Do you agree with Rousseau when he says, "All men have a natural right to what is necessary to them"? What is necessary to all people, and in what sense do they have a right to what is necessary? Who should provide those necessities? Should necessities be provided for everyone or only for people who are unable to provide for themselves? If society will not provide these necessities, does the individual have the right to break the social contract by means of revolution?
4. What seems to be Rousseau's opinion regarding private property or the ownership of property? Beginning with paragraph 59, Rousseau distinguishes between monarchs with sovereignty over people and those with sovereignty over a region, such as France, Italy, or another country. What is Rousseau's view of the property that constitutes a state and

who actually owns it? He mentions that the rights of individual owners must give way to the rights of the community in general. What is your response to this view?

5. Rousseau makes an important distinction between natural liberty and civil liberty. People in a state of nature enjoy natural liberty, and when they bind themselves together into a body politic, they enjoy civil liberty. What are the differences? Define each kind of liberty as carefully as you can, and take a stand on whether you feel civil liberty or natural liberty is superior. How is the conflict between the two forms of liberty felt today?

6. **CONNECTIONS**   Rousseau's thinking emphasizes the role played by the common people in any civil society. How does that emphasis compare with Machiavelli's thinking? Consider the attitudes each writer has toward the essential goodness of people and the essential responsibilities of the monarch or government leader. In what ways is Lao-tzu closer in thinking to Rousseau or Machiavelli?

THOMAS JEFFERSON
The Declaration of Independence

THOMAS JEFFERSON (1723–1826) authored one of the most memorable statements in American history: the Declaration of Independence. He composed the work in 1776 under the watchful eyes of Benjamin Franklin, John Adams, and the rest of the Continental Congress, which spent two and a half days going over every word. Although the substance of the document was developed in committee, Jefferson, because of the grace of his writing style, was selected to craft the actual wording.

Jefferson rose to eminence in a time of great political upheaval. By the time he took a seat in the Virginia legislature in 1769, the colony was already on the course toward revolution. His pamphlet "A Summary View of the Rights of British America" (1774) brought him to the attention of those who were agitating for independence and established him as an ardent republican and revolutionary. In 1779 he was elected governor of Virginia. After the Revolutionary War he moved into the national political arena as the first secretary of state (1790–1793). He then served as Adams's vice president (1797–1801) and was himself elected president in 1801. Perhaps one of his greatest achievements during his two terms in office was his negotiation of the Louisiana Purchase, in which the United States acquired 828,000 square miles of land west of the Mississippi from France for about $15 million.

One of the fundamental paradoxes of Jefferson's personal and political life has been his attitude toward slavery. Like most wealthy Virginians, Jefferson owned slaves. However, in 1784 he tried to abolish slavery in the western territories that were being added to the United States. His "Report on Government for the Western Territory" failed by one vote. Some historians have also speculated that Jefferson had an affair with Sally Hemmings, a mulatto slave who traveled with him abroad, and fathered several of her children.

However unclear his personal convictions, many of Jefferson's accomplishments, which extend from politics to agriculture and mechanical invention, still stand. One of the most versatile Americans of any generation, he wrote a book, *Notes on Virginia* (1782), designed and built Monticello, his famous homestead in Virginia, and in large part founded and designed the University of Virginia (1819).

Despite their revolutionary nature, the ideas Jefferson expressed in the Declaration of Independence were not entirely original. Rousseau's republican philosophies greatly influenced the work. When Jefferson states in the second paragraph that "all men are created equal, that they are endowed by their Creator with certain unalienable rights," he reflects Rousseau's emphasis on the political equality of men and on protecting certain fundamental rights (see Rousseau beginning with paragraph 39, p. 63). Jefferson also wrote that "Governments are instituted among Men, deriving their just powers from the consent of the governed." This is one of Rousseau's primary points, although it took Jefferson to immortalize it in these words.

JEFFERSON'S RHETORIC

Jefferson's techniques include the use of the periodic sentence, which was especially typical of the age. The first sentence of the Declaration of Independence is periodic — that is, it is long and carefully balanced, and the main point comes at the end. Such sentences are not popular today, although an occasional periodic sentence can still be powerful in contemporary prose. Jefferson's first sentence says (in paraphrase): When one nation must sever its relations with a parent nation . . . and stand as an independent nation itself . . . the causes ought to be explained. Moreover, the main body of the Declaration of Independence lists the "causes" that lead to the final and most important element of the sentence. Causal analysis was a method associated with legal thought and reflects his training in eighteenth-century legal analysis. One understood things best when one understood their causes.

The periodic sentence demands certain qualities of balance and parallelism that all good writers should heed. The first sentence in paragraph 2 demonstrates both qualities. The balance is achieved by making each part of the sentence roughly the same length. The parallelism is achieved by linking words in repetition (they are in roman type in the analysis below). Note how the "truths" mentioned in the first clause are enumerated in the succession of noun clauses beginning with "that"; "Rights" are enumerated in the final clause:

> We hold these truths to be self evident,
>   *that* all men are created equal,
>   *that* they are endowed by their Creator with certain unalienable Rights,
>   *that* among these are Life, Liberty and the pursuit of Happiness.

Parallelism is one of the greatest stylistic techniques available to a writer sensitive to rhetoric. It is a natural technique: Many untrained writers and speakers develop it on their own. The periodicity of the sentences and the balance of their parallelism suggest thoughtfulness, wisdom, and control.

Parallelism creates a natural link to the useful device of enumeration, or listing. Many writers using this technique establish their purpose from the outset — "I wish to address three important issues . . ." — and then number them: "First, I want to say . . . Second . . . ," and so on. Jefferson devotes paragraphs 3 through 29 to enumerating the "causes" he mentions in paragraph 1. Each one constitutes a separate paragraph; thus, each has separate weight and importance. Each begins with "He" or "For" and is therefore in parallel structure. The technique of repetition of the same words at the beginning of successive lines is called *anaphora*. Jefferson's use of anaphora here is one of the best known and most effective in all literature. The "He" referred to is Britain's King George III (1738 – 1820), who is never mentioned by name. Congress is opposed not to a personality but to the sovereign of a nation that is oppressing the United States and a tyrant who is not dignified by being named. The "For" introduces grievous acts the king has given his assent to; these are offenses against the colonies.

However, Jefferson does not develop the causes in detail. We do not have specific information about what trade was cut off by the British, what taxes were imposed without consent, or how King George waged war or abdicated government in the colonies. Presumably, Jefferson's audience knew the details and was led by the twenty-seven paragraphs to observe how numerous the causes were. And all are serious; any one alone was enough cause for revolution. The effect of Jefferson's enumeration is to illustrate the patience of the colonies up to this point and to tell the world that the colonies have finally lost patience on account of the reasons listed. The Declaration of Independence projects the careful meditations and decisions of exceptionally calm, patient, and reasonable people.

The Declaration of Independence

In Congress, July 4, 1776

The Unanimous Declaration of the Thirteen United States of America

When in the Course of human events, it becomes necessary for 1 one people to dissolve the political bands which have connected them with another, and to assume among the Powers of the earth, the separate and equal station to which the Laws of Nature and of Nature's God entitle them, a decent respect to the opinions of mankind requires that they should declare the causes which impel them to the separation.

We hold these truths to be self-evident, that all men are created 2 equal, that they are endowed by their Creator with certain inalienable Rights, that among these are Life, Liberty and the pursuit of Happiness. That to secure these rights, Governments are instituted among Men, deriving their just powers from the consent of the governed. That whenever any Form of Government becomes destructive of these ends, it is the Right of the People to alter or to abolish it, and to institute new Government, laying its foundation on such principles and organizing its powers in such form, as to them shall seem most likely to effect their Safety and Happiness. Prudence, indeed, will dictate that Governments long established should not be changed for light and transient causes; and accordingly all experience hath shown, that mankind are more disposed to suffer, while evils are sufferable, than to right themselves by abolishing the forms to which they are accustomed. But when a long train of abuses and usurpations, pursuing invariably the same Object evinces a design to reduce them under absolute Despotism, it is their right, it is their duty, to throw off such Government, and to provide new Guards for their future security. — Such has been the patient sufferance of these Colonies; and such is now the necessity which constrains them to alter their former Systems of Government. The history of the present King of Great Britain is a history of repeated injuries and usurpations, all having in direct object the establishment of an absolute Tyranny over these States. To prove this, let Facts be submitted to a candid world.

He has refused his Assent to Laws, the most wholesome and 3 necessary for the public good.

He has forbidden his Governors to pass Laws of immediate and 4 pressing importance, unless suspended in their operation till his Assent should be obtained; and when so suspended, he has utterly neglected to attend to them.

He has refused to pass other laws for the accommodation of 5 large districts of people, unless those people would relinquish the right of Representation in the Legislature, a right inestimable to them and formidable to tyrants only.

He has called together legislative bodies at places unusual, un- 6 comfortable, and distant from the depository of their Public Records, for the sole purpose of fatiguing them into compliance with his measures.

He has dissolved Representative Houses repeatedly, for oppos- 7 ing with manly firmness his invasions on the rights of the people.

He has refused for a long time, after such dissolutions, to cause 8 others to be elected; whereby the Legislative Powers, incapable of Annihilation, have returned to the People at large for their exercise; the State remaining in the mean time exposed to all the dangers of invasion from without, and convulsions within.

He has endeavoured to prevent the population of these States;[1] 9 for that purpose obstructing the Laws for Naturalization of Foreigners; refusing to pass others to encourage their migration hither, and raising the conditions of new Appropriations of Lands.

He has obstructed the Administration of Justice, by refusing his 10 Assent to Laws for establishing Judiciary Powers.

He has made Judges dependent on his Will alone, for the tenure 11 of their offices, and the amount and payment of their salaries.

He has erected a multitude of New Offices, and sent hither 12 swarms of Officers to harass our People, and eat out their substance.

He has kept among us, in times of peace, Standing Armies with- 13 out the Consent of our legislature.

He has affected to render the Military independent of and supe- 14 rior to the Civil Power.

He has combined with others to subject us to a jurisdiction for- 15 eign to our constitution, and unacknowledged by our laws; giving his Assent to their acts of pretended Legislation:

For quartering large bodies of armed troops among us: 16

For protecting them, by a mock Trial, from Punishment for any 17 Murders which they should commit on the Inhabitants of these States:

For cutting off our Trade with all parts of the world: 18

For imposing taxes on us without our Consent: 19

---

[1] **prevent the population of these States** This meant limiting emigration to the Colonies, thus controlling their growth.

For depriving us in many cases, of the benefits of Trial by Jury: 20

For transporting us beyond Seas to be tried for pretended of-   21
fences:

For abolishing the free System of English Laws in a neighbour-   22
ing Province, establishing therein an Arbitrary government, and enlarging its Boundaries so as to render it at once an example and fit
instrument for introducing the same absolute rule into these
Colonies:

For taking away our Charters, abolishing our most valuable   23
Laws, and altering fundamentally the Forms of our Governments:

For suspending our own Legislatures, and declaring themselves   24
invested with Power to legislate for us in all cases whatsoever.

He has abdicated Government here, by declaring us out of his   25
Protection and waging War against us.

He has plundered our seas, ravaged our Coasts, burnt our   26
towns, and destroyed the lives of our people.

He is at this time transporting large armies of foreign mercenar-   27
ies to compleat the works of death, desolation and tyranny, already
begun with circumstances of Cruelty & perfidy scarcely paralleled in
the most barbarous ages, and totally unworthy the Head of a civilized nation.

He has constrained our fellow Citizens taken Captive on the high   28
Seas to bear Arms against their Country, to become the executioners
of their friends and Brethren, or to fall themselves by their Hands.

He has excited domestic insurrections amongst us, and has en-   29
deavoured to bring on the inhabitants of our frontiers, the merciless
Indian Savages, whose known rule of warfare, is an undistinguished
destruction of all ages, sexes and conditions.

In every stage of these Oppressions We have Petitioned for Re-   30
dress in the most humble terms: Our repeated Petitions have been
answered only by repeated injury. A Prince, whose character is thus
marked by every act which may define a Tyrant, is unfit to be the
ruler of a free People.

Nor have We been wanting in attention to our British brethren.   31
We have warned them from time to time of attempts by their legislature to extend an unwarrantable jurisdiction over us. We have reminded them of the circumstances of our emigration and settlement
here. We have appealed to their native justice and magnanimity, and
we have conjured them by the ties of our common kindred to dis-
avow these usurpations, which, would inevitably interrupt our connections and correspondence. They too have been deaf to the voice
of justice and of consanguinity. We must, therefore, acquiesce in the
necessity, which denounces our Separation, and hold them, as we
hold the rest of mankind, Enemies in War, in Peace Friends.

We, therefore, the Representatives of the United States of America, in General Congress, Assembled, appealing to the Supreme Judge of the world for the rectitude of our intentions, do, in the Name, and by Authority of the good People of these Colonies, solemnly publish and declare, That these United Colonies are, and of Right ought to be Free and Independent States, that they are Absolved from all Allegiance to the British Crown, and that all political connection between them and the State of Great Britain, is and ought to be totally dissolved; and that as Free and Independent States, they have full Power to levy War, conclude Peace, contract Alliances, establish Commerce, and to do all other Acts and Things which Independent States may of right do. And for the support of this Declaration, with a firm reliance on the Protection of Divine Providence, we mutually pledge to each other our Lives, our Fortunes and our sacred Honor. 32

QUESTIONS FOR CRITICAL READING

1. What laws of nature does Jefferson refer to in paragraph 1?
2. What do you think Jefferson feels is the function of government (para. 2)?
3. What does Jefferson say about women? Is there any way you can determine his views from reading this document? Does he appear to favor a patriarchal system?
4. Find at least one use of parallel structure in the Declaration. What key terms are repeated in identical or equivalent constructions?
5. Which causes listed in paragraphs 3 through 29 are the most serious? Are any trivial? Which ones are serious enough to cause a revolution?
6. What do you consider to be the most graceful sentence in the entire Declaration? Where is it placed in the Declaration? What purpose does it serve there?
7. In what ways does the king's desire for stable government interfere with Jefferson's sense of his own independence?

SUGGE5TIONS FOR WRITING

1. Jefferson defines the inalienable rights of a citizen as "Life, Liberty and the pursuit of Happiness." Do you think these are indeed unalienable rights? Answer this question by including some sentences that use parallel structure and repeat key terms in similar constructions. Be certain that you define each of these rights both for yourself and for our time.

2. Write an essay discussing what you feel the function of government should be. Include at least three periodic sentences (underline them). You may first want to establish Jefferson's view of government and then compare or contrast it with your own.

3. Jefferson envisioned a government that allowed its citizens to exercise their rights to life, liberty, and the pursuit of happiness. Has Jefferson's revolutionary vision been achieved in America? Begin with a definition of these three key terms: "life," "liberty," and "the pursuit of happiness." Then, for each term use examples — drawn from current events, your own experience, American history — to take a clear and well-argued stand on whether the nation has achieved Jefferson's goal.

4. Slavery was legal in America in 1776, and Jefferson reluctantly owned slaves. He never presented his plan for gradual emancipation of the slaves to Congress because he realized that Congress would never approve it. But Jefferson and Franklin did finance a plan to buy slaves and return them to Africa, where in 1821 returning slaves founded the nation of Liberia. Agree or disagree with the following statement and defend your position: the ownership of slaves by the people who wrote the Declaration of Independence invalidates it. You may wish to read the relevant chapters on Jefferson and slavery in Merrill D. Peterson's *Thomas Jefferson and the New Nation* (1970).

5. What kind of government does Jefferson seem to prefer? In what ways would his government differ from that of the king he is reacting against? Is he talking about an entirely different system or about the same system but with a different kind of "prince" at the head? How would Jefferson protect the individual against the whim of the state, while also protecting the state against the whim of the individual?

6. **CONNECTIONS**   Write an essay in which you examine the ways that Jefferson agrees or disagrees with Lao-tzu's conception of human nature and of government. How does Jefferson share Lao-tzu's commitment to judicious inactivity? What evidence is there that the king subscribes to it? Describe the similarities and differences between Jefferson's views and those of Lao-tzu.

7. **CONNECTIONS**   What principles does Jefferson share with Jean-Jacques Rousseau? Compare the fundamental demands of the Declaration of Independence with Rousseau's conceptions of liberty and independence. How would Rousseau have reacted to this Declaration?

HANNAH ARENDT
Ideology and Terror:
A Novel Form of Government

HANNAH ARENDT (1906–1975) was born and educated in Germany, earning her doctorate from the University of Heidelberg when she was twenty-two years old. She left Germany for Paris in 1933, the year after Hitler came to power and early in the development of Nazi ideology. In New York City she worked with Jewish relief groups and in 1940 married Heinrich Bluecher, a professor of philosophy. Arendt joined the faculty of the University of Chicago in 1963 and then taught as a visiting professor at a number of universities, eventually settling at the New School for Social Research in New York.

The Origins of Totalitarianism, from which this selection is excerpted, was first published in 1951 and solidified Arendt's reputation as an important political philosopher. She began work on the book in 1945, after Nazism was defeated in Europe, and finished most of it by 1949, during the period of growing tension between the United States and Russia that began the Cold War. Much of the book analyzes the politics of ideology in fascist and communist countries. Arendt went on to write a number of other influential works, such as *The Human Condition* (1958) and *Crises of the Republic* (1972), both of which address the problems she saw connected with a decline in moral values in modern society. One of her most controversial books, *Eichmann in Jerusalem* (1963), examined Adolf Eichmann, head of the Gestapo's Jewish section, who was tried and executed in Jerusalem. She observed that the nature of Eichmann's evil was essentially banal — that his crime was going along with orders without taking the time to assess them critically.

Her last work, *The Life of the Mind,* was not completed, although two of its planned three volumes were published posthumously in 1978.

"Ideology and Terror: A Novel Form of Government" is part of one of the last chapters in *The Origins of Totalitarianism.* The first part of the book sets forth a brief history of modern anti-Semitism because the rise of totalitarianism in Germany was based in large part on Hitler's belief that the Aryan race was biologically and morally more evolved than all other races. In this selection Hannah Arendt shows how the totalitarian state derives its power from propagating a set of ideas, or ideology, such as the view that one race is superior to all others. Once that premise is accepted, she demonstrates, then any and all atrocities against people of other races can be permitted and promoted.

In two instances, describing the ideology of fascist Germany and the ideology of communist Russia, Arendt demonstrates the ways in which the uncritical acceptance of an ideology provides the core of power for totalitarian states. In the case of Germany, racism led to the theory that if some races are inferior and debased then they must be destroyed for the good of humanity — a theory that was put into brutal practice by the Nazis. Arendt shows how this view derives from a misunderstanding of Darwin's theories of the survival of the fittest (see Darwin's "Natural Selection," p. 397). In the case of communist Russia, totalitarianism depended on the "scientific" theory of history put forth by Karl Marx (see Marx's "Communist Manifesto," p. 209) that insisted on class struggle and the need of the most "progressive class" to destroy the less progressive classes. Marx was referred to as the "Darwin of history" in part because his views attempted to employ the same scientific logic as Darwin's theories of biology. According to Arendt, both the Nazi and Communist totalitarian regimes then claimed those laws of biology or history as the justification for their own brutal acts of terror.

ARENDT'S RHETORIC

Arendt's rhetorical approach is careful and thorough. However, she is not conclusively logical throughout. It is not that she is illogical but rather that she avoids the mistakes of the ideologies she critiques. For example, she does not establish one inviolable principle as her logical premise and then argue from it relentlessly.

Instead, she offers a descriptive analysis of the forms of totalitarianism that have dominated the twentieth century. She tries to

show that the absolute acceptance of racist and classist views results in terrorism. She examines the nature of government in terms
of its normal expectations of lawfulness and claims that totalitarian
governments make their ideology the law and thereby destroy lawfulness. As she says, in most forms of government the laws tell us
what we must not do, while totalitarian governments tell us what
we must do.

Arendt's paragraphs are long and carefully developed. In each
she analyzes her terms and the circumstances she mentions. For
example, she begins paragraph 10 with "In the interpretation of totalitarianism, all laws have become laws of movement." She then
explains that Nazi ideology fastened onto a law of nature while
communism fastened onto a law of history. In both cases these
laws are "in motion" — meaning they describe a process of continuing development and change.

The concept of terror, which goes beyond simple fear, is developed by Arendt in several places. According to Arendt, terror is the
essence of the totalitarian state, and without it, the state collapses.
Individual liberty and freedom are erased by the terror of the totalitarian state, and in this sense the values that Rousseau and Jefferson argue for are irrelevant. In some states, such as the state that
Machiavelli imagined, terror might be useful for controlling the opposition. But in the totalitarian state it controls everyone. As
Arendt says, "Terror becomes total when it becomes independent
of all opposition; it rules supreme when nobody any longer stands
in its way" (para. 13).

Ideology and Terror:
A Novel Form of Government

In the preceding chapters we emphasized repeatedly that the   1
means of total domination are not only more drastic but that totalitarianism differs essentially from other forms of political oppression
known to us such as despotism, tyranny and dictatorship. Wherever
it rose to power, it developed entirely new political institutions and
destroyed all social, legal and political traditions of the country. No
matter what the specifically national tradition or the particular spiritual source of its ideology, totalitarian government always transformed classes into masses, supplanted the party system, not by
one-party dictatorships, but by a mass movement, shifted the center

of power from the army to the police, and established a foreign policy openly directed toward world domination. Present totalitarian governments have developed from one-party systems; whenever these became truly totalitarian, they started to operate according to a system of values so radically different from all others, that none of our traditional legal, moral, or common sense utilitarian categories could any longer help us to come to terms with, or judge, or predict their course of action.

If it is true that the elements of totalitarianism can be found by 2 retracing the history and analyzing the political implications of what we usually call the crisis of our century, then the conclusion is unavoidable that this crisis is no mere threat from the outside, no mere result of some aggressive foreign policy of either Germany or Russia, and that it will no more disappear with the death of Stalin than it disappeared with the fall of Nazi Germany. It may even be that the true predicaments of our time will assume their authentic form — though not necessarily the cruelest — only when totalitarianism has become a thing of the past.

It is in the line of such reflections to raise the question whether 3 totalitarian government, born of this crisis and at the same time its clearest and only unequivocal symptom, is merely a makeshift arrangement, which borrows its methods of intimidation, its means of organization and its instruments of violence from the well-known political arsenal of tyranny, despotism and dictatorships, and owes its existence only to the deplorable, but perhaps accidental failure of the traditional political forces — liberal or conservative, national or socialist, republican or monarchist, authoritarian or democratic. Or whether, on the contrary, there is such a thing as the *nature* of totalitarian government, whether it has its own essence and can be compared with and defined like other forms of government such as Western thought has known and recognized since the times of ancient philosophy. If this is true, then the entirely new and unprecedented forms of totalitarian organization and course of action must rest on one of the few basic experiences which men can have whenever they live together, and are concerned with public affairs. If there is a basic experience which finds its political expression in totalitarian domination, then, in view of the novelty of the totalitarian form of government, this must be an experience which, for whatever reason, has never before served as the foundation of a body politic and whose general mood — although it may be familiar in every other respect — never before has pervaded, and directed the handling of, public affairs.

If we consider this in terms of the history of ideas, it seems ex- 4 tremely unlikely. For the forms of government under which men live have been very few; they were discovered early, classified by the Greeks and have proved extraordinarily long-lived. If we apply these findings, whose fundamental idea, despite many variations, did not change in the two and a half thousand years that separate Plato from Kant,[1] we are tempted at once to interpret totalitarianism as some modern form of tyranny, that is a lawless government where power is wielded by one man. Arbitrary power, unrestricted by law, wielded in the interest of the ruler and hostile to the interests of the governed, on one hand, fear as the principle of action, namely fear of the people by the ruler and fear of the ruler by the people, on the other — these have been the hallmarks of tyranny throughout our tradition.

Instead of saying that totalitarian government is unprecedented,   5 we could also say that it has exploded the very alternative on which all definitions of the essence of governments have been based in political philosophy, that is the alternative between lawful and lawless government, between arbitrary and legitimate power. That lawful government and legitimate power, on one side, lawlessness and arbitrary power on the other, belonged together and were inseparable has never been questioned. Yet, totalitarian rule confronts us with a totally different kind of government. It defies, it is true, all positive laws, even to the extreme of defying those which it has itself established (as in the case of the Soviet Constitution of 1936, to quote only the most outstanding example) or which it did not care to abolish (as in the case of the Weimar Constitution which the Nazi government never revoked). But it operates neither without guidance of law nor is it arbitrary, for it claims to obey strictly and unequivocally those laws of Nature or of History from which all positive laws always have been supposed to spring.

It is the monstrous, yet seemingly unanswerable claim of totali-   6 tarian rule that, far from being "lawless," it goes to the sources of authority from which positive laws received their ultimate legitimation, that far from being arbitrary it is more obedient to these suprahuman forces than any government ever was before, and that far from wielding its power in the interest of one man, it is quite prepared to sacrifice everybody's vital immediate interests to the execution of what it assumes to be the law of History or the law of Nature. Its defiance of positive laws claims to be a higher form of legitimacy which, since it is inspired by the sources themselves, can do

---

[1] **Immanuel Kant (1724 – 1804)** Modern philosopher who some rank with Plato (p. 275). Kant suggested that individuals should live as if a universal law could be derived from their behavior. Like Plato, Kant reflected on forms of government.

away with petty legality. Totalitarian lawfulness pretends to have
found a way to establish the rule of justice on earth — something
which the legality of positive law admittedly could never attain. The
discrepancy between legality and justice could never be bridged because the standards of right and wrong into which positive law
translates its own source of authority — "natural law" governing the
whole universe, or divine law revealed in human history, or customs
and traditions expressing the law common to the sentiments of all
men — are necessarily general and must be valid for a countless and
unpredictable number of cases, so that each concrete individual case
with its unrepeatable set of circumstances somehow escapes it.

Totalitarian lawfulness, defying legality and pretending to estab-   7
lish the direct reign of justice on earth, executes the law of History
or of Nature without translating it into standards of right and wrong
for individual behavior. It applies the law directly to mankind without bothering with the behavior of men. The law of Nature or the
law of History, if properly executed, is expected to produce
mankind as its end product; and this expectation lies behind the
claim to global rule of all totalitarian governments. Totalitarian policy claims to transform the human species into an active unfailing
carrier of a law to which human beings otherwise would only passively and reluctantly be subjected. If it is true that the link between
totalitarian countries and the civilized world was broken through
the monstrous crimes of totalitarian regimes, it is also true that this
criminality was not due to simple aggressiveness, ruthlessness, warfare and treachery, but to a conscious break of that *consensus iuris*[2]
which, according to Cicero, constitutes a "people," and which, as international law, in modern times has constituted the civilized world
insofar as it remains the foundation-stone of international relations
even under the conditions of war. Both moral judgment and legal
punishment presuppose this basic consent; the criminal can be
judged justly only because he takes part in the *consensus iuris,* and
even the revealed law of God can function among men only when
they listen and consent to it.

At this point the fundamental difference between the totalitarian   8
and all other concepts of law comes to light. Totalitarian policy does
not replace one set of laws with another, does not establish its own
consensus iuris, does not create, by one revolution, a new form of legality. Its defiance of all, even its own positive laws implies that it
believes it can do without any *consensus iuris* whatever, and still not
resign itself to the tyrannical state of lawlessness, arbitrariness and

---

[2] **Consensus iuris** A general agreement about the laws that people must obey.

fear. It can do without the *consensus iuris* because it promises to release the fulfillment of law from all action and will of man; and it promises justice on earth because it claims to make mankind itself the embodiment of the law.

This identification of man and law, which seems to cancel the discrepancy between legality and justice that has plagued legal thought since ancient times, has nothing in common with the *lumen naturale*[3] or the voice of conscience, by which Nature or Divinity as the sources of authority for the *ius naturale*[4] or the historically revealed commands of God, are supposed to announce their authority in man himself. This never made man a walking embodiment of the law, but on the contrary remained distinct from him as the authority which demanded consent and obedience. Nature or Divinity as the source of authority for positive laws were thought of as permanent and eternal; positive laws were changing and changeable according to circumstances, but they possessed a relative permanence as compared with the much more rapidly changing actions of men; and they derived this permanence from the eternal presence of their source of authority. Positive laws, therefore, are primarily designed to function as stabilizing factors for the ever changing movements of men.

In the interpretation of totalitarianism, all laws have become laws of movement. When the Nazis talked about the law of nature or when the Bolsheviks talk about the law of history, neither nature nor history is any longer the stabilizing source of authority for the actions of mortal men; they are movements in themselves. Underlying the Nazis' belief in race laws as the expression of the law of nature in man, is Darwin's idea of man as the product of a natural development which does not necessarily stop with the present species of human beings, just as under the Bolsheviks' belief in class-struggle as the expression of the law of history lies Marx's notion of society as the product of a gigantic historical movement which races according to its own law of motion to the end of historical times when it will abolish itself.

The difference between Marx's historical and Darwin's naturalistic approach has frequently been pointed out, usually and rightly in favor of Marx. This has led us to forget the great and positive interest Marx took in Darwin's theories; Engels[5] could not think of a greater

---

[3] **lumen naturale** Natural light — like common sense or individual conscience — that informs the individual about how to behave.

[4] **ius naturale** Natural law, thought to be common to all people, derived from nature rather than society.

[5] **Friedrich Engels (1820 – 1895)** Collaborator with Karl Marx on the *Communist Manifesto* (1848). He was the son of a textile mill owner and used some of his fortune to help Marx write *Das Capital* (1867 – 1894). He lived most of his life in England.

compliment to Marx's scholarly achievements than to call him the "Darwin of history." If one considers, not the actual achievement, but the basic philosophies of both men, it turns out that ultimately the movement of history and the movement of nature are one and the same. Darwin's introduction of the concept of development into nature, his insistence that, at least in the field of biology, natural movement is not circular but unilinear, moving in an infinitely progressing direction, means in fact that nature is, as it were, being swept into history, that natural life is considered to be historical. The "natural" law of the survival of the fittest is just as much a historical law and could be used as such by racism as Marx's law of the survival of the most progressive class. Marx's class struggle, on the other hand, as the driving force of history is only the outward expression of the development of productive forces which in turn have their origin in the "labor-power" of men. Labor, according to Marx, is not a historical but a natural-biological force — released through man's "metabolism with nature" by which he conserves his individual life and reproduces the species. Engels saw the affinity between the basic convictions of the two men very clearly because he understood the decisive role which the concept of development played in both theories. The tremendous intellectual change which took place in the middle of the last century consisted in the refusal to view or accept anything "as it is" and in the consistent interpretation of everything as being only a stage of some further development. Whether the driving force of this development was called nature or history is relatively secondary. In these ideologies, the term "law" itself changed its meaning: from expressing the framework of stability within which human actions and motions can take place, it became the expression of the motion itself.

Totalitarian politics which proceeded to follow the recipes of 12 ideologies has unmasked the true nature of these movements insofar as it clearly showed that there could be no end to this process. If it is the law of nature to eliminate everything that is harmful and unfit to live, it would mean the end of nature itself if new categories of the harmful and unfit-to-live could not be found; if it is the law of history that in a class struggle certain classes "wither away," it would mean the end of human history itself if rudimentary new classes did not form, so that they in turn could "wither away" under the hands of totalitarian rulers. In other words, the law of killing by which totalitarian movements seize and exercise power would remain a law of the movement even if they ever succeeded in making all of humanity subject to their rule.

By lawful government we understand a body politic in which 13 positive laws are needed to translate and realize the immutable *ius naturale* or the eternal commandments of God into standards of right and wrong. Only in these standards, in the body of positive laws of each country, do the *ius naturale* or the Commandments of God achieve their political reality. In the body politic of totalitarian government, this place of positive laws is taken by total terror, which is designed to translate into reality the law of movement of history or nature. Just as positive laws, though they define transgressions, are independent of them — the absence of crimes in any society does not render laws superfluous but, on the contrary, signifies their most perfect rule — so terror in totalitarian government has ceased to be a mere means for the suppression of opposition, though it is also used for such purposes. Terror becomes total when it becomes independent of all opposition; it rules supreme when nobody any longer stands in its way. If lawfulness is the essence of non-tyrannical government and lawlessness is the essence of tyranny, then terror is the essence of totalitarian domination.

Terror is the realization of the law of movement; its chief aim is   14
to make it possible for the force of nature or of history to race freely through mankind, unhindered by any spontaneous human action. As such, terror seeks to "stabilize" men in order to liberate the forces of nature or history. It is this movement which singles out the foes of mankind against whom terror is let loose, and no free action of either opposition or sympathy can be permitted to interfere with the elimination of the "objective enemy" of History or Nature, of the class or the race. Guilt and innocence become senseless notions; "guilty" is he who stands in the way of the natural or historical process which has passed judgment over "inferior races," over individuals "unfit to live," over "dying classes and decadent peoples." Terror executes these judgments, and before its court, all concerned are subjectively innocent: the murdered because they did nothing against the system, and the murderers because they do not really murder but execute a death sentence pronounced by some higher tribunal. The rulers themselves do not claim to be just or wise, but only to execute historical or natural laws; they do not apply laws, but execute a movement in accordance with its inherent law. Terror is lawfulness, if law is the law of the movement of some suprahuman force, Nature or History.

Terror as the execution of a law of movement whose ultimate   15
goal is not the welfare of men or the interest of one man but the fabrication of mankind, eliminates individuals for the sake of the species, sacrifices the "parts" for the sake of the "whole." The suprahuman force of Nature or History has its own beginning and its own end, so that it can be hindered only by the new beginning and the individual end which the life of each man actually is.

Positive laws in constitutional government are designed to erect   16
boundaries and establish channels of communication between men
whose community is continually endangered by the new men born
into it. With each new birth, a new beginning is born into the world,
a new world has potentially come into being. The stability of the
laws corresponds to the constant motion of all human affairs, a motion which can never end as long as men are born and die. The laws
hedge in each new beginning and at the same time assure its freedom of movement, the potentiality of something entirely new and
unpredictable; the boundaries of positive laws are for the political
existence of man what memory is for his historical existence: they
guarantee the pre-existence of a common world, the reality of some
continuity which transcends the individual life span of each generation, absorbs all new origins and is nourished by them.

Total terror is so easily mistaken for a symptom of tyrannical gov-   17
ernment because totalitarian government in its initial stages must behave like a tyranny and raze the boundaries of man-made law. But
total terror leaves no arbitrary lawlessness behind it and does not rage
for the sake of some arbitrary will or for the sake of despotic power of
one man against all, least of all for the sake of a war of all against all. It
substitutes for the boundaries and channels of communication between individual men a band of iron which holds them so tightly together that it is as though their plurality had disappeared into One
Man of gigantic dimensions. To abolish the fences of laws between
men — as tyranny does — means to take away man's liberties and destroy freedom as a living political reality; for the space between men as
it is hedged in by laws, is the living space of freedom. Total terror uses
this old instrument of tyranny but destroys at the same time also the
lawless, fenceless wilderness of fear and suspicion which tyranny
leaves behind. This desert, to be sure, is no longer a living space of
freedom, but it still provides some room for the fear-guided movements and suspicion-ridden actions of its inhabitants.

By pressing men against each other, total terror destroys the   18
space between them; compared to the condition within its iron
band, even the desert of tyranny, insofar as it is still some kind of
space, appears like a guarantee of freedom. Totalitarian government
does not just curtail liberties or abolish essential freedoms; nor does
it, at least to our limited knowledge, succeed in eradicating the love
for freedom from the hearts of man. It destroys the one essential
prerequisite of all freedom which is simply the capacity of motion
which cannot exist without space.

Total terror, the essence of totalitarian government, exists neither   19
for nor against men. It is supposed to provide the forces of nature or
history with an incomparable instrument to accelerate their move-

ment. This movement, proceeding according to its own law, cannot in the long run be hindered; eventually its force will always prove more powerful than the most powerful forces engendered by the actions and the will of men. But it can be slowed down and is slowed down almost inevitably by the freedom of man, which even totalitarian rulers cannot deny, for this freedom — irrelevant and arbitrary as they may deem it — is identical with the fact that men are being born and that therefore each of them *is* a new beginning, begins, in a sense, the world anew. From the totalitarian point of view, the fact that men are born and die can be only regarded as an annoying interference with higher forces. Terror, therefore, as the obedient servant of natural or historical movement has to eliminate from the process not only freedom in any specific sense, but the very source of freedom which is given with the fact of the birth of man and resides in his capacity to make a new beginning. In the iron band of terror, which destroys the plurality of men and makes out of many the One who unfailingly will act as though he himself were part of the course of history or nature, a device has been found not only to liberate the historical and natural forces, but to accelerate them to a speed they never would reach if left to themselves. Practically speaking, this means that terror executes on the spot the death sentences which Nature is supposed to have pronounced on races or individuals who are "unfit to live," or History on "dying classes," without waiting for the slower and less efficient processes of nature or history themselves.

In this concept, where the essence of government itself has become motion, a very old problem of political thought seems to have found a solution similar to the one already noted for the discrepancy between legality and justice. If the essence of government is defined as lawfulness, and if it is understood that laws are the stabilizing forces in the public affairs of men (as indeed it always has been since Plato invoked Zeus, the god of the boundaries, in his *Laws*), then the problem of movement of the body politic and the actions of its citizens arises. Lawfulness sets limitations to actions, but does not inspire them; the greatness, but also the perplexity of laws in free societies is that they only tell what one should not, but never what one should do. The necessary movement of a body politic can never be found in its essence if only because this essence — again since Plato — has always been defined with a view to its permanence. Duration seemed one of the surest yardsticks for the goodness of a government. It is still for Montesquieu[6] the supreme proof for the badness

20

---

[6] **Baron de Montesquieu (1689 – 1755)** French legal authority. He developed the concept of the balance of powers in state government — balancing the monarch against the parliament. His most important book is *The Spirit of Laws* (1748).

of tyranny that only tyrannies are liable to be destroyed from within, to decline by themselves, whereas all other governments are destroyed through exterior circumstances. Therefore what the definition of governments always needed was what Montesquieu called a "principle of action" which, different in each form of government, would inspire government and citizens alike in their public activity and serve as a criterion, beyond the merely negative yardstick of lawfulness, for judging all action in public affairs. Such guiding principles and criteria of action are, according to Montesquieu, honor in a monarchy, virtue in a republic and fear in a tyranny.

In a perfect totalitarian government, where all men have become 21 One Man, where all action aims at the acceleration of the movement of nature or history, where every single act is the execution of a death sentence which Nature or History has already pronounced, that is, under conditions where terror can be completely relied upon to keep the movement in constant motion, no principle of action separate from its essence would be needed at all. Yet as long as totalitarian rule has not conquered the earth and with the iron band of terror made each single man a part of one mankind, terror in its double function as essence of government and principle, not of action, but of motion, cannot be fully realized. Just as lawfulness in constitutional government is insufficient to inspire and guide men's actions, so terror in totalitarian government is not sufficient to inspire and guide human behavior.

While under present conditions totalitarian domination still 22 shares with other forms of government the need for a guide for the behavior of its citizens in public affairs, it does not need and could not even use a principle of action strictly speaking, since it will eliminate precisely the capacity of man to act. Under conditions of total terror not even fear can any longer serve as an advisor of how to behave, because terror chooses its victims without reference to individual actions or thoughts, exclusively in accordance with the objective necessity of the natural or historical process. Under totalitarian conditions, fear probably is more widespread than ever before; but fear has lost its practical usefulness when actions guided by it can no longer help to avoid the dangers man fears. The same is true for sympathy or support of the regime; for total terror not only selects its victims according to objective standards; it chooses its executioners with as complete a disregard as possible for the candidate's conviction and sympathies. The consistent elimination of conviction as a motive for action has become a matter of record since the great purges in Soviet Russia and the satellite countries. The aim of totalitarian education has never been to instill convictions but to destroy the capacity to form any. The introduction of purely objective criteria into the selective system of the SS troops was Himmler's great organizational invention; he selected the candidates from photographs according to purely racial criteria. Nature itself decided, not only who was to be eliminated, but also who was to be trained as an executioner.

No guiding principle of behavior, taken itself from the realm of   23
human action, such as virtue, honor, fear, is necessary or can be useful to set into motion a body politic which no longer uses terror as a means of intimidation, but whose essence *is* terror. In its stead, it has introduced an entirely new principle into public affairs that dispenses with human will to action altogether and appeals to the craving need for some insight into the law of movement according to which the terror functions and upon which, therefore, all private destinies depend.

The inhabitants of a totalitarian country are thrown into and   24
caught in the process of nature or history for the sake of accelerating its movement; as such, they can only be executioners or victims of its inherent law. The process may decide that those who today eliminate races and individuals or the members of dying classes and decadent peoples are tomorrow those who must be sacrificed. What totalitarian rule needs to guide the behavior of its subjects is a preparation to fit each of them equally well for the role of executioner and the role of victim. This two-sided preparation, the substitute for a principle of action, is the ideology.

Ideologies — isms which to the satisfaction of their adherents   25
can explain everything and every occurrence by deducing it from a single premise — are a very recent phenomenon and, for many decades, played a negligible role in political life. Only with the wisdom of hindsight can we discover in them certain elements which have made them so disturbingly useful for totalitarian rule. Not before Hitler and Stalin were the great political potentialities of the ideologies discovered.

Ideologies are known for their scientific character: they combine   26
the scientific approach with results of philosophical relevance and pretend to be scientific philosophy. The word "ideology" seems to imply that an idea can become the subject matter of a science just as animals are the subject matter of zoology, and that the suffix *-logy* in ideology, as in zoology, indicates nothing but the *logoi*, the scientific statements made on it. If this were true, an ideology would indeed be a pseudo-science and a pseudo-philosophy, transgressing at the same time the limitations of science and the limitations of philosophy. Deism, for example, would then be the ideology which treats the idea of God, with which philosophy is concerned, in the scien-

tific manner of theology for which God is a revealed reality. (A theology which is not based on revelation as a given reality but treats God as an idea would be as mad as a zoology which is no longer sure of the physical, tangible existence of animals.) Yet we know that this is only part of the truth. Deism, though it denies divine revelation, does not simply make "scientific" statements on a God which is only an "idea," but uses the idea of God in order to explain the course of the world. The "ideas" of isms — race in racism, God in deism, etc. — never form the subject matter of the ideologies and the suffix -logy never indicates simply a body of "scientific" statements.

An ideology is quite literally what its name indicates: it is the   27
logic of an idea. Its subject matter is history, to which the "idea" is applied; the result of this application is not a body of statements about something that is, but the unfolding of a process which is in constant change. The ideology treats the course of events as though it followed the same "law" as the logical exposition of its "idea." Ideologies pretend to know the mysteries of the whole historical process — the secrets of the past, the intricacies of the present, the uncertainties of the future — because of the logic inherent in their respective ideas.

Ideologies are never interested in the miracle of being. They are   28
historical, concerned with becoming and perishing, with the rise and fall of cultures, even if they try to explain history by some "law of nature." The word "race" in racism does not signify any genuine curiosity about the human races as a field for scientific exploration, but is the "idea" by which the movement of history is explained as one consistent process.

The "idea" of an ideology is neither Plato's eternal essence grasped   29
by the eyes of the mind nor Kant's regulative principle of reason but has become an instrument of explanation. To an ideology, history does not appear in the light of an idea (which would imply that history is seen sub specie[7] of some ideal eternity which itself is beyond historical motion) but as something which can be calculated by it. What fits the "idea" into this new role is its own "logic," that is a movement which is the consequence of the "idea" itself and needs no outside factor to set it into motion. Racism is the belief that there is a motion inherent in the very idea of race, just as deism is the belief that a motion is inherent in the very notion of God.

The movement of history and the logical process of this notion   30
are supposed to correspond to each other, so that whatever hap-

---

[7] **Sub specie** As a kind of.

pens, happens according to the logic of one "idea." However, the only possible movement in the realm of logic is the process of deduction from a premise. Dialectical logic, with its process from thesis through antithesis to synthesis which in turn becomes the thesis of the next dialectical movement, is not different in principle, once an ideology gets hold of it; the first thesis becomes the premise and its advantage for ideological explanation is that this dialectical device can explain away factual contradictions as stages of one identical, consistent movement.

As soon as logic as a movement of thought — and not as a nec-   31
essary control of thinking — is applied to an idea, this idea is transformed into a premise. Ideological world explanations performed this operation long before it became so eminently fruitful for totalitarian reasoning. The purely negative coercion of logic, the prohibition of contradictions, became "productive" so that a whole line of thought could be initiated, and forced upon the mind, by drawing conclusions in the manner of mere argumentation. This argumentative process could be interrupted neither by a new idea (which would have been another premise with a different set of consequences) nor by a new experience. Ideologies always assume that one idea is sufficient to explain everything in the development from the premise, and that no experience can teach anything because everything is comprehended in this consistent process of logical deduction. The danger in exchanging the necessary insecurity of philosophical thought for the total explanation of an ideology and its *Weltanschauung,*[8] is not even so much the risk of falling for some usually vulgar, always uncritical assumption as of exchanging the freedom inherent in man's capacity to think for the strait jacket of logic with which man can force himself almost as violently as he is forced by some outside power.

The *Weltanschauungen* and ideologies of the nineteenth century   32
are not in themselves totalitarian, and although racism and communism have become the decisive ideologies of the twentieth century they were not, in principle, any "more totalitarian" than the others; it happened because the elements of experience on which they were originally based — the struggle between the races for world domination, and the struggle between the classes for political power in the respective countries — turned out to be politically more important than those of other ideologies. In this sense the ideological victory of racism and communism over all other isms was decided before the totalitarian movements took hold of precisely these ideologies. On

---

[8] **Weltanschauung** World view.

the other hand, all ideologies contain totalitarian elements, but these are fully developed only by totalitarian movements, and this creates the deceptive impression that only racism and communism are totalitarian in character. The truth is, rather, that the real nature of all ideologies was revealed only in the role that the ideology plays in the apparatus of totalitarian domination. Seen from this aspect, there appear three specifically totalitarian elements that are peculiar to all ideological thinking.

First, in their claim to total explanation, ideologies have the tendency to explain not what is, but what becomes, what is born and passes away. They are in all cases concerned solely with the element of motion, that is, with history in the customary sense of the word. Ideologies are always oriented toward history, even when, as in the case of racism, they seemingly proceed from the premise of nature; here, nature serves merely to explain historical matters and reduce them to matters of nature. The claim to total explanation promises to explain all historical happenings, the total explanation of the past, the total knowledge of the present, and the reliable prediction of the future. Secondly, in this capacity ideological thinking becomes independent of all experience from which it cannot learn anything new even if it is a question of something that has just come to pass. Hence ideological thinking becomes emancipated from the reality that we perceive with our five senses, and insists on a "truer" reality concealed behind all perceptible things, dominating them from this place of concealment and requiring a sixth sense that enables us to become aware of it. The sixth sense is provided by precisely the ideology, that particular ideological indoctrination which is taught by the educational institutions, established exclusively for this purpose, to train the "political soldiers" in the *Ordensburgen* of the Nazis or the schools of the Comintern and the Cominform.[9] The propaganda of the totalitarian movement also serves to emancipate thought from experience and reality; it always strives to inject a secret meaning into every public, tangible event and to suspect a secret intent behind every public political act. Once the movements have come to power, they proceed to change reality in accordance with their ideological claims. The concept of enmity is replaced by that of conspiracy, and this produces a mentality in which reality — real enmity or real friendship — is no longer experienced and understood in its own terms but is automatically assumed to signify something else.

33

---

[9] *Ordensburgen,* **Comintern, Cominform** Institutions of propaganda and political education in Germany and Russia.

Thirdly, since the ideologies have no power to transform reality,   34
they achieve this emancipation of thought from experience through
certain methods of demonstration. Ideological thinking orders facts
into an absolutely logical procedure which starts from an axiomati-
cally accepted premise, deducing everything else from it; that is, it
proceeds with a consistency that exists nowhere in the realm of reality. The deducing may proceed logically or dialectically; in either
case it involves a consistent process of argumentation which, because it thinks in terms of a process, is supposed to be able to comprehend the movement of the suprahuman, natural or historical
processes. Comprehension is achieved by the mind's imitating, either logically or dialectically, the laws of "scientifically" established
movements with which through the process of imitation it becomes
integrated. Ideological argumentation, always a kind of logical deduction, corresponds to the two aforementioned elements of the
ideologies — the element of movement and of emancipation from
reality and experience — first, because its thought movement does
not spring from experience but is self-generated, and, secondly, because it transforms the one and only point that is taken and accepted from experienced reality into an axiomatic premise, leaving
from then on the subsequent argumentation process completely untouched from any further experience. Once it has established its
premise, its point of departure, experiences no longer interfere with
ideological thinking, nor can it be taught by reality.

The device both totalitarian rulers used to transform their re-   35
spective ideologies into weapons with which each of their subjects
could force himself into step with the terror movement was decep-
tively simple and inconspicuous: they took them dead seriously,
took pride the one in his supreme gift for "ice cold reasoning"
(Hitler) and the other in the "mercilessness of his dialectics," and
proceeded to drive ideological implications into extremes of logical
consistency which, to the onlooker, looked preposterously "primitive" and absurd: a "dying class" consisted of people condemned to
death; races that are "unfit to live" were to be exterminated. Whoever agreed that there are such things as "dying classes" and did not
draw the consequence of killing their members, or that the right to
live had something to do with race and did not draw the consequence of killing "unfit races," was plainly either stupid or a coward.
This stringent logicality as a guide to action permeates the whole
structure of totalitarian movements and governments. It is exclusively the work of Hitler and Stalin who, although they did not add
a single new thought to the ideas and propaganda slogans of their
movements, for this reason alone must be considered ideologists of
the greatest importance.

QUESTIONS FOR CRITICAL READING

1. Describe totalitarianism.
2. What role does science or pseudo-science play in the development of totalitarianism?
3. How can racism contribute to producing a totalitarian government?
4. What seem to be the primary goals of totalitarian governments? How do they differ from our own government?
5. How can the main ideas of an ideology proceed from a single premise? (See para. 25.)
6. Where do totalitarian governments operate today? What ideological organizations operate in the manner Arendt describes? What are their basic views?

SUGGESTIONS FOR WRITING

1. Arendt naturally reflected the fears of her own time in this essay. For her the most terrifying and immediate totalitarian governments were Nazi Germany and communist Russia. What evidence do you see in our contemporary world that might suggest totalitarianism is not completely "dead"? What governments seem totalitarian in behavior today? How threatening are they? If you feel totalitarianism is not a threat today, what examples of ideology do you see at work in the modern world? Are there specific threatening ideologies that concern you? Write a brief essay on the existence of totalitarianism or on the threat of ideologies.
2. At the end of paragraph 32 Arendt tells us that "there appear three specifically totalitarian elements that are peculiar to all ideological thinking." She enumerates these in the next two paragraphs. Explain what they are and describe them in terms that you feel your peers would understand. Do you see examples of such elements in the ideological thinking that is represented in your immediate environment? Is it possible that some ideologies do not have these totalitarian elements? Be specific in your answer.
3. What is the role of law in the totalitarian state? Arendt pointed out that in Germany and Russia the laws were rewritten, not abolished, and that constitutions were preserved in unrevised form. What attitudes toward law allowed these governments to do things that other nations saw as breaking international law?
4. **CONNECTIONS** What philosophical differences can you note between Lao-tzu and heads of totalitarian states? What do you think Lao-tzu would have to say about ideologies in general? Is he an ideologue? In what ways might Rousseau and Jefferson be considered ideologues? What is their first premise, and what logical progression must we take once we accept it?

5. **CONNECTIONS**   Although Machiavelli's Prince could easily become a tyrant, is there anything in Machiavelli's advice that encourages the Prince to accept a specific ideology? What are Machiavelli's attitudes toward the law and its relation to the Prince? Would Machiavelli have accepted a totalitarian Prince? How would Arendt evaluate Machiavelli's program? Would she consider him to be promoting an ideology?

PART TWO

JUSTICE

Frederick Douglass
Henry David Thoreau
Martin Luther King, Jr.
Simone de Beauvoir

INTRODUCTION

Ideas of justice have revolved historically around several closely related concepts: moral righteousness, equity of treatment, and reciprocity of action. Justice is an element of interpersonal relations, but philosophers usually link it to the individual's relationship to the state. In the western tradition, the Greek philosopher Plato (428–347 B.C.) was the first to frame the concept of justice in terms of the health of the state. In his work *The Republic* he defined justice both as an overarching ideal and as a practical necessity for the functioning of a harmonious society. In his view, justice was served when each stratum of society (philosopher-rulers, soldiers, and artisans and workers) operated within its own sphere of action and did not interfere with others.

Like Plato, the Greek philosopher Aristotle (384–322 B.C.) viewed the general concept of justice as an important eternal quality that the individual should strive to uphold. He defined general justice as the overarching goal of moral righteousness that ensures a good society, legislative justice as the duty of the individual to comply with the laws of the society (civic virtue), and particular justice as the duty of the judge to redress inequalities in personal transactions. In turn each of these forms of justice works to maintain the overarching ideals of political and economic justice and thus protect the society from collapse. Ironically, although political justice centers on the concept of freedom and liberty, in Aristotle's time warring states enslaved defeated warriors and their families. Aristotle justified this practice by asserting that basic inequalities between people rendered some people natural slaves.

In later centuries, philosophers such as Thomas Hobbes (English, 1588–1679) drew on Aristotle's theories of natural justice — the justice found in a state of nature where the strong always impose their will on the weak. However, Hobbes found that because people actually live in communities with a political structure that leads them to suffer or commit injustices, the concept of justice becomes essentially moral. Hobbes wrestled with the moral parameters of justice and finally concluded that it is impossible to form a universal concept of justice and that justice is whatever laws are most useful and expedient for society.

This tension between justice as a moral ideal and its manifestation in society as practical law has been a hallmark of its evolution as an idea. Indeed, as the writers in this section so eloquently reveal, the laws that are meant to ensure justice within a society often enforce deep injustices. All four authors in this section investigate the relationship between the individual (or group of individuals) and society when the laws codified by that society are seen as unjust: either they enforce unequal treatment where no inherent inequality exists, or they require actions that conflict with individual conscience.

In the excerpt from his *Narrative of the Life of Frederick Douglass, an American Slave,* Douglass links the question of justice to the question of freedom. According to federal and state laws in the early nineteenth century that protected slavery in the South, Douglass was doomed to remain a slave until his dying day, unless his owner freed him or allowed him to purchase his freedom. In recording the circumstances of his life under a government that enforced slave laws — in both the North and the South — at the same time as it advocated independence, Douglass illustrates how deeply the injustice of slavery could damage the individual slave and slave holder.

The question of how the individual should react in the face of unjust laws is taken up by Henry David Thoreau. He refused to pay taxes that would be used in a war against Mexico that he felt was dishonorable, realized that he would have to pay a penalty for his views, and was willing to do so. Thoreau makes a special plea to conscience as a way of dealing with injustice by requiring the individual to place conscience first and law second.

Like Thoreau, Martin Luther King, Jr., was also imprisoned for breaking a law his conscience deemed unjust. In his struggle against the Jim Crow laws enforcing segregation in the South, King acted on his belief that the individual can and should fight laws that treat members of society unjustly. King's *Letter from Birmingham Jail* provides a masterful and moving definition of what makes laws just or unjust. Furthermore, King develops the concept of nonviolent demonstration as a method by which the individual can protest unjust laws.

The tone of Simone de Beauvoir's selection reflects less of the state of crisis that we perceive in Thoreau or King and is less personal than Douglass's piece. But as Douglass clarifies the condition of the African-American slave, Beauvoir clarifies the historical oppression of women. Her voice, like Douglass's, is imbued with reason and calmness. Her purpose is to convince others that the condition of women has changed little since the French Revolution, which, like the American Revolution, promised justice to all.

The writers in this section do not necessarily seek to define justice. Instead, each author illustrates injustice within society and extends the right of any individual — male or female, black or white — to demand just laws and even to break the law when it contradicts the individual's moral conscience. The depth of commitment these writers have to the idea of justice and the rhetorical force of their arguments compel us to respond by evaluating the laws and attitudes that shape our lives.

FREDERICK DOUGLASS
From *Narrative of the Life of Frederick Douglass, an American Slave*

FREDERICK DOUGLASS (1817–1895) was born into slavery in Maryland; he died not only a free man but also a man who commanded the respect of his country, his government, and hosts of supporters. Ironically, it was his owner's wife, Mrs. Hugh Auld, a Northerner, who helped Douglass learn to read and write. Until her husband forcefully convinced her that teaching slaves was "unlawful, as well as unsafe," Mrs. Auld taught Douglass enough so that he could begin his own education — and escape to freedom. Mrs. Auld eventually surpassed her husband in her vehement opposition to having Douglass read, leading Douglass to conclude that slavery had a negative effect on slave and slave holder alike: both suffered the consequences of a political system that was inherently unjust.

The *Narrative* is filled with examples of the injustice of slavery. Douglass had little connection with his family. Separated from his mother, Harriet Bailey, Douglass never knew who his father was. In his *Narrative*, he records the beatings he witnessed as a slave, the conditions under which he lived, and the struggles he felt within himself to be a free man. Douglass himself survived brutal beatings and torture by a professional slave "breaker."

The laws of the time codified the injustices that Douglass and all American slaves suffered. The Fugitive Slave Act of 1793 tightened the hold on all slaves who had gone north in search of freedom. Federal marshalls were enjoined to return slaves to their owners. The Underground Railroad helped so many runaway slaves find their way to Canada that a second Fugitive Slave Act was enacted in 1850 with stiff penalties for those who did not obey the law. In retaliation, many northern states enacted personal freedom laws to counter the Fugitive Slave Act. Eventually, these laws became central to the South's decision to secede. However, Douglass's fate, when he eventually escaped in 1838 by impersonating an African-American seaman (using his papers to board ship), was not secure. Abolitionists in New York helped him find work in shipyards in New Bedford. He changed his name from Auld to Douglass to protect himself, and he began his career as an orator in 1841 at an anti-slavery meeting in Nantucket.

To avoid capture after publication of an early version of his autobiography, Douglass spent two years on a speaking tour of Great Britain and Ireland (1845 – 1847). He then returned to the United States, bought his freedom, and rose to national fame as the founder and editor of the *North Star,* an abolitionist paper published in Rochester, New York. One of his chief concerns was for the welfare of the slaves who had managed to secure their freedom. When the Civil War began, there were no plans to free the slaves, but Douglass managed to help convince Lincoln that it would further the war effort to free them; in 1863 the president delivered the Emancipation Proclamation.

However, the years after the war and Lincoln's death were not good for freed slaves. Terrorist groups in both the North and the South worked to keep them from enjoying freedom, and training programs for ex-slaves that might have been effective were never fully instituted. During this time Douglass worked in various capacities for the government — as assistant secretary of the Santo Domingo Commission, as an official in Washington, D.C., and as U.S. minister to Haiti (1889 – 1891). He was the first African American to become a national figure and to have influence with the government.

DOUGLASS'S RHETORIC

Douglass was basically self-taught, but he knew enough to read the powerful writers of his day. He was a commanding speaker in an age in which eloquence was valued and speakers rewarded handsomely. This excerpt from the *Narrative* — Chapters 6, 7, and 8 — is notable for its clear and direct style. The use of the first-person narrative is as simple as one could wish, yet the feelings projected are sincere and moving.

Douglass's structure is the chronological narrative, telling events in the order in which they occurred. He begins his story at the point of meeting a new mistress, a woman from whom he expected harsh treatment. Because she was new to the concept of slavery, however, she behaved in ways that were unusual, and Douglass remarks on her initially kind attitude. Douglass does not interrupt himself with flashbacks or leaps forward in time but tells the story as it happened. At critical moments, he slows the narrative to describe people or incidents in unusual detail and lets the reader infer from these details the extent of the injustice he suffered.

By today's standards, Douglass may seem formal. His sentences are often longer than those of modern writers, although they are always carefully balanced and punctuated by briefer sentences. Despite his long paragraphs, heavy with example and description, after a century and a half his work remains immediate and moving. No modern reader will have difficulty responding to what Frederick Douglass has to say. His views on justice are as accessible and as powerful now as when they were written.

From *Narrative of the Life of Frederick Douglass, an American Slave*

My new mistress proved to be all she appeared when I first met her at the door, — a woman of the kindest heart and finest feelings. She had never had a slave under her control previously to myself, and prior to her marriage she had been dependent upon her own industry for a living. She was by trade a weaver; and by constant application to her business, she had been in a good degree preserved from the blighting and dehumanizing effects of slavery. I was utterly astonished at her goodness. I scarcely knew how to behave towards her. She was entirely unlike any other white woman I had ever seen. I could not approach her as I was accustomed to approach other white ladies. My early instruction was all out of place. The crouching servility, usually so acceptable a quality in a slave, did not answer when manifested toward her. Her favor was not gained by it; she seemed to be disturbed by it. She did not deem it impudent or unmannerly for a slave to look her in the face. The meanest slave was put fully at ease in her presence, and none left without feeling better for having seen her. Her face was made of heavenly smiles, and her voice of tranquil music.

But, alas! this kind heart had but a short time to remain such.   2
The fatal poison of irresponsible power was already in her hands,
and soon commenced its infernal work. That cheerful eye, under the
influence of slavery, soon became red with rage; that voice, made all
of sweet accord, changed to one of harsh and horrid discord; and
that angelic face gave place to that of a demon.

Very soon after I went to live with Mr. and Mrs. Auld, she very   3
kindly commenced to teach me the A, B, C. After I had learned this,
she assisted me in learning to spell words of three or four letters.
Just at this point of my progress, Mr. Auld found out what was
going on, and at once forbade Mrs. Auld to instruct me further,
telling her, among other things, that it was unlawful, as well as unsafe, to teach a slave to read. To use his own words, further, he said,
"If you give a nigger an inch, he will take an ell.[1] A nigger should
know nothing but to obey his master — to do as he is told to do.
Learning would *spoil* the best nigger in the world. Now," said he, "if
you teach that nigger (speaking of myself) how to read, there would
be no keeping him. It would forever unfit him to be a slave. He
would at once become unmanageable, and of no value to his master.
As to himself, it could do him no good, but a great deal of harm. It
would make him discontented and unhappy." These words sank
deep into my heart, stirred up sentiments within that lay slumber-
ing, and called into existence an entirely new train of thought. It was
a new and special revelation, explaining dark and mysterious things,
with which my youthful understanding had struggled, but struggled
in vain. I now understood what had been to me a most perplexing
difficulty — to wit, the white man's power to enslave the black man.
It was a grand achievement, and I prized it highly. From that moment, I understood the pathway from slavery to freedom. It was just
what I wanted, and I got it at a time when I the least expected it.
Whilst I was saddened by the thought of losing the aid of my kind
mistress, I was gladdened by the invaluable instruction which, by
the merest accident, I had gained from my master. Though conscious of the difficulty of learning without a teacher, I set out with
high hope, and a fixed purpose, at whatever cost of trouble, to learn
how to read. The very decided manner with which he spoke, and
strove to impress his wife with the evil consequences of giving me
instruction, served to convince me that he was deeply sensible of the
truths he was uttering. It gave me the best assurance that I might
rely with the utmost confidence on the results which, he said, would
flow from teaching me to read. What he most dreaded, that I most

---

[1] **ell** A measure about a yard in length.

desired. What he most loved, that I most hated. That which to him was a great evil, to be carefully shunned, was to me a great good, to be diligently sought; and the argument which he so warmly urged, against my learning to read, only served to inspire me with a desire and determination to learn. In learning to read, I owe almost as much to the bitter opposition of my master, as to the kindly aid of my mistress. I acknowledge the benefit of both.

I had resided but a short time in Baltimore before I observed a 4 marked difference, in the treatment of slaves, from that which I had witnessed in the country. A city slave is almost a freeman, compared with a slave on the plantation. He is much better fed and clothed, and enjoys privileges altogether unknown to the slave on the plantation. There is a vestige of decency, a sense of shame, that does much to curb and check those outbreaks of atrocious cruelty so commonly enacted upon the plantation. He is a desperate slaveholder, who will shock the humanity of his nonslaveholding neighbors with the cries of his lacerated slave. Few are willing to incur the odium attaching to the reputation of being a cruel master; and above all things, they would not be known as not giving a slave enough to eat. Every city slaveholder is anxious to have it known of him, that he feeds his slaves well; and it is due to them to say, that most of them do give their slaves enough to eat. There are, however, some painful exceptions to this rule. Directly opposite to us, on Philpot Street, lived Mr. Thomas Hamilton. He owned two slaves. Their names were Henrietta and Mary. Henrietta was about twenty-two years of age, Mary was about fourteen; and of all the mangled and emaciated creatures I ever looked upon, these two were the most so. His heart must be harder than stone, that could look upon these unmoved. The head, neck, and shoulders of Mary were literally cut to pieces. I have frequently felt her head, and found it nearly covered with festering sores, caused by the lash of her cruel mistress. I do not know that her master ever whipped her, but I have been an eye-witness to the cruelty of Mrs. Hamilton. I used to be in Mr. Hamilton's house nearly every day. Mrs. Hamilton used to sit in a large chair in the middle of the room, with a heavy cowskin always by her side, and scarce an hour passed during the day but was marked by the blood of one of these slaves. The girls seldom passed her without her saying, "Move faster, you *black gip!*" at the same time giving them a blow with the cowskin over the head or shoulders, often drawing the blood. She would then say, "Take that, you *black gip!*" — continuing, "If you don't move faster, I'll move you!" Added to the cruel lashings to which these slaves were subjected, they were kept nearly half-starved. They seldom knew what it was to eat a full meal. I have seen Mary contending with the pigs for the offal thrown into the

street. So much was Mary kicked and cut to pieces, that she was oftener called "*pecked*" than by her name.

I lived in Master Hugh's family about seven years. During this   5
time, I succeeded in learning to read and write. In accomplishing
this, I was compelled to resort to various stratagems. I had no regular teacher. My mistress, who had kindly commenced to instruct
me, had, in compliance with the advice and direction of her husband, not only ceased to instruct, but had set her face against my
being instructed by any one else. It is due, however, to my mistress
to say of her, that she did not adopt this course of treatment immediately. She at first lacked the depravity indispensable to shutting
me up in mental darkness. It was at least necessary for her to have
some training in the exercise of irresponsible power, to make her
equal to the task of treating me as though I were a brute.

My mistress was, as I have said, a kind and tender-hearted   6
woman; and in the simplicity of her soul she commenced, when I
first went to live with her, to treat me as she supposed one human
being ought to treat another. In entering upon the duties of a slaveholder, she did not seem to perceive that I sustained to her the relation of a mere chattel, and that for her to treat me as a human being
was not only wrong, but dangerously so. Slavery proved as injurious
to her as it did to me. When I went there, she was a pious, warm,
and tender-hearted woman. There was no sorrow or suffering for
which she had not a tear. She had bread for the hungry, clothes for
the naked, and comfort for every mourner that came within her
reach. Slavery soon proved its ability to divest her of these heavenly
qualities. Under its influence, the tender heart became stone, and
the lamblike disposition gave way to one of tiger-like fierceness. The
first step in her downward course was in her ceasing to instruct me.
She now commenced to practise her husband's precepts. She finally
became even more violent in her opposition than her husband himself. She was not satisfied with simply doing as well as he had commanded; she seemed anxious to do better. Nothing seemed to make
her more angry than to see me with a newspaper. She seemed to
think that here lay the danger. I have had her rush at me with a face
made all up of fury, and snatch from me a newspaper, in a manner
that fully revealed her apprehension. She was an apt woman; and a
little experience soon demonstrated, to her satisfaction, that education and slavery were incompatible with each other.

From this time I was most narrowly watched. If I was in a sepa-   7
rate room any considerable length of time, I was sure to be suspected of having a book, and was at once called to give an account

of myself. All this, however, was too late. The first step had been taken. Mistress, in teaching me the alphabet, had given me the *inch,* and no precaution could prevent me from taking the *ell.*

The plan which I adopted, and the one by which I was most 8 successful, was that of making friends of all the little white boys whom I met in the street. As many of these as I could, I converted into teachers. With their kindly aid, obtained at different times and in different places, I finally succeeded in learning to read. When I was sent to errands, I always took my book with me, and by going one part of my errand quickly, I found time to get a lesson before my return. I used also to carry bread with me, enough of which was always in the house, and to which I was always welcome; for I was much better off in this regard than many of the poor white children in our neighborhood. This bread I used to bestow upon the hungry little urchins, who, in return, would give me that more valuable bread of knowledge. I am strongly tempted to give the names of two or three of those little boys, as a testimonial of the gratitude and af-fection I bear them; but prudence forbids; — not that it would in-jure me, but it might embarrass them; for it is almost an unpardon-able offence to teach slaves to read in this Christian country. It is enough to say of the dear little fellows, that they lived on Philpot Street, very near Durgin and Bailey's ship-yard. I used to talk this matter of slavery over with them. I would sometimes say to them, I wished I could be as free as they would be when they got to be men. "You will be free as soon as you are twenty-one, *but I am a slave for life!* Have not I as good a right to be free as you have?" These words used to trouble them; they would express for me the liveliest sympa-thy, and console me with the hope that something would occur by which I might be free.

I was now about twelve years old, and the thought of being *a* 9 *slave for life* began to bear heavily upon my heart. Just about this time, I got hold of a book entitled "The Columbian Orator." Every opportunity I got, I used to read this book. Among much of other interesting matter, I found in it a dialogue between a master and his slave. The slave was represented as having run away from his master three times. The dialogue represented the conversation which took place between them, when the slave was retaken the third time. In this dialogue, the whole argument in behalf of slavery was brought forward by the master, all of which was disposed of by the slave. The slave was made to say some very smart as well as impressive things in reply to his master — things which had the desired though unexpected effect; for the conversation resulted in the voluntary emancipation of the slave on the part of the master.

In the same book, I met with one of Sheridan's[2] mighty 10
speeches on and in behalf of Catholic emancipation. These were
choice documents to me. I read them over and over again with un-
abated interest. They gave tongue to interesting thoughts of my own
soul, which had frequently flashed through my mind, and died away
for want of utterance. The moral which I gained from the dialogue
was the power of truth over the conscience of even a slaveholder.
What I got from Sheridan was a bold denunciation of slavery, and a
powerful vindication of human rights. The reading of these documents enabled me to utter my thoughts, and to meet the arguments
brought forward to sustain slavery; but while they relieved me of
one difficulty, they brought on another even more painful than the
one of which I was relieved. The more I read, the more I was led to
abhor and detest my enslavers. I could regard them in no other light
than a band of successful robbers, who had left their homes, and
gone to Africa, and stolen us from our homes, and in a strange land
reduced us to slavery. I loathed them as being the meanest as well as
the most wicked of men. As I read and contemplated the subject,
behold! that very discontentment which Master Hugh had predicted
would follow my learning to read had already come, to torment and
sting my soul to unutterable anguish. As I writhed under it, I would
at times feel that learning to read had been a curse rather than a
blessing. It had given me a view of my wretched condition, without
the remedy. It opened my eyes to the horrible pit, but to no ladder
upon which to get out. In moments of agony, I envied my fellow-
slaves for their stupidity. I have often wished myself a beast. I preferred the condition of the meanest reptile to my own. Any thing, no
matter what, to get rid of thinking! It was this everlasting thinking of
my condition that tormented me. There was no getting rid of it. It
was pressed upon me by every object within sight or hearing, ani-
mate or inanimate. The silver trump of freedom had roused my soul
to eternal wakefulness. Freedom now appeared, to disappear no
more forever. It was heard in every sound, and seen in every thing.
It was ever present to torment me with a sense of my wretched condition. I saw nothing without seeing it, I heard nothing without
hearing it, and felt nothing without feeling it. It looked from every
star, it smiled in every calm, breathed in every wind, and moved in
every storm.

I often found myself regretting my own existence, and wishing 11
myself dead; and but for the hope of being free, I have no doubt but
that I should have killed myself, or done something for which I

---

[2] **Richard Brinsley Sheridan (1751 – 1816)** Irish dramatist and orator.

should have been killed. While in this state of mind, I was eager to hear any one speak of slavery. I was a ready listener. Every little while, I could hear something about the abolitionists.[3] It was some time before I found what the word meant. It was always used in such connections as to make it an interesting word to me. If a slave ran away and succeeded in getting clear, or if a slave killed his master, set fire to a barn, or did any thing very wrong in the mind of a slaveholder, it was spoken of as the fruit of *abolition.* Hearing the word in this connection very often, I set about learning what it meant. The dictionary afforded me little or no help. I found it was "the act of abolishing"; but then I did not know what was to be abolished. Here I was perplexed. I did not dare to ask any one about its meaning, for I was satisfied that it was something they wanted me to know very little about. After a patient waiting, I got one of our city papers, containing an account of the number of petitions from the north, praying for the abolition of slavery in the District of Columbia, and of the slave trade between the States. From this time I understood the words *abolition* and *abolitionist,* and always drew near when that word was spoken, expecting to hear something of importance to myself and fellow-slaves. The light broke in upon me by degrees. I went one day down on the wharf of Mr. Waters; and seeing two Irishmen unloading a scow of stone, I went, unasked, and helped them. When we had finished, one of them came to me and asked me if I were a slave. I told him I was. He asked, "Are ye a slave for life?" I told him that I was. The good Irishman seemed to be deeply affected by the statement. He said to the other that it was a pity so fine a little fellow as myself should be a slave for life. He said it was a shame to hold me. They both advised me to run away to the north; that I should find friends there, and that I should be free. I pretended not to be interested in what they said, and treated them as if I did not understand them; for I feared they might be treacherous. White men have been known to encourage slaves to escape, and then, to get the reward, catch them and return them to their masters. I was afraid that these seemingly good men might use me so; but I nevertheless remembered their advice, and from that time I resolved to run away. I looked forward to a time at which it would be safe for me to escape. I was too young to think of doing so immediately; besides, I wished to learn how to write, as I might have occasion to write my own pass. I consoled myself with the hope that I should one day find a good chance. Meanwhile, I would learn to write.

---

[3] **abolitionists** Those who actively opposed slavery.

The idea as to how I might learn to write was suggested to me 12 by being in Durgin and Bailey's ship-yard, and frequently seeing the ship carpenters, after hewing, and getting a piece of timber ready for use, write on the timber the name of that part of the ship for which it was intended. When a piece of timber was intended for the larboard side, it would be marked thus — "L." When a piece was for the starboard side, it would be marked thus — "S." A piece for the larboard side forward, would be marked thus — "L.F." When a piece was for starboard side forward, it would be marked thus — "S.F." For larboard aft, it would be marked thus — "L.A." For starboard aft, it would be marked thus — "S.A." I soon learned the names of these letters, and for what they were intended when placed upon a piece of timber in the ship-yard. I immediately commenced copying them, and in a short time was able to make the four letters named. After that, when I met with any boy who I knew could write, I would tell him I could write as well as he. The next word would be, "I don't believe you. Let me see you try it." I would then make the letters which I had been so fortunate as to learn, and ask him to beat that. In this way I got a good many lessons in writing, which it is quite possible I should never have gotten in any other way. During this time, my copy-book was the board fence, brick wall, and pavement; my pen and ink was a lump of chalk. With these, I learned mainly how to write. I then commenced and continued copying the Italics in Webster's Spelling Book, until I could make them all without looking on the book. By this time, my little Master Thomas had gone to school, and learned how to write, and had written over a number of copy-books. These had been brought home, and shown to some of our near neighbors, and then laid aside. My mistress used to go to class meeting at the Wilk Street meeting-house every Monday afternoon, and leave me to take care of the house. When left thus, I used to spend the time in writing in the spaces left in Master Thomas's copy-book, copying what he had written. I continued to do this until I could write a hand very similar to that of Master Thomas. Thus, after a long, tedious effort for years, I finally succeeded in learning how to write.

In a very short time after I went to live at Baltimore, my old 13 master's youngest son Richard died; and in about three years and six months after his death, my old master, Captain Anthony, died, leaving only his son, Andrew, and daughter, Lucretia, to share his estate. He died while on a visit to see his daughter at Hillsborough. Cut off thus unexpectedly, he left no will as to the disposal of his property. It was therefore necessary to have a valuation of the property, that it might be equally divided between Mrs. Lucretia and Master Andrew.

I was immediately sent for, to be valued with the other property. Here again my feelings rose up in detestation of slavery. I had now a new conception of my degraded condition. Prior to this, I had become, if not insensible to my lot, at least partly so. I left Baltimore with a young heart overborne with sadness, and a soul full of apprehension. I took passage with Captain Rowe, in the schooner Wild Cat, and, after a sail of about twenty-four hours, I found myself near the place of my birth. I had now been absent from it almost, if not quite, five years. I, however, remembered the place very well. I was only about five years old when I left it, to go and live with my old master on Colonel Lloyd's plantation; so that I was now between ten and eleven years old.

We were all ranked together at the valuation. Men and women, 14 old and young, married and single, were ranked with horses, sheep, and swine. There were horses and men, cattle and women, pigs and children, all holding the same rank in the scale of being, and were all subjected to the same narrow examination. Silvery-headed age and sprightly youth, maids and matrons, had to undergo the same indelicate inspection. At this moment, I saw more clearly than ever the brutalizing effects of slavery upon both slave and slaveholder.

After the valuation, then came the division. I have no language 15 to express the high excitement and deep anxiety which were felt among us poor slaves during this time. Our fate for life was now to be decided. We had no more voice in that decision than the brutes among whom we were ranked. A single word from the white men was enough — against all our wishes, prayers, and entreaties — to sunder forever the dearest friends, dearest kindred, and strongest ties known to human beings. In addition to the pain of separation, there was the horrid dread of falling into the hands of Master Andrew. He was known to us all as being a most cruel wretch, — a common drunkard, who had, by his reckless mismanagement and profligate dissipation, already wasted a large portion of his father's property. We all felt that we might as well be sold at once to the Georgia traders, as to pass into his hands; for we knew that that would be our inevitable condition, — a condition held by us all in the utmost horror and dread.

I suffered more anxiety than most of my fellow-slaves. I had 16 known what it was to be kindly treated; they had known nothing of the kind. They had seen little or nothing of the world. They were in very deed men and women of sorrow, and acquainted with grief. Their backs had been made familiar with the bloody lash, so that they had become callous; mine was yet tender; for while at Baltimore I got few whippings, and few slaves could boast of a kinder master and mistress than myself; and the thought of passing out of their hands into those of Master Andrew — a man who, but a few days before, to give me a sample of his bloody disposition, took my little brother by the throat, threw him on the ground, and with the heel of his boot stamped upon his head till the blood gushed from his nose and ears — was well calculated to make me anxious as to my fate. After he had committed this savage outrage upon my brother, he turned to me, and said that was the way he meant to serve me one of these days, — meaning, I suppose, when I came into his possession.

Thanks to a kind Providence, I fell to the portion of Mrs. Lucre-   17
tia, and was sent immediately back to Baltimore, to live again in the family of Master Hugh. Their joy at my return equalled their sorrow at my departure. It was a glad day to me. I had escaped a worse fate than lion's jaws. I was absent from Baltimore, for the purpose of valuation and division, just about one month, and it seemed to have been six.

Very soon after my return to Baltimore, my mistress, Lucretia,   18
died, leaving her husband and child, Amanda; and in a very short time after her death, Master Andrew died. Now all the property of my old master, slaves included, was in the hands of strangers, — strangers who had had nothing to do with accumulating it. Not a slave was left free. All remained slaves, from the youngest to the oldest. If any one thing in my experience, more than another, served to deepen my conviction of the infernal character of slavery, and to fill me with unutterable loathing of slaveholders, it was their base ingratitude to my poor old grandmother. She had served my old master faithfully from youth to old age. She had been the source of all his wealth; she had peopled his plantation with slaves; she had become a great grandmother in his service. She had rocked him in infancy, attended him in childhood, served him through life, and at his death wiped from his icy brow the cold death-sweat, and closed his eyes forever. She was nevertheless left a slave — a slave for life — a slave in the hands of strangers; and in their hands she saw her children, her grandchildren, and her great-grandchildren, divided, like so many sheep, without being gratified with the small privilege of a single word, as to their or her own destiny. And, to cap the climax of their base ingratitude and fiendish barbarity, my grandmother, who was now very old, having outlived my old master and all his children, having seen the beginning and end of all of them, and her present owners finding she was of but little value, her frame already racked with the pains of old age, and complete helplessness fast stealing over her once active limbs, they took her to the woods, built her a little hut, put up a little mud-chimney, and then made her welcome to the privilege of supporting herself there in perfect lone-

liness; thus virtually turning her out to die! If my poor old grandmother now lives, she lives to suffer in utter loneliness; she lives to
remember and mourn over the loss of children, the loss of grandchildren, and the loss of great-grandchildren. They are, in the language of the slave's poet, Whittier,[4] —

> Gone, gone, sold and gone
> To the rice swamp dank and lone,
> Where the slave-whip ceaseless swings,
> Where the noisome insect stings,
> Where the fever-demon strews
> Poison with the falling dews,
> Where the sickly sunbeams glare
> Through the hot and misty air: —
> > Gone, gone, sold and gone
> > To the rice swamp dank and lone,
> > From Virginia hills and waters —
> > Woe is me, my stolen daughters!

The hearth is desolate. The children, the unconscious children, 19
who once sang and danced in her presence, are gone. She gropes her
way, in the darkness of age, for a drink of water. Instead of the
voices of her children, she hears by day the moans of the dove, and
by night the screams of the hideous owl. All is gloom. The grave is at
the door. And now, when weighed down by the pains and aches of
old age, when the head inclines to the feet, when the beginning and
ending of human existence meet, and helpless infancy and painful
old age combine together — at this time, this most needful time, the
time for the exercise of that tenderness and affection which children
only can exercise towards a declining parent — my poor old grandmother, the devoted mother of twelve children, is left all alone, in
yonder little hut, before a few dim embers. She stands — she sits —
she staggers — she falls — she groans — she dies — and there are
none of her children or grandchildren present, to wipe from her
wrinkled brow the cold sweat of death, or to place beneath the sod
her fallen remains. Will not a righteous God visit for these things?

In about two years after the death of Mrs. Lucretia, Master 20
Thomas married his second wife. Her name was Rowena Hamilton.
She was the eldest daughter of Mr. William Hamilton. Master now
lived in St. Michael's. Not long after his marriage, a misunderstanding took place between himself and Master Hugh; and as a means of
punishing his brother, he took me from him to live with himself at

---

[4] **John Greenleaf Whittier (1807 – 1892)** New England abolitionist, journalist, and poet. The poem Douglass cites is "The Farewell" (1835).

St. Michael's. Here I underwent another most painful separation. It, however, was not so severe as the one I dreaded at the division of property; for, during this interval, a great change had taken place in Master Hugh and his once kind and affectionate wife. The influence of brandy upon him, and of slavery upon her, had effected a disastrous change in the characters of both; so that, as far as they were concerned, I thought I had little to lose by the change. But it was not to them that I was attached. It was to those little Baltimore boys that I felt the strongest attachment. I had received many good lessons from them, and was still receiving them, and the thought of leaving them was painful indeed. I was leaving, too, without the hope of ever being allowed to return. Master Thomas had said he would never let me return again. The barrier betwixt himself and brother he considered impassable.

I then had to regret that I did not at least make the attempt to 21 carry out my resolution to run away; for the chances of success are tenfold greater from the city than from the country.

I sailed from Baltimore for St. Michael's in the sloop Amanda, 22 Captain Edward Dodson. On my passage, I paid particular attention to the direction which the steamboats took to go to Philadelphia. I found, instead of going down, on reaching North Point they went up the bay, in a north-easterly direction. I deemed this knowledge of the utmost importance. My determination to run away was again revived. I resolved to wait only so long as the offering of a favorable opportunity. When that came, I was determined to be off.

QUESTIONS FOR CRITICAL READING

1. Douglass describes Mrs. Auld as possessing "the fatal poison of irresponsible power" (para. 2). What precisely does he mean by this?
2. How does the absence of justice undermine the force of law?
3. Why did the slave holders believe learning to read would spoil a slave?
4. What were the results of Douglass's learning to read?
5. How did the slave holders regard their slaves? What differences does Douglass describe in their behavior?

SUGGESTIONS FOR WRITING

1. The society in which Douglass lived was governed by laws established by elected officials who had benefited from the writings of Rousseau and Jefferson, among others. How could they have conceived of their possession of slaves as an expression of justice?

2. What is the most important political issue raised in the essay? Douglass never talks about the law, but he implies a great deal about justice. What is the political truth regarding the law in Maryland at this time? What is the relationship between politics and justice in this essay?

3. One of the defenses of slavery was that it was for the good of the slaves. How might Frederick Douglass have argued against this defense?

4. Douglass assures us that Mrs. Auld was "a kind and tender-hearted woman" (para. 6) when he first went to live with her but that her behavior soon came to resemble that of other slave holders. How did her behavior alter, and what circumstances contributed to the change? Why does Douglass tell us about the change?

5. What, on the whole, is Douglass's attitude toward white people? Examine his statements about them, and establish as far as possible his feelings regarding their character. Is he bitter about his slavery experiences? Does he condemn the society that supported slavery?

6. How effective is the detailed description in the essay? Select the best descriptive passages and analyze them for their effectiveness in context. What does Douglass hope to accomplish by lavishing so much attention on such description?

7. **CONNECTIONS** Which writer on government would Douglass have found most important — Lao-tzu, Machiavelli, Rousseau, or Jefferson? Which would the slave holders agree with? What political ideals does Douglass hold? Trace their sources to one or more of these writers.

8. **CONNECTIONS** Apply the definitions of totalitarianism put forth by Hannah Arendt to the American institution of slavery. How does Douglass's essay describe or reveal the form of government that allowed him to live as a slave?

HENRY DAVID THOREAU
Civil Disobedience

HENRY DAVID THOREAU (1817–1862) began keeping a
journal when he graduated from Harvard in 1837. The journal was
preserved and published, and it shows us the seriousness, determination, and elevation of moral values characteristic of all his work.
He is best known for *Walden* (1854), a record of his departure from
the warm congeniality of Concord, Massachusetts, and the home of
his close friend Ralph Waldo Emerson (1803–1882), for the comparative "wilds" of Walden Pond, where he built a cabin, planted a
garden, and lived simply. In *Walden* Thoreau describes the deaden-
ing influence of ownership and extols the vitality and spiritual
uplift that comes from living close to nature. He also argues that
civilization's comforts sometimes rob a person of independence, integrity, and even conscience.

Thoreau and Emerson were prominent among the group of
writers and thinkers who were referred to as the Transcendentalists. They believed in something that transcended the limits of sensory experience — in other words, something that transcended materialism. Their philosophy was based on the works of Immanuel
Kant (1724–1804), the German idealist philosopher; Samuel Taylor Coleridge (1772–1834), the English poet; and Johann Wolfgang von Goethe (1749–1832), the German dramatist and thinker.
These writers praised human intuition and the capacity to see beyond the limits of common experience.

Their philosophical idealism carried over into the social concerns of the day, expressing itself in works such as *Walden* and
"Civil Disobedience," which was published with the title "Resistance to Civil Government," in 1849, a year after the publication of
The Communist Manifesto. Although Thoreau all but denies his idealism in "Civil Disobedience," it is obvious that after spending a
night in the Concord jail, he realizes he cannot quietly accept his
government's behavior in regard to slavery. He begins to feel that it
is not only appropriate but imperative to disobey unjust laws.

In Thoreau's time the most flagrantly unjust laws were those that supported slavery. The Transcendentalists strongly opposed slavery and spoke out against it. Abolitionists in Massachusetts harbored escaped slaves and helped them move to Canada and freedom. The Fugitive Slave Act, enacted in 1850, the year after "Civil Disobedience" was published, made Thoreau a criminal because he refused to comply with Massachusetts civil authorities when in 1851 they began returning escaped slaves to the South as the law required.

"Civil Disobedience" has been much more influential in the twentieth century than it was in the nineteenth. Mohandas Gandhi (1869 – 1948) claimed that while he was editor of an Indian newspaper in South Africa, it helped to inspire his theories of nonviolent resistance. Gandhi eventually implemented these theories against the British empire and helped win independence for India. In the 1960s, Martin Luther King, Jr., applied the same theories in the fight for racial equality in the United States. Thoreau's essay once again found widespread adherents among the many young men who resisted being drafted into the military to fight in Vietnam because they believed that the war was unjust.

"Civil Disobedience" was written after the Walden experience (which began on July 4, 1845, and ended September 6, 1847). Thoreau quietly returned to Emerson's home and "civilization." His refusal to pay the Massachusetts poll tax — a "per head" tax imposed on all citizens to help support what he considered an unjust war against Mexico — landed him in the Concord jail. He spent just one day and one night there — his aunt paid the tax for him — but the experience was so extraordinary that he began examining it in his journal.

THOREAU'S RHETORIC

Thoreau maintained his journal throughout his life and eventually became convinced that writing was one of the few professions by which he could earn a living. He made more money, however, from lecturing on the lyceum circuit. The lyceum, a New England institution, was a town adult education program, featuring important speakers such as the very successful Emerson and foreign lecturers. Admission fees were very reasonable, and in the absence of other popular entertainment, the lyceum was a popular proving ground for speakers interested in promoting their ideas.

"Civil Disobedience" was first outlined in rough-hewn form in the journal, where the main ideas appear and where experiments in phrasing began. (Thoreau was a constant reviser.) Then in February 1848, Thoreau delivered a lecture on "Civil Disobedience" at the Concord Lyceum urging people of conscience to actively resist a government that acted badly. Finally, the piece was prepared for publication in *Aesthetic Papers,* an intellectual journal edited by Elizabeth Peabody (1804–1894), the sister-in-law of another important New England writer, Nathaniel Hawthorne (1804–1864). There it was refined again, and certain important details were added.

"Civil Disobedience" bears many of the hallmarks of the spoken lecture. For one thing, it is written in the first person and addresses an audience that Thoreau expects will share many of his sentiments but certainly not all his conclusions. His message is to some extent anarchistic, virtually denying an unjust government any authority or respect.

Modern political conservatives generally take his opening quote — "That government is best which governs least" — as a rallying cry against governmental interference in everyday affairs. Such conservatives usually propose reducing government interference by reducing the government's capacity to tax wealth for unpopular causes. In fact, what Thoreau opposes is simply any government that is not totally just, totally moral, and totally respectful of the individual.

The easiness of the pace of the essay also derives from its original form as a speech. Even such locutions as "But to speak practically and as a citizen" (para. 3) connect the essay with its origins. Although Thoreau was not an overwhelming orator — he was short and somewhat homely, an unprepossessing figure — he ensured that his writing achieved what some speakers might have accomplished by means of gesture and theatrics.

Thoreau's language is marked by clarity. He speaks directly to every issue, stating his own position and recommending the position he feels his audience, as reasonable and moral people, should accept. One impressive achievement in this selection is Thoreau's capacity to shape memorable, virtually aphoristic statements that remain "quotable" generations later, beginning with his own quotation from the words of John L. O'Sullivan: "That government is best which governs least." Thoreau calls it a motto, as if it belonged on the great seal of a government or on a coin. It contains an interesting and impressive rhetorical flourish — the device of repeating "govern" and the near rhyme of "best" with "least."

His most memorable statements show considerable attention to the rhetorical qualities of balance, repetition, and pattern. "The only obligation which I have a right to assume is to do at any time what I think right" (para. 4) uses the word "right" in two senses: first as a matter of personal volition; second, as a matter of moral rectitude. One's right, in other words, becomes the opportunity to do right. "For it matters not how small the beginning may seem to be: what is once well done is done forever" (para. 21) also relies on repetition for its effect and balances the concept of a beginning with its capacity to reach out into the future. The use of the rhetorical device of *chiasmus,* a criss-cross relationship between key words, marks "Under a government which imprisons any unjustly, the true place for a just man is also a prison" (para. 22). Here is the pattern:

imprisons . . . unjustly

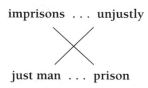

just man . . . prison

Such attention to phrasing is typical of speakers whose expressions must catch and retain the attention of listeners. Audiences do not have the advantage of referring to a text, so the words they hear must be forceful.

Thoreau relies also on analogy — comparing men with machines, people with plants, even the citizen with states considering secession from the Union. His analogies are effective and thus worth examining in some detail. He draws on the analysis of circumstance throughout the essay, carefully examining government actions to determine their qualities and their results. His questions include comments on politics (para. 1), on the Bible (para. 23), on Confucius (para. 24), and finally on his contemporary, Daniel Webster (1782 – 1852) (para. 42), demonstrating a wide range of influence but avoiding the pedantic tone that can come from using quotations too liberally or from citing obscure sources. This essay is simple, direct, and uncluttered. Its enduring influence is in part due to the clarity and grace that characterize Thoreau's writing at its best. Its power derives from Thoreau's demand that citizens act on the basis of conscience.

Civil Disobedience

I heartily accept the motto — "That government is best which 1
governs least,"[1] and I should like to see it acted up to more rapidly
and systematically. Carried out, it finally amounts to this, which also
I believe — "That government is best which governs not at all"; and
when men are prepared for it, that will be the kind of government
which they will have. Government is at best but an expedient; but
most governments are usually, and all governments are sometimes,
inexpedient. The objections which have been brought against a
standing army, and they are many and weighty, and deserve to prevail, may also at last be brought against a standing government. The
standing army is only an arm of the standing government. The government itself, which is only the mode which the people have chosen to execute their will, is equally liable to be abused and perverted
before the people can act through it. Witness the present Mexican
war,[2] the work of comparatively a few individuals using the standing
government as their tool; for in the outset the people would not
have consented to this measure.

This American government — what is it but a tradition, a recent 2
one, endeavoring to transmit itself unimpaired to posterity but each
instant losing some of its integrity? It has not the vitality and force of
a single living man; for a single man can bend it to his will. It is a
sort of wooden gun to the people themselves. But it is not the less
necessary for this; for the people must have some complicated machinery or other, and hear its din, to satisfy that idea of government
which they have. Governments show thus how successfully men can
be imposed on, even impose on themselves, for their own advantage. It is excellent, we must all allow. Yet this government never of
itself furthered any enterprise but by the alacrity with which it got
out of its way. *It* does not keep the country free. *It* does not settle the
West. *It* does not educate. The character inherent in the American
people has done all that has been accomplished; and it would have

---

[1] ... **governs least** John L. O'Sullivan (1813 – 1895) wrote in the *United
States Magazine and Democratic Review* (1837) that "all government is evil, and the
parents of evil. . . . The best government is that which governs least." Thomas Jefferson wrote, "That government is best which governs the least, because its people discipline themselves." Both comments echo the *Tao-te Ching.*

[2] **the present Mexican war (1846 – 1848)** The war was extremely unpopular
in New England because it was an act of a bullying government anxious to grab land
from a weaker nation. The United States had annexed Texas in 1845, precipitating a
welcome retaliation from Mexico.

done somewhat more if the government had not sometimes got in its way. For government is an expedient by which men would fain succeed in letting one another alone; and, as has been said, when it is most expedient the governed are most let alone by it. Trade and commerce, if they were not made of India-rubber, would never manage to bounce over the obstacles which legislators are continually putting in their way; and, if one were to judge these men wholly by the effects of their actions and not partly by their intentions, they would deserve to be classed and punished with those mischievous persons who put obstructions on the railroads.

But to speak practically and as a citizen, unlike those who call   3
themselves no-government men, I ask for, not at once no government, but *at once* a better government. Let every man make known what kind of government would command his respect, and that will be one step toward obtaining it.

After all, the practical reason why, when the power is once in   4
the hands of the people, a majority are permitted, and for a long period continue, to rule is not because they are most likely to be in the right, nor because this seems fairest to the minority but because they are physically the strongest. But a government in which the majority rule in all cases cannot be based on justice, even as far as men understand it. Can there not be a government in which majorities do not virtually decide right and wrong but conscience? — in which majorities decide only those questions to which the rule of expediency is applicable? Must the citizen ever for a moment, or in the least degree, resign his conscience to the legislator? Why has every man a conscience then? I think that we should be men first and subjects afterward. It is not desirable to cultivate a respect for the law, so much as for the right. The only obligation which I have a right to assume is to do at any time what I think right. It is truly enough said that a corporation has no conscience; but a corporation of conscientious men is a corporation *with* a conscience. Law never made men a whit more just; and, by means of their respect for it, even the well-disposed are daily made the agents of injustice. A common and natural result of an undue respect for law is that you may see a file of soldiers, colonel, captain, corporal, privates, powder-monkeys,[3] and all, marching in admirable order over hill and dale to the wars, against their wills, ay, against their common sense and consciences, which makes it very steep marching indeed and produces a palpitation of the heart. They have no doubt that it is a damnable business in which they are concerned; they are all peaceably inclined. Now,

---

[3] **powder-monkeys** The boys who delivered gunpowder to cannons.

what are they? Men at all? or small movable forts and magazines at the service of some unscrupulous man in power? Visit the Navy-Yard,[4] and behold a marine, such a man as an American government can make, or such as it can make a man with its black arts — a mere shadow and reminiscence of humanity, a man laid out alive and standing, and already, as one may say, buried under arms with funeral accompaniments, though it may be —

> Not a drum was heard, not a funeral note,
> As his corse to the rampart we hurried;
> Not a soldier discharged his farewell shot
> O'er the grave where our hero we buried.[5]

The mass of men serve the state thus, not as men mainly, but as   5
machines, with their bodies. They are the standing army, and the militia, jailers, constables, posse comitatus,[6] &c. In most cases there is no free exercise whatever of the judgment or of the moral sense; but they put themselves on a level with wood and earth and stones; and wooden men can perhaps be manufactured that will serve the purpose as well. Such command no more respect than men of straw or a lump of dirt. They have the same sort of worth only as horses and dogs. Yet such as these even are commonly esteemed good citizens. Others — as most legislators, politicians, lawyers, ministers, and office-holders — serve the state chiefly with their heads; and, as they rarely make any moral distinctions, they are as likely to serve the Devil, without *intending* it, as God. A very few, as heroes, patriots, martyrs, reformers in the great sense, and *men,* serve the state with their consciences also and so necessarily resist it for the most part; and they are commonly treated as enemies by it. A wise man will only be useful as a man and will not submit to be "clay" and "stop a hole to keep the wind away," but leave that office to his dust at least:

> I am too high-born to be propertied,
> To be a secondary at control,
> Or useful serving-man and instrument
> To any sovereign state throughout the world.[7]

---

[4] **Navy-Yard** This is apparently the United States Naval yard at Boston.

[5] These lines are from "Burial of Sir John Moore at Corunna" (1817) by the Irish poet Charles Wolfe (1791 – 1823).

[6] **posse comitatus** Literally, the power of the county; it means a law-enforcement group made up of ordinary citizens.

[7] "**clay**," "**stop a hole . . . wind away**," **I am too high-born. . . .** These lines are from Shakespeare; the first is from *Hamlet,* V.i.226 – 227. The verse is from *King John,* V.ii.79 – 82.

He who gives himself entirely to his fellow-men appears to them 6
useless and selfish; but he who gives himself partially to them is pronounced a benefactor and philanthropist.

How does it become a man to behave toward this American 7
government today? I answer, that he cannot without disgrace be associated with it. I cannot for an instant recognize that political organization as *my* government which is the *slave's* government also.

All men recognize the right of revolution; that is, the right to 8
refuse allegiance to, and to resist the government when its tyranny
or its inefficiency are great and unendurable. But almost all say that
such is not the case now. But such was the case, they think, in the
Revolution of '75. If one were to tell me that this was a bad government because it taxed certain foreign commodities brought to its
ports, it is most probable that I should not make an ado about it, for
I can do without them. All machines have their friction; and possibly this does enough good to counterbalance the evil. At any rate, it
is a great evil to make a stir about it. But when the friction comes to
have its machine, and oppression and robbery are organized, I say
let us not have such a machine any longer. In other words, when a
sixth of the population of a nation which has undertaken to be the
refuge of liberty are slaves, and a whole country is unjustly overrun
and conquered by a foreign army and subjected to military law, I
think that it is not too soon for honest men to rebel and revolutionize. What makes this duty the more urgent is the fact that the country so overrun is not our own, but ours is the invading army.

Paley,[8] a common authority with many on moral questions, in 9
his chapter on the "Duty of Submission to Civil Government," resolves all civil obligation into expediency; and he proceeds to say,
"that so long as the interest of the whole society requires it, that is,
so long as the established government cannot be resisted or charged
without public inconveniency, it is the will of God that the established government be obeyed, and no longer. . . . This principle
being admitted, the justice of every particular case of resistance is reduced to a computation of the quantity of the danger and grievance
on the one side, and of the probability and expense of redressing it
on the other." Of this, he says, every man shall judge for himself.
But Paley appears never to have contemplated those cases to which
the rule of expediency does not apply, in which a people, as well as
an individual, must do justice, cost what it may. If I have unjustly

---

[8] **William Paley (1743 – 1805)** An English theologian who lectured widely on
moral philosophy. Paley is famous for *A View of the Evidences of Christianity* (1794).
"Duty of Submission to Civil Government Explained" is Chapter 3 of Book 6 of *The
Principles of Moral and Political Philosophy* (1785).

wrested a plank from a drowning man, I must restore it to him though I drown myself. This, according to Paley, would be inconvenient. But he that would save his life, in such a case, shall lose it. This people must cease to hold slaves and to make war on Mexico, though it cost them their existence as a people.

In their practice, nations agree with Paley; but does anyone 10 think that Massachusetts does exactly what is right at the present crisis?

> A drab of state, a cloth-o'-silver slut,
> To have her train borne up, and her soul trail in the dirt.[9]

Practically speaking, the opponents to a reform in Massachusetts are not a hundred thousand politicians at the South but a hundred thousand merchants and farmers here, who are more interested in commerce and agriculture than they are in humanity, and are not prepared to do justice to the slave and to Mexico, cost what it may. I quarrel not with far-off foes but with those who, near at home, co-operate with, and do the bidding of, those far away, and without whom the latter would be harmless. We are accustomed to say that the mass of men are unprepared; but improvement is slow because the few are not materially wiser or better than the many. It is not so important that many should be as good as you as that there be some absolute goodness somewhere; for that will leaven the whole lump. There are thousands who are in opinion opposed to slavery and to the war who yet in effect do nothing to put an end to them; who, esteeming themselves children of Washington and Franklin, sit down with their hands in their pockets and say that they know not what to do, and do nothing; who even postpone the question of freedom to the question of free trade, and quietly read the prices-current along with the latest advices from Mexico after dinner and, it may be, fall asleep over them both. What is the price-current of an honest man and patriot today? They hesitate and they regret and sometimes they petition; but they do nothing in earnest and with effect. They will wait, well disposed, for others to remedy the evil, that they may no longer have it to regret. At most, they give only a cheap vote, and a feeble countenance and God-speed, to the right, as it goes by them. There are nine hundred and ninety-nine patrons of virtue to one virtuous man. But it is easier to deal with the real possessor of a thing than with the temporary guardian of it.

---

[9] **A drab. . . .** From Cyril Tourneur (1575? – 1626), *Revenger's Tragedy* (1607), IV.iv.70 – 72. "Drab" is an obsolete term for a prostitute. Thoreau quotes the lines to imply that Massachusetts is a "painted lady" with a defiled soul.

All voting is a sort of gaming, like checkers or backgammon,   11
with a slight moral tinge to it, a playing with right and wrong, with
moral questions; and betting naturally accompanies it. The character
of the voters is not staked. I cast my vote, perchance, as I think
right; but I am not vitally concerned that that right should prevail. I
am willing to leave it to the majority. Its obligation, therefore, never
exceeds that of expediency. Even voting *for the right* is *doing* nothing
for it. It is only expressing to men feebly your desire that it should
prevail. A wise man will not leave the right to the mercy of chance,
nor wish it to prevail through the power of the majority. There is
but little virtue in the action of masses of men. When the majority
shall at length vote for the abolition of slavery, it will be because
they are indifferent to slavery, or because there is but little slavery
left to be abolished by their vote. *They* will then be the only slaves.
Only *his* vote can hasten the abolition of slavery who asserts his own
freedom by his vote.

I hear of a convention to be held at Baltimore,[10] or elsewhere,   12
for the selection of a candidate for the Presidency, made up chiefly
of editors, and men who are politicians by profession; but I think,
what is it to any independent, intelligent, and respectable man what
decision they may come to? Shall we not have the advantage of his
wisdom and honesty nevertheless? Can we not count upon some independent votes? Are there not many individuals in the country
who do not attend conventions? But no: I find that the responsible
man, so called, has immediately drifted from his position, and de-
spairs of his country when his country has more reason to despair of
him. He forthwith adopts one of the candidates thus selected as the
only *available* one, thus proving that he is himself *available* for any
purposes of the demagogue. His vote is of no more worth than that
of any unprincipled foreigner or hireling native who may have been
bought. O for a man who is a *man* and, as my neighbor says has a
bone in his back which you cannot pass your hand through! Our
statistics are at fault: the population has been returned too large.
How many *men* are there to a square thousand miles in this country?
Hardly one. Does not America offer any inducement for men to
settle here? The American has dwindled into an Odd Fellow[11] —
one who may be known by the development of his organ of gregari-

---

[10] **Baltimore**   In 1848 the political environment was particularly intense; it was
a seedbed for theoreticians of the Confederacy, which was only beginning to be contemplated seriously.

[11] **Odd Fellow**   The Independent Order of Odd Fellows, a fraternal and benevolent secret society, founded in England in the eighteenth century and first established in the United States in 1819 in Baltimore.

ousness and a manifest lack of intellect and cheerful self-reliance; whose first and chief concern, on coming into the world, is to see that the Almshouses are in good repair; and, before yet he has lawfully donned the virile garb, to collect a fund for the support of the widows and orphans that may be; who, in short, ventures to live only by the aid of the Mutual Insurance Company, which has promised to bury him decently.

It is not a man's duty, as a matter of course, to devote himself to 13 the eradication of any, even the most enormous wrong; he may still properly have other concerns to engage him; but it is his duty, at least, to wash his hands of it and, if he gives it no thought longer, not to give it practically his support. If I devote myself to other pursuits and contemplations, I must first see, at least, that I do not pursue them sitting upon another man's shoulders. I must get off him first, that he may pursue his contemplations too. See what gross inconsistency is tolerated. I have heard some of my townsmen say, "I should like to have them order me out to help put down an insurrection of the slaves, or to march to Mexico — see if I would go"; and yet these very men have each directly by their allegiance and so indirectly, at least, by their money, furnished a substitute. The soldier is applauded who refuses to serve in an unjust war by those who do not refuse to sustain the unjust government which makes the war; is applauded by those whose own act and authority he disregards and sets at naught; as if the State were penitent to that degree that it hired one to scourge it while it sinned, but not to that degree that it left off sinning for a moment. Thus, under the name of Order and Civil Government, we are all made at last to pay homage to and support our own meanness. After the first blush of sin comes its indifference; and from immoral it becomes, as it were, *un*moral, and not quite unnecessary to that life which we have made.

The broadest and most prevalent error requires the most disin- 14 terested virtue to sustain it. The slight reproach to which the virtue of patriotism is commonly liable, the noble are most likely to incur. Those who, while they disapprove of the character and measures of a government, yield to it their allegiance and support, are undoubtedly its most conscientious supporters, and so frequently the most serious obstacles to reform. Some are petitioning the State to dissolve the Union, to disregard the requisitions of the President. Why do they not dissolve it themselves — the union between themselves and the State — and refuse to pay their quota into its treasury? Do not they stand in the same relation to the State that the State does to the Union? And have not the same reasons prevented the State from resisting the Union which have prevented them from resisting the State?

How can a man be satisfied to entertain an opinion merely, and   15
enjoy *it?* Is there any enjoyment in it if his opinion is that he is ag-
grieved? If you are cheated out of a single dollar by your neighbor,
you do not rest satisfied with knowing that you are cheated, or with
saying that you are cheated, or even with petitioning him to pay you
your due; but you take effectual steps at once to obtain the full
amount and see that you are never cheated again. Action from principle, the perception and the performance of right, changes things
and relations; it is essentially revolutionary and does not consist
wholly with anything which was. It not only divides states and
churches, it divides families; ay, it divides the *individual,* separating
the diabolical in him from the divine.

Unjust laws exist: shall we be content to obey them, or shall we   16
endeavor to amend them and obey them until we have succeeded,
or shall we transgress them at once? Men generally, under such a
government as this, think that they ought to wait until they have
persuaded the majority to alter them. They think that if they should
resist the remedy would be worse than the evil. *It* makes it worse.
Why is it not more apt to anticipate and provide for reform? Why
does it not cherish its wise minority? Why does it cry and resist before it is hurt? Why does it not encourage its citizens to be on the
alert to point out its faults and *do* better than it would have them?
Why does it always crucify Christ and excommunicate Copernicus
and Luther[12] and pronounce Washington and Franklin rebels?

One would think that a deliberate and practical denial of its au-   17
thority was the only offence never contemplated by government;
else why has it not assigned its definite, its suitable and proportion-
ate penalty? If a man who has no property refuses but once to earn
nine shillings for the State, he is put in prison for a period unlimited
by any law that I know, and determined only by the discretion of
those who placed him there; but if he should steal ninety times nine
shillings from the State, he is soon permitted to go at large again.

If the injustice is part of the necessary friction of the machine of   18
government, let it go, let it go: perchance it will wear smooth — certainly the machine will wear out. If the injustice has a spring or a
pulley or a rope or a crank exclusively for itself, then perhaps you
may consider whether the remedy will not be worse than the evil;
but if it is of such a nature that it requires you to be the agent of injustice to another, then I say break the law. Let your life be a counter

---

[12] **Nicolaus Copernicus (1473 – 1543) and Martin Luther (1483 – 1546)**
Copernicus revolutionized astronomy and the way humankind perceives the universe; Luther was a religious revolutionary who began the Reformation and created
the first Protestant faith.

friction to stop the machine. What I have to do is to see, at any rate, that I do not lend myself to the wrong which I condemn.

As for adopting the ways which the State has provided for reme- 19 dying the evil, I know not of such ways. They take too much time, and a man's life will be gone. I have other affairs to attend to. I came into this world, not chiefly to make this a good place to live in, but to live in it, be it good or bad. A man has not everything to do, but something; and because he cannot do *everything*, it is not necessary that he should do *something* wrong. It is not my business to be petitioning the Governor or the Legislature any more than it is theirs to petition me; and if they should not hear my petition what should I do then? But in this case the State has provided no way: its very Constitution is the evil. This may seem to be harsh and stubborn and unconciliatory; but it is to treat with the utmost kindness and consideration the only spirit that can appreciate or deserves it. So is all change for the better, like birth and death, which convulse the body.

I do not hesitate to say that those who call themselves Abolition- 20 ists should at once effectually withdraw their support, both in person and property, from the government of Massachusetts, and not wait till they constitute a majority of one before they suffer the right to prevail through them. I think that it is enough if they have God on their side, without waiting for that other one. Moreover, any man more right than his neighbors constitutes a majority of one already.

I meet this American government or its representative, the State 21 government, directly and face to face once a year — no more — in the person of its tax-gatherer; this is the only mode in which a man situated as I am necessarily meets it; and it then says distinctly, Recognize me; and the simplest, the most effectual and, in the present posture of affairs, the indispensablest mode of treating with it on this head, of expressing your little satisfaction with and love for it, is to deny it then. My civil neighbor, the tax-gatherer, is the very man I have to deal with — for it is, after all, with men and not with parchment that I quarrel — and he has voluntarily chosen to be an agent of the government. How shall he ever know well what he is and does as an officer of the government, or as a man, until he is obliged to consider whether he shall treat me, his neighbor, for whom he has respect, as a neighbor and well-disposed man, or as a maniac and disturber of the peace, and see if he can get over this obstruction to his neighborliness without a ruder and more impetuous thought or speech corresponding with his action. I know this well, that if one thousand, if one hundred, if ten men whom I could name — if ten *honest* men only — ay, if *one* HONEST man in this State of Massachusetts, *ceasing to hold slaves,* were actually to withdraw from this copartnership and be locked up in the county jail therefor, it would be the abolition of slavery in America. For it matters not how small the beginning may seem to be: what is once well done is done forever. But we love better to talk about it: that we say is our mission. Reform keeps many scores of newspapers in its service but not one man. If my esteemed neighbor,[13] the State's ambassador, who will devote his days to the settlement of the question of human rights in the Council Chamber, instead of being threatened with the prisons of Carolina, were to sit down the prisoner of Massachusetts, that State which is so anxious to foist the sin of slavery upon her sister — though at present she can discover only an act of inhospitality to be the ground of a quarrel with her — the Legislature would not wholly waive the subject the following winter.

Under a government which imprisons any unjustly, the true place for a just man is also a prison. The proper place today, the only place which Massachusetts has provided for her freer and less desponding spirits is in her prisons, to be put out and locked out of the State by her own act, as they have already put themselves out by their principles. It is there that the fugitive slave and the Mexican prisoner on parole and the Indian come to plead the wrongs of his race should find them; on that separate but more free and honorable ground where the State places those who are not *with* her but *against* her — the only house in a slave State in which a free man can abide with honor. If any think that their influence would be lost there, and their voices no longer afflict the ear of the State, that they would not be as an enemy within its walls, they do not know by how much truth is stronger than error, nor how much more eloquently and effectively he can combat injustice who has experienced a little in his own person. Cast your whole vote, not a strip of paper merely, but your whole influence. A minority is powerless while it conforms to the majority; it is not even a minority then; but it is irresistible when it clogs by its whole weight. If the alternative is to keep all just men in prison or give up war and slavery, the State will not hesitate which to choose. If a thousand men were not to pay their tax-bills this year, that would not be a violent bloody measure, as it would be to pay them, and enable the State to commit violence and shed innocent blood. This is, in fact, the definition of a peaceable revolution, if any such is possible. If the tax-gatherer or any other public

22

---

[13] **esteemed neighbor** Thoreau refers to Samuel Hoar (1778 – 1856), a Massachusetts congressman, who went to South Carolina to protest that state's practice of seizing black seamen from Massachusetts ships and enslaving them. South Carolina threatened Hoar and drove him out of the state. He did not secure the justice he demanded.

officer asks me, as one has done, "But what shall I do?" my answer is, "If you really wish to do anything, resign your office." When the subject has refused allegiance and the officer has resigned his office, then the revolution is accomplished. But even suppose blood should flow. Is there not a sort of blood shed when the conscience is wounded? Through this wound a man's real manhood and immortality flow out, and he bleeds to an everlasting death. I see this blood flowing now.

I have contemplated the imprisonment of the offender rather than the seizure of his goods — though both will serve the same purpose — because they who assert the purest right, and consequently are most dangerous to a corrupt State, commonly have not spent much time in accumulating property. To such the State renders comparatively small service, and a slight tax is wont to appear exorbitant, particularly if they are obliged to earn it by special labor with their hands. If there were one who lived wholly without the use of money, the State itself would hesitate to demand it of him. But the rich man — not to make any invidious comparison — is always sold to the institution which makes him rich. Absolutely speaking, the more money, the less virtue; for money comes between a man and his objects and obtains them for him; and it was certainly no great virtue to obtain it. It puts to rest many questions which he would otherwise be taxed to answer; while the only new question which it puts is the hard but superfluous one, how to spend it. Thus his moral ground is taken from under his feet. The opportunities of living are diminished in proportion as what are called the "means" are increased. The best thing a man can do for his culture when he is rich is to endeavor to carry out those schemes which he entertained when he was poor. Christ answered the Herodians[14] according to their condition. "Show me the tribute-money," said he — and one took a penny out of his pocket — if you use money which has the image of Caesar on it, and which he has made current and valuable, that is, if *you are men of the State* and gladly enjoy the advantages of Caesar's government, then pay him back some of his own when he demands it; "Render therefore to Caesar that which is Caesar's, and to God those things which are God's" — leaving them no wiser than before as to which was which; for they did not wish to know.

When I converse with the freest of my neighbors, I perceive that whatever they may say about the magnitude and seriousness of the

23

24

---

[14] **Herodians** Followers of King Herod who were opposed to Jesus Christ (see Matthew 22:16).

question, and their regard for the public tranquillity, the long and the short of the matter is that they cannot spare the protection of the existing government, and they dread the consequences to their property and families of disobedience to it. For my own part, I should not like to think that I ever rely on the protection of the State. But if I deny the authority of the State when it presents its tax-bill, it will soon take and waste all my property and so harass me and my children without end. This is hard. This makes it impossible for a man to live honestly, and at the same time comfortably, in outward respects. It will not be worth the while to accumulate property; that would be sure to go again. You must hire or squat somewhere and raise but a small crop and eat that soon. You must live within yourself and depend upon yourself always tucked up and ready for a start, and not have many affairs. A man may grow rich in Turkey even, if he will be in all respects a good subject of the Turkish government. Confucius[15] said: "If a state is governed by the principles of reason, poverty and misery are subjects of shame; if a state is not governed by the principles of reason, riches and honors are the subjects of shame." No; until I want the protection of Massachusetts to be extended to me in some distant Southern port, where my liberty is endangered, or until I am bent solely on building up an estate at home by peaceful enterprise, I can afford to refuse allegiance to Massachusetts and her right to my property and life. It costs me less in every sense to incur the penalty of disobedience to the State than it would to obey. I should feel as if I were worth less in that case.

Some years ago the State met me in behalf of the Church and commanded me to pay a certain sum toward the support of a clergyman whose preaching my father attended, but never I myself. "Pay," it said, "or be locked up in the jail." I declined to pay. But, unfortunately, another man saw fit to pay it. I did not see why the schoolmaster should be taxed to support the priest, and not the priest the schoolmaster; for I was not the State's schoolmaster, but I supported myself by voluntary subscription. I did not see why the lyceum should not present its tax-bill and have the State to back its demand, as well as the Church. However, at the request of the selectmen, I condescended to make some such statement as this in writing: — "Know all men by these presents, that I, Henry Thoreau, do not wish to be regarded as a member of any incorporated society which I have not joined." This I gave to the town clerk; and he has it. The

[15] **Confucius (551 – 479 B.C.)** The most important Chinese religious leader. His *Analects* (collection) treated not only religious but moral and political matters as well.

State, having thus learned that I did not wish to be regarded as a member of that church, has never made a like demand on me since; though it said that it must adhere to its original presumption that time. If I had known how to name them, I should then have signed off in detail from all the societies which I never signed on to; but I did not know where to find a complete list.

I have paid no poll-tax[16] for six years. I was put into a jail once on this account, for one night; and, as I stood considering the walls of solid stone, two or three feet thick, the door of wood and iron, a foot thick, and the iron grating which strained the light, I could not help being struck with the foolishness of that institution which treated me as if I were mere flesh and blood and bones, to be locked up. I wondered that it should have concluded at length that this was the best use it could put me to and had never thought to avail itself of my services in some way. I saw that if there was a wall of stone between me and my townsmen, there was a still more difficult one to climb or break through before they could get to be as free as I was. I did not for a moment feel confined, and the walls seemed a great waste of stone and mortar. I felt as if I alone of all my townsmen had paid my tax. They plainly did not know how to treat me but behaved like persons who are underbred. In every threat and in every compliment there was a blunder; for they thought that my chief desire was to stand the other side of that stone wall. I could not but smile to see how industriously they locked the door on my meditations, which followed them out again without let or hindrance, and *they* were really all that was dangerous. As they could not reach me, they had resolved to punish my body; just as boys, if they cannot come at some person against whom they have a spite, will abuse his dog. I saw that the State was half-witted, that it was timid as a lone woman with her silver spoons, and that it did not know its friends from its foes, and I lost all my remaining respect for it and pitied it.   26

Thus the State never intentionally confronts a man's sense, intellectual or moral, but only his body, his senses. It is not armed with superior wit or honesty but with superior physical strength. I was not born to be forced. I will breathe after my own fashion. Let us see who is the strongest. What force has a multitude? They only can force me who obey a higher law than I. They force me to become like themselves. I do not hear of *men* being *forced* to live this way or that by masses of men. What sort of life were that to live? When I meet a gov-   27

---

[16] **poll-tax** A tax levied on every citizen living in a given area; poll means "head," so it is a tax per head. It was about $2 and was used to support the Mexican War.

ernment which says to me, "Your money or your life," why should I be in haste to give it my money? It may be in a great strait and not know what to do: I cannot help that. It must help itself; do as I do. It is not worth the while to snivel about it. I am not responsible for the successful working of the machinery of society. I am not the son of the engineer. I perceive that, when an acorn and a chestnut fall side by side, the one does not remain inert to make way for the other, but both obey their own laws and spring and grow and flourish as best they can till one, perchance, overshadows and destroys the other. If a plant cannot live according to its nature, it dies; and so a man.

The night in prison was novel and interesting enough. The prisoners in their shirt-sleeves were enjoying a chat and the evening air in the doorway when I entered. But the jailer said, "Come, boys, it is time to lock up"; and so they dispersed, and I heard the sound of their steps returning into the hollow apartments. My room-mate was introduced to me by the jailer as "a first-rate fellow and a clever man." When the door was locked, he showed me where to hang my hat and how he managed matters there. The rooms were whitewashed once a month; and this one, at least, was the whitest, most simply furnished, and probably the neatest apartment in the town. He naturally wanted to know where I came from and what brought me there; and when I had told him, I asked him in my turn how he came there, presuming him to be an honest man, of course; and, as the world goes, I believe he was. "Why," said he, "they accuse me of burning a barn; but I never did it." As near as I could discover, he had probably gone to bed in a barn when drunk and smoked his pipe there; and so a barn burnt. He had the reputation of being a clever man, had been there some three months waiting for his trial to come on, and would have to wait as much longer; but he was quite domesticated and contented, since he got his board for nothing and thought that he was well treated. 28

He occupied one window, and I the other; and I saw that if one stayed there long, his principal business would be to look out the window. I had soon read all the tracts that were left there and examined where former prisoners had broken out and where a grate had been sawed off and heard the history of the various occupants of that room; for I found that even here there was a history and a gossip which never circulated beyond the walls of the jail. Probably this is the only house in the town where verses are composed, which afterward printed in a circular form but not published. I was shown quite a long list of verses which were composed by some young men who had been detected in an attempt to escape, who avenged themselves by signing them. 29

I pumped my fellow-prisoner as dry as I could, for fear I should   30
never see him again; but at length he showed me which was my bed
and left me to blow out the lamp.

It was like travelling into a far country, such as I had never ex-   31
pected to behold, to lie there for one night. It seemed to me that I
never had heard the town-clock strike before, nor the evening sounds
of the village; for we slept with the windows open, which were inside
the grating. It was to see my native village in the light of the Middle
Ages, and our Concord was turned into a Rhine stream, and visions of
knights and castles passed before me. They were the voices of old
burghers that I heard in the streets. I was an involuntary spectator and
auditor of whatever was done and said in the kitchen of the adjacent
village-inn — a wholly new and rare experience to me. It was a closer
view of my native town. I was fairly inside of it. I never had seen its institutions before. This is one of its peculiar institutions; for it is a shire
town.[17] I began to comprehend what its inhabitants were about.

In the morning our breakfasts were put through the hole in the   32
door, in small oblong-square tin pans, made to fit, and holding a
pint of chocolate, with brown bread and an iron spoon. When they
called for the vessels again, I was green enough to return what bread
I had left; but my comrade seized it and said that I should lay that
up for lunch or dinner. Soon after he was let out to work at haying
in a neighboring field, whither he went every day, and would not be
back till noon; so he bade me good-day, saying that he doubted if he
should see me again.

When I came out of prison — for someone interfered and paid   33
that tax — I did not perceive that great changes had taken place on the
common, such as he observed who went in a youth and emerged a tottering and gray-headed man; and yet a change had to my eyes come
over the scene — the town and State and country — greater than any
that mere time could effect. I saw yet more distinctly the State in
which I lived. I saw to what extent the people among whom I lived
could be trusted as good neighbors and friends; that their friendship
was for summer weather only; that they did not greatly propose to do
right; that they were a distinct race from me by their prejudices and
superstitions, as the Chinamen and Malays are; that, in their sacrifices
to humanity, they ran no risks, not even to their property; that, after
all, they were not so noble but they treated the thief as he had treated
them and hoped, by a certain outward observance and a few prayers,
and by walking in a particular straight though useless path from time

---

[17] **shire town** A county seat, which means the town would have a court,
county offices, and jails.

to time, to save their souls. This may be to judge my neighbors harshly; for I believe that many of them are not aware that they have such an institution as the jail in their village.

It was formerly the custom in our village, when a poor debtor 34 came out of jail, for his acquaintances to salute him, looking through their fingers, which were crossed to represent the grating of a jail window, "How do ye do?" My neighbors did not thus salute me but first looked at me and then at one another as if I had returned from a long journey. I was put into jail as I was going to the shoemaker's to get a shoe which was mended. When I was let out the next morning I proceeded to finish my errand, and having put on my mended shoe, joined a huckleberry party who were impatient to put themselves under my conduct; and in half an hour — for the horse was soon tackled — was in the midst of a huckleberry field on one of our highest hills two miles off, and then the State was nowhere to be seen.

This is the whole history of "My Prisons."   35

I have never declined paying the highway tax, because I am as 36 desirous of being a good neighbor as I am of being a bad subject; and as for supporting schools I am doing my part to educate my fellow countrymen now. It is for no particular item in the tax-bill that I refuse to pay it. I simply wish to refuse allegiance to the State, to withdraw and stand aloof from it effectually. I do not care to trace the course of my dollar, if I could, till it buys a man or a musket to shoot one with — the dollar is innocent — but I am concerned to trace the effects of my allegiance. In fact, I quietly declare war with the State, after my fashion, though I will still make what use and get what advantage of her I can, as is usual in such cases.

If others pay the tax which is demanded of me from a sympathy 37 with the State, they do but what they have already done in their own case, or rather they abet injustice to a greater extent than the State requires. If they pay the tax from a mistaken interest in the individual taxed, to save his property, or prevent his going to jail, it is because they have not considered wisely how far they let their private feelings interfere with the public good.

This, then, is my position at present. But one cannot be too 38 much on his guard in such a case, lest his action be biassed by obstinacy or an undue regard for the opinions of men. Let him see that he does only what belongs to himself and to the hour.

I think sometimes, Why, this people mean well; they are only 39 ignorant; they would do better if they knew how: why give your neighbors this pain to treat you as they are not inclined to? But I think again, this is no reason why I should do as they do or permit others to suffer much greater pain of a different kind. Again, I sometimes say to myself, When many millions of men, without heat, without ill will, without personal feeling of any kind, demand of you a few shillings only, without the possibility, such is their constitution, of retracting or altering their present demand, and without the possibility, on your side, of appeal to any other millions, why expose yourself to this overwhelming brute force? You do not resist cold and hunger, the winds and the waves, thus obstinately; you quietly submit to a thousand similar necessities. You do not put your head into the fire. But just in proportion as I regard this as not wholly a brute force but partly a human force, and consider that I have relations to those millions as to so many millions of men, and not of mere brute or inanimate things, I see that appeal is possible, first and instantaneously, from them to the Maker of them, and secondly, from them to themselves. But if I put my head deliberately into the fire, there is no appeal to fire or to the Maker of fire, and I have only myself to blame. If I could convince myself that I have any right to be satisfied with men as they are, and to treat them accordingly, and not according, in some respects, to my requisitions and expectations of what they and I ought to be, then, like a good Mussulman[18] and fatalist, I should endeavor to be satisfied with things as they are and say it is the will of God. And, above all, there is this difference between resisting this and a purely brute or natural force, that I can resist this with some effect; but I cannot expect, like Orpheus,[19] to change the nature of the rocks and trees and beasts.

I do not wish to quarrel with any man or nation. I do not wish   40
to split hairs, to make fine distinctions, or set myself up as better than my neighbors. I seek rather, I may say, even an excuse for conforming to the laws of the land. I am but too ready to conform to them. Indeed, I have reason to suspect myself on this head; and each year, as the tax-gatherer comes round, I find myself disposed to review the acts and position of the general and State governments, and the spirit of the people, to discover a pretext for conformity.

> We must affect our country as our parents;
> And if at any time we alienate
> Our love or industry from doing it honor,
> We must respect effects and teach the soul
> Matter of conscience and religion,
> And not desire of rule or benefit.[20]

---

[18] **Mussulman** Muslim; a follower of the religion of Islam.

[19] **Orpheus** In Greek mythology Orpheus was a poet whose songs were so plaintive that they affected animals, trees, and even stones.

[20] **We must affect. . . .** From George Peele (1556–1596), *The Battle of Alcazar* (acted 1588–1589, printed 1594), II.ii. Thoreau added these lines in a later printing of the essay. They emphasize the fact that one is disobedient to the state as one is to a parent — with love and affection and from a cause of conscience. Disobedience is not taken lightly.

I believe that the State will soon be able to take all my work of this sort out of my hands, and then I shall be no better a patriot than my fellow-countrymen. Seen from a lower point of view, the Constitution, with all its faults, is very good; the law and the courts are very respectable; even this State and this American government are, in many respects, very admirable and rare things, to be thankful for, such as a great many have described them; but seen from a point of view a little higher, they are what I have described them; seen from a higher still, and the highest, who shall say what they are, or that they are worth looking at or thinking of at all?

However, the government does not concern me much, and I shall bestow the fewest possible thoughts on it. It is not many moments that I live under a government, even in this world. If a man is thought-free, fancy-free, imagination-free, that which *is not* never for a long time appearing *to be* to him, unwise rulers or reformers cannot fatally interrupt him. 41

I know that most men think differently from myself; but those whose lives are by profession devoted to the study of these or kindred subjects content me as little as any. Statesmen and legislators, standing so completely within the institution, never distinctly and nakedly behold it. They speak of moving society but have no resting-place without it. They may be men of a certain experience and discrimination and have no doubt invented ingenious and even useful systems, for which we sincerely thank them; but all their wit and usefulness lie within certain not very wide limits. They are wont to forget that the world is not governed by policy and expediency. Webster[21] never goes behind government and so cannot speak with authority about it. His words are wisdom to those legislators who contemplate no essential reform in the existing government; but for thinkers, and those who legislate for all time, he never once glances at the subject. I know of those whose serene and wise speculations on this theme would soon reveal the limits of his mind's range and hospitality. Yet, compared with the cheap professions of most reformers, and the still cheaper wisdom and eloquence of politicians in general, his are almost the only sensible and valuable words, and we thank Heaven for him. Comparatively, he is always strong, original, and, above all, practical. Still his quality is not wisdom but prudence. The lawyer's truth is not Truth but consistency, or a consistent expediency. Truth is always in harmony with herself and is not concerned chiefly to reveal the justice that may consist with wrong- 42

---

[21] **Daniel Webster (1782 – 1852)** One of the most brilliant orators of his time. He was secretary of state from 1841 to 1843, which is why Thoreau thinks he cannot be a satisfactory critic of government.

doing. He well deserves to be called, as he has been called, the Defender of the Constitution. There are really no blows to be given by him but defensive ones. He is not a leader but a follower. His leaders are the men of '87.[22] "I have never made an effort," he says, "and never propose to make an effort; I have never countenanced an effort, and never mean to countenance an effort, to disturb the arrangement as originally made, by which the various States came into the Union." Still thinking of the sanction which the Constitution gives to slavery, he says, "Because it was a part of the original compact — let it stand." Notwithstanding his special acuteness and ability, he is unable to take a fact out of its merely political relations and behold it as it lies absolutely to be disposed of by the intellect — what, for instance, it behooves a man to do here in America today with regard to slavery but ventures, or is driven, to make some such desperate answer as the following, while professing to speak absolutely, and as a private man — from which what new and singular code of social duties might be inferred? "The manner," says he, "in which the governments of those States where slavery exists are to regulate it, is for their own consideration, under their responsibility to their constituents, to the general laws of propriety, humanity, and justice, and to God. Associations formed elsewhere, springing from a feeling of humanity, or any other cause, have nothing whatever to do with it. They have never received any encouragement from me, and they never will."[23]

They who know of no purer sources of truth, who have traced   43
up its stream no higher, stand, and wisely stand, by the Bible and the Constitution, and drink at it there with reverence and humility; but they who behold where it comes trickling into this lake or that pool gird up their loins once more and continue their pilgrimage toward its fountain-head.

No man with a genius for legislation has appeared in America.   44
They are rare in the history of the world. There are orators, politicians, and eloquent men by the thousand; but the speaker has not yet opened his mouth to speak who is capable of settling the much-vexed questions of the day. We love eloquence for its own sake and not for any truth which it may utter or any heroism it may inspire. Our legislators have not yet learned the comparative value of free-trade and of freedom, of union, and of rectitude, to a nation. They have no genius or talent for comparatively humble questions of taxation and finance,

---

[22] **men of '87** The men who framed the Constitution in 1787.
[23] These extracts have been inserted since the Lecture was read. [Thoreau's note]

commerce and manufacturers and agriculture. If we were left solely to
the wordy wit of legislators in Congress for our guidance, uncorrected
by the seasonable experience and the effectual complaints of the
people, America would not long retain her rank among the nations.
For eighteen hundred years, though perchance I have no right to say
it, the New Testament has been written; yet where is the legislator
who has wisdom and practical talent enough to avail himself of the
light which it sheds on the science of legislation?

The authority of government, even such as I am willing to sub-   45
mit to — for I will cheerfully obey those who know and can do better than I, and in many things even those who neither know nor can
do so well — is still an impure one: to be strictly just, it must have
the sanction and consent of the governed. It can have no pure right
over my person and property but what I concede to it. The progress
from an absolute to a limited monarchy, from a limited monarchy to
a democracy, is a progress toward a true respect for the individual.
Even the Chinese philosopher[24] was wise enough to regard the individual as the basis of the empire. Is a democracy such as we know it
the last improvement possible in government? Is it not possible to
take a step further towards recognizing and organizing the rights of
man? There will never be a really free and enlightened State until the
State comes to recognize the individual as a higher and independent
power, from which all its own power and authority are derived, and
treats him accordingly. I please myself with imagining a State at last
which can afford to be just to all men and to treat the individual
with respect as a neighbor; which even would not think it inconsistent with its own repose if a few were to live aloof from it, not med-
dling with it, nor embraced by it, who fulfilled all the duties of
neighbors and fellow-men. A State which bore this kind of fruit and
suffered it to drop off as fast as it ripened would prepare the way for
a still more perfect and glorious State, which also I have imagined
but not yet anywhere seen.

QUESTIONS FOR CRITICAL READING

1. How would you characterize the tone of Thoreau's address? Is he
   chastising his audience? Is he praising it? What opinion do you think
   he has of his audience?
2. Explain what Thoreau means when he says, "But a government in
   which the majority rule in all cases cannot be based on justice, even
   as far as men understand it" (para. 4).

---

[24] **Chinese philosopher** Thoreau probably means Confucius.

3. How is injustice "part of the necessary friction of the machine of government" (para. 18)?
4. Why does Thoreau provide us with his "history of prisons" (paras. 28–36)? Describe what being in jail taught Thoreau. Why do you think Thoreau reacted so strongly to being in a local jail for a single day?
5. Choose an example of Thoreau's use of irony, and comment on its effectiveness. (One example appears in para. 25.)
6. How might Thoreau view the responsibility of the majority to a minority within the sphere of government?
7. How clear are Thoreau's concepts of justice? On what are they based?
8. Is it possible that when Thoreau mentions "the Chinese philosopher" (para. 45) he means Lao-tzu? Would Lao-tzu agree that the individual is "the basis of the empire"?

SUGGESTIONS FOR WRITING

1. Thoreau insists, "Law never made men a whit more just" (para. 4). He introduces the concept of conscience as a monitor of law and government. Explain his views on conscience and the conscientious person. How can conscience help create justice? Why is it sometimes difficult for law to create justice?
2. Do you agree with Thoreau when he says, "All voting is a sort of gaming" (para. 11)? Examine his attitude toward elections and the relationship of elections to the kind of justice one can expect from a government.
3. Answer Thoreau's question: "Unjust laws exist: shall we be content to obey them, or shall we endeavor to amend them and obey them until we have succeeded, or shall we transgress them at once?" (para. 16). Thoreau reminds us that the law has been created by the majority and to disobey would put him in a minority—a "wise minority." Why should the wise minority have the right to disobey laws created by the majority?
4. In what ways was the United States government of Thoreau's time built on the individual or on the individual's best interests? In what way is our current government based on the individual's best interests? How can satisfying the individual's best interests be reconciled with satisfying the community's interest? Which would produce more justice?
5. Examine quotations that focus on justice for the individual, and write an essay that establishes the values of the government Thoreau describes. How might that government see its obligations to the governed? How would it treat matters of justice and moral issues? Describe Thoreau's view of the American government of his time in enough detail to give a clear sense of the essay to someone who has not read it.
6. Reread Thoreau's question in 3 above. Answer it in an essay that focuses on issues that are significant to you. Be as practical and cautious

as you feel you should be, and provide your own answer — not the one you feel Thoreau might have given. Then describe the forms that Thoreau's disobedience would be likely to take. What probably would be the limits of his actions?

7. **CONNECTIONS**   Analyze passages from Hannah Arendt's "Ideology and Terror" in relation to what Thoreau says in "Civil Disobedience." Would Arendt have disobeyed a law that was perceived as immoral? Would she have gone to jail to protest unjust laws? During the late 1930s German law would have required Arendt to turn herself in as a Jew, although to do so would have been to face almost certain death. Should she have broken the law?

8. **CONNECTIONS**   Thoreau admits (para. 41) that he is not very concerned with government because he does not have to pay much attention to it. His life goes on regardless of government. He also says that "the authority of government . . . is still an impure one: to be strictly just, it must have the sanction and consent of the governed" (para. 45). How would Jefferson have reacted to Thoreau's attitudes toward government? Would he have agreed with Thoreau's view that it is essentially unimportant to the individual? Does Thoreau derive from Jefferson his view that the success of a government depends on the sanction of the governed? Or did Jefferson have a different idea about the relationship between the government and the governed?

9. **CONNECTIONS**   Thoreau was especially sympathetic to the plight of African-American slaves and would likely have shared the views of Frederick Douglass and Martin Luther King, Jr. What advice might he have given them? Write an essay that applies the basic ideas of "Civil Disobedience" to the circumstances in which Douglass and King found themselves.

MARTIN LUTHER KING, JR.
Letter from Birmingham Jail

MARTIN LUTHER KING, JR., (1929 – 1968) was the most influential civil rights leader in America for a period of more than fifteen years. He was an ordained minister with a doctorate in theology from Boston University. He worked primarily in the South, where he labored steadily to overthrow laws that promoted segregation and to increase the number of black voters registered in southern communities.

From 1958 to 1968 demonstrations and actions opened up opportunities for African Americans who in the South hitherto had been prohibited from sitting in certain sections of buses, using facilities such as water fountains in bus stations, and sitting at luncheon counters with whites. Such laws — unjust and insulting, not to mention unconstitutional — were not challenged by local authorities. Martin Luther King, Jr., who became famous for supporting a program to integrate buses in Montgomery, Alabama, was asked by the Southern Christian Leadership Conference to assist in the fight for civil rights in Birmingham, Alabama, where an SCLC meeting was to be held.

King was arrested as the result of a program of sit-ins at luncheon counters and wrote the letter printed here to a group of clergymen who had criticized his position. King had been arrested before and would be arrested again — resembling Thoreau somewhat in his attitude toward laws that did not conform to moral justice.

King, like Thoreau, was willing to suffer for his views, especially when he found himself faced with punitive laws denying civil rights to all citizens. His is a classic case in which the officers of the government pled that they were dedicated to maintaining a stable civil society, even as they restricted King's individual rights. In 1963, many of the good people to whom King addressed this letter firmly believed that peace and order might be threatened by granting African Americans the true independence and freedom that

King insisted were their rights and indeed were guaranteed under the constitution. This is why King's letter, thirty-five years later, objects to an injustice that was rampant in Douglass's time but was inexcusable in the time of John F. Kennedy.

Eventually, the causes King promoted were victorious. His efforts helped change attitudes in the South and spur legislation that has benefited all Americans. His views concerning nonviolence spread throughout the world, and by the early 1960s he had become famous as a man who stood for human rights and human dignity virtually everywhere. He won the Nobel Peace Prize in 1964.

Although King himself was nonviolent, his program left both him and his followers open to the threat of violence. The sit-ins and voter registration programs spurred countless bombings, threats, and murders by members of the white community. King's life was often threatened, his home bombed, his followers harassed. He was assassinated at the Lorraine Motel in Memphis, Tennessee, on April 4, 1968. But before he died he saw — largely through his own efforts, influence, and example — the face of America change.

KING'S RHETORIC

The most obvious rhetorical tradition King assumes in this important work is that of the books of the Bible that were originally letters, such as Paul's Epistle to the Ephesians and his several letters to the Corinthians. Many of Paul's letters were written while he was in prison in Rome, and he established a moral position that could inspire the citizens who received the letters. At the same time Paul carried out the most important work of the early Christian church — spreading the word of Jesus to those who wished to be Christians but who needed clarification and encouragement.

It is not clear that the clergymen who received King's letter fully appreciated the rhetorical tradition he drew upon — but they were men who preached from the Bible and certainly should have understood it. The text itself alludes to the mission of Paul and to his communications to his people. King works with this rhetorical tradition not only because it is effective but because it resonates with the deepest aspect of his calling — spreading the gospel of Christ. Brotherhood and justice were his message.

King's tone is one of utmost patience with his critics. He seems bent on winning them over to his point of view, just as he seems confident that — because they are, like him, clergymen — their goodwill should help them see the justice of his views.

His method is that of careful reasoning, focusing on the substance of their criticism, particularly on their complaints that his actions were "unwise and untimely" (para. 1). King takes each of those charges in turn and carefully analyzes it against his position and then follows with the clearest possible statement of his own views and why he feels they are worth adhering to. The "Letter from Birmingham Jail" is a model of close and reasonable analysis of a very complex situation. It succeeds largely because it remains concrete, treating one issue after another carefully, refusing to be caught up in passion or posturing. Above all, King remains grounded in logic, convinced that his arguments will in turn convince his audience.

Letter from Birmingham Jail

April 16, 1963

MY DEAR FELLOW CLERGYMEN:[1]

While confined here in the Birmingham city jail, I came across 1
your recent statement calling my present activities "unwise and untimely." Seldom do I pause to answer criticism of my work and ideas. If I sought to answer all the criticisms that cross my desk, my secretaries would have little time for anything other than such correspondence in the course of the day, and I would have no time for constructive work. But since I feel that you are men of genuine good will and that your criticisms are sincerely set forth, I want to try to answer your statement in what I hope will be patient and reasonable terms.

I think I should indicate why I am here in Birmingham, since 2
you have been influenced by the view which argues against "outsiders coming in." I have the honor of serving as president of the

---

[1] This response to a published statement by eight fellow clergymen from Alabama (Bishop C. C. J. Carpenter, Bishop Joseph A. Durick, Rabbi Hilton L. Grafman, Bishop Paul Hardin, Bishop Holan B. Harmon, the Reverend George M. Murray, the Reverend Edward V. Ramage, and the Reverend Earl Stallings) was composed under somewhat constricting circumstances. Begun on the margins of the newspaper in which the statement appeared while I was in jail, the letter was continued on scraps of writing paper supplied by a friendly Negro trusty, and concluded on a pad my attorneys were eventually permitted to leave me. Although the text remains in substance unaltered, I have indulged in the author's prerogative of polishing it for publication. [King's note]

Southern Christian Leadership Conference, an organization operating in every southern state, with headquarters in Atlanta, Georgia. We have some eighty-five affiliated organizations across the South, and one of them is the Alabama Christian Movement for Human Rights. Frequently we share staff, educational, and financial resources with our affiliates. Several months ago the affiliate here in Birmingham asked us to be on call to engage in a nonviolent direct-action program if such were deemed necessary. We readily consented, and when the hour came we lived up to our promise. So I, along with several members of my staff, am here because I was invited here. I am here because I have organizational ties here.

But more basically, I am in Birmingham because injustice is 　3 here. Just as the prophets of the eighth century B.C. left their villages and carried their "thus saith the Lord" far beyond the boundaries of their home towns, and just as the Apostle Paul left his village of Tarsus[2] and carried the gospel of Jesus Christ to the far corners of the Greco-Roman world, so am I compelled to carry the gospel of freedom beyond my own home town. Like Paul, I must constantly respond to the Macedonian call for aid.[3]

Moreover, I am cognizant of the interrelatedness of all communities and states. I cannot sit idly by in Atlanta and not be concerned 　4 about what happens in Birmingham. Injustice anywhere is a threat to justice everywhere. We are caught in an inescapable network of mutuality, tied in a single garment of destiny. Whatever affects one directly, affects all indirectly. Never again can we afford to live with the narrow, provincial, "outside agitator" idea. Anyone who lives inside the United States can never be considered an outsider anywhere within its bounds.

You deplore the demonstrations taking place in Birmingham. 　5 But your statement, I am sorry to say, fails to express a similar concern for the conditions that brought about the demonstrations. I am sure that none of you would want to rest content with the superficial kind of social analysis that deals merely with effects and does not grapple with underlying causes. It is unfortunate that demonstrations are taking place in Birmingham, but it is even more unfortunate that the city's white power structure left the Negro community with no alternative.

---

[2] **village of Tarsus** Birthplace of St. Paul (? – A.D. 67), in Asia Minor, present-day Turkey, close to Syria.
[3] **the Macedonian call for aid** The citizens of Philippi, in Macedonia (northern Greece), were among the staunchest Christians. Paul went to their aid frequently; he also had to resolve occasional bitter disputes within the Christian community there (see Philippians 2:2 – 14).

In any nonviolent campaign there are four basic steps: collec-   6
tion of the facts to determine whether injustices exist; negotiation;
self-purification; and direct action. We have gone through all these
steps in Birmingham. There can be no gainsaying the fact that racial
injustice engulfs this community. Birmingham is probably the most
thoroughly segregated city in the United States. Its ugly record of
brutality is widely known. Negroes have experienced grossly unjust
treatment in the courts. There have been more unsolved bombings
of Negro homes and churches in Birmingham than in any other city
in the nation. These are the hard brutal facts of the case. On the
basis of these conditions, Negro leaders sought to negotiate with the
city fathers. But the latter consistently refused to engage in good-
faith negotiation.

Then, last September, came the opportunity to talk with leaders   7
of Birmingham's economic community. In the course of the negotia-
tions, certain promises were made by the merchants — for example,
to remove the stores' humiliating racial signs. On the basis of these
promises, the Reverend Fred Shuttlesworth and the leaders of the
Alabama Christian Movement for Human Rights agreed to a morato-
rium on all demonstrations. As the weeks and months went by, we
realized that we were the victims of a broken promise. A few signs,
briefly removed, returned; the others remained.

As in so many past experiences, our hopes had been blasted,   8
and the shadow of deep disappointment settled upon us. We had no
alternative except to prepare for direct action, whereby we would
present our very bodies as a means of laying our case before the conscience of the local and the national community. Mindful of the
difficulties involved, we decided to undertake a process of self-
purification. We began a series of workshops on nonviolence, and
we repeatedly asked ourselves: "Are you able to accept blows without retaliating?" "Are you able to endure the ordeal of jail?" We decided to schedule our direct-action program for the Easter season,
realizing that except for Christmas, this is the main shopping period
of the year. Knowing that a strong economic-withdrawal program
would be the by-product of direct action, we felt that this would be
the best time to bring pressure to bear on the merchants for the
needed change.

Then it occurred to us that Birmingham's mayoral election was   9
coming up in March, and we speedily decided to postpone action
until after election day. When we discovered that the Commissioner
of Public Safety, Eugene "Bull" Connor, had piled up enough votes
to be in the run-off, we decided again to postpone action until the
day after the run-off so that the demonstrations could not be used to
cloud the issues. Like many others, we waited to see Mr. Connor de-

feated, and to this end we endured postponement after postponement. Having aided in this community need, we felt that our direct-
action program could be delayed no longer.

You may well ask, "Why direct action? Why sit-ins, marches,   10
and so forth? Isn't negotiation a better path?" You are quite right in
calling for negotiation. Indeed, this is the very purpose of direct action. Nonviolent direct action seeks to create such a crisis and foster
such a tension that a community which has constantly refused to
negotiate is forced to confront the issue. It seeks so to dramatize the
issue that it can no longer be ignored. My citing the creation of tension as part of the work of the nonviolent resister may sound rather
shocking. But I must confess that I am not afraid of the word "tension." I have earnestly opposed violent tension, but there is a type of
constructive, nonviolent tension which is necessary for growth. Just
as Socrates[4] felt that it was necessary to create a tension in the mind
so that individuals could rise from the bondage of myths and half
truths to the unfettered realm of creative analysis and objective ap-
praisal, so must we see the need for nonviolent gadflies to create the
kind of tension in society that will help men rise from the dark
depths of prejudice and racism to the majestic heights of understanding and brotherhood.

The purpose of our direct-action program is to create a situation   11
so crisis-packed that it will inevitably open the door to negotiation. I
therefore concur with you in your call for negotiation. Too long has
our beloved Southland been bogged down in a tragic effort to live in
monologue rather than dialogue.

One of the basic points in your statement is that the action that I   12
and my associates have taken in Birmingham is untimely. Some have
asked: "Why didn't you give the new city administration time to
act?" The only answer that I can give to this query is that the new
Birmingham administration must be prodded about as much as the
outgoing one, before it will act. We are sadly mistaken if we feel that
the election of Albert Boutwell as mayor will bring the millennium[5]
to Birmingham. While Mr. Boutwell is a much more gentle person

---

[4]**Socrates (470? – 399 B.C.)** The "tension in the mind" King refers to is created
by the question-answer technique known as the Socratic method. By posing questions in the beginning of the paragraph, King shows his willingness to share
Socrates' rhetorical techniques. Socrates was imprisoned and killed for his civil disobedience (see para. 21). He was the greatest of the Greek philosophers.

[5]**the millennium** A reference to Revelation 20, according to which the second
coming of Christ will be followed by 1,000 years of peace, when the devil will be in-
capacitated. After this will come a final battle between good and evil, followed by the
Last Judgment.

than Mr. Connor, they are both segregationists, dedicated to maintenance of the status quo. I have hoped that Mr. Boutwell will be reasonable enough to see the futility of massive resistance to desegregation. But he will not see this without pressure from devotees of civil rights. My friends, I must say to you that we have not made a single gain in civil rights without determined legal and nonviolent pressure. Lamentably, it is an historical fact that privileged groups seldom give up their privileges voluntarily. Individuals may see the moral light and voluntarily give up their unjust posture; but, as Reinhold Niebuhr[6] has reminded us, groups tend to be more immoral than individuals.

We know through painful experience that freedom is never voluntarily given by the oppressor; it must be demanded by the oppressed. Frankly, I have yet to engage in a direct-action campaign that was "well timed" in the view of those who have not suffered unduly from the disease of segregation. For years now I have heard the word "Wait!" It rings in the ear of every Negro with piercing familiarity. This "Wait" has almost always meant "Never." We must come to see, with one of our distinguished jurists, that "justice too long delayed is justice denied."[7]   13

We have waited for more than 340 years for our constitutional   14 and God-given rights. The nations of Asia and Africa are moving with jetlike speed toward gaining political independence, but we still creep at horse-and-buggy pace toward gaining a cup of coffee at a lunch counter. Perhaps it is easy for those who have never felt the stinging darts of segregation to say, "Wait." But when you have seen vicious mobs lynch your mothers and fathers at will and drown your sisters and brothers at whim; when you have seen hate-filled policemen curse, kick, and even kill your black brothers and sisters; when you see the vast majority of your twenty million Negro brothers smothering in an airtight cage of poverty in the midst of an affluent society; when you suddenly find your tongue twisted and your speech stammering as you seek to explain to your six-year-old daughter why she can't go to the public amusement park that has just been advertised on television, and see tears welling up in her

---

[6]**Reinhold Niebuhr (1892–1971)** Protestant American philosopher who urged church members to put their beliefs into action against social injustice. He urged Protestantism to develop and practice a code of social ethics and wrote in *Moral Man and Immoral Society* (1932) of the point King mentions here.

[7]**"justice too long delayed is justice denied"** Chief Justice Earl Warren's expression in 1954 was adapted from English writer Walter Savage Landor's phrase "Justice delayed is justice denied."

eyes when she is told that Funtown is closed to colored children, and see ominous clouds of inferiority beginning to form in her little mental sky, and see her beginning to distort her personality by developing an unconscious bitterness toward white people; when you have to concoct an answer for a five-year-old son who is asking, "Daddy, why do white people treat colored people so mean?"; when you take a cross-country drive and find it necessary to sleep night after night in the uncomfortable corners of your automobile because no motel will accept you; when you are humiliated day in and day out by nagging signs reading "white" and "colored"; when your first name becomes "nigger," your middle name becomes "boy" (however old you are) and your last name becomes "John," and your wife and mother are never given the respected title "Mrs."; when you are harried by day and haunted by night by the fact that you are a Negro, living constantly at tiptoe stance, never quite knowing what to expect next, and are plagued with inner fears and outer resentments; when you are forever fighting a degenerating sense of "nobodiness" — then you will understand why we find it difficult to wait. There comes a time when the cup of endurance runs over, and men are no longer willing to be plunged into the abyss of despair. I hope, sirs, you can understand our legitimate and unavoidable impatience.

You express a great deal of anxiety over our willingness to break   15
laws. This is certainly a legitimate concern. Since we so diligently urge people to obey the Supreme Court's decision of 1954 outlawing segregation in the public schools, at first glance it may seem rather paradoxical for us consciously to break laws. One may well ask: "How can you advocate breaking some laws and obeying others?" The answer lies in the fact that there are two types of laws: just and unjust. I would be the first to advocate obeying just laws. One has not only a legal but a moral responsibility to obey just laws. Conversely, one has a moral responsibility to disobey unjust laws. I would agree with St. Augustine[8] that "an unjust law is no law at all."

Now, what is the difference between the two? How does one de-   16
termine whether a law is just or unjust? A just law is a manmade code that squares with the moral law or the law of God. An unjust law is a code that is out of harmony with the moral law. To put it in the terms of St. Thomas Aquinas:[9] An unjust law is a human law that is not rooted in eternal law and natural law. Any law that uplifts

---

[8] **St. Augustine (354 – 430)** Early bishop of the Christian Church who deeply influenced the spirit of Christianity for many centuries.

[9] **St. Thomas Aquinas (1225 – 1274)** The greatest of the medieval Christian philosophers and one of the greatest church authorities.

human personality is just. Any law that degrades human personality is unjust. All segregation statutes are unjust because segregation distorts the soul and damages the personality. It gives the segregator a false sense of superiority and the segregated a false sense of inferiority. Segregation, to use the terminology of the Jewish philosopher Martin Buber,[10] substitutes an "I-it" relationship for an "I-thou" relationship and ends up relegating persons to the status of things. Hence segregation is not only politically, economically, and sociologically unsound, it is morally wrong and sinful. Paul Tillich[11] has said that sin is separation. Is not segregation an existential expression of man's tragic separation, his awful estrangement, his terrible sinfulness? Thus it is that I can urge men to obey the 1954 decision of the Supreme Court, for it is morally right; and I can urge them to disobey segregation ordinances, for they are morally wrong.

Let us consider a more concrete example of just and unjust   17
laws. An unjust law is a code that a numerical or power majority group compels a minority group to obey but does not make binding on itself. This is *difference* made legal. By the same token, a just law is a code that a majority compels a minority to follow and that it is willing to follow itself. This is *sameness* made legal.

Let me give another explanation. A law is unjust if it is inflicted   18
on a minority that, as a result of being denied the right to vote, had no part in enacting or devising the law. Who can say that the legislature of Alabama which set up that state's segregation laws was democratically elected? Throughout Alabama all sorts of devious methods are used to prevent Negroes from becoming registered voters, and there are some counties in which, even though Negroes constitute a majority of the population, not a single Negro is registered. Can any law enacted under such circumstances be considered democratically structured?

Sometimes a law is just on its face and unjust in its application.   19
For instance, I have been arrested on a charge of parading without a permit. Now, there is nothing wrong in having an ordinance which requires a permit for a parade. But such an ordinance becomes un-

---

[10] **Martin Buber (1878 – 1965)** Jewish theologian. *I and Thou* (1923) is his most famous book (see the excerpt on p. 661).

[11] **Paul Tillich (1886 – 1965)** An important twentieth-century Protestant theologian who held that Christianity was reasonable and effective in modern life. Tillich saw sin as an expression of man's separation from God, from himself, and from his fellow man. King sees the separation of the races as a further manifestation of man's sinfulness. Tillich, who was driven out of Germany by the Nazis, stresses the need for activism and the importance of action in determining moral vitality, just as King does.

just when it is used to maintain segregation and to deny citizens the First Amendment privilege of peaceful assembly and protest.

I hope you are able to see the distinction I am trying to point out.   20
In no sense do I advocate evading or defying the law, as would the rabid segregationist. That would lead to anarchy. One who breaks an unjust law must do so openly, lovingly, and with a willingness to accept the penalty. I submit that an individual who breaks a law that conscience tells him is unjust, and who willingly accepts the penalty of imprisonment in order to arouse the conscience of the community over its injustice, is in reality expressing the highest respect for law.

Of course, there is nothing new about this kind of civil disobe-   21
dience. It was evidenced subliminally in the refusal of Shadrach, Meshach, and Abednego to obey the laws of Nebuchadnezzar,[12] on the ground that a higher moral law was at stake. It was practiced superbly by the early Christians, who were willing to face hungry lions and the excruciating pain of chopping blocks rather than submit to certain unjust laws of the Roman Empire. To a degree, academic freedom is a reality today because Socrates practiced civil disobedience. In our own nation, the Boston Tea Party represented a massive act of civil disobedience.

We should never forget that everything Adolf Hitler did in Ger-   22
many was "legal" and everything the Hungarian freedom fighters[13] did in Hungary was "illegal." It was "illegal" to aid and comfort a Jew in Hitler's Germany. Even so, I am sure that, had I lived in Germany at the time, I would have aided and comforted my Jewish brothers. If today I lived in a Communist country where certain principles dear to the Christian faith are suppressed, I would openly advocate disobeying that country's antireligious laws.

I must make two honest confessions to you, my Christian and   23
Jewish brothers. First, I must confess that over the past few years I have been gravely disappointed with the white moderate. I have almost reached the regrettable conclusion that the Negro's great stumbling block in his stride toward freedom is not the White Citizen's Counciler[14] or the Ku Klux Klanner, but the white moderate, who is

---

[12] **Nebuchadnezzar (c. 630 – 562 B.C.)** Chaldean king who twice attacked Jerusalem. He ordered Shadrach, Meshach, and Abednego to worship a golden image. They refused, were cast into a roaring furnace, and were saved by God (see Daniel 1:7 – 3:30).

[13] **Hungarian freedom fighters** The Hungarians rose in revolt against Soviet rule in 1956. Russian tanks put down the uprising with great force that shocked the world. Many freedom fighters died, and many others escaped to the West.

[14] **White Citizen's Counciler** White Citizen's Councils organized in southern states in 1954 to fight school desegregation as ordered by the Supreme Court in May 1954. The councils were not as secret or violent as the Klan; they were also ineffective.

more devoted to "order" than to justice; who prefers a negative peace which is the absence of tension to a positive peace which is the presence of justice; who constantly says, "I agree with you in the goal you seek, but I cannot agree with your methods of direct action"; who paternalistically believes he can set the timetable for another man's freedom; who lives by a mythical concept of time and who constantly advises the Negro to wait for a "more convenient season." Shallow understanding from people of good will is more frustrating than absolute misunderstanding from people of ill will. Lukewarm acceptance is much more bewildering than outright rejection.

I had hoped that the white moderate would understand that law 24 and order exist for the purpose of establishing justice and that when they fail in this purpose they become the dangerously structured dams that block the flow of social progress. I had hoped that the white moderate would understand that the present tension in the South is a necessary phase of the transition from an obnoxious negative peace, in which the Negro passively accepted his unjust plight, to a substantive and positive peace, in which all men will respect the dignity and worth of human personality. Actually, we who engage in nonviolent direct action are not the creators of tension. We merely bring to the surface the hidden tension that is already alive. We bring it out in the open, where it can be seen and dealt with. Like a boil that can never be cured so long as it is covered up but must be opened with all its ugliness to the natural medicines of air and light, injustice must be exposed, with all the tension its exposure creates, to the light of human conscience and the air of national opinion, before it can be cured.

In your statement you assert that our actions, even though 25 peaceful, must be condemned because they precipitate violence. But is this a logical assertion? Isn't this like condemning a robbed man because his possession of money precipitated the evil act of robbery? Isn't this like condemning Socrates because his unswerving commitment to truth and his philosophical inquiries precipitated the act by the misguided populace in which they made him drink hemlock? Isn't this like condemning Jesus because his unique God-consciousness and never-ceasing devotion to God's will precipitated the evil act of crucifixion? We must come to see that, as the federal courts have consistently affirmed, it is wrong to urge an individual to cease his efforts to gain his basic constitutional rights because the quest may precipitate violence. Society must protect the robbed and punish the robber.

I had also hoped that the white moderate would reject the myth 26 concerning time in relation to the struggle for freedom. I have just received a letter from a white brother in Texas. He writes: "All Christians know that the colored people will receive equal rights eventually, but it is possible that you are in too great a religious hurry. It has taken Christianity almost two thousand years to accomplish what it has. The teachings of Christ take time to come to earth." Such an attitude stems from a tragic misconception of time, from the strangely irrational notion that there is something in the very flow of time that will inevitably cure all ills. Actually, time itself is neutral; it can be used either destructively or constructively. More and more I feel that the people of ill will have used time much more effectively than have the people of good will. We will have to repent in this generation not merely for the hateful words and actions of the bad people, but for the appalling silence of the good people. Human progress never rolls in on wheels of inevitability; it comes through the tireless efforts of men willing to be co-workers with God, and without this hard work, time itself becomes an ally of the forces of social stagnation. We must use time creatively, in the knowledge that the time is always ripe to do right. Now is the time to make real the promise of democracy and transform our pending national elegy into a creative psalm of brotherhood. Now is the time to lift our national policy from the quicksand of racial injustice to the solid rock of human dignity.

You speak of our activity in Birmingham as extreme. At first I   27 was rather disappointed that fellow clergymen would see my nonviolent efforts as those of an extremist. I began thinking about the fact that I stand in the middle of two opposing forces in the Negro community. One is a force of complacency, made up in part of Negroes who, as a result of long years of oppression, are so drained of self-respect and a sense of "somebodiness" that they have adjusted to segregation; and in part of a few middle-class Negroes who, because of a degree of academic and economic security and because in some ways they profit by segregation, have become insensitive to the problems of the masses. The other force is one of bitterness and hatred, and it comes perilously close to advocating violence. It is expressed in the various black nationalist groups that are springing up across the nation, the largest and best known being Elijah Muhammad's Muslim movement.[15] Nourished by the Negro's frustration

---

[15] **Elijah Muhammad's Muslim movement** The Black Muslim movement, which began in the 1920s but flourished in the 1960s under its leader, Elijah Muhammad (1897–1975). Among notable figures who became Black Muslims were the poet Imamu Amiri Baraka (b. 1934), the world championship prizefighter Muhammad Ali (b. 1942), and the controversial reformer and religious leader Malcolm X (1925–1965). King saw their rejection of white society (and consequently brotherhood) as a threat.

over the continued existence of racial discrimination, this movement is made up of people who have lost faith in America, who have absolutely repudiated Christianity, and who have concluded that the white man is an incorrigible "devil."

I have tried to stand between these two forces, saying that we   28
need emulate neither the "do-nothingism" of the complacent nor the hatred and despair of the black nationalist. For there is the more excellent way of love and nonviolent protest. I am grateful to God that, through the influence of the Negro church, the way of nonviolence became an integral part of our struggle.

If this philosophy had not emerged, by now many streets of the   29
South would, I am convinced, be flowing with blood. And I am further convinced that if our white brothers dismiss as "rabble-rousers" and "outside agitators" those of us who employ nonviolent direct action, and if they refuse to support our nonviolent efforts, millions of Negroes will, out of frustration and despair, seek solace and security in black nationalist ideologies — a development that would inevitably lead to a frightening racial nightmare.[16]

Oppressed people cannot remain oppressed forever. The yearn-   30
ing for freedom eventually manifests itself, and that is what has happened to the American Negro. Something within has reminded him of his birthright of freedom, and something without has reminded him that it can be gained. Consciously or unconsciously, he has been caught up by the *Zeitgeist*,[17] and with his black brothers of Africa and his brown and yellow brothers of Asia, South America, and the Caribbean, the United States Negro is moving with a sense of great urgency toward the promised land of racial justice. If one recognizes this vital urge that has engulfed the Negro community, one should readily understand why public demonstrations are taking place. The Negro has many pent-up resentments and latent frustrations, and he must release them. So let him march; let him make prayer pilgrimages to the city hall; let him go on freedom rides[18] — and try to understand why he must do so. If his repressed emotions are not released in nonviolent ways, they will seek expression

---

[16] **a frightening racial nightmare** The black uprisings of the 1960s in all major American cities, and the conditions that led to them, were indeed a racial nightmare. King's prophecy was quick to come true.

[17] *Zeitgeist* German word for the intellectual, moral, and cultural spirit of the times.

[18] **freedom rides** In 1961 the Congress of Racial Equality (CORE) organized rides of whites and blacks to test segregation in southern buses and bus terminals with interstate passengers. More than 600 federal marshalls were needed to protect the riders, most of whom were arrested.

through violence; this is not a threat but a fact of history. So I have not said to my people, "Get rid of your discontent." Rather, I have tried to say that this normal and healthy discontent can be channeled into the creative outlet of nonviolent direct action. And now this approach is being termed extremist.

But though I was initially disappointed at being categorized as an   31
extremist, as I continued to think about the matter I gradually gained a measure of satisfaction from the label. Was not Jesus an extremist for love: "Love your enemies, bless them that curse you, do good to them that hate you, and pray for them which despitefully use you, and persecute you." Was not Amos an extremist for justice: "Let justice roll down like waters and righteousness like an ever-flowing stream." Was not Paul an extremist for the Christian gospel: "I bear in my body the marks of the Lord Jesus." Was not Martin Luther an extremist: "Here I stand; I cannot do otherwise, so help me God." And John Bunyan: "I will stay in jail to the end of my days before I make a butchery of my conscience." And Abraham Lincoln: "This nation cannot survive half slave and half free." And Thomas Jefferson:[19] "We hold these truths to be self-evident, that all men are created equal. . . ." So the question is not whether we will be extremists, but what kind of extremists we will be. Will we be extremists for hate or for love? Will we be extremists for the preservation of injustice or for the extension of justice? In that dramatic scene on Calvary's hill three men were crucified. We must never forget that all three were crucified for the same crime — the crime of extremism. Two were extremists for immorality, and thus fell below their environment. The other, Jesus Christ, was an extremist for love, truth, and goodness, and thereby rose above his environment. Perhaps the South, the nation, and the world are in dire need of creative extremists.

I had hoped that the white moderate would see this need. Per-   32
haps I was too optimistic; perhaps I expected too much. I suppose I should have realized that few members of the oppressor race can understand the deep groans and passionate yearnings of the oppressed race, and still fewer have the vision to see that injustice must be rooted out by strong, persistent, and determined action. I am

---

[19] **Amos, Old Testament prophet (8th century B.C.); Paul (? – A.D. 67); Martin Luther (1483 – 1546); John Bunyan (1628 – 1688); Abraham Lincoln (1809 – 1865); and Thomas Jefferson (1743 – 1826)** These figures are all noted for religious, moral, or political innovations that changed the world. Amos was a prophet who favored social justice; Paul argued against Roman law; Luther began the Reformation of the Christian Church; Bunyan was imprisoned for preaching the gospel according to his own understanding; Jefferson drafted the Declaration of Independence.

thankful, however, that some of our white brothers in the South have grasped the meaning of this social revolution and committed themselves to it. They are still all too few in quantity, but they are big in quality. Some — such as Ralph McGill, Lillian Smith, Harry Golden, James McBride Dabbs, Ann Braden, and Sarah Patton Boyle — have written about our struggle[20] in eloquent and prophetic terms. Others have marched with us down nameless streets of the South. They have languished in filthy, roach-infested jails, suffering the abuse and brutality of policemen who view them as "dirty nigger-lovers." Unlike so many of their moderate brothers and sisters, they have recognized the urgency of the moment and sensed the need for powerful "action" antidotes to combat the disease of segregation.

Let me take note of my other major disappointment. I have been   33 so greatly disappointed with the white church and its leadership. Of course, there are some notable exceptions. I am not unmindful of the fact that each of you has taken some significant stands on this issue. I commend you, Reverend Stallings, for your Christian stand on this past Sunday, in welcoming Negroes to your worship service on a nonsegregated basis. I commend the Catholic leaders of this state for integrating Spring Hill College several years ago.

But despite these notable exceptions, I must honestly reiterate   34 that I have been disappointed with the church. I do not say this as one of those negative critics who can always find something wrong with the church. I say this as a minister of the gospel, who loves the church; who was nurtured in its bosom; who has been sustained by its spiritual blessings and who will remain true to it as long as the cord of life shall lengthen.

When I was suddenly catapulted into the leadership of the bus   35 protest in Montgomery, Alabama, a few years ago, I felt we would be supported by the white church. I felt that the white ministers, priests, and rabbis of the South would be among our strongest allies. Instead, some have been outright opponents, refusing to understand the freedom movement and misrepresenting its leaders; all too many others have been more cautious than courageous and have remained silent behind the anesthetizing security of stained-glass windows.

In spite of my shattered dreams, I came to Birmingham with the   36 hope that the white religious leadership of this community would

---

[20] **written about our struggle** These are all prominent southern writers who expressed their feelings regarding segregation in the South. Some of them, like Smith and Golden, wrote very popular books with a wide influence. Some, like McGill and Smith, were severely rebuked by white southerners.

see the justice of our cause and, with deep moral concern, would serve as the channel through which our just grievances could reach the power structure. I had hoped that each of you would understand. But again I have been disappointed. . . .

There was a time when the church was very powerful — in the   37 time when the early Christians rejoiced at being deemed worthy to suffer for what they believed. In those days the church was not merely a thermometer that recorded the ideas and principles of popular opinion; it was a thermostat that transformed the mores of society. Whenever the early Christians entered a town, the people in power became disturbed and immediately sought to convict the Christians for being "disturbers of the peace" and "outside agitators." But the Christians pressed on, in the conviction that they were "a colony of heaven," called to obey God rather than man. Small in number, they were big in commitment. They were too God intoxicated to be "astronomically intimidated." By their effort and example they brought an end to such ancient evils as infanticide and gladiatorial contests.

Things are different now. So often the contemporary church is a   38 weak, ineffectual voice with an uncertain sound. So often it is an archdefender of the status quo. Far from being disturbed by the presence of the church, the powerful structure of the average community is consoled by the church's silent — and often even vocal — sanction of things as they are.

But the judgment of God is upon the church as never before. If   39 today's church does not recapture the sacrificial spirit of the early church, it will lose its authenticity, forfeit the loyalty of millions, and be dismissed as an irrelevant social club with no meaning for the twentieth century. Every day I meet young people whose disappointment with the church has turned into outright disgust.

Perhaps I have once again been too optimistic. Is organized reli-   40 gion too inextricably bound to the status quo to save our nation and the world? Perhaps I must turn my faith to the inner spiritual church, the church within the church, as the true *ekklesia*[21] and the hope of the world. But again I am thankful to God that some noble souls from the ranks of organized religion have broken loose from the paralyzing chains of conformity and joined us as active partners in the struggle for freedom. They have left their secure congregations and walked the streets of Albany, Georgia, with us. They have gone down the highways of the South on torturous rides for free-

---

[21] ***ekklesia*** Greek word for "church" meaning not just the institution but the spirit of the church.

dom. Yes, they have gone to jail with us. Some have been dismissed from their churches, have lost the support of their bishops and fellow ministers. But they have acted in the faith that right defeated is stronger than evil triumphant. Their witness has been the spiritual salt that has preserved the true meaning of the gospel in these troubled times. They have carved a tunnel of hope through the dark mountain of disappointment.

I hope the church as a whole will meet the challenge of this decisive hour. But even if the church does not come to the aid of justice, I have no despair about the future. I have no fear about the outcome of our struggle in Birmingham, even if our motives are at present misunderstood. We will reach the goal of freedom in Birmingham and all over the nation, because the goal of America is freedom. Abused and scorned though we may be, our destiny is tied up with America's destiny. Before the pilgrims landed at Plymouth, we were here. Before the pen of Jefferson etched the majestic words of the Declaration of Independence across the pages of history, we were here. For more than two centuries our forebears labored in this country without wages; they made cotton king; they built the homes of their masters while suffering gross injustice and shameful humiliation — and yet out of a bottomless vitality they continued to thrive and develop. If the inexpressible cruelties of slavery could not stop us, the opposition we now face will surely fail. We will win our freedom because the sacred heritage of our nation and the eternal will of God are embodied in our echoing demands.

Before closing I feel impelled to mention one other point in your statement that has troubled me profoundly. You warmly commended the Birmingham police force for keeping "order" and "preventing violence." I doubt that you would have so warmly commended the police force if you had seen its dogs sinking their teeth into unarmed, nonviolent Negroes. I doubt that you would so quickly commend the policemen if you were to observe their ugly and inhumane treatment of Negroes here in the city jail; if you were to watch them push and curse old Negro women and young Negro girls; if you were to see them slap and kick old Negro men and young boys; if you were to observe them, as they did on two occasions, refuse to give us food because we wanted to sing our grace together. I cannot join you in your praise of the Birmingham police department.

It is true that the police have exercised a degree of discipline in handling the demonstrators. In this sense they have conducted themselves rather "nonviolently" in public. But for what purpose? To preserve the evil system of segregation. Over the past few years I have consistently preached that nonviolence demands that the means we use must be as pure as the ends we seek. I have tried to make clear that it is wrong to use immoral means to attain moral ends. But now I must affirm that it is just as wrong, or perhaps even more so, to use moral means to preserve immoral ends. Perhaps Mr. Connor and his policemen have been rather nonviolent in public, as was Chief Pritchett in Albany, Georgia, but they have used the moral means of nonviolence to maintain the immoral end of racial injustice. As T. S. Eliot[22] has said, "The last temptation is the greatest treason: To do the right deed for the wrong reason."

I wish you had commended the Negro sit-inners and demon- 44
strators of Birmingham for their sublime courage, their willingness to suffer, and their amazing discipline in the midst of great provocation. One day the South will recognize its real heroes. They will be the James Merediths,[23] with the noble sense of purpose that enables them to face jeering and hostile mobs, and with the agonizing loneliness that characterizes the life of the pioneer. They will be old, oppressed, battered Negro women, symbolized in a seventy-two-year-old woman in Montgomery, Alabama, who rose up with a sense of dignity and with her people decided not to ride segregated buses, and who responded with ungrammatical profundity to one who inquired about her weariness: "My feets is tired, but my soul is at rest." They will be the young high school and college students, the young ministers of the gospel and a host of their elders, courageously and nonviolently sitting in at lunch counters and willingly going to jail for conscience' sake. One day the South will know that when these disinherited children of God sat down at lunch counters, they were in reality standing up for what is best in the American dream and for the most sacred values in our Judaeo-Christian heritage, thereby bringing our nation back to those great wells of democracy which were dug deep by the founding fathers in their formulation of the Constitution and the Declaration of Independence.

Never before have I written so long a letter. I'm afraid it is much 45
too long to take your precious time. I can assure you that it would

---

[22] **Thomas Stearns Eliot (1888–1965)** Renowned as one of the twentieth century's major poets, Eliot was born in the United States, but in 1927 became a British subject and a member of the Church of England. Many of his poems focused on religious and moral themes. These lines are from Eliot's play *Murder in the Cathedral,* about Saint Thomas à Becket (1118–1170), the archbishop of Canterbury, who was martyred for his opposition to King Henry II.

[23] **the James Merediths** James Meredith (b. 1933) was the first black to become a student at the University of Mississippi. His attempt to register for classes in 1962 created the first important confrontation between federal and state authorities, when Governor Ross Barnett personally blocked Meredith's entry to the university. Meredith graduated in 1963 and went on to study law at Columbia University.

have been much shorter if I had been writing from a comfortable desk, but what else can one do when he is alone in a narrow jail cell, other than write long letters, think long thoughts, and pray long prayers?

If I have said anything in this letter that overstates the truth and indicates an unreasonable impatience, I beg you to forgive me. If I have said anything that understates the truth and indicates my having a patience that allows me to settle for anything less than brotherhood, I beg God to forgive me.

I hope this letter finds you strong in the faith. I also hope that circumstances will soon make it possible for me to meet each of you, not as an integrationist or a civil rights leader but as a fellow clergyman and a Christian brother. Let us all hope that the dark clouds of racial prejudice will soon pass away and the deep fog of misunderstanding will be lifted from our fear-drenched communities, and in some not too distant tomorrow the radiant stars of love and brotherhood will shine over our great nation with all their scintillating beauty.

> Yours in the cause of
> Peace and Brotherhood,
> MARTIN LUTHER KING, JR.

QUESTIONS FOR CRITICAL READING

1. Define "nonviolent direct action" (para. 2). In what areas of human experience is it best implemented? Is politics its best area of application? What are the four steps in a nonviolent campaign?

2. Do you agree that "law and order exist for the purpose of establishing justice" (para. 24)? Why? Describe how law and order either do or do not establish justice in your community. Compare notes with your peers.

3. King describes an unjust law as "a code that a numerical or power majority group compels a minority group to obey but does not make binding on itself" (para. 17). Devise one or two other definitions of an unjust law. What unjust laws currently on the books do you disagree with?

4. What do you think is the best-written paragraph in the essay? Why?

5. King cites "tension" in paragraph 10 and elsewhere as a beneficial force. Do you agree? What kind of tension does he mean?

6. In what ways was King an extremist (paras. 30–31)?

7. In his letter, to what extent does King consider the needs of women? Would he feel that issues of women's rights are unrelated to issues of racial equality?

8. According to King, how should a government function in relation to the needs of the individual? Does he feel, like Thoreau's "Chinese philosopher," that the empire is built on the individual?

SUGGESTIONS FOR WRITING

1. Write a brief letter protesting an injustice that you feel may not be entirely understood by people you respect. Clarify the nature of the injustice, the reasons that people hold an unjust view, and the reasons your views should be accepted. Consult King's letter, and use his techniques.
2. In paragraph 43, King says, "I have consistently preached that nonviolence demands that the means we use must be as pure as the ends we seek." What exactly does he mean by this? Define the ends he seeks and the means he approves. Do you agree with him on this point? If you have read the selection from Machiavelli, contrast their respective views. Which view seems more reasonable to you?
3. The first part of the letter defends King's journey to Birmingham as a Christian to help his fellows gain justice. He challenges the view that he is an outsider, using such expressions as "network of mutuality" and "garment of destiny" (para. 4). How effective is his argument? Examine the letter for other expressions that justify King's intervention on behalf of his brothers and sisters. Using his logic describe other social areas where you might be justified in acting on your own views on behalf of humanity. Do you expect your endeavors would be welcomed? Are there any areas where you think it would be wrong to intervene in?
4. In paragraphs 15–22, King discusses two kinds of laws — those that are morally right and those that are morally wrong. Which laws did King regard as morally right? Which laws did he consider morally wrong? Analyze one or two current laws that you feel are morally wrong. Be sure to be fair in describing the laws and establishing their nature. Then explain why you feel they are morally wrong. Would you feel justified in breaking these laws? Would you feel prepared, as King was, to pay the penalties demanded of one who breaks the law?
5. Compare King's letter with sections of Paul's letters to the faithful in the New Testament. Either choose a single letter, such as the Epistle to the Romans, or select passages from Romans, the two letters to the Corinthians, the Galatians, the Ephesians, the Thessalonians, or the Philippians. How did Paul and King agree and disagree about brotherly love, the mission of Christ, the mission of the church, concern for the law, and the duties of the faithful? Inventory the New Testament letters and King's letter carefully for concrete evidence of similar or contrary positions.
6. **CONNECTIONS** To what extent do Martin Luther King, Jr.'s, views about government coincide with those of Lao-tzu? Is there a legitimate

comparison to be made between King's policy of nonviolent resistance and Lao-tzu's judicious inactivity? To what extent would King have agreed with Lao-tzu's views? Would Lao-tzu have supported King's position in his letter, or would he have interpreted events differently?

7. **CONNECTIONS** King cites conscience as a guide to obeying just laws and defying unjust laws. How close is his position to that of Thoreau? Do you think that he had read Thoreau's "Civil Disobedience" as an important document regarding justice and injustice? Compare and contrast the positions of these two writers.

SIMONE DE BEAUVOIR
From *The Second Sex*

SIMONE DE BEAUVOIR (1908 – 1986) was one of the most important post – World War II French intellectuals. Her work was basically philosophical, and she herself taught philosophy and lived for a time with one of France's preeminent existentialist philosophers, Jean-Paul Sartre (1905 – 1980). The two attractive, independent, and brilliant leftist thinkers represented the ideal couple to many intellectuals, although recent biographical studies have demonstrated that Beauvoir's ambitions were subjugated to those of Sartre.

She prepared as a teacher at the École Normale Superieure and taught in Marseilles, Rouen, and Paris, all the while writing novels, memoirs, and essays. Her best-known book remains *Le Deuxième Sexe* (1949), published in English in 1953 as *The Second Sex,* which is considered a beacon for the feminist movement. When Beauvoir first began work on this book, French women were not permitted to vote and did not win the right to vote until 1945. In *The Second Sex* she discusses the implications of women's being cast as the Other, the alienated of society. Beauvoir frequently discussed the implications of defining women in relation to men — as what men are not rather than as something in and of themselves.

According to Beauvoir, a person is not born a woman but makes herself a woman. Such a suggestion implies, as Beauvoir develops here, that the individual is shaped and formed by social convention, especially conventions associated with gender. The selection reprinted here from *The Second Sex* is part of a larger discussion of the history of women, much of which is omitted from the English translation of the book. In her work Beauvoir examined the roles that women were restricted to in important periods of

Translated by H. M. Parshley.

173

European history. Although criticized for her concern with only
middle-income women, in this selection she considers the occasional female monarchs as well as peasant farming women.

Beauvoir concentrates on the history of women since the
French Revolution, demonstrating that although social circumstances changed drastically in France after 1789, the lot of women
remained much the same. Her review of the condition of women
preceded most other important feminist writings of the second half
of the twentieth century, and many of its concerns anticipate issues
that have remained constant in feminist writing, such as equal pay
for equal work. The question of justice for women is implicit in
every line of this discussion. Beauvoir does not discuss how
women will achieve justice but rather reminds us that men will not
grant women justice until it is in men's interest to do so.

BEAUVOIR'S RHETORIC

In this essay Beauvoir presents a perspective that she believes
has not been adequately established — that of women in general.
At the time that she wrote this piece, Simone de Beauvoir was not
known as a feminist. Indeed, in the late forties and early fifties few
modern feminists were known in the United States or in France.
Long before Beauvoir aligned herself with certain militant feminists in the 1970s, *The Second Sex* provided a rallying cry, a treatise that examined with great authority the representation of
women in many different intellectual and cultural arenas. For that
reason, the book became a memorable document of great political
power. Its rhetoric is not patterned or self-conscious but simple
and straightforward. The calm, reasonable, direct style enforces the
selection's persuasiveness.

Beauvoir's history of women is, after all, argumentative, and
her purpose is to persuade us that women have been treated unjustly in modern history. Part of her rhetorical method is to point
to the historical status of women, including those of enormous
achievement. She points to the fact that women "have been able to
stir up wars," but "not to propose battle tactics" (para. 4). In other
words, "Through them certain events have been set off, but the
women have been pretexts rather than agents."

To a large extent, Beauvoir attributes women's lack of personal
development to the institution of marriage and household responsibilities such as food preparation and child care that most women
with families accept. She also argues that most modern women
seem to comply with the arrangement that ultimately imprisons

them: a young woman desires marriage because she sees herself "not in accordance with her true nature in itself, but as man defines her."

Beauvoir has drawn criticism for her description of women's behavior. She was accused by writers such as the poet Stevie Smith of standing aside from the mass of women as if she were in a special separate category. Some readers and close friends felt that her relationship with Sartre, in which they saw her treated as an absolute equal intellectually, gave her a distorted view of the nature of women's subjection and gave her writing a cool, overly reserved, intellectual quality.

In fact, this piece is reserved. Beauvoir makes no effort to appeal to our emotions by raging against the oppression of men or by offering us a case study of female suffering. Her careful balancing of detail and fact, however, ultimately makes a powerful and unassailable case. Even her unexpected pairing of free love and adultery (para. 3) demonstrates a form of injustice and the manner in which women have become accustomed to its presence in everyday life. Beauvoir's rational tone throughout the essay is one of the rhetorical hallmarks of *The Second Sex* and has helped establish it as a seminal text.

From *The Second Sex*

If we cast a general glance over this history, we see several conclusions that stand out from it. And this one first of all: the whole of feminine history has been man-made. Just as in America there is no Negro problem, but rather a white problem; just as "anti-semitism is not a Jewish problem: it is our problem"; so the woman problem has always been a man's problem. We have seen why men had moral prestige along with physical strength from the start; they created values, mores, religions; never have women disputed this empire with them. Some isolated individuals — Sappho, Christine de Pisan, Mary Wollstonecraft, Olympe de Gouges[1] — have protested against the harshness of their destiny, and occasionally mass demonstrations have been made; but neither the Roman matrons uniting

---

[1] **Sappho** (c. 610 – c. 580 B.C.), **Christine de Pisan** (1364 – 1431), **Mary Wollstonecraft** (1759 – 1797), **Olympe de Gouges** (1748 – 1793) Prolific writers of poems, essays, novels, and plays.

against the Oppian law nor the Anglo-Saxon suffragettes could have succeeded with their pressure unless the men had been quite disposed to submit to it. Men have always held the lot of woman in their hands; and they have determined what it should be, not according to her interest, but rather with regard to their own projects, their fears, and their needs. When they revered the Goddess Mother, it was because they feared Nature; when the bronze tool allowed them to face Nature boldly, they instituted the patriarchate; then it became the conflict between family and State that defined woman's status; the Christian's attitude toward God, the world, and his own flesh was reflected in the situation to which he consigned her; what was called in the Middle Ages "the quarrel of women" was a quarrel between clerics and laymen over marriage and celibacy; it was the social regime founded on private property that entailed the guardianship of the married woman, and it is the technological evolution accomplished by men that has emancipated the women of today. It was a transformation in masculine ethics that brought about a reduction in family size through birth control and partially freed woman from bondage to maternity. Feminism itself was never an autonomous movement: it was in part an instrument in the hands of politicians, in part an epiphenomenon[2] reflecting a deeper social drama. Never have women constituted a separate caste, nor in truth have they ever as a sex sought to play a historic role. The doctrines that object to the advent of woman considered as flesh, life, immanence, the Other, are masculine ideologies in no way expressing feminine aspirations. The majority of women resign themselves to their lot without attempting to take any action; those who have tried to change it have intended not to be confined within the limits of their peculiarity and cause it to triumph, but to rise above it. When they have intervened in the course of world affairs, it has been in accord with men, in masculine perspectives.

This intervention, in general, has been secondary and episodic. The classes in which women enjoyed some economic independence and took part in production were the oppressed classes, and as women workers they were enslaved even more than the male workers. In the ruling classes woman was a parasite and as such was subjected to masculine laws. In both cases it was practically impossible for woman to take action. The law and the mores did not always coincide, and between them the equilibrium was established in such a manner that woman was never concretely free. In the ancient

_____

[2] **epiphenomenon** A secondary factor, appearing along with the original. In this case, feminism is not the primary political issue but is associated with it.

Roman Republic economic conditions gave the matron concrete powers, but she had no legal independence. Conditions were often similar for woman in peasant civilizations and among the lower commercial middle class: mistress-servant in the house, but socially a minor. Inversely, in epochs of social disintegration woman is set free; but in ceasing to be man's vassal, she loses her fief; she has only a negative liberty, which is expressed in license and dissipation. So it was with woman during the decline of Rome, the Renaissance, the eighteenth century, the Directory (1795–9). Sometimes she succeeded in keeping busy, but found herself enslaved; or she was set free and no longer knew what to do with herself. One remarkable fact among others is that the married woman had her place in society but enjoyed no rights therein; whereas the unmarried female, honest woman or prostitute, had all the legal capacities of a man, but up to this century was more or less excluded from social life.

From this opposition of legal rights and social custom has resulted, among other things, this curious paradox: free love is not forbidden by law, whereas adultery is an offense; but very often the young girl who "goes wrong" is dishonored, whereas the misconduct of the wife is viewed indulgently; and in consequence many young women from the seventeenth century to our own day have married in order to be able to take lovers freely. By means of this ingenious system the great mass of women is held closely in leading strings: exceptional circumstances are required if a feminine personality is to succeed in asserting itself between these two series of restraints, theoretical or concrete. The women who have accomplished works comparable to those of men are those exalted by the power of social institutions above all sexual differentiation. Queen Isabella, Queen Elizabeth, Catherine the Great were neither male nor female — they were sovereigns. It is remarkable that their femininity, when socially abolished, should have no longer meant inferiority: the proportion of queens who had great reigns is infinitely above that of great kings. Religion works the same transformation: Catherine of Siena, St. Theresa,[3] quite beyond any physiological consideration, were sainted souls; the life they led, secular and mystic, their acts, and their writings rose to heights that few men have ever reached.

It is quite conceivable that if other women fail to make a deep impression upon the world, it is because they are tied down in their

---

[3] **Catherine of Siena (1347–1380), St. Theresa (Teresa of Avila, 1515–1582)** Writers who were influential in religion and religious politics. Catherine wrote the *Dialogue* (1378), and Teresa wrote *The Book of Her Life* (1565) (see p. 629), *The Way of Perfection* (1583), *The Interior Castle* (1588), *Spiritual Relations* (1588), and *Exclamations of the Soul to God* (1588).

situation. They can hardly take a hand in affairs in other than a negative and oblique manner. Judith, Charlotte Corday, Vera Zasulich
were assassins; the *Frondeuses*[4] were conspirators; during the Revolution, during the Commune, women battled beside the men against
the established order. Against a liberty without rights, without powers, woman has been permitted to rise in refusal and revolt, while
being forbidden to participate in positively constructive effort; at the
most she may succeed in joining men's enterprises through an indirect road. Aspasia, Mme de Maintenon, the Princess des Ursins[5]
were counselors who were listened to seriously — yet somebody had
to be willing to listen to them. Men are glad to exaggerate the extent
of these influences when they wish to convince woman that she has
chosen the better part; but as a matter of fact, feminine voices are
silent when it comes to concrete action. They have been able to stir
up wars, not to propose battle tactics; they have directed politics
hardly more than in the degree that politics is reduced to intrigue;
the true control of the world has never been in the hands of women;
they have not brought their influence to bear upon technique or
economy, they have not made and unmade states, they have not discovered new worlds. Through them certain events have been set off,
but the women have been pretexts rather than agents. The suicide of
Lucretia[6] has had value only as a symbol. Martyrdom remains open
to the oppressed; during the Christian persecutions, on the morrow
of social or national defeats, women have played this part of witness;
but never has a martyr changed the face of the world. Even when
women have started things and made demonstrations, these moves
have taken on weight only when a masculine decision has effectively
extended them. The American women grouped around Harriet
Beecher Stowe[7] aroused public opinion violently against slavery; but

---

[4] **Judith (biblical figure in the Apocryphal Book of Judith), Charlotte Corday (1768 – 1793), Vera Zasulich (1849 – 1919), *Frondeuses* (heroines of the
French revolution from the Fronde party)** Judith beheaded Holofernes. Corday
killed the French revolutionary leader Jean-Paul Marat. Zasulich was an early Marxist who shot General Trepov, governor of St. Petersburg, in 1878.

[5] **Aspasia (5th cent. B.C.), Mme de Maintenon (Françoise d'Aubigné,
1635 – 1719), the Princess des Ursins (Marie-Anne de la Trémoille, 1642 –
1722)** Aspasia was the mistress of the Greek ruler Pericles. Madame de Maintenon
was the second wife of Louis XIV. The Princess des Ursins was a French noblewoman who exerted great influence over the King of Spain.

[6] **Lucretia** Roman matron who killed herself after telling her husband and Brutus that she was raped by the tyrant Tarquinius. Brutus then killed Tarquinius. Thus
she is linked in legend with the overthrow of kingly power in Rome.

[7] **Harriet Beecher Stowe (1811 – 1896)** Author of the novel *Uncle Tom's
Cabin.*

the true reasons for the War of Secession were not of a sentimental order. The "woman's day" of March 8, 1917 may perhaps have precipitated the Russian Revolution — but it was only a signal.

Most female heroines are oddities: adventuresses and originals 5 notable less for the importance of their acts than for the singularity of their fates. Thus if we compare Joan of Arc, Mme Roland, Flora Tristan, with Richelieu, Danton, Lenin,[8] we see that their greatness is primarily subjective: they are exemplary figures rather than historical agents. The great man springs from the masses and he is propelled onward by circumstances; the masses of women are on the margin of history, and circumstances are an obstacle for each individual, not a springboard. In order to change the face of the world, it is first necessary to be firmly anchored in it; but the women who are firmly rooted in society are those who are in subjection to it; unless designated for action by divine authority — and then they have shown themselves to be as capable as men — the ambitious woman and the heroine are strange monsters. It is only since women have begun to feel themselves at home on the earth that we have seen a Rosa Luxemburg, a Mme Curie[9] appear. They brilliantly demonstrate that it is not the inferiority of women that has caused their historical insignificance: it is rather their historical insignificance that has doomed them to inferiority.[10]

This fact is glaringly clear in the domain in which women have 6 best succeeded in asserting themselves — that is, the domain of culture. Their lot has been deeply bound up with that of arts and letters; among the ancient Germans the functions of prophetess and priestess were already appropriate to women. Because of woman's marginal position in the world, men will turn to her when they strive through culture to go beyond the boundaries of their universe and gain access to something other than what they have known. Courtly mysticism, humanist curiosity, the taste for beauty which flourished in the Italian Renaissance, the preciosity of the seven-

---

[8] **Joan of Arc (1412 – 1431), Mme Jeanne-Marie Roland (1759 – 1793), Flora Tristan (1803 – 1844), Duc de Richelieu (1585 – 1642), Danton (1759 – 1794), Vladimir Ilyich Lenin (1870 – 1924)** Figures important for their political or revolutionary activity.

[9] **Rosa Luxemburg (1871 – 1919), Mme Curie (Marja Sklodowska, 1867 – 1934)** Luxemburg was a German revolutionary Marxist writer. Curie discovered radium.

[10] It is remarkable that out of a thousand statues in Paris (excepting the queens that for a purely architectural reason form the corbel of the Luxembourg) there should be only ten raised to women. Three are consecrated to Joan of Arc. The others are statues of Mme de Ségur, George Sand, Sarah Bernhardt, Mme Boucicault and the Baroness de Hirsch, Maria Deraismes, and Rosa Bonheur. [Beauvoir's note]

teenth century, the progressive idealism of the eighteenth — all brought about under different forms an exaltation of femininity. Woman was thus the guiding star of poetry, the subject matter of the work of art; her leisure allowed her to consecrate herself to the pleasures of the spirit: inspiration, critic, and public of the writer, she became his rival; she it was who often made prevail a mode of sensibility, an ethic that fed masculine hearts, and thus she intervened in her own destiny — the education of women was in large part a feminine conquest. And yet, however important this collective role of the intellectual woman may have been, the individual contributions have been in general of less value. It is because she has not been engaged in action that woman has had a privileged place in the domains of thought and of art; but art and thought have their living springs in action. To be situated at the margin of the world is not a position favorable for one who aims at creating anew: here again, to emerge beyond the given, it is necessary first to be deeply rooted in it. Personal accomplishment is almost impossible in the human categories that are maintained collectively in an inferior situation. "Where would you have one go, with skirts on?" Marie Bashkirtsev wanted to know. And Stendhal said: "All the geniuses who are born *women* are lost to the public good." To tell the truth, one is not born a genius: one becomes a genius; and the feminine situation has up to the present rendered this becoming practically impossible.

The antifeminists obtain from the study of history two contra- 7 dictory arguments: (1) women have never created anything great; and (2) the situation of woman has never prevented the flowering of great feminine personalities. There is bad faith in these two statements; the successes of a privileged few do not counterbalance or excuse the systematic lowering of the collective level; and that these successes are rare and limited proves precisely that circumstances are unfavorable for them. As has been maintained by Christine de Pisan, Poulain de la Barre, Condorcet, John Stuart Mill, and Stendhal,[11] in no domain has woman ever really had her chance. That is why a great many women today demand a new status; and once again their demand is not that they be exalted in their femininity: they wish that in themselves, as in humanity in general, transcendence may prevail over immanence; they wish to be accorded at last

---

[11] Christine de Pisan (1365–1431), Poulain de la Barre (1647–1723), Condorcet (1743–1794), John Stuart Mill (1806–1893), Stendhal (Marie-Henri Beyle, 1783–1842) De Pisan wrote *The Book of the City of Ladies* (1405), among other influential works. De la Barre authored *The Equality of the Sexes* (1673). Condorcet was a French revolutionary and an editor of the *Encyclopédie*. Mill authored *Utilitarianism* (1863) and an essay on granting the vote to women. Stendhal wrote *The Red and the Black* (1831).

the abstract rights and concrete possibilities without the concurrence of which liberty is only a mockery.[12]

This wish is on the way to fulfillment. But the period in which 8
we live is a period of transition; this world, which has always belonged to the men, is still in their hands; the institutions and the values of the patriarchal civilization still survive in large part. Abstract rights are far from being completely granted everywhere to women: in Switzerland they do not yet vote; in France the law of 1942 maintains in attenuated form the privileges of the husband. And abstract rights, as I have just been saying, have never sufficed to assure to woman a definite hold on the world: true equality between the two sexes does not exist even today.

In the first place, the burdens of marriage weigh much more 9
heavily upon woman than upon man. We have noted that servitude to maternity has been reduced by the use — admitted or clandestine — of birth control; but the practice has not spread everywhere nor is it invariably used. Abortion being officially forbidden, many women either risk their health in unsupervised efforts to abort or find themselves overwhelmed by their numerous pregnancies. The care of children like the upkeep of the home is still undertaken almost exclusively by woman. Especially in France the antifeminist tradition is so tenacious that a man would feel that he was lowering himself by helping with tasks hitherto assigned to women. The result is that it is more difficult for woman than for man to reconcile her family life with her role as worker. Whenever society demands this effort, her life is much harder than her husband's.

Consider for example the lot of peasant women. In France they 10
make up the majority of women engaged in productive labor; and they are generally married. Customs vary in different regions: the Norman peasant woman presides at meals, whereas the Corsican woman does not sit at table with the men; but everywhere, playing a most important part in the domestic economy, she shares the man's responsibilities, interests, and property; she is respected and often is in effective control — her situation recalls that of woman in the old agricultural communities. She often has more moral prestige than her husband, but she lives in fact a much harder life. She has exclusive care of garden, sheepfold, pigpen, and so on, and shares in the

---

[12] Here again the antifeminists take an equivocal line. Now, regarding abstract liberty as nothing, they expatiate on the great concrete role that the enslaved woman can play in the world — what then, is she asking for? Again, they disregard the fact that negative license opens no concrete possibilities, and they reproach women who are abstractly emancipated for not having produced evidence of their abilities. [Beauvoir's note]

hard labor of stablework, planting, plowing, weeding, and haying; she spades, reaps, picks grapes, and sometimes helps load and unload wagons with hay, wood, and so forth. She cooks, keeps house, does washing, mending, and the like. She takes on the heavy duties of maternity and child care. She gets up at dawn, feeds the poultry and other small livestock, serves breakfast to the men, goes to work in field, wood, or garden; she draws water, serves a second meal, washes the dishes, works in the fields until time for dinner, and afterward spends the evening mending, cleaning, shelling corn, and what not. Having no time to care for her own health, even when pregnant, she soon gets misshapen; she is prematurely withered and worn out, gnawed by sickness. The compensations man finds in occasional social life are denied to her: he goes in town on Sundays and market days, meets other men, drinks and plays cards in cafés, goes hunting and fishing. She stays at home on the farm and knows no leisure. Only the well-off peasant women, who have servants or can avoid field labor, lead a well-balanced life: they are socially honored and at home exert a great deal of authority without being crushed by work. But for the most part rural labor reduces woman to the condition of a beast of burden.

The businesswoman and the female employer who runs a small 11 enterprise have always been among the privileged; they are the only women recognized since the Middle Ages by the Code as having civil rights and powers. Female grocers, dairy dealers, landladies, tobacconists have a position equivalent to man's; as spinsters or widows, they can in themselves constitute a legal firm; married, they have the same independence as their husbands. Fortunately their work can be carried on in the place where they live, and usually it is not too absorbing.

Things are quite otherwise for the woman worker or employee, 12 the secretary, the saleswoman, all of whom go to work outside the home. It is much more difficult for them to combine their employment with household duties, which would seem to require at least three and a half hours a day, with six hours on Sunday — a good deal to add to the hours in factory or office. As for the learned professions, even if lawyers, doctors, and professors obtain some housekeeping help, the home and children are for them also a burden that is a heavy handicap. In America domestic work is simplified by ingenious gadgets; but the elegant appearance required of the workingwoman imposes upon her another obligation, and she remains responsible for house and children.

Furthermore, the woman who seeks independence through 13 work has less favorable possibilities than her masculine competitors. Her wages in most jobs are lower than those of men; her tasks are less specialized and therefore not so well paid as those of skilled laborers; and for equal work she does not get equal pay. Because of the fact that she is a newcomer in the universe of males, she has fewer chances for success than they have. Men and women alike hate to be under the orders of a woman; they always show more confidence in a man; to be a woman is, if not a defect, at least a peculiarity. In order to "arrive," it is well for a woman to make sure of masculine backing. Men unquestionably occupy the most advantageous places, hold the most important posts. It is essential to emphasize the fact that men and women, economically speaking, constitute two castes.[13]

The fact that governs woman's actual condition is the obstinate survival of extremely antique traditions into the new civilization that is just appearing in vague outline. That is what is misunderstood by hasty observers who regard woman as not up to the possibilities now offered to her or again who see in these possibilities only dangerous temptations. The truth is that her situation is out of equilibrium, and for that reason it is very difficult for her to adapt herself to it. We open the factories, the offices, the faculties to woman, but we continue to hold that marriage is for her a most honorable career, freeing her from the need of any other participation in the collective life. As in primitive civilizations, the act of love is on her part a service for which she has the right to be more or less directly paid. Except in the Soviet Union,[14] modern woman is everywhere permitted to regard her body as capital for exploitation. Prostitution is tolerated,[15] gallantry encouraged. And the married woman is empowered

[14]

---

[13] In America the great fortunes often fall finally into women's hands: younger than their husbands, they survive them and inherit from them; but by that time they are aged and rarely have the initiative to make new investments; they are enjoyers of income rather than proprietors. It is really men who handle the capital funds. At any rate, these privileged rich women make up only a tiny minority. In America, much more than in Europe, it is almost impossible for a woman to reach a high position as lawyer, doctor, etc. [Beauvoir's note]

[14] At least according to official doctrine. [Beauvoir's note]

[15] In Anglo-Saxon countries prostitution has never been regulated. Up to 1900 English and American common law did not regard it as an offense except when it made public scandal and created disorder. Since that date repression has been more or less rigorously imposed, more or less successfully, in England and in the various states of the United States, where legislation in the matter is very diverse. In France, after a long campaign for abolition, the law of April 13, 1946 ordered the closing of licensed brothels and the intensifying of the struggle against procuring: "Holding that the existence of these houses is incompatible with the essential principles of human dignity and the role awarded to woman in modern society." But prostitution continues none the less to carry on. It is evident that the situation cannot be modified by negative and hypocritical measures. [Beauvoir's note]

to see to it that her husband supports her; in addition she is clothed in a social dignity far superior to that of the spinster. The mores are far from conceding to the latter sexual possibilities equivalent to those of the bachelor male; in particular maternity is practically forbidden her, the unmarried mother remaining an object of scandal. How, indeed, could the myth of Cinderella not keep all its validity? Everything still encourages the young girl to expect fortune and happiness from some Prince Charming rather than to attempt by herself their difficult and uncertain conquest. In particular she can hope to rise, thanks to him, into a caste superior to her own, a miracle that could not be bought by the labor of her lifetime. But such a hope is a thing of evil because it divides her strength and her interests; this division is perhaps woman's greatest handicap. Parents still raise their daughter with a view to marriage rather than to furthering her personal development; she sees so many advantages in it that she herself wishes for it; the result is that she is often less specially trained, less solidly grounded than her brothers, she is less deeply involved in her profession. In this way she dooms herself to remain in its lower levels, to be inferior; and the vicious circle is formed: this professional inferiority reinforces her desire to find a husband.

Every benefit always has as its bad side some burden; but if the   15
burden is too heavy, the benefit seems no longer to be anything more than a servitude. For the majority of laborers, labor is today a thankless drudgery, but in the case of woman this is not compensated for by a definite conquest of her social dignity, her freedom of behavior, or her economic independence; it is natural enough for many woman workers and employees to see in the right to work only an obligation from which marriage will deliver them. Because of the fact that she has taken on awareness of self, however, and because she can also free herself from marriage through a job, woman no longer accepts domestic subjection with docility. What she would hope is that the reconciliation of family life with a job should not require of her an exhausting, difficult performance. Even then, as long as the temptations of convenience exist — in the economic inequality that favors certain individuals and the recognized right of woman to sell herself to one of these privileged men — she will need to make a greater moral effort than would a man in choosing the road of independence. It has not been sufficiently realized that the temptation is also an obstacle, and even one of the most dangerous. Here it is accompanied by a hoax, since in fact there will be only one winner out of thousands in the lottery of marriage. The present epoch invites, even compels women to work; but it flashes before their eyes paradises of idleness and delight: it exalts the winners far above those who remain tied down to earth.

The privileged place held by men in economic life, their social usefulness, the prestige of marriage, the value of masculine backing, all this makes women wish ardently to please men. Women are still, for the most part, in a state of subjection. It follows that woman sees herself and makes her choices not in accordance with her true nature it itself, but as man defines her.

QUESTIONS FOR CRITICAL READING

1. How strongly does our society still feel that for a woman marriage is "a most honorable career, freeing her from the need of any other participation in the collective life" (para. 14)?
2. Do you agree that "modern woman is everywhere permitted to regard her body as capital for exploitation" (para.14)? How does such an exploitation affect women's equality?
3. To what extent is the burden of children and home an impediment to women's achieving equality with men?
4. Is Beauvoir correct in complaining that "Men and women alike hate to be under the orders of a woman; they always show more confidence in a man" (para. 13)? If you think this is true, what are the reasons? Have things changed in the workplace since 1949?
5. Do men and women economically "constitute two castes" (para. 13)?
6. How has birth control — totally unknown in its modern forms in 1949 — changed the balance of power between men and women (para. 9)?

SUGGESTIONS FOR WRITING

1. Beauvoir complains (para. 14) that "the obstinate survival of extremely antique traditions into the new civilization" has caused women to overvalue marriage and to think that a Prince Charming will provide fortune and happiness. Examine the "antique traditions" surviving in today's culture that work to create inequality between men and women. Look especially at those traditions that tend to make women want the very thing that prevents their growth.
2. If you disagree with Beauvoir's analysis of the condition of women, use her own rhetorical methods to establish an alternative view. Offer a review of the history of women that demonstrates their achievement and their ability to establish themselves as men's equal in social circumstances.
3. Examine the antifeminist arguments that Beauvoir represents (para. 7). Is her review of their arguments reasonable? Would antifeminists think of the state of contemporary women as a result of injustice? Would

Beauvoir think so? Which of the arguments against Beauvoir seem most powerful?

4. What are the most important sources of injustice toward women? Are they biological, a result of the fact that women must bear children? Are they social, a result of the fact that men assume privileges in marriage that they will not accord women? Are they economic, a result of different economic opportunities for members of "different castes" (para. 13)? Or are they legal, a result of legal institutions such as marriage and suffrage (the right to vote) that always favor men because they are founded by men? Explain your answer.

5. Beauvoir suggests that women have "best succeeded" in asserting themselves in "the domain of culture" (para. 6). In what ways is woman still "the guiding star of poetry, the subject matter of the work of art"? For "poetry" you may substitute song lyrics or another art form, such as film. If you agree that women continue to succeed in the domain of culture, to what do you attribute the success of women in this area? Does it suit men to permit them this success? Why?

6. Are most female heroines "oddities" (para. 5)? Consider the most successful women in modern life. How are they oddities in the sense that Beauvoir suggests?

7. **CONNECTIONS** Compare Beauvoir's arguments with the position assumed by Martin Luther King, Jr., or Frederick Douglass. Each of these men defends a minority's right to justice, but Beauvoir argues in favor of the rights of a numerical majority: after two world wars many millions more women than men inhabited Europe. How does such a fact change our attitude toward the injustices complained about by Beauvoir?

PART THREE

WEALTH

Adam Smith
Karl Marx
John Kenneth Galbraith
Robert B. Reich

INTRODUCTION

Ancient writers talk about wealth in terms of a surplus of necessary or desirable goods and products. After the invention of coins — which historians attribute to the Lydians, whose civilization flourished in the eastern Mediterranean region from 800 to 200 B.C. — wealth also became associated with money. However, the relationship of wealth to money has long been debated. According to Aristotle, people misunderstand wealth when they think of it as "only a quantity of coin." For him, money was useful primarily as a means of representing and purchasing goods but was not sustaining in and of itself.

Writers such as Aristotle have argued that wealth benefits the state by ensuring stability, growth, security, and cultural innovations and that it benefits the individual by providing leisure time, mobility, and luxury. Most societies, however, have struggled with the problems caused by unequal distribution of wealth, either among individuals or between citizens and the state. The Spartan leader Lycurgus is said to have tackled the problem in the ninth century B.C. by convincing the inhabitants of the Greek city-state of Sparta that they needed to redistribute their wealth. Land and household goods were redistributed among the citizens, and Lycurgus was hailed as a hero. However, Lycurgus's model has not been the norm in subsequent civilizations, and questions about the nature of wealth and its role and distribution in society have persisted.

The selections in this section present ideas on wealth from a variety of perspectives. Adam Smith reviews the relationship between wealth and money while examining eighteenth-century mercantile practices. Karl Marx expounds on what he feels are the corrosive effects of excessive wealth on the individual and on the problems caused by unequal distribution of wealth between laborers and business owners. John Kenneth Galbraith and Robert B. Reich further investigate the problems that an unequal distribution of wealth poses for society as a whole.

Adam Smith, in "Of the Principle of the Commercial or Mercantile System," is interested in establishing what wealth is, beyond his statement that "Wealth is power." For him such a statement needed little examination. In the 1770s his England was amassing considerable wealth, and the power the British nation wielded around the globe was so extensive as to be obvious to anyone. But it was not as obvious in his time as it is in ours that money — rather than cattle or corn — was the appropriate measure of wealth. His view is that money, like other things, is a commodity whose value fluctuates. Therefore, his position fluctuates slightly when he tries to establish the measure of wealth.

Smith emphasizes foreign trade to an extent that was novel in his own time. The late eighteenth century saw countries reaping fortunes from the expansion of trade and exploration. The wealth of exploring and seafaring nations such as Spain and Portugal rose immensely as a result of discoveries of gold and silver in the Americas. But England, Holland, and other mercantile traders reaped even greater fortunes by establishing commercial empires that lasted after the American mines were relatively depleted. Smith's focus is on the commercial nature of England's economy and the implications for sustained wealth. His forward-looking emphasis on foreign trade reveals him to be a modern thinker describing how capitalist nations function in international trade.

Karl Marx's *Communist Manifesto* clarifies the relationship between a people's condition and the economic system in which they live. Marx saw that capitalism provided opportunities for the wealthy and powerful to take advantage of labor. He argued that because labor cannot efficiently sell its product, management can keep labor in perpetual economic bondage.

Marx knew poverty firsthand, but one of his close associates, Friedrich Engels, who collaborated on portions of the *Manifesto,* was the son of a factory owner and so was able to observe closely how the rich can oppress the poor. For both of them, the economic system of capitalism produced a class struggle between the rich (bourgeoisie) and the laboring classes (proletariat).

John Kenneth Galbraith's selection, "The Position of Poverty," dates from the middle of the twentieth century and addresses an issue that earlier thinkers avoided — the question of poverty. It is not that earlier writers were unaware that poverty existed — most mention it in passing — but their main concern was the accumulation and preservation of wealth. Galbraith, in his study of the economics of contemporary America, also focuses on wealth; the title of his most famous book is *The Affluent Society* (1958). He, however, points toward something greater than the issue of attaining affluence. His concern is with the allocation of the wealth that American society has produced. His fears that selfishness and waste will dominate the affluent society have led him to write about what he considers the most important social issue related to economics: poverty and its effects. If Smith was correct in seeing wealth as appropriate subject matter for economic study, then Galbraith has pointed to the opposite of wealth as being equally worthy of close examination.

Robert B. Reich, formerly a lecturer at Harvard University until he was appointed secretary of labor in the first Clinton administration, has taught courses in economics and published widely. His 1991 book, *The Work of Nations,* echoes the title of Adam Smith's eighteenth-century masterpiece of capitalist theory, *The Wealth of Nations*. While Reich's views on labor are distinct from Smith's, his essay focuses on labor with the same intensity Smith brings to money. His views consider how worldwide economic developments will affect labor in the next decades. According to Reich, labor falls into three groups — routine workers, in-person servers, and symbolic analysts — each of which will fare differently in the coming years.

Most of these theorists agree that a healthy economy can relieve the misery and suffering of a population. Most agree that wealth and plenty are preferable to impoverishment and want. But some are also concerned with the effects of materialism and greed on the spiritual life of a nation. Galbraith sees a society with enormous power to bring about positive social change, the capacity to make positive moral decisions. But Galbraith, for all his optimism, reminds us that we have made very little progress in an area of social concern that has been a focus of thought and action for a generation.

ADAM SMITH
Of the Principle of the Commercial or Mercantile System

ADAM SMITH (1723–1790) was born in Kirkcaldy, on the east coast of Scotland. He attended Glasgow University and took a degree from Oxford, after which he gave a successful series of lectures on rhetoric in his hometown, which resulted in his appointment as professor of logic at Glasgow in 1751. A year later he moved to a professorship in moral philosophy that had been vacated by Thomas Craggie, one of his former teachers. He held this position for twelve years. Smith's early reputation was built entirely on his work in moral philosophy, which included theology, ethics, justice, and political economy.

In many ways Adam Smith's views are striking in their modernity; in fact, his work continues to inform our understanding of current economic trends. His classic and best-known book, *An Inquiry into the Nature and Causes of the Wealth of Nations* (1776), examines the economic system of the modern nation that has reached, as England had, the commercial level of progress. According to Smith, a nation has to pass through a number of levels of culture — from hunter-gatherer to modern commercial — on its way to becoming modern. In this sense, he was something of an evolutionist in economics.

Wealth of Nations is quite different in both tone and concept from his earlier success, *Theory of Moral Sentiments* (1759). The earlier work postulated a social order based, in part, on altruism — an order where individuals aid one another — whereas *Wealth of Nations* asserts that the best economic results are obtained when individuals work for their own interests and their own gain. This kind of effort, Smith assures us, results in the general improvement of a society because the industry of the individual benefits everyone in the nation by producing more wealth: the greater the wealth of the nation, the better the lot of every individual in the nation.

"Of the Principle of the Commercial or Mercantile System" examines wealth, money, and the problems of trading commodities and money. It addresses foreign trade as well as the fundamental value of money. There is no question that Smith is an ardent capitalist who feels an almost messianic need to spread its doctrine. He maintained throughout his life that *Wealth of Nations* was one with his writings on moral and social issues and that when his work was complete it would include the basic elements of any society.

One subject that Smith explores is the relation of wealth and money, and his attitude is essentially very much the modern view: "wealth and money, in short, are, in common language, considered as in every respect synonymous" (para. 1). Rich countries "abound in money," and he seems to agree with John Locke that gold and silver are "the most solid and substantial part of the moveable wealth of a nation" (para. 3). In eighteenth-century England money was generally metal, and silver was the standard. Even today British money is based on the pound sterling. However, in another section of his book, Smith measures value in terms of labor and corn and not of gold and silver. Corn was the staple grain of England at that time. The cost of corn responded to inflation and deflation, just as the cost of labor responded to supply and demand. Ultimately, he felt that the best yardstick of value was the cost of labor, but even that cost, like others, is conveniently measured in terms of money.

Smith's discussion is especially interesting because he commodifies money. As he puts it, the wheat merchant brings his harvest to the town to buy money with it. If money is silver, then the abundance or shortage of silver will affect its value, just as the abundance or shortage of wheat will affect its value. Smith pays close attention to foreign trade because certain nations fear having their gold and silver leave their shores and thus impoverish the nation. He points out that under Europe's modern economic system silver spent abroad for goods consumed at home did not impoverish the nation. Further, unless silver could be spent abroad, it would be impossible to buy raw materials, manufacture goods, and then sell them abroad at a profit. This procedure was — especially for England at the time — the core of the commercial economic system.

Smith's practicality is notable. Even if a nation tried to keep its silver and gold at home, he notes, it would be impossible to control smuggling, since it was much easier to smuggle an ounce of gold than the amount of tea that the gold would purchase. But Smith's optimism, based perhaps on England's commercial success, insisted on open foreign trade and a willingness to let the value of money fluctuate. Despite his declaration that "It would be too ridiculous to go about seriously to prove, that wealth does not consist in money, or in gold and silver; but in what money purchases, and is valuable only for purchasing" (para. 17), his overall implication is that money is only a convenience. As he says, it is the "known and established instrument of commerce" (para. 18) and therefore is convenient for establishing wealth. Smith closes his comments by saying, "It is not for its own sake that men desire money, but for the sake of what they can purchase with it" (para. 18).

His analysis of economic circumstances in his own time was aided by research in the field. He traveled on the Continent from 1764 to 1766 as a private tutor to the duke of Buccleuch, and thus his references to French towns and their economic character have the weight of observation to give them substance. He also implies that his English contemporaries are much more industrious than their predecessors and also that the wealth of England is greater than that of other European nations.

SMITH'S RHETORIC

This selection is a tightly reasoned work that examines the function of money in a commercial economy. In earlier sections of *Wealth of Nations* Smith examines various values in society, particularly the value of labor and goods. He saw essentially two great economies in England at his time — the commercial, based in trade among individuals and nations, and the agricultural, based on the production of crops. This section focuses entirely on commerce and champions the views of one of the scholars he quotes — Thomas Mun, who not only wrote about foreign trade but became enormously wealthy practicing it.

Smith bases some of his theories on the assumption that consumable goods are the basic items that affect the wealth of the nation. He even says that the amount of money that can circulate in a nation is directly connected with the quantity of consumable goods available for sale. The weekly updates on our own gross national product are reminders that Smith's theories are not far from the ones that govern our own economy. Yet in this essay his energies are given over to demonstrating the validity of his arguments. His method is close reasoning.

Smith's prose is clear, balanced, and marked by careful use of parallelism — some of the qualities we find in Thomas Jefferson's prose. The balance and parallelism make many of his most important statements memorable, quotable, and almost aphoristic. In paragraph 1 of Book II, Chapter 3, of *Wealth of Nations,* we find this statement: "A man grows rich by employing a multitude of manufacturers: he grows poor by maintaining a multitude of menial servants." Two independent clauses, one on the subject of growing rich, the other on the subject of growing poor, are paralleled with one another, balanced almost perfectly in their structure.

Smith makes deliberate stylistic choices, and his appreciation of the aphorism is clear from one of his own: "To grow rich is to get money" (para. 1). Elsewhere he says, "Wealth . . . is power" (Bk. I, ch. 5). Above all, Smith wants to convince us that he is a rational man who reasons carefully to demonstrate the truth.

Of the Principle of the Commercial or Mercantile System

That wealth consists in money, or in gold and silver, is a popu- 1
lar notion which naturally arises from the double function of money, as the instrument of commerce, and as the measure of value. In consequence of its being the instrument of commerce, when we have money we can more readily obtain whatever else we have occasion for, than by means of any other commodity. The great affair, we always find, is to get money. When that is obtained, there is no difficulty in making any subsequent purchase. In consequence of its being the measure of value, we estimate that of all other commodities by the quantity of money which they will exchange for. We say of a rich man that he is worth a great deal, and of a poor man that he is worth very little money. A frugal man, or a man eager to be rich, is said to love money; and a careless, a generous, or a profuse man, is said to be indifferent about it. To grow rich is to get money; and wealth and money, in short, are, in common language, considered as in every respect synonymous.

A rich country, in the same manner as a rich man, is supposed 2
to be a country abounding in money; and to heap up gold and silver in any country is supposed to be the readiest way to enrich it. For some time after the discovery of America, the first enquiry of the

Spaniards, when they arrived upon any unknown coast, used to be, if there was any gold or silver to be found in the neighbourhood? By the information which they received, they judged whether it was worth while to make a settlement there, or if the country was worth the conquering. Plano Carpino, a monk sent ambassador from the king of France to one of the sons of the famous Gengis Khan, says that the Tartars used frequently to ask him, if there was plenty of sheep and oxen in the kingdom of France? Their enquiry had the same object with that of the Spaniards. They wanted to know if the country was rich enough to be worth the conquering. Among the Tartars, as among all other nations of shepherds, who are generally ignorant of the use of money, cattle are the instruments of commerce and the measures of value. Wealth, therefore, according to them, consisted in cattle, as according to the Spaniards it consisted in gold and silver. Of the two, the Tartar notion, perhaps, was the nearest to the truth.

Mr. Locke[1] remarks a distinction between money and other   3
moveable goods. All other moveable goods, he says, are of so consumable a nature that the wealth which consists in them cannot be much depended on, and a nation which abounds in them one year may, without any exportation, but merely by their own waste and extravagance, be in great want of them the next. Money, on the contrary, is a steady friend, which, though it may travel about from hand to hand, yet if it can be kept from going out of the country, is not very liable to be wasted and consumed. Gold and silver, therefore, are, according to him, the most solid and substantial part of the moveable wealth of a nation, and to multiply those metals ought, he thinks, upon that account, to be the great object of its political œconomy.

Others admit that if a nation could be separated from all the   4
world, it would be of no consequence how much, or how little money circulated in it. The consumable goods which were circulated by means of this money, would only be exchanged for a greater or a smaller number of pieces; but the real wealth or poverty of the country, they allow, would depend altogether upon the abundance or scarcity of those consumable goods. But it is otherwise, they think, with countries which have connections with foreign nations, and which are obliged to carry on foreign wars, and to maintain fleets and armies in distant countries. This, they say, cannot be done, but by sending abroad money to pay them with; and a nation

---

[1] **John Locke** English philosopher (1632 – 1704) who wrote, among other works, *Observations on Silver Money* (1695).

cannot send much money abroad, unless it has a good deal at home. Every such nation, therefore, must endeavour in time of peace to accumulate gold and silver, that, when occasion requires, it may have wherewithal to carry on foreign wars.

In consequence of these popular notions, all the different nations of Europe have studied, though to little purpose, every possible means of accumulating gold and silver in their respective countries. Spain and Portugal, the proprietors of the principal mines which supply Europe with those metals, have either prohibited their exportation under the severest penalties, or subjected it to a considerable duty. The like prohibition seems anciently to have made a part of the policy of most other European nations. It is even to be found, where we should least of all expect to find it, in some old Scotch acts of parliament, which forbid under heavy penalties the carrying gold or silver *forth of the kingdom*. The like policy anciently took place both in France and England.

When those countries became commercial, the merchants found this prohibition, upon many occasions, extremely inconvenient. They could frequently buy more advantageously with gold and silver than with any other commodity, the foreign goods which they wanted, either to import into their own, or to carry to some other foreign country. They remonstrated, therefore, against this prohibition as hurtful to trade.

They represented, first, that the exportation of gold and silver in order to purchase foreign goods, did not always diminish the quantity of those metals in the kingdom. That, on the contrary, it might frequently increase that quantity; because, if the consumption of foreign goods was not thereby increased in the country, those goods might be re-exported to foreign countries, and, being there sold for a large profit, might bring back much more treasure than was originally sent out to purchase them. Mr. Mun compares this operation of foreign trade to the seed-time and harvest of agriculture.

> If we only behold [says he] the actions of the husbandman in the seed-time, when he casteth away much good corn into the ground, we shall account him rather a madman than a husbandman. But when we consider his labours in the harvest, which is the end of his endeavours, we shall find the worth and plentiful increase of his actions.[2]

---

[2] From Thomas Mun (1571–1641), *England's Treasure by Forraign Trade, or the Ballance of our Forraign Trade is the Rule of our Treasure* (1664). The work was written in 1630.

They represented, secondly, that this prohibition could not hin- 8
der the exportation of gold and silver, which, on account of the
smallness of their bulk in proportion to their value, could easily be
smuggled abroad. That this exportation could only be prevented by
a proper attention to, what they called, the balance of trade. That
when the country exported to a greater value than it imported, a balance became due to it from foreign nations, which was necessarily
paid to it in gold and silver, and thereby increased the quantity of
those metals in the kingdom. But that when it imported to a greater
value than it exported, a contrary balance became due to foreign nations, which was necessarily paid to them in the same manner, and
thereby diminished that quantity. That in this case to prohibit the
exportation of those metals could not prevent it, but only by making
it more dangerous, render it more expensive. That the exchange was
thereby turned more against the country which owed the balance,
than it otherwise might have been; the merchant who purchased a
bill upon the foreign country being obliged to pay the banker who
sold it, not only for the natural risk, trouble and expence of sending
the money thither, but for the extraordinary risk arising from the
prohibition. But that the more the exchange was against any country, the more the balance of trade became necessarily against it; the
money of that country becoming necessarily of so much less value,
in comparison with that of the country to which the balance was
due. That if the exchange between England and Holland, for example, was five per cent. against England, it would require a hundred
and five ounces of silver in England to purchase a bill for a hundred
ounces of silver in Holland; that a hundred and five ounces of silver
in England, therefore, would be worth only a hundred ounces of silver in Holland, and would purchase only a proportionable quantity
of Dutch goods: but that a hundred ounces of silver in Holland, on
the contrary, would be worth a hundred and five ounces in England,
and would purchase a proportionable quantity of English goods:
that the English goods which were sold to Holland would be sold so
much cheaper; and the Dutch goods which were sold to England, so
much dearer, by the difference of the exchange; that the one would
draw so much less Dutch money to England, and the other so much
more English money to Holland, as this difference amounted to: and
that the balance of trade, therefore, would necessarily be so much
more against England, and would require a greater balance of gold
and silver to be exported to Holland.

Those arguments were partly solid and partly sophistical. They 9
were solid so far as they asserted that the exportation of gold and silver in trade might frequently be advantageous to the country. They

were solid too, in asserting that no prohibition could prevent their exportation, when private people found any advantage in exporting them. But they were sophistical in supposing, that either to preserve or to augment the quantity of those metals required more the attention of government, than to preserve or to augment the quantity of any other useful commodities, which the freedom of trade, without any such attention, never fails to supply in the proper quantity. They were sophistical too, perhaps, in asserting that the high price of exchange necessarily increased, what they called, the unfavourable balance of trade, or occasioned the exportation of a greater quantity of gold and silver. That high price, indeed, was extremely disadvantageous to the merchants who had any money to pay in foreign countries. They paid so much dearer for the bills which their bankers granted them upon those countries. But though the risk arising from the prohibition might occasion some extraordinary expence to the bankers, it would not necessarily carry any more money out of the country. This expence would generally be all laid out in the country, in smuggling the money out of it, and could seldom occasion the exportation of a single six-pence beyond the precise sum drawn for. The high price of exchange too would naturally dispose the merchants to endeavour to make their exports nearly balance their imports, in order that they might have this high exchange to pay upon as small a sum as possible. The high price of exchange, besides, must necessarily have operated as a tax, in raising the price of foreign goods, and thereby diminishing their consumption. It would tend, therefore, not to increase, but to diminish, what they called the unfavourable balance of trade, and consequently the exportation of gold and silver.

Such as they were, however, those arguments convinced the 10 people to whom they were addressed. They were addressed by merchants to parliaments, and to the councils of princes, to nobles, and to country gentlemen; by those who were supposed to understand trade, to those who were conscious to themselves that they knew nothing about the matter. That foreign trade enriched the country, experience demonstrated to the nobles and country gentlemen, as well as to the merchants; but how, or in what manner, none of them well knew. The merchants knew perfectly in what manner it enriched themselves. It was their business to know it. But to know in what manner it enriched the country, was no part of their business. This subject never came into their consideration, but when they had occasion to apply to their country for some change in the laws relating to foreign trade. It then became necessary to say something about the beneficial effects of foreign trade, and the manner in which those effects were obstructed by the laws as they then stood.

To the judges who were to decide the business, it appeared a most satisfactory account of the matter, when they were told that foreign trade brought money into the country, but that the laws in question hindered it from bringing so much as it otherwise would do. Those arguments therefore produced the wished-for effect. The prohibition of exporting gold and silver was in France and England confined to the coin of those respective countries. The exportation of foreign coin and of bullion was made free. In Holland, and in some other places, this liberty was extended even to the coin of the country. The attention of government was turned away from guarding against the exportation of gold and silver, to watch over the balance of trade, as the only cause which could occasion any augmentation or diminution of those metals. From one fruitless care it was turned away to another care much more intricate, much more embarrassing, and just equally fruitless. The title of Mun's book, *England's Treasure by Foreign Trade,* became a fundamental maxim in the political œconomy, not of England only, but of all other commercial countries. The inland or home trade, the most important of all, the trade in which an equal capital affords the greatest revenue, and creates the greatest employment to the people of the country, was considered as subsidiary only to foreign trade. It neither brought money into the country, it was said, nor carried any out of it. The country therefore could never become either richer or poorer by means of it, except so far as its prosperity or decay might indirectly influence the state of foreign trade.

11 A country that has no mines of its own must undoubtedly draw its gold and silver from foreign countries, in the same manner as one that has no vineyards of its own must draw its wines. It does not seem necessary, however, that the attention of government should be more turned towards the one than towards the other object. A country that has wherewithal to buy wine, will always get the wine which it has occasion for; and a country that has wherewithal to buy gold and silver, will never be in want of those metals. They are to be bought for a certain price like all other commodities, and as they are the price of all other commodities, so all other commodities are the price of those metals. We trust with perfect security that the freedom of trade, without any attention of government, will always supply us with the wine which we have occasion for: and we may trust with equal security that it will always supply us with all the gold and silver which we can afford to purchase or to employ, either in circulating our commodities, or in other uses.

12 The quantity of every commodity which human industry can either purchase or produce, naturally regulates itself in every country according to the effectual demand, or according to the demand of

those who are willing to pay the whole rent, labour and profits which must be paid in order to prepare and bring it to market. But no commodities regulate themselves more easily or more exactly according to this effectual demand than gold and silver; because, on account of the small bulk and great value of those metals, no commodities can be more easily transported from one place to another, from the places where they are cheap, to those where they are dear, from the places where they exceed, to those where they fall short of this effectual demand. If there were in England, for example, an effectual demand for an additional quantity of gold, a packet-boat could bring from Lisbon, or from wherever else it was to be had, fifty tuns of gold, which could be coined into more than five millions of guineas. But if there were an effectual demand for grain to the same value, to import it would require, at five guineas a tun, a million of tuns of shipping, or a thousand ships of a thousand tuns each. The navy of England would not be sufficient.

When the quantity of gold and silver imported into any country 13 exceeds the effectual demand, no vigilance of government can prevent their exportation. All the sanguinary laws of Spain and Portugal are not able to keep their gold and silver at home. The continual importations from Peru and Brazil exceed the effectual demand of those countries, and sink the price of those metals there below that in the neighbouring countries. If, on the contrary, in any particular country their quantity fell short of the effectual demand, so as to raise their price above that of the neighbouring countries, the government would have no occasion to take any pains to import them. If it were even to take pains to prevent their importation, it would not be able to effectuate it. Those metals, when the Spartans had got wherewithal to purchase them, broke through all the barriers which the laws of Lycurgus[3] opposed to their entrance into Lacedemon. All the sanguinary laws of the customs are not able to prevent the importation of the teas of the Dutch and Gottenburgh East India companies; because somewhat cheaper than those of the British company. A pound of tea, however, is about a hundred times the bulk of one of the highest prices, sixteen shillings, that is commonly paid for it in silver, and more than two thousand times the bulk of the same price in gold, and consequently just so many times more difficult to smuggle.

---

[3] **Lycurgus** Quasi-legendary Spartan leader (fl. 8th cent. B.C.) known as "the law-giver," he made Sparta a powerful unified state. Lacedemon was a rival state. Lycurgus was believed to have recalled gold and silver, replaced it with iron "money," and redistributed the wealth. See Plutarch's *Lives*.

It is partly owing to the easy transportation of gold and silver   14
from the places where they abound to those where they are wanted,
that the price of those metals does not fluctuate continually like that
of the greater part of other commodities, which are hindered by
their bulk from shifting their situation, when the market happens
to be either over or under-stocked with them. The price of those
metals, indeed, is not altogether exempted from variation, but the
changes to which it is liable are generally slow, gradual, and uniform. In Europe, for example, it is supposed, without much foundation, perhaps, that, during the course of the present and preceding
century, they have been constantly, but gradually, sinking in their
value, on account of the continual importations from the Spanish
West Indies. But to make any sudden change in the price of gold
and silver, so as to raise or lower at once, sensibly and remarkably,
the money price of all other commodities, requires such a revolution
in commerce as that occasioned by the discovery of America.

If, notwithstanding all this, gold and silver should at any time   15
fall short in a country which has wherewithal to purchase them,
there are more expedients for supplying their place, than that of almost any other commodity. If the materials of manufacture are
wanted, industry must stop. If provisions are wanted, the people
must starve. But if money is wanted, barter will supply its place,
though with a good deal of inconveniency. Buying and selling upon
credit, and the different dealers compensating their credits with one
another, once a month or once a year, will supply it with less inconveniency. A well-regulated paper money will supply it, not only
without any inconveniency, but, in some cases, with some advantages. Upon every account, therefore, the attention of government
never was so unnecessarily employed, as when directed to watch
over the preservation or increase of the quantity of money in any
country.

No complaint, however, is more common than that of a scarcity   16
of money. Money, like wine, must always be scarce with those who
have neither wherewithal to buy it, nor credit to borrow it. Those
who have either, will seldom be in want either of the money, or of
the wine which they have occasion for. This complaint, however, of
the scarcity of money, is not always confined to improvident spend-
thrifts. It is sometimes general through a whole mercantile town,
and the country in its neighbourhood. Over-trading is the common
cause of it. Sober men, whose projects have been disproportioned to
their capitals, are as likely to have neither wherewithal to buy
money, nor credit to borrow it, as prodigals whose expence has
been disproportioned to their revenue. Before their projects can be
brought to bear, their stock is gone, and their credit with it. They

run about everywhere to borrow money, and every body tells them that they have none to lend. Even such general complaints of the scarcity of money do not always prove that the usual number of gold and silver pieces are not circulating in the country, but that many people want those pieces who have nothing to give for them. When the profits of trade happen to be greater than ordinary, over-trading becomes a general error both among great and small dealers. They do not always send more money abroad than usual, but they buy upon credit both at home and abroad, an unusual quantity of goods, which they send to some distant market, in hopes that the returns will come in before the demand for payment. The demand comes before the returns, and they have nothing at hand, with which they can either purchase money, or give solid security for borrowing. It is not any scarcity of gold and silver, but the difficulty which such people find in borrowing, and which their creditors find in getting payment, that occasions the general complaint of the scarcity of money.

It would be too ridiculous to go about seriously to prove, that   17 wealth does not consist in money, or in gold and silver; but in what money purchases, and is valuable only for purchasing. Money, no doubt, makes always a part of the national capital; but it has already been shown that it generally makes but a small part, and always the most unprofitable part of it.

It is not because wealth consists more essentially in money than   18 in goods, that the merchant finds it generally more easy to buy goods with money, than to buy money with goods; but because money is the known and established instrument of commerce, for which every thing is readily given in exchange, but which is not always with equal readiness to be got in exchange for every thing. The greater part of goods besides are more perishable than money, and he may frequently sustain a much greater loss by keeping them. When his goods are upon hand too, he is more liable to such demands for money as he may not be able to answer, than when he has got their price in his coffers. Over and above all this, his profit arises more directly from selling than from buying, and he is upon all these accounts generally much more anxious to exchange his goods for money, than his money for goods. But though a particular merchant, with abundance of goods in his warehouse, may sometimes be ruined by not being able to sell them in time, a nation or country is not liable to the same accident. The whole capital of a merchant frequently consists in perishable goods destined for purchasing money. But it is but a very small part of the annual produce of the land and labour of a country which can ever be destined for purchasing gold and silver from their neighbours. The far greater part is circulated and consumed among themselves; and even of the surplus which is sent abroad, the greater part is generally destined for the purchase of other foreign goods. Though gold and silver, therefore, could not be had in exchange for the goods destined to purchase them, the nation would not be ruined. It might, indeed, suffer some loss and inconveniency, and be forced upon some of those expedients which are necessary for supplying the place of money. The annual produce of its land and labour, however, would be the same, or very nearly the same, as usual, because the same, or very nearly the same consumable capital would be employed in maintaining it. And though goods do not always draw money so readily as money draws goods, in the long-run they draw it more necessarily than even it draws them. Goods can serve many other purposes besides purchasing money, but money can serve no other purpose besides purchasing goods. Money, therefore, necessarily runs after goods, but goods do not always or necessarily run after money. The man who buys, does not always mean to sell again, but frequently to use or to consume; whereas he who sells, always means to buy again. The one may frequently have done the whole, but the other can never have done more than the one-half of his business. It is not for its own sake that men desire money, but for the sake of what they can purchase with it.

QUESTIONS FOR CRITICAL READING

1. In terms of wealth, what is the relationship between money and goods?
2. In paragraph 15 Smith notes that a potential shortage of money could possibly halt trade and suggests the remedy of using paper money. Do you think that Smith would have understood and approved of our contemporary use of paper money that is not backed by gold or silver?
3. What are the advantages of gold and silver money over paper money?
4. Why is wealth not measured in what money purchases? See para. 17.
5. What does Smith mean when he implies that Portugal and Spain, by prohibiting export of gold and silver, take part in an ancient policy that existed before nations "became commercial"? See paragraphs 5, 6, and 7 for his discussion.

SUGGESTIONS FOR WRITING

1. Smith says that it is merchants' business to know how foreign trade will affect their own wealth, "But to know in what manner it enriched the country, was no part of their business" (para. 10). Is this statement

true today? Examine the context in which he makes this statement, and fashion an argument defending or attacking his position.

2. In discussing foreign trade, Smith says that nations without gold and silver mines may have wine to sell for gold and silver and thereby acquire the metal (para. 11). In other words, a nation with natural resources has the opportunity to create wealth. How can England or Japan, which has few natural resources, accumulate wealth? What is responsible for their wealth?

3. Examine the economic issues behind this statement: "The man who buys, does not always mean to sell again, but frequently to use or to consume; whereas he who sells, always means to buy again" (para. 18). What are the implications of the statement for understanding the nature of wealth? How does it clarify the relationship between goods and money?

4. Adam Smith was a moral philosopher as well as a brilliant economic thinker. Write an essay that analyzes Smith's views of the morality of wealth. At the same time, compare his views with your own. Is there a clear position that Smith or any of us ought to take on the moral issues involved in creating great wealth? Assuming that the wealth is created legally, would there be any reason to argue for its inherent moral value, either positive or negative? Find passages in Smith that demonstrate his awareness of moral questions concerning wealth.

5. **CONNECTIONS**   Compare Adam Smith's attitudes toward wealth with those of Karl Marx in *Communist Manifesto*. Imagine Smith and Marx debating the question of whether it is better to promote great wealth in a nation or to ensure that great wealth can never be permitted for even the most industrious individual. What good results might Smith assume would arise from the production of wealth? What bad things might Marx assume would arise from the production of wealth?

6. **CONNECTIONS**   Which writer is closer in spirit to the principles that Thomas Jefferson upheld: Adam Smith or Karl Marx? Smith praises capital in all its forms, while Marx blames capital for the miseries of the people. Where would Jefferson stand in relation to these writers and which of his principles would each of these writers take in defense of his own position? Is the right to amass great wealth guaranteed in Jefferson's demand that people be permitted the pursuit of happiness?

KARL MARX
The Communist Manifesto

KARL MARX (1818–1883) was born in Germany to Jewish parents who converted to Lutheranism. A scholarly man, Marx studied literature and philosophy, ultimately earning a doctorate in philosophy at the University of Jena. After being denied a university position however, he turned to make a living from journalism.

Soon after beginning his journalistic career, Marx came into conflict with Prussian authorities because of his radical social views, and after a period of exile in Paris he moved to Brussels. After several more moves, Marx found his way to London, where he finally settled in absolute poverty; his friend Friedrich Engels (1820–1895) contributed money to prevent his and his family's starvation. During this time in London, Marx wrote the books for which he is famous while writing for and editing newspapers. His contributions to the *New York Daily Tribune* number over 300 items between the years 1851 and 1862.

Marx is best known for his theories of socialism, as expressed in *The Communist Manifesto* (1848) — which, like much of his important work, was written with Engels's help — and in the three-volume *Das Kapital (Capital),* the first volume of which was published in 1867. In his own lifetime he was not well known, nor were his ideas widely debated. Yet he was part of an ongoing movement composed mainly of intellectuals. Vladimir Lenin (1870–1924) was a disciple whose triumph in the Russian Revolution of 1917 catapulted Marx to the forefront of world thought. Since 1917 Marx's thinking has been scrupulously analyzed, debated, and argued. Capitalist thinkers have found him unconvincing, whereas

Translated by Samuel Moore. Part III of *The Communist Manifesto,* "Socialist and Communist Literature," is omitted here.

Communist thinkers have found him a prophet and keen analyst of social structures.

In England, Marx's studies centered on the concept of an ongoing class struggle between those who owned property — the bourgeoisie — and those who owned nothing but whose work produced wealth — the proletariat. Marx was concerned with the forces of history, and his view of history was that it is progressive and, to an extent, inevitable. This view is prominent in *The Communist Manifesto,* particularly in Marx's review of the overthrow of feudal forms of government by the bourgeoisie. He thought it inevitable that the bourgeoisie and the proletariat would engage in a class struggle, from which the proletariat would emerge victorious. In essence, Marx took a materialist position. He denied the providence of God in the affairs of humans and defended the view that economic institutions evolve naturally and that, in their evolution, they control the social order. Thus, communism was an inevitable part of the process, and in the Manifesto he worked to clarify the reasons for its inevitability.

One of Marx's primary contentions was that capital is "not a personal, it is a social power" (para. 78). Thus, according to Marx, the "past dominates the present" (para. 83), since the accumulation of past capital determines how people will live in the present society. Capitalist economists, however, see capital as a personal power, but a power that, as John Kenneth Galbraith might say, should be used in a socially responsible way.

MARX'S RHETORIC

The selection included here omits one section, the least important for the modern reader. The first section has a relatively simple rhetorical structure that depends on comparison. The title, "Bourgeois and Proletarians," tells us that the section will clarify the nature of each class and then go on to make some comparisons and contrasts. These concepts were by no means as widely discussed or thought about in 1848 as they are today, so Marx is careful to define his terms. At the same time, he establishes his theories regarding history by making further comparisons with class struggles in earlier ages.

Marx's style is simple and direct. He moves steadily from point to point, establishing his views on the nature of classes, on the nature of bourgeois society, and on the questions of industrialism and

its effects on modern society. He considers wealth, worth, nationality, production, agriculture, and machinery. Each point is dealt
with in turn, usually in its own paragraph.

The organization of the next section, "Proletarians and Communists" (paras. 60 – 133), is not, despite its title, comparative in
nature. Rather, with the proletariat defined as the class of the future, Marx tries to show that the Communist cause is the proletarian cause. In the process, Marx uses a clever rhetorical strategy. He
assumes that he is addressed by an antagonist — presumably a
bourgeois or a proletarian who is in sympathy with the bourgeoisie. He then proceeds to answer each popular complaint
against communism. He shows that it is not a party separate from
other workers' parties (para. 61). He clarifies the question of abolishing existing property relations (paras. 68 – 93). He emphasizes
the antagonism between capital and wage labor (para. 76); he discusses the disappearance of culture (para. 94); he clarifies the
questions of the family (paras. 98 – 100) and of the exploitation of
children (para. 101). He brings up the new system of public education (paras. 102 – 04). He raises the touchy issue of the "community of women" (paras. 105 – 10), as well as the charge that Communists want to abolish nations (paras. 111 – 15). He brushes aside
religion (para. 116). When he is done with the complaints, he gives
us a rhetorical signal: "But let us have done with the bourgeois objections to Communism" (para. 126).

The rest of the second section contains a brief summary, and
then Marx presents his ten-point program (para. 131). The structure is simple, direct, and effective. In the process of answering the
charges against communism, Marx is able to clarify exactly what it
is and what it promises. In contrast to his earlier arguments, the
ten points of his Communist program seem clear, easy, and (again
by contrast) almost acceptable. While the style is not dashing (despite a few memorable lines), the rhetorical structure is extraordinarily effective for the purposes at hand.

In the last section (paras. 135 – 45), in which Marx compares
the Communists with other reform groups such as those agitating
for redistribution of land and other agrarian reforms, he indicates
that the Communists are everywhere fighting alongside existing
groups for the rights of people who are oppressed by their societies. As Marx says, "In short, the Communists everywhere support every revolutionary movement against the existing social and
political order of things" (para. 141). Nothing could be a more
plain and direct declaration of sympathies.

The Communist Manifesto

A specter is haunting Europe — the specter of Communism. All 1
the Powers of old Europe have entered into a holy alliance to exorcise this specter; Pope and Czar, Metternich[1] and Guizot,[2] French
Radicals[3] and German police-spies.

Where is the party in opposition that has not been decried as 2
communistic by its opponents in power? Where the Opposition that
has not hurled back the branding reproach of Communism against
the more advanced opposition parties, as well as against its reactionary adversaries?

Two things result from this fact. 3

I. Communism is already acknowledged by all European Pow- 4
ers to be itself a Power.

II. It is high time that Communists should openly, in the face of 5
the whole world, publish their views, their aims, their tendencies,
and meet this nursery tale of the specter of Communism with a
Manifesto of the party itself.

To this end, Communists of various nationalities have assem- 6
bled in London and sketched the following Manifesto, to be published in the English, French, German, Italian, Flemish and Danish
languages.

Bourgeois and Proletarians[4]

The history of all hitherto existing society is the history of class 7
struggles.

Freeman and slave, patrician and plebeian, lord and serf, guild- 8
master and journeyman, in a word, oppressor and oppressed, stood
in constant opposition to one another, carried on uninterrupted,

---

[1] **Prince Klemens von Metternich (1773 – 1859)** Foreign minister of Austria
(1809 – 1848) who had a hand in establishing the peace after the final defeat in
1815 of Napoleon (1769 – 1821); Metternich was highly influential in the crucial
Congress of Vienna (1814 – 1815).

[2] **François Pierre Guizot (1787 – 1874)** Conservative French statesman, author, and philosopher. Like Metternich, he was opposed to communism.

[3] **French Radicals** Actually middle-class liberals who wanted a return to a republic in 1848 after the eighteen-year reign of Louis-Philippe (1773 – 1850), the
"citizen king."

[4] By bourgeoisie is meant the class of modern Capitalists, owners of the means
of social production and employers of wage labor. By proletariat, the class of modern
wage laborers who, having no means of production of their own, are reduced to selling their labor-power in order to live. [Engels's note]

now hidden, now open fight, a fight that each time ended, either in a revolutionary re-constitution of society at large, or in the common ruin of the contending classes.

In the earlier epochs of history we find almost everywhere a 9 complicated arrangement of society into various orders, a manifold gradation of social rank. In ancient Rome we have patricians, knights, plebeians, slaves; in the Middle Ages, feudal lords, vassals, guild-masters, journeymen, apprentices, serfs; in almost all of these classes, again, subordinate gradations.

The modern bourgeois society that has sprouted from the ruins 10 of feudal society, has not done away with class antagonisms. It has but established new classes, new conditions of oppression, new forms of struggle in place of the old ones.

Our epoch, the epoch of the bourgeoisie, possesses, however, 11 this distinctive feature; it has simplified the class antagonisms. Society as a whole is more and more splitting up into two great hostile camps, into two great classes directly facing each other: Bourgeoisie and Proletariat.

From the serfs of the Middle Ages sprang the chartered burghers 12 of the earliest towns. From these burgesses the first elements of the bourgeoisie were developed.

The discovery of America, the rounding of the Cape,[5] opened 13 up fresh ground for the rising bourgeoisie. The East Indian and Chinese markets, the colonization of America, trade with the colonies, the increase in the means of exchange and in commodities generally, gave to commerce, to navigation, to industry, an impulse never before known, and thereby, to the revolutionary element in the tottering feudal society, a rapid development.

The feudal system of industry, under which industrial produc- 14 tion was monopolized by closed guilds, now no longer sufficed for the growing wants of the new market. The manufacturing system took its place. The guild-masters were pushed on one side by the manufacturing middle-class: division of labor between the different corporate guilds vanished in the face of division of labor in each single workshop.

Meantime the markets kept ever growing, the demand ever ris- 15 ing. Even manufacture no longer sufficed. Thereupon, steam and machinery revolutionized industrial production. The place of manufacture was taken by the giant, Modern Industry, the place of the in-

---

[5] **the Cape** The Cape of Good Hope, at the southern tip of Africa. This was a main sea route for trade with India and the Orient. Europe profited immensely from the opening up of these new markets in the sixteenth century.

dustrial middle-class, by industrial millionaires, the leaders of whole industrial armies, the modern bourgeois.

Modern industry has established the world market, for which 16 the discovery of America paved the way. This market has given an immense development to commerce, to navigation, to communication by land. This development has, in its turn, reacted on the extension of industry; and in proportion as industry, commerce, navigation, railways extended, in the same proportion the bourgeoisie developed, increased its capital, and pushed into the background every class handed down from the Middle Ages.

We see, therefore, how the modern bourgeoisie is itself the 17 product of a long course of development, of a series of revolutions in the modes of production and of exchange.

Each step in the development of the bourgeoisie was accompa- 18 nied by a corresponding political advance of that class. An oppressed class under the sway of the feudal nobility, an armed and self-governing association in the medieval commune,[6] here independent urban republic (as in Italy and Germany), there taxable "third estate"[7] of the monarchy (as in France), afterwards, in the period of manufacture proper, serving either the semi-feudal or the absolute monarchy as a counterpoise against nobility, and, in fact, corner stone of the great monarchies in general, the bourgeoisie has at last, since the establishment of Modern Industry and of the world-market, conquered for itself, in the modern representative State, exclusive political sway. The executive of the modern State is but a committee for managing the common affairs of the whole bourgeoisie.

The bourgeoisie, historically, has played a most revolutionary part. 19

The bourgeoisie, wherever it has got the upper hand, has put an 20 end to all feudal, patriarchal, idyllic relations. It has pitilessly torn asunder the motley feudal ties that bound man to his "natural superiors," and has left no other nexus between man and man than naked self-interest, than callous "cash payment." It has drowned the most heavenly ecstasies of religious fervor,[8] of chivalrous enthusi-

------

[6] **the medieval commune** Refers to the growth in the eleventh century of towns whose economy was highly regulated by mutual interest and agreement.

[7] **"third estate"** The clergy was the first estate, the aristocracy the second estate, and the bourgeoisie the third estate.

[8] **religious fervor** This and other terms in this sentence contain a compressed historical observation. "Religious fervor" refers to the Middle Ages; "chivalrous enthusiasm" refers to the rise of the secular state and to the military power of knights; "Philistine sentimentalism" refers to the development of popular arts and literature in the sixteenth, seventeenth, and eighteenth centuries. The word "Philistine" refers to those who were generally uncultured, that is, the general public. "Sentimentalism" is a code word for the encouragement of emotional response rather than rational thought.

asm, of Philistine sentimentalism, in the icy water of egotistical calculation. It has resolved personal worth into exchange value, and in place of the numberless indefeasible chartered freedoms, has set up that single, unconscionable freedom — Free Trade. In one word, for exploitation, veiled by religious and political illusions, it has substituted naked, shameless, direct, brutal exploitation.

The bourgeoisie has stripped of its halo every occupation hith- 21 erto honored and looked up to with reverent awe. It has converted the physician, the lawyer, the priest, the poet, the man of science, into its paid wage laborers.

The bourgeoisie has torn away from the family its sentimental 22 veil, and has reduced the family relation to a mere money relation.

The bourgeoisie has disclosed how it came to pass that the bru- 23 tal display of vigor in the Middle Ages, which reactionists so much admire, found its fitting complement in the most slothful indolence. It has been the first to show what man's activity can bring about. It has accomplished wonders far surpassing Egyptian pyramids, Roman aqueducts and Gothic cathedrals; it has conducted expeditions that put in the shade all former Exoduses of nations and crusades.

The bourgeoisie cannot exist without constantly revolutionizing 24 the instruments of production, and thereby the relations of production, and with them the whole relations of society. Conservation of the old modes of production in unaltered form was, on the contrary, the first condition of existence for all earlier industrial classes. Constant revolutionizing of production, uninterrupted disturbance of all social conditions, everlasting uncertainty and agitation distinguish the bourgeois epoch from all earlier ones. All fixed, fast frozen relations, with their train of ancient and venerable prejudices and opinions, are swept away, all new formed ones become antiquated before they can ossify. All that is solid melts into the air, all that is holy is profaned, and man is at last compelled to face with sober senses, his real conditions of life, and his relations with his kind.

The need of a constantly expanding market for its prod- 25 ucts chases the bourgeoisie over the whole surface of the globe. It must nestle everywhere, settle everywhere, establish connections everywhere.

The bourgeoisie has through its exploitation of the world- 26 market given a cosmopolitan character to production and consumption in every country. To the great chagrin of reactionists, it has drawn from under the feet of industry the national ground on which it stood. All old-established national industries have been destroyed or are daily being destroyed. They are dislodged by new industries, whose introduction becomes a life and death question for all civilized nations, by industries that no longer work up indigenous raw material, but raw material drawn from the remotest zones; industries whose products are consumed, not only at home, but in every quarter of the globe. In place of the old wants, satisfied by the productions of the country, we find new wants, requiring for their satisfaction the products of distant lands and climes. In place of the old local and national seclusion and self-sufficiency, we have intercourse in every direction, universal interdependence of nations. And as in material, so also in intellectual production. The intellectual creations of individual nations become common property. National onesidedness and narrowmindedness become more and more impossible, and from the numerous national and local literatures there arises a world-literature.

The bourgeoisie, by the rapid improvement of all instruments of production, by the immensely facilitated means of communication, draws all, even the most barbarian nations into civilization. The cheap prices of its commodities are the heavy artillery with which it batters down all Chinese walls, with which it forces the barbarians' intensely obstinate hatred of foreigners to capitulate. It compels all nations, on pain of extinction, to adopt the bourgeois mode of production; it compels them to introduce what it calls civilization into their midst, i.e., to become bourgeois themselves. In a word, it creates a world after its own image.

The bourgeoisie has subjected the country to the rule of the towns. It has created enormous cities, has greatly increased the urban population as compared with the rural and has thus rescued a considerable part of the population from the idiocy of rural life. Just as it has made the country dependent on the towns, so it has made barbarian and semi-barbarian countries dependent on civilized ones, nations of peasants on nations of bourgeois, the East on the West.

The bourgeoisie keeps more and more doing away with the scattered state of the population, of the means of production, and of property. It has agglomerated population, centralized means of production, and has concentrated property in a few hands. The necessary consequence of this was political centralization. Independent, or but loosely connected provinces, with separate interests, laws, governments, and systems of taxation, became lumped together in one nation, with one government, one code of laws, one national class interest, one frontier and one customs tariff.

The bourgeoisie, during its rule of scarce one hundred years, has created more massive and more colossal productive forces than have all preceding generations together. Subjection of Nature's forces to man, machinery, application of chemistry to industry and agriculture, steam-navigation, railways, electric telegraphs, clearing of whole continents for cultivation, canalization of rivers, whole populations conjured out of the ground — what earlier century had even a presentiment that such productive forces slumbered in the lap of social labor?

We see then: the means of production and of exchange on whose foundation the bourgeoisie built itself up, were generated in feudal society. At a certain stage in the development of these means of production and of exchange, the conditions under which feudal society produced and exchanged, the feudal organization of agriculture and manufacturing industry, in one word, the feudal relations of property became no longer compatible with the already developed productive forces; they became so many fetters. They had to burst asunder; they were burst asunder. **31**

Into their place stepped free competition, accompanied by a social and political constitution adapted to it, and by the economical and political sway of the bourgeois class. **32**

A similar movement is going on before our own eyes. Modern bourgeois society with its relations of production, of exchange and of property, a society that has conjured up such gigantic means of production and of exchange, is like the sorcerer, who is no longer able to control the powers of the nether world whom he has called up by his spells. For many a decade past, the history of industry and commerce is but the history of the revolt of modern productive forces against modern conditions of production, against the property relations that are the conditions for the existence of the bourgeoisie and of its rule. It is enough to mention the commercial crises that by their periodical return put on its trial, each time more threateningly, the existence of the entire bourgeois society. In these crises a great part not only of the existing products, but also of the previously created productive forces, are periodically destroyed. In these crises there breaks out an epidemic that, in all earlier epochs, would have seemed an absurdity — the epidemic of overproduction. Society suddenly finds itself put back into a state of momentary barbarism; it appears as if a famine, a universal war of devastation, had cut off the supply of every means of subsistence; industry and commerce seem to be destroyed; and why? Because there is too much civilization, too much means of subsistence, too much industry, too much commerce. The productive forces at the disposal of society no longer tend to further the development of the conditions of the bourgeois property; on the contrary, they have become too powerful for these conditions by which they are fettered, and as soon as they overcome these fetters they bring disorder into the whole of bourgeois society, endanger the existence of bourgeois property. The **33** conditions of bourgeois society are too narrow to comprise the wealth created by them. And how does the bourgeoisie get over these crises? On the one hand by enforced destruction of a mass of productive forces; on the other, by the conquest of new markets, and by the more thorough exploitation of the old ones. That is to say, by paving the way for more extensive and more destructive crises, and by diminishing the means whereby crises are prevented.

The weapons with which the bourgeoisie felled feudalism to the   34 ground are now turned against the bourgeoisie itself.

But not only has the bourgeoisie forged the weapons that bring   35 death to itself; it has also called into existence the men who are to wield those weapons — the modern working class — the proletarians.

In proportion as the bourgeoisie, i.e., capital, is developed, in   36 the same proportion is the proletariat, the modern working class, developed, a class of laborers who live only so long as they find work, and who find work only so long as their labor increases capital. These laborers, who must sell themselves piecemeal, are a commodity, like every other article of commerce, and are consequently exposed to all the vicissitudes of competition, to all the fluctuations of the market.

Owing to the extensive use of machinery and to division of   37 labor, the work of the proletarians has lost all individual character, and, consequently, all charm for the workman. He becomes an appendage of the machine, and it is only the most simple, most monotonous and most easily acquired knack that is required of him. Hence, the cost of production of a workman is restricted almost entirely to the means of subsistence that he requires for his maintenance, and for the propagation of his race. But the price of a commodity, and also of labor, is equal to its cost of production. In proportion, therefore, as the repulsiveness of the work increases the wage decreases. Nay more, in proportion as the use of machinery and division of labor increases, in the same proportion the burden of toil increases, whether by prolongation of the working hours, by increase of the work enacted in a given time, or by increased speed of the machinery, etc.

Modern industry has converted the little workshop of the patri-   38 archal master into the great factory of the industrial capitalist. Masses of laborers, crowded into factories, are organized like soldiers. As privates of the industrial army they are placed under the command of a perfect hierarchy of officers and sergeants. Not only are they the slaves of the bourgeois class and of the bourgeois state, they are daily and hourly enslaved by the machine, by the overlooker, and, above all, by the individual bourgeois manufacturer himself. The more openly this despotism proclaims gain to be its end and aim, the more petty, the more hateful and the more embittering it is.

The less the skill and exertion or strength implied in manual   39
labor, in other words, the more modern industry becomes developed, the more is the labor of men superseded by that of women. Differences of age and sex have no longer any distinctive social validity for the working class. All are instruments of labor, more or less expensive to use, according to their age and sex.

No sooner is the exploitation of the laborer by the manufac-   40
turer, so far at an end, that he receives his wages in cash, than he is set upon by the other portions of the bourgeoisie, the landlord, the shopkeeper, the pawnbroker, etc.

The lower strata of the middle class — the small trades-people,   41
shopkeepers and retired tradesmen generally, the handicraftsmen and peasants — all these sink gradually into the proletariat, partly because their diminutive capital does not suffice for the scale on which Modern Industry is carried on, and is swamped in the competition with the large capitalists, partly because their specialized skill is rendered worthless by new methods of production. Thus the proletariat is recruited from all classes of the population.

The proletariat goes through various stages of development.   42
With its birth begins its struggle with the bourgeoisie. At first the contest is carried on by individual laborers, then by the workpeople of a factory, then by the operatives of one trade, in one locality, against the individual bourgeois who directly exploits them. They direct their attacks not against the bourgeois conditions of production, but against the instruments of production themselves; they destroy imported wares that compete with their labor, they smash to pieces machinery, they set factories ablaze, they seek to restore by force the vanished status of the workman of the Middle Ages.

At this stage the laborers still form an incoherent mass scattered   43
over the whole country, and broken up by their mutual competition. If anywhere they unite to form more compact bodies, this is not yet the consequence of their own active union, but of the union of the bourgeoisie, which class, in order to attain its own political ends, is compelled to set the whole proletariat in motion, and is moreover yet, for a time, able to do so. At this stage, therefore, the proletarians do not fight their enemies, but the enemies of their enemies, the remnants of absolute monarchy, the landowners, the non-industrial bourgeois, the petty bourgeoisie. Thus the whole historical movement is concentrated in the hands of the bourgeoisie, every victory so obtained is a victory for the bourgeoisie.

But with the development of industry the proletariat not only   44
increases in number; it becomes concentrated in greater masses, its
strength grows and it feels that strength more. The various interests
and conditions of life within the ranks of the proletariat are more
and more equalized, in proportion as machinery obliterates all distinctions of labor, and nearly everywhere reduces wages to the same
low level. The growing competition among the bourgeois, and the
resulting commercial crisis, make the wages of the workers even
more fluctuating. The unceasing improvement of machinery, ever
more rapidly developing, makes their livelihood more and more
precarious; the collisions between individual workmen and individual bourgeois take more and more the character of collisions between two classes. Thereupon the workers begin to form combinations (Trades' Unions)[9] against the bourgeois; they club together in
order to keep up the rate of wages; they found permanent associations in order to make provision beforehand for these occasional re-
volts. Here and there the contest breaks out into riots.

Now and then the workers are victorious, but only for a time.   45
The real fruit of their battle lies not in the immediate result but in
the ever-expanding union of workers. This union is helped on by
the improved means of communication that are created by modern
industry, and that places the workers of different localities in contact
with one another. It was just this contact that was needed to centralize the numerous local struggles, all of the same character, into one
national struggle between classes. But every class struggle is a political struggle. And that union, to attain which the burghers of the
Middle Ages with their miserable highways, required centuries, the
modern proletarians, thanks to railways, achieve in a few years.

This organization of the proletarians into a class, and conse-   46
quently into a political party, is continually being upset again by the
competition between the workers themselves. But it ever rises up
again, stronger, firmer, mightier. It compels legislative recognition of
particular interests of the workers by taking advantage of the divisions among the bourgeoisie itself. Thus the ten hours' bill in England[10] was carried.

---

[9] **combinations (Trades' Unions)** The labor movement was only beginning in
1848. It consisted of trades' unions that started as social clubs but soon began agitating for labor reform. They represented an important step in the growth of socialism
in Europe.

[10] **the ten hours' bill in England** This bill (1847) was an important labor reform. It limited the working day for women and children in factories to only ten
hours, at a time when it was common for some people to work sixteen hours a day.
The bill's passage was a result of political division, not of benevolence on the managers' part.

Altogether collisions between the classes of the old society fur- 47
ther, in many ways, the course of development of the proletariat.
The bourgeoisie finds itself involved in a constant battle. At first
with the aristocracy; later on, with those portions of the bourgeoisie
itself whose interests have become antagonistic to the progress of industry; at all times, with the bourgeoisie of foreign countries. In all
these battles it sees itself compelled to appeal to the proletariat, to
ask for its help, and thus, to drag it into the political arena. The
bourgeoisie itself, therefore, supplies the proletariat with its own elements of political and general education; in other words, it furnishes
the proletariat with weapons for fighting the bourgeoisie.

Further, as we have already seen, entire sections of the ruling 48
classes are, by the advance of industry, precipitated into the proletariat, or are at least threatened in their conditions of existence.
These also supply the proletariat with fresh elements of enlightenment and progress.

Finally, in times when the class-struggle nears the decisive hour, 49
the process of dissolution going on within the ruling class — in fact,
within the whole range of an old society — assumes such a violent,
glaring character that a small section of the ruling class cuts itself
adrift and joins the revolutionary class, the class that holds the future
in its hands. Just as, therefore, at an earlier period, a section of the nobility went over to the bourgeoisie, so now a portion of the bourgeoisie goes over to the proletariat, and in particular, a portion of the
bourgeois ideologists, who have raised themselves to the level of comprehending theoretically the historical movements as a whole.

Of all the classes that stand face to face with the bourgeoisie 50
today the proletariat alone is a really revolutionary class. The other
classes decay and finally disappear in the face of modern industry;
the proletariat is its special and essential product.

The lower middle class, the small manufacturer, the shop- 51
keeper, the artisan, the peasant, all these fight against the bourgeoisie, to save from extinction their existence as fractions of the
middle class. They are therefore not revolutionary, but conservative.
Nay, more; they are reactionary, for they try to roll back the wheel
of history. If by chance they are revolutionary, they are so only in
view of their impending transfer into the proletariat; they thus defend not their present, but their future interests; they desert their
own standpoint to place themselves at that of the proletariat.

The "dangerous class," the social scum, that passively rotting 52
mass thrown off by the lowest layers of old society, may, here and
there, be swept into the movement by a proletarian revolution; its
conditions of life, however, prepare it far more for the part of a
bribed tool of reactionary intrigue.

In the conditions of the proletariat, those of the old society at   53
large are already virtually swamped. The proletarian is without
property; his relation to his wife and children has no longer anything in common with the bourgeois family relations; modern industrial labor, modern subjection to capital, the same in England as
in France, in America as in Germany, has stripped him of every trace
of national character. Law, morality, religion, are to him so many
bourgeois prejudices, behind which lurk in ambush just as many
bourgeois interests.

All the preceding classes that got the upper hand sought to for-   54
tify their already acquired status by subjecting society at large to
their conditions of appropriation. The proletarians cannot become
masters of the productive forces of society, except by abolishing
their own previous mode of appropriation, and thereby also every
other previous mode of appropriation. They have nothing of their
own to secure and to fortify; their mission is to destroy all previous
securities for and insurances of individual property.

All previous historical movements were movements of minori-   55
ties, or in the interest of minorities. The proletarian movement is the
self-conscious, independent movement of the immense majority.
The proletariat, the lowest stratum of our present society, cannot
stir, cannot raise itself up without the whole superincumbent strata
of official society being sprung into the air.

Though not in substance, yet in form, the struggle of the prole-   56
tariat with the bourgeoisie is at first a national struggle. The proletariat of each country must, of course, first of all settle matters with
its own bourgeoisie.

In depicting the most general phases of the development of the   57
proletariat, we traced the more or less veiled civil war, raging within
existing society, up to the point where that war breaks out into open
revolution, and where the violent overthrow of the bourgeoisie, lays
the foundations for the sway of the proletariat.

Hitherto every form of society has been based, as we have al-   58
ready seen, on the antagonism of oppressing and oppressed classes.
But in order to oppress a class, certain conditions must be assured to
it under which it can, at least, continue its slavish existence. The
serf, in the period of serfdom, raised himself to membership in the
commune, just as the petty bourgeois, under the yoke of feudal ab-
solutism, managed to develop into a bourgeois. The modern laborer,
on the contrary, instead of rising with the progress of industry, sinks
deeper and deeper below the conditions of existence of his own
class. He becomes a pauper, and pauperism develops more rapidly
than population and wealth. And here it becomes evident that the
bourgeoisie is unfit any longer to be the ruling class in society, and

to impose its conditions of existence upon society as an over-riding law. It is unfit to rule, because it is incompetent to assure an existence to its slave within his slavery, because it cannot help letting him sink into such a state that it has to feed him, instead of being fed by him. Society can no longer live under this bourgeoisie; in other words, its existence is no longer compatible with society.

The essential condition for the existence, and for the sway of the bourgeois class, is the formation and augmentation of capital; the condition for capital is wage labor. Wage labor rests exclusively on competition between the laborers. The advance of industry, whose involuntary promoter is the bourgeoisie, replaces the isolation of the laborers, due to competition, by their involuntary combination, due to association. The development of Modern Industry, therefore, cuts from under its feet the very foundation on which the bourgeoisie produces and appropriates products. What the bourgeoisie therefore produces, above all, are its own grave diggers. Its fall and the victory of the proletariat are equally inevitable. 59

Proletarians and Communists

In what relation do the Communists stand to the proletarians as a whole? 60

The Communists do not form a separate party opposed to other working class parties. 61

They have no interests separate and apart from those of the proletariat as a whole. 62

They do not set up any sectarian principles of their own, by which to shape and mold the proletarian movement. 63

The Communists are distinguished from the other working class parties by this only: 1. In the national struggles of the proletarians of the different countries, they point out and bring to the front the common interests of the entire proletariat, independently of all nationality. 2. In the various stages of development which the struggle of the working class against the bourgeoisie has to pass through, they always and everywhere represent the interests of the movement as a whole. 64

The Communists, therefore, are on the one hand practically the most advanced and resolute section of the working class parties of every country, that section which pushes forward all others; on the other hand, theoretically, they have over the great mass of the proletariat the advantage of clearly understanding the line of march, the conditions, and the ultimate general results of the proletarian movement. 65

The immediate aim of the Communists is the same as that of all 66
the other proletarian parties: formation of the proletariat into a class,
overthrow of the bourgeois of supremacy, conquest of political
power by the proletariat.

The theoretical conclusions of the Communists are in no way 67
based on ideas or principles that have been invented or discovered
by this or that would-be universal reformer.

They merely express, in general terms, actual relations springing 68
from an existing class struggle, from a historical movement going on
under our very eyes. The abolition of existing property relations is
not at all a distinctive feature of Communism.

All property relations in the past have continually been sub- 69
ject to historical change consequent upon the change in historical
conditions.

The French Revolution, for example, abolished feudal property 70
in favor of bourgeois property.

The distinguishing feature of Communism is not the abolition 71
of property generally, but the abolition of bourgeois property. But
modern bourgeois private property is the final and most complete
expression of the system of producing and appropriating products,
that is based on class antagonism, on the exploitation of the many
by the few.

In this sense, the theory of the Communists may be summed up 72
in the single sentence: Abolition of private property.

We Communists have been reproached with the desire of abol- 73
ishing the right of personally acquiring property as the fruit of a
man's own labor, which property is alleged to be the groundwork of
all personal freedom, activity and independence.

Hard won, self-acquired, self-earned property! Do you mean the 74
property of the petty artisan and of the small peasant, a form of
property that preceded the bourgeois form? There is no need to
abolish that; the development of industry has to a great extent already destroyed it, and is still destroying it daily.

Or do you mean modern bourgeois private property?   75

But does wage labor create any property for the laborer? Not a 76
bit. It creates capital, i.e., that kind of property which exploits wage
labor, and which cannot increase except upon condition of getting a
new supply of wage labor for fresh exploitation. Property, in its present form, is based on the antagonism of capital and wage labor. Let
us examine both sides of this antagonism.

To be a capitalist is to have not only a purely personal, but a so- 77
cial status in production. Capital is a collective product, and only by
the united action of many members, nay, in the last resort, only by
the united action of all members of society, can it be set in motion.

Capital is therefore not a personal, it is a social power. 78

When, therefore, capital is converted into common property, 79
into the property of all members of society, personal property is not
thereby transformed into social property. It is only the social character of the property that is changed. It loses its class character.

Let us now take wage labor. 80

The average price of wage labor is the minimum wage, i.e., that 81
quantum of the means of subsistence which is absolutely requisite to
keep the laborer in bare existence as a laborer. What, therefore, the
wage laborer appropriates by means of his labor, merely suffices to
prolong and reproduce a bare existence. We by no means intend to
abolish this personal appropriation of the products of labor, an appropriation that is made for the maintenance and reproduction of
human life, and that leaves no surplus wherewith to command the
labor of others. All that we want to do away with is the miserable
character of this appropriation, under which the laborer lives merely
to increase capital and is allowed to live only in so far as the interests
of the ruling class require it.

In bourgeois society, living labor is but a means to increase ac- 82
cumulated labor. In Communist society accumulated labor is but a
means to widen, to enrich, to promote the existence of the laborer.

In bourgeois society, therefore, the past dominates the present; 83
in Communist society the present dominates the past. In bourgeois
society, capital is independent and has individuality, while the living
person is dependent and has no individuality.

And the abolition of this state of things is called by the bour- 84
geois abolition of individuality and freedom! And rightly so. The
abolition of bourgeois individuality, bourgeois independence and
bourgeois freedom is undoubtedly aimed at.

By freedom is meant, under the present bourgeois conditions of 85
production, free trade, free selling and buying.

But if selling and buying disappears, free selling and buying dis- 86
appears also. This talk about free selling and buying, and all the
other "brave words" of our bourgeoisie about freedom in general
have a meaning, if any, only in contrast with restricted selling and
buying, with the fettered traders of the Middle Ages, but have no
meaning when opposed to the Communistic abolition of buying and
selling, of the bourgeois conditions of production, and of the bourgeoisie itself.

You are horrified at our intending to do away with private prop- 87
erty. But in your existing society private property is already done
away with for nine-tenths of the population; its existence for the few
is solely due to its non-existence in the hands of those nine-tenths.
You reproach us, therefore, with intending to do away with a form

of property, the necessary condition for whose existence is the non-existence of any property for the immense majority of society.

In one word, you reproach us with intending to do away with 88 your property. Precisely so: that is just what we intend.

From the moment when labor can no longer be converted into 89 capital, money, or rent, into a social power capable of being monopolized, i.e., from the moment when individual property can no longer be transformed into bourgeois property, into capital, from that moment, you say, individuality vanishes.

You must, therefore, confess that by "individual" you mean no 90 other person than the bourgeois, than the middle-class owner of property. This person must, indeed, be swept out of the way and made impossible.

Communism deprives no man of the power to appropriate the 91 products of society: all that it does is to deprive him of the power to subjugate the labor of others by means of such appropriation.

It has been objected that upon the abolition of private property 92 all work will cease and universal laziness will overtake us.

According to this, bourgeois society ought long ago to have 93 gone to the dogs through sheer idleness; for those of its members who work acquire nothing, and those who acquire anything do not work. The whole of this objection is but another expression of the tautology: that there can no longer be any wage labor when there is no longer any capital.

All objections urged against the Communistic mode of produc- 94 ing and appropriating material products have, in the same way, been urged against the Communistic modes of producing and appropriating intellectual products. Just as, to the bourgeois, the disappearance of class property is the disappearance of production itself, so the disappearance of class culture is to him identical with the disappearance of all culture.

That culture, the loss of which he laments, is, for the enormous 95 majority, a mere training to act as a machine.

But don't wrangle with us so long as you apply, to our intended 96 abolition of bourgeois property, the standard of your bourgeois notions of freedom, culture, law, etc. Your very ideas are but the outgrowth of the conditions of your bourgeois production and bourgeois property, just as your jurisprudence is but the will of your class made into a law for all, a will whose essential character and direction are determined by the economical conditions of existence of your class.

The selfish misconception that induces you to transform into 97 eternal laws of nature and of reason the social forms springing from your present mode of production and form of property — historical relations that rise and disappear in the progress of production — this misconception you share with every ruling class that has preceded you. What you see clearly in the case of ancient property, what you admit in the case of feudal property, you are of course forbidden to admit in the case of your own bourgeois form of property.

Abolition of the family! Even the most radical flare up at this infamous proposal of the Communists.   98

On what foundation is the present family, the bourgeois family, based? On capital, on private gain. In its completely developed form this family exists only among the bourgeoisie. But this state of things finds its complement in the practical absence of the family among the proletarians, and in public prostitution.   99

The bourgeois family will vanish as a matter of course when its complement vanishes, and both will vanish with the vanishing of capital.   100

Do you charge us with wanting to stop the exploitation of children by their parents? To this crime we plead guilty.   101

But, you will say, we destroy the most hallowed of relations when we replace home education by social.   102

And your education! Is not that also social, and determined by the social conditions under which you educate; by the intervention, direct or indirect, of society by means of schools, etc.? The Communists have not invented the intervention of society in education; they do but seek to alter the character of that intervention, and to rescue education from the influence of the ruling class.   103

The bourgeois clap-trap about the family and education, about the hallowed correlation of parent and child, become all the more disgusting, the more, by the action of Modern Industry, all family ties among the proletarians are torn asunder and their children transformed into simple articles of commerce and instruments of labor.   104

But you Communists would introduce community of women, screams the whole bourgeoisie chorus.   105

The bourgeois sees in his wife a mere instrument of production. He hears that the instruments of production are to be exploited in common, and, naturally, can come to no other conclusion, than that the lot of being common to all will likewise fall to the women.   106

He has not even a suspicion that the real point aimed at is to do away with the status of women as mere instruments of production.   107

For the rest, nothing is more ridiculous than the virtuous indignation of our bourgeois at the community of women which, they pretend, is to be openly and officially established by the Communists. The Communists have no need to introduce community of women, it has existed almost from time immemorial.   108

Our bourgeois, not content with having the wives and daugh- 109
ters of their proletarians at their disposal, not to speak of common
prostitutes, take the greatest pleasure in seducing each others' wives.

Bourgeois marriage is in reality a system of wives in common, 110
and thus, at the most, what the Communists might possibly be reproached with, is that they desire to introduce, in substitution for a
hypocritically concealed, an openly legalized community of women.
For the rest, it is self-evident that the abolition of the present system
of production must bring with it the abolition of the community of
women springing from that system, i.e., of prostitution both public
and private.

The Communists are further reproached with desiring to abol- 111
ish countries and nationalities.

The working men have no country. We cannot take from them 112
what they don't possess. Since the proletariat must first of all acquire
political supremacy, must rise to be the leading class of the nation,
must constitute itself the nation, it is, so far, itself national, though
not in the bourgeois sense of the word.

National differences and antagonisms between peoples are daily 113
more and more vanishing, owing to the development of the bourgeoisie, to freedom of commerce, to the world-market, to uniformity
in the mode of production and in the conditions of life corresponding thereto.

The supremacy of the proletariat will cause them to vanish still 114
faster. United action, of the leading civilized countries at least, is one
of the first conditions for the emancipation of the proletariat.

In proportion as the exploitation of one individual by another is 115
put an end to, the exploitation of one nation by another will also be
put an end to. In proportion as the antagonism between classes
within the nation vanishes, the hostility of one nation to another will
come to an end.

The charges against Communism made from a religious, a 116
philosophical, and generally, from an ideological standpoint, are not
deserving of serious examination.

Does it require deep intuition to comprehend that man's ideas, 117
views and conceptions, in one word, man's consciousness, changes
with every change in the conditions of his material existence, in his
social relations and in his social life?

What else does the history of ideas prove than that intellectual 118
production changes in character in proportion as material production is changed? The ruling ideas of each age have ever been the
ideas of its ruling class.

When people speak of ideas that revolutionize society they do 119
but express the fact that within the old society the elements of a new

one have been created, and that the dissolution of the old ideas keeps even pace with the dissolution of the old conditions of existence.

When the ancient world was in its last throes the ancient reli- 120 gions were overcome by Christianity. When Christian ideas succumbed in the 18th century to rationalist ideas, feudal society fought its deathbattle with the then revolutionary bourgeoisie. The ideas of religious liberty and freedom of conscience merely gave expression to the sway of free competition within the domain of knowledge.

"Undoubtedly," it will be said, "religious, moral, philosophical 121 and judicial ideas have been modified in the course of historical development. But religion, morality, philosophy, political science, and law, constantly survived this change.

"There are, besides, eternal truths such as Freedom, Justice, etc., 122 that are common to all states of society. But Communism abolishes eternal truths, it abolishes all religion and all morality, instead of constituting them on a new basis; it therefore acts in contradiction to all past historical experience."

What does this accusation reduce itself to? The history of all 123 past society has consisted in the development of class antagonisms, antagonisms that assumed different forms at different epochs.

But whatever form they may have taken, one fact is common to 124 all past ages, viz., the exploitation of one part of society by the other. No wonder, then, that the social consciousness of past ages, despite all the multiplicity and variety it displays, moves within certain common forms, or general ideas, which cannot completely vanish except with the total disappearance of class antagonisms.

The Communist revolution is the most radical rupture with tra- 125 ditional property relations; no wonder that its development involves the most radical rupture with traditional ideas.

But let us have done with the bourgeois objections to Com- 126 munism.

We have seen above that the first step in the revolution by the 127 working class is to raise the proletariat to the position of ruling class, to win the battle of democracy.

The proletariat will use its political supremacy to wrest, by de- 128 grees, all capital from the bourgeoisie, to centralize all instruments of production in the hands of the State, i.e., of the proletariat organized as a ruling class; and to increase the total productive forces as rapidly as possible.

Of course, in the beginning, this cannot be effected except by 129 means of despotic inroads on the rights of property, and on the conditions of bourgeois production; by means of measures, therefore, which appear economically insufficient and untenable, but which in the course of the movement outstrip themselves, necessitate further inroads upon the old social order, and are unavoidable as a means of entirely revolutionizing the mode of production.

These measures will of course be different in different countries. 130

Nevertheless in the most advanced countries the following will 131 be pretty generally applicable:

1. Abolition of property in land and application of all rents of land to public purposes.
2. A heavy progressive or graduated income tax.
3. Abolition of all right of inheritance.
4. Confiscation of the property of all emigrants and rebels.
5. Centralization of credit in the hands of the State, by means of a national bank with State capital and an exclusive monopoly.
6. Centralization of the means of communication and transport in the hands of the State.
7. Extension of factories and instruments of production owned by the State; the bringing into cultivation of waste lands, and the improvement of the soil generally in accordance with a common plan.
8. Equal liability of all to labor. Establishment of industrial armies, especially for agriculture.
9. Combination of agriculture with manufacturing industries; gradual abolition of the distinction between town and country by a more equable distribution of the population over the country.
10. Free education for all children in public schools. Abolition of children's factory labor in its present form. Combination of education with industrial production, etc., etc.

When, in the course of development, class distinctions have dis- 132 appeared, and all production has been concentrated in the hands of a vast association of the whole nation, the public power will lose its political character. Political power, properly so called, is merely the organized power of one class for oppressing another. If the proletariat during its contest with the bourgeoisie is compelled, by the force of circumstances, to organize itself as a class, if, by means of a revolution, it makes itself the ruling class, and, as such, sweeps away by force the old conditions of production, then it will, along with these conditions, have swept away the conditions for the existence of class antagonism, and of classes generally, and will thereby have abolished its own supremacy as a class.

In place of the old bourgeois society, with its classes and class 133
antagonisms, we shall have an association in which the free development of each is the condition for the free development of all. . . .

Position of the Communists in Relation to the Various Existing Opposition Parties

[The preceding section] has made clear the relations of the 134
Communists to the existing working class parties, such as the
Chartists in England and the Agrarian Reforms[11] in America.

The Communists fight for the attainment of the immediate 135
aims, for the enforcement of the momentary interests of the working
class; but in the movement of the present they also represent and
take care of the future of that movement. In France the Communists
ally themselves with the Social-Democrats[12] against the conservative
and radical bourgeoisie, reserving, however, the right to take up a
critical position in regard to phrases and illusions traditionally
handed down from the great Revolution.

In Switzerland they support the Radicals,[13] without losing sight 136
of the fact that this party consists of antagonistic elements, partly
of Democratic Socialists, in the French sense, partly of radical
bourgeois.

In Poland they support the party that insists on an agrarian rev- 137
olution, as the prime condition for national emancipation, that party
which fomented the insurrection of Cracow in 1846.[14]

In Germany they fight with the bourgeoisie whenever it acts 138
in a revolutionary way, against the absolute monarchy, the feudal
squirearchy, and the petty bourgeoisie.

---

[11] **Agrarian Reforms** Agrarian reform was a very important issue in America
after the Revolution. The Chartists were a radical English group established in 1838;
they demanded political and social reforms. They were among the more violent revolutionaries of the day. Agrarian reform, redistribution of the land, was slow to
come, and the issue often sparked violence between social classes.

[12] **Social-Democrats** In France in the 1840s, a group that proposed the ideal
of labor reform through the establishment of workshops supplied with government
capital.

[13] **Radicals** By 1848, European Radicals, taking their name from the violent
revolutionaries of the French Revolution (1789–1799), were a nonviolent group
content to wait for change.

[14] **the insurrection of Cracow in 1846** Cracow was an independent city in
1846. The insurrection was designed to join Cracow with Poland and to further
large-scale social reforms.

But they never cease for a single instant to instill into the work- 139
ing class the clearest possible recognition of the hostile antagonism
between bourgeoisie and proletariat, in order that the German
workers may straightway use, as so many weapons against the bourgeoisie, the social and political conditions that the bourgeoisie must
necessarily introduce along with its supremacy, and in order that,
after the fall of the reactionary classes in Germany, the fight against
the bourgeoisie itself may immediately begin.

The Communists turn their attention chiefly to Germany, be- 140
cause that country is on the eve of a bourgeois revolution,[15] that is
bound to be carried out under more advanced conditions of European civilization, and with a more developed proletariat, than that of
England was in the seventeenth and of France in the eighteenth century, and because the bourgeois revolution in Germany will be but
the prelude to an immediately following proletarian revolution.

In short, the Communists everywhere support every revolution- 141
ary movement against the existing social and political order of
things.

In all these movements they bring to the front, as the leading 142
question in each, the property question, no matter what its degree of
development at the time.

Finally, they labor everywhere for the union and agreement of 143
the democratic parties of all countries.

The Communists disdain to conceal their views and aims. They 144
openly declare that their ends can be attained only by the forcible
overthrow of all existing social conditions. Let the ruling classes
tremble at a Communistic revolution. The proletarians have nothing
to lose but their chains. They have a world to win.

Working men of all countries, unite!   145

---

[15] **on the eve of a bourgeois revolution** Ferdinand Lassalle (1825 – 1864) developed the German labor movement and was in basic agreement with Marx, who
was nevertheless convinced that Lassalle's approach was wrong. The environment in
Germany seemed appropriate for revolution, in part because of its fragmented political structure and in part because no major revolution had yet occurred there.

QUESTIONS FOR CRITICAL READING

1. Begin by establishing your understanding of the terms "bourgeois" and
   "proletarian." Does Marx make a clear distinction between the terms?
   Are such terms applicable to American society today? Which of these
   groups, if any, do you feel that you belong to?

2. Marx makes the concept of social class fundamental to his theories. Can "social class" be easily defined? Are social classes evident in our society? Are they engaged in a struggle of the sort Marx assumes to be inevitable?

3. What are Marx's views about the value of work in the society he describes? What is his attitude toward wealth?

4. Marx says that every class struggle is a political struggle. Do you agree?

5. Examine the first part. Which class gets more paragraphs — the bourgeoisie or the proletariat? Why?

6. Is the modern proletariat a revolutionary class?

7. Is Marx's analysis of history clear? Try to summarize his views on the progress of history.

8. Is capital a social force, or is it a personal force? Do you think of your savings (either now or in the future) as belonging to you alone or as in some way belonging to your society?

9. What, in Marx's view, is the responsibility of wealthy citizens?

SUGGESTIONS FOR WRITING

1. Defend or attack Marx's statement: "The executive of the modern State is but a committee for managing the common affairs of the whole bourgeoisie" (para. 18). Is this generally true? Take three "affairs of the whole bourgeoisie" and test each one in turn.

2. Examine Marx's statements regarding women. Refer especially to paragraphs 39, 98, 105, and 110. Does he imply that his views are in conflict with his general society? After you have a list of his statements, see if you can establish exactly what he is recommending. Do you approve of his recommendations?

3. Marx's program of ten points is listed in paragraph 131. Using the technique that Marx himself uses — taking each point in its turn, clarifying the problems with the point, and finally deciding for or against the point — evaluate his program. Which points do you feel are most beneficial to society? Which are detrimental to society? What is your overall view of the general worth of the program? Do you think it would be possible to put such a program into effect?

4. All Marx's views are predicated on the present nature of property ownership and the changes that communism will institute. He claims, for example, that a rupture with property relations "involves the most radical rupture with traditional ideas" (para. 125). And he discusses in depth his proposal for the rupture of property relations (paras. 68–93). Clarify traditional property relations — what can be owned and by whom — and then contrast with these the proposals Marx makes. Establish your own views as you go along. Include your reasons for taking issue or expressing agreement with Marx. What kinds of property relations do you see around you? What kinds are most desirable for a healthy society?

5. What is the responsibility of the state toward the individual in the kind of economic circumstances that Marx describes? How can the independence of individuals who have amassed great wealth and wish to operate freely be balanced against the independence of those who are poor and have no wealth to manipulate? What kinds of abuse are possible in such circumstances, and what remedies can a state achieve through altering the economic system? What specific remedies does Marx suggest? Are they workable?

6. Do you feel that Marx's suggestions are desirable? Or that they are likely to produce the effects he desires? Critics sometimes complain about Marx's misunderstanding of human nature. Do you feel he has an adequate understanding of human nature? What do you see as impediments to the full success of his program?

7. **CONNECTIONS** Hannah Arendt suggests that Marx invokes a law of history in insisting that there will be a clash between people from different economic classes. Examine this document to see how much of Arendt's position can be defended by reference to Marx. How were Marx's views used to produce a totalitarian state in the Soviet Union? In other words, is Arendt's analysis of Marx accurate?

8. **CONNECTIONS** Marx's philosophy differs from that of Robert B. Reich. How would Marx respond to Reich's analysis of the future of labor in the next few decades? Would Marx see signs of a coming class struggle in the distinctions Reich draws between the routine workers, the in-person servers, and the symbolic analysts? Does Reich's essay take any of Marx's theories into account?

JOHN KENNETH GALBRAITH
The Position of Poverty

JOHN KENNETH GALBRAITH (b. 1908) was born in Canada but has been an American citizen since 1937. He grew up on a farm in Ontario and took his first university degree in agricultural science. This background may have contributed to the success of his many books on subjects such as economics, the State Department, Indian art, and government, which have always explained complex concepts with a clarity easily grasped by laypeople. Sometimes he has been criticized for oversimplifying issues, but on the whole, he has made a brilliant success of writing with wit and humor about perplexing and sometimes troubling issues.

Galbraith was professor of economics at Harvard University for many years. During the presidential campaigns of Adlai Stevenson in 1952 and 1956, he assisted the Democrats as a speechwriter and economics adviser. He performed the same tasks for John F. Kennedy in 1960. Kennedy appointed Galbraith ambassador to India, a post that he maintained for a little over two years, including the period during which India and China fought a border war. His experiences in India resulted in *Ambassador's Journal: A Personal Account of the Kennedy Years* (1969). Kennedy called Galbraith his finest ambassadorial appointment.

Galbraith's involvement with politics was somewhat unusual for an academic economist at that time. It seems to have stemmed from strongly held personal views on the social issues of his time. One of the most important contributions of his best-known and probably most significant book, *The Affluent Society* (1958; rev. eds. 1969, 1976, 1984), was its analysis of America's economic ambitions. He pointed out that at that time the economy was entirely tied up in the measurement and growth of the gross national prod-

---

From *The Affluent Society*.

uct. Economists and government officials concentrated on boosting output, a goal that he felt was misdirected because it would result in products that people really did not need and that would not benefit them. Creating artificial needs for things that had no ultimate value and building in a "planned obsolescence" seemed to him to be wasteful and ultimately destructive.

Galbraith suggested that America concentrate on genuine needs and satisfy them immediately. He was deeply concerned about the environment and suggested that clean air was a priority that took precedence over industry. He supported development of the arts and stressed the importance of improving housing across the nation. His effort was directed at trying to help Americans change certain basic values by giving up the pursuit of useless consumer novelties and substituting a program of genuine social development. The commitment to consumer products as the basis of the economy naturally argued against a redirection of effort toward the solution of social problems.

Galbraith is so exceptionally clear in his essay that little commentary is needed to establish its importance. He is insightful in clarifying two kinds of poverty: case poverty and insular poverty. Case poverty is restricted to an individual and his or her family and often seems to be caused by alcoholism, ignorance, mental deficiency, discrimination, or specific handicaps. It is an individual, not a group, disorder. Insular poverty affects a group in a given area — an "island" within the larger society. He points to poverty in Appalachia and in the slums of major cities, where most of the people in those "islands" are at or below the poverty level. Insular poverty is linked to the environment, and its causes are somehow derived from that environment.

Galbraith's analysis is perceptive and influential, and while little or no progress has been made in solving the problem of poverty since 1959, he assures us that there are steps that can be taken to help eradicate it. Such steps demand the nation's will, however, and he warns that the nation may lack the will. He also reasons that because the poor are a minority, few politicians make them a campaign issue. Actually, he was wrong. Kennedy in 1960, Lyndon Johnson in 1964, and Jimmy Carter in 1976 made programs for the poor central among their governmental concerns. Because of the war in Vietnam and other governmental policies, however, the 1960s and early 1970s were a time of staggering inflation, wiping out any of the advances the poor had made. The extent to which this is true is observable in the income figures for 1959, which seem so low as to conjure up the last century rather than the midtwentieth century.

GALBRAITH'S RHETORIC

The most important rhetorical achievement of the piece is its style. This is an example of the elevated plain style: a clear, direct, and basically simple approach to language that only occasionally admits a somewhat learned vocabulary — as in the use of a very few words such as "opulent," "unremunerative," and "ineluctable." Most of the words he uses are ordinary ones.

He breaks the essay into six carefully numbered sections. In this way he highlights its basic structure and informs us that he has clearly separated its elements into related groups so that he can speak directly to aspects of his subject rather than to the entire topic. This rhetorical technique of division contributes to clarity and confers a sense of authority on the writer.

Galbraith relies on statistical information that the reader can examine if necessary. This information is treated in the early stages of the piece as a prologue. Once such information has been given, Galbraith proceeds in the manner of a logician establishing premises and deriving the necessary conclusions. The subject is sober and sobering, involving issues that are complex, uncertain, and difficult, but the style is direct, confident, and essentially simple. This is the secret of the success of the book from which this selection comes. *The Affluent Society* has been translated into well over a dozen languages and has been a best-seller around the globe, and despite the fact that its statistical information is outdated, it remains an influential book. Its fundamental insights are such that it is likely to be relevant to the economy of the United States for generations to come.

The Position of Poverty

"The study of the causes of poverty," Alfred Marshall[1] observed 1
at the turn of the century, "is the study of the causes of the degradation of a large part of mankind." He spoke of contemporary England
as well as of the world beyond. A vast number of people both in
town and country, he noted, had insufficient food, clothing and
house-room; they were: "Overworked and undertaught, weary and
careworn, without quiet and without leisure." The chance of their
succor, he concluded, gave to economic studies, "their chief and
their highest interest."

No contemporary economist would be likely to make such an 2
observation about the United States. Conventional economic discourse makes obeisance to the continued existence of some poverty.
"We must remember that we still have a great many poor people." In
the nineteen-sixties, poverty promised, for a time, to become a subject of serious political concern. Then war came and the concern
evaporated or was displaced. For economists of conventional mood,
the reminders that the poor still exist are a useful way of allaying un-
easiness about the relevance of conventional economic goals. For
some people, wants must be synthesized. Hence, the importance of
the goods to them is not *per se* very high. So much may be con-
ceded. But others are far closer to physical need. And hence we must
not be cavalier about the urgency of providing them with the most
for the least. The sales tax may have merit for the opulent, but it still
bears heavily on the poor. The poor get jobs more easily when the
economy is expanding. Thus, poverty survives in economic discourse partly as a buttress to the conventional economic wisdom.

The privation of which Marshall spoke was, a half century ago, 3
the common lot at least of all who worked without special skill. As a
general affliction, it was ended by increased output which, however
imperfectly it may have been distributed, nevertheless accrued in
substantial amount to those who worked for a living. The result was
to reduce poverty from the problem of a majority to that of a minority. It ceased to be a general case and became a special case. It is this
which has put the problem of poverty into its peculiar modern form.

For poverty does survive. In part, it is a physical matter; those 4
afflicted have such limited and insufficient food, such poor clothing,
such crowded, cold and dirty shelter that life is painful as well as

---

[1] **Alfred Marshall (1842 – 1924)** An English economist whose *Principles of
Economics* (1890) was long a standard text and is still relied on by some economists
for its theories of costs, value, and distribution.

comparatively brief. But just as it is far too tempting to say that, in matters of living standards, everything is relative, so it is wrong to rest everything on absolutes. People are poverty-stricken when their income, even if adequate for survival, falls radically behind that of the community. Then they cannot have what the larger community regards as the minimum necessary for decency; and they cannot wholly escape, therefore, the judgment of the larger community that they are indecent. They are degraded for, in the literal sense, they live outside the grades or categories which the community regards as acceptable.

Since the first edition of this book appeared, and one hopes   5
however slightly as a consequence, the character and dimension of this degradation have become better understood. There have also been fulsome promises that poverty would be eliminated. The performance on these promises has been less eloquent.

The degree of privation depends on the size of the family, the   6
place of residence — it will be less with given income in rural areas than in the cities — and will, of course, be affected by changes in living costs. The Department of Health, Education and Welfare has established rough standards, appropriately graded to family size, location and changing prices, to separate the poor from the less poor and the affluent. In 1972, a non-farm family of four was deemed poor if it had an income of $4275; a couple living otherwise than on a farm was called poor if it had less than $2724 and an unattached individual if receiving less than $2109. A farm family of four was poor with less than $3639; of two with less than $2315.[2]

By these modest standards, 24.5 million households, including   7
individuals and families, were poor in 1972 as compared with 13.4 million in 1959. Because of the increase in population, and therewith in the number of households, in these years the reduction in the number of poor households, as a proportion of all households, was rather greater — from 24 percent in 1959 to 12 percent in 1972.[3]

One can usually think of the foregoing deprivation as falling   8
into two broad categories. First, there is what may be called *case* poverty. This one encounters in every community, rural or urban, however prosperous that community or the times. Case poverty is the poor farm family with the junk-filled yard and the dirty children playing in the bare dirt. Or it is the gray-black hovel beside the railroad tracks. Or it is the basement dwelling in the alley.

---

[2] *Statistical Abstract of the United States,* 1974, p. 389. [Galbraith's note]
[3] *Statistical Abstract,* 1974, p. 389. [Galbraith's note]

Case poverty is commonly and properly related to some charac- 9
teristic of the individuals so afflicted. Nearly everyone else has mastered his environment; this proves that it is not intractable. But some
quality peculiar to the individual or family involved — mental deficiency, bad health, inability to adapt to the discipline of industrial
life, uncontrollable procreation, alcohol, discrimination involving a
very limited minority, some educational handicap unrelated to community shortcoming, or perhaps a combination of several of these
handicaps — has kept these individuals from participating in the
general well-being.

Second, there is what may be called *insular* poverty — that 10
which manifests itself as an "island" of poverty. In the island, everyone or nearly everyone is poor. Here, evidently, it is not easy to explain matters by individual inadequacy. We may mark individuals
down as intrinsically deficient in social performance; it is not proper .
or even wise so to characterize an entire community. The people of
the island have been frustrated by some factor common to their
environment.

Case poverty exists. It has also been useful to those who have 11
needed a formula for keeping the suffering of others from causing
suffering to themselves. Since this poverty is the result of the deficiencies, including the moral shortcomings, of the persons concerned, it is possible to shift the responsibility to those involved.
They are worthless and, as a simple manifestation of social justice,
they suffer for it. Or, at a somewhat higher level of social perception
and compassion, it means that the problem of poverty is sufficiently
solved by private and public charity. This rescues those afflicted
from the worst consequences of their inadequacy or misfortune; no
larger social change or reorganization is suggested. Except as it may
be insufficient in its generosity, the society is not at fault.

Insular poverty yields to no such formulas. In earlier times, 12
when agriculture and extractive industries were the dominant
sources of livelihood, something could be accomplished by shifting
the responsibility for low income to a poor natural endowment and
thus, in effect, to God. The soil was thin and stony, other natural resources absent and hence the people were poor. And, since it is the
undoubted preference of many to remain in the vicinity of the place
of their birth, a homing instinct that operates for people as well as
pigeons, the people remained in the poverty which heaven had de-
creed for them. It is an explanation that is nearly devoid of empirical
application. Connecticut is very barren and stony and incomes are
very high. Similarly Wyoming. West Virginia is well watered with
rich mines and forests and the people are very poor. The South is
much favored in soil and climate and similarly poor and the very

richest parts of the South, such as the Mississippi-Yazoo Delta, have long had a well-earned reputation for the greatest deprivation. Yet so strong is the tendency to associate poverty with natural causes that even individuals of some modest intelligence will still be heard, in explanation of insular poverty, to say, "It's basically a poor country." "It's a pretty barren region."

Most modern poverty is insular in character and the islands are 13 the rural and urban slums. From the former, mainly in the South, the southern Appalachians and Puerto Rico, there has been until recent times a steady flow of migrants, some white but more black, to the latter. Grim as life is in the urban ghetto, it still offers more hope, income and interest than in the rural slum. Largely in consequence of this migration, the number of poor farm families — poor by the standards just mentioned — declined between 1959 and 1973 from 1.8 million to 295,000. The decline in the far larger number of poor non-farm households in these years was only from 6.5 million to 4.5 million.[4]

This is not the place to provide a detailed profile of this poverty. 14 More than half of the poor households are headed by a woman, although in total women head only 9 percent of families. Over 30 percent are black, another 10 percent are of Spanish origin. A very large proportion of all black households (31 percent in 1973 as compared with 8 percent of whites) fall below the poverty line. Especially on the farms, where the young have departed for the cities, a disproportionate number of the poor are old. More often than not, the head of the household is not in the labor force at all.

But the more important characteristic of insular poverty is 15 forces, common to all members of the community, which restrain or prevent participation in economic life at going rates of return. These restraints are several. Race, which acts to locate people by their color rather than by the proximity to employment, is obviously one. So are poor educational facilities. (And this effect is further exaggerated when the poorly educated, endemically a drug on the labor market, are brought together in dense clusters by the common inadequacy of the schools available to blacks and the poor.) So is the disintegration of family life in the slum which leaves households in the hands of women. Family life itself is in some measure a manifestation of affluence. And so, without doubt, is the shared sense of helplessness and rejection and the resulting demoralization which is the product of the common misfortune.

---

[4] U.S. Department of Commerce, *Current Population Reports,* "Consumer Income," Series P-60, No. 98 (Washington, D.C.: U.S. Government Printing Office, 1975). [Galbraith's note]

The most certain thing about this poverty is that it is not reme- 16
died by a general advance in income. Case poverty is not remedied
because the specific individual inadequacy precludes employment
and participation in the general advance. Insular poverty is not directly alleviated because the advance does not remove the specific
frustrations of environment to which the people of these islands are
subject. This is not to say that it is without effect. If there are jobs
outside the ghetto or away from the rural slum, those who are qualified, and not otherwise constrained, can take them and escape. If
there are no such jobs, none can escape. But it remains that advance
cannot improve the position of those who, by virtue of self or environment, cannot participate.

With the transition of the very poor from a majority to a com- 17
parative minority position, there has been a change in their political
position. Any tendency of a politician to identify himself with those
of the lowest estate usually brought the reproaches of the well-to-do.
Political pandering and demagoguery were naturally suspected. But,
for the man so reproached, there was the compensating advantage of
alignment with a large majority. Now any politician who speaks for
the very poor is speaking for a small and generally inarticulate minority. As a result, the modern liberal politician regularly aligns
himself not with the poverty-ridden members of the community but
with the far more numerous people who enjoy the far more affluent
income of (say) the modern trade union member or the intellectual.
Ambrose Bierce, in *The Devil's Dictionary*, called poverty "a file provided for the teeth of the rats of reform."[5] It is so no longer. Reform
now concerns itself with the needs of people who are relatively well-
to-do — whether the comparison be with their own past or with
those who are really at the bottom of the income ladder.

In consequence, a notable feature of efforts to help the very 18
poor is their absence of any very great political appeal.[6] Politicians
have found it possible to be indifferent where they could not be de-
risory. And very few have been under a strong compulsion to support these efforts.

The concern for inequality and deprivation had vitality only so 19
long as the many suffered while a few had much. It did not survive
as a decisive political issue in a time when the many had much even

---

[5] **Ambrose Bierce (1842 – 1914?)** A southern American writer noted for satir-
ical writings such as the one quoted.

[6] This was true of the Office of Economic Opportunity — the so-called poverty
program — and was ultimately the reason for its effective demise. [Galbraith's note]

though others had much more. It is our misfortune that when inequality declined as an issue, the slate was not left clean. A residual and in some ways rather more hopeless problem remained.

An affluent society, that is also both compassionate and rational 20 would, no doubt, secure to all who needed it the minimum income essential for decency and comfort. The corrupting effect on the human spirit of unearned revenue has unquestionably been exaggerated as, indeed, have the character-building values of hunger and privation. To secure to each family a minimum income, as a normal function of the society, would help ensure that the misfortunes of parents, deserved or otherwise, were not visited on their children. It would help ensure that poverty was not self-perpetuating. Most of the reaction, which no doubt would be adverse, is based on obsolete attitudes. When poverty was a majority phenomenon, such action could not be afforded. A poor society, as this essay has previously shown, had to enforce the rule that the person who did not work could not eat. And possibly it was justified in the added cruelty of applying the rule to those who could not work or whose efficiency was far below par. An affluent society has no similar excuse for such rigor. It can use the forthright remedy of providing income for those without. Nothing requires such a society to be compassionate. But it no longer has a high philosophical justification for callousness.

The notion that income is a remedy for indigency has a certain 21 forthright appeal.[7] As elsewhere argued, it would also ease the problems of economic management by reducing the reliance on production as a source of income. The provision of such a basic source of income must henceforth be the first and the strategic step in the attack on poverty.

But it is only one step. In the past, we have suffered from the 22 supposition that the only remedy for poverty lies in remedies that allow people to look after themselves — to participate in the economy. Nothing has better served the conscience of people who wished to avoid inconvenient or expensive action than an appeal, on this issue, to Calvinist precept — "The only sound way to solve the problem of poverty is to help people help themselves." But this does not mean that steps to allow participation and to keep poverty from being self-perpetuating are unimportant. On the contrary. It requires that the investment in children from families presently afflicted be as little below normal as possible. If the children of poor

---

[7] As earlier noted, in the first edition, the provision of guaranteed income was discussed but dismissed as "beyond reasonable hope." [Galbraith's note]

families have first-rate schools and school attendance is properly enforced; if the children, though badly fed at home, are well nourished
at school; if the community has sound health services, and the physical well-being of the children is vigilantly watched; if there is opportunity for advanced education for those who qualify regardless of
means; and if, especially in the case of urban communities, housing
is ample and housing standards are enforced, the streets are clean,
the laws are kept, and recreation is adequate — then there is a
chance that the children of the very poor will come to maturity
without inhibiting disadvantage. In the case of insular poverty, this
remedy requires that the services of the community be assisted from
outside. Poverty is self-perpetuating partly because the poorest communities are poorest in the services which would eliminate it. To
eliminate poverty efficiently, we must, indeed, invest more than pro-
portionately in the children of the poor community. It is there that
high quality schools, strong health services, special provision for nutrition and recreation are most needed to compensate for the very
low investment which families are able to make in their own
offspring.

The effect of education and related investment in individuals is   23
to help them overcome the restraints that are imposed by their environment. These need also to be attacked even more directly — by
giving the mobility that is associated with plentiful, good and readily
available housing, by provision of comfortable, efficient and economical mass transport, by making the environment pleasant and
safe, and by eliminating the special health handicaps that afflict the
poor.

Nor is case poverty entirely resistant to such remedies. Much   24
can be done to treat those characteristics which cause people to reject or be rejected by the modern industrial society. Educational deficiencies can be overcome. Mental deficiencies can be treated. Physical handicaps can be remedied. The limiting factor is not a lack of
knowledge of what can be done. Overwhelmingly, it is a shortage of
money.

It will be clear that, to a remarkable extent, the remedy for   25
poverty leads to the same requirements as those for social balance.
The restraints that confine people to the ghetto are those that result
from insufficient investment in the public sector. And the means to
escape from these constraints and to break their hold on subsequent
generations just mentioned — better nutrition and health, better education, more and better housing, better mass transport, an environment more conducive to effective social participation — all, with

rare exceptions, call for massively greater investment in the public sector. In recent years, the problems of the urban ghetto have been greatly discussed but with little resultant effect. To a certain extent, the search for deeper social explanations of its troubles has been motivated by the hope that these (together with more police) might lead to solutions that would somehow elide the problem of cost. It is an idle hope. The modern urban household is an extremely expensive thing. We have not yet taken the measure of the resources that must be allocated to its public tasks if it is to be agreeable or even tolerable. And first among the symptoms of an insufficient allocation is the teeming discontent of the modern ghetto.

A further feature of these remedies is to be observed. Their con-   26
sequence is to allow participation in the economic life of the larger community — to make people and the children of people who are now idle productive. This means that they will add to the total output of goods and services. We see once again that even by its own terms the present preoccupation with the private sector of the economy as compared with the whole spectrum of human needs is inefficient. The parallel with investment in the supply of trained and educated manpower discussed above will be apparent.

But increased output of goods is not the main point. Even to the   27
most intellectually reluctant reader, it will now be evident that enhanced productive efficiency is not the motif of this volume. The very fact that increased output offers itself as a by-product of the effort to eliminate poverty is one of the reasons. No one would be called up to write at such length on a problem so easily solved as that of increasing production. The main point lies elsewhere. Poverty — grim, degrading and ineluctable — is not remarkable in India. For few, the fate is otherwise. But in the United States, the survival of poverty is remarkable. We ignore it because we share with all societies at all times the capacity for not seeing what we do not wish to see. Anciently this has enabled the nobleman to enjoy his dinner while remaining oblivious to the beggars around his door. In our own day, it enables us to travel in comfort by Harlem and into the lush precincts of midtown Manhattan. But while our failure to notice can be explained, it cannot be excused. "Poverty," Pitt[8] exclaimed, "is no disgrace but it is damned annoying." In the contemporary United States, it is not annoying but it is a disgrace.

---

[8] **William Pitt, the Younger (1759 – 1806)** British prime minister from 1783 to 1801 and, briefly, again in 1804 and 1805.

QUESTIONS FOR CRITICAL READING

1. What is the fundamental difference between the attitude Alfred Marshall held toward the poor (para. 1) and the attitude contemporary economists hold?
2. Galbraith avoids a specific definition of poverty because he says it changes from society to society. How would you define poverty as it exists in our society? What are its major indicators?
3. According to Galbraith, what is the relationship of politics to poverty?
4. What, according to this essay, seem to be the causes of poverty?
5. Clarify the distinctions Galbraith makes between case poverty and insular poverty. Are they reasonable distinctions?
6. Does Galbraith oversimplify the issues of poverty in America?
7. Galbraith first published this piece in 1958. How much have attitudes toward poverty changed since then? What kinds of progress seem to have been made toward eradicating poverty?

SUGGESTIONS FOR WRITING

1. In paragraph 4, Galbraith says, "People are poverty-stricken when their income, even if adequate for survival, falls radically behind that of the community. Then they cannot have what the larger community regards as the minimum necessary for decency; and they cannot wholly escape, therefore, the judgment of the larger community that they are indecent. They are degraded for, in the literal sense, they live outside the grades or categories which the community regards as acceptable." Examine what he says here, and explain what he means. Is this an accurate description of poverty? How would you amend it? If you accept his description of poverty, what public policy would you recommend to deal with it? What would be the consequences of accepting Galbraith's description?
2. Galbraith points out some anomalies of poverty and place. For example, he notes that West Virginia is rich in resources but that its people have been notable for their poverty. Connecticut, on the other hand, is poor in resources, with stony, untillable land, and its people have been notable for their wealth. Some economists have also pointed out that, when the Americas were settled, South America had gold, had lush tropics that yielded food and fruit for the asking, and held the promise of immense wealth. North America had a harsh climate, stubborn soil conditions, and dense forests that needed clearing. Yet North America has less poverty now than does South America. Write a brief essay in which you consider whether what is said above is too simplified to be useful. If it is not, what do you think is the reason for the economic distinctions that Galbraith and others point out?
3. What personal experiences have you had with poverty? Are you familiar with examples of case poverty? If so, describe them in such a way as

to help others understand them. What causes produced the poverty? What is the social situation of the people in your examples? How might they increase their wealth?

4. Examine the newspapers for the last several days, and look through back issues of magazines such as *Time, Newsweek,* the *New Republic,* the *New Leader,* or *U.S. News & World Report.* How many stories does each devote to the question of poverty? Present a survey of the views you find, and compare them with Galbraith's. How much agreement or disagreement is there? Would the level of the nation's concern with poverty please Galbraith?

5. Write a brief essay about current political attitudes toward poverty. If possible, gather some recent statements made by politicians. Analyze them to see how closely they tally with Galbraith's concerns and views. Do any specific politicians act as spokespeople for the poor?

6. Galbraith says that poverty has undergone a dramatic change in our society: once most people were poor and only a few were affluent, and now most people are affluent and only a few are poor. Is Galbraith correct in this assessment? Interview your parents and grandparents and their friends to establish or disprove the validity of Galbraith's claim, and then explain what you feel are the problems the poor face as a result of their current minority status. If possible, during your interviews ask what feelings your parents and their friends have about the poor. What feelings do you have? Are they shared by your friends?

7. **CONNECTIONS** What might Adam Smith have said about Galbraith's examination of poverty? How might Smith interpret the relationship of poverty to wealth? How would he suggest relieving poverty? Does Smith take a sympathetic attitude to those who are impoverished? Does Galbraith?

ROBERT B. REICH

Why the Rich Are Getting Richer and the Poor, Poorer

ROBERT B. REICH (b. 1946), University Professor in the Heller Graduate School at Brandeis University, who served as secretary of labor in the first Clinton administration, holds a graduate degree from Yale Law School, and unlike his former colleagues in the John F. Kennedy School of Government at Harvard, he does not hold a Ph.D. in economics. Nonetheless, he has written numerous books on economics and has been a prominent lecturer for a dozen years. *The Work of Nations* (1991), from which this essay comes, is the distillation of many years' analysis of modern economic trends.

As a college student, Reich was an activist but not a radical. In 1968 he was a Rhodes scholar, studying at Oxford University with Bill Clinton and a number of others who are now influential American policymakers. Reich is a specialist in policy studies — that is, the relationship of governmental policy to the economic health of the nation. Unlike those who champion free trade and unlimited expansion, Reich questions the existence of free trade by pointing to the effect of government taxation on business enterprise. Taxation — like many governmental policies regarding immigration, tariffs, and money supply — directly shapes the behavior of most companies. Reich feels that government must establish and execute an industrial policy that will benefit the nation.

While organized labor groups, such as industrial unions, have rejected much of his theorizing about labor, Reich has developed a reputation as a conciliator who can see opposite sides of a question and resolve them. He is known for his denunciation of mergers, lawsuits, takeovers, and other deals that he believes simply churn money around rather than produce wealth. He feels that such maneuvers enrich a few predatory people but do not benefit labor in

251

general — and, indeed, that the debt created by such deals harms labor in the long run.

In *The Next American Frontier* (1983) Reich insists that government, unions, and businesses must cooperate to create a workable program designed to improve the economy. Trusting to chance and free trade, he argues, will not work in the current economy. He also has said that the old assembly-line methods must give way to what he calls "flexible production," involving smaller, customized runs of products for specific markets.

Reich's *The Work of Nations,* whose title draws on Adam Smith's classic *The Wealth of Nations* (1776), examines the borderless nature of contemporary corporations. Multinational corporations are a reality, and as he points out in the following essay, their flexibility makes it possible for them to thrive by moving manufacturing plants from nation to nation. The reasons for moving are sometimes connected to lower wages but more often are connected to the infrastructure of a given nation. Reliable roads, plentiful electricity, well-educated workers, low crime rates, and political stability are all elements that make a location attractive to a multinational corporation.

REICH'S RHETORIC

The structure of "Why the Rich Are Getting Richer and the Poor, Poorer" is built on a metaphor: that of boats rising or falling with the tide. As Reich notes, "All Americans used to be in roughly the same economic boat" (para. 2), and when the economic tide rose, most people rose along with it. However, today "national borders no longer define our economic fate"; Reich therefore views Americans today as being in different boats, depending on their role in the economy, and his essay follows the fates of three distinct kinds of workers.

Examining the routine worker, he observes, "The boat containing routine producers is sinking rapidly" (para. 3). As he demonstrates, the need for routine production has declined in part because of improvements in production facilities. Much labor-intensive work has been replaced by machines. Modern factories often scramble to locate in places where production costs are lowest. People in other nations work at a fraction of the hourly rate of American workers, and since factories are relatively cheap to establish, they can be easily moved.

Reich continues the boat metaphor with "in-person servers." The boat that carries these workers, he says, "is sinking as well, but somewhat more slowly and unevenly" (para. 20). Workers in restau-

rants, retail outlets, car washes, and other personal service industries often work part-time and have few health or other benefits.
Their jobs are imperiled by machines as well, although not as much
as manufacturing jobs are. Although the outlook for such workers is
buoyed by a declining population, which will reduce competition for
their jobs, increased immigration may cancel this benefit.

Finally, Reich argues that the "vessel containing America's
symbolic analysts is rising" (para. 28). This third group contains
the population that identifies and solves problems and brokers
ideas. "Almost everyone around the world is buying the skills and
insights of Americans who manipulate oral and visual symbols"
(para. 33). Engineers, consultants, marketing experts, publicists,
and those in entertainment fields all manage to cross national
boundaries and prosper at a rate that is perhaps startling. As a result of an expanding world market, symbolic analysts do not depend only on the purchasing power of routine and in-service workers. Instead, they rely on the same global web that dominates the
pattern of corporate structure.

Reich's essay follows the fate of these three groups in turn to
establish the pattern of change and expectation that will shape
America's economic future. His metaphor is deftly handled, and he
includes details, examples, facts, and careful references to support
his position.

Why the Rich Are Getting Richer
and the Poor, Poorer

The division of labour is limited by the extent of the market.
— ADAM SMITH,
*An Inquiry into the Nature
and Causes of the Wealth of Nations* (1776)

Regardless of how your job is officially classified (manufactur-   1
ing, service, managerial, technical, secretarial, and so on), or the industry in which you work (automotive, steel, computer, advertising,
finance, food processing), your real competitive position in the
world economy is coming to depend on the function you perform in
it. Herein lies the basic reason why incomes are diverging. The fortunes of routine producers are declining. In-person servers are also
becoming poorer, although their fates are less clear-cut. But sym-

bolic analysts — who solve, identify, and broker new problems — are, by and large, succeeding in the world economy.

All Americans used to be in roughly the same economic boat. 2 Most rose or fell together as the corporations in which they were employed, the industries comprising such corporations, and the national economy as a whole became more productive — or languished. But national borders no longer define our economic fates. We are now in different boats, one sinking rapidly, one sinking more slowly, and the third rising steadily.

The boat containing routine producers is sinking rapidly. Recall 3 that by midcentury routine production workers in the United States were paid relatively well. The giant pyramidlike organizations at the core of each major industry coordinated their prices and investments — avoiding the harsh winds of competition and thus maintaining healthy earnings. Some of these earnings, in turn, were reinvested in new plant and equipment (yielding ever-larger-scale economies); another portion went to top managers and investors. But a large and increasing portion went to middle managers and production workers. Work stoppages posed such a threat to high-volume production that organized labor was able to exact an ever-larger premium for its cooperation. And the pattern of wages established within the core corporations influenced the pattern throughout the national economy. Thus the growth of a relatively affluent middle class, able to purchase all the wondrous things produced in high volume by the core corporations.

But, as has been observed, the core is rapidly breaking down into 4 global webs which earn their largest profits from clever problem-solving, -identifying, and brokering. As the costs of transporting standard things and of communicating information about them continue to drop, profit margins on high-volume, standardized production are thinning, because there are few barriers to entry. Modern factories and state-of-the-art machinery can be installed almost anywhere on the globe. Routine producers in the United States, then, are in direct competition with millions of routine producers in other nations. Twelve thousand people are added to the world's population every hour, most of whom, eventually, will happily work for a small fraction of the wages of routine producers in America.[1]

---

[1] The reader should note, of course, that lower wages in other areas of the world are of no particular attraction to global capital unless workers there are sufficiently productive to make the labor cost of producing *each unit* lower there than in higher-wage regions. Productivity in many low-wage areas of the world has improved due to the ease with which state-of-the-art factories and equipment can be installed there. [Reich's note]

The consequence is clearest in older, heavy industries, where 5 high-volume, standardized production continues its ineluctable move to where labor is cheapest and most accessible around the world. Thus, for example, the Maquiladora factories cluttered along the Mexican side of the U.S. border in the sprawling shanty towns of Tijuana, Mexicali, Nogales, Agua Prieta, and Ciudad Juárez — factories owned mostly by Americans, but increasingly by Japanese — in which more than a half million routine producers assemble parts into finished goods to be shipped into the United States.

The same story is unfolding worldwide. Until the late 1970s, 6 AT&T had depended on routine producers in Shreveport, Louisiana, to assemble standard telephones. It then discovered that routine producers in Singapore would perform the same tasks at a far lower cost. Facing intense competition from other global webs, AT&T's strategic brokers felt compelled to switch. So in the early 1980s they stopped hiring routine producers in Shreveport and began hiring cheaper routine producers in Singapore. But under this kind of pressure for ever lower high-volume production costs, today's Singaporean can easily end up as yesterday's Louisianan. By the late 1980s, AT&T's strategic brokers found that routine producers in Thailand were eager to assemble telephones for a small fraction of the wages of routine producers in Singapore. Thus, in 1989, AT&T stopped hiring Singaporeans to make telephones and began hiring even cheaper routine producers in Thailand.

The search for ever lower wages has not been confined to heavy 7 industry. Routine data processing is equally footloose. Keypunch operators located anywhere around the world can enter data into computers, linked by satellite or transoceanic fiber-optic cable, and take it out again. As the rates charged by satellite networks continue to drop, and as more satellites and fiber-optic cables become available (reducing communication costs still further), routine data processors in the United States find themselves in ever more direct competition with their counterparts abroad, who are often eager to work for far less.

By 1990, keypunch operators in the United States were earning, 8 at most, $6.50 per hour. But keypunch operators throughout the rest of the world were willing to work for a fraction of this. Thus, many potential American data-processing jobs were disappearing, and the wages and benefits of the remaining ones were in decline. Typical was Saztec International, a $20-million-a-year data-processing firm headquartered in Kansas City, whose American strategic brokers contracted with routine data processors in Manila and with American-owned firms that needed such data-processing services. Compared with the average Philippine income of $1,700 per year, data-entry operators working for Saztec earn the princely sum of $2,650. The remainder of Saztec's employees were American problem-solvers and -identifiers, searching for ways to improve the worldwide system and find new uses to which it could be put.[2]

By 1990, American Airlines was employing over 1,000 data   9
processors in Barbados and the Dominican Republic to enter names and flight numbers from used airline tickets (flown daily to Barbados from airports around the United States) into a giant computer bank located in Dallas. Chicago publisher R. R. Donnelley was sending entire manuscripts to Barbados for entry into computers in preparation for printing. The New York Life Insurance Company was dispatching insurance claims to Castleisland, Ireland, where routine producers, guided by simple directions, entered the claims and determined the amounts due, then instantly transmitted the computations back to the United States. (When the firm advertised in Ireland for twenty-five data-processing jobs, it received six hundred applications.) And McGraw-Hill was processing subscription renewal and marketing information for its magazines in nearby Galway. Indeed, literally millions of routine workers around the world were receiving information, converting it into computer-readable form, and then sending it back — at the speed of electronic impulses — whence it came.

The simple coding of computer software has also entered into   10
world commerce. India, with a large English-speaking population of technicians happy to do routine programming cheaply, is proving to be particularly attractive to global webs in need of this service. By 1990, Texas Instruments maintained a software development facility in Bangalore, linking fifty Indian programmers by satellite to TI's Dallas headquarters. Spurred by this and similar ventures, the Indian government was building a teleport in Poona, intended to make it easier and less expensive for many other firms to send their routine software design specifications for coding.[3]

This shift of routine production jobs from advanced to develop-   11
ing nations is a great boon to many workers in such nations who otherwise would be jobless or working for much lower wages. These workers, in turn, now have more money with which to purchase symbolic-analytic services from advanced nations (often embedded within all sorts of complex products). The trend is also beneficial to everyone around the world who can now obtain high-volume,

[2] John Maxwell Hamilton, "A Bit Player Buys into the Computer Age," *New York Times Business World,* December 3, 1989, p. 14. [Reich's note]

[3] Udayan Gupta, "U.S.-Indian Satellite Link Stands to Cut Software Costs," *Wall Street Journal,* March 6, 1989, p. B2. [Reich's note]

standardized products (including information and software) more cheaply than before.

But these benefits do not come without certain costs. In particu-   12
lar the burden is borne by those who no longer have good-paying routine production jobs within advanced economies like the United States. Many of these people used to belong to unions or at least benefited from prevailing wage rates established in collective bargaining agreements. But as the old corporate bureaucracies have flattened into global webs, bargaining leverage has been lost. Indeed, the tacit national bargain is no more.

Despite the growth in the number of new jobs in the United   13
States, union membership has withered. In 1960, 35 percent of all nonagricultural workers in America belonged to a union. But by 1980 that portion had fallen to just under a quarter, and by 1989 to about 17 percent. Excluding government employees, union membership was down to 13.4 percent.[4] This was a smaller proportion even than in the early 1930s, before the National Labor Relations Act created a legally protected right to labor representation. The drop in membership has been accompanied by a growing number of collective bargaining agreements to freeze wages at current levels, reduce wage levels of entering workers, or reduce wages overall. This is an important reason why the long economic recovery that began in 1982 produced a smaller rise in unit labor costs than any of the eight recoveries since World War II — the low rate of unemployment during its course notwithstanding.

Routine production jobs have vanished fastest in traditional   14
unionized industries (autos, steel, and rubber, for example), where average wages have kept up with inflation. This is because the jobs of older workers in such industries are protected by seniority; the youngest workers are the first to be laid off. Faced with a choice of cutting wages or cutting the number of jobs, a majority of union members (secure in the knowledge that there are many who are junior to them who will be laid off first) often have voted for the latter.

Thus the decline in union membership has been most striking   15
among young men entering the work force without a college education. In the early 1950s, more than 40 percent of this group joined unions; by the late 1980s, less than 20 percent (if public employees are excluded, less than 10 percent).[5] In steelmaking, for example, al-

---

[4] *Statistical Abstract of the United States* (Washington, D.C.: U.S. Government Printing Office, 1989), p. 416, table 684. [Reich's note]

[5] Calculations from Current Population Surveys by L. Katz and A. Revenga, "Changes in the Structure of Wages: U.S. and Japan," National Bureau of Economic Research, September 1989. [Reich's note]

though many older workers remained employed, almost half of all routine steelmaking jobs in America vanished between 1974 and 1988 (from 480,000 to 260,000). Similarly with automobiles: During the 1980s, the United Auto Workers lost 500,000 members — one-third of their total at the start of the decade. General Motors alone cut 150,000 American production jobs during the 1980s (even as it added employment abroad). Another consequence of the same phenomenon: the gap between the average wages of unionized and nonunionized workers widened dramatically — from 14.6 percent in 1973 to 20.4 percent by end of the 1980s.[6] The lesson is clear. If you drop out of high school or have no more than a high school diploma, do not expect a good routine production job to be awaiting you.

16   Also vanishing are lower- and middle-level management jobs involving routine production. Between 1981 and 1986, more than 780,000 foremen, supervisors, and section chiefs lost their jobs through plant closings and layoffs.[7] Large numbers of assistant division heads, assistant directors, assistant managers, and vice presidents also found themselves jobless. GM shed more than 40,000 white-collar employees and planned to eliminate another 25,000 by the mid-1990s.[8] As America's core pyramids metamorphosed into global webs, many middle-level routine producers were as obsolete as routine workers on the line.

17   As has been noted, foreign-owned webs are hiring some Americans to do routine production in the United States. Philips, Sony, and Toyota factories are popping up all over — to the self-congratulatory applause of the nation's governors and mayors, who have lured them with promises of tax abatements and new sewers, among other amenities. But as these ebullient politicians will soon discover, the foreign-owned factories are highly automated and will become far more so in years to come. Routine production jobs account for a small fraction of the cost of producing most items in the United States and other advanced nations, and this fraction will continue to decline sharply as computer-integrated robots take over. In 1977 it took routine producers thirty-five hours to assemble an automobile in the United States; it is estimated that by the mid-1990s,

---

[6] U.S. Department of Commerce, Bureau of Labor Statistics, "Wages of Unionized and Non-Unionized Workers," various issues. [Reich's note]

[7] U.S. Department of Labor, Bureau of Labor Statistics, "Reemployment Increases Among Displaced Workers," *BLS News,* USDL 86-414, October 14, 1986, table 6. [Reich's note]

[8] *Wall Street Journal,* February 16, 1990, p. A5. [Reich's note]

Japanese-owned factories in America will be producing finished automobiles using only eight hours of a routine producer's time.[9]

The productivity and resulting wages of American workers who   18
run such robotic machinery may be relatively high, but there may not be many such jobs to go around. A case in point: in the late 1980s, Nippon Steel joined with America's ailing Inland Steel to build a new $400 million cold-rolling mill fifty miles west of Gary, Indiana. The mill was celebrated for its state-of-the-art technology, which cut the time to produce a coil of steel from twelve days to about one hour. In fact, the entire plant could be run by a small team of technicians, which became clear when Inland subsequently closed two of its old cold-rolling mills, laying off hundreds of routine workers. Governors and mayors take note: your much-ballyhooed foreign factories may end up employing distressingly few of your constituents.

Overall, the decline in routine jobs has hurt men more than   19
women. This is because the routine production jobs held by men in high-volume metal-bending manufacturing industries had paid higher wages than the routine production jobs held by women in textiles and data processing. As both sets of jobs have been lost, American women in routine production have gained more equal footing with American men — equally poor footing, that is. This is a major reason why the gender gap between male and female wages began to close during the 1980s.

The second of the three boats, carrying in-person servers, is   20
sinking as well, but somewhat more slowly and unevenly. Most in-person servers are paid at or just slightly above the minimum wage and many work only part-time, with the result that their take-home pay is modest, to say the least. Nor do they typically receive all the benefits (health care, life insurance, disability, and so forth) garnered by routine producers in large manufacturing corporations or by symbolic analysts affiliated with the more affluent threads of global webs.[10] In-person servers are sheltered from the direct effects of global competition and, like everyone else, benefit from access to lower-cost products from around the world. But they are not immune to its indirect effects.

---

[9] Figures from the International Motor Vehicles Program, Massachusetts Institute of Technology, 1989. [Reich's note]

[10] The growing portion of the American labor force engaged in in-person services, relative to routine production, thus helps explain why the number of Americans lacking health insurance increased by at least 6 million during the 1980s. [Reich's note]

For one thing, in-person servers increasingly compete with for-   21
mer routine production workers, who, no longer able to find well-
paying routine production jobs, have few alternatives but to seek in-
person service jobs. The Bureau of Labor Statistice estimates that of
the 2.8 million manufacturing workers who lost their jobs during
the early 1980s, fully one-third were rehired in service jobs paying
at least 20 percent less.[11] In-person servers must also compete with
high school graduates and dropouts who years before had moved
easily into routine production jobs but no longer can. And if demographic predictions about the American work force in the first
decades of the twenty-first century are correct (and they are likely to
be, since most of the people who will comprise the work force are
already identifiable), most new entrants into the job market will be
black or Hispanic men, or women — groups that in years past have
possessed relatively weak technical skills. This will result in an even
larger number of people crowding into in-person services. Finally,
in-person servers will be competing with growing numbers of immigrants, both legal and illegal, for whom in-person services will comprise the most accessible jobs. (It is estimated that between the mid-
1980s and the end of the century, about a quarter of all workers
entering the American labor force will be immigrants.[12])

Perhaps the fiercest competition that in-person servers face   22
comes from labor-saving machinery (much of it invented, designed,
fabricated, or assembled in other nations, of course). Automated
tellers, computerized cashiers, automatic car washes, robotized
vending machines, self-service gasoline pumps, and all similar gadgets substitute for the human beings that customers once encountered. Even telephone operators are fast disappearing, as electronic
sensors and voice simulators become capable of carrying on conversations that are reasonably intelligent and always polite. Retail sales
workers — among the largest groups of in-person servers — are similarly imperiled. Through personal computers linked to television
screens, tomorrow's consumers will be able to buy furniture, appliances, and all sorts of electronic toys from their living rooms — examining the merchandise from all angles, selecting whatever color,
size, special features, and price seem most appealing, and then
transmitting the order instantly to warehouses from which the selections will be shipped directly to their homes. So, too, with financial
transactions, airline and hotel reservations, rental car agreements,

---

[11] U.S. Department of Labor, Bureau of Labor Statistics, "Reemployment Increases Among Disabled Workers," October 14, 1986. [Reich's note]

[12] Federal Immigration and Naturalization Service, *Statistical Yearbook* (Washington, D.C.: U.S. Government Printing Office, 1986, 1987). [Reich's note]

and similar contracts, which will be executed between consumers in their homes and computer banks somewhere else on the globe.[13]

Advanced economies like the United States will continue to   23 generate sizable numbers of new in-person service jobs, of course, the automation of older ones notwithstanding. For every bank teller who loses her job to an automated teller, three new jobs open for aerobics instructors. Human beings, it seems, have an almost insatiable desire for personal attention. But the intense competition nevertheless ensures that the wages of in-person servers will remain relatively low. In-person servers — working on their own, or else dispersed widely amid many small establishments, filling all sorts of personal-care niches — cannot readily organize themselves into labor unions or create powerful lobbies to limit the impact of such competition.

In two respects, demographics will work in favor of in-person   24 servers, buoying their collective boat slightly. First, as has been noted, the rate of growth of the American work force is slowing. In particular, the number of young workers is shrinking. Between 1985 and 1995, the number of the eighteen- to twenty-four-year-olds will have declined by 17.5 percent. Thus, employers will have more incentive to hire and train in-person servers whom they might previously have avoided. But this demographic relief from the competitive pressures will be only temporary. The cumulative procreative energies of the postwar baby-boomers (born between 1946 and 1964) will result in a new surge of workers by 2010 or thereabouts.[14] And immigration — both legal and illegal — shows every sign of increasing in years to come.

Next, by the second decade of the twenty-first century, the   25 number of Americans aged sixty-five and over will be rising precipitously, as the baby-boomers reach retirement age and live longer. Their life expectancies will lengthen not just because fewer of them will have smoked their way to their graves and more will have eaten better than their parents, but also because they will receive all sorts of expensive drugs and therapies designed to keep them alive — barely. By 2035, twice as many Americans will be elderly as in 1988, and the number of octogenarians is expected to triple. As these decaying baby-boomers ingest all the chemicals and receive all the treatments, they will need a great deal of personal attention. Millions

---

[13] See Claudia H. Deutsch, "The Powerful Push for Self-Service," *New York Times,* April 9, 1989, section 3, p. 1. [Reich's note]

[14] U.S. Bureau of the Census, Current Population Reports, Series P-23, no. 138, tables 2-1, 4-6. See W. Johnson, A. Packer, et al., *Workforce 2000: Work and Workers for the 21st Century* (Indianapolis: Hudson Institute, 1987). [Reich's note]

of deteriorating bodies will require nurses, nursing-home operators, hospital administrators, orderlies, home-care providers, hospice aides, and technicians to operate and maintain all the expensive machinery that will monitor and temporarily stave off final disintegration. There might even be a booming market for euthanasia specialists. In-person servers catering to the old and ailing will be in strong demand.[15]

One small problem: the decaying baby-boomers will not have   26 enough money to pay for these services. They will have used up their personal savings years before. Their Social Security payments will, of course, have been used by the government to pay for the previous generation's retirement and to finance much of the budget deficits of the 1980s. Moreover, with relatively fewer young Americans in the population, the supply of housing will likely exceed the demand, with the result that the boomers' major investments — their homes — will be worth less (in inflation-adjusted dollars) when they retire than they planned for. In consequence, the huge cost of caring for the graying boomers will fall on many of the same people who will be paid to care for them. It will be like a great sump pump: in-person servers of the twenty-first century will have an abundance of health-care jobs, but a large portion of their earnings will be devoted to Social Security payments and income taxes, which will in turn be used to pay their salaries. The net result: no real improvement in their standard of living.

The standard of living of in-person servers also depends, in-   27 directly, on the standard of living of the Americans they serve who are engaged in world commerce. To the extent that *these* Americans are richly rewarded by the rest of the world for what they contribute, they will have more money to lavish upon in-person services. Here we find the only form of "trickle-down" economics that has a basis in reality. A waitress in a town whose major factory has just been closed is unlikely to earn a high wage or enjoy much job security; in a swank resort populated by film producers and banking moguls, she is apt to do reasonably well. So, too, with nations. In-person servers in Bangladesh may spend their days performing roughly the same tasks as in-person servers in the United States, but have a far lower standard of living for their efforts. The difference comes in the value that their customers add to the world economy.

---

[15] The Census Bureau estimates that by the year 2000, at least 12 million Americans will work in health services — well over 6 percent of the total work force. [Reich's note]

Unlike the boats of routine producers and in-person servers, 28 however, the vessel containing America's symbolic analysts is rising. Worldwide demand for their insights is growing as the ease and speed of communicating them steadily increases. Not every symbolic analyst is rising as quickly or as dramatically as every other, of course; symbolic analysts at the low end are barely holding their own in the world economy. But symbolic analysts at the top are in such great demand worldwide that they have difficulty keeping track of all their earnings. Never before in history has opulence on such a scale been gained by people who have earned it, and done so legally.

Among symbolic analysts in the middle range are American sci- 29 entists and researchers who are busily selling their discoveries to global enterprise webs. They are not limited to American customers. If the strategic brokers in General Motors' headquarters refuse to pay a high price for a new means of making high-strength ceramic engines dreamed up by a team of engineers affiliated with Carnegie Mellon University in Pittsburgh, the strategic brokers of Honda or Mercedes-Benz are likely to be more than willing.

So, too, with the insights of America's ubiquitous management 30 consultants, which are being sold for large sums to eager entrepreneurs in Europe and Latin America. Also, the insights of America's energy consultants, sold for even larger sums to Arab sheikhs. American design engineers are providing insights to Olivetti, Mazda, Siemens, and other global webs; American marketers, techniques for learning what worldwide consumers will buy; American advertisers, ploys for ensuring that they actually do. American architects are issuing designs and blueprints for opera houses, art galleries, museums, luxury hotels, and residential complexes in the world's major cities; American commercial property developers, marketing these properties to worldwide investors and purchasers.

Americans who specialize in the gentle art of public relations are 31 in demand by corporations, governments, and politicians in virtually every nation. So, too, are American political consultants, some of whom, at this writing, are advising the Hungarian Socialist Party, the remnant of Hungary's ruling Communists, on how to salvage a few parliamentary seats in the nation's first free election in more than forty years. Also at this writing, a team of American agricultural consultants is advising the managers of a Soviet farm collective employing 1,700 Russians eighty miles outside Moscow. As noted, American investment bankers and lawyers specializing in financial circumnavigations are selling their insights to Asians and Europeans who are eager to discover how to make large amounts of money by moving large amounts of money.

Developing nations, meanwhile, are hiring American civil engi-   32
neers to advise on building roads and dams. The present thaw in the
Cold War will no doubt expand these opportunities. American engineers from Bechtel (a global firm notable for having employed both
Caspar Weinberger and George Shultz for much larger sums than either earned in the Reagan administration) have begun helping the So-
viets design and install a new generation of nuclear reactors. Nations
also are hiring American bankers and lawyers to help them renegoti-
ate the terms of their loans with global banks, and Washington lobby-
ists to help them with Congress, the Treasury, the World Bank, the
IMF, and other politically sensitive institutions. In fits of obvious des-
peration, several nations emerging from communism have even hired
American economists to teach them about capitalism.

Almost everyone around the world is buying the skills and in-   33
sights of Americans who manipulate oral and visual symbols — mu-
sicians, sound engineers, film producers, makeup artists, directors,
cinematographers, actors and actresses, boxers, scriptwriters, songwriters, and set designers. Among the wealthiest of symbolic analysts are Steven Spielberg, Bill Cosby, Charles Schulz, Eddie Murphy, Sylvester Stallone, Madonna, and other star directors and
performers — who are almost as well known on the streets of Dres-
den and Tokyo as in the Back Bay of Boston. Less well rewarded but
no less renowned are the unctuous anchors on Turner Broadcast-
ing's Cable News, who appear daily, via satellite, in places ranging
from Vietnam to Nigeria. Vanna White is the world's most-watched
game-show hostess. Behind each of these familiar faces is a collection of American problem-solvers, -identifiers, and brokers who
train, coach, advise, promote, amplify, direct, groom, represent, and
otherwise add value to their talents.[16]

There are also the insights of senior American executives who   34
occupy the world headquarters of global "American" corporations
and the national or regional headquarters of global "foreign" corporations. Their insights are duly exported to the rest of the world
through the webs of global enterprise. IBM does not export many
machines from the United States, for example. Big Blue makes machines all over the globe and services them on the spot. Its prime
American exports are symbolic and analytic. From IBM's world
headquarters in Armonk, New York, emanate strategic brokerage

---

[16] In 1989, the entertainment business summoned to the United States $5.5
billion in foreign earnings — making it among the nation's largest export industries,
just behind aerospace. U.S. Department of Commerce, International Trade Commission, "Composition of U.S. Exports," various issues. [Reich's note]

and related management services bound for the rest of the world. In return, IBM's top executives are generously rewarded.

The most important reason for this expanding world market 35 and increasing global demand for the symbolic and analytic insights of Americans has been the dramatic improvement in worldwide communication and transportation technologies. Designs, instructions, advice, and visual and audio symbols can be communicated more and more rapidly around the globe, with ever-greater precision and at ever-lower cost. Madonna's voice can be transported to billions of listeners, with perfect clarity, on digital compact discs. A new invention emanating from engineers in Battelle's laboratory in Columbus, Ohio, can be sent almost anywhere via modem, in a form that will allow others to examine it in three dimensions through enhanced computer graphics. When face-to-face meetings are still required — and videoconferencing will not suffice — it is relatively easy for designers, consultants, advisers, artists, and executives to board supersonic jets and, in a matter of hours, meet directly with their worldwide clients, customers, audiences, and employees.

With rising demand comes rising compensation. Whether in the 36 form of licensing fees, fees for service, salaries, or shares in final profits, the economic result is much the same. There are also nonpecuniary rewards. One of the best-kept secrets among symbolic analysts is that so many of them enjoy their work. In fact, much of it does not count as work at all, in the traditional sense. The work of routine producers and in-person servers is typically monotonous; it causes muscles to tire or weaken and involves little independence or discretion. The "work" of symbolic analysts, by contrast, often involves puzzles, experiments, games, a significant amount of chatter, and substantial discretion over what to do next. Few routine producers or in-person servers would "work" if they did not need to earn the money. Many symbolic analysts would "work" even if money were no object.

At midcentury, when America was a national market dominated 37 by core pyramid-shaped corporations, there were constraints on the earnings of people at the highest rungs. First and most obviously, the market for their services was largely limited to the borders of the nation. In addition, whatever conceptual value they might contribute was small relative to the value gleaned from large scale — and it was dependent on large scale for whatever income it was to summon. Most of the problems to be identified and solved had to do with enhancing the efficiency of production and improving the flow of materials, parts, assembly, and distribution. Inventors searched for the rare breakthrough revealing an entirely new product to be made in high volume; management consultants, executives, and engineers thereafter tried to speed and synchronize its manufacture, to better achieve scale efficiencies; advertisers and marketers sought then to whet the public's appetite for the standard item that emerged. Since white-collar earnings increased with larger scale, there was considerable incentive to expand the firm; indeed, many of America's core corporations grew far larger than scale economies would appear to have justified.

By the 1990s, in contrast, the earnings of symbolic analysts 38 were limited neither by the size of the national market nor by the volume of production of the firms with which they were affiliated. The marketplace was worldwide, and conceptual value was high relative to value added from scale efficiencies.

There had been another constraint on high earnings, which also 39 gave way by the 1990s. At midcentury, the compensation awarded to top executives and advisers of the largest of America's core corporations could not be grossly out of proportion to that of low-level production workers. It would be unseemly for executives who engaged in highly visible rounds of bargaining with labor unions, and who routinely responded to government requests to moderate prices, to take home wages and benefits wildly in excess of what other Americans earned. Unless white-collar executives restrained themselves, moreover, blue-collar production workers could not be expected to restrain their own demands for higher wages. Unless both groups exercised restraint, the government could not be expected to forbear from imposing direct controls and regulations.

At the same time, the wages of production workers could not be 40 allowed to sink too low, lest there be insufficient purchasing power in the economy. After all, who would buy all the goods flowing out of American factories if not American workers? This, too, was part of the tacit bargain struck between American managers and their workers.

Recall the oft-repeated corporate platitude of the era about the 41 chief executive's responsibility to carefully weigh and balance the interests of the corporation's disparate stakeholders. Under the stewardship of the corporate statesman, no set of stakeholders — least of all white-collar executives — was to gain a disproportionately large share of the benefits of corporate activity; nor was any stakeholder — especially the average worker — to be left with a share that was disproportionately small. Banal though it was, this idea helped to maintain the legitimacy of the core American corporation in the eyes of most Americans, and to ensure continued economic growth.

But by the 1990s, these informal norms were evaporating, just   42
as (and largely because) the core American corporation was vanishing. The links between top executives and the American production
worker were fading: an ever-increasing number of subordinates and
contractees were foreign, and a steadily growing number of American routine producers were working for foreign-owned firms. An
entire cohort of middle-level managers, who had once been deemed
"white collar," had disappeared; and, increasingly, American executives were exporting their insights to global enterprise webs.

As the American corporation itself became a global web almost   43
indistinguishable from any other, its stakeholders were turning into
a large and diffuse group, spread over the world. Such global stakeholders were less visible, and far less noisy, than national stakeholders. And as the American corporation sold its goods and services all
over the world, the purchasing power of American workers became
far less relevant to its economic survival.

Thus have the inhibitions been removed. The salaries and bene-   44
fits of America's top executives, and many of their advisers and consultants, have soared to what years before would have been unimaginable heights, even as those of other Americans have declined.

QUESTIONS FOR CRITICAL READING

1. What are symbolic analysts? Give some examples from your own expe-
    rience.
2. What is the apparent relationship between higher education and an
    educated worker's prospects for wealth?
3. To what extent do you agree or disagree with Reich's description and
    analysis of routine workers and in-service workers?
4. If Reich's analysis is correct, which gender or social groups are likely to
    be most harmed by modern economic circumstances in America?
    Which are most likely to become wealthy? Why?
5. Are symbolic analysts inherently more valuable to our society than
    routine or in-service workers? Why do symbolic analysts command so
    much more wealth?
6. Which of the three groups Reich mentions do you see as having the
    greatest potential for growth in the next thirty years?

SUGGESTIONS FOR WRITING

1. Judging from the views that Reich holds about decreasing job opportu-
    nities for all three groups of workers, how will increased immigration

affect the American economy? Is immigration a hopeful sign? Is it a danger to the economy? How do most people seem to perceive the effect of increased immigration?

2. To what extent do you think Reich is correct about the growing wealth of symbolic analysts? He says, "Never before in history has opulence on such a scale been gained by people who have earned it, and done so legally" (para. 28). Do you see yourself as a symbolic analyst? How do you see your future in relation to the three economic groups Reich describes?

3. Reich says, "Few routine producers or in-person servers would 'work' if they did not need to earn the money. Many symbolic analysts would 'work' even if money were no object" (para. 36). Is this true? Examine your own experience — along with the experience of others you know — and defend or attack this view. How accurate do you consider Reich to be in his analysis of the way various workers view their work?

4. Describe the changes that have taken place in the American economy in the last forty years, according to this essay. How have they affected the way Americans work and the work that Americans can expect to find? How have your personal opportunities been broadened or narrowed by the changes? Do you feel the changes have been good for the country or not? Why?

5. Reich's view of the great success of Japanese corporations and of their presence as manufacturing giants in the United States and elsewhere is largely positive. He has pointed out elsewhere that Honda and other manufacturers in the United States provide jobs and municipal income that would otherwise go to other nations. What is your view of the presence of large Japanese corporations in the United States? What is your view of other nations' manufacturing facilities in the United States?

6. Why are the rich getting richer and the poor poorer? Examine the kinds of differences between the rich and the poor that Reich describes. Is the process of increasing riches for the rich and increasing poverty for the poor inevitable, or will it begin to change in the near future?

7. **CONNECTIONS** Reich's book title is modeled on Adam Smith's. What attitudes and views does he share with Adam Smith? Smith approves of wealth. Is that true of Reich? Reich explains why the rich are getting richer and the poor are getting poorer. Does Reich seem to share Galbraith's concerns for those in poverty? How could the nation help improve the ratio of rich and poor? Could it eradicate the problem of poverty entirely?

PART FOUR

MIND

Plato
Moses Maimonides
Sigmund Freud
Carl Jung
Karen Horney
Howard Gardner

INTRODUCTION

Ideas about the nature of the human mind have abounded throughout history. Philosophers and scientists have sought to discern the mind's components and functions and have distinguished humans from other animals according to the qualities associated with the mind, such as reason and self-awareness. The ancient Greeks formulated the concept of the psyche (from which we derive the term *psychology*) as the center of consciousness and reason as well as emotions. During the Renaissance, René Descartes (1596 – 1650) concluded *Cogito ergo sum* (I think, therefore I am) and proposed that the mind was the source of human identity and that reason was the key to comprehending the material world. Influenced by Descartes, John Locke (1632 – 1704) developed a theory of the mind as a *tabula rasa* or blank slate that was shaped entirely by external experiences. The selections in this section further explore these questions about the nature of the mind and its relationship to consciousness, knowledge, intellect, and the other means by which we work to understand ourselves and our world.

The first selection, by Plato, contains one of the most formative ideas about the nature of mind. Plato posited that the world of sensory experience is not the real world and that our senses are in fact incapable of experiencing reality. In Plato's view, reality is an ideal that exists only in an environment something akin to the concept of heaven. He suggested that people are born with knowledge of that reality. The infant, in other words, possesses the ideas of reality to start with, having gained them from heaven and retaining them in memory. For Plato, education was the process by which students regained such "lost" memories and made them part of their conscious understanding. Although he never uses the terms *conscious* and *unconscious* in describing the mind, Plato's views foreshadow the later theories of psychologists such as William James (1842 – 1910), Sigmund Freud, and Carl Jung.

The nature of human knowledge also intrigued Moses Maimonides, a medieval thinker whose work centered mostly in north Africa. He lived in an Islamic society and was well versed in Arab studies and Arab culture, although he wrote primarily on Jewish topics, especially religious texts. He was qualified to be a rabbi but earned his living in Cairo as a physician. In *The Guide for the Perplexed,* Maimonides discusses philosophy, theology, and science in his effort to approach religion from a rational perspective. In the process, he examines the question of the limitations of the human intellect. Like Plato, he argues that the world perceived through the senses is not a complete reality and that certain realms of knowledge exist that the mind cannot fully comprehend. However, he is more interested in the educational circumstances that limit the development of the mind than in the mind's inherent limits. Thus, he focuses on what he believes to be the proper educational approach to assimilating the knowledge that lies within human understanding.

Sigmund Freud, one of the founders of psychoanalysis, is perhaps most famous for his studies of the unconscious. His theories regarding the relationship of the conscious mind to the unconscious mind have become central to the thinking of many modern psychiatrists. His essay from *The Interpretation of Dreams* presents the main outlines of his theory that dreams are products of the psychical activity of the individual and that they offer insight into the content of the unconscious. Until Freud's time, the primary thinking about dreams ignored a connection with the conscious mind of the wakeful individual. Books on the subject had long treated all dreams as categorical and assumed that a meaning could be assigned to a dream based on its structure rather than on the life of the individual. Freud's careful analysis of dreams demonstrates that the dream is connected to the conscious mind of the dreamer and therefore must be interpreted in terms of the individual's life.

Carl Jung began his studies with Freud's views of the content of the unconscious, but one of his analyses led him in a novel direction. He concluded that some of the content of the unconscious mind could not have begun in the conscious mind because it was not the product of the individual's conscious experience. Jung reasoned that certain images present in the unconscious were common to all members of a culture. He called these images *archetypal* because they seemed fundamental and universal, such as the archetype of the father and the archetype of the mother. He then hypothesized that part of the mind's content is derived from cultural history. Unlike Freud, Jung saw the unconscious as containing images that represented deep instinctual longings belonging to an entire culture, not just to the individual.

A contemporary of both Freud and Jung, Karen Horney incorporates ideas from both these thinkers while advancing her theories on the relations between men and women. "The Distrust Between the Sexes" describes certain habits of mind that may be thought of as culturally induced but that may also reflect genuine differences in individual minds. Like Jung, Horney argues that if the culture has produced an archetypal male and an archetypal female, no matter what the experiences of the individual, the unconscious registers those archetypes. Horney also talks about culturally induced behavior that begins in "formative years," but since she is a follower of Freud, she does not propose that the distinctions are as clearly gender-linked as Jung insists that archetypes are culturally linked. However, some of her theories about how one sex views the other imply that gender plays a significant role in forming attitudes. In this sense, certain of Horney's views are interpretable in Jungian terms.

Howard Gardner's interest is intelligence, which he approaches from a pluralist point of view. His idea of seven distinct intelligences, as opposed to the conventional views as represented by standardized IQ tests, is at once traditional and revolutionary. In drawing on the model of ancient Greek education, he urges us to examine the virtues of all seven forms of intelligence and not rely on the logical-mathematical model that dominates contemporary education. Gardner notes that certain forms of intelligence are culturally linked, but he leaves open the question of whether they are gender-linked.

These essays approach the problem of mind from different positions and are concerned with different questions of consciousness, thought, limitation, and intelligence. They raise some of the most basic questions concerning the mind, such as, What are its components? What can it know? What should we most value in its function? In answering these questions, each essay provides us with ideas that provoke more thought and still more questions.

PLATO
The Allegory of the Cave

PLATO (428 – 347 B.C.) was born into an aristocratic, probably Athenian family and educated according to the best precepts
available. He eventually became a student of Socrates and later involved himself closely with Socrates' work and teaching. Plato was
not only Socrates' finest student but also the student who immortalized Socrates in his works. Most of Plato's works are philosophical essays in which Socrates speaks as a character in a dialogue
with one or more students or listeners.

Both Socrates and Plato lived in turbulent times. In 404 B.C.
Athens was defeated by Sparta and its government taken over by
tyrants. Political life in Athens became dangerous. Plato felt, however, that he could effect positive change in Athenian politics until,
in 399 B.C., Socrates was tried unjustly for corrupting the youth of
Athens and sentenced to death. After that, Plato withdrew from
public life and devoted himself to writing and to the Academy he
founded in an olive grove in Athens. The Academy endured for almost a thousand years, which tells us how greatly Plato's thought
was valued.

Although it is not easy to condense Plato's views, he may be
said to have held the world of sense perception to be inferior to the
world of ideal entities that exist only in a pure spiritual realm.
These ideals, or forms, Plato argued, are perceived directly by
everyone before birth and then dimly remembered here on earth.
But the memory, dim as it is, enables people to understand what
the senses perceive, despite the fact that the senses are unreliable
and their perceptions imperfect.

This view of reality has long been important to philosophers
because it gives a philosophical basis to antimaterialistic thought.

From *The Republic*. Translated and glossed by Benjamin Jowett.

It values the spirit first and frees people from the tyranny of sensory perception and sensory reward. In the case of love, Plato held that Eros leads individuals to revere the body and its pleasures; but the thrust of his teaching is that the body is a metaphor for spiritual delights. Plato maintains that the body is only a starting point, which eventually can lead to both spiritual fulfillment and the appreciation of true beauty.

On the one hand, "The Allegory of the Cave" is a discussion of politics: *The Republic,* from which it is taken, is a treatise on justice and the ideal government. On the other hand, it has long stood as an example of the notion that if we rely on our perceptions to know the truth about the world, then we will know very little about it. In order to live ethically, it is essential to know what is true and, therefore, what is important to us beyond the world of sensory perception.

Plato's allegory has been persuasive for centuries and remains at the center of thought that attempts to counter the pleasures of the sensual life. Most religions aim for spiritual enlightenment and praise the qualities of the soul, which lies beyond perception. Thus, it comes as no surprise that Christianity and other religions have developed systems of thought that bear a close resemblance to his. Later refinements of his thought, usually called Neo-Platonism, have been influential even into modern times.

PLATO'S RHETORIC

Two important rhetorical techniques are at work in the following selection. The first and more obvious — at least on one level — is the device of the allegory, a story in which the characters and situations actually represent people and situations in another context. It is a difficult technique to sustain, although Aesop's fables were certainly successful in using animals to represent people and their foibles. The advantage of the technique is that a complex and sometimes unpopular argument can be fought and won before the audience realizes that an argument is under way. The disadvantage of the technique is that the terms of the allegory may only approximate the situation it represents; thus, the argument may fail to be convincing.

The second rhetorical technique Plato uses is the dialogue. In fact, this device is a hallmark of Plato's work, since most of his writings are called dialogues. The *Symposium, Apology, Phaedo, Crito, Meno,* and most of his famous works are written in dialogue form. Usually Socrates is speaking to a student or a friend about highly abstract issues, asking questions that require simple answers. Slowly, the questioning proceeds to elucidate the answers to complex issues.

This question-and-answer technique basically constitutes the Socratic method. Socrates analyzes the answer to each question, examines its implications, and then asserts the truth. The method works partly because Plato believes that people do not learn things but remember them. That is, people originate from heaven, where they knew the truth; they already possess knowledge and must recover it by means of the dialogue. Socrates' method is ideally suited to that purpose.

Beyond these techniques, however, we must look at Plato's style. It is true that he is working with difficult ideas, but his style is so clear, simple, and direct that few people would have trouble understanding what he is saying at any given moment. Considering the influence this work has had on world thought and the reputation Plato had earned by the time he came to write *The Republic,* its style is remarkably plain and accessible. Plato's respect for rhetoric and its proper uses is part of the reason he can express himself with such impressive clarity.

The Allegory of the Cave

SOCRATES, GLAU- CON. *The den, the prisoners: the light at a distance;*

And now, I said, let me show in a figure how 1 far our nature is enlightened or unenlightened: — Behold! human beings living in an underground den, which has a mouth open towards the light and reaching all along the den; here they have been from their childhood, and have their legs and necks chained so that they cannot move, and can only see before them, being prevented by the chains from turning round their heads. Above and behind them a fire is blazing at a distance, and between the fire and the prisoners there is a raised way; and you will see, if you look, a low wall built along the way, like the screen which marionette players have in front of them, over which they show the puppets.

I see. 2

the low wall,
and the moving
figures of which
the shadows
are seen on the
opposite wall of
the den.

And do you see, I said, men passing along the 3
wall carrying all sorts of vessels, and statues and
figures of animals made of wood and stone and
various materials, which appear over the wall?
Some of them are talking, others silent.

You have shown me a strange image, and they 4
are strange prisoners.

Like ourselves, I replied; and they see only 5
their own shadows, or the shadows of one another,
which the fire throws on the opposite wall of the
cave?

True, he said; how could they see anything but 6
the shadows if they were never allowed to move
their heads?

And of the objects which are being carried in 7
like manner they would only see the shadows?

Yes, he said.   8

And if they were able to converse with one an- 9
other, would they not suppose that they were naming what was actually before them?

Very true.   10

The prisoners
would mistake
the shadows
for realities.

And suppose further that the prison had an 11
echo which came from the other side, would they
not be sure to fancy when one of the passers-by
spoke that the voice which they heard came from
the passing shadow?

No question, he replied.   12

To them, I said, the truth would be literally 13
nothing but the shadows of the images.

That is certain.   14

And now look again, and see what will natu- 15
rally follow if the prisoners are released and dis-
abused of their error. At first, when any of them is
liberated and compelled suddenly to stand up and
turn his neck round and walk and look towards
the light, he will suffer sharp pains; the glare will
distress him, and he will be unable to see the reali-

And when
released, they
would still
persist in
maintaining
the superior
truth of the
shadows.

ties of which in his former state he had seen the
shadows; and then conceive some one saying to
him, that what he saw before was an illusion, but
that now, when he is approaching nearer to being
and his eye is turned towards more real existence,
he has a clearer vision — what will be his reply?
And you may further imagine that his instructor is

pointing to the objects as they pass and requiring him to name them, — will he not be perplexed? Will he not fancy that the shadows which he formerly saw are truer than the objects which are now shown to him?

Far truer. 16

And if he is compelled to look straight at the 17 light, will he not have a pain in his eyes which will make him turn away to take refuge in the objects of vision which he can see, and which he will conceive to be in reality clearer than the things which are now being shown to him?

True, he said. 18

When dragged upwards, they would be dazzled by excess of light.

And suppose once more, that he is reluctantly 19 dragged up a steep and rugged ascent, and held fast until he is forced into the presence of the sun himself, is he not likely to be pained and irritated? When he approaches the light his eyes will be dazzled, and he will not be able to see anything at all of what are now called realities.

Not all in a moment, he said. 20

He will require to grow accustomed to the 21 sight of the upper world. And first he will see the shadows best, next the reflections of men and other objects in the water, and then the objects themselves; then he will gaze upon the light of the moon and the stars and the spangled heaven; and he will see the sky and the stars by night better than the sun or the light of the sun by day?

Certainly. 22

At length they will see the sun and understand his nature.

Last of all he will be able to see the sun, and 23 not mere reflections of him in the water, but he will see him in his own proper place, and not in another; and he will contemplate him as he is.

Certainly. 24

He will then proceed to argue that this is he 25 who gives the season and the years, and is the guardian of all that is in the visible world, and in a certain way the cause of all things which he and his fellows have been accustomed to behold?

Clearly, he said, he would first see the sun and 26 then reason about him.

And when he remembered his old habitation, 27 and the wisdom of the den and his fellow prison-

They would then pity their old companions of the den.

ers, do you not suppose that he would felicitate himself on the change, and pity them?

Certainly, he would.   28

And if they were in the habit of conferring   29
honors among themselves on those who were quickest to observe the passing shadows and to re-mark which of them went before, and which fol-lowed after, and which were together; and who were therefore best able to draw conclusions as to the future, do you think that he would care for such honors and glories, or envy the possessors of them? Would he not say with Homer,

> Better to be the poor servant of a poor master,

and to endure anything, rather than think as they do and live after their manner?

Yes, he said, I think that he would rather suffer   30
anything than entertain these false notions and live in this miserable manner.

Imagine once more, I said, such an one coming   31
suddenly out of the sun to be replaced in his old situation; would he not be certain to have his eyes full of darkness?

To be sure, he said.   32

But when they returned to the den, they would see much worse than those who had never left it.

And if there were a contest, and he had to   33
compete in measuring the shadows with the pris-oners who had never moved out of the den, while his sight was still weak, and before his eyes had be-come steady (and the time which would be needed to acquire this new habit of sight might be very considerable), would he not be ridiculous? Men would say of him that up he went and down he came without his eyes; and that it was better not even to think of ascending; and if any one tried to loose another and lead him up to the light, let them only catch the offender, and they would put him to death.

No question, he said.   34

The prison is the world of sight, the light of the fire is the sun.

This entire allegory, I said, you may now ap-   35
pend, dear Glaucon, to the previous argument; the prison house is the world of sight, the light of the fire is the sun, and you will not misapprehend me if you interpret the journey upwards to be the as-cent of the soul into the intellectual world accord-

ing to my poor belief, which, at your desire, I have expressed — whether rightly or wrongly God knows. But, whether true or false, my opinion is that in the world of knowledge the idea of good appears last of all, and is seen only with an effort; and, when seen, is also inferred to be the universal author of all things beautiful and right, parent of light and of the lord of light in this visible world, and the immediate source of reason and truth in the intellectual; and that this is the power upon which he who would act rationally either in public or private life must have his eye fixed.

I agree, he said, as far as I am able to under- 36 stand you.

Moreover, I said, you must not wonder that 37 those who attain to this beatific vision are unwilling to descend to human affairs; for their souls are ever hastening into the upper world where they desire to dwell; which desire of theirs is very natural, if our allegory may be trusted.

Yes, very natural. 38

Nothing extraordinary in the philosopher being unable to see in the dark.

And is there anything surprising in one who 39 passes from divine contemplations to the evil state of man, misbehaving himself in a ridiculous manner; if, while his eyes are blinking and before he has become accustomed to the surrounding darkness, he is compelled to fight in courts of law, or in other places, about the images or the shadows of images of justice, and is endeavoring to meet the conceptions of those who have never yet seen absolute justice?

Anything but surprising, he replied. 40

The eyes may be blinded in two ways, by excess or by defect of light.

Anyone who has common sense will remem- 41 ber that the bewilderments of the eyes are of two kinds, and arise from two causes, either from coming out of the light or from going into the light, which is true of the mind's eye, quite as much as of the bodily eye; and he who remembers this when he sees anyone whose vision is perplexed and weak, will not be too ready to laugh; he will first ask whether that soul of man has come out of the brighter life, and is unable to see because unaccustomed to the dark, or having turned from darkness to the day is dazzled by excess of light. And he will count the one happy in his condition and state of being, and he will pity the other; or, if he have a mind to laugh at the soul which comes from below into the light, there will be more reason in this than in the laugh which greets him who returns from above out of the light into the den.

That, he said, is a very just distinction.   42

The conversion of the soul is the turning round the eye from darkness to light.

But then, if I am right, certain professors of education must be wrong when they say that they can put a knowledge into the soul which was not there before, like sight into blind eyes.   43

They undoubtedly say this, he replied.   44

Whereas, our argument shows that the power and capacity of learning exists in the soul already; and that just as the eye was unable to turn from darkness to light without the whole body, so too the instrument of knowledge can only by the movement of the whole soul be turned from the world of becoming into that of being, and learn by degrees to endure the sight of being, and of the brightest and best of being, or in other words, of the good.   45

Very true.   46

And must there not be some art which will effect conversion in the easiest and quickest manner; not implanting the faculty of sight, for that exists already, but has been turned in the wrong direction, and is looking away from the truth?   47

Yes, he said, such an art may be presumed.   48

The virtue of wisdom has a divine power which may be turned either towards good or towards evil.

And whereas the other so-called virtues of the soul seem to be akin to bodily qualities, for even when they are not originally innate they can be implanted later by habit and exercise, the virtue of wisdom more than anything else contains a divine element which always remains, and by this conversion is rendered useful and profitable; or, on the other hand, hurtful and useless. Did you never observe the narrow intelligence flashing from the keen eye of a clever rogue — how eager he is, how clearly his paltry soul sees the way to his end; he is the reverse of blind, but his keen eyesight is forced into the service of evil, and he is mischievous in proportion to his cleverness?   49

Very true, he said.   50

But what if there had been a circumcision of 51
such natures in the days of their youth; and they
had been severed from those sensual pleasures,
such as eating and drinking, which, like leaden
weights, were attached to them at their birth, and
which drag them down and turn the vision of their
souls upon the things that are below — if, I say,
they had been released from these impediments
and turned in the opposite direction, the very same
faculty in them would have seen the truth as
keenly as they see what their eyes are turned to
now.

Neither the uneducated nor the over-educated will be good servants of the State.

Very likely. 52

Yes, I said; and there is another thing which is 53
likely, or rather a necessary inference from what
has preceded, that neither the uneducated and un-
informed of the truth, nor yet those who never
make an end of their education, will be able ministers of State; not the former, because they have no
single aim of duty which is the rule of all their actions, private as well as public; nor the latter, because they will not act at all except upon compulsion, fancying that they are already dwelling apart
in the islands of the blessed.

Very true, he replied. 54

Then, I said, the business of us who are the 55
founders of the State will be to compel the best
minds to attain that knowledge which we have already shown to be the greatest of all — they must
continue to ascend until they arrive at the good;
but when they have ascended and seen enough we
must not allow them to do as they do now.

What do you mean? 56

Men should as-cend to the upper world, but they should also return to the lower.

I mean that they remain in the upper world: 57
but this must not be allowed; they must be made to
descend again among the prisoners in the den, and
partake of their labors and honors, whether they
are worth having or not.

But is not this unjust? he said; ought we to give 58
them a worse life, when they might have a better?

You have again forgotten, my friend, I said, the 59
intention of the legislator, who did not aim at making any one class in the State happy above the rest;
the happiness was to be in the whole State, and he

held the citizens together by persuasion and necessity, making them benefactors of the State, and therefore benefactors of one another; to this end he created them, not to please themselves, but to be his instruments in binding up the State.

True, he said, I had forgotten.   60

The duties of philosophers.

Observe, Glaucon, that there will be no injus- 61
tice in compelling our philosophers to have a care and providence of others; we shall explain to them that in other States, men of their class are not obliged to share in the toils of politics: and this is reasonable, for they grow up at their own sweet will, and the government would rather not have them. Being self-taught, they cannot be expected to show any gratitude for a culture which they have never received. But we have brought you into the world to be rulers of the hive, kings of yourselves and of the other citizens, and have educated you far better and more perfectly than they have been educated, and you are better able to share in the double duty. Wherefore each of you, when his turn comes, must go down to the general underground abode, and get the habit of seeing in the dark.

Their obligations to their country will induce them to take part in her government.

When you have acquired the habit, you will see ten thousand times better than the inhabitants of the den, and you will know what the several images are, and what they represent, because you have seen the beautiful and just and good in their truth. And thus our State, which is also yours, will be a reality, and not a dream only, and will be administered in a spirit unlike that of other States, in which men fight with one another about shadows only and are distracted in the struggle for power, which in their eyes is a great good. Whereas the truth is that the State in which the rulers are most reluctant to govern is always the best and most quietly governed, and the State in which they are most eager, the worst.

Quite true, he replied.   62

And will our pupils, when they hear this, 63
refuse to take their turn at the toils of State, when they are allowed to spend the greater part of their time with one another in the heavenly light?

They will be willing but not anxious to rule.

Impossible, he answered; for they are just 64 men, and the commands which we impose upon them are just; there can be no doubt that every one of them will take office as a stern necessity, and not after the fashion of our present rulers of State.

The statesman must be provided with a better life than that of a ruler; and then he will not covet office.

Yes, my friend, I said; and there lies the point. 65 You must contrive for your future rulers another and a better life than that of a ruler, and then you may have a well-ordered State; for only in the State which offers this, will they rule who are truly rich, not in silver and gold, but in virtue and wisdom, which are the true blessings of life. Whereas if they go to the administration of public affairs, poor and hungering after their own private advantage, thinking that hence they are to snatch the chief good, order there can never be; for they will be fighting about office, and the civil and domestic broils which thus arise will be the ruin of the rulers themselves and of the whole State.

Most true, he replied. 66

And the only life which looks down upon the 67 life of political ambition is that of true philosophy. Do you know of any other?

Indeed, I do not, he said. 68

QUESTIONS FOR CRITICAL READING

1. What is the relationship between Socrates and Glaucon? Are they equal in intellectual authority? Are they concerned with the same issues?
2. How does the allegory of the prisoners in the cave watching shadows on a wall relate to us today? What shadows do we see, and how do they distort our sense of what is real?
3. Are we prisoners in the same sense that Plato's characters are?
4. If Plato is right that the material world is an illusion, how would too great a reliance on materialism affect ethical decisions?
5. What ethical issues, if any, are raised by Plato's allegory?
6. In paragraph 49, Plato states that the virtue of wisdom "contains a divine element." What is "a divine element"? What does this statement seem to mean? Do you agree with Plato?
7. What distinctions does Plato make between the public and the private? Would you make the same distinctions (see paras. 53 – 55)?

SUGGESTIONS FOR WRITING

1. Analyze the allegory of the cave for its strengths and weaknesses. Consider what the allegory implies for people living in a world of the senses and for what might lie behind that world. To what extent are people like (or unlike) the figures in the cave? To what extent is the world we know like the cave?

2. Socrates ends the dialogue by saying that after rulers of the state have served their term, they must be able to look forward to a better life than that of being rulers. He and Glaucon agree that only one life "looks down upon the life of political ambition" — "that of true philosophy" (para. 67). What is the life of true philosophy? Is it superior to that of governing (or anything else)? How would you define its superiority? What would its qualities be? What would its concerns be? Would you be happy leading such a life?

3. In what ways would depending on the material world for one's highest moral values affect ethical behavior? What is the connection between ethics and materialism? Write a brief essay that defends or attacks materialism as a basis for ethical action. How can people aspire to the good if they root their greatest pleasures in the senses? What alternatives do modern people have if they choose to base their actions on nonmaterialistic, or spiritual, values? What are those values? How can they guide our ethical behavior? Do you think they should?

4. In paragraph 61, Socrates outlines a program that would assure Athens of having good rulers and good government. Clarify exactly what the program is, what its problems and benefits are, and how it could be put into action. Then decide whether the program would work. You may consider whether it would work for our time, for Socrates' time, or both. If possible, use examples (hypothetical or real) to bolster your argument.

5. Socrates states unequivocally that Athens should compel the best and the most intelligent young men to be rulers of the state. Review his reasons for saying so, consider what his concept of the state is, and then take a stand on the issue. Is it right to compel the best and most intelligent young people to become rulers? If so, would it be equally proper to compel those well suited for the professions of law, medicine, teaching, or religion to follow those respective callings? Would an ideal society result if all people were forced to practice the calling for which they had the best aptitude?

6. **CONNECTIONS** Plato has a great deal to say about goodness as it relates to government. Compare his views with those of Lao-tzu and Machiavelli. Which of those thinkers would Plato have agreed with most? How did he influence that person? In comparing these three writers and their political views, consider the nature of goodness they required in a ruler. Do you think that we hold similar attitudes today in our expectations for the goodness of our government?

MOSES MAIMONIDES
On the Limits of Man's Intellect

MOSES MAIMONIDES (1135 – 1204) was known in his own time as Rabbi Moses Ben Maimon. He was born in Córdoba, Spain, when Arabs ruled most of Spain, a period of great advances in learning, music, and art. A scholar in a scholarly society, Maimonides was educated by his father in Judaism and the study of Jewish texts, medicine, and philosophy.

However, it was also a time of religious tension, and Maimonides' concerns for his faith forced him to move several times. The more conservative Arab factions who gained control of Córdoba made it difficult for Jews to practice their religion. As a result, Maimonides moved first to Fez in North Africa and then later to Cairo, where he did most of his important work. He wrote several studies of Jewish texts but is best known for *The Guide for the Perplexed* (1190), from which this selection comes. From 1166 to his death, he lived in Cairo, where he dominated the Jewish Community and influenced its scholars and thinkers. During this time his father died, and his brother, who was supporting the family, was lost at sea with the family fortune. To make a living, Maimonides turned to medicine and became prominent as a healer. He was offered a position at the English court, which he refused, and instead remained physician to Saladin (1137 – 1193), the brilliant sultan of Egypt.

In the selection that follows, Maimonides discusses the nature and limits of the human mind. His purpose is to examine the ways in which we learn, the impediments to learning, and the qualities that are necessary to learning. Underlying all his concerns, however, is a fundamental religious faith that he assumes is shared by his readers. His belief in God is firm and critical to all his thinking.

From *The Guide for the Perplexed.* Translated by M. Friedländer.

Earlier chapters in the *Guide* discuss the nature of God and the nature of belief. The chapters that appear here, 31 through 34, address the mind's limitations. Maimonides gives several examples of the limits of the mind — the fact that we cannot know the number of the stars, whether it is even or odd; that we cannot know the number of animals, and so forth (para. 2). Modern physicists likewise point to the limitations of the mind when they postulate a ten-dimensional universe that cannot be fathomed by minds limited by our familiar four-dimensional universe (counting time as a dimension).

Maimonides focuses in this selection on questions of metaphysics, a term used in early philosophy to imply all that is not contained in the study of physics, and emphasizes the study of nonmaterial things, such as the mind itself. Theology is sometimes included in metaphysics, but in this selection, Maimonides concentrates on the nature of the mind and its qualities. His considerations are pragmatic: he discusses the problems that individuals of various ages have in approaching complex studies and argues that, for various reasons, individuals are naturally limited or limit themselves in their quest for intellectual perfection. He also discusses the role of desire in relation to the role of progressive comprehension of difficult studies. In Maimonides' view, it is not enough to want to know something, such as a foreign language, but it is also necessary to be willing to master each step that leads toward the goal of knowledge.

Maimonides felt that one progressed naturally in learning and that it might be disastrous to take studies out of their proper order. For example, he advises against beginning with metaphysics because the science demands maturity and prior learning and says that one "who begins with Metaphysics, will not only become confused in matters of religion, but will fall into complete infidelity" (para. 10). Maimonides, in this selection, concentrates on gaining knowledge while also commenting on the kind of knowledge that is not obtainable to any human.

One troubling detail for the modern reader is Maimonides' references to exclusively male students and his emphasis on females as being unworthy to listen to disputation. In twelfth-century Arab society, women were prohibited from attaining educations similar to those of men because of strictly adhered to religious beliefs. Maimonides did not question the Jewish and Arab traditions that supported his views. Likewise, in the Christian world of the Middle Ages women were prohibited from receiving the same education available for men.

MAIMONIDES' RHETORIC

Like most philosophers of his time (and the following centuries), Maimonides agreed that one derived true knowledge by means of logical analysis — what he called disputation. He felt that some things, such as the sun's light, were known based on evidence of the senses, but that other things were known only by logical argument. In this selection, Maimonides deals with both kinds of knowledge but emphasizes the things we know by means of logical reasoning. He sometimes pauses to say, "I will now proceed to explain the reasons..." for whatever he is about to declare as true and then marshals the reasons.

Because he cannot always argue directly, he resorts to a highly effective means of argument based on analogy. He refers to the method as the employment of the simile or metaphor. When he compares knowledge to food, he employs one of the most common "figures" in medieval discussions of the mind (para. 8). Just as a moderate amount of some food is nourishing, overconsumption of the same food can cause illness. Likewise, a moderate amount of knowledge can make the individual wise, whereas too much too soon becomes indigestible and will confuse the individual. Maimonides uses this argument to defend his view that beginners should start with perceptible studies that can be mastered easily and subjects that are more palpable, such as logic, mathematics, and the physical sciences (para. 17), before attempting metaphysics. Maimonides establishes a basic truth for his argument by relying on analogy when he says that "mental perception" is similar to "physical perception" (para. 4). Just as the senses have limits of distance — we cannot see things far away — so the mental faculties have their limitations, and to try to work past them is to court "imperfection": "Ideas founded on mere imagination will prevail over you, you will incline toward defects... on account of the confusion which troubles the mind" (para. 6).

In addition to the considerable use of analogy, simile, and metaphor — which he credits the Bible with using extensively — Maimonides quotes frequently from the Old Testament to bolster the view he defends. He also refers to contemporary thinkers who may have been familiar to his original readers. These references to undisputed authorities are conclusive to his argument and make it possible for him to avoid detailed logical disputation. Not all of these quotations may seem relevant to the modern reader, but their combined force would have been convincing to his readers.

Another rhetorical device that helps Maimonides organize his thoughts is enumeration. He begins Chapter 34 with, "There are five reasons why instruction should not begin with Metaphysics" (para. 13), and then devotes specific paragraphs to each of those five reasons. He argues that first, metaphysics is very difficult, and it is not sensible to start with the most difficult study. Second, the intelligence of the young is "at first insufficient" (para. 15). Third, "The preparatory studies are of long duration" (para. 16), and people get worn out easily. To prove this point, Maimonides offers a simile: "He who approaches metaphysical problems without proper preparation is like a person who journeys towards a certain place, and on the road falls into a deep pit" (para. 19). Fourth, it is important for the individual to attain some moral perfection before beginning the study of metaphysics — and in those who are stirred by physical needs, such perfection is unlikely. Fifth, the needs involved in providing one's livelihood are such that they distract the individual from study.

Thus, Maimonides reasons that the study of metaphysics is reserved for the select few and is not for the "common people" (para. 25). As he writes, "It is not for the beginner, and he should abstain from it, as the little child has to abstain from taking solid food and from carrying heavy weights" (para. 25).

On the Limits of Man's Intellect

Chapter XXXI

Know that for the human mind there are certain objects of perception which are within the scope of its nature and capacity; on the other hand, there are, amongst things which actually exist, certain objects which the mind can in no way and by no means grasp: the gates of perception are closed against it. Further, there are things of which the mind understands one part, but remains ignorant of the other; and when man is able to comprehend certain things, it does not follow that he must be able to comprehend everything. This also applies to the senses: they are able to perceive things, but not at every distance; and all other powers of the body are limited in a similar way. A man can, e.g., carry two kikkar, but he cannot carry ten kikkar. How individuals of the same species surpass each other in these sensations and in other bodily faculties is universally known, but there is a limit to them, and their power cannot extend to every distance or to every degree.

All this is applicable to the intellectual faculties of man. There is a considerable difference between one person and another as regards these faculties, as is well known to philosophers. While one man can discover a certain thing by himself, another is never able to understand it, even if taught by means of all possible expressions and metaphors, and during a long period; his mind can in no way grasp it, his capacity is insufficient for it. This distinction is not unlimited. A boundary is undoubtedly set to the human mind which it cannot pass. There are things (beyond that boundary) which are acknowledged to be inaccessible to human understanding, and man does not show any desire to comprehend them, being aware that such knowledge is impossible, and that there are no means of overcoming the difficulty; e.g., we do not know the number of stars in heaven, whether the number is even or odd; we do not know the number of animals, minerals, or plants, and the like. There are other things, however, which man very much desires to know, and strenuous efforts to examine and to investigate them have been made by thinkers of all classes, and at all times. They differ and disagree, and constantly raise new doubts with regard to them, because their minds are bent on comprehending such things, that is to say, they are moved by desire; and every one of them believes that he has discovered the way leading to a true knowledge of the thing, although human reason is entirely unable to demonstrate the fact by convincing evidence. — For a proposition which can be proved by evidence is not subject to dispute, denial, or rejection; none but the ignorant would contradict it, and such contradiction is called "denial of a demonstrated proof." Thus you find men who deny the spherical form of the earth, or the circular form of the line in which the stars move, and the like; such men are not considered in this treatise. This confusion prevails mostly in metaphysical subjects, less in problems relating to physics, and is entirely absent from the exact sciences. Alexander Aphrodisius said that there are three causes which prevent men from discovering the exact truth: first, arrogance and vainglory; secondly, the subtlety, depth, and difficulty of any subject which is being examined; thirdly, ignorance and want of capacity to comprehend what might be comprehended. These causes are enumerated by Alexander. At the present time there is a fourth cause not mentioned by him, because it did not then prevail, namely, habit and training. We naturally like what we have been accustomed to, and are attracted towards it. This may be observed amongst villagers; though they rarely enjoy the benefit of a douche or bath, and have few enjoyments, and pass a life of privation, they

dislike town life and do not desire its pleasures, preferring the inferior things to which they are accustomed, to the better things to
which they are strangers; it would give them no satisfaction to live in
palaces, to be clothed in silk, and to indulge in baths, ointments,
and perfumes.

The same is the case with those opinions of man to which he   3
has been accustomed from his youth; he likes them, defends them,
and shuns the opposite views. This is likewise one of the causes
which prevent men from finding truth, and which make them cling
to their habitual opinions. Such is, e.g., the case with the vulgar notions with respect to the corporeality of God, and many other metaphysical questions, as we shall explain. It is the result of long familiarity with passages of the Bible, which they are accustomed to
respect and to receive as true, and the literal sense of which implies
the corporeality of God and other false notions; in truth, however,
these words were employed as figures and metaphors for reasons to
be mentioned below. Do not imagine that what we have said of the
insufficiency of our understanding and of its limited extent is an assertion founded only on the Bible; for philosophers likewise assert
the same, and perfectly understand it, without having regard to any
religion or opinion. It is a fact which is only doubted by those who
ignore things fully proved. This chapter is intended as an introduction to the next.

Chapter XXXII

You must consider, when reading this treatise, that mental per-   4
ception, because connected with matter, is subject to conditions
similar to those to which physical perception is subject. That is to
say, if your eye looks around, you can perceive all that is within the
range of your vision; if, however, you overstrain your eye, exerting it
too much by attempting to see an object which is too distant for
your eye, or to examine writings or engravings too small for your
sight, and forcing it to obtain a correct perception of them, you will
not only weaken your sight with regard to that special object, but
also for those things which you otherwise are able to perceive: your
eye will have become too weak to perceive what you were able to
see before you exerted yourself and exceeded the limits of your
vision.

The same is the case with the speculative faculties of one who   5
devotes himself to the study of any science. If a person studies too
much and exhausts his reflective powers, he will be confused, and
will not be able to apprehend even that which had been within the

power of his apprehension. For the powers of the body are all alike in this respect.

The mental perceptions are not exempt from a similar condi- 6 tion. If you admit the doubt, and do not persuade yourself to believe that there is a proof for things which cannot be demonstrated, or to try at once to reject and positively to deny an assertion the opposite of which has never been proved, or attempt to perceive things which are beyond your perception, then you have attained the highest degree of human perfection, then you are like R. Akibha,[1] who "in peace entered [the study of these theological problems], and came out in peace." If, on the other hand, you attempt to exceed the limit of your intellectual power, or at once to reject things as impossible which have never been proved to be impossible, or which are in fact possible, though their possibility be very remote, then you will be like Elisha Aher;[2] you will not only fail to become perfect, but you will become exceedingly imperfect. Ideas founded on mere imagination will prevail over you, you will incline toward defects, and toward base and degraded habits, on account of the confusion which troubles the mind, and of the dimness of its light, just as weakness of sight causes invalids to see many kinds of unreal images, especially when they have looked for a long time at dazzling or at very minute objects.

Respecting this it has been said, "Hast thou found honey? eat so 7 much as is sufficient for thee, lest thou be filled therewith, and vomit it" (Prov. xxv. 16). Our Sages also applied this verse to Elisha Aher.

How excellent is this simile! In comparing knowledge to food 8 (as we observed in chap. xxx.), the author of Proverbs mentions the sweetest food, namely, honey, which has the further property of irritating the stomach, and of causing sickness. He thus fully describes the nature of knowledge. Though great, excellent, noble and perfect, it is injurious if not kept within bounds or not guarded properly; it is like honey which gives nourishment and is pleasant, when eaten in moderation, but is totally thrown away when eaten immoderately. Therefore, it is not said "lest thou be filled and loathe it," but "lest thou vomit it." The same idea is expressed in the words, "It is not good to eat much honey" (Prov. xxv. 27); and in the words, "Neither make thyself over-wise; why shouldst thou destroy thyself?" (Eccles. vii. 16); comp. "Keep thy foot when thou goest to the house of God" (ibid. v. I). The same subject is alluded to in the words of David,

---

[1]**R. Akibha** Aqiva' Ben Yosef (c.40 – 135 A.D.), Palestinian scholar.
[2]**Elisha Aher** Elisha ben Vayah, (known as Aher, the other) flourished in the second century A.D. He was a Palestinian scholar who doubted the unity of God.

"Neither do I exercise myself in great matters, or in things too high for me" (Ps. cxxxi. 2), and in the sayings of our Sages: "Do not inquire into things which are too difficult for thee, do not search what is hidden from thee; study what you are allowed to study, and do not occupy thyself with mysteries." They meant to say, Let thy mind only attempt things which are within human perception; for the study of things which lie beyond man's comprehension is extremely injurious, as has been already stated. This lesson is also contained in the Talmudical passage, which begins, "He who considers four things," etc., and concludes, "He who does not regard the honour of his Creator"; here also is given the advice which we have already mentioned, viz., that man should not rashly engage in speculation with false conceptions, and when he is in doubt about anything, or unable to find a proof for the object of his inquiry, he must not at once abandon, reject and deny it; he must modestly keep back, and from regard to the honour of his Creator, hesitate [from uttering an opinion] and pause. This has already been explained.

It was not the object of the Prophets and our Sages in these utter- 9 ances to close the gate of investigation entirely, and to prevent the mind from comprehending what is within its reach, as is imagined by simple and idle people, whom it suits better to put forth their ignorance and incapacity as wisdom and perfection, and to regard the distinction and wisdom of others as irreligion and imperfection, thus taking darkness for light and light for darkness. The whole object of the Prophets and the Sages was to declare that a limit is set to human reason where it must halt. Do not criticise the words used in this chapter and in others in reference to the mind, for we only intended to give some idea of the subject in view, not to describe the essence of the intellect; for other chapters have been dedicated to this subject.

Chapter XXXIII

You must know that it is very injurious to begin with this 10 branch of philosophy, viz., Metaphysics; or to explain [at first] the sense of the similes occurring in prophecies, and interpret the metaphors which are employed in historical accounts and which abound in the writings of the Prophets. On the contrary, it is necessary to initiate the young and to instruct the less intelligent according to their comprehension; those who appear to be talented and to have capacity for the higher method of study, i.e., that based on proof and on true logical argument, should be gradually advanced towards perfection, either by tuition or by self-instruction. He, however, who begins with Metaphysics, will not only become confused in matters of religion, but will fall into complete infidelity. I compare such a person to an infant fed with wheaten bread, meat and wine; it will undoubtedly die, not because such food is naturally unfit for the human body, but because of the weakness of the child, who is unable to digest the food, and cannot derive benefit from it. The same is the case with the true principles of science. They were presented in enigmas, clad in riddles, and taught by all wise men in the most mysterious way that could be devised, not because they contain some secret evil, or are contrary to the fundamental principles of the Law (as fools think who are only philosophers in their own eyes), but because of the incapacity of man to comprehend them at the beginning of his studies: only slight allusions have been made to them to serve for the guidance of those who are capable of understanding them. These sciences were, therefore, called Mysteries (*sodoth*), and Secrets of the Law (*sitre torah*), as we shall explain.

This also is the reason why "the Torah speaks the language of man," as we have explained, for it is the object of the Torah to serve as a guide for the instruction of the young, of women, and of the common people; and as all of them are incapable to comprehend the true sense of the words, tradition was considered sufficient to convey all truths which were to be established; and as regards ideals, only such remarks were made as would lead towards a knowledge of their existence, though not to a comprehension of their true essence. When a man attains to perfection, and arrives at a knowledge of the "Secrets of the Law," either through the assistance of a teacher or by self-instruction, being led by the understanding of one part to the study of the other, he will belong to those who faithfully believe in the true principles, either because of conclusive proof, where proof is possible, or by forcible arguments, where argument is admissible; he will have a true notion of those things which he previously received in similes and metaphors, and he will fully understand their sense. We have frequently mentioned in this treatise the principle of our Sages "not to discuss the *Ma'aseh Mercabah*[3] even in the presence of one pupil, except he be wise and intelligent; and then only the headings of the chapters according to the capacity of the pupil, and on two conditions, first, that he be wise, i.e., that he should have successfully gone through the preliminary studies, and secondly that he be intelligent, talented, clear-headed, and of quick perception, that is, "have a mind of his own," as our Sages termed it.

_____

[3] **Ma'aseh Mercabah** The study of metaphysics.

I will now proceed to explain the reasons why we should not in- 12
struct the multitude in pure metaphysics, or begin with describing
to them the true essence of things, or with showing them that a
thing must be as it is, and cannot be otherwise. This will form the
subject of the next chapter; and I proceed to say —

Chapter XXXIV

There are five reasons why instruction should not begin with 13
Metaphysics, but should at first be restricted to pointing out what is
fitted for notice and what may be made manifest to the multitude.

First Reason. — The subject itself is difficult, subtle and pro- 14
found, "Far off and exceeding deep, who can find it out?" (Eccles.
vii. 24). The following words of Job may be applied to it: "Whence
then cometh wisdom? and where is the place of understanding?"
(Job xxvii. 20). Instruction should not begin with abstruse and difficult subjects. In one of the similes contained in the Bible, wisdom
is compared to water, and amongst other interpretations given by
our Sages of this simile, occurs the following: He who can swim may
bring up pearls from the depth of the sea, he who is unable to swim
will be drowned, therefore only such persons as have had proper instruction should expose themselves to the risk.

Second Reason. — The intelligence of man is at first insufficient; 15
for he is not endowed with perfection at the beginning, but at first
possesses perfection only *in potentiâ,* not in fact. Thus it is said, "And
man is born a wild ass" (Job xi. 12). If a man possesses a certain faculty *in potentiâ,* it does not follow that it must become in him a reality. He may possibly remain deficient either on account of some obstacle, or from want of training in practices which would turn the
possibility into a reality. Thus it is distinctly stated in the Bible, "Not
many are wise" (Job xxxii. 9); also our Sages say, "I noticed how few
were those who attained to a higher degree of perfection." There are
many things which obstruct the path to perfection, and which keep
man away from it. Where can he find sufficient preparation and
leisure to learn all that is necessary in order to develop that perfection which he has *in potentiâ?*

Third Reason. — The preparatory studies are of long duration, 16
and man, in his natural desire to reach the goal, finds them frequently too wearisome, and does not wish to be troubled by them.
Be convinced that, if man were able to reach the end without
preparatory studies, such studies would not be preparatory but tire-
some and utterly superfluous. Suppose you awaken any person,
even the most simple, as if from sleep, and you say to him, Do you

not desire to know what the heavens are, what is their number and
their form; what beings are contained in them; what the angels are;
how the creation of the whole world took place; what is its purpose,
and what is the relation of its various parts to each other; what is the
nature of the soul; how it enters the body; whether it has an independent existence, and if so, how it can exist independently of the
body; by what means and to what purpose, and similar problems.
He would undoubtedly say "Yes," and show a natural desire for the
true knowledge of these things; but he will wish to satisfy that desire
and to attain to that knowledge by listening to a few words from
you. Ask him to interrupt his usual pursuits for a week, till he learn
all this, he would not do it, and would be satisfied and contented
with imaginary and misleading notions; he would refuse to believe
that there is anything which requires preparatory studies and perse-
vering research.

You, however, know how all these subjects are connected together; for there is nothing else in existence but God and His works,
the latter including all existing things besides Him; we can only obtain
a knowledge of Him through His works; His works give evidence of
His existence, and show what must be assumed concerning Him, that
is to say, what must be attributed to Him either affirmatively or nega-
tively. It is thus necessary to examine all things according to their
essence, to infer from every species such true and well established
propositions as may assist us in the solution of metaphysical problems. Again, many propositions based on the nature of numbers and
the properties of geometrical figures, are useful in examining things
which must be negatived in reference to God, and these negations will
lead us to further inferences. You will certainly not doubt the necessity of studying astronomy and physics, if you are desirous of comprehending the relation between the world and Providence as it is in reality, and not according to imagination. There are also many subjects of
speculation, which, though not preparing the way for metaphysics,
help to train the reasoning power, enabling it to understand the nature of a proof, and to test truth by characteristics essential to it. They
remove the confusion arising in the minds of most thinkers, who confound accidental with essential properties, and likewise the wrong
opinions resulting therefrom. We may add, that although they do not
form the basis for metaphysical research, they assist in forming a correct notion of these things, and are certainly useful in many other
things connected with that discipline. Consequently he who wishes to
attain to human perfection, must therefore first study Logic, next the
various branches of Mathematics in their proper order, then Physics,
and lastly Metaphysics. We find that many who have advanced to a
certain point in the study of these disciplines become weary, and stop;

17

that others, who are endowed with sufficient capacity, are interrupted in their studies by death, which surprises them while still engaged with the preliminary course. Now, if no knowledge whatever had been given to us by means of tradition, and if we had not been brought to the belief in a thing through the medium of similes, we would have been bound to form a perfect notion of things with their essential characteristics, and to believe only what we could prove: a goal which could only be attained by long preparation. In such a case most people would die, without having known whether there was a God or not, much less that certain things must be asserted about Him, and other things denied as defects. From such a fate not even "one of a city or two of a family" (Jer. iii. 14) would have escaped.

As regards the privileged few, "the remnant whom the Lord calls" (Joel iii. 5), they only attain the perfection at which they aim after due preparatory labour. The necessity of such a preparation and the need of such a training for the acquisition of real knowledge, has been plainly stated by King Solomon in the following words: "If the iron be blunt, and he do not whet the edge, then must he put to more strength; and it is profitable to prepare for wisdom" (Eccles. x. 10); "Hear counsel, and receive instruction, that thou mayest be wise in thy latter end" (Prov. xix. 20). 18

There is still another urgent reason why the preliminary disciplines should be studied and understood. During the study many doubts present themselves, and the difficulties, or the objections raised against certain assertions, are soon understood, just as the demolition of a building is easier than its erection; while, on the other hand, it is impossible to prove an assertion, or to remove any doubts, without having recourse to several propositions taken from these preliminary studies. He who approaches metaphysical problems without proper preparation is like a person who journeys towards a certain place, and on the road falls into a deep pit, out of which he cannot rise, and he must perish there; if he had not gone forth, but had remained at home, it would have been better for him. 19

Solomon has expatiated in the book of Proverbs on sluggards and their indolence, by which he figuratively refers to indolence in the search after wisdom. He thus speaks of a man who desires to know the final results, but does not exert himself to understand the preliminary disciplines which lead to them, doing nothing else but desire. "The desire of the slothful killeth him; for his hands refuse to labour. He coveteth greedily all the day long; but the righteous giveth, and spareth not" (Prov. xxi. 25, 26); that is to say, if the desire killeth the slothful, it is because he neglects to seek the thing which might satisfy his desire, he does nothing but desire, and hope to obtain a thing without using the means to reach it. It would be 20 better for him were he without that desire. Observe how the end of the simile throws light on its beginning. It concludes with the words "but the righteous giveth, and spareth not"; the antithesis of "righteous" and "slothful" can only be justified on the basis of our interpretation. Solomon thus indicates that only such a man is righteous who gives to everything its due portion; that is to say, who gives to the study of a thing the whole time required for it, and does not devote any part of that time to another purpose. The passage may therefore be paraphrased thus: "And the righteous man devotes his ways to wisdom, and does not withhold any of them." Comp. "Give not thy strength unto women" (Prov. xxxi. 3).

The majority of scholars, that is to say, the most famous in science, are afflicted with this failing, viz., that of hurrying at once to the final results, and of speaking about them, without treating of the preliminary disciplines. Led by folly or ambition to disregard those preparatory studies, for the attainment of which they are either incapable or too idle, some scholars endeavour to prove that these are injurious or superfluous. On reflection the truth will become obvious.   21

The Fourth Reason is taken from the physical constitution of man. It has been proved that moral conduct is a preparation for intellectual progress, and that only a man whose character is pure, calm and steadfast, can attain to intellectual perfection; that is, acquire correct conceptions. Many men are naturally so constituted that all perfection is impossible; e.g., he whose heart is very warm and is himself very powerful, is sure to be passionate, though he tries to counteract that disposition by training; he whose testicles are warm, humid, and vigorous, and the organs connected therewith are surcharged, will not easily refrain from sin, even if he makes great efforts to restrain himself. You also find persons of great levity and rashness, whose excited manners and wild gestures prove that their constitution is in disorder, and their temperament so bad that it cannot be cured. Such persons can never attain to perfection; it is utterly useless to occupy oneself with them on such a subject [as Metaphysics]. For this science is, as you know, different from the science of Medicine and of Geometry, and, from the reason already mentioned, it is not every person who is capable of approaching it. It is impossible for a man to study it successfully without moral preparation; he must acquire the highest degree of uprightness and integrity, "for the froward is an abomination to the Lord, but His secret is with the righteous" (Prov. iii. 32). Therefore it was considered inadvisable to teach it to young men; nay, it is impossible for them to comprehend it, on account of the heat of their blood and the flame of youth, which confuses their minds; that heat, which causes all the disorder, must first disappear; they must have become moderate and settled, humble in their hearts, and subdued in   22 their temperament; only then will they be able to arrive at the highest degree of the perception of God, i.e., the study of Metaphysics, which are called *Ma'aseh Mercabah*. Compare "The Lord is nigh unto them that are of a broken heart" (Ps. xxxiv. 18); "I dwell in the high and lofty place, with him also that is of a contrite and humble spirit; to revive the spirit of the humble, and to revive the heart of the contrite ones" (Isa. lvii. 15).

Therefore the rule, "the headings of the sections may be con- 23 fided to him," is further restricted in the Talmud, in the following way: The headings of the sections must only be handed down to an Ab-bet-din (President of the Court), whose heart is full of care, i.e., in whom wisdom is united with humility, meekness, and a great dread of sin. It is further stated there: "The secrets of the Law can only be communicated to a counsellor, scholar, and good orator." These qualities can only be acquired if the physical constitution of the student favour their development. You certainly know that some persons, though exceedingly able, are very weak in giving counsel, while others are ready with proper counsel and good advice in social and political matters. A person so endowed is called "counsellor" and may be unable to comprehend purely abstract notions, even such as are similar to common sense. He is unacquainted with them, and has no talent whatever for them; we apply to him the words: "Wherefore is there a price in the hand of a fool to get wisdom, seeing he hath no heart to it?" (Prov. xvii. 16). Others are intelligent and naturally clear-sighted, able to convey complicated ideas in concise and well chosen language, — such a person is called "a good orator," but he has not been engaged in the pursuit of science, or has not acquired any knowledge of it. Those who have actually acquired a knowledge of the sciences, are called "wise in arts" (or "scholars"); the Hebrew term for "wise in arts" — *ḥakam ḥarashim* — has been explained in the Talmud as implying, that when such a man speaks, all become, as it were, speechless.

Now, consider how, in the writings of the Rabbis, the admission 24 of a person into discourses on metaphysics is made dependent on distinction in social qualities, and study of philosophy, as well as on the possession of clearsightedness, intelligence, eloquence, and ability to communicate things by slight allusions. If a person satisfies these requirements, the secrets of the Law are confided to him. In the same place we also read the following passage: — R. Jochanan[4]

----

[4] **R. Jochanan** Yohanan Ha-Sandelar (fl. second century A.D.), a student of R. Akibha and an important interpreter of the Bible.

said to R. Elasar,[5] "Come, I will teach you *Ma'aseh Mercabah*." The reply was, "I am not yet old," or in other words, I have not yet become old, I still perceive in myself the hot blood and the rashness of youth. You learn from this that, in addition to the above-named good qualities, a certain age is also required. How, then, could any person speak on these metaphysical themes in the presence of ordinary people, of children, and of women!

Fifth Reason. — Man is disturbed in his intellectual occupation 25 by the necessity of looking after the material wants of the body, especially if the necessity of providing for wife and children be superadded; much more so if he seeks superfluities in addition to his ordinary wants, for by custom and bad habits these become a powerful motive. Even the perfect man to whom we have referred, if too busy with these necessary things, much more so if busy with unnecessary things, and filled with a great desire for them — must weaken or altogether lose his desire for study, to which he will apply himself with interruption, lassitude, and want of attention. He will not attain to that for which he is fitted by his abilities, or he will acquire imperfect knowledge, a confused mass of true and false ideas. For these reasons it was proper that the study of Metaphysics should have been exclusively cultivated by privileged persons, and not entrusted to the common people. It is not for the beginner, and he should abstain from it, as the little child has to abstain from taking solid food and from carrying heavy weights.

---

[5] **R. Elasar** R. El'azar (fl. second century A.D.), a student of Yohanan. When he taught metaphysics, "fire fell from Heaven, the trees burst into song."

QUESTIONS FOR CRITICAL READING

1. How would you restate Maimonides' basic views on the progress of learning for most people?
2. What are Maimonides' views about the nature and limitations of the human mind? How would you agree or disagree with his points?
3. How much of an impediment to learning is "the hot blood and the rashness of youth" (para. 24)?
4. Do you think a good "moral constitution" is a requirement of serious learning? Why or why not?
5. Why do you think Maimonides uses the statement "wisdom is compared with water" in paragraph 14?
6. Which of the analogies is your favorite? Defend your choice.

SUGGESTIONS FOR WRITING

1. Maimonides argues that advanced studies are for the privileged people in his society. In his time, few people could hope for an education of any kind, and the vast majority were illiterate. Today most people are literate, and many in our own society continue their education with college and postgraduate studies. To what extent do you agree or disagree with Maimonides' suggestion that advanced studies be restricted to the few?

2. This selection is an extended argument against instructing young students in metaphysics. Examine the argument to determine how effective it is. What are the principal parts of the argument, and which are most effective? Which parts of the argument are less effective? How does your experience in education reinforce or contradict Maimonides' argument?

3. What are the advantages and disadvantages of using simile in the fashion Maimonides does in this selection? It is clear that he believes the technique to be especially powerful and useful. Is he correct? What are its particular strengths for the modern reader? Why is it useful, and why does it appeal to different kinds of readers? What are the dangers involved in relying on analogy to conduct a serious argument?

4. Maimonides seems to make the perfection of the individual the central goal of education. How common is such an attitude toward perfection among today's students? What term might better describe the ambitions of the modern student? In what ways are Maimonides' student and the student of today alike? How are they different?

5. **CONNECTIONS**   How do Maimonides' ideals of education relate to Howard Gardner's views of the seven forms of intelligence that should be developed in schools? How would Gardner interpret Maimonides' concept of perfection? How would Maimonides regard Gardner's treating the varieties of intelligence as relatively equal in value? Would Gardner agree with Maimonides' view that few people can understand advanced studies?

6. **CONNECTIONS**   Examine Maimonides' concepts of intellectual limitation in relation to Plato's allegory of the cave. In what ways would Plato agree with the sense that there are things that the intellect cannot comprehend? What are each author's respective solutions for learning to live with those limitations? Is it possible to determine whether or not Maimonides had read Plato's allegory?

SIGMUND FREUD
From *The Interpretation of Dreams*

SIGMUND FREUD (1856 – 1939) is, in the minds of many, the founder of modern psychiatry. He developed the psychoanalytic method: the examination of the mind using dream analysis, the analysis of the unconscious through free association, and the correlation of findings with attitudes toward sexuality and sexual development. His theories changed the way people treated neurosis and most other mental disorders. Today we use terms he either invented or championed, such as *psychoanalysis, penis envy, Oedipus complex,* and *wish-fulfillment.*

Freud was born in Freiberg, Moravia (now the Czech Republic), and moved to Vienna, Austria, when he was four. He pursued a medical career and soon began exploring neurology, which stimulated him to begin his psychoanalytic methods. *The Interpretation of Dreams* (1899) is one of his first important books. It was followed in rapid succession by a number of ground-breaking studies: *The Psychopathology of Everyday Life* (1904), *Three Essays on the Theory of Sexuality* (1905), *Totem and Taboo* (1913), *Beyond the Pleasure Principle* (1920), and *Civilization and Its Discontents* (1930). Freud's personal life was essentially uneventful in Vienna until he was put under house arrest by the Nazis in 1938. He was released and moved to London, where he died the following year.

As a movement, psychoanalysis shocked most of the world by postulating a superego, which establishes high standards of personal behavior; an ego, which corresponds to the apparent personality; an id, which includes the deepest primitive forces of life; and

From *The Interpretation of Dreams.* Translated by James Strachey.

an unconscious, into which thoughts and memories we cannot face are repressed or sublimated. The origin of much mental illness, the theory presumes, lies in the inability of the mind to find a way to sublimate — express in harmless and often creative ways — the painful thoughts that have been repressed. Dreams and unconscious actions sometimes act as releases or harmless expressions of these thoughts and memories.

Before Freud's work, books that interpreted details and classic dreams existed, but they assumed dreams were universal in importance rather than personal. In *The Interpretation of Dreams,* Freud reviews these historical approaches to dreams, and draws the revolutionary conclusion that dreams can be interpreted as important personal psychological events. The second part of Freud's book offers a sample interpretation of one of his own dreams concerning injections given to a patient named Irma (he refers to the analysis in this selection). In that analysis he shows how his dream reveals his own uncertainties about his patient.

Freud's theory of the dream as wish-fulfillment is first introduced in this chapter and is developed further in the last section of his book. In this chapter he explores evidence indicating that dreams express the unfulfilled wishes of the individual. He offers a number of examples from his own dreams as well as from dreams of family members. He also makes some interesting observations about the dreams of children, with examples from his own children's dreams. His examples are familiar and pertinent to his family circumstances, but they are universal enough to help readers interpret their own dreams.

FREUD'S RHETORIC

Freud's style is simple and direct in this chapter. His language is relaxed, clear, and familiar, as is the material he introduces, since most of it comes from his own family's experiences. He tells us about his trips, his mountain walks, his family around him, and their desires and hopes. He states that when they are disappointed, their dreams supply the pleasures that they were denied.

Freud's basic effort is that of argumentation — although his style is so unthreatening that for many readers the argument will be invisible. Freud expects to convince his readers by the method of supplying a number of examples and offering analyses of the examples. Once the reader has read through these analyzed examples, he or she is expected to be convinced that dreams are, indeed, wish-fulfillments. Freud was unable to offer examples of dream analyses from other analysts because, as he tells us in the early part of his book, no other analyst approaches dreams as he does. He does offer us a dream or two from nonfamily members, but the analyses are his own.

One interesting rhetorical device that seems to underlie the entire selection is a simple metaphor expressed in the opening paragraph, where he likens the reader's present position to someone who has ascended a mountain top and paused to enjoy the view. The heights, attainable only through effort, are a metaphor for the exertions of the psychoanalyst that raise the sights of the patient or the reader. Only from the promontory can one see the true topography of the locale, and Freud's work takes us to that promontory. Moreover, several of the examples Freud later uses are also drawn from mountain climbing — walks by himself and others through the foothills leading to the mountain. He tells of his child growing impatient with the foothills because he wishes to gain the mountain top immediately. All this is a convenient metaphor for the preparations that the analyst must make to understand the truth about the meaning of dreams.

In a letter Freud wrote to an associate while he was working on the book, he describes his rhetorical approach in the following manner: "The whole thing is planned on the model of an imaginary walk. First comes the dark wood of the authorities (who cannot see the trees), where there is no clear view and it is easy to go astray. Then there is a cavernous defile through which I lead my readers — my specimen dream with its peculiarities, its details, its indiscretions and its bad jokes — and then, all at once, the high ground and the open prospect" (August 6, 1899).

Not all of Freud's writing is as approachable as this example. But when Freud writes about universal experiences, his style is often clear and direct. In large part because of Freud's rhetorical skill, the concept of the dream as wish-fulfillment has become part of our language.

From *The Interpretation of Dreams*

When, after passing through a narrow defile, we suddenly   1
emerge upon a piece of high ground, where the path divides and the finest prospects open up on every side, we may pause for a moment and consider in which direction we shall first turn our steps. Such is the case with us, now that we have surmounted the first interpreta-

tion of a dream. We find ourselves in the full daylight of a sudden discovery. Dreams are not to be likened to the unregulated sounds that rise from a musical instrument struck by the blow of some external force instead of by a player's hand; they are not meaningless, they are not absurd; they do not imply that one portion of our store of ideas is asleep while another portion is beginning to wake. On the contrary, they are psychical phenomena of complete validity — fulfillments of wishes; they can be inserted into the chain of intelligible waking mental acts; they are constructed by a highly complicated activity of the mind.

But no sooner have we begun to rejoice at this discovery than   2 we are assailed by a flood of questions. If, as we are told by dream-interpretation, a dream represents a fulfilled wish, what is the origin of the remarkable and puzzling form in which the wish-fulfillment is expressed? What alteration have the dream-thoughts undergone before being changed into the manifest dream which we remember when we wake up? How does that alteration take place? What is the source of the material that has been modified into the dream? What is the source of the many peculiarities that are to be observed in the dream-thoughts — such, for instance, as the fact that they may be mutually contradictory? Can a dream tell us anything new about our internal psychical processes? Can its content correct opinions we have held during the day?

I propose that for the moment we should leave all these ques-   3 tions on one side and pursue our way further along one particular path. We have learnt that a dream can represent a wish as fulfilled. Our first concern must be to enquire whether this is a universal characteristic of dreams or whether it merely happened to be the content of the particular dream (the dream of Irma's injection) which was the first that we analyzed. For even if we are prepared to find that every dream has a meaning and a psychical value, the possibility must remain open of this meaning not being the same in every dream. Our first dream was the fulfillment of a wish; a second one might turn out to be a fulfilled fear; the content of a third might be a reflection; while a fourth might merely reproduce a memory. Shall we find other wishful dreams besides this one? Or are there perhaps no dreams but wishful ones?

It is easy to prove that dreams often reveal themselves without   4 any disguise as fulfillments of wishes; so that it may seem surprising that the language of dreams was not understood long ago. For instance, there is a dream that I can produce in myself as often as I like — experimentally, as it were. If I eat anchovies or olives or any other highly salted food in the evening, I develop thirst during the night which wakes me up. But my waking is preceded by a dream; and this always has the same content, namely, that I am drinking. I dream I am swallowing down water in great gulps, and it has the delicious taste that nothing can equal but a cool drink when one is parched with thirst. Then I wake up and have to have a real drink. This simple dream is occasioned by the thirst which I become aware of when I wake. The thirst gives rise to a wish to drink, and the dream shows me that wish fulfilled. In doing so it is performing a function — which it was easy to divine. I am a good sleeper and not accustomed to be woken by any physical need. If I can succeed in appeasing my thirst by *dreaming* that I am drinking, then I need not wake up in order to quench it. This, then, is a dream of convenience. Dreaming has taken the place of action, as it often does elsewhere in life. Unluckily my need for water to quench my thirst cannot be satisfied by a dream in the same way as my thirst for revenge against my friend Otto and Dr. M.; but the good intention is there in both cases. Not long ago this same dream of mine showed some modification. I had felt thirsty even before I fell asleep, and I had emptied a glass of water that stood on the table beside my bed. A few hours later during the night I had a fresh attack of thirst, and this had inconvenient results. In order to provide myself with some water I should have had to get up and fetch the glass standing on the table by my wife's bed. I therefore had an appropriate dream that my wife was giving me a drink out of a vase; this vase was an Etruscan cinerary urn which I had brought back from a journey to Italy and had since given away. But the water in it tasted so salty (evidently because of the ashes in the urn) that I woke up. It will be noticed how conveniently everything was arranged in this dream. Since its only purpose was to fulfil a wish, it could be completely egoistical. A love of comfort and convenience is not really compatible with consideration for other people. The introduction of the cinerary urn was probably yet another wish-fulfillment. I was sorry that the vase was no longer in my possession — just as the glass of water on my wife's table was out of my reach. The urn with its ashes fitted in, too, with the salty taste in my mouth which had now grown stronger and which I knew was bound to wake me.

Dreams of convenience like these were very frequent in my 5 youth. Having made it a practice as far back as I can remember to work late into the night, I always found it difficult to wake early. I used then to have a dream of being out of bed and standing by the washing stand; after a while I was no longer able to disguise from myself the fact that I was really still in bed, but in the meantime I had had a little more sleep. A slothful dream of this kind, which was expressed in a particularly amusing and elegant form, has been reported to me by a young medical colleague who seems to share my liking for sleep. The landlady of his lodgings in the neighborhood of the hospital had strict instructions to wake him in time every morning but found it no easy job to carry them out. One morning sleep seemed peculiarly sweet. The landlady called through the door: "Wake up, Herr Pepi! It's time to go to the hospital!" In response to this he had a dream that he was lying in bed in a room in the hospital, and that there was a card over the bed on which was written: "Pepi H., medical student, age 22." While he was dreaming, he said to himself "As I'm already *in* the hospital, there's no need for me to go there" — and turned over and went on sleeping. In this way he openly confessed the motive for his dream.

Here is another dream in which once again the stimulus pro-   6 duced its effect during actual sleep. One of my women patients, who had been obliged to undergo an operation on her jaw which had taken an unfavorable course, was ordered by her doctors to wear a cooling apparatus on the side of her face day and night. But as soon as she fell asleep she used to throw it off. One day, after she had once more thrown the apparatus on the floor, I was asked to speak to her seriously about it. "This time I really couldn't help it," she answered. "It was because of a dream I had in the night. I dreamed I was in a box at the opera and very much enjoying the performance. But Herr Karl Meyer was in the nursing home and complaining bitterly of pains in his jaw. So I told myself that as I hadn't any pain I didn't need the apparatus; and I threw it away." The dream of this poor sufferer seems almost like a concrete representation of a phrase that sometimes forces its way on to people's lips in unpleasant situations: "I must say I could think of something more agreeable than this." The dream gives a picture of this more agreeable thing. The Herr Karl Meyer on to whom the dreamer transplanted her pains was the most indifferent young man of her acquaintance that she could call to mind.

The wish-fulfillment can be detected equally easily in some   7 other dreams which I have collected from normal people. A friend of mine, who knows my theory of dreams and has told his wife of it, said to me one day: "My wife has asked me to tell you that she had a dream yesterday that she was having her period. You can guess what that means." I could indeed guess it. The fact that this young married woman dreamed that she was having her period meant that she had missed her period. I could well believe that she would have been glad to go on enjoying her freedom a little longer before shouldering the burden of motherhood. It was a neat way of announcing her first pregnancy. Another friend of mine wrote and told me that, not long before, his wife had dreamed that she had noticed some milk stains on the front of her vest. This too was an announcement of pregnancy, but not of a first one. The young mother was wishing that she might have more nourishment to give her second child than she had had for her first.

A young woman had been cut off from society for weeks on end while she nursed her child through an infectious illness. After the child's recovery, she had a dream of being at a party at which, among others, she met Alphonse Daudet, Paul Bourget, and Marcel Prévost;[1] they were all most affable to her and highly amusing. All of the authors resembled their portraits, except Marcel Prévost, of whom she had never seen a picture; and he looked like . . . the disinfection officer who had fumigated the sick room the day before and who had been her first visitor for so long. Thus it seems possible to give a complete translation of the dream: "It's about time for something more amusing than this perpetual sick-nursing."

These examples will perhaps be enough to show that dreams which can only be understood as fulfillments of wishes and which bear their meaning upon their faces without disguise are to be found under the most frequent and various conditions. They are mostly short and simple dreams, which afford a pleasant contrast to the confused and exuberant compositions that have in the main attracted the attention of the authorities. Nevertheless, it will repay us to pause for a moment over these simple dreams. We may expect to find the very simplest forms of dreams in *children,* since there can be no doubt that their psychical productions are less complicated than those of adults. Child psychology, in my opinion, is destined to perform the same useful services for adult psychology that the investigation of the structure or development of the lower animals has performed for research into the structure of the higher classes of animals. Few deliberate efforts have hitherto been made to make use of child psychology for this purpose.

The dreams of young children are frequently pure wish-fulfillments and are in that case quite uninteresting compared with the dreams of adults. They raise no problems for solution; but on the other hand they are of inestimable importance in proving that, in their essential nature, dreams represent fulfillments of wishes. I have been able to collect a few instances of such dreams from material provided by my own children.

I have to thank an excursion which we made from Aussee to the lovely village of Hallstatt in the summer of 1896 for two dreams:

---

[1] **Alphonse Daudet (1840 – 1897), Paul Bourget (1852 – 1935), and Marcel Prévost (1862 – 1941)** All French novelists.

One of these was dreamed by my daughter, who was then eight and a half, and the other by her brother of five and a quarter. I must explain by way of preamble that we had been spending the summer on a hillside near Aussee, from which, in fine weather, we enjoyed a splendid view of the Dachstein. The Simony Hütte could be clearly distinguished through a telescope. The children made repeated attempts at seeing it through the telescope — I cannot say with what success. Before our excursion, I had told the children that Hallstatt lay at the foot of the Dachstein. They very much looked forward to the day. From Hallstatt we walked up the Echerntal, which delighted the children with its succession of changing landscapes. One of them, however, the five-year-old boy, gradually became fretful. Each time a new mountain came into view he asked if that was the Dachstein and I had to say, "No, only one of the foothills." After he had asked the question several times, he fell completely silent; and he refused point blank to come with us up the steep path to the waterfall. I thought he was tired. But next morning he came to me with a radiant face and said: "Last night I dreamed we were at the Simony Hütte." I understood him then. When I had spoken about the Dachstein, he had expected to climb the mountain in the course of our excursion to Hallstatt and to find himself at close quarters with the hut which there had been so much talk about in connection with the telescope. But when he found that he was being fobbed off with foothills and a waterfall, he felt disappointed and out of spirits. The dream was a compensation. I tried to discover its details, but they were scanty: "You have to climb up steps for six hours" — which was what he had been told.

The same excursion stirred up wishes in the eight-and-a-half-year-old girl as well — wishes which had to be satisfied in a dream. We had taken our neighbor's twelve-year-old son with us to Hallstatt. He was already a full-blown gallant, and there were signs that he had engaged the young lady's affections. Next morning she told me the following dream: "Just fancy! I had a dream that Emil was one of the family and called you 'Father' and 'Mother' and slept with us in the big room like the boys. Then Mother came in and threw a handful of big bars of chocolate, wrapped up in blue and green paper, under our beds." Her brothers, who have evidently not inherited a faculty for understanding dreams, followed the lead of the authorities and declared that the dream was nonsense. The girl herself defended one part of the dream at least; and it throws light on the theory of neuroses to learn *which* part. "Of course it's nonsense Emil being one of the family; but the part about the bars of chocolate isn't." It had been precisely on that point that I had been in the dark, but the girl's mother now gave me the explanation. On their way home from the station the children had stopped in front of a slot machine from which they were accustomed to obtain bars of chocolate of that very kind, wrapped in shiny metallic paper. They had wanted to get some; but their mother rightly decided that the day had already fulfilled enough wishes and left this one over to be fulfilled by the dream. I myself had not observed the incident. But the part of the dream which had been proscribed by my daughter was immediately clear to me. I myself had heard our well-behaved guest telling the children on the walk to wait till Father and Mother caught up with them. The little girl's dream turned this temporary kinship into permanent adoption. Her affection was not yet able to picture any other forms of companionship than those which were represented in the dream and which were based on her relation to her brothers. It was of course impossible to discover without questioning her why the bars of chocolate were thrown under the beds.

A friend of mine has reported a dream to me which was very   13
much like my son's. The dreamer was an eight-year-old girl. Her father had started off with several children on a walk to Dornbach, with the idea of visiting the Rohrer Hütte. As it was getting late, however, he had turned back, promising the children to make up for the disappointment another time. On their way home they had passed the sign post that marks the path up to the Hameau. The children had then asked to be taken up to the Hameau; but once again for the same reason they had to be consoled with the promise of another day. Next morning the eight-year-old girl came to her father and said in satisfied tones: "Daddy, I dreamed last night that you went with us to the Rohrer Hütte and the Hameau." In her impatience she had anticipated the fulfillment of her father's promises.

Here is an equally straightforward dream, provoked by the   14
beauty of the scenery at Aussee in another of my daughters, who was at that time three and a quarter. She had crossed the lake for the first time, and the crossing had been too short for her: When we reached the landing-stage she had not wanted to leave the boat and had wept bitterly. Next morning she said: "Last night I went on the lake." Let us hope that her dream-crossing had been of a more satisfying length.

My eldest boy, then eight years old, already had dreams of his   15
fantasies coming true: He dreamed that he was driving in a chariot with Achilles and that Diomede was the charioteer. As may be guessed, he had been excited the day before by a book on the legends of Greece which had been given to his elder sister.

If I may include words spoken by children in their sleep under   16
the heading of dreams, I can at this point quote one of the most

youthful dreams in my whole collection. My youngest daughter, then nineteen months old, had had an attack of vomiting one morning and had consequently been kept without food all day. During the night after this day of starvation she was heard calling out excitedly in her sleep: "Anna Fweud, stwawbewwies, wild stwawbewwies, omblet, pudden!" At that time she was in the habit of using her own name to express the idea of taking possession of something. The menu included pretty well everything that must have seemed to her to make up a desirable meal. The fact that strawberries appeared in it in two varieties was a demonstration against the domestic health regulations. It was based upon the circumstance, which she had no doubt observed, that her nurse had attributed her indisposition to a surfeit of strawberries. She was thus retaliating in her dream against this unwelcome verdict.

Though we think highly of the happiness of childhood because 17 it is still innocent of sexual desires, we should not forget what a fruitful source of disappointment and renunciation, and consequently what a stimulus to dreaming, may be provided by the other of the two great vital instincts. Here is another instance of this. My nephew, aged 22 months, had been entrusted with the duty of congratulating me on by birthday and of presenting me with a basket of cherries, which are still scarcely in season at that time of year. He seems to have found the task a hard one, for he kept on repeating "Chewwies in it" but could not be induced to hand the present over. However, he found a means of compensation. He had been in the habit every morning of telling his mother that he had a dream of the "white soldier" — a Guards officer in his white cloak whom he had once gazed at admiringly in the street. On the day after his birthday sacrifice he awoke with a cheerful piece of news, which could only have originated from a dream: "Hermann eaten all the chewwies!"

I do not myself know what animals dream of. But a proverb, to 18 which my attention was drawn by one of my students, does claim to know. "What," asks the proverb, "do geese dream of?" And it replies: "Of maize." The whole theory that dreams are wish-fulfillments is contained in these two phrases.

It will be seen that we might have arrived at our theory of the 19 hidden meaning of dreams most rapidly merely by following linguistic usage. It is true that common language sometimes speaks of dreams with contempt. (The phrase "*Träume sind Schäume* [Dreams are froth]" seems intended to support the scientific estimate of dreams.) But, on the whole, ordinary usage treats dreams above all as the blessed fulfillers of wishes. If ever we find our expectation surpassed by the event, we exclaim in our delight: "I should never have imagined such a thing even in my wildest dreams."

QUESTIONS FOR CRITICAL READING

1. Why is it important to consider dreams as related to waking mental events?
2. What do you think dreams reveal about the way your mind works? How does your view compare to Freud's?
3. How do the dreams Freud mentions seem to fulfill wishes?
4. Do your own dreams seem to be wish-fulfillment dreams? Give some examples, and see how the dreams are analyzed by others.
5. How useful is it to rely on the dreams of oneself and one's family to develop a theory of dreams? Does Freud convince you that his theory is viable?
6. Freud says, "We may expect to find the very simplest forms of dreams in *children*" (para. 9). Why do you agree or disagree with him on this point?
7. In paragraph 4 Freud mentions "dreams of convenience." What are they? Have you had such dreams?

SUGGESTIONS FOR WRITING

1. What does Freud's theory of dreams tell us about the nature of the human mind? Freud insists that dreams are important psychic events that are a product of the individual's mind and are not something impressed on the mind by outside sources. If they are mental events that need to be analyzed to be understood, what can be inferred about the mind that created them?
2. In paragraph 3 Freud mentions a dream he calls "a fulfilled fear." Examine your own dreams for a few evenings, write down a dream that fits this description, and offer your own interpretation of the dream.
3. Freud says that compared with the dreams of adults, the dreams of children seem to be "pure" wish-fulfillments. Collect some dreams from children, and analyze them. Decide whether they are as obviously wish-fulfillments as Freud's examples are.
4. Do animals dream? Freud raises this interesting question late in the discussion. Have you any evidence to suggest that animals dream? If so, write a brief essay that examines the possible content of an animal's dream. What might be the likely function of the dream in the animal's psychic life?
5. Which of your dreams do you believe is definitely not a wish-fulfillment dream? Describe it carefully, and analyze it in relation to your life. If you prove it is not a wish-fulfillment dream, what does that imply about Freud's views?
6. **CONNECTIONS** Plato's concerns in his "Allegory of the Cave" point to a level of reality that humans cannot reach because of the limitations of sensory apprehension. Is it also true that the dream world represents a level of reality that is impossible to reach because of the limitations of

the conscious, waking mind? Which part of the mind — the conscious or the unconscious — does Freud seem to regard as primary in his discussion? Is there the sense that he regards one or the other as possessing a greater "reality"? How do his views fit those of Plato?

7. **CONNECTIONS**   The mountain metaphor that Freud uses may be compared with Maimonides' concern for the proper preparation of individuals for the study of metaphysics. The dream, being a mental event, belongs to the area of metaphysics. What similarities do you see between Maimonides' intellectual method and that of Freud?

CARL JUNG
The Personal and the Collective Unconscious

CARL GUSTAV JUNG (1875 – 1961), Freud's most famous disciple, was a Swiss physician who collaborated with Freud from 1907 to 1912, when the two argued about the nature of the unconscious. Jung's *Psychology of the Unconscious* (1912) posits an unconscious that is composed of more than the ego, superego, and id. According to Jung, an additional aspect of the unconscious is a collection of archetypal images that can be inherited by members of the same group. Experience clarifies these images, but the images in turn direct experience.

In one of his essays on the collective unconscious, Jung asserts that the great myths express the archetypes of actions and heroes stored in the unconscious by elucidating them for the individual and society. These archetypes represent themselves in mythic literature in images, such as the great father or the great mother, or in patterns of action, such as disobedience and self-sacrifice. They transcend social barriers and exemplify themselves similarly in most people in any given cultural group. For Jung, the individual must adapt to the archetypes that reveal themselves in the myths in order to be psychically healthy.

Like Freud, Jung postulates a specific model of the way the mind works: he claims the existence not only of a conscious mind — which all of us can attest to from experience and common sense — but also of an unconscious component to the mind. He argues that we are unaware of the content of our unconscious mind except, perhaps, in dreams (which occur when we are unconscious),

Translated by Cary F. Baynes (London and New York, 1931), republished in *Psyche and Symbol* (New York, 1958).

which Freud and others insist speak to us in symbols rather than in direct language. Jung also acknowledges the symbolic nature of the unconscious, but disagrees with the source of the content of the unconscious mind.

In "The Personal and the Collective Unconscious" (1916), Jung describes the pattern of psychological transference that most psychoanalysts experience with their patients. In the case presented here, the patient's problems were associated with her father, and the transference was the normal one of conceiving of the doctor — in this case, Jung — in terms of the father. When this transference occurs, the patient often is cured of the problems that brought her to the psychoanalyst, but in this case the transference was incomplete. Jung offers a detailed analysis of the dreams that revealed the problems with the transference and describes the intellectual state of the woman whose dreams form the basis of the discussion. She is intelligent, conscious of the mechanism of transference, and careful about her own inner life. Yet the dream that Jung analyzes had a content that he could not relate to her personal life.

In an attempt to explain his inability to analyze the woman's dream strictly in terms of her personal life, Jung reexamines Freud's definition of the unconscious. As Jung explains Freud's view, the unconscious is a repository for material that is produced by the conscious mind and later repressed so as not to interfere with the function of the conscious mind. Thus, painful memories and unpleasant fears are often repressed and rarely become problems because they are sublimated — transformed into harmless activity, often dreams — and released. According to Freud, the material in the unconscious mind develops solely from personal experience.

Jung, however, argues that personal experiences form only part of the individual's unconscious, what he calls the "personal unconscious" (para. 17). For the patient in this essay, the images in the dream that he and the patient at first classified as a transference dream (in which the doctor became the father/lover figure) had qualities that could not be explained fully by transference. Instead, the dream seemed to represent a primordial figure, a god. From this, Jung develops the view that such a figure is cultural in nature and not personal. Nothing in the patient's life pointed to her concern for a god of the kind that developed in her dream. Jung proposes that the images that comprised the content of her dream were not a result of personal experience or education but, instead, were inherited. Jung defines this portion of the unconscious as the "collective unconscious" (para. 19).

Jung's theories proved unacceptable to Freud. After their collaboration ended, Jung studied the world's myths and mythic systems, including alchemy and occult literature. In them he saw many of the archetypal symbols that he felt were revealed in dreams — including symbolic quests, sudden transformations, dramatic or threatening landscapes, and images of God. His conclusions were that this literature, most or all of which was suppressed or rejected by modern religions such as Christianity, was a repository for the symbols of the collective unconscious — at least of western civilization and perhaps of other civilizations.

JUNG'S RHETORIC

Like Freud, Jung tells a story. His selection is a narrative beginning with a recapitulation of Freud's view of the unconscious. Jung tells us that according to the conventional view the contents of the unconscious have passed "the threshold of consciousness" (para. 2): in other words they were once in the conscious mind of the individual. However, Jung also asserts that "the unconscious contains components that have *not yet* reached the threshold of the conscious" (para. 3). At least two questions arise from this assertion: what is that content, and where did it come from?

Jung then provides the "example" (para. 5) of the woman whose therapy he was conducting. He tells us, as one would tell a story, about the woman's treatment and how such treatment works in a general sense. He explains the phenomenon of transference, claiming that "a successful transference can . . . cause the whole neurosis to disappear" (para. 5). Near the end of this patient's treatment he analyzed her dreams and found something he did not expect. He relates the narrative of the dream (para. 10), which includes the image of a superhuman father figure in a field of wheat swaying in the wind. From this he concludes that the image of the dream is not the doctor/father/lover figure that is common to transference — and that the patient was thoroughly aware of — but something of an entirely different order. He connects it to an archetype of God and proceeds to an analysis that explains the dream in terms of a collective unconscious whose content is shared by groups of people rather than created by the individual alone.

Jung's rhetorical strategy here is an argument proceeding from both example and analysis. The example is given in detail, along with enough background to make it useful to the reader. Then the example is narrated carefully, and its content is examined through a process of analysis familiar to those in psychiatry.

Some of the material in this selection is relatively challenging because Jung uses technical language and some occasionally obscure references. However, the simplicity of the technique of narrative, telling a story of what happened, makes the selection intelligible, even though it deals with highly complex and controversial ideas.

The Personal and the Collective Unconscious

In Freud's view, as most people know, the contents of the unconscious are limited to infantile tendencies which are repressed because of their incompatible character. Repression is a process that begins in early childhood under the moral influence of the environment and lasts throughout life. Through analysis the repressions are removed and the repressed wishes made conscious. 1

According to this theory, the unconscious contains only those parts of the personality which could just as well be conscious and are in fact suppressed only through upbringing. Although from one point of view the infantile tendencies of the unconscious are the most conspicuous, it would nonetheless be incorrect to define or evaluate the unconscious entirely in these terms. The unconscious has still another side to it: it includes not only repressed contents, but also all psychic material that lies below the threshold of consciousness. It is impossible to explain the subliminal nature of all this material on the principle of repression; otherwise, through the removal of repressions, a man would acquire a phenomenal memory which would thenceforth forget nothing. 2

We therefore emphatically say that in addition to the repressed material the unconscious contains all those psychic components that have fallen below the threshold, including subliminal sense perceptions. Moreover we know, from abundant experience as well as for theoretical reasons, that the unconscious also contains components that have *not yet* reached the threshold of consciousness. These are the seeds of future conscious contents. Equally we have reason to suppose that the unconscious is never at rest in the sense of being inactive, but is continually engaged in grouping and regrouping its contents. Only in pathological cases can this activity be regarded as completely autonomous; normally it is co-ordinated with the conscious mind in a compensatory relationship. 3

It is to be assumed that all these contents are personal in so far as they are acquired during the individual's life. Since this life is lim- 4 ited, the number of acquired contents in the unconscious must also be limited. This being so, it might be thought possible to empty the unconscious either by analysis or by making a complete inventory of unconscious contents, on the ground that the unconscious cannot produce anything more than is already known and accepted in the conscious mind. We should also have to infer, as already indicated, that if one could stop the descent of conscious contents into the unconscious by doing away with repression, unconscious productivity would be paralyzed. This is possible only to a very limited extent, as we know from experience. We urge our patients to hold fast to repressed contents that have been re-associated with consciousness, and to assimilate them into their plan of life. But this procedure, as we may daily convince ourselves, makes no impression on the unconscious, since it calmly continues to produce dreams and fantasies which, according to Freud's original theory, must arise from personal repressions. If in such cases we pursue our observations systematically and without prejudice, we shall find material which, although similar in form to the previous personal contents, yet seems to contain allusions that go far beyond the personal sphere.

Casting about in my mind for an example to illustrate what I   5
have just said, I have a particularly vivid memory of a woman patient with a mild hysterical neurosis which, as we expressed it in those days, had its principal cause in a "father complex." By this we wanted to denote the fact that the patient's peculiar relationship to her father stood in her way. She had been on very good terms with her father, who had since died. It was a relationship chiefly of feeling. In such cases it is usually the intellectual function that is developed, and this later becomes the bridge to the world. Accordingly our patient became a student of philosophy. Her energetic pursuit of knowledge was motivated by her need to extricate herself from the emotional entanglement with her father. This operation may succeed if her feelings can find an outlet on the new intellectual level, perhaps in the formation of an emotional tie with a suitable man, equivalent to the former tie. In this particular case, however, the transition refused to take place, because the patient's feelings remained suspended, oscillating between her father and a man who was not altogether suitable. The progress of her life was thus held up, and that inner disunity so characteristic of a neurosis promptly made its appearance. The so-called normal person would probably be able to break the emotional bond in one or the other direction by a powerful act of will, or else — and this is perhaps the more usual thing — he would come through the difficulty unconsciously, on the smooth path of instinct, without ever being aware of the sort of conflict that lay behind his headaches or other physical discomforts.

But any weakness of instinct (which may have many causes) is enough to hinder a smooth unconscious transition. Then all progress is delayed by conflict, and the resulting stasis of life is equivalent to a neurosis. In consequence of the standstill, psychic energy flows off in every conceivable direction, apparently quite uselessly. For instance, there are excessive innervations of the sympathetic system, which lead to nervous disorders of the stomach and intestines; or the vagus (and consequently the heart) is stimulated; or fantasies and memories, uninteresting enough in themselves, become overvalued and prey on the conscious mind (mountains out of molehills). In this state a new motive is needed to put an end to the morbid suspension. Nature herself paves the way for this, unconsciously and indirectly, through the phenomenon of the transference (Freud). In the course of treatment the patient transfers the father imago to the doctor, thus making him, in a sense, the father, and in the sense that he is *not* the father, also making him a substitute for the man she cannot reach. The doctor therefore becomes both a father and a kind of lover — in other words, the object of conflict. In him the opposites are united, and for this reason he stands for a quasi-ideal solution of the conflict. Without in the least wishing it, he draws upon himself an overvaluation that is almost incredible to the outsider, for to the patient he seems like a savior or a god. This way of speaking is not altogether so laughable as it sounds. It is indeed a bit much to be a father and lover at once. Nobody could possibly stand up to it in the long run, precisely because it is too much of a good thing. One would have to be a demigod at least to sustain such a role without a break, for all the time one would have to be the giver. To the patient in the state of transference, this provisional solution naturally seems ideal, but only at first; in the end she comes to a standstill that is just as bad as the neurotic conflict was. Fundamentally, nothing has yet happened that might lead to a real solution. The conflict has merely been transferred. Nevertheless a successful transference can — at least temporarily — cause the whole neurosis to disappear, and for this reason it has been very rightly recognized by Freud as a healing factor of first-rate importance, but, at the same time, as a provisional state only, for although it holds out the possibility of a cure, it is far from being the cure itself.

This somewhat lengthy discussion seemed to me essential if my example was to be understood, for my patient had arrived at the state of transference and had already reached the upper limit where the standstill begins to make itself disagreeable. The question now arose: what next? I had of course become the complete savior, and the thought of having to give me up was not only exceedingly distasteful to the patient, but positively terrifying. In such a situation "sound common sense" generally comes out with a whole repertory of admonitions: "you simply must," "you really ought," "you just cannot," etc. So far as sound common sense is, happily, not too rare and not entirely without effect (pessimists, I know, exist), a rational motive can, in the exuberant feeling of health you get from transference, release so much enthusiasm that a painful sacrifice can be risked with a mighty effort of will. If successful — and these things sometimes are — the sacrifice bears blessed fruit, and the erstwhile patient leaps at one bound into the state of being practically cured. The doctor is generally so delighted that he fails to tackle the theoretical difficulties connected with this little miracle.

If the leap does not succeed — and it did not succeed with my 7 patient — one is then faced with the problem of severing the transference. Here "psychoanalytic" theory shrouds itself in a thick darkness. Apparently we are to fall back on some nebulous trust in fate: somehow or other the matter will settle itself. "The transference stops automatically when the patient runs out of money," as a slightly cynical colleague once remarked to me. Or the ineluctable demands of life make it impossible for the patient to linger on in the transference — demands which compel the involuntary sacrifice, sometimes with a more or less complete relapse as a result. (One may look in vain for accounts of such cases in the books that sing the praises of psychoanalysis!)

To be sure, there are hopeless cases where nothing helps; but 8 there are also cases that do not get stuck and do not inevitably leave the transference situation with bitter hearts and sore heads. I told myself, at this juncture with my patient, that there must be a clear and respectable way out of the impasse. My patient had long since run out of money — if indeed she ever possessed any — but I was curious to know what means nature would devise for a satisfactory way out of the transference deadlock. Since I never imagined that I was blessed with that "sound common sense" which always knows exactly what to do in every tangled situation, and since my patient knew as little as I, I suggested to her that we could at least keep an eye open for any movements coming from a sphere of the psyche uncontaminated by our superior wisdom and our conscious plannings. That meant first and foremost her dreams.

Dreams contain images and thought associations which we do 9 not create with conscious intent. They arise spontaneously without our assistance and are representatives of a psychic activity withdrawn from our arbitrary will. Therefore the dream is, properly speaking, a highly objective, natural product of the psyche, from which we might expect indications, or at least hints, about certain basic trends in the psychic process. Now, since the psychic process, like any other life process, is not just a causal sequence, but is also a process with a teleological orientation,[1] we might expect dreams to give us certain indicia about the objective causality as well as about the objective tendencies, because they are nothing less than self-portraits of the psychic life process.

On the basis of these reflections, then, we subjected the dreams   10
to a careful examination. It would lead too far to quote word for word all the dreams that now followed. Let it suffice to sketch their main character: the majority referred to the person of the doctor, that is to say, the actors were unmistakably the dreamer herself and her doctor. The latter, however, seldom appeared in this natural shape, but was generally distorted in a remarkable way. Sometimes his figure was of supernatural size, sometimes he seemed to be extremely aged, then again he resembled her father, but was at the same time curiously woven into nature, as in the following dream: *Her father (who in reality was of small stature) was standing with her on a hill that was covered with wheat fields. She was quite tiny beside him, and he seemed to her like a giant. He lifted her up from the ground and held her in his arms like a little child. The wind swept over the wheat fields, and as the wheat swayed in the wind, he rocked her in his arms.*

From this dream and from others like it I could discern various   11
things. Above all I got the impression that her unconscious was holding unshakably to the idea of my being the father-lover, so that the fatal tie we were trying to undo appeared to be doubly strengthened. Moreover one could hardly avoid seeing that the unconscious placed a special emphasis on the supernatural, almost "divine" nature of the father-lover, thus accentuating still further the overvaluation occasioned by the transference. I therefore asked myself whether the patient had still not understood the wholly fantastic character of her transference, or whether perhaps the unconscious could never be reached by understanding at all, but must blindly and idiotically pursue some nonsensical chimera. Freud's idea that the unconscious can "do nothing but wish," Schopenhauer's[2] blind and aimless Will, the gnostic demi-urge who in his vanity deems himself perfect and then in the blindness of his limitation creates something lamentably imperfect — all these pessimistic suspicions of an essentially negative background to the world and the soul came threateningly near. And indeed there would be nothing to set against this except a well-meaning "you ought," reinforced by a

---

[1] **teleological orientation** Possessing a sense of design; directed toward an end or purpose.
[2] **Arthur Schopenhauer (1788 – 1860)** German pessimistic philosopher.

stroke of the ax that would cut down the whole phantasmagoria for good and all.

But as I turned the dreams over and over in my mind, there 12 dawned on me another possibility. I said to myself: it cannot be denied that the dreams continue to speak in the same old metaphors with which our conversations have made both doctor and patient sickeningly familiar. But the patient has an undoubted understanding of her transference fantasy. She knows that I appear to her as a semidivine father-lover, and she can, at least intellectually, distinguish this from my factual reality. Therefore the dreams are obviously reiterating the conscious standpoint minus the conscious criticism, which they completely ignore. They reiterate the conscious contents, not *in toto*, but insist on the fantastic standpoint as opposed to "sound common sense."

I naturally asked myself what was the source of this obstinacy 13 and what was its purpose? That it must have some purposive meaning I was convinced, for there is no truly living thing that does not have a final meaning, that can in other words be explained as a mere leftover from antecedent facts. But the energy of the transference is so strong that it gives one the impression of a vital instinct. That being so, what is the purpose of such fantasies? A careful examination and analysis of the dreams, especially of the one just quoted, revealed a very marked tendency — in contrast to conscious criticism, which always seeks to reduce things to human proportions — to endow the person of the doctor with superhuman attributes. He had to be gigantic, primordial, huger than the father, like the wind that sweeps over the earth — was he then to be made into a god? Or, I said to myself, was it rather the case that the unconscious was trying to *create* a god out of the person of the doctor, as it were to free a vision of God from the veils of the personal, so that the transference to the person of the doctor was no more than a misunderstanding on the part of the conscious mind, a stupid trick played by "sound common sense"? Was the urge of the unconscious perhaps only apparently reaching out towards the person, but in a deeper sense towards a god? Could the longing for a god be a *passion* welling up from our darkest, instinctual nature, a passion unswayed by any outside influences, deeper and stronger perhaps than the love for a human person? Or was it perhaps the highest and truest meaning of that inappropriate love we call transference, a little bit of real *Gottesminne*,[3] that has been lost to consciousness ever since the fifteenth century?

---

[3] **Gottesminne** Love of God.

No one will doubt the reality of a passionate longing for a   14
human person; but that a fragment of religious psychology, an historical anachronism, indeed something of a medieval curiosity — we
are reminded of Mechtild of Magdeburg[4] — should come to light as
an immediate living reality in the middle of the consulting room,
and be expressed in the prosaic figure of the doctor, seems almost
too fantastic to be taken seriously.

A genuinely scientific attitude must be unprejudiced. The sole   15
criterion for the validity of an hypothesis is whether or not it possesses an heuristic — i.e., explanatory — value. The question now is,
can we regard the possibilities set forth above as a valid hypothesis?
There is no a priori[5] reason why it should not be just as possible that
the unconscious tendencies have a goal beyond the human person,
as that the unconscious can "do nothing but wish." Experience alone
can decide which is the more suitable hypothesis.

This new hypothesis was not entirely plausible to my very criti-   16
cal patient. The earlier view that I was the father-lover, and as such
presented an ideal solution of the conflict, was incomparably more
attractive to her way of feeling. Nevertheless her intellect was sufficiently clear to appreciate the theoretical possibility of the new hypothesis. Meanwhile the dreams continued to disintegrate the person of the doctor and swell them to ever vaster proportions.
Concurrently with this there now occurred something which at first
I alone perceived, and with the utmost astonishment, namely a kind
of subterranean undermining of the transference. Her relations with
a certain friend deepened perceptibly, notwithstanding the fact that
consciously she still clung to the transference. So that when the time
came for leaving me, it was no catastrophe, but a perfectly reasonable parting. I had the privilege of being the only witness during the
process of severance. I saw how the transpersonal control point developed — I cannot call it anything else — a *guiding function* and step
by step gathered to itself all the former personal overvaluations;
how, with this afflux of energy, it gained influence over the resisting
conscious mind without the patient's consciously noticing what was
happening. From this I realized that the dreams were not just fantasies, but self-representations of unconscious developments which
allowed the psyche of the patient gradually to grow out of the pointless personal tie.

---

[4] **Mechtild of Magdeburg** Thirteenth-century German mystic, writer, and
saint.

[5] **a priori** Based on theory rather than on experiment or evidence.

This change took place, as I showed, through the unconscious   17
development of a transpersonal control point; a virtual goal, as it
were, that expressed itself symbolically in a form which can only be
described as a vision of God. The dreams swelled the human person
of the doctor to superhuman proportions, making him a gigantic
primordial father who is at the same time the wind, and in whose
protecting arms the dreamer rests like an infant. If we try to make
the patient's conscious, and traditionally Christian, idea of God responsible for the divine image in the dreams, we would still have to
lay stress on the distortion. In religious matters the patient had a
critical and agnostic attitude, and her idea of a possible deity had
long since passed into the realm of the inconceivable, i.e., had dwindled into a complete abstraction. In contrast to this, the god-image
of the dreams corresponded to the archaic conception of a nature
demon, something like Wotan.[6] *Theos to pneûma,* "God is spirit," is
here translated back into its original form where *pneûma* means
"wind": God is the wind, stronger and mightier than man, an invisible breath-spirit. As in the Hebrew ruach, so in Arabic *ruh* means
breath and spirit. Out of the purely personal form the dreams developed an archaic god-image that is infinitely far from the conscious
idea of God. It might be objected that this is simply an infantile
image, a childhood memory. I would have no quarrel with this assumption if we were dealing with an old man sitting on a golden
throne in heaven. But there is no trace of any sentimentality of that
kind; instead, we have a primitive conception that can correspond
only to an archaic mentality. These primitive conceptions, of which
I have given a large number of examples in my *Symbols of Transformation,* tempt one to make, in regard to unconscious material, a distinction very different from that between "preconscious" and "unconscious" or "subconscious" and "unconscious." The justification
for these distinctions need not be discussed here. They have a definite value and are worth refining further as points of view. The fundamental distinction which experience has forced upon me merely
claims the value of a further point of view. From what has been said
it is clear that we have to distinguish in the unconscious a layer
which we may call the *personal unconscious.* The materials contained
in this layer are of a personal nature in so far as they have the character partly of acquisitions derived from the individual's life and
partly of psychological factors which could just as well be conscious.
It is readily understandable that incompatible psychological ele-

---

[6] **Wotan** Supreme God; character in Richard Wagner's *Ring* cycle of operas.

ments are liable to repression and therefore become unconscious; but on the other hand we also have the possibility of making and keeping the repressed contents conscious, once they have been recognized. We recognize them as personal contents because we can discover their effects, or their partial manifestation, or their specific origin in our personal past. They are the integral components of the personality, they belong to its inventory, and their loss to consciousness produces an inferiority in one or the other respect — an inferiority, moreover, that has the psychological character not so much of an organic mutilation or an inborn defect as of a want which gives rise to a feeling of moral resentment. The sense of moral inferiority always indicates that the missing element is something which, one feels, should not be missing, or which could be made conscious if only one took enough trouble. The feeling of moral inferiority does not come from a collision with the generally accepted and, in a sense, arbitrary moral law, but from the conflict with one's own self which, for reasons of psychic equilibrium, demands that the deficit be redressed. Whenever a sense of moral inferiority appears, it shows that there is not only the demand to assimilate an unconscious component, but also the possibility of assimilating it. In the last resort it is a man's moral qualities which force him, either through direct recognition of the necessity to do so, or indirectly through a painful neurosis, to assimilate his unconscious self and to keep himself fully conscious. Whoever progresses along this road of realizing the unconscious self must inevitably bring into consciousness the contents of the personal unconscious, thus widening the scope of his personality. I should add at once that this "widening" primarily concerns the moral consciousness, one's self-knowledge, for the unconscious contents that are released and brought into consciousness by analysis are usually unpleasant — which is precisely why these wishes, memories, tendencies, plans, etc., were repressed. These are the contents that are brought to light in much the same way by a thorough confession, though to a much more limited extent. The rest comes out as a rule in dream analysis. It is often very interesting to watch how the dreams fetch up the essential points, bit by bit and with the nicest choice. The total material that is added to consciousness causes a considerable widening of the horizon, a deepened self-knowledge which, more than anything else, is calculated to humanize a man and make him modest. But even self-knowledge, assumed by all wise men to be the best and most efficacious, has different effects on different characters. We make very remarkable discoveries in this respect in practical analysis, but I shall deal with this question in the next chapter.

As my example of the archaic idea of God shows, the uncon-   18
scious seems to contain other things besides personal acquisitions
and belongings. My patient was quite unconscious of the derivation
of "spirit" from "wind," or of the parallelism between the two. This
content was not the product of her thinking, nor had she ever been
taught it. The critical passage in the New Testament was inaccessible
to her — *to pneûma pneî hopou thelei* — since she knew no Greek. If
we must take it as a wholly personal acquisition, it might be a case
of so-called cryptomnesia,[7] the unconscious recollection of a
thought which the dreamer had once read somewhere. I have nothing against such a possibility in this particular case; but I have seen a
sufficient number of other cases — many of them are to be found in
the book mentioned above — where cryptomnesia can be excluded
with certainty. Even if it were a case of cryptomnesia, which seems
to me very improbable, we should still have to explain what the pre-
disposition was that caused just this image to be retained and later,
as Semon puts it, "ecphorated" (*ekphoreîn,* Latin *efferre,* "to produce"). In any case, cryptomnesia or no cryptomnesia, we are dealing with a genuine and thoroughly primitive god image that grew
up in the unconscious of a civilized person and produced a living effect — an effect which might well give the psychologist of religion
food for reflection. There is nothing about this image that could be
called personal: it is a wholly collective image, the ethnic origin of
which has long been known to us. Here is an historical image of
world-wide distribution that has come into existence again through
a natural psychic function. This is not so very surprising, since my
patient was born into the world with a human brain which presumably still functions today much as it did of old. We are dealing with
a reactivated archetype, as I have elsewhere called these primordial
images. These ancient images are restored to life by the primitive,
analogical mode of thinking peculiar to dreams. It is not a question
of inherited ideas, but of inherited thought patterns.

In view of these facts we must assume that the unconscious con-   19
tains not only personal, but also impersonal, collective components
in the form of inherited categories or archetypes. I have therefore
advanced the hypothesis that at its deeper levels the unconscious
possesses collective contents in a relatively active state. That is why I
speak of the collective unconscious.

---

[7] Cf. Théodore Flournoy, *Des Indes à la planète Mars: Étude sur un cas de som-
nambulisme avec glossolalie* (Paris and Geneva, 1900; trans. by D. B. Vermilye as *From
India to the Planet Mars,* New York, 1900), and Jung, "Psychology and Pathology of
So-called Occult Phenomena," *Coll. Works,* Vol. 1, pp. 81ff. [Jung's note]

QUESTIONS FOR CRITICAL READING

1. What is Jung's view of the relationship of the unconscious mind to the conscious mind? How does it compare to Freud's?
2. What is repression? Why does repression work as it does?
3. How does transference work in psychoanalytic treatment? Is it a good thing or not?
4. What is unusual about Jung's patient's dream? What about it can he not fit into a normal pattern of transference?
5. What is the distinction between the personal unconscious and the collective unconscious?
6. Do you agree that "Dreams contain images and thought associations which we do not create with conscious intent" (para. 9)? Why or why not?

SUGGESTIONS FOR WRITING

1. Jung talks about common sense and its limitations. For some people, common sense denies the existence of an unconscious mind. Relying on Jung, your own personal experiences, and any other sources you choose, defend the existence of an unconscious mind. At the same time, do your best to explain the content of the unconscious and why it is important to the individual.
2. With reference to your own dreams, argue for or against the belief that dreams are products of the conscious mind. Have you had dreams whose content did not pass the "threshold" of your conscious mind?
3. Although the adult Jung was not religious, as the son of a Swiss pastor he was well acquainted with religion. In paragraph 13, Jung asserts that his patient's dream reveals a fundamental human longing for God. As he puts it, "Could the longing for a god be a *passion* welling up from our darkest, instinctual nature?" Examine the possibility that such a psychological phenomenon has affected your attitude toward religion and religious belief.
4. Jung suggests that mythic literature maintains some of the images that make up the collective unconscious of a group of people. Select a myth (consult Ovid's *Metamorphosis,* Grimm's fairy tales, or the Greek myths, or choose a pattern of mythic behavior repeated in popular films), and analyze the instinctual longing it represents for us. What does the myth reveal about our culture?
5. **CONNECTIONS** Maimonides says a great deal about simile and metaphor and their value in communicating difficult truths. To what extent do dreams use simile and metaphor to communicate with the conscious mind? What are the primary ways by which the unconscious mind communicates with the conscious mind?

KAREN HORNEY
The Distrust Between the Sexes

KAREN HORNEY (1885 – 1952) was a distinguished psychiatrist who developed her career somewhat independently of the influence of Sigmund Freud. In her native Germany, she taught in the Berlin Psychoanalytic Institute from the end of World War I until 1932, a year before Hitler came to power. She was influenced by Freud's work — as was every other psychoanalyst — but she found that, although brilliant, it did not satisfactorily explain important issues in female sexuality.

In Germany, Horney's early research was centered on questions about female psychology. This selection, first published in German in 1931, is part of these early studies. Horney's conclusion was that penis envy, like many other feminine psychological issues, was determined by cultural factors and that these issues were not purely psychological or libidinal in origin. She thought Freud oversimplified female sexuality and that the truth, demonstrated through her own analysis, was vastly different. She began a significant theoretical shift that saw neurosis as a product of both psychological and cultural conflicts rather than of psychological stress alone.

In 1932, Horney emigrated to America, where she began writing a distinguished series of publications on neurosis. Her career in Chicago was remarkable. Not only did she found the American Institute for Psychoanalysis (1941) and the *American Journal of Psychoanalysis,* she also wrote such important books as *The Neurotic Personality of Our Time* (1937), *New Ways in Psychoanalysis* (1939), and *Self-Analysis* (1942). Her work was rooted in cultural studies, and one of her principal arguments was that neuroses, including sexual problems, are caused by cultural influences and pressures that the individual simply cannot deal with. Freud thought the reverse, placing the causal force of neuroses in sexuality.

From *Feminine Psychology* (1967).

Her studies constantly brought her back to the question of interpersonal relations, and she saw neurotic patterns developed in childhood as the main cause of many failed relationships. The selection focuses particularly on the relationship that individuals establish with their mother or their father. Her insistence that childhood patterns affect adult behavior is consonant with Freudianism; however, her interpretations of those patterns are somewhat different. Like Jung, she looks toward anthropological studies of tribal behavior for help in interpreting the behavior of modern people.

Horney claims that the distrust between the sexes cannot be explained away as existing only in individuals but is a widespread phenomenon that arises out of psychological forces present in men and women. She discusses a number of cultural practices in primitive peoples in an effort to suggest that even without modern cultural trappings, the two sexes suffer anxieties in their relationships. She also looks at the individual in a family setting, showing that normal expectations of child-parent relations can sometimes be frustrated, with seriously harmful results.

In addition, she examines the nature of culture, reminding us that early societies were often matriarchal — that is, centered not on men and their activities but on women. Her views about matriarchy, that the mystery of a woman is connected to her biologically creative nature, are quite suggestive in psychological terms. The envy as she sees it is on the part of men, who compensate for their inability to create life by spending their energies creating "state, religion, art, and science" (para. 14).

Horney speaks directly about sexual matters and about what she sees as male anxieties. She holds that there are distinct areas of conflict between men and women and that they are psychological in origin.

HORNEY'S RHETORIC

This is an expository essay, establishing the truth of hypothesis by pointing to a range of evidence from a variety of sources. Horney's view is that the distrust between the sexes is the result of cultural forces of which the individual is only dimly aware. In this sense, she aligns herself with the Freudians, who constantly point to influences on the individual that are subconscious in nature and, therefore, not part of the individual's self-awareness.

In a sense, her essay is itself an analysis of the relationship between men and women, with a look back at the history of culture.

Her technique — a review of older societies — establishes that the current nature of the relationship between men and women is colored by the fact that most modern societies are dominated by patriarchal institutions. In ancient times, however, societies may well have been matriarchal.

This selection was originally delivered as a lecture to the German Women's Medical Association in November 1930, and most of the audience was female. Consequently, the nature of the imagery, the frankness of the discourse, and the cultural focus concern issues that would have a distinct impact on women. On reading this essay, it becomes clear that Karen Horney is speaking with a particular directness that she might have modified for a mixed audience.

Her method of writing is analytical, as she says several times. She is searching for causes within the culture as well as within the individual. Her range of causal analysis includes the comparative study of cultures (ethnology) as well as personal psychology. Her capacity to call on earlier writers and cultures reveals her enormous scope of knowledge and also helps convince the reader of the seriousness of her inquiry.

The Distrust Between the Sexes

As I begin to talk to you today about some problems in the relationship between the sexes, I must ask you not to be disappointed. I will not concern myself primarily with the aspect of the problem that is most important to the physician. Only at the end will I briefly deal with the question of therapy. I am far more concerned with pointing out to you several psychological reasons for the distrust between the sexes.

The relationship between men and women is quite similar to that between children and parents, in that we prefer to focus on the positive aspects of these relationships. We prefer to assume that love is the fundamentally given factor and that hostility is an accidental and avoidable occurrence. Although we are familiar with slogans such as "the battle of the sexes" and "hostility between the sexes," we must admit that they do not mean a great deal. They make us overfocus on sexual relations between men and women, which can very easily lead us to a too one-sided view. Actually, from our recollection of numerous case histories, we may conclude that love relationships are quite easily destroyed by overt or covert hostility. On the other hand we are only too ready to blame such difficulties on individual misfortune, on incompatibility of the partners, and on social or economic causes.

The individual factors, which we find causing poor relations between men and women, may be the pertinent ones. However, because of the great frequency, or better, the regular occurrence of disturbances in love relations, we have to ask ourselves whether the disturbances in the individual cases might not arise from a common background; whether there are common denominators for this easily and frequently arising suspiciousness between the sexes?   3

It is almost impossible to attempt within the framework of a brief lecture to give you a complete survey of so large a field. I therefore will not even mention such factors as the origin and effects of such social institutions as marriage. I merely intend to select at random some of the factors that are psychologically understandable and pertain to the causes and effects of the hostility and tension between the sexes.   4

I would like to start with something very commonplace — namely, that a good deal of this atmosphere of suspiciousness is understandable and even justifiable. It apparently has nothing to do with the individual partner, but rather with the intensity of the affects[1] and with the difficulty of taming them.   5

We know or may dimly sense, that these affects can lead to ecstasy, to being beside oneself, to surrendering oneself, which means a leap into the unlimited and the boundless. This is perhaps why real passion is so rare. For like a good businessman, we are loath to put all our eggs in one basket. We are inclined to be reserved and ever ready to retreat. Be that as it may, because of our instinct for self preservation, we all have a natural fear of losing ourselves in another person. That is why what happens to love, happens to education and psychoanalysis; everybody thinks he knows all about them, but few do. One is inclined to overlook how little one gives of oneself, but one feels all the more this same deficiency in the partner, the feeling of "You never really loved me." A wife who harbors suicidal thoughts because her husband does not give her all his love, time, and interest, will not notice how much of her own hostility, hidden vindictiveness, and aggression are expressed through her attitude. She will feel only despair because of her abundant "love," while at the same time she will feel most intensely and see most clearly the lack of love in her partner. Even Strindberg[2] [who was a   6

---

[1] **affects** Feelings, emotions, or passions.
[2] **August Strindberg** (1849 – 1912) A Swedish playwright and novelist whose dark portraits of women were influenced by his misogyny (hatred of women).

misogynist] defensively managed to say on occasion that he was no woman hater, but that women hated and tortured him.

Here we are not dealing with pathological phenomena at all. In pathological cases we merely see a distortion and exaggeration of a general and normal occurrence. Anybody, to a certain extent, will be inclined to overlook his own hostile impulses, but under pressure of his own guilty conscience, may project them onto the partner. This process must, of necessity, cause some overt or covert distrust of the partner's love, fidelity, sincerity, or kindness. This is the reason why I prefer to speak of distrust between the sexes and not of hatred; for in keeping with our own experience we are more familiar with the feeling of distrust.

A further, almost unavoidable, source of disappointment and distrust in our normal love life derives from the fact that the very intensity of our feelings of love stirs up all of our secret expectations and longings for happiness, which slumber deep inside us. All our unconscious wishes, contradictory in their nature and expanding boundlessly on all sides, are waiting here for their fulfillment. The partner is supposed to be strong, and at the same time helpless, to dominate us and be dominated by us, to be ascetic and to be sensuous. He should rape us and be tender, have time for us exclusively and also be intensely involved in creative work. As long as we assume that he could actually fulfill all these expectations, we invest him with the glitter of sexual overestimation. We take the magnitude of such overvaluation for the measure of our love, while in reality it merely expresses the magnitude of our expectations. The very nature of our claims makes their fulfillment impossible. Herein lies the origin of the disappointments with which we may cope in a more or less effective way. Under favorable circumstances we do not even have to become aware of the great number of our disappointments, just as we have not been aware of the extent of our secret expectations. Yet there remain traces of distrust in us, as in a child who discovers that his father cannot get him the stars from the sky after all.

Thus far, our reflections certainly have been neither new nor specifically analytical and have often been better formulated in the past. The analytical approach begins with the question: What special factors in human development lead to the discrepancy between expectations and fulfillment and what causes them to be of special significance in particular cases? Let us start with a general consideration. There is a basic difference between human and animal development — namely, the long period of the infant's helplessness and dependency. The paradise of childhood is most often an illusion with which adults like to deceive themselves. For the child, however, this paradise is inhabited by too many dangerous monsters. Unpleasant experiences with the opposite sex seem to be unavoidable. We need only recall the capacity that children possess, even in their very early years, for passionate and instinctive sexual desires similar to those of adults and yet different from them. Children are different in the aims of their drives, but above all, in the pristine integrity of their demands. They find it hard to express their desires directly, and where they do, they are not taken seriously. Their seriousness sometimes is looked upon as being cute, or it may be overlooked or rejected. In short, children will undergo painful and humiliating experiences of being rebuffed, being betrayed, and being told lies. They also may have to take second place to a parent or a sibling, and they are threatened and intimidated when they seek, in playing with their own bodies, those pleasures that are denied them by adults. The child is relatively powerless in the face of all this. He is not able to ventilate his fury at all, or only to a minor degree, nor can he come to grips with the experience by means of intellectual comprehension. Thus, anger and aggression are pent up within him in the form of extravagant fantasies, which hardly reach the daylight of awareness, fantasies that are criminal when viewed from the standpoint of the adult, fantasies that range from taking by force and stealing, to those about killing, burning, cutting to pieces, and choking. Since the child is vaguely aware of these destructive forces within him, he feels, according to the talion law,[3] equally threatened by the adults. Here is the origin of those infantile anxieties of which no child remains entirely free. This already enables us to understand better the fear of love of which I have spoke before. Just here, in this most irrational of all areas, the old childhood fears of a threatening father or mother are reawakened, putting us instinctively on the defensive. In other words, the fear of love will always be mixed with the fear of what we might do to the other person, or what the other person might do to us. A lover in the Aru Islands,[4] for example, will never make a gift of a lock of hair to his beloved, because should an argument arise, the beloved might burn it, thus causing the partner to get sick.

I would like to sketch briefly how childhood conflicts may affect   10
the relationship to the opposite sex in later life. Let us take as an example a typical situation: The little girl who was badly hurt through some great disappointment by her father, will transform her innate

---

[3] **talion law** Law that demands that the criminal be given the same punishment as was suffered by the victim — an eye for an eye.

[4] **Aru Islands** Islands in Indonesia that were especially interesting for modern anthropologists.

instinctual wish to receive from the man, into a vindictive one of taking from him by force. Thus the foundation is laid for a direct line of development to a later attitude, according to which she will not only deny her maternal instincts, but will have only one drive, i.e., to harm the male, to exploit him, and to suck him dry. She has become a vampire. Let us assume that there is a similar transformation from the wish to receive to the wish to take away. Let us further assume that the latter wish was repressed due to anxiety from a guilty conscience; then we have here the fundamental constellation for the formation of a certain type of woman who is unable to relate to the male because she fears that every male will suspect her of wanting something from him. This really means that she is afraid that he might guess her repressed desires. Or by completely projecting onto him her repressed wishes, she will imagine that every male merely intends to exploit her, that he wants from her only sexual satisfaction, after which he will discard her. Or let us assume that a reaction formation of excessive modesty will mask the repressed drive for power. We then have the type of woman who shies away from demanding or accepting anything from her husband. Such a woman, however, due to the return of the repressed, will react with depression to the nonfulfillment of her unexpressed, and often unformulated, wishes. She thus unwittingly jumps from the frying pan into the fire, as does her partner, because a depression will hit him much harder than direct aggression. Quite often the repression of aggression against the male drains all her vital energy. The woman then feels helpless to meet life. She will shift the entire responsibility for her helplessness onto the man, robbing him of the very breath of life. Here you have the type of woman who, under the guise of being helpless and childlike, dominates her man.

These are examples that demonstrate how the fundamental attitude of women toward men can be disturbed by childhood conflicts. In an attempt to simplify matters, I have stressed only one point, which, however, seems crucial to me — the disturbance in the development of motherhood. 11

I shall now proceed to trace certain traits of male psychology. I do not wish to follow individual lines of development, though it might be very instructive to observe analytically how, for instance, even men who consciously have a very positive relationship with women and hold them in high esteem as human beings, harbor deep within themselves a secret distrust of them; and how this distrust relates back to feelings toward their mothers, which they experienced in their formative years. I shall focus rather on certain typical attitudes of men toward women and how they have appeared during various eras of history and in different cultures, not only as 12 regards sexual relationships with women, but also, and often more so, in nonsexual situations, such as in their general evaluation of women.

I shall select some random examples, starting with Adam and Eve. Jewish culture, as recorded in the Old Testament, is outspokenly patriarchal. This fact reflects itself in their religion, which has no maternal goddesses; in their morals and customs, which allow the husband the right to dissolve the marital bond simply by dismissing his wife. Only by being aware of this background can we recognize the male bias in two incidents of Adam's and Eve's history. First of all, woman's capacity to give birth is partly denied and partly devaluated: Eve was made of Adam's rib and a curse was put on her to bear children in sorrow. In the second place, by interpreting her tempting Adam to eat of the tree of knowledge as a sexual temptation, woman appears as the sexual temptress, who plunges man into misery. I believe that these two elements, one born out of resentment, the other out of anxiety, have damaged the relationship between the sexes from the earliest times to the present. Let us follow this up briefly. Man's fear of woman is deeply rooted in sex, as is shown by the simple fact that it is only the sexually attractive woman of whom he is afraid and who, although he strongly desires her, has to be kept in bondage. Old women, on the other hand, are held in high esteem, even by cultures in which the young woman is dreaded and therefore suppressed. In some primitive cultures the old woman may have the decisive voice in the affairs of the tribe; among Asian nations also she enjoys great power and prestige. On the other hand, in primitive tribes woman is surrounded by taboos during the entire period of her sexual maturity. Women of the Arunta tribe are able to magically influence the male genitals. If they sing to a blade of grass and then point it at a man or throw it at him, he becomes ill or loses his genitals altogether. Women lure him to his doom. In a certain East African tribe, husband and wife do not sleep together, because her breath might weaken him. If a woman of a South African tribe climbs over the leg of a sleeping man, he will be unable to run; hence the general rule of sexual abstinence two to five days prior to hunting, warfare, or fishing. Even greater is the fear of menstruation, pregnancy, and childbirth. Menstruating women are surrounded by extensive taboos — a man who touches a menstruating woman will die. There is one basic thought at the bottom of all this: Woman is a mysterious being who communicates with spirits and thus has magic powers that she can use to hurt the male. He must therefore protect himself against her powers by keeping her subjugated. Thus the Miri in Bengal do not permit their women to eat the flesh of the tiger, lest they become too strong. The

13

Watawela of East Africa keep the art of making fire a secret from their women, lest women become their rulers. The Indians of California have ceremonies to keep their women in submission; a man is disguised as a devil to intimidate the women. The Arabs of mecca exclude women from religious festivities to prevent familiarity between women and their overlords. We find similar customs during the Middle Ages — the Cult of the Virgin[5] side by side with the burning of witches; the adoration of "pure" motherliness, completely divested of sexuality, next to the cruel destruction of the sexually seductive woman. Here again is the implication of underlying anxiety, for the witch is in communication with the devil. Nowadays, with our more humane forms of aggression, we burn women only figuratively, sometimes with undisguised hatred, sometimes with apparent friendliness. In any case "The Jew must burn."[6] In friendly and secret autos-da-fé,[7] many nice things are said about women, but it is just unfortunate that in her God-given natural state, she is not the equal of the male. Möbius[8] pointed out that the female brain weighs less than the male one, but the point need not be made in so crude a way. On the contrary, it can be stressed that woman is not at all inferior, only different, but that unfortunately she has fewer or none of those human or cultural qualities that man holds in such high esteem. She is said to be deeply rooted in the personal and emotional spheres, which is wonderful; but unfortunately, this makes her incapable of exercising justice and objectivity, therefore disqualifying her for positions in law and government and in the spiritual community. She is said to be at home only in the realm of eros. Spiritual matters are alien to her innermost being, and she is at odds with cultural trends. She therefore is, as Asians frankly state, a second-rate

---

[5] **Cult of the Virgin** During the Medieval period (c. 700 – 1300), the Roman Catholic Church promoted a strong emotional attachment to the Virgin Mary, which resulted in the production of innumerable paintings and sculptures. Horney points out the irony of venerating the mother of God while tormenting human women by burning them at the stake.

[6] **"The Jew must burn."** This is a quote from *Nathan the Wise* by the eighteenth-century German author Gotthold Ephraim Lessing, a humanist and a spokesman for enlightenment and rationality. The expression became a colloquialism. It meant no matter how worthy and well-intentioned his acts, by virtue of being a Jew, a man was guilty. [Translator's note]

[7] **autos-da-fé** Literally, acts of faith. It was a term used to refer to the hearing at which the Holy Inquisition gave its judgment on a case of heresy, and its most common use is to refer to the burning of heretics at the stake.

[8] **Paul Julius Möbius** (1853 – 1907) German neurologist and student of the pathological traits of geniuses such as Rousseau, Goethe, Schopenhauer, and Nietzsche.

being. Woman may be industrious and useful but is, alas, incapable of productive and independent work. She is, indeed, prevented from real accomplishment by the deplorable, bloody tragedies of menstruation and childbirth. And so every man silently thanks his God, just as the pious Jew does in his prayers, that he was not created a woman.

Man's attitude toward motherhood is a large and complicated   14 chapter. One is generally inclined to see no problem in this area. Even the misogynist is obviously willing to respect woman as a mother and to venerate her motherliness under certain conditions, as mentioned above regarding the Cult of the Virgin. In order to obtain a clearer picture, we have to distinguish between two attitudes: men's attitudes toward motherliness, as represented in its purest form in the Cult of the Virgin, and their attitude toward motherhood as such, as we encounter it in the symbolism of the ancient mother goddesses. Males will always be in favor of motherliness, as expressed in certain spiritual qualities of women, i.e., the nurturing, selfless, self-sacrificing mother; for she is the ideal embodiment of the woman who could fulfill all his expectations and longings. In the ancient mother goddesses, man did not venerate motherliness in the spiritual sense, but rather motherhood in its most elemental meaning. Mother goddesses are earthy goddesses, fertile like the soil. They bring forth new life and they nurture it. It was this life-creating power of woman, an elemental force, that filled man with admiration. And this is exactly the point where problems arise. For it is contrary to human nature to sustain appreciation without resentment toward capabilities that one does not possess. Thus, a man's minute share in creating new life became, for him, an immense incitement to create something new on his part. He has created values of which he might well be proud. State, religion, art, and science are essentially his creations, and our entire culture bears the masculine imprint.

However, as happens elsewhere, so it does here; even the great-   15 est satisfactions or achievements, if born out of sublimation, cannot fully make up for something for which we are not endowed by nature. Thus there has remained an obvious residue of general resentment of men against women. This resentment expresses itself, also in our times, in men's distrustful defensive maneuvers against the threat of women's invasion of their domains; hence their tendency to devalue pregnancy and childbirth and to overemphasize male genitality. This attitude does not express itself in scientific theories alone, but is also of far-reaching consequence for the entire relationship between the sexes, and for sexual morality in general. Motherhood, especially illegitimate motherhood, is very insufficiently protected by laws — with the one exception of a recent attempt at improvement in Russia. Conversely, there is ample opportunity for the fulfillment of the male's sexual needs. Emphasis on irresponsible sexual indulgence, and devaluation of women to an object of purely physical needs, are further consequences of this masculine attitude.

From Bachofen's[9] investigations we know that this state of the cultural supremacy of the male has not existed since the beginning of time, but that women once occupied a central position. This was the era of the so-called matriarchy, when law and custom were centered around the mother. Matricide was then, as Sophocles[10] showed in the *Eumenides,* the unforgivable crime, while patricide, by comparison, was a minor offense. Only in recorded historical times have men begun, with minor variations, to play the leading role in the political, economical, and judicial fields, as well as in the area of sexual morality. At present we seem to be going through a period of struggle in which women once more dare to fight for their equality. This is a phase, the duration of which we are not yet able to survey.   16

I do not want to be misunderstood as having implied that all disaster results from male supremacy and that relations between the sexes would improve if women were given the ascendancy. However, we must ask ourselves why there should have to be any power struggle at all between the sexes. At any given time, the more powerful side will create an ideology suitable to help maintain its position and to make this position acceptable to the weaker one. In this ideology the differentness of the weaker one will be interpreted as inferiority, and it will be proven that these differences are unchangeable, basic, or God's will. It is the function of such an ideology to deny or conceal the existence of a struggle. Here is one of the answers to the question raised initially as to why we have so little awareness of the fact that there is a struggle between the sexes. It is in the interest of men to obscure this fact; and the emphasis they place on their ideologies has caused women, also, to adopt these theories. Our attempt at resolving these rationalizations and at examining these ideologies as to their fundamental driving forces, is merely a step on the road taken by Freud.[11]   17

---

[9] **J. J. Bachofen (1815 – 1887)** One of the earliest German ethnologists who proposed, in 1861, that a pattern of matriarchy — in which the female was the dominant figure in society — had existed in the earliest societies.

[10] **Sophocles (496? – 406 B.C.)** A great Greek tragedian. However, Horney is probably referring to Aeschylus (525 – 456 B.C.), who wrote the *Eumenides,* the play she mentions.

[11] **Sigmund Freud (1856 – 1939)** See the introduction to his selection in this part.

I believe that my exposition shows more clearly the origin of re- 18
sentment than the origin of dread, and I therefore want to discuss
briefly the latter problem. We have seen that the male's dread of the
female is directed against her as a sexual being. How is this to be understood? The clearest aspect of this dread is revealed by the Arunta
tribe. They believe that the woman has the power to magically influence the male genital. This is what we mean by castration anxiety in
analysis. It is an anxiety of psychogenic origin that goes back to feelings of guilt and old childhood fears. Its anatomical-psychological
nucleus lies in the fact that during intercourse the male has to en-
trust his genitals to the female body, that he presents her with his
semen and interprets this as a surrender of vital strength to the
woman, similar to his experiencing the subsiding of erection after
intercourse as evidence of having been weakened by the woman. Although the following idea has not been thoroughly worked through
yet, it is highly probable, according to analytical and ethnological
data, that the relationship to the mother is more strongly and directly associated with the fear of death than the relationship to the
father. We have learned to understand the longing for death as the
longing for reunion with the mother. In African fairy tales it is a
woman who brings death into the world. The great mother goddesses also brought death and destruction. It is as though we were
possessed by the idea that the one who gives life is also capable of
taking it away. There is a third aspect of the male's dread of the female that is more difficult to understand and to prove, but that can
be demonstrated by observing certain recurrent phenomena in the
animal world. We can see that the male is quite frequently equipped
with certain specific stimulants for attracting the female, or with
specific devices for seizing her during sexual union. Such arrangements would be incomprehensible if the female animal possessed
equally urgent or abundant sexual needs as does the male. As a matter of fact, we see that the female rejects the male unconditionally,
after fertilization has occurred. Although examples taken from the
animal world may be applied to human beings only with the greatest of caution, it is permissible, in this context, to raise the following
question: Is it possible that the male is sexually dependent on the female to a higher degree than the woman is on him, because in
women part of the sexual energy is linked to generative processes?
Could it be that men, therefore, have a vital interest in keeping
women dependent on them? So much for the factors that seem to be
at the root of the great power struggle between men and women, insofar as they are of a psychogenic nature and related to the male.

That many-faceted thing called love succeeds in building 19
bridges from the loneliness on this shore to the loneliness on the

other one. These bridges can be of great beauty, but they are rarely built for eternity and frequently they cannot tolerate too heavy a burden without collapsing. Here is the other answer to the question posed initially of why we see love between the sexes more distinctly than we see hate — because the union of the sexes offers us the greatest possibilities for happiness. We therefore are naturally inclined to overlook how powerful are the destructive forces that continually work to destroy our chances for happiness.

We might ask in conclusion, how can analytical insights contribute to diminish the distrust between the sexes? There is no uniform answer to this problem. The fear of the power of the affects and the difficulty in controlling them in a love relationship, the resulting conflict between surrender and self-preservation, between the I and the Thou[12] is an entirely comprehensible, unmitigatable, and as it were, normal phenomenon. The same thing applies in essence to our readiness for distrust, which stems from unresolved childhood conflicts. These childhood conflicts, however, can vary greatly in intensity, and will leave behind traces of variable depth. Analysis not only can help in individual cases to improve the relationship with the opposite sex, but it can also attempt to improve the psychological conditions of childhood and forestall excessive conflicts. This, of course, is our hope for the future. In the momentous struggle for power, analysis can fulfill an important function by uncovering the real motives of this struggle. This uncovering will not eliminate the motives, but it may help to create a better chance for fighting the struggle on its own ground instead of relegating it to peripheral issues.

20

---

[12] **the I and the Thou** A reference to Martin Buber's book *I and Thou* (see page 661). Buber (1878 – 1965), a Jewish theologian and philosopher, is associated with modern existentialism.

QUESTIONS FOR CRITICAL READING

1. Do you agree that there is hostility between the sexes? What evidence can you cite?
2. What are some of the most important childhood experiences that can affect adult behavior toward the opposite sex?
3. This selection was originally a lecture delivered in Germany in 1930. To what extent are its concerns no longer relevant? To what extent are they still relevant?
4. Do you think this essay could promote better relations between men and women?

5. What kinds of expectations do women seem to have of men, and vice versa? Do these expectations tend to contribute to hostility in specific ways? Consider Horney's description of expectations in paragraph 8.

6. How do the examples of behavior in primitive cultures contribute to an understanding of the relationship between the sexes in our culture?

7. Is Horney pessimistic or optimistic about relationships between the sexes?

SUGGESTIONS FOR WRITING

1. In paragraph 9, Horney says that unpleasant experiences with the opposite sex are unavoidable. In your experience, is this true? What unpleasant experiences have you had with the opposite sex? What unpleasant experiences have you observed?

2. Horney mentions that the intensity of our feelings can stir up secret longings for, and expectations of, the opposite sex (para. 8). What kinds of secret expectations do you feel each sex might have about the other in a relationship? Why would such expectations remain secret? Does such secrecy contribute to problems? Does it contribute to hostility?

3. Deep in the essay, in paragraph 14, Horney mentions envy as contributing to the hostility between the sexes. She says, "For it is contrary to human nature to sustain appreciation without resentment toward capabilities that one does not possess." Do you agree with her? Do you think envy may have something to do with the hostility between the sexes? Examine your own experience to see whether you recall instances of envy on your part toward a member of the opposite sex (or vice versa).

4. At one point, Horney says, "Man's fear of woman is deeply rooted in sex" (para. 13). Do you think this is true? Is woman's fear of man similarly rooted? Examine this question by comparing two men's magazines and two women's magazines to determine what they reveal about the psychology of men and women. Compare their visual material, particularly photographs of members of the opposite sex. Also compare the fiction, and look for signs of a specifically male or female form of fantasy. Compare the advertising to identify the interests of men and women — and try to relate these to psychological concerns.

5. Horney is very direct in her discussion of male dominance in society, saying not only that it exists but asking, "Could it be that men, therefore, have a vital interest in keeping women dependent on them?" (para. 18). Conduct an interview with one man and one woman. Find out whether they have the same or different feelings about this question. Ask them if they see an effort on the part of men to keep women dependent, and then ask them what form any such dependency takes. Do they agree? Where do you stand on this issue?

6. At one point, Horney discusses how different men are from women. Write an essay in which you show the extent to which women are dif-

ferent from men. If possible, sample others' opinions and see if they note important differences. To what extent would differences between men and women contribute toward hostility?

7. What are the most important psychic phenomena in Horney's discussion? Her concerns are primarily cultural, but she also describes a psychological situation that has its root in mental experience. What are the most important mental experiences, and how do they manifest themselves in the mental life of individuals?

8. **CONNECTIONS** Jung discusses the personal and collective unconscious. Horney's argument is that there are personal and cultural aspects to the development of the minds of men and women. How close is Horney to Jung's position regarding what is personal and what is cultural in gender distinction? Does Jung's or Freud's work with dreams clarify the distinctions?

HOWARD GARDNER
A Rounded Version: The Theory of Multiple Intelligences

HOWARD GARDNER (b. 1943), professor of education and adjunct professor of psychology at Harvard University, is codirector of Harvard's Project Zero, a program dedicated to improving education in schools by emphasizing creativity in thinking and problem solving. By emphasizing the arts and the newer electronic technologies associated with learning, the program cultivates a "culture of thinking" in the classroom as opposed to a culture of rote learning. Gardner has received a MacArthur Foundation award (1981), which supported his research for five years, and has won a number of important awards in the field of education, including the Grawemeyer Award in Education (1990), given for the first time to an American. Among his many books are *Leading Minds: An Anatomy of Leadership* (1995) and *Extraordinary Minds: Portraits of Exceptional Individuals and an Examination of Our Extraordinariness* (1997).

Perhaps the most important and best-known product of Project Zero is the theory of multiple intelligences, which Gardner first published in *Frames of Mind* (1983). In that book, he noted that the general attitude toward intelligence centers on the IQ (intelligence quotient) test that Alfred Binet (1857–1911) devised. Binet believed that intelligence is measurable and that IQ tests result in numerical scores that are reliable indicators of a more or less permanent basic intelligence. Gardner offered several objections to that view. One was that IQ predictors might point to achievement in schools and colleges but did not point to achievement in life. Scores of middling students performed at extraordinary levels in business, politics, and other walks of life, while high-achieving students often settled for middling careers. The reports on high-

From *Multiple Intelligences: The Theory in Practice.*

performing executives indicated a considerable intelligence at work, but it was not necessarily the kind of intelligence that could be measured by the Binet tests.

Gardner also was intrigued by findings that local regions of the brain controlled specific functions of the mind. For example, studies had established that certain regions of the brain were specialized for language functions, while others were specialized for physical movement, music, mathematics, and other skills. When those portions of the brain suffered damage, as with stroke or accident, the functions for which they were specialized were adversely affected. These observations, which were plentiful in the work of neurologists during and after World War II, led Gardner to propose the existence of a variety of intelligences rather than only one.

As he explains in the following essay from his book *Multiple Intelligences: The Theory in Practice* (1993), his studies led him to propose seven distinct intelligences. The first is linguistic, which naturally includes language. This intelligence applies not only to learning languages but also to using language well — as, for example, in the case of poets and writers. The second is logical-mathematical, which refers to the applications of mathematics and of logical reasoning. Our society uses these verbal-mathematical forms of intelligence as the practical measure of intelligence: the SATs, for instance, depend almost entirely on measuring these forms.

Gardner adds five more forms of intelligence. Spatial intelligence concerns the ways in which we perceive and imagine spatial relations. Some people, such as architects and sculptors, are clearly more gifted than others at imagining space. Musical intelligence is seen as distinct from other forms of intelligence if only because some people, such as child prodigies, are apparently born with superior musical abilities. Bodily-kinesthetic intelligence shows up in dancers and athletes, like Mikhail Barishnikov and Jackie Joyner-Kersee, who perform extraordinarily with their bodies. But bodily-kinesthetic intelligence also applies to detailed physical work, such as the manipulations necessary for the work of surgeons, dentists, and craftspeople, such as weavers, potters, metalworkers, and jewelers.

Finally, Gardner also defines two kinds of personal intelligence that are difficult to isolate and study but that he feels must be regarded as forms of intelligence. Interpersonal intelligence concerns the way we get along with other people. People with a high interpersonal intelligence might be salespeople, teachers, politicians, or evangelists. They respond to others and are sensitive to their needs and their concerns. They understand cooperation, compromise, and respect for other people's views. The second kind of personal intelligence — intrapersonal — refers to how one understands oneself. The self-knowledge to recognize one's strengths and weaknesses and to avoid an inflated sense of self-importance constitutes a high degree of intrapersonal intelligence.

Gardner sees all these intelligences working together in the individual. As he says, when one of them dominates, the individual can appear freakish, as the person with autism who easily multiplies huge numbers in his head but cannot relate to other human beings. Because the individual must nurture all these intelligences to develop into a complete person, Gardner is working to revise educational practices to reflect all varieties of intelligence.

Greeks in the time of Plato and Aristotle seem to have understood much of what Gardner says. They included music and dance, for example, in the curriculum of their schools. They developed linguistic and interpersonal skills in the teaching of rhetoric and made logic and mathematics central to their teaching. One of Socrates' most famous statements, in fact — "Know thyself" — admonishes us to develop intrapersonal intelligence.

GARDNER'S RHETORIC

Rather than open the essay by describing the multiple intelligences, Gardner starts with a dramatic scene and a hypothetical story. He describes "Two eleven-year-old children" who take an IQ test and then are regarded in special ways by their teachers: one is expected to do well in school, while the other is expected to do less well. The expectations are met. But years later the student with the lower IQ is vastly more successful in business than the student who scored higher. Why is this so? The rest of the essay answers that implied rhetorical question.

One of the most important devices Gardner relies on is enumeration. He has seven different kinds of intelligence to discuss and takes each one in turn. The reader is not aware of a special range of importance to the seven forms of intelligence: the first, musical intelligence, is not necessarily the most important or the first to be recognized in an individual. Bodily-kinesthetic is not necessarily less important because it comes after musical intelligence. By placing logical-mathematical intelligence in the middle of the sequence, Gardner suggests that this form of intelligence, which our society traditionally treats as first in importance, should take its place beside a range of intelligences that are all more or less equal in value.

Just as important as the use of enumeration is Gardner's use of parallelism in the structure of each of the intelligences he enumerates. For each he offers a subhead that identifies the specific intelligence and then a "sketch with a thumbnail biography" that helps establish the nature of the intelligence. Then Gardner discusses the details of each intelligence and suggests ways in which it may relate to other forms of intelligence. This method has the advantage of extreme clarity. Likewise, paralleling examples and quotations in describing each intelligence makes the point over and over and ultimately produces a convincing argument without the appearance of argument.

Gardner makes another important rhetorical decision regarding the size and nature of the paragraphs. Modern readers, conditioned by newspapers and magazines, expect paragraphs to be short and direct. Gardner's paragraphs reflect a decision to communicate with a general reading audience rather than an audience of specialists or specially educated readers. For that reason, a single subject may sometimes be discussed in two or more adjacent paragraphs, with the paragraph break acting as a "breather" (see paras. 18 – 19 and 21 – 22).

All these rhetorical devices aid the reader in absorbing complex material. Gardner's primary efforts in this essay are communication. He keeps his language simple, his sentences direct, and his paragraphs brief. For the modern reader, this is a recipe for understanding.

A Rounded Version: The Theory of Multiple Intelligences

Coauthored by Joseph Walters

Two eleven-year-old children are taking a test of "intelligence." 1 They sit at their desks laboring over the meanings of different words, the interpretation of graphs, and the solutions to arithmetic problems. They record their answers by filling in small circles on a single piece of paper. Later these completed answer sheets are scored objectively: the number of right answers is converted into a standardized score that compares the individual child with a population of children of similar age.

The teachers of these children review the different scores. They   2
notice that one of the children has performed at a superior level; on all sections of the test, she answered more questions correctly than did her peers. In fact, her score is similar to that of children three to four years older. The other child's performance is average — his scores reflect those of other children his age.

A subtle change in expectations surrounds the review of these   3
test scores. Teachers begin to expect the first child to do quite well during her formal schooling, whereas the second should have only moderate success. Indeed these predictions come true. In other words, the test taken by the eleven-year-olds serves as a reliable predictor of their later performance in school.

How does this happen? One explanation involves our free use of   4
the word "intelligence": the child with the greater "intelligence" has the ability to solve problems, to find the answers to specific questions, and to learn new material quickly and efficiently. These skills in turn play a central role in school success. In this view, "intelligence" is a singular faculty that is brought to bear in any problem-solving situation. Since schooling deals largely with solving problems of various sorts, predicting this capacity in young children predicts their future success in school.

"Intelligence," from this point of view, is a general ability that is   5
found in varying degrees in all individuals. It is the key to success in solving problems. This ability can be measured reliably with standardized pencil-and-paper tests that, in turn, predict future success in school.

What happens after school is completed? Consider the two indi-   6
viduals in the example. Looking further down the road, we find that the "average" student has become a highly successful mechanical engineer who has risen to a position of prominence in both the professional community of engineers as well as in civic groups in his community. His success is no fluke — he is considered by all to be a talented individual. The "superior" student, on the other hand, has had little success in her chosen career as a writer; after repeated rejections by publishers, she has taken up a middle management position in a bank. While certainly not a "failure," she is considered by her peers to be quite "ordinary" in her adult accomplishments. So what happened?

This fabricated example is based on the facts of intelligence test-   7
ing. IQ tests predict school performance with considerable accuracy, but they are only an indifferent predictor of performance in a profes-

sion after formal schooling.[1] Furthermore, even as IQ tests measure only logical or logical-linguistic capacities, in this society we are nearly "brain-washed" to restrict the notion of intelligence to the capacities used in solving logical and linguistic problems.

To introduce an alternative point of view, undertake the following "thought experiment." Suspend the usual judgment of what constitutes intelligence and let your thoughts run freely over the capabilities of humans — perhaps those that would be picked out by the proverbial Martian visitor. In this exercise, you are drawn to the brilliant chess player, the world-class violinist, and the champion athlete; such outstanding performers deserve special consideration. Under this experiment, a quite different view of *intelligence* emerges. Are the chess player, violinist, and athlete "intelligent" in these pursuits? If they are, then why do our tests of "intelligence" fail to identify them? If they are not "intelligent," what allows them to achieve such astounding feats? In general, why does the contemporary construct "intelligence" fail to explain large areas of human endeavor? 8

In this chapter we approach these problems through the theory of multiple intelligences (MI). As the name indicates, we believe that human cognitive competence is better described in terms of a set of abilities, talents, or mental skills, which we call "intelligences." All normal individuals possess each of these skills to some extent; individuals differ in the degree of skill and in the nature of their combination. We believe this theory of intelligence may be more humane and more veridical than alternative views of intelligence and that it more adequately reflects the data of human "intelligent" behavior. Such a theory has important educational implications, including ones for curriculum development. 9

What Constitutes an Intelligence?

The question of the optimal definition of intelligence looms large in our inquiry. Indeed, it is at the level of this definition that the theory of multiple intelligences diverges from traditional points of view. In a traditional view, intelligence is defined operationally as the ability to answer items on tests of intelligence. The inference from the test scores to some underlying ability is supported by statistical techniques that compare responses of subjects at different ages; the apparent correlation of these test scores across ages and across different tests corroborates the notion that the general faculty 10

---

[1] Jencks, C. (1972). *Inequality*. New York: Basic Books. [Gardner's note]

of intelligence, *g*, does not change much with age or with training or experience. It is an inborn attribute or faculty of the individual.

Multiple intelligences theory, on the other hand, pluralizes the   11
traditional concept. An intelligence entails the ability to solve problems or fashion products that are of consequence in a particular cultural setting or community. The problem-solving skill allows one to approach a situation in which a goal is to be obtained and to locate the appropriate route to that goal. The creation of a *cultural* product is crucial to such functions as capturing and transmitting knowledge or expressing one's views or feelings. The problems to be solved range from creating an end for a story to anticipating a mating move in chess to repairing a quilt. Products range from scientific theories to musical compositions to successful political campaigns.

MI theory is framed in light of the biological origins of each   12
problem-solving skill. Only those skills that are universal to the human species are treated. Even so, the biological proclivity to participate in a particular form of problem solving must also be coupled with the cultural nurturing of that domain. For example, language, a universal skill, may manifest itself particularly as writing in one culture, as oratory in another culture, and as the secret language of anagrams in a third.

Given the desire of selecting intelligences that are rooted in biol-   13
ogy, and that are valued in one or more cultural settings, how does one actually identify an "intelligence"? In coming up with our list, we consulted evidence from several different sources: knowledge about normal development and development in gifted individuals; information about the breakdown of cognitive skills under conditions of brain damage; studies of exceptional populations, including prodigies, idiots savants, and autistic children; data about the evolution of cognition over the millennia; cross-cultural accounts of cognition; psychometric studies, including examinations of correlations among tests; and psychological training studies, particularly measures of transfer and generalization across tasks. Only those candidate intelligences that satisfied all or a majority of the criteria were selected as bona fide intelligences. A more complete discussion of each of these criteria for an "intelligence" and the seven intelligences that have been proposed so far, is found in *Frames of mind.*[2] This book also considers how the theory might be disproven and compares it to competing theories of intelligence.

---

[2] Gardner, H. (1983). *Frames of mind: The theory of multiple intelligences.* New York: Basic Books. [Gardner's note]

In addition to satisfying the aforementioned criteria, each intel- 14
ligence must have an identifiable core operation or set of operations.
As a neutrally based computational system, each intelligence is acti-
vated or "triggered" by certain kinds of internally or externally presented information. For example, one core of musical intelligence is
the sensitivity to pitch relations, whereas one core of linguistic intelligence is the sensitivity to phonological features.

An intelligence must also be susceptible to encoding in a symbol 15
system — a culturally contrived system of meaning, which captures
and conveys important forms of information. Language, picturing,
and mathematics are but three nearly worldwide symbol systems
that are necessary for human survival and productivity. The relationship of a candidate intelligence to a human symbol system is no
accident. In fact, the existence of a core computational capacity anticipates the existence of a symbol system that exploits that capacity.
While it may be possible for an intelligence to proceed without an
accompanying symbol system, a primary characteristic of human intelligence may well be its gravitation toward such an embodiment.

The Seven Intelligences

Having sketched the characteristics and criteria of an intelli- 16
gence, we turn now to a brief consideration of each of the seven intelligences. We begin each sketch with a thumbnail biography of a
person who demonstrates an unusual facility with that intelligence.
These biographies illustrate some of the abilities that are central to
the fluent operation of a given intelligence. Although each biography
illustrates a particular intelligence, we do not wish to imply that in
adulthood intelligences operate in isolation. Indeed, except for ab-
normal individuals, intelligences always work in concert, and any
sophisticated adult role will involve a melding of several of them.
Following each biography we survey the various sources of data that
support each candidate as an "intelligence."

Musical Intelligence

When he was three years old, Yehudi Menuhin was smuggled into
the San Francisco Orchestra concerts by his parents. The sound of
Louis Persinger's violin so entranced the youngster that he insisted on a violin for his birthday and Louis Persinger as his
teacher. He got both. By the time he was ten years old, Menuhin
was an international performer.[3]

------

[3] Menuhin, Y. (1977). *Unfinished journey*. New York: Knopf. [Gardner's note]

Violinist Yehudi Menuhin's musical intelligence manifested it- 17
self even before he had touched a violin or received any musical
training. His powerful reaction to that particular sound and his
rapid progress on the instrument suggest that he was biologically
prepared in some way for that endeavor. In this way evidence from
child prodigies supports our claim that there is a biological link to a
particular intelligence. Other special populations, such as autistic
children who can play a musical instrument beautifully but who
cannot speak, underscore the independence of musical intelligence.

A brief consideration of the evidence suggests that musical skill 18
passes the other tests for an intelligence. For example, certain parts
of the brain play important roles in perception and production of
music. These areas are characteristically located in the right hemisphere, although musical skill is not as clearly "localized," or located
in a specifiable area, as language. Although the particular susceptibility of musical ability to brain damage depends on the degree of
training and other individual differences, there is clear evidence for
"amusia" or loss of musical ability.

Music apparently played an important unifying role in Stone 19
Age (Paleolithic) societies. Birdsong provides a link to other species.
Evidence from various cultures supports the notion that music is a
universal faculty. Studies of infant development suggest that there is
a "raw" computational ability in early childhood. Finally, musical
notation provides an accessible and lucid symbol system.

In short, evidence to support the interpretation of musical ability 20
as an "intelligence" comes from many different sources. Even though
musical skill is not typically considered an intellectual skill like mathematics, it qualifies under our criteria. By definition it deserves consideration; and in view of the data, its inclusion is empirically justified.

Bodily-Kinesthetic Intelligence

Fifteen-year-old Babe Ruth played third base. During one game
his team's pitcher was doing very poorly and Babe loudly criticized him from third base. Brother Mathias, the coach, called out,
"Ruth, if you know so much about it, YOU pitch!" Babe was surprised and embarrassed because he had never pitched before, but
Brother Mathias insisted. Ruth said later that at the very moment
he took the pitcher's mound, he KNEW he was supposed to be a
pitcher and that it was "natural" for him to strike people out. Indeed, he went on to become a great major league pitcher (and, of
course, attained legendary status as a hitter).[4]

---

[4] Connor, A. (1982). *Voices from Cooperstown.* New York: Collier. (Based on a
quotation taken from *The Babe Ruth story,* Babe Ruth & Bob Considine. New York:
Dutton, 1948.) [Gardner's note]

Like Menuhin, Babe Ruth was a child prodigy who recognized   21
his "instrument" immediately upon his first exposure to it. This
recognition occurred in advance of formal training.

Control of bodily movement is, of course, localized in the motor   22
cortex, with each hemisphere dominant or controlling bodily movements on the contra-lateral side. In right-handers, the dominance
for such movement is ordinarily found in the left hemisphere. The
ability to perform movements when directed to do so can be impaired even in individuals who can perform the same movements
reflexively or on a nonvoluntary basis. The existence of specific
apraxia constitutes one line of evidence for a bodily-kinesthetic intelligence.

The evolution of specialized body movements is of obvious ad-   23
vantage to the species, and in humans this adaptation is extended
through the use of tools. Body movement undergoes a clearly defined developmental schedule in children. And there is little question of its universality across cultures. Thus it appears that bodily-
kinesthetic "knowledge" satisfies many of the criteria for an
intelligence.

The consideration of bodily-kinesthetic knowledge as "problem   24
solving" may be less intuitive. Certainly carrying out a mime sequence or hitting a tennis ball is not solving a mathematical equation. And yet, the ability to use one's body to express an emotion (as
in a dance), to play a game (as in a sport), or to create a new product
(as in devising an invention) is evidence of the cognitive features of
body usage. The specific computations required to solve a particular
bodily-kinesthetic *problem,* hitting a tennis ball, are summarized by
Tim Gallwey:

> At the moment the ball leaves the server's racket, the brain calcu-
> lates approximately where it will land and where the racket will
> intercept it. This calculation includes the initial velocity of the
> ball, combined with an input for the progressive decrease in ve-
> locity and the effect of wind and after the bounce of the ball. Si-
> multaneously, muscle orders are given: not just once, but con-
> stantly with refined and updated information. The muscles must
> cooperate. A movement of the feet occurs, the racket is taken
> back, the face of the racket kept at a constant angle. Contact is
> made at a precise point that depends on whether the order was
> given to hit down the line or cross-court, an order not given until
> after a split-second analysis of the movement and balance of the
> opponent.
>
> To return an average serve, you have about one second to do
> this. To hit the ball at all is remarkable and yet not uncommon.

The truth is that everyone who inhabits a human body possesses a remarkable creation.[5]

Logical-Mathematical Intelligence. In 1983 Barbara McClin- 25 tock won the Nobel Prize in medicine or physiology for her work in microbiology. Her intellectual powers of deduction and observation illustrate one form of logical-mathematical intelligence that is often labeled "scientific thinking." One incident is particularly illuminating. While a researcher at Cornell in the 1920s McClintock was faced one day with a problem: while *theory* predicted 50-percent pollen sterility in corn, her research assistant (in the "field") was finding plants that were only 25- to 30-percent sterile. Disturbed by this discrepancy, McClintock left the cornfield and returned to her office where she sat for half an hour, thinking:

> Suddenly I jumped up and ran back to the (corn) field. At the top of the field (the others were still at the bottom) I shouted "Eureka, I have it! I know what the 30% sterility is!" . . . They asked me to prove it. I sat down with a paper bag and a pencil and I started from scratch, which I had not done at all in my laboratory. It had all been done so fast; the answer came and I ran. Now I worked it out step by step — it was an intricate series of steps — and I came out with [the same result]. [They] looked at the material and it was exactly as I'd said it was; it worked out exactly as I had diagrammed it. Now, why did I know, without having done it on paper? Why was I so sure?[6]

This anecdote illustrates two essential facts of the logical- 26 mathematical intelligence. First, in the gifted individual, the process of problem solving is often remarkably rapid — the successful scientist copes with many variables at once and creates numerous hypotheses that are each evaluated and then accepted or rejected in turn.

The anecdote also underscores the *nonverbal* nature of the intel- 27 ligence. A solution to a problem can be constructed *before* it is articulated. In fact, the solution process may be totally invisible, even to the problem solver. This need not imply, however, that discoveries of this sort — the familiar "Aha!" phenomenon — are mysterious, intuitive, or unpredictable. The fact that it happens more frequently to some people (perhaps Nobel Prize winners) suggests the oppo-

[5] Gallwey, T. (1976). *Inner tennis.* New York: Random House. [Gardner's note]

[6] Keller, E. (1983). *A feeling for the organism* (p. 104). Salt Lake City: W. H. Freeman. [Gardner's note]

site. We interpret this as the work of theological-mathematical intelligence.

Along with the companion skill of language, logical-mathematical 28 reasoning provides the principal basis for IQ tests. This form of intelligence has been heavily investigated by traditional psychologists, and it is the archetype of "raw intelligence" or the problem-solving faculty that purportedly cuts across domains. It is perhaps ironic, then, that the actual mechanism by which one arrives at a solution to a logical-mathematical problem is not as yet properly understood.

This intelligence is supported by our empirical criteria as well. 29 Certain areas of the brain are more prominent in mathematical calculation than others. There are idiots savants who perform great feats of calculation even though they remain tragically deficient in most other areas. Child prodigies in mathematics abound. The development of this intelligence in children has been carefully documented by Jean Piaget and other psychologists.

Linguistic Intelligence

> At the age of ten, T. S. Eliot created a magazine called "Fireside" to which he was the sole contributor. In a three-day period during his winter vacation, he created eight complete issues. Each one included poems, adventure stories, a gossip column, and humor. Some of this material survives and it displays the talent of the poet.[7]

As with the logical intelligence, calling linguistic skill an "intelli- 30 gence" is consistent with the stance of traditional psychology. Linguistic intelligence also passes our empirical tests. For instance, a specific area of the brain, called "Broca's Area," is responsible for the production of grammatical sentences. A person with damage to this area can understand words and sentences quite well but has difficulty putting words together in anything other than the simplest of sentences. At the same time, other thought processes may be entirely unaffected.

The gift of language is universal, and its development in chil- 31 dren is strikingly constant across cultures. Even in deaf populations where a manual sign language is not explicitly taught, children will often "invent" their own manual language and use it surreptitiously! We thus see how an intelligence may operate independently of a specific input modality or output channel.

---

[7] Soldo, J. (1982). Jovial juvenilia: T. S. Eliot's first magazine. *Biography, 5,* 25–37. [Gardner's note]

Spatial Intelligence

Navigation around the Caroline Islands in the South Seas is accomplished without instruments. The position of the stars, as viewed from various islands, the weather patterns, and water color are the only sign posts. Each journey is broken into a series of segments; and the navigator learns the position of the stars within each of these segments. During the actual trip the navigator must envision mentally a reference island as it passes under a particular star and from that he computes the number of segments completed, the proportion of the trip remaining, and any corrections in heading that are required. The navigator cannot *see* the islands as he sails along; instead he maps their locations in his mental "picture" of the journey.[8]

Spatial problem solving is required for navigation and in the use 32 of the notational system of maps. Other kinds of spatial problem solving are brought to bear in visualizing an object seen from a different angle and in playing chess. The visual arts also employ this intelligence in the use of space.

Evidence from brain research is clear and persuasive. Just as the 33 left hemisphere has, over the course of evolution, been selected as the site of linguistic processing in right-handed persons, the right hemisphere proves to be the site most crucial for spatial processing. Damage to the right posterior regions causes impairment of the ability to find one's way around a site, to recognize faces or scenes, or to notice fine details.

Patients with damage specific to regions of the right hemisphere 34 will attempt to compensate for their spacial deficits with linguistic strategies. They will try to reason aloud, to challenge the task, or even make up answers. But such nonspatial strategies are rarely successful.

Blind populations provide an illustration of the distinction be- 35 tween the spatial intelligence and visual perception. A blind person can recognize shapes by an indirect method: running a hand along the object translates into length of time of movement, which in turn is translated into the size of the object. For the blind person, the perceptual system of the tactile modality parallels the visual modality in the seeing person. The analogy between the spatial reasoning of the blind and the linguistic reasoning of the deaf is notable.

There are few child prodigies among visual artists, but there are 36 idiots savants such as Nadia.[9] Despite a condition of severe autism,

---

[8] Gardner, H. (1983). *Frames of mind: The theory of multiple intelligences.* New York: Basic Books. [Gardner's note]

[9] Selfe, L. (1977). *Nadia: A case of extraordinary drawing in an autistic child.* New York: Academic Press. [Gardner's note]

this preschool child made drawings of the most remarkable representational accuracy and finesse.

Interpersonal Intelligence.   With little formal training in special education and nearly blind herself, Anne Sullivan began the intimidating task of instructing a blind and deaf seven-year-old Helen Keller. Sullivan's efforts at communication were complicated by the child's emotional struggle with the world around her. At their first meal together, this scene occurred:

> Annie did not allow Helen to put her hand into Annie's plate and take what she wanted, as she had been accustomed to do with her family. It became a test of wills — hand thrust into plate, hand firmly put aside. The family, much upset, left the dining room. Annie locked the door and proceeded to eat her breakfast while Helen lay on the floor kicking and screaming, pushing and pulling at Annie's chair. [After half an hour] Helen went around the table looking for her family. She discovered no one else was there and that bewildered her. Finally, she sat down and began to eat her breakfast, but with her hands. Annie gave her a spoon. Down on the floor it clattered, and the contest of wills began anew.[10]

Anne Sullivan sensitively responded to the child's behavior. She wrote home: "The greatest problem I shall have to solve is how to discipline and control her without breaking her spirit. I shall go rather slowly at first and try to win her love."

In fact, the first "miracle" occurred two weeks later, well before the famous incident at the pumphouse. Annie had taken Helen to a small cottage near the family's house, where they could live alone. After seven days together, Helen's personality suddenly underwent a profound change — the therapy had worked:

> My heart is singing with joy this morning. A miracle has happened! The wild little creature of two weeks ago has been transformed into a gentle child.[11]

It was just two weeks after this that the first breakthrough in Helen's grasp of language occurred; and from that point on, she progressed with incredible speed. The key to the miracle of language was Anne Sullivan's insight into the *person* of Helen Keller.

37

38

39

40

---

[10] Lash, J. (1980). *Helen and teacher: The story of Helen Keller and Anne Sullivan Macy* (p. 52). New York: Delacorte. [Gardner's note]

[11] Lash (p. 54). [Gardner's note]

Interpersonal intelligence builds on a core capacity to notice 41
distinctions among others; in particular, contrasts in their moods,
temperaments, motivations, and intentions. In more advanced
forms, this intelligence permits a skilled adult to read the intentions
and desires of others, even when these have been hidden. This skill
appears in a highly sophisticated form in religious or political leaders, teachers, therapists, and parents. The Helen Keller – Anne Sullivan story suggests that this interpersonal intelligence does not depend on language.

All indices in brain research suggest that the frontal lobes play a 42
prominent role in interpersonal knowledge. Damage in this area can
cause profound personality changes while leaving other forms of
problem solving unharmed — a person is often "not the same person" after such an injury.

Alzheimer's disease, a form of presenile dementia, appears to at- 43
tack posterior brain zones with a special ferocity, leaving spatial,
logical, and linguistic computations severely impaired. Yet, Alzheimer's patients will often remain well groomed, socially proper,
and continually apologetic for their errors. In contrast, Pick's disease, another variety of presenile dementia that is more frontally oriented, entails a rapid loss of social graces.

Biological evidence for interpersonal intelligence encompasses 44
two additional factors often cited as unique to humans. One factor is
the prolonged childhood of primates, including the close attachment to the mother. In those cases where the mother is removed
from early development, normal interpersonal development is in serious jeopardy. The second factor is the relative importance in humans of social interaction. Skills such as hunting, tracking, and
killing in prehistoric societies required participation and cooperation of large numbers of people. The need for group cohesion, leadership, organization, and solidarity follows naturally from this.

Intrapersonal Intelligence.   In an essay called "A Sketch of the 45
Past," written almost as a diary entry, Virginia Woolf discusses the
"cotton wool of existence" — the various mundane events of life.
She contrasts this "cotton wool" with three specific and poignant
memories from her childhood: a fight with her brother, seeing a particular flower in the garden, and hearing of the suicide of a past visitor:

> These are three instances of exceptional moments. I often tell
> them over, or rather they come to the surface unexpectedly. But
> now for the first time I have written them down, and I realize

something that I have never realized before. Two of these moments ended in a state of despair. The other ended, on the contrary, in a state of satisfaction.

The sense of horror (in hearing of the suicide) held me powerless. But in the case of the flower, I found a reason; and was thus able to deal with the sensation. I was not powerless.

Though I still have the peculiarity that I receive these sudden shocks, they are now always welcome; after the first surprise, I always feel instantly that they are particularly valuable. And so I go on to suppose that the shock-receiving capacity is what makes me a writer. I hazard the explanation that a shock is at once in my case followed by the desire to explain it. I feel that I have had a blow; but it is not, as I thought as a child, simply a blow from an enemy hidden behind the cotton wool of daily life; it is or will become a revelation of some order; it is a token of some real thing behind appearances; and I make it real by putting it into words.[12]

This quotation vividly illustrates the intrapersonal intelligence — knowledge of the internal aspects of a person: access to one's own feeling life, one's range of emotions, the capacity to effect discriminations among these emotions and eventually to label them and to draw upon them as a means of understanding and guiding one's own behavior. A person with good intrapersonal intelligence has a viable and effective model of himself or herself. Since this intelligence is the most private, it requires evidence from language, music, or some other more expressive form of intelligence if the observer is to detect it at work. In the above quotation, for example, linguistic intelligence is drawn upon to convey intrapersonal knowledge; it embodies the interaction of intelligences, a common phenomenon to which we will return later.   46

We see the familiar criteria at work in the intrapersonal intelligence. As with the interpersonal intelligence, the frontal lobes play a central role in personality change. Injury to the lower area of the frontal lobes is likely to produce irritability or euphoria; while injury to the higher regions is more likely to produce indifference, listlessness, slowness, and apathy — a kind of depressive personality. In such "frontal-lobe" individuals, the other cognitive functions often remain preserved. In contrast, among aphasics who have recovered sufficiently to describe their experiences, we find consistent testimony: while there may have been a diminution of general alertness and considerable depression about the condition, the individual in no way felt himself to be a different person. He recognized his own needs, wants, and desires and tried as best he could to achieve them.   47

---

[12] Woolf, V. (1976). *Moments of being* (pp. 69–70). Sussex: The University Press. [Gardner's note]

The autistic child is a prototypical example of an individual 48
with impaired intrapersonal intelligence; indeed, the child may not
even be able to refer to himself. At the same time, such children
often exhibit remarkable abilities in the musical, computational,
spatial, or mechanical realms.

Evolutionary evidence for an intrapersonal faculty is more diffi- 49
cult to come by, but we might speculate that the capacity to transcend the satisfaction of instinctual drives is relevant. This becomes
increasingly important in a species not perennially involved in the
struggle for survival.

In sum, then, both interpersonal and intrapersonal faculties pass 50
the tests of an intelligence. They both feature problem-solving endeavors with significance for the individual and the species. Interpersonal intelligence allows one to understand and work with others; intrapersonal intelligence allows one to understand and work
with oneself. In the individual's sense of self, one encounters a
melding of inter- and intrapersonal components. Indeed, the sense
of self emerges as one of the most marvelous of human inven-
tions — a symbol that represents all kinds of information about a
person and that is at the same time an invention that all individuals
construct for themselves.

Summary: The Unique Contributions
of the Theory

As human beings, we all have a repertoire of skills for solving 51
different kinds of problems. Our investigation has begun, therefore,
with a consideration of these problems, the contexts they are found
in, and the culturally significant products that are the outcome. We
have not approached "intelligence" as a reified human faculty that is
brought to bear in literally any problem setting; rather, we have
begun with the problems that humans *solve* and worked back to the
"intelligences" that must be responsible.

Evidence from brain research, human development, evolution, 52
and cross-cultural comparisons was brought to bear in our search
for the relevant human intelligences: a candidate was included only
if reasonable evidence to support its membership was found across
these diverse fields. Again, this tack differs from the traditional one:
since no candidate faculty is *necessarily* an intelligence, we could
choose on a motivated basis. In the traditional approach to "intelligence," there is no opportunity for this type of empirical decision.

We have also determined that these multiple human faculties, 53
the intelligences, are to a significant extent *independent*. For example,
research with brain-damaged adults repeatedly demonstrates that

particular faculties can be lost while others are spared. This independence of intelligences implies that a particularly high level of ability in one intelligence, say mathematics, does not require a similarly high level in another intelligence, like language or music. This independence of intelligences contrasts sharply with traditional measures of IQ that find high correlations among test scores. We speculate that the usual correlations among subtests of IQ tests come about because all of these tasks in fact measure the ability to respond rapidly to items of a logical-mathematical or linguistic sort; we believe that these correlations would be substantially reduced if one were to survey in a contextually appropriate way the full range of human problem-solving skills.

Until now, we have supported the fiction that adult roles depend 54 largely on the flowering of a single intelligence. In fact, however, nearly every cultural role of any degree of sophistication requires a combination of intelligences. Thus, even an apparently straightforward role, like playing the violin, transcends a reliance on simple musical intelligence. To become a successful violinist requires bodily-kinesthetic dexterity and the interpersonal skills of relating to an audience and, in a different way, choosing a manager; quite possibly it involves an intrapersonal intelligence as well. Dance requires skills in bodily-kinesthetic, musical, interpersonal, and spatial intelligences in varying degrees. Politics requires an interpersonal skill, a linguistic facility, and perhaps some logical aptitude. Inasmuch as nearly every cultural role requires several intelligences, it becomes important to consider individuals as a collection of aptitudes rather than as having a singular problem-solving faculty that can be measured directly through pencil-and-paper tests. Even given a relatively small number of such intelligences, the diversity of human ability is created through the differences in these profiles. In fact, it may well be that the "total is greater than the sum of the parts." An individual may not be particularly gifted in any intelligence; and yet, because of a particular combination or blend of skills, he or she may be able to fill some niche uniquely well. Thus it is of paramount importance to assess the particular combination of skills that may earmark an individual for a certain vocational or avocational niche.

QUESTIONS FOR CRITICAL READING

1. In the heading beginning paragraph 10, Gardner asks, "What Constitutes an Intelligence?" After reading this essay, how would you answer that question? How effectively does Gardner answer it?

2. What is the relation of culture to intelligence? See paragraph 11.
3. Why does society value logical-mathematical intelligence so highly? Do you feel it is reasonable to do so? Why?
4. What relationship do you see between intelligence and problem solving? What relationship do you see between education and problem solving?
5. Do you think that education can increase these seven forms of intelligence? What evidence can you cite that intelligence is not fixed but can be altered by experience?
6. Why is it important "to assess the particular combination of skills that may earmark an individual" (para. 54)?

SUGGESTIONS FOR WRITING

1. Gardner says that his theory of MI (multiple intelligences) was shaped by his observations of "the biological origins of each problem-solving skill" (para. 12). Why is this important to his theory? How has he connected each of the intelligences to a biological origin? What biological issues are not fully accounted for in the theory of multiple intelligences?
2. In which of these seven forms of intelligence do you excel? Describe your achievements in these forms by giving specific examples that help your reader relate your abilities to the intelligences you have cited. Now that you have identified your primary intelligence, what implications do they suggest for your later life?
3. Gardner is keenly interested in reforming education in light of his discovery of multiple intelligences. How could education be altered to best accommodate seven forms of intelligence? What would be done differently in schools? Who would benefit from the differences you propose? How would society in general benefit from those differences?
4. Describe a problem-solving situation that demands two or more of the intelligences that Gardner describes. If possible, draw your example from your own experience or the experience of someone you know. Describe how the several intelligences work together to help solve the problem.
5. In some discussions of the forms of intelligence, commentators add an eighth — the naturalist's ability to recognize fine distinctions and patterns in the natural world. What might be the biological origin for that intelligence? In what cultural context might that intelligence be crucial? Do you feel that there is such an intelligence as the naturalist or that it is included in other forms of intelligence?
6. **CONNECTIONS**   What relationship do you see between Plato's discussion of the soul and Gardner's discussion of intelligence? See paragraphs 40 – 55 in Plato. Which of Gardner's intelligences does Socrates seem to favor in Plato's dialogue?
7. **CONNECTIONS**   Which writers in this section of the book could best adapt Gardner's theories to their own? Consider Plato's discussion

of the cave and the concerns of Maimonides on the limits of intelligence. How could Gardner have benefited from Maimonides' theories? What are the limits of the seven intelligences? How might Karen Horney have used Gardner's theories to explain the different ways in which the sexes regard each other? Do the different sexes excel in different forms of intelligence? How might Gardner or Horney defend or argue against such a view?

PART FIVE

NATURE

Francis Bacon
Charles Darwin
Stephen Jay Gould
Michio Kaku
Richard Dawkins

INTRODUCTION

Ideas of nature — of the world that exists outside human invention — have formed the core of human inquiry since the beginning of society. Early civilizations viewed nature as a willfully creative and destructive force and structured their religions around gods and goddesses who personified components of the natural world. For example, many early Egyptian and Greek religions worshipped a sun god, such as Ra or Apollo, and performed rituals meant to gain the favor of these gods.

This affiliation of nature with divine forces was gradually joined by a new approach: scientific inquiry. The basic premise of scientific inquiry was that the physical world could be understood through careful observation and described through consistent and logical rules. Lucretius, a prominent Roman thinker who lived during the first century B.C., wrote one of the first treatises on natural science. In his work *On the Nature of Things,* he argued that nature should be viewed in purely materialistic terms and that the universe was composed of minute pieces of matter or "atoms." During the Renaissance the pursuit of a scientific understanding of the world culminated with Nicolaus Copernicus's (1473 – 1543) heliocentric (sun-centered) model of the universe. In the seventeenth century Sir Isaac Newton (1642 – 1727) further developed these methods of objective observation while formulating his laws of physics. Although nature was still believed to be the creation of a divine force, its workings were gradually becoming more and more accessible to human understanding. In the process, humans began to reevaluate their own place in nature.

The five writers in this section offer various ideas on nature, from the origin of life to the structure of the universe. Many of their theories were contended in their time and continue to be debated and rethought, but they share the underlying mission of deciphering the forces that shape our world and our lives.

At the time Bacon wrote, before the advent of sophisticated scientific instruments, most scientists relied on their five senses and their theoretical preconceptions to investigate the workings of the world around them. In "The Four Idols" Bacon raises questions about these modes of scientific inquiry by asking, What casts of mind are essential to gaining knowledge? What prevents us from understanding nature clearly? By thus critiquing traditional presumptions and methods of investigation, Bacon challenges his readers to examine nature with new mental tools.

In "Natural Selection," Charles Darwin proposes a theory that is still controversial. While on a voyage around South America in the

HMS *Beagle,* Darwin observed remarkable similarities in the structures of various animals. He approached these discoveries with the advantages of a good education, a deep knowledge of the Bible and theology (he was trained as a minister), and a systematic and inquiring mind. Ultimately, he developed his theories of evolution to explain the significance of resemblances he detected among his scientific samples of insects and flowers and other forms of life. Explaining the nature of nature forms the underpinnings of Darwin's work.

Stephen Jay Gould, in "Nonmoral Nature," examines the results of the kind of thinking that Bacon deplored in the seventeenth century but that nevertheless flourished in the nineteenth century. Interpreting the world of nature as if it were fashioned by someone with the same prejudices as the Victorian scientist — usually also a minister — led people to see good and evil in animal and insect behavior. Even today most of us see the world in such terms. To Gould, however, the world is the world; moral issues relate to people, not to dolphins or sharks. For him, thinking like a naturalist means achieving detachment: how we approach the evidence before us, in other words, is as important as what we actually observe. Gould wants us to give up anthropomorphic ways of interpreting evidence in favor of a more rational approach. As he demonstrates, this is not easy to achieve.

Puzzling out the most current thinking in theoretical physics requires speculation that borders on what Michio Kaku calls craziness. The question he raises about a new theory of the universe is not whether it seems rational but whether it is crazy enough to be possible. Kaku is a theoretical physicist who helped develop the superstring theory, which he hopes will reconcile the quantum theory and the theory of relativity. Both of these theories explain a great deal about the universe, but each falls short in accounting for all four fundamental forces. The superstring theory, which asserts that the atom is composed of strings of energy vibrating at different frequencies, apparently reconciles the theories and permits physicists to develop mathematical equations that accurately predict physical events.

Richard Dawkins, sometimes described as an "ultra-Darwinist," probes into the microbiology of evolution, examining the genetic material that permits us to begin to trace the origin of species — including our own species, *Homo sapiens.* He finds the lines of descent stretch back to the continent of his birth, Africa, where he postulates the existence of African Eve, the female from which we all have descended. Although his method is complex and his results are not absolutely certain, Dawkins is confident that, regardless of whether we descend from a single female who lived in Africa some two hundred thousand years ago, we did descend from life that has its origin in Africa. His examination of details of our genetic code depends on sophisticated instruments and understanding that did not exist only a few years ago.

Although Francis Bacon probably would not understand the astonishing theories that the other writers in this section discuss, he would appreciate the methods they used to reason about their hypotheses and to establish their conclusions. All these writers are joined in their desire to understand the workings of nature and in their profound respect for the questions that remain.

FRANCIS BACON
The Four Idols

FRANCIS BACON, Lord Verulam (1561 – 1626), lived during one of the most exciting times in history. Among his contemporaries were the essayist Michel de Montaigne; the playwrights Christopher Marlowe and William Shakespeare; the adventurer Sir Francis Drake; and Queen Elizabeth I, in whose reign he held several high offices. He became lord high chancellor of England in 1618 but fell from power in 1621 through a complicated series of events, among which was his complicity in a bribery scheme. His so-called crimes were minor, but he paid dearly for them. His book *Essayes* (1597) was exceptionally popular during his lifetime, and when he found himself without a proper job, he devoted himself to what he declared to be his own true work, writing about philosophy and science.

His purpose in *Novum Organum* (The New Organon), published in 1620, was to replace the old organon, or instrument of thought, Aristotle's treatises on logic and thought. Despite Aristotle's pervasive influence on sixteenth- and seventeenth-century minds — his texts were used in virtually all schools and colleges — Bacon thought that Aristotelian deductive logic produced error. In *Novum Organum* he tried to set the stage for a new attitude toward logic and scientific inquiry. He proposed a system of reasoning usually referred to as induction. This quasi-scientific method involves collecting and listing observations from nature. Once a mass of observations is gathered and organized, Bacon believed, the truth about what is observed will become apparent.

Bacon is often mistakenly credited with having invented the scientific method of inquiring into nature, but although he was right about the need for collecting and observing, he was wrong about their outcome. After all, one could watch an infinite number of apples (and oranges, too) fall to the ground without ever having the

---

From *Novum Organum.*

slightest sense of why they do so. What Bacon failed to realize — and he died before he could get close enough to scientific observation to realize it — is the creative function of the scientist as expressed in the hypothesis. The hypothesis — an educated guess about why something happens — is then tested by the kinds of observations Bacon recommended.

Nonetheless, "The Four Idols" is a brilliant work. It does establish the requirements for the kind of observation that produces true scientific knowledge. Bacon despaired of any thoroughly objective inquiry in his own day, in part because no one paid attention to the ways in which the idols strangled thought, observation, and imagination. He realized that the would-be natural philosopher was foiled even before he began. Bacon was a farsighted man. He was correct about the failures of science in his time; and he was correct, moreover, in his assessment that advancement would depend on sensory perception and on aids to perception, such as microscopes and telescopes. The real brilliance of "The Four Idols" lies in Bacon's focus not on what is observed but on the instrument of observation, the human mind. Only when the instrument is freed of error can we rely on its observations.

BACON'S RHETORIC

Bacon was trained during the great age of rhetoric, and his prose (even though in this case it is translated from Latin) shows the clarity, balance, and organization that characterize the prose writing of seventeenth-century England. The most basic device Bacon uses is enumeration: stating clearly that there are four idols and implying that he will treat each one in turn.

Enumeration is one of the most common and most reliable rhetorical devices. The listener hears a speaker say "I have only three things I want to say today," and is alerted to listen for all three, while feeling secretly grateful that there are only three. When encountering complex material, the reader is always happy to have such "road signs" as "The second aspect of this question is. . . ."

"The Four Idols," after a three-paragraph introduction, proceeds with a single paragraph devoted to each idol, so that we have an early definition of each and a sense of what to look for. Paragraphs 8 to 16 cover only the issues related to the Idols of the Tribe: the problems all people have simply because they are people. Paragraphs 17 to 22 consider the Idols of the Cave, those particular fixations individuals have because of their special backgrounds or limitations. Paragraphs 23 to 26 address the questions related to Idols of the Marketplace, particularly those that deal with the way people misuse words and abuse definitions. The remainder of the selection treats the Idols of the Theater, which relate entirely to philosophic systems and preconceptions — all of which tend to narrow the scope of research and understanding.

Enumeration is used within each of these groups of paragraphs as well. Bacon often begins a paragraph with such statements as "There is one principal . . . distinction between different minds" (para. 19). Or he says, "The idols imposed by words on the understanding are of two kinds" (para. 24). The effect is to ensure clarity where confusion could easily reign.

As an added means of achieving clarity, Bacon sets aside a single paragraph — the last — to summarize the main points that he has made, in the order in which they were made.

Within any section of this selection, Bacon depends on observation, example, and reason to make his points. When he speaks of a given idol, he defines it, gives several examples to make it clearer, discusses its effects on thought, and then dismisses it as dangerous. He then goes on to the next idol. Where appropriate, in some cases he names those who are victims of a specific idol. In each case he tries to be thorough, explanatory, and convincing.

Not only is this work a landmark in thought; it is also, because of its absolute clarity, a beacon. We can still profit from its light.

The Four Idols

The idols[1] and false notions which are now in possession of the human understanding, and have taken deep root therein, not only so beset men's minds that truth can hardly find entrance, but even after entrance obtained, they will again in the very instauration[2] of the sciences meet and trouble us, unless men being forewarned of the danger fortify themselves as far as may be against their assaults.   1

There are four classes of idols which beset men's minds. To these for distinction's sake I have assigned names — calling the first   2

---

[1] **idols** By this term Bacon means phantoms or illusions. The Greek philosopher Democritus spoke of *eidola*, tiny representations of things that impressed themselves on the mind (see note 21).

[2] **instauration** Institution.

class *Idols of the Tribe*; the second, *Idols of the Cave*; the third, *Idols of the Marketplace*; the fourth, *Idols of the Theater*.

The formation of ideas and axioms by true induction[3] is no 3
doubt the proper remedy to be applied for the keeping off and clearing away of idols. To point them out, however, is of great use; for the doctrine of idols is to the interpretation of nature what the doctrine of the refutation of sophisms[4] is to common logic.

The *Idols of the Tribe* have their foundation in human nature itself, and in the tribe or race of men. For it is a false assertion that the sense of man is the measure of things. On the contrary, all perceptions as well of the sense as of the mind are according to the measure of the individual and not according to the measure of the universe. And the human understanding is like a false mirror, which, receiving rays irregularly, distorts and discolors the nature of things by mingling its own nature with it.

The *Idols of the Cave* are the idols of the individual man. For 5
everyone (besides the errors common to human nature in general) has a cave or den of his own, which refracts[5] and discolors the light of nature; owing either to his own proper and peculiar nature; or to his education and conversation with others; or to the reading of books, and the authority of those whom he esteems and admires; or to the differences of impressions, accordingly as they take place in a mind preoccupied and predisposed or in a mind indifferent and settled; or the like. So that the spirit of man (according as it is meted out to different individuals) is in fact a thing variable and full of perturbation,[6] and governed as it were by chance. Whence it was well observed by Heraclitus[7] that men look for sciences in their own lesser worlds, and not in the greater or common world.

There are also idols formed by the intercourse and association of 6
men with each other, which I call *Idols of the Marketplace,* on ac-

---

[3] **induction** Bacon championed induction as the method by which new knowledge is developed. As he saw it, induction involved a patient gathering and categorizing of facts in the hope that a large number of them would point to the truth. As a process of gathering evidence from which inferences are drawn, induction is contrasted with Aristotle's method, *deduction,* according to which a theory is established and the truth deduced. Deduction places the stress on the authority of the expert; induction places the stress on the facts themselves.

[4] **sophisms** Apparently intelligent statements that are wrong; false wisdom.

[5] **refracts** Deflects, bends back, alters.

[6] **perturbation** Uncertainty, disturbance. In astronomy, the motion caused by the gravity of nearby planets.

[7] **Heraclitus (535? – 475? B.C.)** Greek philosopher who believed that there was no reality except in change; all else was illusion. He also believed that fire was the basis of all the world and that everything we see is a transformation of it.

count of the commerce and consort of men there. For it is by discourse that men associate; and words are imposed according to the apprehension of the vulgar.[8] And therefore the ill and unfit choice of words wonderfully obstructs the understanding. Nor do the definitions or explanations wherewith in some things learned men are wont[9] to guard and defend themselves, by any means set the matter right. But words plainly force and overrule the understanding, and throw all into confusion and lead men away into numberless empty controversies and idle fancies.

Lastly, there are idols which have immigrated into men's minds 7 from the various dogmas of philosophies, and also from wrong laws of demonstration.[10] These I call *Idols of the Theater*; because in my judgment all the received systems[11] are but so many stage-plays, representing worlds of their own creation after an unreal and scenic fashion. Nor is it only of the systems now in vogue, or only of the ancient sects and philosophies, that I speak; for many more plays of the same kind may yet be composed and in like artificial manner set forth; seeing that errors the most widely different have nevertheless causes for the most part alike. Neither again do I mean this only of entire systems, but also of many principles and axioms in science, which by tradition, credulity, and negligence, have come to be received.

But of these several kinds of idols I must speak more largely and 8 exactly, that the understanding may be duly cautioned.

The human understanding is of its own nature prone to suppose 9 the existence of more order and regularity in the world than it finds. And though there be many things in nature which are singular and unmatched, yet it devises for them parallels and conjugates and relatives[12] which do not exist. Hence the fiction that all celestial bodies move in perfect circles; spirals and dragons being (except in name) utterly rejected. Hence too the element of fire with its orb is brought in, to make up the square with the other three which the sense perceives. Hence also the ratio of density[13] of the so-called elements is

---

[8] **vulgar** Common people.

[9] **wont** Accustomed.

[10] **laws of demonstration** Bacon may be referring to Aristotle's logical system of syllogism and deduction.

[11] **received systems** Official or authorized views of scientific truth.

[12] **parallels and conjugates and relatives** A reference to the habit of assuming that phenomena are regular and ordered, consisting of squares, triangles, circles, and other regular shapes.

[13] **ratio of density** The false assumption that the relationship of mass or weight to volume was ten to one. This is another example of Bacon's complaint, establishing a convenient regular "relative" or relationship.

arbitrarily fixed at ten to one. And so on of other dreams. And these fancies affect not dogmas only, but simple notions also.

The human understanding when it has once adopted an opin- 10 ion (either as being the received opinion or as being agreeable to itself) draws all things else to support and agree with it. And though there be a greater number and weight of instances to be found on the other side, yet these it either neglects and despises, or else by some distinction sets aside and rejects; in order that by this great and pernicious predetermination the authority of its former conclusions may remain inviolate. And therefore it was a good answer that was made by one who when they showed him hanging in a temple a picture of those who had paid their vows as having escaped shipwreck, and would have him say whether he did not now acknowledge the power of the gods — "Ay," asked he again, "but where are they painted that were drowned after their vows?" And such is the way of all superstition, whether in astrology, dreams, omens, divine judgments, or the like; wherein men having a delight in such vanities, mark the events where they are fulfilled, but where they fail, though this happen much oftener, neglect and pass them by. But with far more subtlety does this mischief insinuate itself into philosophy and the sciences; in which the first conclusion colors and brings into conformity with itself all that come after, though far sounder and better. Besides, independently of that delight and vanity which I have described, it is the peculiar and perpetual error of the human intellect to be more moved and excited by affirmatives than by negatives; whereas it ought properly to hold itself indifferently disposed towards both alike. Indeed, in the establishment of any true axiom, the negative instance is the more forcible of the two.

The human understanding is moved by those things most 11 which strike and enter the mind simultaneously and suddenly, and so fill the imagination; and then it feigns and supposes all other things to be somehow, though it cannot see how, similar to those few things by which it is surrounded. But for that going to and fro to remote and heterogeneous instances, by which axioms are tried as in the fire,[14] the intellect is altogether slow and unfit, unless it be forced thereto by severe laws and overruling authority.

---

[14] **tried as in the fire** Trial by fire is a figure of speech representing thorough, rigorous testing even to the point of risking what is tested. An axiom is a statement of apparent truth that has not yet been put to the test of examination and investigation.

The human understanding is unquiet; it cannot stop or rest, and 12
still presses onward, but in vain. Therefore it is that we cannot conceive of any end or limit to the world, but always as of necessity it
occurs to us that there is something beyond. Neither again can it be
conceived how eternity has flowed down to the present day; for that
distinction which is commonly received of infinity in time past and
in time to come can by no means hold; for it would thence follow
that one infinity is greater than another, and that infinity is wasting
away and tending to become finite. The like subtlety arises touching
the infinite divisibility of lines,[15] from the same inability of thought
to stop. But this inability interferes more mischievously in the discovery of causes:[16] for although the most general principles in nature ought to be held merely positive, as they are discovered, and
cannot with truth be referred to a cause; nevertheless, the human
understanding being unable to rest still seeks something prior in the
order of nature. And then it is that in struggling towards that which
is further off, it falls back upon that which is more nigh at hand;
namely, on final causes: which have relation clearly to the nature of
man rather than to the nature of the universe, and from this source
have strangely defiled philosophy. But he is no less an unskilled and
shallow philosopher who seeks causes of that which is most general,
than he who in things subordinate and subaltern[17] omits to do so.

The human understanding is no dry light, but receives an infu- 13
sion from the will and affections;[18] whence proceed sciences which
may be called "sciences as one would." For what a man had rather
were true he more readily believes. Therefore he rejects difficult
things from impatience of research; sober things, because they narrow hope; the deeper things of nature, from superstition; the light of

---

[15] **infinite divisibility of lines** This gave rise to the paradox of Zeno, the
Greek philosopher of the fifth century B.C. who showed that it was impossible to get
from one point to another because one had to pass the midpoint of the line determined by the two original points, and then the midpoint of the remaining distance,
and then of that remaining distance, down to an infinite number of points. By using
accepted truths to "prove" an absurdity about motion, Zeno actually hoped to prove
that motion itself did not exist. This is the "subtlety" or confusion Bacon says is produced by the "inability of thought to stop."

[16] **discovery of causes** Knowledge of the world was based on four causes: efficient (who made it?), material (what is it made of?), formal (what is its shape?), and
final (what is its purpose?). The scholastics concentrated their thinking on the first
and last, while the "middle causes," related to matter and shape, were the proper
subject matter of science because they alone yielded to observation. (See para. 34.)

[17] **subaltern** Lower in status.

[18] **will and affections** Human free will and emotional needs and responses.

experience, from arrogance and price, lest his mind should seem to be occupied with things mean and transitory; things not commonly believed, out of deference to the opinion of the vulgar. Numberless in short are the ways, and sometimes imperceptible, in which the affections color and infect the understanding.

But by far the greatest hindrance and aberration of the human understanding proceeds from the dullness, incompetency, and deceptions of the senses; in that things which strike the sense outweigh things which do not immediately strike it, though they be more important. Hence it is that speculation commonly ceases where sight ceases; insomuch that of things invisible there is little or no observation. Hence all the working of the spirits[19] enclosed in tangible bodies lies hid and unobserved of men. So also all the more subtle changes of form in the parts of coarser substances (which they commonly call alteration, though it is in truth local motion through exceedingly small spaces) is in like manner unobserved. And yet unless these two things just mentioned be searched out and brought to light, nothing great can be achieved in nature, as far as the production of works is concerned. So again the essential nature of our common air, and of all bodies less dense than air (which are very many) is almost unknown. For the sense by itself is a thing infirm and erring; neither can instruments for enlarging or sharpening the senses do much; but all the truer kind of interpretation of nature is effected by instances and experiments fit and apposite;[20] wherein the sense decides touching the experiment only, and the experiment touching the point in nature and the thing itself.   14

The human understanding is of its own nature prone to abstractions and gives a substance and reality to things which are fleeting. But to resolve nature into abstractions is less to our purpose than to dissect her into parts; as did the school of Democritus,[21] which went further into nature than the rest. Matter rather than forms should be the object of our attention, its configurations and changes of configuration, and simple action, and law of action or motion; for forms are figments of the human mind, unless you will call those laws of action forms.   15

Such then are the idols which I call *Idols of the Tribe;* and which take their rise either from the homogeneity of the substance of the   16

---

[19] **spirits** The soul or animating force.

[20] **apposite** Appropriate; well related.

[21] **Democritus (460? – 370? B.C.)** Greek philosopher who thought the world was composed of atoms. Bacon felt such "dissection" to be useless because it was impractical. Yet Democritus's concept of the *eidola,* the mind's impressions of things, may have contributed to Bacon's idea of "the idol."

human spirit,[22] or from its preoccupation, or from it narrowness, or from its restless motion, or from an infusion of the affections, or from the incompetency of the senses, or from the mode of impression.

The *Idols of the Cave* take their rise in the peculiar constitution, 17 mental or bodily, of each individual; and also in education, habit, and accident. Of this kind there is a great number and variety; but I will instance those the pointing out of which contains the most important caution, and which have most effect in disturbing the clearness of the understanding.

Men become attached to certain particular sciences and specula- 18 tions, either because they fancy themselves the authors and inventors thereof, or because they have bestowed the greatest pains upon them and become most habituated to them. But men of this kind, if they betake themselves to philosophy and contemplations of a general character, distort and color them in obedience to their former fancies; a thing especially to be noticed in Aristotle,[23] who made his natural philosophy[24] a mere bondservant to his logic, thereby rendering it contentious and well nigh useless. The race of chemists[25] again out of a few experiments of the furnace have built up a fantastic philosophy, framed with reference to a few things; and Gilbert[26] also, after he had employed himself most laboriously in the study and observation of the loadstone, proceeded at once to construct an entire system in accordance with his favorite subject.

There is one principal and, as it were, radical distinction between 19 different minds, in respect of philosophy and the sciences, which is this: that some minds are stronger and apter to mark the differences of things, others to mark their resemblances. The steady and acute mind can fix its contemplations and dwell and fasten on the subtlest distinctions: the lofty and discursive mind recognizes and puts together the finest and most general resemblances. Both kinds however easily err in excess, by catching the one at gradations, the other at shadows.

---

[22] **human spirit** Human nature.

[23] **Aristotle (384 – 322 B.C.)** Greek philosopher whose *Organon* (system of logic) dominated the thought of Bacon's time. Bacon sought to overthrow Aristotle's hold on science and thought.

[24] **natural philosophy** The scientific study of nature in general — biology, zoology, geology, etc.

[25] **chemists** Alchemists had developed a "fantastic philosophy" from their experimental attempts to transmute lead into gold.

[26] **William Gilbert (1544 – 1603)** An English scientist who studied magnetism and codified many laws related to magnetic fields. He was particularly ridiculed by Bacon for being too narrow in his researches.

There are found some minds given to an extreme admiration of   20
antiquity, others to an extreme love and appetite for novelty; but
few so duly tempered that they can hold the mean, neither carping
at what has been well laid down by the ancients, nor despising what
is well introduced by the moderns. This however turns to the great
injury of the sciences and philosophy; since these affectations of antiquity and novelty are the humors[27] of partisans rather than judgments; and truth is to be sought for not in the felicity of any age,
which is an unstable thing, but in the light of nature and experience,
which is eternal. These factions therefore must be abjured,[28] and
care must be taken that the intellect be not hurried by them into assent.

Contemplations of nature and of bodies in their simple form   21
break up and distract the understanding, while contemplations of
nature and bodies in their composition and configuration overpower
and dissolve the understanding: a distinction well seen in the school
of Leucippus[29] and Democritus as compared with the other philosophies. For that school is so busied with the particles that it hardly at-
tends to the structure; while the others are so lost in admiration of
the structure that they do not penetrate to the simplicity of nature.
These kinds of contemplation should therefore be alternated and
taken by turns; that so the understanding may be rendered at once
penetrating and comprehensive, and the inconveniences above mentioned, with the idols which proceed from them, may be avoided.

Let such then be our provision and contemplative prudence for   22
keeping off and dislodging the *Idols of the Cave,* which grow for the
most part either out of the predominance of a favorite subject, or out
of an excessive tendency to compare or to distinguish, or out of par-
tiality for particular ages, or out of the largeness or minuteness of
the objects contemplated. And generally let every student of nature
take this as a rule — that whatever his mind seizes and dwells upon
with peculiar satisfaction is to be held in suspicion, and that so
much the more care is to be taken in dealing with such questions to
keep the understanding even and clear.

But the *Idols of the Marketplace* are the most troublesome of all: 23
idols which have crept into the understanding through the alliances
of words and names. For men believe that their reason governs
words; but it is also true that words react on the understanding; and

---

[27] **humors** Used in a medical sense to mean a distortion caused by imbalance.
[28] **abjured** Renounced, sworn off, repudiated.
[29] **Leucippus (fifth century B.C.)** Greek philosopher; teacher of Democritus
and inventor of the atomistic theory. His works survive only in fragments.

this it is that has rendered philosophy and the sciences sophistical and inactive. Now words, being commonly framed and applied according to the capacity of the vulgar, follow those lines of division which are most obvious to the vulgar understanding. And whenever an understanding of greater acuteness or a more diligent observation would alter those lines to suit the true divisions of nature, words stand in the way and resist the change. Whence it comes to pass that the high and formal discussions of learned men end oftentimes in disputes about words and names; with which (according to the use and wisdom of the mathematicians) it would be more prudent to begin, and so by means of definitions reduce them to order. Yet even definitions cannot cure this evil in dealing with natural and material things; since the definitions themselves consist of words, and those words beget others: so that it is necessary to recur to individual instances, and those in due series and order; as I shall say presently when I come to the method and scheme for the formation of notions and axioms.[30]

The idols imposed by words on the understanding are of two   24
kinds. They are either names of things which do not exist (for as there are things left unnamed through lack of observation, so likewise are there names which result from fantastic suppositions and to which nothing in reality responds), or they are names of things which exist, but yet confused and ill-defined, and hastily and irregularly derived from realities. Of the former kind are Fortune, the Prime Mover, Planetary Orbits, Element of Fire, and like fictions which owe their origin to false and idle theories.[31] And this class of idols is more easily expelled, because to get rid of them it is only necessary that all theories should be steadily rejected and dismissed as obsolete.

But the other class, which springs out of a faulty and unskillful   25
abstraction, is intricate and deeply rooted. Let us take for example such a word as *humid*; and see how far the several things which the word is used to signify agree with each other; and we shall find the word *humid* to be nothing else than a mark loosely and confusedly applied to denote a variety of actions which will not bear to be reduced to any constant meaning. For it both signifies that which easily spreads itself round any other body; and that which in itself is in-

---

[30] **notions and axioms** Conceptions and definitive statements of truth.

[31] **idle theories** These are things that cannot be observed and thus do not exist. Fortune is fate; the Prime Mover is God or some "first" force; the notion that planets orbited the sun was considered as "fantastic" as these others or as the idea that everything was made up of fire and its many permutations.

determinate and cannot solidize; and that which readily yields in every direction; and that which easily divides and scatters itself; and that which easily unites and collects itself; and that which readily flows and is put in motion; and that which readily clings to another body and wets it; and that which is easily reduced to a liquid, or being solid easily melts. Accordingly when you come to apply the word — if you take it in one sense, flame is humid; if in another, air is not humid; if in another, fine dust is humid; if in another, glass is humid. So that it is easy to see that the notion is taken by abstraction only from water and common and ordinary liquids, without any due verification.

There are however in words certain degrees of distortion and error. One of the least faulty kinds is that of names of substances, especially of lowest species and well-deduced (for the notion of *chalk* and of *mud* is good, of *earth* bad);[32] a more faulty kind is that of actions, as *to generate, to corrupt, to alter;* the most faulty is of qualities (except such as are the immediate objects of the sense), as *heavy, light, rare, dense,* and the like. Yet in all these cases some notions are of necessity a little better than others, in proportion to the greater variety of subjects that fall within the range of the human sense.   26

But the *Idols of the Theater* are not innate, nor do they steal into the understanding secretly, but are plainly impressed and received into the mind from the play-books of philosophical systems and the perverted rules of demonstration.[33] To attempt refutations in this case would be merely inconsistent with what I have already said: for since we agree neither upon principles nor upon demonstrations, there is no place for argument. And this is so far well, inasmuch as it leaves the honor of the ancients untouched. For they are no wise disparaged — the question between them and me being only as to the way. For as the saying is, the lame man who keeps the right road outstrips the runner who takes a wrong one. Nay, it is obvious that when a man runs the wrong way, the more active and swift he is the further he will go astray.   27

But the course I propose for the discovery of sciences is such as leaves but little to the acuteness and strength of wits, but places all wits[34] and understandings nearly on a level. For as in the drawing of   28

---

[32] *earth* **bad** Chalk and mud were useful in manufacture; hence they were terms of approval. *Earth* is used here in the sense we use *dirt*, as in "digging in the dirt."

[33] **perverted rules of demonstration** Another complaint against Aristotle's logic as misapplied in Bacon's day.

[34] **wits** Intelligence, reasoning powers.

a straight line or perfect circle, much depends on the steadiness and practice of the hand, if it be done by aim of hand only, but if with the aid of rule or compass, little or nothing; so is it exactly with my plan. But though particular confutations[35] would be of no avail, yet touching the sects and general divisions of such systems I must say something; something also touching the external signs which show that they are unsound; and finally something touching the causes of such great infelicity and of such lasting and general agreement in error; that so the access to truth may be made less difficult, and the human understanding may the more willingly submit to its purgation and dismiss its idols.

Idols of the Theater, or of systems, are many, and there can be and perhaps will be yet many more. For were it not that now for many ages men's minds have been busied with religion and theology; and were it not that civil governments, especially monarchies, have been averse to such novelties, even in matters speculative; so that men labor therein to the peril and harming of their fortunes — not only unrewarded, but exposed also to contempt and envy; doubtless there would have arisen many other philosophical sects like to those which in great variety flourished once among the Greeks. For as on the phenomena of the heavens many hypotheses may be constructed, so likewise (and more also) many various dogmas may be set up and established on the phenomena of philosophy. And in the plays of this philosophical theater you may observe the same thing which is found in the theater of the poets, that stories invented for the stage are more compact and elegant, and more as one would wish them to be, than true stories out of history. 29

In general, however, there is taken for the material of philosophy either a great deal out of a few things, or a very little out of many things; so that on both sides philosophy is based on too narrow a foundation of experiment and natural history, and decides on the authority of too few cases. For the rational school of philosophers[36] snatches from experience a variety of common instances, neither duly ascertained nor diligently examined and weighed, and leaves all the rest to meditation and agitation of wit. 30

---

[35] **confutations** Specific counterarguments. Bacon means that he cannot offer particular arguments against each scientific sect; thus he offers a general warning.

[36] **rational school of philosophers** Platonists who felt that human reason alone could discover the truth and that experiment was unnecessary. Their observation of experience produced only a "variety of common instances" from which they reasoned.

There is also another class of philosophers,[37] who having be-   31
stowed much diligent and careful labor on a few experiments, have
thence made bold to educe and construct systems; wresting all other
facts in a strange fashion to conformity therewith.

And there is yet a third class,[38] consisting of those who out of   32
faith and veneration mix their philosophy with theology and traditions; among whom the vanity of some has gone so far aside as to
seek the origin of sciences among spirits and genii.[39] So that this
parent stock of errors — this false philosophy — is of three kinds;
the sophistical, the empirical, and the superstitious. . . .

But the corruption of philosophy by superstition and an admix-   33
ture of theology is far more widely spread, and does the greatest
harm, whether to entire systems or to their parts. For the human understanding is obnoxious to the influence of the imagination no less
than to the influence of common notions. For the contentious and
sophistical kind of philosophy ensnares the understanding; but this
kind, being fanciful and tumid[40] and half poetical, misleads it more
by flattery. For there is in man an ambition of the understanding, no
less than of the will, especially in high and lofty spirits.

Of this kind we have among the Greeks a striking example in   34
Pythagoras, though he united with it a coarser and more cumbrous
superstition; another in Plato and his school,[41] more dangerous and
subtle. It shows itself likewise in parts of other philosophies, in the
introduction of abstract forms and final causes and first causes, with
the omission in most cases of causes intermediate, and the like.
Upon this point the greatest caution should be used. For nothing is
so mischievous as the apotheosis of error; and it is a very plague of
the understanding for vanity to become the object of veneration. Yet
in this vanity some of the moderns have with extreme levity indulged so far as to attempt to found a system of natural philosophy

---

[37] **another class of philosophers** William Gilbert (1544–1603) experimented tirelessly with magnetism, from which he derived numerous odd theories.
Though Gilbert was a true scientist, Bacon thought of him as limited and on the
wrong track.

[38] **a third class** Pythagoras (580?–500? B.C.) was a Greek philosopher who
experimented rigorously with mathematics and a tuned string. He is said to have developed the musical scale. His theory of reincarnation, or the transmigration of
souls, was somehow based on his travels in India and his work with scales. The superstitious belief in the movement of souls is what Bacon complains of.

[39] **genii** Oriental demons or spirits; a slap at Pythagoras, who traveled in the
Orient.

[40] **tumid** Overblown, swollen.

[41] **Plato and his school** Plato's religious bent was further developed by Plotinus (A.D. 205–270) in his *Enneads*. Although Plotinus was not a Christian, his Neo-
platonism was welcomed as a philosophy compatible with Christianity.

on the first chapter of Genesis, on the book of Job, and other parts of the sacred writings; seeking for the dead among the living: which also makes the inhibition and repression of it the more important, because from this unwholesome mixture of things human and divine there arises not only a fantastic philosophy but also an heretical religion. Very meet it is therefore that we be sober-minded, and give to faith that only which is faith's. . . .

So much concerning the several classes of Idols, and their equipage: all of which must be renounced and put away with a fixed and solemn determination, and the understanding thoroughly freed and cleansed; the entrance into the kingdom of man, founded on the sciences, being not much other than the entrance into the kingdom of heaven, whereunto none may enter except as a little child. 35

QUESTIONS FOR CRITICAL READING

1. Which of Bacon's idols is the most difficult to understand? Do your best to define it.
2. Which of these idols do we still need to worry about? Why? What dangers does it present?
3. What does Bacon mean by saying that our senses are weak (para. 14)? In what ways do you agree or disagree with that statement?
4. Occasionally Bacon says something that seems a bit like an aphorism (see the introduction to Machiavelli, p. 35). Find at least one such expression in this selection. On examination, does the expression have as much meaning as it seems to have?
5. What kind of readers did Bacon expect for this piece? What clues does his way of communicating provide regarding the nature of his anticipated readers?

SUGGESTIONS FOR WRITING

1. Which of Bacon's idols most seriously affects the way you as a person observe nature? Using enumeration, arrange the idols in order of their effect on your own judgment. If you prefer, you may write about which idol you believe is most effective in slowing investigation into nature.
2. Is it true, as Bacon says in paragraph 10, that people are in general more excited by affirmation than by negation? Do we really stress the positive and deemphasize the negative in the conduct of our general affairs? Find at least three instances in which people seem to gravitate toward the positive or the negative in various everyday situations. Try

to establish whether Bacon has, in fact, described what is a habit of mind.

3. In paragraph 13, Bacon states that the "will and affections" enter into matters of thought. By this he means that our understanding of what we observe is conditioned by what we want and what we feel. Thus, when he says, "For what a man had rather were true he more readily believes," he tells us that people tend to believe what they want to believe. Test this statement by means of observation. Find out, for example, how many older people are convinced that the world is deteriorating, how many younger people feel that there is a plot on the part of older people to hold them back, how many women feel that men consciously oppress women, and how many men feel that feminists are not as feminine as they should be. What other beliefs can you discover that seem to have their origin in what people want to believe rather than in what is true?

4. Bacon's views on religion have always been questionable. He grew up in a very religious time, but his writings rarely discuss religion positively. In this work he talks about giving "to faith that only which is faith's" (para. 34). He seems to feel that scientific investigation is something quite separate from religion. Examine the selection carefully to determine what you think Bacon's view on this question is. Then take a stand on the issue of the relationship between religion and science. Should science be totally independent of religious concerns? Should religious issues control scientific experimentation? What does Bacon mean when he complains about the vanity of founding "a system of natural philosophy on the first chapter of Genesis, on the book of Job, and other parts of the sacred writings" (para. 34)? "Natural philosophy" means biology, chemistry, physics, and science in general. Are Bacon's complaints justified? Would his complaints be relevant today?

5. **CONNECTIONS** How has the reception of Darwin's work been affected by a general inability of the public to see beyond Bacon's four idols? Read both Darwin's essay and that of Stephen Jay Gould. Which of those two writers is more concerned with the lingering effects of the four idols? Do you feel that the effects have seriously affected people's beliefs regarding Darwinian theory?

6. **CONNECTIONS** What do Maimonides and Bacon agree on regarding the limitations of the human intellect? Does Maimonides perceive the limitations that Bacon refers to in his discussion? Which of the four idols does Maimonides seem aware of? On the other hand, in what ways does Bacon disagree with Maimonides regarding the absolute limits of the mind? What does their difference in focus — Maimonides on metaphysics, Bacon on physics — imply for their expectations for the mind's capacity to know the truth about nature?

CHARLES DARWIN
Natural Selection

CHARLES DARWIN (1809 – 1882) was trained as a minister
in the Church of England, but he was also the grandson of one of
England's greatest horticulturists, Erasmus Darwin. Partly as a way
of putting off ordination in the church and partly because of his
natural curiosity, Darwin found himself performing the functions
of a naturalist on HMS *Beagle,* which was engaged in scientific ex-
plorations around South America during the years 1831 to 1836.
Darwin's book *Journal of Researches into the Geology and Natural
History of the Various Countries Visited by H. M. S. Beagle, 1832 – 36*
(1839) details the experiences he had and offers us some views of
his self-education as a naturalist.

His journeys on the *Beagle* led him to note variations in species
of animals he found in various separate locales, particularly between remote islands and the mainland. Varieties — his term for
any visible (or invisible) differences in markings, coloration, size
or shape of appendages, organs, or bodies — were of some peculiar
use, he believed, for animals in the environment in which he found
them. He was not certain about the use of these varieties, and he
did not know whether the changes that created the varieties resulted from the environment or from some chance operation of nature. Ultimately, he concluded that varieties in nature were caused
by three forces: (1) natural selection, in which varieties occur spontaneously by chance but are then "selected" for because they are
aids to survival; (2) direct action of the environment, in which non-

From *On the Origin of Species by Means of Natural Selection.* This text is from the
first edition, published in 1859. In the five subsequent editions, Darwin hedged
more and more on his theory, often introducing material in defense against objections. The first edition is vigorous and direct; this edition jolted the worlds of science
and religion out of their complaisance. In later editions, this chapter was titled "Natural Selection; or, Survival of the Fittest."

adaptive varieties do not survive because of climate, food conditions, or the like; and (3) the effects of use or disuse of a variation (for example, the short beak of a bird in para. 9). Darwin later regarded sexual selection, which figures prominently in this work, as less significant.

The idea of evolution — the gradual change of species through some kind of modification of varieties — had been in the air for many years when Darwin began his work. The English scientists W. C. Wells in 1813 and Patrick Matthew in 1831 had both proposed theories of natural selection, although Darwin was unaware of their work. Alfred Russel Wallace (1823 – 1913), a younger English scientist, revealed in 1858 that he was about to propose the same theory of evolution as was Darwin. They jointly published brief versions of their theories in 1858, and the next year Darwin rushed the final version of his book *On the Origin of Species by Means of Natural Selection* to press.

Darwin did not mention human beings as part of the evolutionary process in *On the Origin of Species;* because he was particularly concerned about the probable adverse reactions of theologians, he merely promised later discussion of that subject. It came in *The Descent of Man and Selection in Relation to Sex* (1871), the companion to *On the Origin of Species.*

When Darwin returned to England after completing his researches on the *Beagle,* he supplemented his knowledge with information gathered from breeders of pigeons, livestock, dogs, and horses. This research, it must be noted, involved relatively few samples and was conducted according to comparatively unscientific practices. Yet although limited, it corresponded with his observations of nature. Humans could and did cause changes in species; Darwin's task was to show that nature — through the process of natural selection — could do the same thing.

The Descent of Man stirred up a great deal of controversy between the church and Darwin's supporters. Not since the Roman Catholic Church denied the fact that the earth went around the sun, which Galileo proved scientifically by 1632 (and was placed under house arrest for his pains), had there been a more serious confrontation between science and religion. Darwin was ridiculed by ministers and doubted by older scientists; but his views were stoutly defended by younger scientists, many of whom had arrived at similar conclusions. In the end, Darwin's views were accepted by the Church of England, and when he died in 1882 he was lionized and buried at Westminster Abbey in London. Only recently has controversy concerning his work arisen again.

DARWIN'S RHETORIC

Despite the complexity of the material it deals with, Darwin's writing is fluent, smooth, and stylistically sophisticated and keeps the reader engaged. Darwin's rhetorical method depends entirely on the yoking of thesis and demonstration. He uses definition frequently, but most often he uses testimony, gathering information and instances, both real and imaginary, from many different sources.

Interestingly enough, Darwin claimed that he used Francis Bacon's method of induction in his researches, gathering evidence of many instances of a given phenomenon, from which the truth — or a natural law — emerges. In fact, Darwin did not quite follow this path. Like most modern scientists, he established a hypothesis after a period of observation, and then he looked for evidence that confirmed or refuted the hypothesis. He was careful to include examples that argued against his view, but like most scientists, he emphasized the importance of the supportive samples.

Induction plays a part in the rhetoric of this selection in that it is dominated by examples from bird breeding, birds in nature, domestic farm animals and their breeding, and botany, including the breeding of plants and the interdependence of certain insects and certain plants. Erasmus Darwin was famous for his work with plants, and it is natural that such observations would play an important part in his grandson's thinking.

The process of natural selection is carefully discussed, particularly in paragraph 8 and thereafter. Darwin emphasizes its positive nature and its differences from selection by human breeders. The use of comparison, which appears frequently in the selection, is most conspicuous in these paragraphs. He postulates a nature in which the fittest survive because they are best adapted for survival, but he does not dwell on the fate of those who are unfit individuals. It was left to later writers, often misapplying his theories, to do that.

Natural Selection

How will the struggle for existence . . . act in regard to variation? Can the principle of selection, which we have seen is so potent in the hands of man, apply in nature? I think we shall see that it can act most effectually. Let it be borne in mind in what an endless number of strange peculiarities our domestic productions, and, in a lesser degree, those under nature, vary; and how strong the hereditary tendency is. Under domestication, it may be truly said that the whole organization becomes in some degree plastic.[1] Let it be borne in mind how infinitely complex and close-fitting are the mutual relations of all organic beings to each other and to their physical conditions of life. Can it, then, be thought improbable, seeing that variations useful to man have undoubtedly occurred, that other variations useful in some way to each being in the great and complex battle of life, should sometimes occur in the course of thousands of generations? If such do occur, can we doubt (remembering that many more individuals are born than can possibly survive) that individuals having any advantage, however slight, over others, would have the best chance of surviving and or procreating their kind? On the other hand, we may feel sure that any variation in the least degree injurious would be rigidly destroyed. This preservation of favorable variations and the rejection of injurious variations, I call Natural Selection. Variations neither useful nor injurious would not be affected by natural selection, and would be left a fluctuating element, as perhaps we see in the species called polymorphic.[2]

We shall best understand the probable course of natural selection by taking the case of a country undergoing some physical change, for instance, of climate. The proportional numbers of its inhabitants would almost immediately undergo a change, and some species might become extinct. We may conclude, from what we have seen of the intimate and complex manner in which the inhabitants of each country are bound together, that any change in the numerical proportions of some of the inhabitants, independently of the change of climate itself, would most seriously affect many of the others. If the country were open on its borders, new forms would certainly immigrate, and this also would seriously disturb the relations of some of the former inhabitants. Let it be remembered how powerful the influence of a single introduced tree or mammal has been shown to be. But in the case of an island, or of a country partly surrounded by barriers, into which new and better adapted forms could not freely enter, we should then have places in the economy of nature which would assuredly be better filled up, if some of the original inhabitants were in some manner modified; for, had the area been open to immigration, these same places would have been seized on by intruders. In such case, every slight modification,

---

[1] **plastic** Capable of being shaped and changed.
[2] **species called polymorphic** Species that have more than one form over the course of their lives, such as butterflies.

which in the course of ages chanced to arise, and which in any way favored the individuals of any of the species, by better adapting them to their altered conditions, would tend to be preserved; and natural selection would thus have free scope for the work of improvement.

We have reason to believe . . . that a change in the conditions of 3 life, by specially acting on the reproductive system, causes or increases variability; and in the foregoing case the conditions of life are supposed to have undergone a change, and this would manifestly be favorable to natural selection, by giving a better chance of profitable variations occurring; and unless profitable variations do occur, natural selection can do nothing. Not that, as I believe, any extreme amount of variability is necessary; as man can certainly produce great results by adding up in any given direction mere individual differences, so could Nature, but far more easily, from having incomparably longer time at her disposal. Nor do I believe that any great physical change, as of climate, or any unusual degree of isolation to check immigration, is actually necessary to produce new and unoccupied places for natural selection to fill up by modifying and improving some of the varying inhabitants. For as all the inhabitants of each country are struggling together with nicely balanced forces, extremely slight modifications in the structure or habits of one inhabitant would often give it an advantage over others; and still further modifications of the same kind would often still further increase the advantage. No country can be named in which all the native inhabitants are now so perfectly adapted to each other and to the physical conditions under which they live, that none of them could anyhow be improved; for in all countries, the natives have been so far conquered by naturalized productions, that they have allowed foreigners to take firm possession of the land. And as foreigners have thus everywhere beaten some of the natives, we may safely conclude that the natives might have been modified with advantage, so as to have better resisted such intruders.

As man can produce and certainly has produced a great result 4 by his methodical and unconscious means of selection, what may not nature effect? Man can act only on external and visible characters; nature cares nothing for appearances, except in so far as they may be useful to any being. She can act on every internal organ, on every shade of constitutional difference, on the whole machinery of life. Man selects only for his own good; Nature only for that of the being which she tends. Every selected character is fully exercised by her; and the being is placed under well-suited conditions of life. Man keeps the natives of many climates in the same country; he seldom exercises each selected character in some peculiar and fitting manner; he feeds a long and a short beaked pigeon on the same food; he does not exercise a long-backed or long-legged quadruped in any peculiar manner; he exposes sheep with long and short wool to the same climate. He does not allow the most vigorous males to struggle for the females. He does not rigidly destroy all inferior animals, but protects during each varying season, as far as lies in his power, all his productions. He often begins his selection by some half-monstrous form; or at least by some modification prominent enough to catch the eye, or to be plainly useful to him. Under nature, the slightest difference of structure or constitution may well turn the nicely balanced scale in the struggle for life, and so be preserved. How fleeting are the wishes and efforts of man! how short his time! and consequently how poor will his products be, compared with those accumulated by nature during whole geological periods. Can we wonder, then, that nature's productions should be far "truer" in character than man's productions; that they should be infinitely better adapted to the most complex conditions of life, and should plainly bear the stamp of far higher workmanship?

It may be said that natural selection is daily and hourly scruti-   5
nizing, throughout the world, every variation, even the slightest; rejecting that which is bad, preserving and adding up all that is good; silently and insensibly working, whenever and wherever opportunity offers, at the improvement of each organic being in relation to its organic and inorganic conditions of life. We see nothing of these slow changes in progress, until the hand of time has marked the long lapse of ages, and then so imperfect is our view into long past geological ages, that we only see that the forms of life are now different from what they formerly were.

Although natural selection can act only through and for the   6
good of each being, yet characters and structures, which we are apt to consider as of very trifling importance, may thus be acted on. When we see leaf-eating insects green, and bark-feeders mottled-grey; the alpine ptarmigan white in winter, the red-grouse the color of heather, and the black-grouse that of peaty earth, we must believe that these tints are of service to these birds and insects in preserving them from danger. Grouse, if not destroyed at some period of their lives, would increase in countless numbers; they are known to suffer largely from birds of prey; and hawks are guided by eyesight to their prey — so much so that on parts of the Continent[3] persons are warned not to keep white pigeons, as being the most liable to de-

---

[3] **Continent** European continent; the contiguous land mass of Europe, which excludes the British Isles.

struction. Hence I can see no reason to doubt that natural selection might be most effective in giving the proper color to each kind of grouse, and in keeping that color, when once acquired, true and constant. Nor ought we to think that the occasional destruction of an animal of any particular color would produce little effect; we should remember how essential it is in a flock of white sheep to destroy every lamb with the faintest trace of black. In plants, the down on the fruit and the color of the flesh are considered by botanists as characters of the most trifling importance; yet we hear from an excellent horticulturist, Downing,[4] that in the United States, smooth-skinned fruits suffer far more from a beetle, a curculio,[5] than those with down; that purple plums suffer far more from a certain disease than yellow plums; whereas another disease attacks yellow-fleshed peaches far more than those with other colored flesh. If, with all the aids of art, these slight differences make a great difference in cultivating the several varieties, assuredly, in a state of nature, where the trees would have to struggle with other trees and with a host of enemies, such differences would effectually settle which variety, whether a smooth or downy, a yellow or purple fleshed fruit, should succeed.

In looking at many small points of difference between species, 7 which, as far as our ignorance permits us to judge, seem to be quite unimportant, we must not forget that climate, food, etc., probably produce some slight and direct effect. It is, however, far more necessary to bear in mind that there are many unknown laws of correlation[6] of growth, which, when one part of the organization is modified through variation and the modifications are accumulated by natural selection for the good of the being, will cause other modifications, often of the most unexpected nature.

As we see that those variations which under domestication appear at any particular period of life, tend to reappear in the offspring at the same period — for instance, in the seeds of the many varieties of our culinary and agricultural plants; in the caterpillar and cocoon stages of the varieties of the silkworm; in the eggs of poultry, and in the color of the down of their chickens; in the horns of our sheep and cattle when nearly adult — so in a state of nature, natural selection will be enabled to act on and modify organic beings at any age,

---

[4] **Andrew Jackson Downing (1815–1852)** American horticulturist and specialist in fruit and fruit trees.

[5] **curculio** A weevil.

[6] **laws of correlation** In certain plants and animals, one condition relates to another, as in the case of blue-eyed white cats, which are always deaf; the reasons are not clear but have to do with genes and their locations.

by the accumulation of profitable variations at that age, and by their inheritance at a corresponding age. If it profit a plant to have its seeds more and more widely disseminated by the wind, I can see no greater difficulty in this being effected through natural selection than in the cotton-planter increasing and improving by selection the down in the pods on his cotton-trees. Natural selection may modify and adapt the larva of an insect to a score of contingencies, wholly different from those which concern the mature insect. These modifications will no doubt effect, through the laws of correlation, the structure of the adult; and probably in the case of those insects which live only for a few hours, and which never feed, a large part of their structure is merely the correlated result of successive changes in the structure of their larvae. So, conversely, modifications in the adult will probably often affect the structure of the larva; but in all cases natural selection will ensure that modifications consequent on other modifications at a different period of life, shall not be in the least degree injurious: for if they became so, they would cause the extinction of the species.

Natural selection will modify the structure of the young in rela-   9 tion to the parent, and of the parent in relation to the young. In social animals it will adapt the structure of each individual for the benefit of the community; if each in consequence profits by the selected change. What natural selection cannot do is to modify the structure of one species, without giving it any advantage, for the good of another species; and though statements to this effect may be found in works of natural history, I cannot find one case which will bear investigation. A structure used only once in an animal's whole life, if of high importance to it, might be modified to any extent by natural selection; for instance, the great jaws possessed by certain insects, and used exclusively for opening the cocoon — or the hard tip to the beak of nestling birds, used for breaking the egg. It has been asserted that of the best short-beaked tumbler-pigeons, more perish in the egg than are able to get out of it; so that fanciers[7] assist in the act of hatching. Now, if nature had to make the beak of a full-grown pigeon very short for the bird's own advantage, the process of modification would be very slow, and there would be simultaneously the most rigorous selection of the young birds within the egg, which had the most powerful and hardest beaks, for all with weak beaks would inevitably perish; or, more delicate and more easily broken shells might be selected, the thickness of the shell being known to vary like every other structure.

---

[7] **fanciers** Amateurs who raise and race pigeons.

Sexual Selection

Inasmuch as peculiarities often appear under domestication in   10
one sex and become hereditarily attached to that sex, the same fact
probably occurs under nature, and if so, natural selection will be able
to modify one sex in its functional relations to the other sex, or in relation to wholly different habits of life in the two sexes, as is sometimes the case with insects. And this leads me to say a few words on
what I call Sexual Selection. This depends, not on a struggle for existence, but on a struggle between the males for possession of the females; the result is not death to the unsuccessful competitor, but few
or no offspring. Sexual selection is, therefore, less rigorous than natural selection. Generally, the most vigorous males, those which are
best fitted for their places in nature, will leave most progeny. But in
many cases, victory will depend not on general vigor, but on having
special weapons, confined to the male sex. A hornless stag or spurless
cock would have a poor chance of leaving offspring. Sexual selection
by always allowing the victor to breed might surely give indomitable
courage, length to the spur, and strength to the wing to strike in the
spurred leg, as well as the brutal cock fighter,[8] who knows well that he
can improve his breed by careful selection of the best cocks. How low
in the scale of nature this law of battle descends, I know not; male al-
ligators have been described as fighting, bellowing, and whirling
round, like Indians in a wardance, for the possession of the females;
male salmons have been seen fighting all day long; male stag-beetles
often bear wounds from the huge mandibles[9] of other males. The war
is, perhaps, severest between the males of polygamous animals,[10] and
these seem oftenest provided with special weapons. The males of carnivorous animals are already well armed; though to them and to others, special means of defense may be given through means of sexual
selection, as the mane to the lion, the shoulder-pad to the boar, and
the hooked jaw to the male salmon; for the shield may be as important
for victory as the sword or spear.

Among birds, the contest is often of a more peaceful character.   11
All those who have attended to the subject believe that there is the
severest rivalry between the males of many species to attract, by
singing, the females. The rock-thrush of Guiana,[11] birds of paradise,
and some others, congregate; and successive males display their gor-

---

[8] **brutal cock fighter** Cockfights were a popular spectator sport in England,
especially for gamblers; but many people considered them a horrible brutality.

[9] **mandibles** Jaws.

[10] **polygamous animals** Animals that typically have more than one mate.

[11] **Guyana** Formerly British Guiana, on the northeast coast of South America.

geous plumage and perform strange antics before the females, which standing by as spectators, at last choose the most attractive partner. Those who have closely attended to birds in confinement well know that they often take individual preferences and dislikes: thus Sir R. Heron[12] has described how one pied peacock was eminently attractive to all his hen birds. It may appear childish to attribute any effect to such apparently weak means: I cannot here enter on the details necessary to support this view; but if man can in a short time give elegant carriage and beauty to his bantams,[13] according to his standard of beauty, I can see no good reason to doubt that female birds, by selecting, during thousands of generations, the most melodious or beautiful males, according to their standard of beauty, might produce a marked effect. I strongly suspect that some well-known laws with respect to the plumage of male and female birds, in comparison with the plumage of the young, can be explained on the view of plumage having been chiefly modified by sexual selection, acting when the birds have come to the breeding age or during the breeding season; the modifications thus produced being inherited at corresponding ages or seasons, either by the males alone, or by the males and females; but I have not space here to enter on this subject.

Thus it is, as I believe, that when the males and females of any animal have the same general habits of life, but differ in structure, color, or ornament, such differences have been mainly caused by sexual selection; that is, individual males have had, in successive generations, some slight advantage over other males, in their weapons, means of defense, or charms; and have transmitted these advantages to their male offspring. Yet, I would not wish to attribute all such sexual differences to this agency: for we see peculiarities arising and becoming attached to the male sex in our domestic animals (as the wattle in male carriers, horn-like protuberances in the cocks of certain fowls, etc.), which we cannot believe to be either useful to the males in battle, or attractive to the females. We see analogous cases under nature, for instance, the tuft of hair on the breast of the turkey-cock, which can hardly be either useful or ornamental to this bird; indeed, had the tuft appeared under domestication, it would have been called a monstrosity.

12

---

[12] **Sir Robert Heron (1765–1854)** English politician who maintained a menagerie of animals.
[13] **bantams** Cocks bred for fighting.

Illustrations of the Action of Natural Selection

In order to make it clear how, as I believe, natural selection acts, 13 I must beg permission to give one or two imaginary illustrations. Let us take the case of a wolf, which preys on various animals, securing some by craft, some by strength, and some by fleetness; and let us suppose that the fleetest prey, a deer for instance, had from any change in the country increased in numbers, or that other prey had decreased in numbers, during that season of the year when the wolf is hardest pressed for food. I can under such circumstances see no reason to doubt that the swiftest and slimmest wolves would have the best chance of surviving, and so be preserved or selected, provided always that they retained strength to master their prey at this or at some other period of the year, when they might be compelled to prey on other animals. I can see no more reason to doubt this, than that man can improve the fleetness of his greyhounds by careful and methodical selection, or by that unconscious selection which results from each man trying to keep the best dogs without any thought of modifying the breed.

Even without any change in the proportional numbers of the ani- 14 mals on which our wolf preyed, a cub might be born with an innate tendency to pursue certain kinds of prey. Nor can this be thought very improbable; for we often observe great differences in the natural tendencies of our domestic animals; one cat, for instance, taking to catch rats, another mice; one cat, according to Mr. St. John,[14] bringing home winged game, another hares or rabbits, and another hunting on marshy ground and almost nightly catching woodcocks or snipes. The tendency to catch rats rather than mice is known to be inherited. Now, if any slight innate change of habit or of structure benefited an individual wolf, it would have the best chance of surviving and of leaving offspring. Some of its young would probably inherit the same habits or structure, and by the repetition of this process, a new variety might be formed which would either supplant or coexist with the parent-form of wolf. Or, again, the wolves inhabiting a mountainous district, and those frequenting the lowlands, would naturally be forced to hunt different prey; and from the continued preservation of the individuals best fitted for the two sites, two varieties might slowly be formed. These varieties would cross and blend where they met; but

---

[14] **Charles George William St. John (1809 – 1856)** An English naturalist whose book *Wild Sports and Natural History of the Highlands* was published in 1846.

to this subject of intercrossing we shall soon have to return. I may add, that, according to Mr. Pierce,[15] there are two varieties of the wolf inhabiting the Catskill Mountains in the United States, one with a light greyhound-like form, which pursues deer, and the other more bulky, with shorter legs, which more frequently attacks the shepherd's flocks.

Let us now take a more complex case. Certain plants excrete a sweet juice, apparently for the sake of eliminating something injurious from their sap; this is effected by glands at the base of the stipules[16] in some Leguminosæ, and at the back of the leaf of the common laurel. This juice, though small in quantity, is greedily sought by insects. Let us now suppose a little sweet juice or nectar to be excreted by the inner bases of the petals of a flower. In this case insects in seeking the nectar would get dusted with pollen, and would certainly often transport the pollen from one flower to the stigma of another flower. The flowers of two distinct individuals of the same species would thus get crossed; and the act of crossing, we have good reason to believe (as will hereafter be more fully alluded to), would produce very vigorous seedlings, which consequently would have the best chance of flourishing and surviving. Some of these seedlings would probably inherit the nectar-excreting power. Those individual flowers which had the largest glands or nectaries, and which excreted most nectar, would be oftenest visited by insects, and would be oftenest crossed; and so in the long-run would gain the upper hand. Those flowers, also, which had their stamens and pistils[17] placed, in relation to the size and habits of the particular insects which visited them, so as to favor in any degree the transportal of their pollen from flower to flower, would likewise be favored or selected. We might have taken the case of insects visiting flowers for the sake of collecting pollen instead of nectar; and as pollen is formed for the sole object of fertilization, its destruction appears a simple loss to the plant; yet if a little pollen were carried, at first occasionally and then habitually, by the pollen-devouring insects from flower to flower, and a cross thus effected, although nine-tenths of the pollen were destroyed, it might still be a great gain to the plant; and those individuals which produced more and more pollen, and had larger and larger anthers,[18] would be selected.

15

---

[15] **Pierce** Unidentified.

[16] **stipules** Spines at the base of a leaf.

[17] **stamens and pistils** Sexual organs of plants. The male and female organs appear together in the same flower.

[18] **anthers** An anther is that part of the stamen that contains pollen.

When our plant, by this process of the continued preservation   16
or natural selection of more and more attractive flowers, had been
rendered highly attractive to insects, they would, unintentionally on
their part, regularly carry pollen from flower to flower; and that they
can most effectually do this, I could easily show by many striking instances. I will give only one — not as a very striking case, but as
likewise illustrating one step in the separation of the sexes of plants,
presently to be alluded to. Some holly-trees bear only male flowers,
which have four stamens producing rather a small quantity of
pollen, and a rudimentary pistil; other holly-trees bear only female
flowers; these have a full-sized pistil, and four stamens with shriv-
elled anthers, in which not a grain of pollen can be detected. Having
found a female tree exactly sixty yards from a male tree, I put the
stigmas[19] of twenty flowers, taken from different branches, under
the microscope, and on all, without exception, there were pollen-
grains, and on some a profusion of pollen. As the wind had set for
several days from the female to the male tree, the pollen could not
thus have been carried. The weather had been cold and boisterous,
and therefore not favorable to bees; nevertheless every female flower
which I examined had been effectually fertilized by the bees, accidentally dusted with pollen, having flown from tree to tree in search
of nectar. But to return to our imaginary case: as soon as the plant
had been rendered so highly attractive to insects that pollen was regularly carried from flower to flower, another process might commence. No naturalist doubts the advantage of what has been called
the "physiological division of labor"; hence we may believe that it
would be advantageous to a plant to produce stamens alone in one
flower or on one whole plant, and pistils alone in another flower or
on another plant. In plants under culture and placed under new
conditions of life, sometimes the male organs and sometimes the female organs become more or less impotent; now if we suppose this
to occur in ever so slight a degree under nature, then as pollen is already carried regularly from flower to flower, and as a more complete separation of the sexes of our plant would be advantageous on
the principle of the division of labor, individuals with this tendency
more and more increased, would be continually favored or selected,
until at last a complete separation of the sexes would be effected.

Let us now turn to the nectar-feeding insects in our imaginary   17
case: we may suppose the plant of which we have been slowly increasing the nectar by continued selection, to be a common plant;
and that certain insects depended in main part on its nectar for food.

---

[19] **stigmas** Where the plant's pollen develops.

I could give many facts, showing how anxious bees are to save time; for instance, their habit of cutting holes and sucking the nectar at the bases of certain flowers, which they can, with a very little more trouble, enter by the mouth. Bearing such facts in mind, I can see no reason to doubt that an accidental deviation in the size and form of the body, or in the curvature and length of the proboscis,[20] etc., far too slight to be appreciated by us, might profit a bee or other insect, so that an individual so characterized would be able to obtain its food more quickly, and so have a better chance of living and leaving descendants. Its descendants would probably inherit a tendency to a similar slight deviation of structure. The tubes of the corollas[21] of the common red and incarnate clovers (Trifolium pratense and incarnatum) do not on a hasty glance appear to differ in length; yet the hive-bee can easily suck the nectar out of the incarnate clover, but not out of the common red clover, which is visited by humble-bees[22] alone; so that whole fields of the red clover offer in vain an abundant supply of precious nectar to the hive-bee. Thus it might be a great advantage to the hive-bee to have a slightly longer or differently constructed proboscis. On the other hand, I have found by experiment that the fertility of clover greatly depends on bees visiting and moving parts of the corolla, so as to push the pollen on to the stigmatic surface. Hence, again, if humble-bees were to become rare in any country, it might be a great advantage to the red clover to have a shorter or more deeply divided tube to its corolla, so that the hive-bee could visit its flowers. Thus I can understand how a flower and a bee might slowly become, either simultaneously or one after the other, modified and adapted in the most perfect manner to each other, by the continued preservation of individuals presenting mutual and slightly favorable deviations of structure.

I am well aware that this doctrine of natural selection, exemplified in the above imaginary instances, is open to the same objections which were at first urged against Sir Charles Lyell's noble views[23] on "the modern changes of the earth, as illustrative of geology"; but we now very seldom hear the action, for instance, of the coast-waves, called a trifling and insignificant cause, when applied to the excavation of gigantic valleys or to the formation of the longest lines of in-

18

---

[20] **proboscis** Snout.

[21] **corollas** Inner set of floral petals.

[22] **humble-bees** Bumblebees.

[23] **Sir Charles Lyell's noble views** Lyell (1797 – 1875) was an English geologist whose landmark work, *Principles of Geology* (1830 – 1833), Darwin read while on the *Beagle*. The book inspired Darwin, and the two scientists became friends. Lyell was shown portions of *On the Origin of Species* while Darwin was writing it.

land cliffs. Natural selection can act only by the preservation and accumulation of infinitesimally small inherited modifications, each
profitable to the preserved being; and as modern geology has almost
banished such views as the excavation of a great valley by a single
diluvial[24] wave, so will natural selection, if it be a true principle,
banish the belief of the continued creation of new organic beings, or
of any great and sudden modification in their structure.

---

[24] **diluvial** Pertaining to a flood. Darwin means that geological changes, such
as those that caused the Grand Canyon, were no longer thought of as being created
instantly by flood (or other catastrophes) but were considered to have developed
over a long period of time, as he imagines happened in the evolution of the species.

QUESTIONS FOR CRITICAL READING

1. Darwin's metaphor "battle of life" (para. 1) introduces issues that
   might be thought extraneous to a scientific inquiry. What is the danger
   of using such a metaphor? What is the advantage of doing so?
2. Many religious groups reject Darwin's concept of natural selection, but
   they heartily accept human selection in the form of controlled breeding. Why would there be such a difference between the two?
3. Do you feel that the theory of natural selection is a positive force?
   Could it be directed by divine power?
4. There is no reference to human beings in this work. How might the
   principles at work on animals also work on people? Do you think that
   Darwin assumes this?
5. When this chapter was published in a later edition, Darwin added to
   its title "Survival of the Fittest." What issues or emotions does that new
   title raise that "Natural Selection" does not?

SUGGESTIONS FOR WRITING

1. In paragraph 13, Darwin uses imaginary examples. Compare the value
   of his genuine examples and these imaginary ones. How effective is the
   use of imaginary examples in an argument? What requirements should
   an imaginary example meet to be forceful in an argument? Do you find
   Darwin's imaginary examples to be strong or weak?
2. From paragraph 14 on, Darwin discusses the process of modification
   of a species through its beginning in the modification of an individual.
   Explain, insofar as you understand the concept, how a species could
   be modified by a variation occurring in just one individual. In your explanation, use Darwin's rhetorical technique of the imaginary example.

3. Write an essay that takes as its thesis statement the following sentence from paragraph 18: "Natural selection can act only by the preservation and accumulation of infinitesimally small inherited modifications, each profitable to the preserved being." Be sure to examine the work carefully for other statements by Darwin that add strength, clarity, and meaning to this one. You may also employ the Darwinian device of presenting "imaginary instances" in your essay.

4. A controversy exists concerning the Darwinian theory of evolution. Explore the *Readers' Guide to Periodical Literature and the Internet* for up-to-date information on the creationist-evolutionist conflict in schools. Look up either or both terms to see what articles you can find. Define the controversy and take a stand on it. Use your knowledge of natural selection gained from this piece. Remember, too, that Darwin was trained as a minister of the church and was concerned about religious opinion.

5. When Darwin wrote this piece, he believed that sexual selection was of great importance in evolutionary changes in species. Assuming that this belief is true, establish the similarities between sexual selection in plants and animals and sexual selection, as you have observed it, in people. Paragraphs 10 to 12 discuss this issue. Darwin does not discuss human beings, but it is clear that physical and stylistic distinctions between the sexes have some bearing on selection. Assuming that to be true, what qualities in people (physical and mental) are likely to survive? Why?

6. **CONNECTIONS** Which of Francis Bacon's four idols would have made it most difficult for Darwin's contemporaries to accept the theory of evolution, despite the mass of evidence he presented? Do the idols interfere with people's ability to evaluate evidence?

7. **CONNECTIONS** In "Ideology and Terror: A Novel Form of Government," Hannah Arendt claims that the social applications of Darwinian views are central to the efficient operation of a terrorist government. Now that you have read Darwin's ideas on natural selection and his comments on the survival of species, can you verify that Arendt's views are reasonable and probable? Describe how one could construct a political ideology using the ideas in Darwin's selection.

STEPHEN JAY GOULD
Nonmoral Nature

STEPHEN JAY GOULD (b. 1941) is Alexander Agassiz professor of zoology at Harvard University, where his field of interest centers on the special evolutionary problems related to species of Bahamian snails. He decided to become a paleontologist when he was five years old, after he visited the American Museum of Natural History in New York City with his father and first saw reconstructed dinosaurs.

Gould has become well known for essays on science written with the clarity needed to explain complex concepts to a general audience and also informed by a superb scientific understanding. His articles for *Natural History* magazine have been widely quoted and collected in book form. His books have won both praise and prizes. With works such as *Ever Since Darwin* (1977), *The Panda's Thumb* (1980), *The Mismeasure of Man* (1981), *The Flamingo's Smile* (1985), *Bully for Brontosaurus* (1991), *Eight Little Piggies* (1993), and *Dinosaur in a Haystack* (1995), Gould has pointed to the significance of the work of the scientist he most frequently cites, Charles Darwin. His books have been celebrated around the world, and in 1981 Gould won a MacArthur Fellowship — a stipend of more than $38,000 a year for five years that permitted him to do any work he wished.

"Nonmoral Nature" examines a highly controversial issue — the religious "reading" of natural events. Gould opposes the position of creationists who insisted that the Bible's version of creation be taught in science courses as scientific fact. Moreover, he views the account of the creation in Genesis as religious, not scientific, and points out that Darwin (who was trained as a minister) did not see a conflict between his theories and religious beliefs.

From *Natural History*, vol. 91, no. 2. 1982.

Gould's primary point in this selection is that the behavior of animals in nature — with ruthless and efficient predators inflicting pain on essentially helpless prey — has presented theologians with an exacting dilemma: if God is good and if creation reveals his goodness, why do nature's victims suffer?

Gould examines in great detail specific issues that plagued nineteenth-century theologians. One of these, the behavior of the ichneumon wasp, an efficient wasp that plants its egg in a host caterpillar or aphid, is his special concern. Gould describes the behavior of the ichneumon in detail to make it plain that the total mechanism of the predatory, parasitic animal is complex, subtle, and brilliant. The ichneumon paralyzes its host and then eats it from the inside out, taking care not to permit a victim to die until the last morsel is consumed. He also notes that because there are so many species of ichneumons, their behavior cannot be regarded as an isolated phenomenon.

It is almost impossible to read this selection without developing respect for the predator, something that was extremely difficult, if not impossible, for nineteenth-century theologians to do. Their problem, Gould asserts, was that they anthropomorphized the behavior of these insects. That is, they thought of them in human terms. The act of predation was seen as comparable to the acts of human thugs who toy with their victims, or as Gould puts it, the acts of executioners in Renaissance England who inflicted as much pain as possible on traitors before killing them. This model is the kind of lens through which the behavior of predators was interpreted and understood.

Instead of an anthropocentric — human-centered — view, Gould suggests a scientific view that sees the behavior of predators as sympathetically as that of victims. In this way, he asserts, the ichneumon — and nature — will be seen as nonmoral, and the act of predation seen as neither good nor evil. The concept of evil, he says, is limited to human beings. The world of nature is unconcerned with it, and if we apply morality to nature, we see nature as merely a reflection of our own beliefs and values. Instead, he wishes us to conceive of nature as he thinks it is, something apart from strictly human values.

GOULD'S RHETORIC

Gould's writing is distinguished for its clarity and directness. In this essay, he relies on the testimony of renowned authorities, establishing at once a remarkable breadth of interest and revealing considerably detailed learning about his subject. He explores a number of theories with sympathy and care, demonstrating their limits before offering his own views.

Since his field of interest is advanced biology, he runs the risk of losing the general reader. To avoid doing this, he could have oversimplified his subject, but he does not: he does not shrink from using Latin classifications to identify his subject matter, but he defines each specialized term when he first uses it. He clarifies each opposing argument and demonstrates, in his analysis, its limitations and potential.

Instead of using a metaphor to convince us of a significant fact or critical opinion, Gould "deconstructs" a metaphor that was once in wide use — that the animal world, like the human world, is ethical. He reveals the metaphor to us, shows how it has affected belief, and then asks us to reject it in favor of seeing the world as it actually is. Although maintaining the metaphor is inviting and can be irresistible, Gould says we must resist it.

Gould also makes widespread use of the rhetorical device of metonymy, in which a part of something stands for the whole. Thus, the details of nature, which is God's creation, are made to reflect the entirety, which is God. Therefore, the behavior of the ichneumon comes to stand for the nature of God; and because the ichneumon's behavior is adjudged evil by those who think that animal behavior is metaphorically like that of people, there is a terrible contradiction that cannot be rationalized by theological arguments.

Gould shows us just how difficult the problem of the theologian is. Then he shows us a way out. But his way out depends on the capacity to think in a new way, a change that some may not be able to achieve.

Nonmoral Nature

When the Right Honorable and Reverend Francis Henry, earl of 1
Bridgewater,[1] died in February, 1829, he left £8,000 to support a series of books "on the power, wisdom and goodness of God, as manifested in the creation." William Buckland,[2] England's first official
academic geologist and later dean of Westminster, was invited to
compose one of the nine Bridgewater Treatises. In it he discussed
the most pressing problem of natural theology: If God is benevolent
and the Creation displays his "power, wisdom and goodness," then
why are we surrounded with pain, suffering, and apparently senseless cruelty in the animal world?

Buckland considered the depredation of "carnivorous races" as 2
the primary challenge to an idealized world in which the lion might
dwell with the lamb. He resolved the issue to his satisfaction by arguing that carnivores actually increase "the aggregate of animal enjoyment" and "diminish that of pain." The death of victims, after all, is
swift and relatively painless, victims are spared the ravages of decrepi-
tude and senility, and populations do not outrun their food supply to
the greater sorrow of all. God knew what he was doing when he made
lions. Buckland concluded in hardly concealed rapture:

> The appointment of death by the agency of carnivora, as the ordi-
> nary termination of animal existence, appears therefore in its main
> results to be a dispensation of benevolence; it deducts much from
> the aggregate amount of the pain of universal death; it abridges,
> and almost annihilates, throughout the brute creation, the misery
> of disease, and accidental injuries, and lingering decay; and im-
> poses such salutary restraint upon excessive increase of numbers,
> that the supply of food maintains perpetually a due ratio to the
> demand. The result is, that the surface of the land and depths of
> the waters are ever crowded with myriads of animated beings, the
> pleasures of whose life are co-extensive with its duration; and
> which throughout the little day of existence that is allotted to
> them, fulfill with joy the functions for which they were created.

We may find a certain amusing charm in Buckland's vision 3
today, but such arguments did begin to address "the problem of

---

[1] **Reverend Francis Henry, earl of Bridgewater (1756 – 1829)** He was the
eighth and last earl of Bridgewater. He was also a naturalist and a Fellow at All Souls
College, Oxford, before he became earl of Bridgewater in 1823. On his death, he left
a fund to be used for the publication of the Bridgewater Treatises, essay discussions
of the moral implications of scientific research and discoveries.

[2] **William Buckland (1784 – 1856)** An English clergyman and also a geologist. His essay "Geology and Mineralogy" was a Bridgewater Treatise in 1836.

evil" for many of Buckland's contemporaries — how could a benevolent God create such a world of carnage and bloodshed? Yet these
claims could not abolish the problem of evil entirely, for nature includes many phenomena far more horrible in our eyes than simple
predation. I suspect that nothing evokes greater disgust in most of
us than slow destruction of a host by an internal parasite — slow ingestion, bit by bit, from the inside. In no other way can I explain
why *Alien,* an uninspired, grade-C, formula horror film, should have
won such a following. That single scene of Mr. Alien, popping forth
as a baby parasite from the body of a human host, was both sicker-
ing and stunning. Our nineteenth-century forebears maintained
similar feelings. Their greatest challenge to the concept of a benevolent deity was not simple predation — for one can admire quick and
efficient butcheries, especially since we strive to construct them ourselves — but slow death by parasitic ingestion. The classic case,
treated at length by all the great naturalists, involved the so-called
ichneumon fly. Buckland had sidestepped the major issue.

The ichneumon fly, which provoked such concern among nat-   4
ural theologians, was a composite creature representing the habits of
an enormous tribe. The Ichneumonoidea are a group of wasps, not
flies, that include more species than all the vertebrates combined
(wasps, with ants and bees, constitute the order Hymenoptera; flies,
with their two wings — wasps have four — form the order Diptera).
In addition, many related wasps of similar habits were often cited
for the same grisly details. Thus, the famous story did not merely
implicate a single aberrant species (perhaps a perverse leakage from
Satan's realm), but perhaps hundreds of thousands of them — a
large chunk of what could only be God's creation.

The ichneumons, like most wasps, generally live freely as adults   5
but pass their larval life as parasites feeding on the bodies of other
animals, almost invariably members of their own phylum, Arthro-
poda. The most common victims are caterpillars (butterfly and moth
larvae), but some ichneumons prefer aphids and others attack spiders. Most hosts are parasitized as larvae, but some adults are attacked, and many tiny ichneumons inject their brood directly into
the egg of their host.

The free-flying females locate an appropriate host and then con-   6
vert it to a food factory for their own young. Parasitologists speak of
ectoparasitism when the uninvited guest lives on the surface of its
host, and endoparasitism when the parasite dwells within. Among
endoparasitic ichneumons, adult females pierce the host with their
ovipositor and deposit eggs within it. (The ovipositor, a thin tube
extending backward from the wasp's rear end, may be many times
as long as the body itself.) Usually, the host is not otherwise incon-

venienced for the moment, at least until the eggs hatch and the ichneumon larvae begin their grim work of interior excavation. Among
ectoparasites, however, many females lay their eggs directly upon
the host's body. Since an active host would easily dislodge the egg,
the ichneumon mother often simultaneously injects a toxin that paralyzes the caterpillar or other victim. The paralysis may be permanent, and the caterpillar lies, alive but immobile, with the agent of
its future destruction secure on its belly. The egg hatches, the helpless caterpillar twitches, the wasp larva pierces and begins its grisly
feast.

Since a dead and decaying caterpillar will do the wasp larva no 7
good, it eats in a pattern that cannot help but recall, in our inappropriate, anthropocentric interpretation, the ancient English penalty
for treason — drawing and quartering, with its explicit object of ex-
tracting as much torment as possible by keeping the victim alive and
sentient. As the king's executioner drew out and burned his client's
entrails, so does the ichneumon larva eat fat bodies and digestive organs first, keeping the caterpillar alive by preserving intact the essential heart and central nervous system. Finally, the larva completes
its work and kills its victim, leaving behind the caterpillar's empty
shell. Is it any wonder that ichneumons, not snakes or lions, stood
as the paramount challenge to God's benevolence during the heyday
of natural theology?

As I read through the nineteenth- and twentieth-century litera- 8
ture on ichneumons, nothing amused me more than the tension between an intellectual knowledge that wasps should not be described
in human terms and a literary or emotional inability to avoid the familiar categories of epic and narrative, pain and destruction, victim
and vanquisher. We seem to be caught in the mythic structures of
our own cultural sagas, quite unable, even in our basic descriptions,
to use any other language than the metaphors of battle and conquest. We cannot render this corner of natural history as anything
but story, combining the themes of grim horror and fascination and
usually ending not so much with pity for the caterpillar as with admiration for the efficiency of the ichneumon.

I detect two basic themes in most epic descriptions: the strug- 9
gles of prey and the ruthless efficiency of parasites. Although we acknowledge that we witness little more than automatic instinct or
physiological reaction, still we describe the defenses of hosts as
though they represented conscious struggles. Thus, aphids kick and
caterpillars may wriggle violently as wasps attempt to insert their
ovipositors. The pupa of the tortoise-shell butterfly (usually considered an inert creature silently awaiting its conversion from duckling
to swan) may contort its abdominal region so sharply that attacking

wasps are thrown into the air. The caterpillars of *Hapalia,* when attacked by the wasp *Apanteles machaeralis,* drop suddenly from their leaves and suspend themselves in air by a silken thread. But the wasp may run down the thread and insert its eggs nonetheless. Some hosts can encapsulate the injected egg with blood cells that aggregate and harden, thus suffocating the parasite.

J. H. Fabre,[3] the great nineteenth-century French entomologist, 10 who remains to this day the preeminently literate natural historian of insects, made a special study of parasitic wasps and wrote with an unabashed anthropocentrism about the struggles of paralyzed victims (see his books *Insect Life* and *The Wonders of Instinct*). He describes some imperfectly paralyzed caterpillars that struggle so violently every time a parasite approaches that the wasp larvae must feed with unusual caution. They attach themselves to a silken strand from the roof of their burrow and descend upon a safe and exposed part of the caterpillar:

> The grub is at dinner: head downwards, it is digging into the limp belly of one of the caterpillars. . . . At the least sign of danger in the heap of caterpillars, the larva retreats . . . and climbs back to the ceiling, where the swarming rabble cannot reach it. When peace is restored, it slides down [its silken cord] and returns to table, with its head over the viands and its rear upturned and ready to withdraw in case of need.

In another chapter, he describes the fate of a paralyzed cricket: 11

> One may see the cricket, bitten to the quick, vainly move its antennae and abdominal styles, open and close its empty jaws, and even move a foot, but the larva is safe and searches its vitals with impunity. What an awful nightmare for the paralyzed cricket!

Fabre even learned to feed some paralyzed victims by placing a 12 syrup of sugar and water on their mouthparts — thus showing that they remained alive, sentient, and (by implication) grateful for any palliation of their inevitable fate. If Jesus, immobile and thirsting on the cross, received only vinegar from his tormentors, Fabre at least could make an ending bittersweet.

The second theme, ruthless efficiency of the parasites, leads to 13 the opposite conclusion — grudging admiration for the victors. We learn of their skill in capturing dangerous hosts often many times larger than themselves. Caterpillars may be easy game, but the

---

[3] **Jean-Henri Fabre** (1823 – 1915) A French entomologist whose patient study of insects earned him the nickname "the Virgil of Insects." His writings are voluminous and, at times, elegant.

psammocharid wasps prefer spiders. They must insert their ovipositors in a safe and precise spot. Some leave a paralyzed spider in its
own burrow. *Planiceps hirsutus,* for example, parasitizes a California
trapdoor spider. It searches for spider tubes on sand dunes, then
digs into nearby sand to disturb the spider's home and drive it out.
When the spider emerges, the wasp attacks, paralyzes its victim,
drags it back into its own tube, shuts and fastens the trapdoor, and
deposits a single egg upon the spider's abdomen. Other psammocharids will drag a heavy spider back to a previously prepared
cluster of clay or mud cells. Some amputate a spider's legs to make
the passage easier. Others fly back over water, skimming a buoyant
spider along the surface.

Some wasps must battle with other parasites over a host's body.   14
Rhyssella curvipes can detect the larvae of wood wasps deep within
alder wood and drill down to its potential victims with its sharply
ridged ovipositor. *Pseudorhyssa alpestris,* a related parasite, cannot
drill directly into wood since its slender ovipositor bears only rudimentary cutting ridges. It locates the holes made by *Rhyssella,* inserts
its ovipositor, and lays an egg on the host (already conveniently paralyzed by *Rhyssella*), right next to the egg deposited by its relative.
The two eggs hatch at about the same time, but the larva of
Pseudorhyssa has a bigger head bearing much larger mandibles.
Pseudorhyssa seizes the smaller *Rhyssella* larva, destroys it, and proceeds to feast upon a banquet already well prepared.

Other praises for the efficiency of mothers invoke the themes of   15
early, quick, and often. Many ichneumons don't even wait for their
hosts to develop into larvae, but parasitize the egg directly (larval
wasps may then either drain the egg itself or enter the developing
host larva). Others simply move fast. *Apanteles militaris* can deposit
up to seventy-two eggs in a single second. Still others are doggedly
persistent. *Aphidius gomezi* females produce up to 1,500 eggs and
can parasitize as many as 600 aphids in a single working day. In a
bizarre twist upon "often," some wasps indulge in polyembryony, a
kind of iterated supertwinning. A single egg divides into cells that
aggregate into as many as 500 individuals. Since some polyembry-
onic wasps parasitize caterpillars much larger than themselves and
may lay up to six eggs in each, as many as 3,000 larvae may develop
within, and feed upon, a single host. These wasps are endoparasites
and do not paralyze their victims. The caterpillars writhe back and
forth, not (one suspects) from pain, but merely in response to the
commotion induced by thousands of wasp larvae feeding within.

The efficiency of mothers is matched by their larval offspring. I   16
have already mentioned the pattern of eating less essential parts first,
thus keeping the host alive and fresh to its final and merciful dis-

patch. After the larva digests every edible morsel of its victim (if only to prevent later fouling of its abode by decaying tissue), it may still use the outer shell of its host. One aphid parasite cuts a hole in the belly of its victim's shell, glues the skeleton to a leaf by sticky secretions from its salivary gland, and then spins a cocoon to pupate within the aphid's shell.

In using inappropriate anthropocentric language in this romp through the natural history of ichneumons, I have tried to emphasize just why these wasps became a preeminent challenge to natural theology—the antiquated doctrine that attempted to infer God's essence from the products of his creation. I have used twentieth-century examples for the most part, but all themes were known and stressed by the great nineteenth-century natural theologians. How then did they square the habits of these wasps with the goodness of God? How did they extract themselves from this dilemma of their own making?   17

The strategies were as varied as the practitioners; they shared only the theme of special pleading for an a priori doctrine[4]—they knew that God's benevolence was lurking somewhere behind all these tales of apparent horror. Charles Lyell[5] for example, in the first edition of his epochal *Principles of Geology* (1830 – 1833), decided that caterpillars posed such a threat to vegetation that any natural checks upon them could only reflect well upon a creating deity, for caterpillars would destroy human agriculture "did not Providence put causes in operation to keep them in due bounds."   18

The Reverend William Kirby,[6] rector of Barham and Britain's foremost entomologist, chose to ignore the plight of caterpillars and focused instead upon the virtue of mother love displayed by wasps in provisioning their young with such care.   19

> The great object of the female is to discover a proper nidus for her eggs. In search of this she is in constant motion. Is the caterpillar

---

[4] **an a priori doctrine** *A priori* means beforehand, and Gould refers to those who approach a scientific situation with a preestablished view in mind. He is suggesting that such an approach prevents the kind of objectivity and fairness that scientific examination is supposed to produce.

[5] **Charles Lyell (1797 – 1875)** An English geologist who established the glacial layers of the Eocene (dawn of recent), Miocene (less recent), and Pliocene (more recent) epochs during his excavations of Tertiary period strata in Italy. He was influential in urging Darwin to publish his theories. His work is still respected.

[6] **The Reverend William Kirby (1759 – 1850)** An English specialist in insects. He was the author of a Bridgewater Treatise, *On the power, wisdom, and goodness of God, as manifested in the creation of animals, and in their history, habits, and instincts* (2 vols., 1835).

of a butterfly or moth the appropriate food for her young? You see her alight upon the plants where they are most usually to be met with, run quickly over them, carefully examining every leaf, and, having found the unfortunate object of her search, insert her sting into its flesh, and there deposit an egg. . . . The active Ichneumon braves every danger, and does not desist until her courage and address have insured subsistence for one of her future progeny.

Kirby found this solicitude all the more remarkable because the   20
female wasp will never see her child and enjoy the pleasures of parenthood. Yet her love compels her to danger nonetheless:

A very large proportion of them are doomed to die before their young come into existence. But in these the passion is not extinguished. . . . When you witness the solicitude with which they provide for the security and sustenance of their future young, you can scarcely deny to them love for a progeny they are never destined to behold.

Kirby also put in a good word for the marauding larvae, praising   21
them for their forbearance in eating selectively to keep their caterpillar prey alive. Would we all husband our resources with such care!

In this strange and apparently cruel operation one circumstance is truly remarkable. The larva of the Ichneumon, though every day, perhaps for months, it gnaws the inside of the caterpillar, and though at last it has devoured almost every part of it except the skin and intestines, carefully all this time it avoids injuring the vital organs, as if aware that its own existence depends on that of the insect upon which it preys! . . . What would be the impression which a similar instance amongst the race of quadrupeds would make upon us? If, for example, an animal . . . should be found to feed upon the inside of a dog, devouring only those parts not essential to life, while it cautiously left uninjured the heart, arteries, lungs, and intestines — should we not regard such an instance as a perfect prodigy, as an example of instinctive forebearance almost miraculous? [The last three quotes come from the 1856, and last pre-Darwinian, edition of Kirby and Spence's *Introduction to Entomology*.]

This tradition of attempting to read moral meaning from nature   22
did not cease with the triumph of evolutionary theory after Darwin published *On the Origin of Species* in 1859 — for evolution could be read as God's chosen method of peopling our planet, and ethical messages might still populate nature. Thus, St. George Mivart,[7] one

---

[7] **St. George Mivart (1827–1900)** English anatomist and biologist who examined the comparative anatomies of insect-eating and meat-eating animals. A convert to Roman Catholicism in 1844, he was unable to reconcile religious and evolutionary theories and was excommunicated from the Catholic Church in 1900.

of Darwin's most effective evolutionary critics and a devout Catholic, argued that "many amiable and excellent people" had been misled by the apparent suffering of animals for two reasons. First, however much it might hurt, "physical suffering and moral evil are simply incommensurable." Since beasts are not moral agents, their feelings cannot bear any ethical message. But secondly, lest our visceral sensitivities still be aroused, Mivart assures us that animals must feel little, if any, pain. Using a favorite racist argument of the time — that "primitive" people suffer far less than advanced and cultured people — Mivart extrapolated further down the ladder of life into a realm of very limited pain indeed: Physical suffering, he argued,

> depends greatly upon the mental condition of the sufferer. Only during consciousness does it exist, and only in the most highly organized men does it reach its acme. The author has been assured that lower races of men appear less keenly sensitive to physical suffering than do more cultivated and refined human beings. Thus only in man can there really be any intense degree of suffering, because only in him is there that intellectual recollection of past moments and that anticipation of future ones, which constitute in great part the bitterness of suffering. The momentary pang, the present pain, which beasts endure, though real enough, is yet, doubtless, not to be compared as to its intensity with the suffering which is produced in man through his high prerogative of self-consciousness [from *Genesis of Species,* 1871].

It took Darwin himself to derail this ancient tradition — in that   23 gentle way so characteristic of his radical intellectual approach to nearly everything. The ichneumons also troubled Darwin greatly and he wrote of them to Asa Gray[8] in 1860:

> I own that I cannot see as plainly as others do, and as I should wish to do, evidence of design and beneficence on all sides of us. There seems to me too much misery in the world. I cannot persuade myself that a beneficent and omnipotent God would have designedly created the Ichneumonidae with the express intention

---

[8] **Asa Gray (1810 – 1888)** America's greatest botanist. His works, which are still considered important, are *Structural Botany* (1879; originally published in 1842 as *Botanical Text-Book*), *The Elements of Botany* (1836), *How Plants Grow* (1858), and *How Plants Behave* (1872). Gray was a serious critic of Darwin and wrote a great number of letters to him, but he was also a firm believer in Darwinian evolution. Since he was also a well-known member of an evangelical Protestant faith, he was effective in countering religious attacks on Darwin by showing that there is no conflict between Darwinism and religion.

of their feeding within the living bodies of Caterpillars, or that a cat should play with mice.

Indeed, he had written with more passion to Joseph Hooker[9] in 1856: "What a book a devil's chaplain might write on the clumsy, wasteful, blundering, low, and horribly cruel works of nature!" [24]

This honest admission — that nature is often (by our standards) cruel and that all previous attempts to find a lurking goodness behind everything represent just so much absurd special pleading — can lead in two directions. One might retain the principle that nature holds moral messages for humans, but reverse the usual perspective and claim that morality consists in understanding the ways of nature and doing the opposite. Thomas Henry Huxley[10] advanced this argument in his famous essay on *Evolution and Ethics* (1893): [25]

> The practice of that which is ethically best — what we call goodness or virtue — involves a course of conduct which, in all respects, is opposed to that which leads to success in the cosmic struggle for existence. In place of ruthless self-assertion it demands self-restraint; in place of thrusting aside, or treading down, all competitors, it requires that the individual shall not merely respect, but shall help his fellows. . . . It repudiates the gladiatorial theory of existence. . . . Laws and moral precepts are directed to the end of curbing the cosmic process.

The other argument, more radical in Darwin's day but common now, holds that nature simply is as we find it. Our failure to discern the universal good we once expected does not record our lack of insight or ingenuity but merely demonstrates that nature contains no moral messages framed in human terms. Morality is a subject for philosophers, theologians, students of the humanities, indeed for all thinking people. The answers will not be read passively from nature; they do not, and cannot, arise from the data of science. The factual state of the world does not teach us how we, with our powers for good and evil, should alter or preserve it in the most ethical manner. [26]

---

[9] **Joseph Hooker (1817 – 1911)** English botanist who studied flowers in exotic locations such as Tasmania, the Antarctic, New Zealand, and India. He was, along with Charles Lyell, a friend of Darwin and one of those who urged him to publish *On the Origin of Species*. He was the director of London's Kew Gardens from 1865 to 1885.

[10] **Thomas Henry Huxley (1825 – 1895)** An English naturalist who, quite independent of organizations and formal support, became one of the most important scientists of his time. He searched for a theory of evolution that was based on a rigorous examination of the facts and found, in Darwin's work, the theory that he could finally respect. He was a strong champion of Darwin.

Darwin himself tended toward this view, although he could not, 27
as a man of his time, thoroughly abandon the idea that laws of nature might reflect some higher purpose. He clearly recognized that
the specific manifestations of those laws — cats playing with mice,
and ichneumon larvae eating caterpillars — could not embody ethical messages, but he somehow hoped that unknown higher laws
might exist "with the details, whether good or bad, left to the working out of what we may call chance."

Since ichneumons are a detail, and since natural selection is a 28
law regulating details, the answer to the ancient dilemma of why
such cruelty (in our terms) exists in nature can only be that there
isn't any answer — and that the framing of the question "in our
terms" is thoroughly inappropriate in a natural world neither made
for us nor ruled by us. It just plain happens. It is a strategy that
works for ichneumons and that natural selection has programmed
into their behavioral repertoire. Caterpillars are not suffering to
teach us something; they have simply been outmaneuvered, for
now, in the evolutionary game. Perhaps they will evolve a set of adequate defenses sometime in the future, thus sealing the fate of ichneumons. And perhaps, indeed probably, they will not.

Another Huxley, Thomas's grandson Julian,[11] spoke for this po- 29
sition, using as an example — yes, you guessed it — the ubiquitous
ichneumons:

> Natural selection, in fact, though like the mills of God in grinding
> slowly and grinding small, has few other attributes that a civilized
> religion would call divine. . . . Its products are just as likely to be
> aesthetically, morally, or intellectually repulsive to us as they are
> to be attractive. We need only think of the ugliness of *Sacculina* or
> a bladderworm, the stupidity of a rhinoceros or a stegosaur, the
> horror of a female mantis devouring its mate or a brood of ichneu-
> mon flies slowly eating out a caterpillar.

It is amusing in this context, or rather ironic since it is too serious to be
amusing, that modern creationists accuse evolutionists of preaching a
specific ethical doctrine called secular humanism and thereby demand
equal time for their unscientific and discredited views. If nature is nonmoral, then evolution cannot teach any ethical theory at all. The assumption that it can has abetted a panoply of social evils that ideologues falsely read into nature from their beliefs — eugenics and
(misnamed) social Darwinism prominently among them. Not only did

---

[11] **Thomas's grandson Julian** Julian Huxley (1887 – 1975), an English biologist and a brother of the novelist Aldous Huxley.

Darwin eschew any attempt to discover an antireligious ethic in nature, he also expressly stated his personal bewilderment about such deep issues as the problem of evil. Just a few sentences after invoking the ichneumons, and in words that express both the modesty of this splendid man and the compatibility, through lack of contact, between science and true religion, Darwin wrote to Asa Gray,

> I feel most deeply that the whole subject is too profound for the human intellect. A dog might as well speculate on the mind of Newton. Let each man hope and believe what he can.

QUESTIONS FOR CRITICAL READING

1. What does Gould reveal to us about the nature of insect life?
2. What scientific information does Gould provide that is most valuable in explaining how nature works?
3. What does it mean to anthropomorphize nature? What are some concrete results of doing so?
4. Describe the reaction you have to the process by which the ichneumon wasp parasitizes its host.
5. How might the behavior of the ichneumon wasp put at stake any genuine religious questions of today?
6. What counterassertions can you make to Gould's view that nature is nonmoral?

SUGGESTIONS FOR WRITING

1. In a brief essay, try to answer the question Gould examines in paragraph 1: "Why are we surrounded with pain, suffering, and apparently senseless cruelty in the animal world?"
2. Is the fact of such pain, suffering, and apparently senseless cruelty a religious issue? If so, in what way? If not, demonstrate why.
3. In paragraph 17, Gould describes natural theology as "the antiquated doctrine that attempted to infer God's essence from the products of his creation." Is this a reasonable description of natural theology as you understand it? What can a theology that bases its claims in an observation of nature claim about the essence of God? What kind of religion would support a theology that was based on the behavior of natural life, including ichneumons?
4. Gould points out that even after having established his theory of evolution, Darwin could not "thoroughly abandon the idea that laws of nature might reflect some higher purpose" (para. 27). Assuming that you agree with Darwin but also acknowledge the problems that Gould pre-

sents, clarify what the higher purpose of a nature such as Gould describes might be. Does Gould's description of the behavior of the ichneumon (or any other) predator in any way compromise the idea that nature has a higher purpose? Does Gould hold that it has a higher purpose?

5. **CONNECTIONS**   Compare this essay with Francis Bacon's "The Four Idols." What intellectual issues do the two essays share? What common ground do they share regarding attitudes toward science and religion? What might Francis Bacon have decided about the ultimate ethical issues raised by a consideration of the ichneumon? Do you think that Bacon would have held the same views about the ichneumon's predatory powers as did the nineteenth-century theologians? That is, would he have conceived of nature in ethical/moral terms?

6. **CONNECTIONS**   Why would Gould's scientific subject matter involve issues of morality to a greater extent than, say, the subject matter of Francis Bacon, Charles Darwin, or Richard Dawkins? Is it possible that the study of physics or chemistry is less fundamentally concerned with moral issues than the study of biology is? One result of Darwin's concerns is the possibility that apes and humans are related. Is this point less worthy of consideration from a moral viewpoint than the behavior of the ichneumon wasp? What are the major moral issues in science that you have observed from examining these writers?

MICHIO KAKU
The Theory of the Universe?

MICHIO KAKU (b. 1947) was born and raised in San Jose, California, took his undergraduate degree at Harvard, and returned to California for his Ph.D. in physics at Berkeley in 1972. Since 1973 he has been professor of theoretical physics at the City University of New York, publishing widely on superstring theory (which he discusses in this selection), supergravity, and string field theory. Kaku is also deeply concerned about the practical ramifications of theoretical physics and has written several books on the dangers of nuclear war. He remains active in groups that advocate disarmament.

"The Theory of the Universe?" (1992), from *Mysteries of Life and the Universe,* edited by William H. Shore, is a condensation of ideas that Kaku has explained in greater detail in several of his books. The best-selling *Hyperspace* (1994) is one of the most useful and clear discussions of the "craziness" of modern theories of physics. Kaku shows us that modern research by contemporary physicists has produced a view of the natural world that virtually defies common sense, just as facts such as the earth is not flat and the earth moves around the sun rather than the sun around the earth contradict common sense. Unfortunately, common sense does not help us understand modern physics or the truth about the world of the atom. Since we cannot directly perceive the atom or the molecule, we require sophisticated equipment to make their nature become evident. Interestingly, Francis Bacon insisted in *Novum Organum* that until better tools were evolved, people would not be able to see the truth about the complexities of nature.

In an early chapter of *Hyperspace,* Kaku tells a story about being a young boy and watching fish in a small pond. He realized that for the carp, it was inconceivable that he or anything outside the water in which they swam should exist. Their perceptions were limited entirely to the watery environment they called home. The

431

same is true for people. Our environment may seem larger and more capacious than a pond, but we, like the carp, are limited in our perceptions. Plato realized this when he postulated his allegory of the cave and theorized that our profoundly limited sensory apparatus prevents us from even imagining experiences beyond what we know from our senses.

In Kaku's "The Theory of the Universe?" we come across a similar anomaly. We are used to living in the three dimensions of space and the added dimension of time, and we find it impossible to imagine a fifth dimension. To an extent, this echoes some of Maimonides' concerns about the limits of the human mind. To resolve conflicts between the major theories of explaining the universe — the quantum theory and the theory of relativity — we need a mathematics that postulates more than four dimensions. Fortunately, mathematics describes what our natural senses regard as inconceivable. According to Kaku, ten dimensions are needed to resolve conflicts in modern theories and accurately predict the behavior of subatomic particles. Kaku's explanation of this phenomenon defies common sense — but, as one theoretician has said, it is a theory that may be crazy enough to explain the true nature of nature.

Kaku explains the superstring theory as "tiny strings of energy" that have an infinite number of vibrations, thus explaining why protons that collide in super colliders seem to release so many particles. The quantum theory explains the universe in terms of tiny quantities of energy exchanged between something that has energy and something that needs it. The theory of relativity explains the universe by describing a space-time continuum (an endless fabric of space and time) that is distorted and warped, producing the illusion that energy is exchanged. The string theory implies that everything in the universe is created by "tiny strings of energy" that vibrate and then produce what appear to be quanta to quantum mechanics theorists and the fabric of space-time to relativists. Even with the patient clarifications that mark the writing of Michio Kaku, the theory defies common sense. But that's the point. If it did not, it would not be able to describe the truth about nature any more than the theory of a flat earth does.

KAKU'S RHETORIC

Michio Kaku uses the journalistic technique of short paragraphs. He does not use the journalistic technique of writing a lead and trying to get a "hook" for the reader to hold onto, but he does write a selection that could be included as a feature story in a newspaper. His terminology, except where it must be technical, is clear and not jargon. He avoids explanations that might confuse his readers and chooses simple analogies and examples to explain even very complex ideas.

He begins on a personal note by talking about himself as a child and the results of his curiosity. He was taken by the story of the life of Albert Einstein and wished to emulate him even if he had to become a physicist in order to do it. In the process of explaining his own ambitions, he begins to explain the outlines of the theories that Einstein developed and worked on until his death. As he tells us, Einstein died with papers on his desk relating to the unified field theory, what Kaku calls "the Holy Grail of physics." The quest image is central to Kaku's rhetorical strategy. In medieval lore, the Holy Grail was the cup that Jesus Christ drank from at the Last Supper, and it would produce great joy and miraculous blessings to the nation that possessed it. Crusaders attempting to win the Holy Land from Islamic rule hoped that the Grail would be found by the effort of true believers.

Unfortunately, many fraudulent examples of the Grail surfaced, and the true grail has never been identified. The theory of the universe may be something like the Grail in that it may never be realized, either. If Michio Kaku is correct in his superstring theory, then in a sense he is the golden knight who has brought blessings on humanity. Fortunately, Professor Kaku does not press the Holy Grail image any further than he needs to, but it helps us realize the magnitude of his theoretical efforts to explain theories that baffle perceptions.

One of Kaku's most useful rhetorical techniques is the subhead. This, too, is conventional in journalism, but it is used in other kinds of writing as well. In this essay subheads serve as welcome guideposts: "The Four Fundamental Forces" guides us to an understanding of the four forces in the universe, "Two Great Theories" prepares us to grapple with the quantum theory and the theory of relativity, "Superstrings" finally brings us to Kaku's own theory, "Ten-Dimensional Hyperspace" introduces the complexities of other dimensions, and other subheads lead us carefully through his step-by-step descriptions.

The essay is not an argument. Kaku is not trying to convert quantum theorists or relativists to his new view. Instead, he is interested primarily in describing the choices that permit the reader to participate in the discussion. To be sure, he believes that the superstring has the capacity to explain the workings of nature and the universe. But since it cannot be proved experimentally and is likely to remain theoretical, he hopes merely to describe the theory. When more work is done on it and more analysis is available, the theory may or may not hold up. But for the moment, Kaku tells us, common sense is out, and "craziness" is the new paradigm in modern physics.

The Theory of the Universe?

When I was a child of eight, I heard a story that will stay with me for the rest of my life. I remember my schoolteachers telling us about a great scientist who had just died. They talked about him with great reverence, calling him one of the greatest scientists in all history. They said that very few people could understand his ideas, but that his discoveries had changed the entire world and everything around us.   1

But what most intrigued me about this man was that he had died before he could complete his greatest discovery. They said he had spent years on this theory, but he died with unfinished papers still sitting on his desk.   2

I was fascinated by the story. To a child, this was a great mystery. What was his unfinished work? What problem could possibly be so difficult and so important that such a great scientist would dedicate years of his life to its pursuit?   3

Curious, I decided to learn all I could about Albert Einstein[1] and his unfinished theory. Some of the happiest moments of my childhood were spent quietly reading every book I could find about this great man and his ideas. When I exhausted the books in our local library, I began to scour libraries and bookstores across the city and state, eagerly searching for more clues. I soon learned that this story was far more exciting than any murder mystery and more important than anything I could ever imagine. I decided that I would try to get to the root of this mystery, even if I had to become a theoretical physicist to do it.   4

Gradually, I began to appreciate the magnitude of his unfinished quest. I learned that Einstein had three great theories. The first two, the special and the general theories of relativity, led to the development of the atomic bomb and to our present-day conceptions   5

---

[1] **Albert Einstein (1879 – 1955)** Generally thought to be the greatest modern physicist, he devised the general theory of relativity.

of black holes and the Big Bang. These two theories by themselves earned him his reputation as the greatest scientist since Isaac Newton.[2]

However, Einstein was not satisfied. The third, which he called the *unified field theory*, was to have been his crowning achievement. It was to be the theory of the universe, the Holy Grail of physics that would finally unify all physical laws into one simple framework. It was to have been the ultimate goal of all physics, the theory to end all theories. 6

Sadly, it consumed Einstein for the last thirty years of his life; he spent many lonely years in a frustrating pursuit of the greatest theory of all time. But he wasn't alone; I learned that some of the greatest minds of the twentieth century, such as Werner Heisenberg and Wolfgang Pauli,[3] also struggled with this problem and ultimately gave up. 7

Given the fruitless search that has stumped these and other Nobel Prize winners for half a century, most physicists agree that the Theory of Everything must be a radical departure from everything that has been tried before. For example, when Niels Bohr,[4] founder of modern atomic theory, once listened to Pauli's explanation of his own version of the unified field theory, Bohr finally stood up and said, "We are all agreed that your theory is absolutely crazy. But what divides us is whether your theory is crazy enough." 8

Today, however, after decades of false starts and frustrating dead ends, many of the world's leading physicists think that they have finally found the theory "crazy enough" to be the unified field theory. Scores of physicists in the world's major research laboratories now believe we have at last found the Theory of Everything. 9

The theory that has generated so much excitement is called the *superstring theory*. Nearly every science publication in the world has featured major stories on the superstring theory, interviewing some of its pioneers, such as John Schwarz, Michael Green, and Yoichiro Nambu. (*Discover* magazine even featured it twice on its cover). My book *Beyond Einstein: The Cosmic Search for the Theory of the Universe* was the first attempt to explain this fabulous theory to the lay audience. 10

---

[2] **Isaac Newton (1642–1727)** One of the greatest scientists of the eighteenth century, famous for developing the theory of gravity.

[3] **Werner Heisenberg (1901–1976) and Wolfgang Pauli (1900–1958)** Heisenberg was the German physicist famous for the Heisenberg uncertainty principle that says anything you observe is disturbed by the act of observation. Pauli was an Austrian physicist who pioneered quantum theories.

[4] **Niels Bohr (1885–1962)** Danish physicist who applied quantum theory to the atom and participated in developing the atomic bomb.

Naturally, any theory that claims to have solved the most intimate 11
secrets of the universe will be the center of intense controversy. Even
Nobel Prize winners have engaged in heated discussions about the validity of the superstring theory. In fact, over this theory we are witnessing the liveliest debate in theoretical physics in decades.

To understand the power of the superstring theory and why it is 12
heralded as the theory of the universe (and to understand the delicious controversy that it has stirred up), it is necessary to understand that there are four forces that control everything in the known
universe, and that the superstring theory gives us the first (and only)
description that can unite all four forces in a single framework.

The Four Fundamental Forces

Over two thousand years ago, the ancient Greeks thought that 13
all matter in the universe could be reduced to four elements: air,
water, earth, and fire. Today, after centuries of research, we know
that these substances are actually composites; they in turn are made
of smaller atoms and subatomic particles held together by just four
and only four fundamental forces.

Gravity is the force that keeps our feet anchored to the spinning 14
earth and binds the solar system and the galaxies together. If the
force of gravity could somehow be turned off, we would be immediately flung into outer space at approximately a thousand miles per
hour. Furthermore, if gravity did not hold the Sun together, it
would explode in a catastrophic burst of energy. Without gravity,
the Earth and the planets would spin out into freezing deep space
and the galaxies would fly apart.

Electromagnetism is the force that lights up our cities and ener- 15
gizes our household appliances. The electronic revolution, which
has given us the light bulb, TV, the telephone, the computer, radio,
radar, the microwave, and the dishwasher, is a byproduct of the
electromagnetic force. Without this force, our civilization would be
wrenched several hundred years into the past, into a primitive world
lit by candlelight and camp fires.

The strong nuclear force is the force that powers the Sun. With- 16
out the nuclear force, the stars would flicker out and the heavens
would go dark. Without the Sun, all life on Earth would perish as
the oceans turned to solid ice. The nuclear force not only makes life
on Earth possible, it is also the devastating force unleashed by a hy-
drogen bomb, which can be compared to a piece of the Sun brought
down to Earth.

The weak nuclear force is the force responsible for radioactive 17
decay. The weak force is harnessed in modern hospitals in the form
of radioactive tracers used in nuclear medicine. For example, dramatic color pictures of the living brain as it thinks and experiences
emotions are made possible by the decay of radioactive sugar in the
brain.

It is no exaggeration to say that the mastery of each of these four 18
fundamental forces has changed every aspect of human civilization.
For example, when Newton tried to solve his theory of gravitation,
he was forced to develop a new mathematics and formulate his celebrated laws of motion. These laws of mechanics in turn helped to
usher in the Industrial Revolution.

Furthermore, the mastery of the electromagnetic force by math- 19
ematical physicist James Maxwell[5] in the 1860s has revolutionized
our way of life. Whenever there is a power blackout, we are forced
to live much like our forebears in the last century. Today, over half
of the world's industrial wealth is connected, in some way or other,
to the electromagnetic force, without which modern civilization is
unthinkable.

Similarly, when the nuclear force was unleashed with the 20
atomic bomb, human history for the first time faced a new and
frightening set of possibilities, including the total annihilation of all
life on Earth. With the nuclear force, we could finally understand
the enormous engine that lies within the Sun and the stars, but we
could also glimpse for the first time the end of humanity itself.

Thus, whenever scientists unravel the secrets of one of the four 21
fundamental forces, they irrevocably alter the course of modern civilization. Some of the greatest breakthroughs in the history of the sciences can be traced back to the gradual understanding of these
forces.

Given their importance the next question is, Can these four fun- 22
damental forces be united into one super force? Are they but diverse
manifestations of a deeper reality?

Two Great Theories

At present there are two physical frameworks that have partially 23
explained the mysterious features of these four fundamental forces.
Remarkably, these two formalisms, the *quantum theory* and *general*

---

[5]**James Maxwell (1831 – 1879)** English physicist whose experiments with
electromagnetism led to modern theories of electricity and quantum theory.

relativity, allow us to explain the *sum total of all physical knowledge* at the fundamental level. Without exception.

All the laws of physics and chemistry, which can fill entire li-   24
braries with technical journals and books, can in principle be derived from these two fundamental theories — making these the most
successful physical theories of all time, withstanding the test of
thousands of experiments and challenges.

Ironically, these two fundamental frameworks are diametrically   25
opposed to each other. The quantum theory, for example, is the theory of the microcosm, with unparalleled success at describing the
subatomic world. The theory of relativity, by contrast, is a theory of
the macrocosmic world, the world of galaxies, superclusters, black
holes, and Creation itself.

The quantum theory explains three of the four forces (the weak   26
and strong nuclear forces, and the electromagnetic force) by postulating the exchange of tiny packets of energy, called *quanta.* When a
flashlight is turned on, for example, it emits trillions upon trillions
of photons, or quanta, of light. Lasers, radar waves, and microwaves
all can be described by postulating that they are caused by the
movement of these tiny quanta of energy. Likewise, the weak force
is governed by the exchange of subatomic particles called *W-bosons.*
The strong nuclear force, in turn, binds protons together by the exchange of *gluons.*

However, the quantum theory stands in sharp contrast to Ein-   27
stein's general theory of relativity, which postulates an entirely different physical picture to explain the force of gravity.

Imagine, for the moment, dropping a heavy shotput on a large   28
bedspread. The shotput will, of course, sink deeply into the bedspread. Now imagine shooting a small marble across the bed. Since
the bed is warped, the marble will execute a curved path. However,
for a person viewing the marble from a great distance, it will appear
that the shotput is exerting an invisible "force" on the marble, forcing it to move in a curved path. In other words, we can now replace
the clumsy concept of a "force" with the more elegant concept of a
bending of space itself. We now have an entirely new definition of
this "force." It is nothing but the byproduct of the warping of space.

In the same way that a marble moves on a curved bedspread,   29
the Earth moves around the Sun in a curved path, because space-
time itself is curved. In this new picture, gravity is not a "force" but a
byproduct of the warping of space-time. In some sense, gravity does
not exist; what moves the planets and stars is the distortion of space
and time.

However, the problem that has stubbornly resisted solution for   30
fifty years is that these two frameworks do not resemble each other

in any way. The quantum theory reduces "forces" to the exchange of discrete packets of energy, or quanta, while Einstein's theory of gravity, by contrast, explains the cosmic forces holding the galaxies together by postulating the smooth deformation of the fabric of space-time. This is the root of the problem, that the quantum theory and general relativity have two different physical pictures (packets of energy versus smooth space-time continua) and different mathematics to describe them. This sad state of affairs can be compared to Mother Nature having two hands, neither of which communicates with the other.

All attempts by the greatest minds of the twentieth century at   31 merging the quantum theory with the theory of gravity have failed. Unquestionably, the greatest problem facing physicists today is the unification of these two physical frameworks into one theory.

Superstrings

Today, however, many physicists think that we have finally   32 solved this long-standing problem. A new theory, which is certainly "crazy enough" to be correct, has astounded the world's physics community. But it has also raised a storm of controversy, with Nobel Prize winners adamantly taking opposite sides of the issue.

This is the superstring theory, which postulates that all matter   33 and energy can be reduced to tiny strings of energy vibrating in a ten-dimensional universe.

Edward Witten,[6] of the Institute for Advanced Study at Prince-   34 ton, who some claim is the successor to Einstein, has said that superstring theory will dominate the world of physics for the next fifty years, in the same way that the quantum theory has dominated physics for the last half century.

As Einstein once said, all great physical theories can be repre-   35 sented by simple pictures. Similarly, superstring theory can be explained visually. Imagine a violin string, for example. The note A is no more fundamental than the note B. What is fundamental is the violin string itself. By studying vibrations or harmonies on a violin string, one can calculate the infinite number of possible frequencies that can exist.

Similarly, the superstring can also vibrate in different frequen-   36 cies. Each frequency, in turn, corresponds to a subatomic particle, or a quantum. This explains why there appears to be an infinite

---

[6] **Edward Witten (b. 1931)** Physicist at Princeton University.

number of particles. According to this theory, our bodies, which are made of subatomic particles, can be described by the resonances of trillions upon trillions of tiny strings.

In summary, the "notes" of the superstring are the subatomic parti- 37
cles, the "harmonies" of the superstring are the laws of physics, and the universe can be compared to a "symphony" of vibrating superstrings.

As the string vibrates, however, it causes the surrounding space- 38
time continuum to warp around it. Miraculously enough, a detailed calculation shows that the superstring forces the space-time contin-uum to be distorted exactly as Einstein originally predicted. Thus, we now have a harmonious description that merges the theory of quanta with the theory of space-time continua.

Ten-Dimensional Hyperspace

The superstring theory represents perhaps the most radical de- 39
parture from ordinary physics in decades. But its most controversial prediction is that the universe originally began in ten dimensions. To its supporters, the prediction of a ten-dimensional universe has been a conceptual tour de force introducing a startling, breathtaking math-ematics into the world of physics. To its critics, however, the intro-duction of ten-dimensional hyperspace borders on science fiction.

To understand these higher dimensions, we must remember 40
that it takes three numbers to locate every point in the universe, from the tip of your nose to the ends of the universe.

For example, if you want to meet some friends for lunch in 41
Manhattan, you say that you will meet them at the building at the corner of Forty-second and Fifth Avenue, on the thirty-seventh floor. It takes two numbers to locate your position on a map, and one number to specify the distance above the map.

However, the existence of the fourth spatial dimension has been 42
a lively area of debate since the time of the Greeks. Ptolemy,[7] in fact, even gave a "proof" that more than three dimensions cannot exist. Ptolemy reasoned that only three straight lines that are mutually perpendicular can be drawn (for example, the three perpendicular lines making up a corner of a room). Since a fourth straight line cannot be drawn perpendicular to each of the other three axes — ergo! — the fourth dimension cannot exist.

---

[7] **Ptolemy (fl. A.D. 127–145)** Alexandrian astronomer who described the earth as the center of the universe. His theories held until the sixteenth century, when challenged by Copernicus.

What Ptolemy actually proved was that it is impossible for us to 43
visualize the fourth dimension. Although computers routinely manipulate equations in *n*-dimensional space, humans are incapable of visualizing more than three dimensions.

The reason for this unfortunate accident has to do with biology 44
rather than physics. Human evolution put a premium on being able to visualize objects moving in three dimensions, such as lunging saber-tooth tigers and charging mammoths.

Since tigers do not attack us in the fourth dimension, there was 45
no evolutionary correction pressure to develop a brain with the ability to visualize four dimensions.

From a mathematical point of view, however, adding higher di- 46
mensions has a distinct advantage: It allows us to describe more forces. There is more "room" in higher dimensions to insert the electromagnetic force into the gravitational force. (In this picture, light becomes a vibration in the fourth dimension.) In other words, adding more dimensions to a theory always allows us to unify more laws of physics.

A simple analogy may help. The ancients were once puzzled by 47
the weather. Why does it get colder as we go north? Why do the winds blow to the west? What is the origin of the seasons? To the ancients, these were mysteries that could not be solved.

The key to these puzzles, of course, is to leap into the third di- 48
mension, to go *up* into outer space, to see that the Earth is actually a sphere rotating around a tilted axis. In one stroke, these mysteries of the weather — the seasons, the winds, the temperature patterns, etc. — become transparent.

Likewise, the superstring is able to accommodate a large num- 49
ber of forces because it has more "room" in its equations to do so.

What Happened Before the Big Bang?

One of the nagging problems of Einstein's old theory of gravity 50
was that it did not explain the origin of the Big Bang.

The ten-dimensional superstring theory, however, gives us a 51
compelling explanation according to which the universe originally started as a perfect ten-dimensional universe with nothing in it.

However, this ten-dimensional universe was not stable. The 52
original ten-dimensional space-time finally "cracked" into two pieces, four- and six-dimensional universes. The six-dimensional universe collapsed into a tiny ball, while the remaining four-dimensional universe inflated at an enormous rate.

The four-dimensional universe (ours) expanded rapidly, even- 53
tually creating the Big Bang, while the six-dimensional universe
wrapped itself into a ball and collapsed down to infinitesimal size.

The Big Bang is now viewed as a rather minor aftershock of a 54
more cataclysmic collapse: the breaking of a ten-dimensional universe into four- and six-dimensional universes.

In principle, it also explains why we cannot measure the six- 55
dimensional universe: it has shrunk down to a size smaller than an
atom.

Re-Creating Creation

Although the superstring theory has been called the most sensa- 56
tional discovery in theoretical physics in the past decades, its critics
have focused on its weakest point, that it is almost impossible to
test. The energy at which the four fundamental forces merge into a
single unified force is the fabulous *Planck energy,*[8] which is a billion
billion times greater than the energy found in a proton.

Even if all the nations of the Earth were to band together and 57
single-mindedly build the biggest atom smasher in all history, it
would still not be enough to test this theory.

Because of this, some physicists have scoffed at the idea that su- 58
perstring theory can be considered a legitimate theory. Nobel laureate Sheldon Glashow,[9] for example, has compared the superstring
theory to the former President Reagan's Star Wars program because
it is untestable and drains the best scientific talent.

The reason the theory cannot be tested is rather simple. The The- 59
ory of Everything is necessarily a theory of Creation. It must explain
everything, from the origin of the Big Bang down to that of the lilies of
the field. To test this theory on Earth, therefore, means to re-create
Creation of Earth, which is impossible with present-day technology.

The SSC: Biggest Experiment of All Time

These questions about unifying the fundamental forces may not 60
be academic if the largest scientific machine ever, the SSC,[10] is built
to test some of our ideas about the instant of Creation. (Although

---

[8] *Planck energy* Max Planck (1858–1947) postulated the quantum theory
by establishing a quantum of energy emitted by radiating objects. Planck formulated
the basis of quantum theory.

[9] **Sheldon Glashow (b. 1932)** Nobel prize-winning physicist at Harvard.

[10] **SSC** Superconducting super-collider, a huge machine designed for splitting
the atom.

the SSC was originally approved by the Reagan administration, because of its enormous cost, the project is still touch-and-go, depending every year on Congressional funding.)

The SSC is projected to accelerate protons to a staggering energy of tens of trillions of electron volts. When these subatomic particles slam into each other at these fantastic energies, they will generate temperatures that have not been reached since the instant of Creation (although not hot enough to test fully the superstring theory). That is why the super-collider is sometimes called a "window on Creation." 61

The SSC is projected to cost over eight billion dollars (a large amount of money compared to the government's science budget, but insignificant relative to that of the Pentagon). By every measure, it will be a colossal machine. It will consist of a ring of powerful magnets stretched out in a tube over fifty miles in diameter. In fact, one could easily fit the Washington Beltway, which surrounds Washington, D.C., inside the SSC. 62

At present, the SSC is scheduled to be finished near the turn of the century in Texas, near the city of Dallas. When completed, it will employ thousands of physicists and engineers and cost millions of dollars to operate. 63

At the very least, physicists hope that the SSC will find some exotic subatomic particles, such as the Higgs boson and the top quark,[11] in order to complete our present-day understanding of the quantum theory. However, there is also the small chance that physicists might discover "supersymmetric" particles, which are predicted by the superstring theory. In other words, although the superstring theory cannot be tested directly by the SSC, one hopes to find particles (vibrations) predicted by superstring theory among the debris created by smashing protons together. 64

The Parable of the Gemstone

To understand the intense controversy surrounding superstring theory, think of the following parable. 65

Imagine that at the beginning of time there was a beautiful, glittering gemstone. Its perfect symmetries were a sight to behold. How- 66

---

[11]**top quark** The quark is the smallest particle in the atom, but it comes in several "flavors." The top quark, which turned out to be the largest, was one of the last flavors to be discovered experimentally and therefore represented a special challenge. It was discovered in 1995, after this article was written.

ever, it possessed a tiny flaw and became unstable, eventually exploding into thousands of pieces. Imagine that the fragments of the gemstone rained down on a flat, two-dimensional world called Flatland, where there lived a mythical race of beings called Flatlanders.

These Flatlanders were intrigued by the beauty of the fragments, 67 which could be found scattered all over Flatland. The scientists of Flatland postulated that these fragments must have come from a crystal of unimaginable beauty that shattered in a titanic Big Bang. They then decided to embark upon a noble quest to reassemble all the pieces of the gemstone.

After two thousand years of labor by the finest minds of Flat- 68 land, they were finally able to fit many, but certainly not all, of the fragments together in two chunks. The first chunk was called the *quantum,* and the second chunk was called *relativity.*

Although the Flatlanders were rightfully proud of their 69 progress, they were dismayed to find that these two chunks did not fit together. For half a century, the Flatlanders maneuvered the chunks in all possible ways and still could not make them fit.

Finally, some of the younger, more rebellious scientists sug- 70 gested a heretical solution: perhaps these two chunks could fit together if they were moved in a *third dimension.*

This immediately set off the greatest scientific controversy in 71 years. The older scientists scoffed at this idea, because they didn't believe in an unseen third dimension. "What you can't measure doesn't exist," they declared.

Furthermore, even if the third dimension existed, one could cal- 72 culate that the energy necessary to move the pieces *up* off Flatland would exceed all the energy available in Flatland. Thus it was an untestable theory.

However, the younger scientists were undaunted. Using pure 73 mathematics, they could show that these two chunks would likely fit together if they were rotated and moved in the third dimension. The younger scientists claimed that the problem was therefore theoretical rather than experimental. If one could completely solve the equations of the third dimension, one could, in principle, fit the two chunks perfectly together and resolve the problem once and for all.

We Are Not Smart Enough

That is also the conclusion of today's superstring enthusiasts: 74 the fundamental problem is theoretical, not practical. The true problem is in solving the theory completely and then comparing it with present-day experimental data, not in building gigantic atom smashers.

Edward Witten, impressed by the vast new areas of mathematics   75 opened up by the superstring theory, has said that the superstring theory represents "twenty-first-century physics that fell accidentally into the twentieth century."

The superstring theory may very well be twenty-first-century   76 physics, but twenty-first-century mathematics has not yet been discovered.

This situation is not entirely new to the history of physics.   77 When Newton first discovered the universal law of gravitation at the age of twenty-three, he was unable to solve his equation because the mathematics of the seventeenth century was too primitive. He then labored over the next twenty years to develop a new mathematical formalism (calculus) that was powerful enough to solve his universal law of gravitation.

Similarly, the fundamental problem facing the superstring the-   78 ory is theoretical. If we could only sharpen our analytical skills and develop more powerful mathematical tools, perhaps we could solve the superstring theory and end the controversy.

Ironically, the superstring equations stand before us in perfectly   79 well defined form, yet we are too primitive to understand why they work so well, and we are too dim-witted to solve them. The search for the theory of the universe is perhaps finally entering its last phase, awaiting the birth of a new mathematics powerful enough to solve it.

Imagine a child gazing at a TV set. The images and stories con-   80 veyed through the screen are easily understood by the child, yet the electronic wizardry inside the TV set is beyond the child's ken. Likewise, we physicists gaze in wonder at the mathematical sophistication and elegance of the superstring equation and are awed by its power, yet we do not understand why it works.

Perhaps some readers will be inspired by this story to read every   81 book in their libraries about the superstring theory. Perhaps some young reader will be the one to complete this quest for the theory of the universe, begun so many years ago by Einstein.

QUESTIONS FOR CRITICAL READING

1. What was Einstein's unified field theory supposed to accomplish?
2. How does the quantum theory differ from the theory of relativity?
3. What does the superstring theory accomplish that other theories cannot?

4. What are the four fundamental forces in the universe? With which are you most familiar?
5. What are some problems associated with ten-dimensional space? Why can't people envision it? How can it be described?
6. Why is the superstring theory difficult to test?
7. Explain the parable of the gemstone (paras. 64 – 73).

SUGGESTIONS FOR WRITING

1. Comment on the adequacy of the musical metaphor Kaku uses beginning with paragraph 32. He calls subatomic particles "notes," the laws of physics "harmonies," and the universe a "symphony." How well does this explanation work for you? How does the description help intensify the beauty of the universe and the aesthetics of the superstring theory?
2. What questions remain in your mind after having read this selection? What do you feel you need to know more about? What are the limits of the theories that Michio Kaku has described here? What parts of his explanation would you like to have developed even further?
3. The superconducting super-collider (paras. 60 – 64) was being constructed when Kaku wrote this essay. It represents the best chance for scientists to test the superstring theory, but government budget problems have stopped the project, and it is not likely to be resumed. Do you feel that the $8 billion it would cost to build can be justified? How important is it to "prove" a scientific theory about the origins of the universe and its deepest structure?
4. The parable of the gemstone describes Flatlanders, people living in a two-dimensional world. Does it offer us a useful comparison with our own condition in attempting to understand the universe? What analogies would you use to describe our attempts to understand the universe?
5. Write an explanation of the superstring theory for your little brother or sister (or a friend's little brother or sister). Make your explanation as simple and direct as possible. When you have finished writing your description, read it to your intended audience (or give it to the child to read) and write down the questions that occur to your reader. Also, write down your reader's response to the theory. Then, comment on the difficulty or ease of communicating Kaku's theory.
6. Describe the four fundamental forces in the universe. What personal experience do each of us have with these four forces? Do you feel more aware of these forces now that you know that they are the four forces that act on everything in the universe? Why is it possible for people to live their lives almost unaware of these forces? What does our knowledge of them make possible in the modern world?
7. **CONNECTIONS** Compare the theories that Kaku describes here with the situation in which people find themselves in Plato's cave. Is it

possible that Plato was describing a situation similar to the one that we find ourselves in when we face the complexities of the physics of the universe? What, if anything, is Platonic about Kaku's description of the way in which we perceive the universe?

8. **CONNECTIONS** Would Kaku agree with Moses Maimonides in suggesting that the human mind is limited in its capacity to understand the universe? What are the ways in which Kaku feels the mind is limited? How does mathematics help to relieve the mind's limitations concerning the problems of establishing a coherent theory of the universe?

RICHARD DAWKINS
All Africa and Her Progenies

RICHARD DAWKINS (b. 1941) was born in Nairobi, Kenya,
where his father served during the Second World War. He later
studied at Oxford University and took his doctorate there in the
field of ethology, the study of animal behavior. He holds the newly
endowed Charles Simonyi Chair of Public Understanding of Science at Oxford. In that position, he spends much of his time giving
public lectures, appearing on television, and writing about biology
and natural science.

Dawkins has been described as an "ultra-Darwinist," a fervent
apologist for the power of natural selection to have produced the
astonishing variety of life on the planet. His first book, *The Selfish
Gene* (1976), created a controversy because of its unusual application of Darwinian theories. His most startling claim was that natural selection worked on the level of the gene, not just the individual, and that the survival of the fittest involved the survival of the
fittest genes. Some scientists have accused Dawkins of oversimplifying Darwin's theories, but despite this criticism, his views continue to be influential in the fields of genetics and biology.

Dawkins's books are notable for their clarity and for their ability to communicate complex ideas to a general public. In *The Blind
Watchmaker* (1986), Dawkins examines the argument that the apparent design and intention implied in evolution points to the existence of God. Dawkins attempts to demonstrate that the mutations
that produce such evolutionary developments as the eye, hair, and
feathers could have been produced by chance over thirty or forty of
the available several hundred million years of evolution. This book
created another controversy, especially among religious scientists
who argued against him. *River Out of Eden* (1995), from which the

From *River Out of Eden*.

following chapter is drawn, examines the Darwinian view of nature. It concerns not only the evolution of human beings, but the
specialized evolution of many animals.

In "All Africa and Her Progenies," Dawkins primarily presents
the case for the existence of one common ancestor for all human
beings. In the process, Dawkins explores the nature of the genetic
code that marks all individuals and all species. He explains the relationships of species such as humans, primates, horses, and pigs
in terms of the number of different genetic markers they share. Because the genetic markers of specific areas of the genetic code are
the same for individuals of the same species but vary increasingly
as the species become distant, the number of differences between
yeast and horses is greater than the number of differences between
pigs and horses.

DNA — deoxyribonucleic acid — codes genetic material in individuals. Since both mother and father contribute to an individual's DNA, it is exceedingly difficult to trace individuals back to
common ancestors. However, for mitochondria, tiny structures in
each of our cells, genetic material comes only from the female line,
which allows us to trace back relationships along the female line.
Dawkins tells of an experiment using genetic samples from one
hundred thirty-five women from different ethnic groups and locations that suggests that our common ancestor is "African Eve," a female from whom we all descend. Dawkins explains the complexities involved in making such a claim, including his assertion that
all living beings probably trace their lineage back to Africa.

DAWKINS'S RHETORIC

Perhaps because Richard Dawkins spends a considerable
amount of time speaking before live audiences, he often is challenged by scientists and others to defend his views. He spends a lot
of time in *River Out of Eden* explaining people's questions and his
answers. Most of the questions center on the "why" issue: why
does evolution work as it does, and what is the purpose of it all?
Dawkins feels such questions are not relevant and sometimes loses
patience in answering them. As a result, the tone of the early paragraphs in this excerpt can seem impatient. He explains his argumentative style in a footnote to paragraph 2. His first several paragraphs address the question of whether a belief in science is a faith,
the way belief in religion is a faith. Dawkins is abrupt in his manner, using the example of the airplane and the space voyage to the
moon. He categorically defends science as a way to discover the

truth about phenomena and considers faith to be something quite different. Consequently, his tone may seem abrasive and his style brusque, especially when he says, "Show me a cultural relativist at thirty thousand feet and I'll show you a hypocrite."

Apart from the structured argument, Dawkins relies on some of the rhetorical resources that we have seen at work in other writers. The metaphor is one of his most carefully used devices. He speaks of the genealogical tree, reminding us that we have two parents, four grandparents, eight great-grandparents, and so on, until the branches of the tree become overloaded; by the time we trace ourselves back to the time of Caesar, we would have more ancestors than there were people alive. Consequently, he turns the branching metaphor backward and postulates a river as the metaphor for descent. The river picks up material as it goes, and it branches out into separate tributaries that correspond to species and families. He uses the metaphor to help us understand our origins from a single female source.

Because he is communicating with a general audience rather than an audience of scientists, he carefully explains each issue as he proceeds. The difficult is broken down into parts, and connections are made apparent where they might seem hazy. He uses the techniques of narrative and example as much as possible, sometimes interrupting his story with crucial information and explanation about the relationship of individuals to their ancestors and to each other.

However, Dawkins keeps a number of lines of thought going almost simultaneously, and his method of keeping them straight comes clear at the end, when he resorts to the device of enumeration to summarize his major points. He begins paragraph 46 with, "We may come to the following conclusions: First, . . ." and then enumerates and evaluates six conclusions. In some ways, that paragraph serves as a guide to the entire essay.

Dawkins's theory of an African Eve has been received as plausible and probable by many biologists studying genetics. His views are based on modern confirmations of Darwinian theories of natural selection and general evolution of species. His approach is a defense of those views with an effort to demonstrate their implications, at least for our own species.

All Africa and Her Progenies

It is often thought clever to say that science is no more than our 1
modern origin myth. The Jews had their Adam and Eve, the Sumerians their Marduk and Gilgamesh, the Greeks Zeus and the Olympians, the Norsemen their Valhalla. What is evolution, some smart people say, but our modern equivalent of gods and epic heroes, neither better nor worse, neither truer nor falser? There is a fashionable salon philosophy called cultural relativism which holds, in its extreme form, that science has no more claim to truth than tribal myth: science is just the mythology favored by our modern Western tribe. I once was provoked by an anthropologist colleague into putting the point starkly, as follows: Suppose there is a tribe, I said, who believe that the moon is an old calabash tossed into the sky, hanging only just out of reach above the treetops. Do you really claim that our scientific truth — that the moon is about a quarter of a million miles away and a quarter the diameter of the Earth — is no more true than the tribe's calabash? "Yes," the anthropologist said. "We are just brought up in a culture that sees the world in a scientific way. They are brought up to see the world in another way. Neither way is more true than the other."

Show me a cultural relativist at thirty thousand feet and I'll 2
show you a hypocrite. Airplanes built according to scientific principles work. They stay aloft, and they get you to a chosen destination. Airplanes built to tribal or mythological specifications, such as the dummy planes of the cargo cults in jungle clearings or the beeswaxed wings of Icarus, don't.[1] If you are flying to an international congress of anthropologists or literary critics, the reason you will probably get there — the reason you don't plummet into a ploughed field — is that a lot of Western scientifically trained engineers have got their sums right. Western science, acting on good evidence that the moon orbits the Earth a quarter of a million miles away, using Western-designed computers and rockets, has suc-

---

[1] This is not the first time I have used this knock-down argument, and I must stress that it is aimed strictly at people who think like my colleague of the calabash. There are others who, confusingly, also call themselves cultural relativists although their views are completely different and perfectly sensible. To them, cultural relativism just means that you cannot understand a culture if you try to interpret its beliefs in terms of your own culture. You have to see each of the culture's beliefs in the context of the culture's other beliefs. I suspect that this sensible form of cultural relativism is the original one, and that the one I have criticized is an extremist, though alarmingly common, perversion of it. Sensible relativists should work harder at distancing themselves from the fatuous kind. [Dawkins's note]

ceeded in placing people on its surface. Tribal science, believing that the moon is just above the treetops, will never touch it outside of dreams.

I seldom give a public lecture without a member of the audience brightly coming up with something along the same lines as my anthropologist colleague, and it usually elicits a murmuration of approving nods. No doubt the nodders feel good and liberal and unracist. An even more reliable nod-provoker is "Fundamentally, your belief in evolution comes down to faith, and therefore it's no better than somebody else's belief in the Garden of Eden."

Every tribe has had its origin myth — its story to account for the universe, life and humanity. There is a sense in which science does indeed provide the equivalent of this, at least for the educated section of our modern society. Science may even be described as a religion, and I have, not entirely facetiously, published a brief case for science as an appropriate subject for religious-education classes.[2] (In Britain, religious education is a compulsory part of the school curriculum, unlike in the United States, where it is banned for fear of offending any of the plethora of mutually incompatible faiths.) Science shares with religion the claim that it answers deep questions about origins, the nature of life, and the cosmos. But there the resemblance ends. Scientific beliefs are supported by evidence, and they get results. Myths and faiths are not and do not.

Of all origin myths, the Jewish story of the Garden of Eden is so pervasive in our culture that it has bequeathed its name to an important scientific theory about our ancestry, the theory of "African Eve." I am devoting this chapter to African Eve partly because it will enable me to develop the analogy of the river of DNA[3] but also because I want to contrast her, as a scientific hypothesis, with the legendary matriarch of the Garden of Eden. If I succeed, you will find the truth more interesting, maybe even more poetically moving, than the myth. We begin with an exercise in pure reasoning. Its relevance will become clear soon.

You have two parents, four grandparents, eight great-grandparents and so on. With every generation, the number of ancestors doubles. Go back *g* generations and the number of ancestors is 2 multiplied by itself *g* times: 2 to the power *g*. Except that, without leaving our armchair, we can quickly see that it cannot be so. To convince ourselves of this, we have only to go back a little way — say, to the time of Jesus, almost exactly two thousand years ago. If

3

4

5

6

---

[2] *The Spectator* (London), August 6, 1994. [Dawkins's note]

[3] **DNA** Deoxyribonucleic acid, the basic substance of genes.

we assume, conservatively, four generations per century — that is, that people breed on average at the age of twenty-five — two thousand years amounts to a mere eighty generations. The real figure is probably more than this (until recent times, many women bred extremely young), but this is only an armchair calculation, and the point is made regardless of such details. Two multiplied by itself 80 times is a formidable number, a 1 followed by 24 noughts, a trillion American trillions. You had a million million million million ancestors who were contemporaries of Jesus, and so did I! But the total population of the world at that time was a fraction of a negligible fraction of the number of ancestors we have just calculated.

Obviously we have gone wrong somewhere, but where? We did   7 the calculation right. The only thing we got wrong was our assumption about doubling up in every generation. In effect, we forgot that cousins marry. I assumed that we each have eight great-grandparents. But any child of a first-cousin marriage has only six great-grandparents, because the cousins' shared grandparents are in two separate ways great-grandparents to the children. "So what?" you may ask. People occasionally marry their cousins (Charles Darwin's wife, Emma Wedgwood, was his first cousin), but surely it doesn't happen often enough to make a difference? Yes it does, because "cousin" for our purposes includes second cousins, fifth cousins, sixteenth cousins and so forth. When you count cousins as distant as that, every marriage is a marriage between cousins. You sometimes hear people boasting of being a distant cousin of the Queen, but it is rather pompous of them, because we are *all* distant cousins of the Queen, and of everybody else, in more ways than can ever be traced. The only thing special about royalty and aristocrats is that they can do the tracing explicitly. As the fourteenth Earl of Home said when taunted about his title by his political opponent, "I suppose Mr. Wilson, when you come to think of it, is the fourteenth Mr. Wilson."

The upshot of all this is that we are much closer cousins of one   8 another than we normally realize, and we have many fewer ancestors than simple calculations suggest. Seeking to get her reasoning along these lines, I once asked a student to make an educated guess as to how long ago her most recent common ancestor with me might have lived. Looking hard at my face, she unhesitatingly replied, in a slow, rural accent, "Back to the apes." An excusable intuitive leap, but it is approximately 10,000 percent wrong. It would suggest a separation measured in millions of years. The truth is that the most recent ancestor she and I shared would possibly have lived no more than a couple of centuries ago, possibly well after William the Conqueror.[4] Moreover, we were certainly cousins in many different ways simultaneously.

The model of ancestry that led to our erroneously inflated calcu-   9
lation of ancestral numbers was an ever-branching tree, branching and branching again. Turned the other way up, and equally wrong, is a tree model of descent. A typical individual has two children, four grandchildren, eight great-grandchildren and so on down to impossible trillions of descendants a few centuries hence. A far more realistic model of ancestry and descent is the flowing river of genes, which we introduced in the previous chapter. Within its banks, the genes are an ever-rolling stream through time. Currents swirl apart and join again as the genes crisscross down the river of time. Draw out a bucketful at intervals from points spaced out down the length of the river. Pairs of molecules in a bucket will have been companions before, at intervals during their progress down the river, and they will be companions once more. They have also been widely separated in the past, and they will be widely separated again. It is hard to trace the points of contact, but we can be mathematically certain that the contacts happen — mathematically certain that if two genes are out of contact at a particular point, we won't have to travel far in either direction along the river until they touch again.

You may not know that you are a cousin of your husband, but it   10
is statistically likely that you won't have to go far back in your ancestry until you meet a junction with his lineage. Looking in the other direction, toward the future, it might seem obvious that you have a good chance of sharing descendants with your husband or wife. But here is a much more arresting thought. Next time you are with a large group of people — say, in a concert hall or at a football match — look around at the audience and reflect upon the following: if you have any descendants at all in the distant future, there are probably people at the same concert whose hands you could shake as coancestors of your future descendants. Cograndparents of the same children usually know they are coancestors, and this must give them a certain feeling of affinity whether or not they get on personally. They can look at each other and say, "Well, I may not like him much, but his DNA is mingled with mine in our shared grandchild, and we can hope to share descendants into the future, long after we're gone. Surely this creates a bond between us." But my point is that, if you are blessed with distant descendants at all, some of the perfect strangers at the concert hall will probably be your coances-

[4] **William the Conqueror (c. 1028 – 1087)** Duke of Normandy who conquered England and ruled as William I from 1066.

tors. You can survey the auditorium and speculate about which individuals, male or female, are destined to share your descendants and which are not. You and I, whoever you are and whatever your color and sex, may well be coancestors. Your DNA may be destined to mingle with mine. Salutations!

Now suppose we travel back in a time machine, perhaps to a   11
crowd in the Colosseum, or farther back, to market day in Ur, or even farther still. Survey the crowd, just as we imagined for our modern concert audience. Realize that you can divide these long-dead individuals into two and only two categories: those who are your ancestors and those who are not. That is obvious enough, but now we come to a remarkable truth. If your time machine has taken you sufficiently far back, you can divide the individuals you meet into those who are ancestors of every human alive in 1995 and those who are the ancestors of nobody alive in 1995. There are no intermediates. Every individual you set eyes on when you step outside your time machine is either a universal human ancestor or not an ancestor of anybody at all.

This is an arresting thought, but it is trivially easy to prove. All   12
you have to do is move your mental time machine back to a ludicrously long time ago: say, to three hundred fifty million years ago, when our ancestors were lobe-finned fishes with lungs, emerging from the water and becoming amphibians. If a particular fish is my ancestor, it is inconceivable that he is not your ancestor too. If he were not, this would imply that the lineage leading to you and the lineage leading to me had independently, without cross-reference, evolved from fish through amphibian, reptile, mammal, primate, ape and hominid, ending up so similar that we can talk to each other and, if we are of opposite sex, mate with each other. What is true of you and me is true of any pair of humans.

We have proved that if we travel sufficiently far back in time,   13
every individual we encounter must be the ancestor either of all of us or of none of us. But how far is sufficiently far? We clearly don't need to go back to lobe-finned fishes — that was the *reductio ad absurdum*[5] — but how far do we have to go back until we come to a universal ancestor of every human alive in 1995? That's a much more difficult question, and it is the one to which I next want to turn. This one cannot be answered from the armchair. We need real information, measurements from the hard world of particular facts.

Sir Ronald Fisher, the formidable English geneticist and mathe-   14
matician, who could be regarded as Darwin's greatest twentieth-

---

[5] ***reductio ad absurdum*** The point at which things become absurd.

century successor as well as the father of modern statistics, had this to say in 1930:

> It is only the geographical and other barriers to sexual intercourse between different races . . . which prevent the whole of mankind from having had, apart from the last thousand years, a practically identical ancestry. The ancestry of members of the same nation can differ little beyond the last 500 years; at 2000 years the only differences that would seem to remain would be those between distinct ethnographic races; these . . . may indeed be extremely ancient; but this could only be the case if for long ages the diffusion of blood between the separated groups was almost non-existent.

In the terms of our river analogy, Fisher is, in effect, making use 15 of the fact that the genes of all the members of one geographically united race are flowing down the same river. But when it came to his actual figures — five hundred years, two thousand years, the antiquity of the separation of different races — Fisher had to have been making educated guesses. The relevant facts were not available in his time. Now, with the molecular-biology revolution, there is an embarrassment of riches. It is molecular biology that has given us the charismatic African Eve.

The digital river is not the only metaphor that has been used. It 16 is tempting to liken the DNA in each one of us to a family Bible. DNA is a very long piece of text, written, as we saw in the previous chapter, in a four-letter alphabet. The letters have been scrupulously copied from our ancestors, and only from our ancestors, with remarkable fidelity even in the case of very remote ancestors. It should be possible, by comparing the texts preserved in different people, to reconstruct their cousinship and work back to a common ancestor. Distant cousins, whose DNA has had more time to diverge — say, Norwegians and Australian aborigines — should differ in a larger number of words. Scholars do this kind of thing with different versions of biblical documents. Unfortunately, in the case of DNA archives, there is a snag. Sex.

Sex is an archivist's nightmare. Instead of leaving ancestral texts 17 intact but for an occasional inevitable error, sex wantonly and energetically wades in and destroys the evidence. No bull ever abused a china shop as sex abuses the DNA archives. There is nothing like it in biblical scholarship. Admittedly, a scholar seeking to trace the origins of, say, the Song of Solomon is aware that it is not quite what it seems. The Song has oddly disjointed passages, suggesting that it is really fragments of several different poems, only some of them erotic, stitched together. It contains errors — mutations — especially in translation. "Take us the foxes, the little foxes, that spoil the vines" is a mistranslation, even though a lifetime's repetition has given it a haunting appeal of its own, which is unlikely to be matched by the more correct "Catch for us the fruit bats, the little fruit bats . . .":

> For lo, the winter is past, the rain is over and gone. The flowers appear on the earth; the time of the singing of birds is come, and the voice of the turtle is heard in our land.

The poetry is so ravishing that I am reluctant to spoil it by not- 18 ing that here, too, is an undoubted mutation. Reinsert "dove" after "turtle," as the modern translations correctly but leadenly do, and hear the cadence collapse. But these are minor errors, the inevitable, slight degradations we have to expect when documents are not printed in thousands or etched on high-fidelity computer disks but copied and recopied by mortal scribes from scarce and vulnerable papyri.

But now let sex enter the picture. (No, in the sense I mean, sex 19 does not enter the Song of Songs.) Sex, in the sense I mean, amounts to ripping out half of one document, in the form of randomly chosen fragments, and mixing it with the complementarily butchered half of another document. Unbelievable — vandalistic, even — as it sounds, this is exactly what happens whenever a sex cell is made. For instance, when a man makes a sperm cell, the chromosomes that he inherited from his father pair off with the chromosomes that he inherited from his mother, and great chunks of them change places. A child's chromosomes are an irretrievably scrambled mishmash of its grandparents' chromosomes and so on back to distant ancestors. Of the would-be ancient texts, the letters, perhaps the words, may survive intact down the generations. But chapters, pages, even paragraphs are torn up and recombined with such ruthless efficiency that as a means of tracing history they are almost useless. Where ancestral history is concerned, sex is the great cover-up.

We can use DNA archives to reconstruct history wherever sex is 20 safely out of the picture. I can think of two important examples. One is African Eve, and I'll come to her. The other case is the reconstruction of more remote ancestry — looking at relationships among species rather than within species. As we saw in the previous chapter, sexual mixing takes place only within species. When a parental species buds off a daughter species, the river of genes splits into two branches. After they have diverged for a sufficient time, sexual mixing within each river, far from being a hindrance to the genetic archivist, actually helps in the reconstruction of ancestry and cousinships among species. It is only where within-species cousinships are concerned that sex messes up the evidence. Where between-species cousinships are concerned, sex helps because it tends automatically to ensure that each individual is a good genetic sample of the entire species. It doesn't matter which bucketful you haul out of a well-churned river; it will be representative of the water of that river.

DNA texts taken from representatives of different species have   21
indeed been compared, with great success, letter by letter, to construct family trees of species. It is even possible, according to one influential school of thought, to put dates on the branchings. This opportunity follows from the albeit controversial notion of a "molecular clock": the assumption that mutations in any one region of the genetic text occur at a constant rate per million years. We'll return to the molecular-clock hypothesis in a moment.

The "paragraph" in our genes describing the protein called cy-   22
tochrome *c* is 339 letters long. Twelve letter changes separate human cytochrome *c* from the cytochrome *c* of horses, our rather distant cousins. Only one cytochrome *c* letter change separates humans from monkeys (our fairly close cousins), one letter change separates horses from donkeys (their very close cousins) and three letter changes separate horses from pigs (their somewhat more distant cousins). Forty-five letter changes separate humans from yeast and the same number separates pigs from yeast. It is not surprising that these numbers should be the same, because as we follow back the river leading to humans, it joins with the river leading to pigs much more recently than their common river joins the river leading to yeast. There is a little slop in these numbers, however. The number of letter changes in cytochrome *c* separating horses from yeast is not forty-five but forty-six. This does not mean that pigs are closer cousins of yeast than horses are. They are exactly equally close to yeast, as are all vertebrates — and, indeed, all animals. Perhaps an extra change crept into the lineage leading to horses since the time of the rather recent ancestor they share with pigs. That is not important. On the whole, the number of cytochrome *c* letter changes separating pairs of creatures is pretty much what we'd expect from previous ideas of the branching pattern of the evolutionary tree.

The molecular clock theory, as noted, holds that the rate of   23
change of a given piece of text per million years is roughly fixed. Of the forty-six cytochrome *c* letter changes separating horses from yeast, it is assumed that about half of them occurred during evolution from the common ancestor to modern horses and about half of them occurred during evolution from the common ancestor to modern yeast (obviously, the two evolutionary pathways have taken exactly the same number of millions of years to accomplish). At first

this seems a surprising thing to assume. After all, it is pretty likely that the common ancestor resembled yeast more than it resembled a horse. The reconciliation lies in the assumption, increasingly accepted since it was first championed by the eminent Japanese geneticist Motoo Kimura, that the greater part of genetic texts can change freely without the text's meaning being affected.

A good analogy is varying the typeface in a printed sentence. "A   24
horse is *a* mammal." "A **yeast** is *a* **fungus**." The meaning of these sentences comes through loud and clear, even though every word is printed in a different font. The molecular clock ticks away in the equivalent of meaningless font changes, as the millions of years go by. The changes that are subject to natural selection and that describe the difference between a horse and a yeast — the changes in *meaning* of the sentences — are the tip of the iceberg.

Some molecules have a higher clock rate than others. Cy-   25
tochrome *c* evolves relatively slowly: about one letter change every twenty-five million years. This is probably because cytochrome *c*'s vital importance to an organism's survival depends critically upon its detailed shape. Most changes in such a shape-critical molecule are not tolerated by natural selection. Other proteins, such as those called fibrinopeptides, although they are important, work equally well in lots of variant forms. The fibrinopeptides are used in blood clotting, and you can change most of their details without harming their clottability. The mutation rate in these proteins is about one change every six hundred thousand years, a rate more than forty times faster than that for cytochrome *c*. Fibrinopeptides, therefore, are no good for reconstructing ancient ancestry, although they are useful for reconstructing more recent ancestry — for example, within the mammals. There are hundreds of different proteins, each changing at its own characteristic rate per million years and each independently usable for reconstructing family trees. They all yield pretty much the same family tree — which, by the way, is rather good evidence, if evidence were needed, that the theory of evolution is true.

We came into this discussion from the realization that sexual   26
mixing messes up the historical record. We distinguished two ways in which the effects of sex could be escaped. We've just dealt with one of them, following from the fact that sex does not mix genes between species. This opens up the possibility of using DNA sequences to reconstruct remotely ancient family trees of our ancestors that lived long before we became recognizably human. But we've already agreed that if we go back that far we humans are all definitely descended from the same single individual anyway. We wanted to

find out how recently we could still claim common descent with all other humans. To discover that, we have to turn to a different kind of DNA evidence. This is where African Eve comes into the story.

African Eve is sometimes called Mitochondrial Eve. Mitochondria are tiny, lozenge-shaped bodies swarming by the thousands in each one of our cells. They are basically hollow but with a complicated interior structure of membranous baffles. The area afforded by these membranes is much larger than you'd think from the outside appearance of mitochondria, and it is used. The membranes are the production lines of a chemical factory — more precisely, a power station. A carefully controlled chain reaction is strung out along the membranes — a chain reaction involving more stages than those in any human chemical factory. The result is that energy, originating in food molecules, is released in controlled steps and stored in reusable form for burning later, wherever it is needed, anywhere in the body. Without our mitochondria, we'd die in a second.

That's what mitochondria do, but we are here more concerned with where they come from. Originally, in ancient evolutionary history, they were bacteria. This is the remarkable theory championed, by the redoubtable Lynn Margulis of the University of Massachusetts at Amherst, from heterodox origins through grudging interest to triumphant near-universal acceptance today. Two billion years ago, the remote ancestors of mitochondria were free-living bacteria. Together with other bacteria of different kinds, they took up residence inside larger cells. The resulting community of ("prokaryotic") bacteria became the large ("eukaryotic") cell we call our own. Each one of us is a community of a hundred million million mutually dependent eukaryotic cells. Each one of those cells is a community of thousands of specially-tamed bacteria, entirely enclosed within the cell, where they multiply as bacteria will. It has been calculated that if all the mitochondria in a single human body were laid end to end, they would girdle the Earth not once but two thousand times. A single animal or plant is a vast community of communities packed in interacting layers, like a rain forest. As for a rain forest itself, it is a community seething with perhaps ten million species of organisms, every individual member of every species being itself a community of communities of domesticated bacteria. Not only is Dr. Margulis's theory of origins — the cell as an enclosed garden of bacteria — incomparably more inspiring, exciting and uplifting than the story of the Garden of Eden. It has the additional advantage of being almost certainly true.

Like most biologists, I now assume the truth of the Margulis theory, and in this chapter I mention it only to follow up a particular implication: mitochondria have their own DNA, which is confined to a single ring chromosome, as in other bacteria. And now for the point that this has all been leading up to. Mitochondrial DNA does not participate in any sexual mixing, either with the main "nuclear" DNA of the body or with the DNA of other mitochondria. Mitochondria, like many bacteria, reproduce simply by dividing. Whenever a mitochondrion divides into two daughter mitochondria, each daughter gets an identical copy — give or take the odd mutation — of the original chromosome. Now you see the beauty of this, from our point of view as long-distance genealogists. We found that where our ordinary DNA texts are concerned, in every generation sex scrambles the evidence, confusing the contributions from paternal and maternal lines. Mitochondrial DNA is blessedly celibate.

We get our mitochondria from our mother only. Sperms are too   30
small to contain more than a few mitochondria; they have just enough to provide the energy to power their tails as they swim toward the egg, and these mitochondria are cast away with the tail when the sperm head is absorbed in the egg at fertilization. The egg is massive by comparison, and its huge, fluid-filled interior contains a rich culture of mitochondria. This culture seeds the child's body. So whether you are female or male, your mitochondria are all descended from an initial inoculum of your mother's mitochondria. Whether you are male or female, your mitochondria are all descended from your maternal grandmother's mitochondria. None from your father, none from either grandfather, none from your paternal grandmother. The mitochondria constitute an independent record of the past, uncontaminated by the main nuclear DNA, which is equally likely to come from each of four grandparents, each of eight great-grandparents and so on back.

Mitochondrial DNA is uncontaminated, but it is not immune to   31
mutation — to random errors in copying. Indeed, it mutates at a higher rate than our "own" DNA, because (as is the case with all bacteria) it lacks the sophisticated proofreading machinery our cells have evolved over the eons. There will be a few differences between your mitochondrial DNA and mine, and the number of differences will be a measure of how far back our ancestors diverged. Not *any* of our ancestors, but our ancestors in the female female female . . . line. If your mother happens to be a purebred native Australian, or a purebred Chinese, or a purebred !Kung San of the Kalahari, there will be rather a lot of differences between your mitochondrial DNA and mine. It doesn't matter who your father is: he can be an English marquess or a Sioux chieftain, for all the difference it makes to your mitochondria. And the same goes for any of your male ancestors, ever.

So there is a separate mitochondrial Apocrypha,[6] handed down 32
alongside the main family Bible but with the great virtue of going
down the female line only. This is not a sexist point; it would be just
as good if it came down through the male line only. The virtue lies
in its intactness, in its not being chopped and merged in every generation. Consistent descent via either sex but not both is what we, as
DNA genealogists, need. The Y chromosome which, like a surname,
is handed down the male line only, would in theory be just as good,
but it contains too little information to be useful. The mitochondrial
Apocrypha is ideal for dating common ancestors within one species.

Mitochondrial DNA has been exploited by a group of re- 33
searchers associated with the late Allan Wilson in Berkeley, California. In the 1980s, Wilson and his colleagues sampled the sequences
from 135 living women drawn from all around the world — Australian aborigines, New Guinea highlanders, Native Americans, Europeans, Chinese and representatives of various peoples in Africa.
They looked at the numbers of letter differences separating each
woman from each other woman. They gave these numbers to a computer and asked it to construct the most parsimonious family tree it
could find. "Parsimonious" here means doing away as much as possible with the need to postulate coincidence. This requires some explaining.

Think back to our earlier discussion of horses, pigs and yeast, 34
and the analysis of cytochrome *c* letter sequences. You remember
that horses differ from pigs in only three such letters, pigs differ
from yeast in forty-five letters, and horses differ from yeast in forty-
six letters. We made the point that, theoretically, since horses and
pigs are connected to each other by a relatively recent common ancestor, they should be exactly the same distance from yeast. The difference between forty-five and forty-six is an anomaly, something
that in an ideal world would not be there. It may be due to an additional mutation on the route to horses or a reverse mutation on the
route to pigs.

Now, absurd as such an idea is in reality, it is theoretically con- 35
ceivable that pigs are really closer to yeast than they are to horses. It
is theoretically possible that pigs and horses have evolved their close
resemblance to one another (their cytochrome *c* texts are only three
letters apart, and their bodies are basically built to an almost identical mammalian pattern) by massive coincidence. The reason we
don't believe this is that the ways in which pigs resemble horses

---

[6] **Apocrypha** Of uncertain authenticity. A reference to a separate strain, as in
the apocryphal books of the Bible, which some religions do not accept as canonical.

vastly outnumber the ways in which pigs resemble yeast. Admittedly, there is a single DNA letter in which pigs appear closer to yeast than to horses, but this is swamped by millions of resemblances going the other way. The argument is one of parsimony. If we assume that pigs are close to horses, we need to accommodate only one coincidental resemblance. If we try to assume that pigs are close to yeast, we have to postulate a prodigiously unrealistic concatenation of independently acquired coincidental resemblances.

In the cases of horses, pigs and yeast, the parsimony argument is   36
too overwhelming to be in doubt. But in the mitochondrial DNA of different human races there is nothing overwhelming about the resemblances. Parsimony arguments still apply, but they are slight, quantitative arguments, not massive, knock-down arguments. Here's what the computer, in theory, has to do. It has to make a list of all possible family trees relating the 135 women. It then examines this set of possible trees and picks out the most parsimonious one — that is, the one that minimizes the number of coincidental resemblances. We must accept that even the best tree will probably force us to accept a few little coincidences, just as we were forced to accept the fact that, with regard to one DNA letter, yeasts are closer to pigs than to horses. But — in theory, at least — the computer should be able to take that in its stride and announce to us which of the many possible trees is the most parsimonious, the least coincidence-ridden.

That is in theory. In practice, there is a snag. The number of   37
possible trees is greater than you, or I, or any mathematician, can possibly imagine. For horse, pig and yeast there are only three possible trees. The obviously correct one is *[[pig horse] yeast]*, with pig and horse nested together inside the innermost brackets and yeast as the unrelated "outgroup." The other two theoretical trees are *[[pig yeast] horse]* and *[[horse yeast] pig]*. If we add a fourth creature — say, squid — the number of trees goes up to fifteen. I won't list all fifteen, but the true (most parsimonious) one is *[[[pig horse] squid] yeast]*. Again, pig and horse, as close relatives, are cosily nested together in the innermost brackets. Squid is the next to join the club, having a more recent ancestor with the pig/horse lineage than yeast does. Any of the fourteen other trees — for instance, *[[pig squid] [horse yeast]]* — is definitely less parsimonious. It is highly improbable that pig and horse could have independently evolved their numerous resemblances if pig were really a closer cousin to squid and horse were really a closer cousin to yeast.

If three creatures yield three possible trees, and four creatures   38
yield fifteen possible trees, how many possible trees could be constructed for a hundred and thirty-five women? The answer is such a risibly large number that there is no point in writing it out. If the largest and fastest computer in the world were set to work listing all

the possible trees, the end of the world would be upon us before the computer had made a perceptible dent in the task.

Nevertheless, the problem is not hopeless. We are used to taming impossibly large numbers by judicious sampling techniques. We can't count the number of insects in the Amazon Basin, but we can estimate the number by sampling small plots dotted at random through the forest and assuming that these plots are representative. Our computer can't examine all possible trees uniting the 135 women, but it can pull out random samples from the set of all possible trees. If, whenever you draw a sample from the gigabillions of possible trees, you notice that the most parsimonious members of the sample have certain features in common, you can conclude that probably the most parsimonious of all the trees has the same features.

This is what people have done. But it isn't necessarily obvious what is the best way to do it. Just as entomologists might disagree over the most representative way to sample the Brazilian rain forest, so DNA genealogists have used different sampling methods. And unfortunately the results don't always agree. Nevertheless, for what they are worth, I'll present the conclusions the Berkeley group reached in their original analysis of human mitochondrial DNA. Their conclusions were extremely interesting and provocative. According to them, the most parsimonious tree turns out to be firmly rooted in Africa. What this means is that some Africans are more distantly related to other Africans than to anybody in the whole of the rest of the world. The whole of the rest of the world — Europeans, Native Americans, Australian aboriginals, Chinese, New Guineans, Inuits, and all — form one relatively close group of cousins. Some Africans belong in this close group. But other Africans don't. According to this analysis, the most parsimonious tree looks like this: [some Africans [other Africans [yet other Africans [yet other Africans and everybody else]]]]. They therefore concluded that the grand ancestress of all of us lived in Africa: "African Eve." As I have said, this conclusion is controversial. Others have claimed that equally parsimonious trees can be found in which the outermost branches occur outside Africa. They also claim that the Berkeley group obtained the particular results they did partly because of the order in which their computer looked at the possible trees. Obviously, order of looking ought not to matter. Probably most experts would still put their money on Mitochondrial Eve's being African, but they wouldn't do so with any great confidence.

The second conclusion of the Berkeley group is less controversial. No matter where Mitochondrial Eve lived, they were able to estimate when. It is known how fast mitochondrial DNA evolves; you can therefore put an approximate date on each of the branch points on the tree of divergence of mitochondrial DNA. And the branch

39

40

41

point that unites all womankind — the birth date of Mitochondrial Eve — is between a hundred fifty thousand and a quarter of a million years ago.

Whether Mitochondrial Eve was an African or not, it is important 42 to avoid a possible confusion with another sense in which it is undoubtedly true that our ancestors came out of Africa. Mitochondrial Eve is a recent ancestor of all modern humans. She was a member of the species *Homo sapiens*. Fossils of much earlier hominids, *Homo erectus,* have been found outside as well as inside Africa. The fossils of ancestors even more remote than *Homo erectus,* such as *Homo habilis* and various species of *Australopithecus* (including a newly discovered one more than four million years old), have been found only in Africa. So if we are the descendants of an African diaspora within the last quarter of a million years, it is the second African diaspora. There was an earlier exodus, perhaps a million and a half years ago, when *Homo erectus* meandered out of Africa to colonize parts of the Middle East and Asia. The African Eve theory is claiming not that these earlier Asians didn't exist but that they leave no surviving descendants. Whichever way you look at it, we are all, if you go back two million years, Africans. The African Eve theory is claiming in addition that we surviving humans are all Africans if you go back only a few hundred thousand years. It would be possible, if new evidence supported it, to trace all modern mitochondrial DNA back to an ancestress outside Africa ("Asian Eve," say) while at the same time agreeing that our more remote ancestors are to be found only in Africa.

Let's assume, for the moment, that the Berkeley group is right, 43 and examine what their conclusion does and does not mean. The "Eve" sobriquet has had unfortunate consequences. Some enthusiasts have run away with the idea that she must have been a lonely woman, the only woman on Earth, the ultimate genetic bottleneck, even a vindication of Genesis! This is a complete misunderstanding. The correct claim is not that she was the only woman on Earth, nor even that the population was relatively small during her time. Her companions, of both sexes, may have been both numerous and fecund. They may still have numerous descendants alive today. But all descendants of their mitochondria have died out, because their link with us passes, at some point, through a male. In the same way, a noble surname (surnames are linked to Y chromosomes and pass down the male-only line in exact mirror image to mitochondria) can die out, but this doesn't mean that possessors of the surname have no descendants. They may have numerous descendants via pathways other than the male-only pathway. The correct claim is only that Mitochondrial Eve is the most recent woman of whom it can be said that all modern humans are descended from her in the female-only line. There *has* to be *a* woman of whom this claim can be made.

The only argument is over whether she lived here rather than there, at this time rather than at that time. The fact that she did live, in some place and at some time, is certain.

Here is a second misunderstanding — a more common one, 44 which I have heard perpetrated even by leading scientists working in the field of mitochondrial DNA. This is the belief that Mitochondrial Eve is our most recent common ancestor. It is based on a confusion between "most recent common ancestor" and "most recent common ancestor in the purely female line." Mitochondrial Eve is our most recent common ancestor in the purely female line, but there are lots of other ways of being descended from people than in the female line. Millions of other ways. Go back to our calculations of numbers of ancestors (forgetting the complication of cousin marriage, which was the point of the argument before). You have eight great-grandparents but only one of them is in the purely female line. You have sixteen great-great-grandparents but only one of *them* is in the purely female line. Even allowing that cousin marriage reduces the number of ancestors in a given generation, it is still true that there are far, far, far more ways of being an ancestor than just in the female-only line. As we follow our genetic river back through remote antiquity, there were probably lots of Eves and lots of Adams — focal individuals, of whom it is possible to say that all 1995's people are descended from her, or him. Mitochondrial Eve is only one of these. There is no particular reason to think that of all these Eves and Adams, Mitochondrial Eve is the most recent. On the contrary. She is defined in a *particular* way: we are descended from her via a particular pathway through the river of descent. The number of possible pathways to set alongside the female-only pathway is so large that it is mathematically highly unlikely that Mitochondrial Eve is the most recent of these many Eves and Adams. It is special among pathways in one way (being female-only). It would be a remarkable coincidence if it were special among pathways in another way (being the most recent).

An additional point of mild interest is that our most recent com- 45 mon ancestor is somewhat more likely to have been an Adam than an Eve. Harems of females are more likely to occur than harems of males, if only because males are physically capable of having hundreds of children, even thousands. *The Guinness Book of Records* puts the record at over a thousand, achieved by Moulay Ishmael the Bloodthirsty. (Incidentally, Moulay Ishmael might well be adopted by feminists as a general symbol of macho unpleasantness. It is said that his method of mounting a horse was to draw his sword and leap into the saddle, achieving quick release by simultaneously decapitating the slave who held the bridle. Implausible as this is, the fact that the legend comes down to us, together with his reputation for having killed ten thousand men with his own hand, perhaps gives an idea of the kinds of qualities that were admired among men of his type.) Females, even under ideal conditions, cannot have more than a couple of tens of children. A female is more likely than a male to have the average number of children. A few males may have a ludicrously greedy share of the children, which means that other males must have none. If anybody fails to reproduce altogether, it is more likely to be a male than a female. And if anybody garners a disproportionate posterity, it is also likely to be a male. This goes for the most recent common ancestor of all humanity, who is therefore more likely to have been an Adam than an Eve. To take an extreme example, who is more likely to be the ancestor of all present-day Moroccans, Moulay Ishmael the Bloodthirsty or any *one* woman in his unfortunate harem?

We may come to the following conclusions: First, it is necessarily certain that there existed one female, whom we may call Mitochondrial Eve, who is the most recent common ancestor of all modern humans down the female-only pathway. It is also certain that there existed one person, of unknown sex, whom we may call the Focal Ancestor, who is the most recent common ancestor of all modern humans down any pathway. Third, although it is possible that Mitochondrial Eve and the Focal Ancestor are one and the same, it is vanishingly unlikely that this is so. Fourth, it is somewhat more likely that the Focal Ancestor was a male than a female. Fifth, Mitochondrial Eve very probably lived less than a quarter of a million years ago. Sixth, there is disagreement over where Mitochondrial Eve lived, but the balance of informed opinion still favors Africa. Only conclusions five and six depend upon inspection of scientific evidence. The first four can all be worked out by armchair reasoning from common knowledge. 46

But I said that ancestors hold the key to understanding life itself. The story of African Eve is a parochial, human microcosm of a grander and incomparably more ancient epic. We shall again have recourse to the metaphor of the river of genes, our river out of Eden. But we shall follow it back through a time scale incommensurably older than the legendary Eve's thousands of years and African Eve's hundreds of thousands. The river of DNA has been flowing through our ancestors in an unbroken line that spans not less than three thousand million years. 47

QUESTIONS FOR CRITICAL READING

1. What is an origin myth, and how does Dawkins's explanation of human origins conform with other origin myths?

2. Why does Dawkins think his explanation is not a myth?
3. Cite examples of tribal science other than the ones Dawkins gives in his first four paragraphs.
4. What is the difference between Dawkins's river metaphor and the standard family tree metaphor for genealogy? See paragraphs 8 to 10 for some of his discussion.
5. In paragraph 11 Dawkins says that if we could go back to the time of Ur or even earlier, we could divide all the people who were then alive into those who are ancestors of everyone living and those who are not. What implications might that have for contemporary society?
6. Referring to paragraphs 14 and 15, how far back in time would we have to go to search out the mutual ancestry of the entire human race?
7. How does Dawkins put Darwinian theory to work in his analysis of origins?

SUGGESTIONS FOR WRITING

1. Dawkins constructs an argument that asserts we are descended from a common ancestor whom he calls African Eve. Examine his argument, and discuss its strengths and weaknesses. Does the scientific evidence point clearly in the direction that Dawkins has suggested?
2. Explain how Dawkins proposes we use the "DNA archives" to examine ancestorship. He discusses this matter in paragraphs 20 to 25. How do you interpret the information regarding the letter changes in the cytochrome *c* of various animals? What does the closeness or distance from other animals or living things tell us about the reliability of cytochrome *c* to help us understand our relationship to other beings in the world?
3. Explain why mitochondria are more helpful than genes in tracing the ancestry of individuals. For this essay, research the current understanding of mitochondria and their genetic structure.
4. Respond to the theories of Lynn Margulis, discussed in paragraphs 28 to 30. If his assumption is true that all mitochondria were bacteria, then at one level all higher animals have bacteria for ancestors. How could that realization affect some people's beliefs in the nobility of humankind?
5. **CONNECTIONS** Dawkins is referred to as an "ultra-Darwinist." Given your understanding of Darwin's theories of natural selection, do you feel that the ideas Dawkins champions about nature would be warmly received by Darwin? In what ways are Dawkins's theories compatible with Darwin's? How does he go beyond Darwin?
6. **CONNECTIONS** Referring to Hannah Arendt's discussion in Part One of this book, how could Dawkins's development of Darwin's theories support or undermine the racist views of Nazi Germany? How could an ideology be constructed from Dawkins's ideas as they are presented here?

PART SIX

CULTURE

Herodotus
Álvar Núñez Cabeza de Vaca
Ruth Benedict
Margaret Mead
Clifford Geertz

INTRODUCTION

The contemporary concept of culture encompasses the laws, rituals, values, beliefs, and intellectual and artistic endeavors of a society. However, in the past culture was not considered an overarching description of all the components of a society; instead, the idea of culture was often juxtaposed with the idea of civilization. In ancient Rome the word *cultura* was linked with the concepts of knowledge and philosophy while *civis* denoted political citizenship in Rome and thus a sense of superiority to the surrounding non-Roman societies. During the Enlightenment, thinkers such as Rousseau (see Part One) argued for a romantic concept of culture as representing the natural and creative potential of human endeavor, whereas civilization was viewed as representing the artificial and mechanical forces of technology that ultimately resulted in man's alienation from his fellow man. However, for many social critics, by the late nineteenth and early twentieth century the idea of culture had come to include the combination of social, ideological, political, and economic forces that shaped and defined a given society or group.

Perhaps because culture is necessarily a human creation, anthropologists and historians have long examined their own and other cultures for clues to the nature of individual and collective human identities. In fact, it has often been through exposure to different cultures that humans have come to a clearer understanding of their own traditions and philosophies. Michel de Montaigne (1533–1592), one of the most influential of the Renaissance thinkers, was deeply interested in cultures other than that of his native France. Although he himself did not travel extensively, he read widely and studied reports of the contemporary expeditions to North and South America. According to Montaigne, the customs that prevailed in any nation or region should be treated as acceptable and moral for that culture, even if they seem unacceptable for others. He held that moral judgments were a matter of opinion only and resisted judging cultures solely on the customs and mores of his own society.

The question of whether or not it is possible to be objective (and what the concept of objectivity means) is central to the study of culture. As the readings in this section attest, virtually all great travelers, historians, anthropologists, and other students of culture judge and describe foreign societies based on their own cultural standards. However, the urge to understand the traits that are unique to as well as those that are shared among the different societies of the world propels them onward in their studies. In the process we all learn more about ourselves and the people with whom we share our world.

Herodotus traveled widely in the classical world and lived at a time when Greece was at its zenith (he was first published around 425 B.C.). For him, its civilization was the crowning glory of all humankind. In commenting on people who lived in lands that figured in his history of the Persian wars, Herodotus usually relied on his own personal experiences and observations. He records his impressions of Egyptian culture with an eye toward both its similarities with Greek culture (particularly in the names of gods) and its differences. He is painstaking in his efforts to communicate the details of Egyptian culture, ranging from sexual practices and methods of embalming to treatment of animals, sacred and otherwise.

Álvar Núñez Cabeza de Vaca was an early sixteenth-century Spaniard shipwrecked on the coast of Texas at a time when no European had set foot in the region. During his eight-year adventure — filled with harrowing escapes from death and extraordinary accomplishments — he lived among several different tribes of Native Americans. Although he was not always treated well — in some cases he was threatened with death or slavery — he found ways to make himself useful enough that his Native American hosts were willing to feed and house him. Apart from being considered a *curandero,* a faith healer, he also managed to become a trader and traveler among various tribes. In his *Relación,* Cabeza de Vaca systematically recounts the behavior of the Native Americans with whom he lived. He describes them physically and explains the ways they gather food, house themselves, and conduct warfare. In his thoroughness he resembles Herodotus. Interestingly, he spent time with some of the Native American tribes that Ruth Benedict discusses in her reflections on Zuñi and Pueblo culture.

Ruth Benedict's interests center on the ideas involved in shaping cultures. While she was a graduate student in anthropology at Columbia University, she developed her own concepts regarding the psychological makeup of culture. Borrowing the terms *Apollonian* and *Dionysian* from Friedrich Nietzsche, she applied them to various peoples within and outside Pueblo culture. For example, she saw the Pueblo Zuñi as Apollonian — intellectual, cool, reserved — and the Kwakiutl of the Northwest, whom her teacher Franz Boas had studied, as Dionysian — quick tempered, intemperate, given to grand passion. Her application of these terms related more to psychology than to religion. She used Apollonian and Dionysian to describe the apparent mental states of people in the cultures she studied. For example, she spent a considerable amount of time studying the Dobu people in the Pacific, which convinced her that their mental state was neither Apollonian nor Dionysian. Instead, she felt that they displayed qualities associated with schizophrenia. Not all students of culture apply methods of psychology in the field, but it is one of Benedict's special strengths.

Margaret Mead, a student of both Franz Boas and Ruth Benedict, learned seven languages in order to communicate with people in cultures in the South Pacific both before and after World War II. "Women, Sex, and Sin" is a study of attitudes toward women in the culture of the Manus, a people living on the largest of the Admiralty Islands northwest of what is today Papua New Guinea. She reveals a fascinating development in the culture caused largely by the wartime interaction of Manus men with men from Australia and with films from the United States. As she tells us, the men returned to the island of Manus and purposively restructured their society. Few anthropologists have the opportunity that Mead had to study the effects of such an overwhelming change in social behavior. In the process, however, she examines the effects of change on the women themselves and notes that underneath, much has remained the same.

Clifford Geertz reflects on the difficulty of ever being able to report on a culture "from the native's point of view." He establishes relatively quickly that such a venture is essentially impossible. However, he attempts to resolve the problem of how we can know another culture by suggesting that it is possible to study the "symbolic forms" of a culture, its "words, images, institutions, behaviors." He supports his theory by referring to three cultures he has studied closely — Javanese, Balinese, and Moroccan. Each of these is different, and each is instructive. In each case, Geertz discusses some key words in the local language in an effort to demonstrate the specificity of the symbolic forms he studied. His efforts offer us a method by which we can study not only other cultures but also our own.

These essays exemplify the range of thought regarding the possibility of understanding other cultures. At the same time, they offer insight into the ways in which other people lived and continue to live, reminding us that we are part of a larger community of humanity, whose diverse cultures are in a constant state of interaction and change. In addition, the awareness these writers provide can help us understand ourselves as much as we hope to understand others.

HERODOTUS
Observations on Egypt

HERODOTUS (484? to 430 – 420 B.C.) is considered by most to have been the first Greek historian and therefore the first European historian. In his *History* he refers to other writers who kept journals and produced short pieces on historical events, but no one in his time wrote as extensively and comprehensively about historical experience as he did. Herodotus intended his work to be a history of the Persian-Greek wars of the period of 499 to 479 B.C. However, he soon realized that to give a detailed narrative of the wars, he had to provide a great deal of background. Born in Halicarnassus, a Greek city that was controlled by the Persians in what is now Turkey, Herodotus had an interesting perspective on the events he described. His essentially multicultural upbringing seems to have helped him maintain objectivity when talking about people and cultures other than his own.

The entire *History* seems to have been available for Greeks to read some time before 425 B.C., when it is presumed that Herodotus was in Athens. It is clear from the *History* that he was a remarkable traveler. He traveled not only to Egypt but to Libya, Babylonia, Byzantium, and north to parts of modern Germany and Russia. He kept good notes and wrote copiously about his experiences. As he did so, he focused on issues that he thought his readers, who were Greeks, would or should want to know about, revealing not only his own personal interests but the major interests of his audience.

The sections that appear here are from the second (2:45 – 92) of the five books that comprise the *History* and focus on Egyptian culture. Herodotus covers a wide variety of subjects, beginning with sacrifices and animals in an attempt to refute the rumor that Egyptians intended to sacrifice the Greek hero Heracles (who was

---

From *The History*. Translated by David Grene.

said to have instead turned on his host and slaughtered them all). Herodotus laughs at such a story on several grounds. He first claims that the Egyptians do not sacrifice animals (he contradicts himself later) and then argues that it is ridiculous to suppose a single man could slaughter thousands. Because he is a skeptic and defends a rational view of things, he is a remarkable observer of culture. He balances the stories he's heard with the likelihood of their being true.

Herodotus displays great curiosity about the culture of the Egyptians. He seems sympathetic to Egyptian culture and regards it as more ancient than Greek culture and as the source for some Greek practices. This is particularly true in matters concerning religion, which consume much of Herodotus's interest. Herodotus talks extensively about the Egyptian gods, noting that the Egyptians have the same gods that the Greeks have. Thus, the Egyptians have a chief god called Amon, and the Greeks call their chief god Zeus. Egyptian culture, however, had flourished for three thousand years by the time that the Greek order of gods was established in the *Iliad* by Homer and in the *Theogony* (birth of the gods) by Hesiod — less than four hundred years before Herodotus.

Another focus of the *History* is animals, especially sacred animals. Herodotus discusses them at length, especially cats and birds, which enjoyed special privileges in Egyptian society. The crocodile, which is ubiquitous on the Nile, is also examined, particularly sacred crocodiles, which were decorated with jewelry and clothing. Such animals have since been discovered in funerary digs, a fact that lends credence to Herodotus's descriptions.

He reserves special attention for Egyptian funeral and embalming practices, which seem to have been as intriguing to the Greeks of his time as they are to the people of our time. However, he does not describe the embalming of a pharaoh or ruler but rather concentrates on three standard methods of embalming that were available to ordinary citizens. His description sounds strikingly familiar to modern business practices: the most expensive grade of embalming was the most complex and satisfactory, while the least expensive was the most rudimentary. This attention to compelling details is what made Herodotus so widely read in his own day and what gives his work the power to continue to intrigue and inform.

HERODOTUS'S RHETORIC

Herodotus has often been praised for his narrative skills. Even when he recounts details and facts, he puts them in a context by telling a small story about them. Overall the *History* concerns warfare, but throughout the book, Herodotus pauses to do what he does in this section — digress. These digressions take him into interesting areas and permit him to discourse on related subjects before returning to his main topics. Digressions were always welcome in classical literature because they provided the human interest that satisfies people's curiosity.

Herodotus does not construct complex metaphors as he tells his story but moves directly to the things that interest him and gives us the important facts in an efficient manner. When he has an anecdote to tell us, he does so. When something shocking happens, as in the case of the woman who copulates with a goat in the Mendesian province (para. 2), he gives us the facts as he knows them and lets us draw our own conclusions. When he disapproves of a specific practice, he lets us know by his tone or by a telling descriptive term, such as "monstrosity."

His interest in origins informs his style by giving him a focus for most of his observations. He tells us that the gods as the Greeks know them "came from Egypt to Greece" (para. 6). When he sees a distinction in origin he mentions it, such as his reference to statues of Hermes, the messenger of the gods, with erect penises. Those are not from the Egyptians, he tells us, but from the Pelasgians, the people who lived in Greece eight centuries before Herodotus. He does not tell us the function of such statues, just that they did not come from Egypt. His Greek audience would have been familiar enough with them to know what their religious purposes were.

Herodotus acknowledges testimony that he receives from people, often saying things like, "That is what I heard from the priests in Thebes" (para. 11). He clearly distinguishes between what he has been told and what he himself has witnessed. The priests at Thebes told him a story about "two black doves" (para. 11) that flew from Egypt to the countries of Libya and Dodona. He explains that it concerns an ancient story of two women who were stolen by the Phoenicians and sold to each of these countries and later became famous for their divination. Herodotus narrates the story and then analyzes it. His explanation of the story and its background is typical of the way he reveals the hidden significance in the narratives that have been presented to him.

Herodotus's clear, informative style coupled with his astute analysis of cultural practices established him as one of history's first historians and also one of its greatest. His eye for details that both linked the Egyptians to and differentiated them from the Greeks made his work relevant and engrossing to the readers of his day and of ours as well.

Observations on Egypt

The Greeks tell many stories that show no manner of thought. [1] In particular, there is the tale they tell of Heracles[1] to the effect that he came to Egypt and that the Egyptians put garlands on his head and led him in procession, with intent to sacrifice him to Zeus; that for a while he held quiet, but when they brought him near the altar itself and had started the first rites on him, he took himself to his valor and slaughtered them all. In my opinion, the Greeks who tell this story know absolutely nothing about the nature of the Egyptians and their customs. Here is a people for whom the sacrifice of beasts themselves is unholy, except for pigs, bulls, bull-calves — that is, such as are pure — and geese; how could they sacrifice human beings? And furthermore, since Heracles was still only one, and also only a human being, as they themselves say, how can it accord with nature that he should slaughter that many tens of thousands? That is what I have to say about the matter; as I do so, may both gods and heroes view me kindly!

This is why the aforementioned Egyptians do not sacrifice she- [2] goats and he-goats: these people, the Mendesians, reckon Pan to be one of the Eight Gods, and the Eight, they say, were before the Twelve. Both in painting and in sculpture their painters and image-makers make the image of Pan as the Greeks do, with a goat face and a he-goat's legs; it is not that they think the god *is* so — nay, they think him like the other gods; but why he is so depicted it is not pleasant for me to say. The Mendesians regard as holy all goats, but the males more than the females, and the herdsmen that tend these he-goats have more honor than those that tend the others. Of the he-goats there is one in especial, and, when he dies, great mourning is instituted in all the Mendesian province. The he-goat and Pan are both called Mendes in the Egyptian language. In this province, in my time, a monstrosity took place: a he-goat coupled with a woman, plain, for all to see. This was done in the nature of a public exhibition.

The Egyptians think the pig an unclean animal. If any one of the [3] Egyptians, but passing by, touch a pig, he goes to the river and dips himself therein, garments and all. Furthermore, such native-born Egyptians as are swineherds, alone of all people, durst not enter any

---

[1] **Heracles** Hercules. According to Greek tradition, a seer declared Egypt would not recover from a plague of nine years unless there were an annual sacrifice of a foreigner. Heracles was said to be the first foreigner chosen, but he killed King Busiris and escaped. Herodotus scoffs at this myth.

Egyptian shrine; nor is anyone willing to give his daughter in marriage to one of a family of swineherds or to marry one himself from such a family, and so the swineherds marry and are given in marriage only among their own folk. The Egyptians do not think fit to sacrifice the pig to any god except the Moon and Dionysus,[2] and to these they sacrifice at the same time, the very full moon; it is then they sacrifice pigs and taste of their flesh. Why it is that they utterly reject the pig at other festivals and sacrifice it at this one — as to this, there is a story told about the matter by the Egyptians; I know it, but it is not quite suitable to be declared. This is how they make the sacrifice of pigs to the Moon: when the sacrificer makes his sacrifice, he puts together the tip of the tail, the spleen, and the caul and covers them up with all the fat that is about the belly of the beast; he then consecrates it in the fire. The rest of the flesh they eat in the Day of the Full Moon, the day on which they sacrifice the victim, but on no other day will they taste it. The poor people among them, through their poverty, make up pigs of dough and bake these and sacrifice them.

On the eve of the festival of Dionysus, each one of them cuts the throat of his pig in front of the doorway and then gives it, to take away, to the swineherd who has sold it to him. For the rest of the festival in honor of Dionysus, except for the dance choruses, the Egyptians celebrate it almost in everything like the Greeks. But instead of phalluses they have another invention, which are eighteen-inch-high images, controlled by strings, which the women carry round the villages; these images have a penis that nods and in size is not much less than all the rest of the body. Ahead there goes a flute-player, and the women follow, singing in honor of Dionysus. Now why the penis is so much bigger and is the only thing movable in the body — about this there is a sacred story told.

It seems to me that Melampus,[3] son of Amythaon, was not ignorant of this sacrifice; indeed, he seems to have been well versed in it. For it is Melampus who was for the Greeks the expositor of Dionysus — of his name, his sacrifice, and the phallic procession; strictly speaking, he did not put all together and manifest the whole story for them, for there were teachers afterwards who advanced it further. But it was Melampus who instituted the phallic procession to Dionysus, and it was from him that the Greeks learned to do what they do. It is my opinion that Melampus was a clever man who had

---

[2] **Dionysus** Greek god of wine and drama. The great Greek tragedies were performed in March in Athens during the celebration called the City Dionysia in honor of the god Dionysus.

[3] **Melampus** A soothsayer of Argos, said to understand the song of birds.

formed for himself an art of divination, and, having learned from
Egypt, he introduced much that was new to the Greeks, including
the ritual of Dionysus — and he made very little change in it. I will
never believe that the rites in Egypt and those in Greece can resemble each other by coincidence; for in that case the Greek rites would
have been in the Greek fashion, and they would not have been so recently instituted. Nor will I admit that the Egyptians could have
taken these from the Greeks — either these or any other thing of
customary usage. In my opinion, Melampus learned these Dionysiac
rites for the most part from Cadmus, the man of Tyre, and from
those Phoenicians who came with him to the country now called
Boeotia.[4]

The names of nearly all the gods came from Egypt to Greece.   6
That these gods came from the barbarians I found on inquiry to be
true; personally, I believe they came from Egypt. For except for Poseidon and the Dioscuri, as I mentioned before, and also Hera, Hes-
tia, Themis, and the Graces and Nereids, of all the other gods the
names have always existed in Egypt. I say what the Egyptians themselves say. In the case of gods of whom the Egyptians say they do
not know the names, these, I think, were named by the Pelasgians,[5]
except for Poseidon. This god the Greeks learned of from the
Libyans. No other people save the Libyans have had Poseidon's
name established among them from the beginning, and they have always honored him. The Egyptians do not proffer ritual honors to
heroes at all.

These things — and other things besides, which I shall show —   7
the Greeks learned from the Egyptians; but the making of the Hermes statues with the phallus erect, *that* they did not learn from the
Egyptians but from the Pelasgians, and it was the Athenians first of
all the Greeks who took over this practice and, from the Athenians,
all the rest. For the Pelasgians came to settle with the Athenians in
their land when the Athenians themselves were already counted as
Greeks. Thereby the Pelasgians too came to be regarded as Greeks.
Anyone who has been initiated into the rites of the Cabeiri, which
the Samothracians celebrate, taking them from the Pelasgians,
knows what I am talking of. For these Pelasgians, who came to live
with the Athenians, once lived in Samothrace, and it was from them
that the Samothracians took over the orgies. The Athenians, then,
were the first of the Greeks to make the statues of Hermes with the
penis erect, and it was from the Pelasgians they learned it. The Pelas-

---

[4] **Boeotia** District in northeast Greece, including the city of Thebes.
[5] **Pelasgians** Early inhabitants of Greece.

gians tell a holy story about this — matters that are made clear in the Samothracian mysteries.

Formerly the Pelasgians made all their sacrifices with invoca- 8 tions to gods (I know of this from what I heard at Dodona) but put no special title or name on any one of them; for they had not yet heard of any such. They gave them the title "gods" [*theoi*] from the circumstance that they had disposed [*ti-thēmi*, root *thē*] everything in order [*cosmos*] and arranged all. But afterwards, after a great while, they learned the names that came from Egypt — those of the other gods, that is; for the name of Dionysus they learned long after that. And after a time they consulted the oracle at Dodona about the names. This oracle at Dodona was the most ancient oracular place of all among the Greeks, and at that time it was the only one. When the Pelasgians asked the oracle in Dodona whether they should take on the names that came from the barbarians, the oracle bade them use the names. And from that time on they sacrificed using the names of the gods, and afterwards the Greeks received the names from the Pelasgians.

But whence each of these gods came into existence, or whether 9 they were for ever, and what kind of shape they had were not known until the day before yesterday, if I may use the expression; for I believe that Homer and Hesiod[6] were four hundred years before my time — and no more than that. It is they who created for the Greeks their theogony; it is they who gave to the gods the special names for their descent from their ancestors and divided among them their honors, their arts, and their shapes. Those who are spoken of as poets before Homer and Hesiod were, in my opinion, later born. The first part of this that I have said is what the priestesses at Dodona say, but the latter, as concerns Homer and Hesiod, is my own statement.

Concerning the oracles, the one that is among the Greeks and 10 the other in Libya, this is the story that the Egyptians tell. The priests of the Theban Zeus declared that two women, priestesses, were carried away from Thebes by Phoenicians and that they (the Theban priests) had learned that one of them was sold into Libya and the other to the Greeks. These women, they said, were the first to set up places of prophecy among these aforementioned peoples. When I asked them from what source they spoke with such exact

---

[6] **Homer and Hesiod** Ancient Greek poets believed to have lived around 750 B.C. (Homer) and 700 B.C. (Hesiod). Homer wrote *The Iliad* and *The Odyssey*; Hesiod wrote *The Theogony*, about the birth of the Greek gods, and *Works and Days*, about the daily life of Greek peasants. Herodotus's dating of these writers is probably reliable.

knowledge, they said that there had been a great search by their own people after these women, but they could never be found, but that afterwards they had learned about them what they had now told me.

This is what I heard from the priests in Thebes, but the follow- 11 ing is what the priestesses of Dodona had to say. There were, they said, two black doves that flew from Thebes in Egypt, and the one of them came to Libya and the other to themselves at Dodona, and the latter one settled upon an oak tree and with a human voice proclaimed that there should be there, in that place, an oracle of Zeus; they themselves then grasped that this proclamation to them was a thing divine, and because of it they made the place of the ora- cle. The dove that flew to Libya, they say, bade the Libyans also make the oracle of Amon there, and again the Libyans did what it said. The latter is also an oracle of Zeus. These things were told me by the priestesses of Dodona, the eldest of whom is called Promeneia, the second-eldest, Timarete, and the youngest, Nican- dra. The other people of Dodona who are concerned with the shrine agreed in the account of the priestesses.

My judgment of the matter is this: if the Phoenicians sold these 12 women, one to Libya and one to Greece, it seems to me that the woman who was sold into what is now Greece but in those early days was called Pelasgia — the very same land — was sold into Thesprotia; that then, being a slave there, she set up a shrine in honor of Zeus, under an oak that grew there. It was natural that she should do so since she had been a handmaid in the temple of Zeus in Thebes, whence she came, and so she would have remembered that. After she had learned the Greek language, she founded a place of prophecy there. At this point she told the people of Dodona that her sister had been sold into Libya by the very same Phoenicians who had sold herself to them.

I believe that the women were called by the Dodonaeans 13 "doves" because they were barbarians, and so they seemed to the people of Dodona to talk like birds. After a time they said, "The bird spoke with a human voice," as soon as the woman talked compre- hensibly. As long as she talked her own barbarian language, she seemed to them to speak like a bird. How, after all, could a dove speak with a human voice? That they said that the dove was black indicates that the woman was an Egyptian.

The methods of divination at Thebes in Egypt and at Dodona 14 are very similar to one another. Furthermore, divination from sacri- fices came from Egypt. Also, the Egyptians were the first people to organize holy assemblies, processions, and services of the gods, and it was from them that the Greeks learned these things. My proof of this is that the Egyptian practices are clearly very ancient indeed, and the Greek ones only lately established.

The Egyptians hold their assemblies not once a year but very often. The chief of these and the most reverentially celebrated is in honor of Artemis, at the town of Bubastis.[7] The second is at the city of Busiris and is in honor of Isis. In that city there is the greatest shrine of Isis, and the city was established at the center of the Egyptian Delta. Isis is in the Greek tongue Demeter. The third assembly is in the city of Saïs and is in honor of Athena; the fourth is in the city of Heliopolis in honor of Helios; the fifth is in honor of Leto in the city of Buto; and the sixth is in the city of Papremis in honor of Ares.

When they travel to Bubastis, this is what they do. They sail thither, men and women together, and a great number of each in each boat. Some of the women have rattles and rattle them, others play the flute through the entire trip, and the remainder of the women and men sing and clap their hands. As they travel on toward Bubastis and come near some other city, they edge the boat near the bank, and some of the women do as I have described. But others of them scream obscenities in derision of the women who live in that city, and others of them set to dancing, and others still, standing up, throw their clothes open to show their nakedness. This they do at every city along the riverbank. When they come to Bubastis, they celebrate the festival with great sacrifices, and more wine is drunk at that single festival than in all the rest of the year besides. There they throng together, man and woman (but no children), up to the number of seven hundred thousand, as the natives say.

That, then, is what is done there. How, at the city of Busiris, they celebrate the festival in honor of Isis I have already said. But in this festival, after the sacrifice, all the men and all the women, assuredly many tens of thousands of human beings, beat their breasts in lament; but whom it is they lament I may not declare; it would be unholy for me. But those of the Carians who are living in Egypt do even more than this, inasmuch as they cut their foreheads with knives, and thereby it is clear that they are foreigners and not Egyptians.

When the people gather to the city of Saïs, on the night of the sacrifice everyone burns many lamps, under the open sky, around their houses. The lamps are saucers full of oil and of salt and, on top, a wick, which burns all night long; and the name they call the festival is the Festival of the Lamps. Even those of the Egyptians who

15

16

17

18

---

[7] **Bubastis** City in the Nile River delta. The deity Bast was a cat-headed god, and the celebration Herodotus describes was among the most boisterous of Egyptian revels.

do not come to the festival itself keep the night of the festival heedfully, all of them, too, burning lamps; so the lamps burn not only in
the city of Saïs but throughout all Egypt. Why it is that this night
has won light and honor — as to that, there is a sacred story told.

Those who go to Heliopolis and Buto perform the sacrifice only.   19
But in Papremis they perform the sacrifice and the holy rites as elsewhere, but also, when the sun is sinking, some few of the priests remain busied with the service of the image; but the most of them,
with wooden clubs, stand at the entrance of the shrine. More than a
thousand men, who are performing their vows and also carrying
wooden clubs, stand all massed opposite to the first set. The image
itself, in a small wooden gilt shrine, they have conveyed, the day before, to another holy chamber. Those few of the priests who have
been left with the image drag a four-wheeled cart bearing the shrine
and the image within the shrine; but the priests standing at the entrance will not suffer the cart to enter. But the votaries come to the
rescue of the god and strike at those who would keep him out.
There is a sharp battle, then, with the wooden clubs, and they break
one another's heads; and, in my opinion, many die of their wounds,
though the Egyptians tell me that no one *dies*. The natives explain
this festival as follows. They say that Ares'[8] mother dwelt in the temple; Ares himself was reared elsewhere, but, when he came to manhood, he returned and wished to couple with his mother. His
mother's servants would not let him come in but kept him off — for
they had never laid eyes on him before. But the god went and
brought people from another city and handled the servants roughly,
and so he came in to where his mother was. It is from this, they say,
that, at the festival of Ares, blows are part of the ritual.

The Egyptians were the first of mankind to feel religious scru-   20
ples in certain matters — notably, not to lie with women in holy
places nor yet to go into the holy places after lying with a woman
without first washing oneself. For nearly all the rest of mankind, except for the Egyptians and the Greeks, have intercourse in holy
places and rise from intercourse with a woman and go into a shrine
without washing, for they think that men are much as other beasts;
they see the other beasts and the tribes of birds riding one another
in the temples and sacred precincts of the gods. If this were not
pleasing to the god, the beasts would not do it. But this kind of reasoning that they bring forward is one that for me, especially, is distasteful. Still, certainly, the Egyptians, in this and in all other matters
of the holy things, are excessively given to religious scruples.

---

[8] **Ares** Greek name for Mars, god of war.

Egypt, though it marches on the borders of Libya, is not very 21
populous in wild animals. But those that there are, wild or tame, are
all considered sacred, both those that have their living with
mankind and those that do not. But if I were to say why it is that the
animals are dedicated as sacred, my argument would drive me into
talking of matters divine, and the declaration of these is what I
would particularly shun. To the degree that I have spoken of them,
it was with but a touch, and under stress of necessity, that I have
spoken. There is a custom about the animals, and it is this. There are
keepers appointed for the maintenance of the animals, for each kind
separate, and men and women alike are keepers from among the
Egyptians, child succeeding father in this office of honor. In the cities,
each man, discharging his vows, does it thus: they pray to the god
whose beast it is, and they shave off their children's hair, either all
the head or a half or a third, and they weigh the hairs in a scale
against silver. When the scale tips, this sum is given to the keeper of
the beast, and she, up to the value of it, cuts up fish and gives it to
the animal to eat. Such is their arrangement for the animals' maintenance. Whoever kills one of these animals, if the act was willed,
death is his penalty; but, if involuntary, he must pay such fine as the
priests shall determine. But a man who kills an ibis or a hawk,
whether of intent or not, he must die.

There are indeed many animals that have their lives along with 22
the people, but there would be still more if it were not for what happens to the cats. When the female cats give birth, they will no longer
frequent the toms, and the latter, for all their desire to mate with
them, cannot do so. So they contrive the following trick. They steal
and carry off the kittens from their mothers and kill them; but although they kill them, they do not eat them. The females, deprived
of their young and eager to have more, go then, and then only, to
the toms; for cats are a breed with a great love of children. When
there is a fire, something eerie happens to the cats. The Egyptians,
neglecting altogether to quench the fires, stand in a line, with men at
intervals, and heedfully try to save the cats. But the cats slip through
the line and, jumping over the men, leap into the fire. This, when it
happens, causes great grief to the Egyptians. In whoever's house a
cat dies naturally, those who dwell in the house all shave their eyebrows, but only these; if the dead animal is a dog, they shave all
their body and head.

The dead cats are carried away to sacred houses where they are 23
buried, as soon as mummified, in the city of Bubastis. Bitches each
man buries in his own city in holy coffins. Ferrets are treated in the
same way as dogs. Shrewmice and hawks they take to the city of
Buto, ibises to the city of Hermes. Bears are very rare, and wolves are

not much larger than foxes; these they bury wherever they find them lying.

The nature of the crocodile is of this kind: for the four winter 24 months it eats nothing at all; it is a four-footed creature and is of both land and water; that is to say, it lays its eggs on land and hatches them out, and it spends most of the day on dry land but all the night in the water, for the water is warmer than the open air and the dew. Of all the mortal creatures we know, it grows greatest from smallest beginnings. For the eggs it lays are no larger than those of a goose, and the young thing that hatches is in proportion to the egg; but it is born and grows to a length of twenty-three feet or more. It has the eyes of a pig and great teeth and tusks in proportion to its greatness of body. Alone of animals it has no tongue; nor does it move its lower jaw but alone of animals draws its upper jaw toward its lower. It has powerful nails and a scaly skin, which is unbreakable, on its back. It is blind in the water but has the sharpest of sights in the air. As it makes its livelihood in the water, it has a mouth that, inside, teems with leeches. Other birds and animals flee it, but the sandpiper has come to peace terms with it, for the crocodile owes him much. For when the crocodile comes out of the water onto the land, and thereafter opens its mouth, which it is wont to do for the most part toward the west wind, then the sandpiper crawls into its mouth and gulps down the leeches. This is of great benefit to the crocodile, who likes it and does the sandpiper no hurt.

For some of the Egyptians the crocodile is sacred; but for some 25 it is not — in fact, they treat it as an enemy. Those Egyptians who live about Thebes and the lake of Moeris regard them as especially sacred. At each of these places there is one crocodile, selected out of all, who has been trained and is tame, and the people put ornaments of glass and gold into his ears, and he wears bracelets on his front feet; they give him food specially set aside for him, and offerings, and in all treat him so that he has the best of lives. When the animals die, they mummify them and bury them in sacred coffins. But those people who live around Elephantine[9] even eat crocodiles; they do not think them sacred at all. The Egyptians do not use the name "crocodile" for the animal, but "champsa." The Ionians called them crocodiles because they thought their forms like the lizards that in their own country live in the dry-stone walls.

There are many ways of hunting the crocodile, and of every 26 sort. I will tell you about the one that seems most worthwhile relating. The hunter puts his bait, the back of a pig, on a hook and lets it

---

[9] **Elephantine** Island in the Nile near Aswan.

go out into the middle of the stream; he himself stays on the river-bank, where he has a young pig, alive, and he hits the pig. As soon as the crocodile hears the squeal of the pig, he makes for the sound and meets the bait (the dead pig's back) and swallows it down. Then they draw him in. When he has been hauled to land, first of all the hunter smears his eyes with mud. After he has done that, he masters the animal, for the rest, right easily; but if this is not done, he does so only with trouble.

The hippopotamuses are sacred in the province of Papremis but not so among the rest of the Egyptians. This is the kind of form they have: four feet, cloven hooves like cattle, a snub nose, and with the mane of a horse; they show tusks, a horse's tail and voice, and are of the bigness of the greatest ox. Hippopotamus skin is so thick that, when it is dried, men make spearshafts out of it.   27

In the river there are also otters, which the people think are sacred. They also regard as sacred the fish they call the lepidotus and the eel; these, they say, are sacred to the Nile, as, among birds, is the fox-goose.   28

There is another sacred bird, the name of which is the phoenix. I never saw one myself, except in pictures; for indeed it comes but rarely — the people of Heliopolis say only every five hundred years. They say that he comes at the time his father dies. If he is indeed like his pictures, he would be of this kind and this size: he has gold on his wings, which are otherwise mostly red, and the outline and size of him are likest to an eagle. The people say that this bird manages the following contrivance, though for my part I do not believe it. He sets out from Arabia and conveys his father to the shrine of the Sun, and he carries his father emplastered in myrrh and buries him in the Sun's shrine. The manner of his conveyance is this: first he forms an egg of myrrh, of a weight that he is able to carry, and after that he tries carrying it; and when the trial of it is over, he hollows out the egg and stows his father into it, and with more myrrh he plasters over the place he had hollowed out and stowed his father within. When his father lies within it, the weight is then the same as at first; and so, having plastered it over, he carries his father to the shrine of the Sun in Egypt. This is what the bird does, they say.   29

There are also sacred serpents about Thebes that do no harm at all to man. They are small and have two horns growing on the top of their heads; and these, when they die, they bury in the shrine of Zeus, for, they say, they are sacred to that god.   30

There is a place in Arabia just about the city of Buto, and to this place I went to inquire about the winged serpents; and when I came there, I saw the bones and backbones of serpents past all telling for numbers; there were heaps of backbones, great heaps and lesser,   31 and some even lesser than these; and truly many were the heaps. Now this place where the backbones are strewn about is where there is a pass, from narrow mountains into a great plain, and this plain neighbors the plain of Egypt. There is a story that with the coming of spring the winged serpents fly from Arabia into Egypt, and the ibis birds meet the serpents at this pass and will not suffer the snakes to come through, but kill them. It is for this deed that the Arabians say the Egyptians have held the bird in great honor. And the Egyptians themselves agree that they honor the ibis on these grounds.

The form of the ibis is like this: it is wonderfully black all over, 32 has the legs of a crane, and a very hooked beak. In size it is about that of the corn crake. This is the form of the black ones, those that fight the serpents; but those that most frequent the society of men (there are two sorts of ibis) have heads and necks that are bare, and this bird is white-feathered, save for the head, the neck, and the tips of the wings and the tail, all of which are wonderfully black; and the legs and beak of the bird are like the other variety of them. The form of the snakes is that of the water snake, but their wings are not feathered but are pretty much like the wings of the bat. That is all I have to say about animals that are sacred.

Of the Egyptians themselves, those of them who live around the 33 sown part of the country are great in cultivating the memory of mankind and are far the greatest record-keepers of any people with whom I have been in contact. Here is their manner of life: for three days in succession in each month they physic themselves, hunting health with emetics and purges, because they think that from the food that nourishes mankind come all their diseases. Indeed, in general the Egyptians are the healthiest of all men (after the Libyans), and it is because, I think, of their climate; for their seasons do not change much, one from the other. It is in changes that diseases grow most among men, and in no matter does change make such difference as in changes of seasons. They eat bread, which they make of barley grain and call "cyllestis." The wine they use is made of barley, for there are no vines in their country. Some of their fish they dry in the sun and eat raw, but others they eat pickled in brine. Of birds they eat quails and ducks and small birds raw, having pickled them first. But other meats, which, among them, belong to the class of birds or fishes, except for such as are appointed them as sacred, they eat roasted or boiled.

In social gatherings of the wealthy among the Egyptians, when 34 they are done with the dinner, there is a man who carries round the likeness of a dead man in a coffin, very exactly rendered, both in painting and wrought work, and made of wood; in size it is between eighteen inches and three feet. The man shows the figure to each of the diners and says: "Look upon him, drink and enjoy yourself; for even such you shall be when you are dead." That is what they do at banquets.

They follow their fathers' customs and take no others to themselves at all. Among other remarkable customs is their one chant, the Linus Song,[10] which is sung also in Phoenicia and in Cyprus and elsewhere, with different names throughout the nations; but it is agreed that it is the same song that the Greeks, when they sing it, call the Linus Song. There are so many matters at which I marvel among the Egyptians, but certainly one is whence they got the name of the Linus Song. It is clear that they have sung it forever. Linus, in Egyptian, is called Maneros. The Egyptians said that he was the only son of the first king of Egypt and that, dying untimely, he was honored by the Egyptians with this funeral chant and that this was their first and only song.

There is this other custom, which the Egyptians have in common with the Lacedaemonians alone among the Greeks: young men, when they encounter their elders, yield the road to them and step out of the way; also, when the old men approach, the young stand up from their seats. But in *this* they are like none of the Greeks: instead of speaking a greeting to one another in the streets, they do obeisance, dropping the hand to the knee.

They wear linen tunics, with fringes about their legs, which they call "calasiris," and they wear white woolen mantles on top of these again. But they never bring into the temple anything of wool, nor may they be buried in such. That contravenes their religion. In this they agree with those rites that are called Orphic and Bacchic but are in fact Egyptian and Pythagorean. For in the case of these rites, too, whoever has a share in them may not be buried in woolen garments. There is a holy tale about this.

Here are some other discoveries of the Egyptians. They find each month and each day belongs to a god, whichever he may be; and on whatever day a man was born depends what events he will encounter and how he will die and what manner of man he will be. Some of the Greeks who are in the way of poetry have used this. The Egyptians have discovered more monstrous happenings than any other people in the world. When one such happens, they write it down and watch for the outcome, and, if anything like it happens again hereafter, they think that the same result will take place.

35

36

37

38

---

[10] **Linus Song** Linus was a son of Apollo killed by dogs (or in some versions of the myth by Apollo or Heracles) when he was an infant. The song was a powerful lament sung at harvest time.

Their divination is as follows: to no man is the art assigned, and   39
only to certain of the gods. For there is a place of divination of Heracles, and of Apollo, and Athena, and Artemis, and Ares, and Zeus,
and the one they hold in the greatest honor of all, that of Leto in the
city of Buto. However, the methods of divination are not the same in
all these places, but they vary.

About medicine, they order it thus: each doctor is a doctor for   40
one disease and no more. The whole land is full of doctors; there are
some for the eyes, some for the head, and some for the teeth, and
some for the belly, and there are some for the diseases that have no
outward sign.

These are the ways they keen for and bury the dead: when a   41
man that has repute is dead and his household has lost him, then all
the womenkind from that house plaster their head and face with
mud, and afterwards, having left the corpse in the house, they themselves wander through the city, beating their breasts; while so doing,
they wear their clothes girt up and show their breasts, and with
them are all their kindred women; on the other side, the men beat
their breasts, and they too wear their clothes girt up. When they
have done all this, they then carry the corpse to the embalming.

There are those who set themselves to this very trade and make   42
it their special craft. When a corpse is brought them, they show to
those who bring it models of dead men done in wood, imitations,
and painted. The most perfect form of these, they say, belongs to
One whose name I may not mention in connection with such a matter.[11] The second class they show is somewhat inferior to this and
cheaper, and the third cheapest of all. Having so told them, they inquire of them according to what model they wish the dead man prepared. So the people who brought him agree on a price and then go
away, and the others, left in their house, do their embalming. Here
is the proceeding for the most perfect model: first they draw out the
brains with a hooked iron tool through the nostrils, and in place of
what they draw out they pour in drugs. Then, with a sharp
Ethiopian stone knife, they make a cut in the flank and clean out the
belly completely and rinse it with palm wine and chopped-up
spices. Thereafter they fill it with pure ground myrrh, cassia, and
other spices (except for frankincense) and stitch up the anus. Having done this, they embalm the body in saltpeter and hide it away
for seventy days. More days than that one may not embalm it. When

---

[11] **One whose name** . . . Herodotus refers to Osiris. In order to reach the kingdom of the dead and be resurrected, one had to pass the test of Osiris, an Egyptian
god, believed to be judge of the dead.

the seventy days are over, they wash the corpse and wrap up the whole body with bandages of fine linen cut into strips, smearing these with gum, which for the most part the Egyptians use instead of glue. Then the relatives take back the corpse and make a hollow wooden form, man-shaped, and, having so made it, they enclose the corpse within, and, having shut it up, they store it in a coffin chamber, placing it upright against a wall.

That is how they prepare the dead on the dearest plan; but 43 those who preferred the middle form of burial, because they would shun the greatness of the expense, they prepare as follows: they fill their syringes with pure oil of cedar and fill up the belly of the corpse, neither making any incision nor taking out the guts but pumping the drench in through the anus and sealing it up against flowing out again; then they embalm the body for the prescribed days, and on the last day they draw out of the belly the cedar oil they had put in. This has such power that it brings out with itself the guts and the intestines, all dissolved. The saltpeter eats away the flesh, and so what is left of the dead man is a skin only and the bones. When they are done with all this, they give back the body, having done nothing further to it.

The third method of embalmment, which is what prepares the 44 poorer dead, is this: they rinse out the belly with a purge, embalm the body for the seventy days, and, after that, give it back to be carried away.

The wives of distinguished men, when they die, they do not 45 give for embalmment right away, nor yet women who are especially beautiful and of great account. Only when they have been dead three or four days do they hand them over to the embalmers. This is done to prevent the embalmers from copulating with these women. For they say that one of them was caught copulating with a freshly dead woman and that a fellow workman told on him.

Whoever, either of the Egyptians themselves or a foreigner, has 46 been carried off by a crocodile, or has clearly come by his death by the action of the river itself, at whatever city he comes to land must, with the greatest concern, be embalmed and treated as well as ever is possible and be buried in a holy coffin. No one may put a hand on him, either of his relatives or friends, but the burial must be conducted by the very priests of the Nile, inasmuch as they are handling a corpse that is something more than human.

The Egyptians avoid following Greek customs and, to speak in 47 general, the customs of any people other than their own. All the other Egyptians keep to this zealously; but there is one great city, Chemmis, in the Theban province, near Neapolis, in which there is a square temple of Perseus, the son of Danaë, and round it grow palm trees. The gateway of this temple is of very great stones, and on this stand two very huge stone figures. Within this surrounding enclosure there is a shrine, and in it stands an image of Perseus. The people of Chemmis say that Perseus often appears in their country, here and there, and often within the temple, and that a sandal worn by him is discovered, three feet long in size, and that when this appears all Egypt prospers. This is what they say, and they do certain Greek things in honor of Perseus: they hold a gymnastic contest, covering all forms of competition; for prizes they have cattle and clothing and skins. When I asked them why it was that Perseus appeared to them alone and why it was that they alone among the Egyptians set up a gymnastic festival, they said that Perseus came originally from their own city; for Danaus and Lynceus were men of Chemmis, and they sailed away to Greece, and, counting over the generations from them, they come at last to Perseus. He came to Egypt, they say, for the same reason that the Greeks give: to bring the Gorgon's head out of Libya. They said that he came to their country and recognized all his kinsfolk, and that he came to Egypt thoroughly knowing the name of the city of Chemmis because he had heard it from his mother. It was at his bidding, they say, that they celebrated the gymnastic contest.

All these are the customs of the Egyptians who live above the marsh country. Those who live in the marshes have much the same customs as the rest — there, too, each man lives with just one wife, as the Greeks do — but with respect to cheap food they have made certain innovations of their own. When the river is full and floods the plains, there grow in the water many lilies, which the Egyptians call lotus. They pick these and dry them in the sun and then crush the center part of the lotus, which is like a poppy, and make of it loaves, which they bake in the fire. The root of the lotus is also eatable and to some extent sweet; it is round and about the size of an apple. There are other lilies like roses; these grow in the river too, and from them there is a fruit, growing in a calyx, which comes from the root by a separate stem and which is in form most like a wasp's honeycomb. In this there are many seeds, about the size of an olive stone, and these are eaten both fresh and dried. The papyrus, which grows yearly there, they draw out of the marshes; the upper part of it they cut off and use for other purposes, but the lower part, to the length of some eighteen inches, they eat; they sell it, as well. Those who want to have papyrus at its best bake it in a redhot oven and eat it. Some of the people live altogether on fish; they catch these, gut them, and then dry them in the sun and eat them dried.

48

QUESTIONS FOR CRITICAL READING

1. What does Herodotus say about the tradition of religious sacrifice in Egypt? Given what Herodotus says about Egypt, what can you conclude about sacrifice in Greece?
2. Why does Herodotus say, "I will never believe that the rites in Egypt and those in Greece can resemble each other by coincidence" (para. 5)?
3. How did the Pelasgians come to know the names of the gods?
4. What kind of Egyptian religious scruple does Herodotus discuss in paragraph 20?
5. Why does Herodotus talk so much about animals in Egypt?

SUGGESTIONS FOR WRITING

1. What is Herodotus's general attitude toward Egyptian culture? Given that Egypt was exotic and strange to a foreigner, what evidence do you find that reveals his feelings about the culture? What clues suggest he feels Greek culture is superior to Egyptian culture?
2. Judging from this passage, how do the religious practices of the Egyptians and Greeks differ regarding sex and sexuality? Analyze Herodotus to see what he reveals indirectly in his discussion.
3. What does Herodotus say about the practice of divination? What is divination, and what role does it seem to play in Egyptian culture? How is it connected to the beliefs in the gods in either Egypt or Greece?
4. In this excerpt, Herodotus seems to take a special interest in animals. Write a short essay in which you explore his general attitude toward animals and their role in Egyptian culture. What can you tell from his descriptions of Egyptian attitudes toward animals about how different or similar they are to Greek attitudes? Why do you think Herodotus is so particular in his descriptions of animals and their role in Egyptian life?
5. **CONNECTIONS**   How does Herodotus treat the political similarities and differences between Egypt and Greece? How do the political issues raised by Herodotus compare to those raised by Jefferson in *The Declaration of Independence* or by Lao-tzu in the *Tao-te Ching*? What do you think Jefferson's reaction to the Egyptian government Herodotus describes would be? What would Lao-tzu's reaction be?
6. **CONNECTIONS**   Compare Herodotus with either Margaret Mead or Clifford Geertz in terms of their interest in specific behavior in the cultures they examine and their ability to be sympathetic to the culture they examine.

ÁLVAR NÚÑEZ CABEZA DE VACA
From *La Relación*

ÁLVAR NÚÑEZ CABEZA DE VACA (c. 1409 – c. 1560) was
born and died in Spain but is most famous for the years he spent as
one of the first Europeans to explore the American southwest. He
was the treasurer for a three-hundred-man expedition that reached
Tampa, Florida, in 1528. The party continued overland on foot and
then in small boats along the coast. Several boats (including
Cabeza de Vaca's) were shipwrecked, probably on Galveston Island
off of Texas, which he calls the Isle of Ill Fate. Most of the sixty or
so survivors were enslaved by the Native Americans and died
within a few years, but Cabeza de Vaca — along with his companions Castillo, Dorantes, and Estaban, an African slave — managed
to escape inland and survive for eight years. They wandered
through southern Texas and Mexico among nomadic groups for
some six thousand miles until they eventually met up with
Spaniards in a settlement on the Sinalo River in Mexico in 1536.
Cabeza de Vaca wrote the story of his adventures shortly afterward, providing us with the earliest European descriptions of the
manners of the Native Americans of the southwest and offering us
insights into the ways in which the cultures viewed each other.

The chapters of his *La Relación* (1542) that are included here
tell primarily of the months Cabeza de Vaca spent with the Avavares. One of his persistent observations about the Avavares is that
they were almost always hungry and gaunt. In a few encampments
he visited, the Avavares had a surplus of food: for example, in one
community Cabeza de Vaca reports that his companions and he
were offered the hearts of six thousand deer. However, in general,
Cabeza de Vaca's descriptions portray most of the Avavares as

From *The Narrative of Álvar Núñez Cabeza De Vaca.* Translated by Fanny
Bandelier.

thin — sometimes to the point of starvation. The Avavares were best fed when the plant they called *tuna* — the prickly pear cactus — was in season. During that period they ate heartily, grinding the fruit for flour and roasting its leaves. But once the season was done, the community went back to a destitute life. Interestingly, some modern commentators have found this description puzzling because the region was known to have had plentiful sources of food.

Some of the most striking features of Cabeza de Vaca's rhetoric are his declarations of religious faith. Given the nature of Spanish culture in the sixteenth century, such declarations may well have been pro forma, a requirement for his audience. However, his faith may also have been as strong as he says it was. Throughout the physical hardships of his journeys — the grueling hikes and the bouts of near starvation — Cabeza de Vaca kept a firm faith in God and the power of prayer to sustain him.

Most surprising, perhaps, are the descriptions Cabeza de Vaca gives of his own role as a shaman, or traditional healer, within the Avavares community. In many Native American societies, the shaman was a highly esteemed figure who was called on to heal the sick or injured through both prayer and herbal medicines. Archaeo-logical research indicates that shamans were usually better fed and housed than ordinary tribe members. Cabeza de Vaca was appar-ently thrust into this role by the Avavares, who referred to him and his companions as "children of the sun" and ascribed divine pow-ers to them. Ironically, Cabeza de Vaca attributes his Christian faith as the source of the healings he performs. When he offers a re-markable account of raising a man from the dead, he claims that he thinks of Jesus, approaches the man, makes the sign of the cross over him, and later learns that the man has revived.

As with all historical documents, the reader must decide what level of credibility to grant the author; however, it is clear that Cabeza de Vaca's *Relación* offers a look into one of the first interac-tions between two starkly different cultures that would nonethe-less become deeply entwined in the years to come.

CABEZA DE VACA'S RHETORIC

One enduring question about *La Relación* concerns its purpose. Some historians have asserted that it was primarily a political doc-ument designed to support the Spanish official policy that discour-aged taking Native Americans as slaves. Much of the book tells of the kindnesses of the Avavares and their gentleness toward one an-other. When Cabeza de Vaca does describe the warlike qualities of the Avavares, he highlights their intelligent strategies for protecting themselves, such as the description of setting campfires in their homes and then withdrawing to the forest so that enemies would think that they were "at home" and easy targets. Such a stratagem would have been worthy of advanced European military commanders. His careful descriptions of the ways in which they conducted warfare would have been relevant for contemporary readers, since warfare was a norm of European life.

Perhaps even more relevant to the Spaniards of the sixteenth century would have been the usefulness of the document to justify the Spanish conquest of the southwest and Mexico. The Avavares as Cabeza de Vaca portrays them seem a scattered and sometimes helpless group. Their portrait as hungry and sick would make them candidates for colonialization in the name of humanity. Despite his description of their poverty, when Cabeza de Vaca finally found the Spanish settlement and returned to Spain, he reported that he had heard of cities inland that had great wealth in gold. These stories suggest to modern scholars that the Native Americans who told them had already met Europeans and knew what they wanted. By telling them there was gold elsewhere, they would get rid of them. Cabeza de Vaca's reports were directly responsible for Coronado's later expedition in search of the golden cities of the Americas.

Cabeza de Vaca's primary rhetorical device is the narrative, telling what happened where and when and what the circumstances were like. His descriptions are economical and precise. Like Herodotus, Cabeza de Vaca tells us a good deal about customs. He notes how the Avavares greeted him and how they were fearful when they first saw a European. He describes the tasks he performed in the community, explaining that he had to take an active role in the Avavares' life or else he would not eat. When he skinned hides, for example, he was allowed to eat the scrapings, a special reward. He not only provides details about Avavares warfare but describes customs of marriage and customs involving the old, the weak, and the dying. He pays special attention to women and the ways that they are treated by men. In some cases, women are peacemakers, as when they arrange a truce after a raid, but in other cases, women are the cause of war.

Like Herodotus, Cabeza de Vaca remains relevant to us by offering vivid details about the lives of people whose culture is different from ours. The last passage in the selection that follows is perhaps most telling when it states that "All men are curious to know the habits and devices of others," a fact that drives contemporary literature as much as it did the narratives of Cabeza de Vaca's day.

From *La Relación*

Chapter Twenty-two

Early the next day many Indians came and brought five people   1
who were paralyzed and very ill, and they came for Castillo to cure
them. Every one of the patients offered him his bow and arrows,
which he accepted, and by sunset he made the sign of the cross over
each of the sick, recommending them to God, Our Lord, and we all
prayed to Him as well as we could to restore them to health. And
He, seeing there was no other way of getting those people to help
us so that we might be saved from our miserable existence, had
mercy upon us, and in the morning all woke up well and hearty and
went away in such good health as if they never had had any ailment
whatever. This caused them great admiration and moved us to
thanks to Our Lord and to greater faith in His goodness and the
hope that He would save us, guiding us to where we could serve
Him. For myself I may say that I always had full faith in His mercy
and in that He would liberate me from captivity, and always told my
companions so.

When the Indians had gone and taken along those recently   2
cured, we removed to others that were eating *tunas*[1] also, called *Cul-
talchuches* and *Maliacones,* which speak a different language, and
with them were others, called *Coayos* and *Susolas,* and on another
side those called *Atayos,* who were at war with the *Susolas,* and exchanging arrow shots with them every day.

Nothing was talked about in this whole country but of the won-   3
derful cures which God, Our Lord, performed through us, and so
they came from many places to be cured, and after having been with
us two days some Indians of the *Susolas* begged Castillo to go and attend to a man who had been wounded, as well as to others that were
sick and among whom, they said, was one on the point of death.
Castillo was very timid, especially in difficult and dangerous cases,
and always afraid that his sins might interfere and prevent the cures
from being effective. Therefore the Indians told me to go and perform the cure. They liked me, remembering that I had relieved them
while they were out gathering nuts, for which they had given us
nuts and hides. This had happened at the time I was coming to join
the Christians. So I had to go, and Dorantes and Estevanico went
with me.

---

[1] *tunas* The Indian name for prickly pear cactus, whose fruit is edible.

When I came close to their ranches I saw that the dying man we had been called to cure was dead, for there were many people around him weeping and his lodge was torn down, which is a sign that the owner has died. I found the Indian with eyes upturned, without pulse and with all the marks of lifelessness. At least so it seemed to me, and Dorantes said the same. I removed a mat with which he was covered, and as best I could prayed to Our Lord to restore his health, as well as that of all the others who might be in need of it, and after having made the sign of the cross and breathed on him many times they brought his bow and presented it to me, and a basket of ground *tunas,* and took me to many others who were suffering from vertigo. They gave me two more baskets of *tunas,* which I left to the Indians that had come with us. Then we returned to our quarters.

Our Indians to whom I had given the *tunas* remained there, and at night returned telling that the dead man whom I attended to in their presence had resuscitated, rising from his bed, had walked about, eaten and talked to them, and that all those treated by me were well and in very good spirits. This caused great surprise and awe, and all over the land nothing else was spoken of. All who heard it came to us that we might cure them and bless their children, and when the Indians in our company (who were the *Cultalchulches*) had to return to their country, before parting they offered us all the *tunas* they had for their journey, not keeping a single one, and gave us flint stones as long as one and a half palms, with which they cut and that are greatly prized among them. They begged us to remember them and pray to God to keep them always healthy, which we promised to do, and so they left, the happiest people upon earth, having given us the very best they had.

We remained with the *Avavares* Indians for eight months, according to our reckoning of the moons. During that time they came for us from many places and said that verily we were children of the sun. Until then Dorantes and the Negro had not made any cures, but we found ourselves so pressed by the Indians coming from all sides, that all of us had to become medicine men. I was the most daring and reckless of all in undertaking cures. We never treated anyone that did not afterwards say he was well, and they had such confidence in our skill as to believe that none of them would die as long as we were among them.

These Indians and the ones we left behind told us a very strange tale. From their account it may have occurred fifteen or sixteen years ago. They said there wandered then about the country a man, whom they called "Bad Thing," of small stature and with a beard, although they never could see his features clearly, and whenever he would approach their dwellings their hair would stand on end and they began to tremble. In the doorway of the lodge there would then appear a firebrand. That man thereupon came in and took hold of anyone he chose, and with a sharp knife of flint, as broad as a hand and two palms in length, he cut their side, and, thrusting his hand through the gash, took out the entrails, cutting off a piece one palm long, which he threw into the fire. Afterwards he made three cuts in one of the arms, the second one at the place where people are usually bled, and twisted the arm, but reset it soon afterwards. Then he placed his hands on the wounds, and they told us they closed at once. Many times he appeared among them while they were dancing, sometimes in the dress of a woman and again as a man, and whenever he took a notion to do it he would seize the hut or lodge, take it up into the air and come down with it again with a great crash. They also told us how, many a time, they set food before him, but he never would partake of it, and when they asked him where he came from and where he had his home, he pointed to a rent in the earth and said his house was down below.

We laughed very much at those stories, making fun of them, 8 and then, seeing our incredulity they brought to us many of those whom, they said, he had taken, and we saw the scars of his slashes in the places and as they told. We told them he was a demon and explained as best we could that if they would believe in God, Our Lord, and be Christians like ourselves, they would not have to fear that man, nor would he come and do such things unto them, and they might be sure that as long as we were in this country he would not dare to appear again. At this they were greatly pleased and lost much of their apprehension.

The same Indians told us they had seen the Asturian and 9 Figueroa with other Indians further along on the coast, which we had named *of the figs*. All those people had no reckoning by either sun or moon, nor do they count by months and years; they judge of the seasons by the ripening of fruits, by the time when fish die and by the appearance of the stars, in all of which they are very clever and expert. While with them we were always well treated, although our food was never too plentiful, and we had to carry our own water and wood. Their dwellings and their food are like those of the others, but they are much more exposed to starvation, having neither maize nor acorns or nuts. We always went about naked like them and covered ourselves at night with deerskins.

During six of the eighteen months we were with them we suf- 10 fered much from hunger, because they do not have fish either. At the end of that time the *tunas* began to ripen, and without their noticing it we left and went to other Indians further ahead, called

Maliacones, at a distance of one day's travel. Three days after I and the Negro reached there I sent him back to get Castillo and Dorantes, and after they rejoined me we all departed in company of the Indians, who went to eat a small fruit of some trees. On this fruit they subsist for ten or twelve days until the *tunas* are fully ripe. There they joined other Indians called *Arbadaos,* whom we found to be so sick, emaciated and swollen that we were greatly astonished. The Indians with whom we had come went back on the same trail, and we told them that we wished to remain with the others, at which they showed grief. So we remained with the others in the field near their dwellings.

When the Indians saw us they clustered together, after having 11 talked among themselves, and each one of them took the one of us whom he claimed by the hand and they led us to their homes. While with those we suffered more hunger than among any of the others. In the course of a whole day we did not eat more than two handfuls of the fruit, which was green and contained so much milky juice that our mouths were burnt by it. As water was very scarce, whoever ate of them became very thirsty. And we finally grew so hungry that we purchased two dogs, in exchange for nets and other things, and a hide with which I used to cover myself. I have said already that through all that country we went naked, and not being accustomed to it, like snakes we shed our skin twice a year. Exposure to the sun and air covered our chests and backs with big sores that made it very painful to carry the big and heavy loads, the ropes of which cut into the flesh of our arms.

The country is so rough and overgrown that often after we had 12 gathered firewood in the timber and dragged it out, we would bleed freely from the thorns and spines which cut and slashed us wherever they touched. Sometimes it happened that I was unable to carry or drag out the firewood after I had gathered it with much loss of blood. In all that trouble my only relief or consolation was to remember the passion of our Saviour, Jesus Christ, and the blood He shed for me, and to ponder how much greater His sufferings had been from the thorns, than those I was then enduring. I made a contract with the Indians to make combs, arrows, bows and nets for them. Also we made matting of which their lodges are constructed and of which they are in very great need, for, although they know how to make it, they do not like to do any work, in order to be able to go in quest of food. Whenever they work they suffer greatly from hunger.

Again, they would make me scrape skins and tan them, and the 13 greatest luxury I enjoyed was on the day they would give me a skin to scrape, because I scraped it very deep in order to eat the parings, which would last me two or three days. It also happened to us, while being with these Indians and those before mentioned, that we would eat a piece of meat which they gave us, raw, because if we broiled it the first Indian coming along would snatch and eat it; it seemed useless to take any pains, in view of what we might expect; neither were we particular to go to any trouble in order to have it broiled and might just as well eat it raw. Such was the life we led there, and even that scanty maintenance we had to earn through the objects made by our own hands for barter.

Chapter Twenty-three

After we had eaten the dogs it seemed to us that we had enough   14
strength to go further on, so we commended ourselves to the guidance of God, Our Lord, took leave of these Indians, and they put us on the track of others of their language who were nearby. While on our way it began to rain and rained the whole day. We lost the trail and found ourselves in a big forest, where we gathered plenty of leaves of *tunas* which we roasted that same night in an oven made by ourselves, and so much heat did we give them that in the morning they were fit to be eaten. After eating them we recommended ourselves to God again, and left, and struck the trail we had lost.

Issuing from the timber, we met other Indian dwellings, where   15
we saw two women and some boys, who were so frightened at the sight of us that they fled to the forest to call the men that were in the woods. When these came they hid behind trees to peep at us. We called them and they approached in great fear. After we addressed them they told us they were very hungry and that nearby were many of their own lodges, and they would take us to them. So that night we reached a site where there were fifty dwellings, and the people were stupefied at seeing us and showed much fear. After they had recovered from their astonishment they approached and put their hands to our faces and bodies and afterwards to their faces and bodies also. We stayed there that night, and in the morning they brought their sick people, begging us to cross them, and gave us what they had to eat, which were leaves of *tunas* and green *tunas* baked.

For the sake of this good treatment, giving us all they had, con-   16
tent with being without anything for our sake, we remained with them several days, and during that time others came from further on. When those were about to leave we told the first ones that we intended to accompany them. This made them very sad, and they begged us on their knees not to go. But we went and left them in tears at our departure, as it pained them greatly.

Chapter Twenty-four

From the Island of Ill Fate on, all the Indians whom we met as   17
far as to here have the custom of not cohabiting with their wives
when these are pregnant, and until the child is two years old.

Children are nursed to the age of twelve years, when they are   18
old enough to gather their own food. We asked them why they
brought their children up in that way and they replied, it was owing
to the great scarcity of food all over that country, since it was common (as we saw) to be without it two or three days, and even four,
and for that reason they nursed the little ones so long to preserve
them from perishing through hunger. And even if they should survive, they would be very delicate and weak. When one falls sick he
is left to die in the field unless he be somebody's child. Other invalids, if unable to travel, are abandoned; but a son or brother is
taken along.

There is also a custom for husbands to leave their wives if they   19
do not agree, and to remarry whom they please; this applies to the
young men, but after they have had children they stay with their
women and do not leave them.

When, in any village, they quarrel among themselves, they   20
strike and beat each other until worn out, and only then do they
separate. Sometimes their women step in and separate them, but
men never interfere in these brawls. Nor do they ever use bow and
arrow, and after they have fought and settled the question, they take
their lodges and women and go out into the field to live apart from
the others till their anger is over, and when they are no longer angry
and their resentment has passed away they return to the village and
are as friendly again as if nothing had happened. There is no need of
mediation. When the quarrel is between unmarried people they go
to some of the neighbors, who, even if they be enemies, will receive
them well, with great festivities and gifts of what they have, so that,
when pacified, they return to their village wealthy.

They are all warriors and so astute in guarding themselves from   21
an enemy as if trained in continuous wars and in Italy. When in
places where their enemies can offend them, they set their lodges on
the edge of the roughest and densest timber and dig a trench close
to it in which they sleep. The men at arms are hidden by brushwood
and have their loopholes, and are so well covered and concealed
that even at close range they cannot be seen.

To the densest part of the forest they open a very narrow trail   22
and there arrange a sleeping place for their women and children. As
night sets in they build fires in the lodges, so that if there should be
spies about, these would think the people to sleep there. And before

sunrise they light the same fires again. Now, if the town is assaulted, they can attack from ditches, without being seen or discovered.

In case there are no forests wherein they can hide thus and pre-   23
pare their ambushes, they settle on the plain wherever it appears most appropriate, surrounding the place with trenches protected by brushwood. In these they open loopholes through which they can reach the enemy with arrows, and those parapets they build for the night. While I was with the *Aguenes* and these not on their guard, their enemies surprised them at midnight, killing three and wounding a number, so that they fled from their houses to the forest. As soon, however, as they noticed that the others had gone they went back, picked up all the arrows the others had spent and left and followed them as stealthily as possible. That same night they reached the others' dwellings unnoticed, and at sunrise attacked, killing five, besides wounding a great many. The rest made their escape, leaving homes and bows behind, with all their other belongings.

A short time after this the women of those calling themselves   24
Guevenes came, held a parley and made them friends again, but sometimes women are also the cause of war. All those people when they have personal questions and are not of one family, kill each other in a treacherous way and deal most cruelly with one another.

Chapter Twenty-five

Those Indians are the readiest people with their weapons of all   25
I have seen in the world, for when they suspect the approach of an enemy they lie awake all night with their bows within reach and a dozen of arrows, and before one goes to sleep he tries his bow, and should the string not be to his liking he arranges it until it suits him. Often they crawl out of their dwellings so as not to be seen and look and spy in every direction after danger, and if they detect anything, in less than no time are they all out in the field with their bows and arrows. Thus they remain until daybreak, running hither and thither whenever they see danger or suspect their enemies might approach. When day comes they unstring their bows until they go hunting.

The string of their bows are made of deer sinews. They fight in a   26
crouching posture, and while shooting at each other talk and dart from one side to the other to dodge the arrows of the foe. In this way they receive little damage from our crossbows and muskets. On the contrary, the Indians laugh at those weapons, because they are not dangerous to them on the plains over which they roam. They are only good in narrows and in swamps.

Horses are what the Indians dread most, and by means of which 27
they will be overcome.

Whoever has to fight Indians must take great care not to let 28
them think he is disheartened or that he covets what they own; in
war they must be treated very harshly, for should they notice either
fear or greed, they are the people who know how to abide their time
for revenge and to take courage from the fears of their enemy. After
spending all their arrows, they part, going each his own way, and
without attempting pursuit, although one side might have more
men than the other; such is their custom.

Many times they are shot through and through with arrows, but 29
do not die from the wounds as long as the bowels or heart are not
touched; on the contrary, they recover quickly. Their eyesight, hearing and senses in general are better, I believe, than those of any
other men upon earth. They can stand, and have to stand, much
hunger, thirst and cold, being more accustomed and used to it than
others. This I wished to state here, since, besides that all men are curious to know the habits and devices of others, such as might come
in contact with those people should be informed of their customs
and deeds, which will be of no small profit to them.

QUESTIONS FOR CRITICAL READING

1. What is Cabeza de Vaca's attitude toward his remarkable cures?
2. How does Cabeza de Vaca reveal his feelings about the Avavares? Does
   he seem to respect them, or is he suspicious of them?
3. How does Cabeza de Vaca know "the dying man" of paragraph 4 is
   dead? What clues about how he was resuscitated can you derive from
   his description?
4. What do the Avavares do when their sick and dying are cured? How
   does Cabeza de Vaca benefit from praying for the sick?
5. Why did the Avavares feel "that none of them would die as long as we
   were among them" (para. 6)?

SUGGESTIONS FOR WRITING

1. Try to explain the amazing record of success for the cures performed
   by Cabeza de Vaca and his companions. To answer this question, you
   may want to research the practices of shamanism, and determine
   which practices Cabeza de Vaca seems to perform during his cures.
2. Why is it possible for Cabeza de Vaca to establish a trade among the
   Indians? What kinds of things does he trade? Does he seem to derive
   satisfaction from his travels?

3. What do you make of the story of the "Bad Thing" who has a beard and carries a flint knife two palms in length (paras. 7 and 8)? There was no source of flint near the Avavares, and even their arrowheads were tiny because the rocks were unsuitable for the purpose of making points. How does Cabeza de Vaca treat the story? Have we such stories in our own culture?

4. Examine this selection for its religious content. Is the religious devotion of Cabeza de Vaca convincing? What seem to be the religious beliefs of the Avavares?

5. What can you tell about the general daily life of the Avavares from this selection? From paragraph 17 onward, Cabeza de Vaca tells us about interesting details of life that he has witnessed. How much does he seem to sympathize with the specifics of the Avavares' behavior? At what points does he seem impatient with the Avavares' ways?

6. **CONNECTIONS**   Compare the tone of Herodotus's examination of Egyptian life with Cabeza de Vaca's examination of the way the Avavares live. Would Cabeza de Vaca have been aware of Herodotus's *History*? What does Cabeza de Vaca do that Herodotus would have approved of? Which writer makes you more aware of his personality?

7. **CONNECTIONS**   Judging from what Cabeza de Vaca tells us about the ways in which the Avavares' culture functions, what can you tell about its political nature? Rousseau spoke often of individuals in a state of nature and may have been thinking of North American Indians. Would Rousseau have praised the political structures that Cabeza de Vaca witnessed?

RUTH BENEDICT
The Pueblos of New Mexico

RUTH BENEDICT (1887 – 1948) studied anthropology at Columbia University under the supervision of Franz Boas and received her Ph.D. there in 1923. She is renowned for her work with
Native North Americans and for her many distinguished books,
such as *The Concept of the Guardian Spirit in North America* (1923);
Tales of the Cochiti Indians (1931); *Patterns of Culture* (1934; *Race,
Science, and Politics* (1940); and *The Chrysanthemum and the Sword*
(1946). Like Boas, she insists that cultures are not determined by
race, biology, or geography but instead grow individually in response to their own personal experiences and history, developing
traditions that make them distinct in behavior.

In her researches on southwestern Native Americans, Benedict
developed an interesting psychological model of cultures. She suggested that the cultures she studied had developed psychological
models that correspond with certain well-known psychological
types for individuals. For example, she uses the two general types
that Friedrich Nietzsche refers to in his essay "Apollonianism and
Dionysianism." For her the Zuñi of the Southwest are Apollonian — by which she means that they are intellectual, rational,
cool, and reserved. The northwestern tribes of the Kwakiutl are,
she felt, Dionysian — by which she means given to intoxication,
emotion, and celebration. She also sees patterns of paranoia and
schizophrenia in the "psychological personalities" of some cultures, such as the Dobu of Melanesia, whom she also studied. The
Dobu have an especially difficult time getting along together because of ingrained distrust of their fellow Dobu.

From *Patterns of Culture* (1934).

511

Benedict uses these psychological portraits drawn specifically
from Nietzsche with the understanding that they should not be applied absolutely, but with respect for variations. Her point is that
cultures develop much as individuals develop, in response to the
historical tradition: "A culture, like an individual, is a more or less
consistent pattern of thought and action. Within each culture there
come into being characteristic purposes not necessarily shared by
other types of society." Despite her use of the Nietzschean terms,
Benedict felt that there is no way to establish a typology of cultures. The terms were designed only to establish a useful characterization to help explain the ways of the culture. Benedict believed,
along with Boas and others, that one's own culture provides the
lens through which one observes others. Consequently, Benedict
warns us, our capacity to truly see and understand other peoples
whose values and basic concepts are foreign is limited.

Nonetheless, Benedict provides us with a view of the Zuñi that
helps us gain some sense of their culture, particularly in terms of
its distinctions. The question of whether we can truly understand
other cultures always underlies her work. She accepts our limitations but presses onward to help us expand our perspective. Her
technique is to concentrate on clear exposition and description so
that we see what is of importance to the culture.

Much of her emphasis is on the vision quest associated with religion and religious rites. She reminds us that religion and ritual
are central to the culture of the Native American, and she goes into
great detail about both. "We cannot understand the Pueblo configuration of culture without a certain acquaintance with their customs," she explains. Benedict tells us a great deal about the distinctions between the Pueblo — or Zuñi — and their surrounding
neighbors, emphasizing that although Zuñi live extremely close to
groups in Mexico and New Mexico whose environments are essentially identical, the cultures are essentially distinct.

The distinction between the Apollonian and Dionysian becomes a convenient symbol for her to establish basic differences of
attitude, especially toward the role of the individual in the society.
In Zuñi, individualism is not promoted. The social group works together and devotes much of its energy to elaborate religious ceremonies that must be performed with letter-perfect accuracy to ensure their effectiveness. Other Native American cultures promote
individualism in sometimes complex ways. For example, the emphasis on the vision quest — a solitary experience usually conducted in remote areas with the aid of natural drugs — is common
among all the groups that surround Zuñi but totally foreign to
Zuñi. It is not part of their cultural heritage despite the fact that
the drugs, such as peyote, are easily available.

BENEDICT'S RHETORIC

The passage reprinted here is marked by the use of comparison. At first Benedict compares the Zuñi with nearby tribes; then she introduces the Nietzschean terms that are themselves borrowed from Greek culture. The implied comparison with Greece is one of Benedict's subjects, but she soon moves back to the question of how the Zuñi compare with their neighbors.

Benedict's greatest skill as a writer is clarity. Her writing is concrete, with specific references to places and events. She is forced to write without naming individuals, a limitation that ordinarily cripples the style of many prose writers. But she sometimes introduces individuals through their activities — for example, preparing for marriage and setting out on a quest. The point of this strategy is to reduce our reliance on the individual as a measure of things. The Zuñi do not rely on the individual, and neither does Benedict. She attempts to show us the customs of the people so that we can come closer to understanding their culture.

By beginning with the description of experiences common to our own culture, such as courtship and marriage, Benedict concretizes her writing and piques our interest immediately. However, Benedict soon moves on to describe events and concerns essentially exotic to our culture. The connection, for example, between drugs and the religious quest for visions that will guide the individual, and perhaps the group, for a lifetime is quite unlike any experience we are likely to have: our cultural use of drugs is either medicinal or recreational, not spiritual.

Finally, Benedict clarifies the issues behind the vision quest and those that separate the questers from Zuñi. She focuses clearly on the careful and accurate description of Zuñi customs. Her ability to remain concrete even in the face of her refusal to describe the individual experience of members of Zuñi is remarkable.

The Pueblos of New Mexico

No other aspect of existence seriously competes in Zuñi interest   1
with the dances and the religious observances. Domestic affairs like
marriage and divorce are casually and individually arranged. Zuñi is
a strongly socialized culture and not much interested in those things
that are matters for the individual to attend to. Marriage is arranged
almost without courtship. Traditionally girls had few opportunities
for speaking to a boy alone, but in the evening when all the girls car-

ried the water-jars on their heads to the spring for water, a boy might waylay one and ask for a drink. If she liked him she gave it to him. He might ask her also to make him a throwing stick for the rabbit hunt, and give her afterwards the rabbits he had killed. Boys and girls were supposed to have no other meetings, and certainly there are many Zuñi women today who were married with no more preliminary sex experience than this.

When the boy decides to ask her father for the girl, he goes to her house. As in every Zuñi visit, he first tastes the food that is set before him, and the father says to him as he must say to every visitor, "Perhaps you came for something." The boy answers, "Yes, I came thinking of your daughter." The father calls his daughter, saying, "I cannot speak for her. Let her say." If she is willing, the mother goes into the next room and makes up the pallet and they retire together. Next day she washes his hair. After four days she dresses in her best clothes and carries a large basket of fine corn flour to his mother's house as a present. There are no further formalities and little social interest is aroused in the affair.

If they are not happy together, and think of separating, especially if they have no children that have lived, the wife will make a point of going to serve at the ceremonial feasts. When she has a tête-à-tête with some eligible man they will arrange a meeting. In Zuñi it is never thought to be difficult for a woman to acquire a new husband. There are fewer women than men, and it is more dignified for a man to live with a wife than remain in his mother's house. Men are perennially willing. When the woman is satisfied that she will not be left husbandless, she gathers together her husband's possessions and places them on the doorsill, in olden times on the roof by the hatchway. There are not many: his extra pair of moccasins, his dance skirt and sash, if he has them, his box of precious feathers for prayer-sticks, his paint-pots for prayer-sticks and for refurbishing masks. All his more important ceremonial possessions he has never brought from his mother's house. When he comes home in the evening he sees the little bundle, picks it up and cries, and returns with it to his mother's house. He and his family weep and are regarded as unfortunate. But the rearrangement of living-quarters is the subject of only fleeting gossip. There is rarely an interplay of deep feeling. Husbands and wives abide by the rules, and these rules hardly provide for violent emotions, either of jealousy or of revenge, or of an attachment that refuses to accept dismissal.

In spite of the casual nature of marriage and divorce, a very large proportion of Zuñi marriages endure through the greater part of a lifetime. Bickering is not liked, and most marriages are peaceful. The permanence of Zuñi marriages is the more striking because marriage, instead of being the social form behind which all the forces of tradition are massed, as in our culture, cuts directly across the most strongly institutionalized social bond in Zuñi.

This is the matrilineal family, which is ceremonially united in its 5 ownership and care of the sacred fetishes.[1] To the women of the household, the grandmother and her sisters, her daughters and their daughters, belong the house and the corn that is stored in it. No matter what may happen to marriages, the women of the household remain with the house for life. They present a solid front. They care for and feed the sacred objects that belong to them. They keep their secrets together. Their husbands are outsiders, and it is their brothers, married now into the houses of other clans, who are united with the household in all affairs of moment. It is they who return for all the retreats when the sacred objects of the house are set out before the altar. It is they, not the women, who learn the word-perfect ritual of their sacred bundle and perpetuate it. A man goes always, for all important occasions, to his mother's house, which, when she dies, becomes his sister's house, and if his marriage breaks up, he returns to the same stronghold.

This blood-relationship group, rooted in the ownership of the 6 house, united in the care of sacred objects, is the important group in Zuñi. It has permanence and important common concerns. But it is not the economically functioning group. Each married son, each married brother, spends his labour upon the corn which will fill his wife's storeroom. Only when his mother's or sister's house lacks male labour does he care for the cornfield of his blood-relationship group. The economic group is the household that lives together, the old grandmother and her husband, her daughters and their husbands. These husbands count in the economic group, though in the ceremonial group they are outsiders.

For women there is no conflict. They have no allegiance of any 7 kind to their husbands' groups. But for all men there is double allegiance. They are husbands in one group and brothers in another. Certainly in the more important families, in those which care for permanent fetishes, a man's allegiance as brother has more social weight than his allegiance as husband. In all families a man's position derives, not, as with us, from his position as breadwinner, but from his rôle in relation to the sacred objects of the household. The husband, with no such relationship to the ceremonial possessions of his wife's house to trade upon, only gradually attains to position in the household as his children grow to maturity. It is as their father,

---

[1] **fetishes** Objects believed to have power for magic.

not as provider or as their mother's husband, that he finally attains
some authority in the household where he may have lived for
twenty years.

Economic affairs are always as comparatively unimportant in 8
Zuñi as they are in determining the family alignments. Like all the
Pueblos, and perhaps in greater degree than the rest, Zuñi is rich. It
has gardens and peach orchards and sheep and silver and turquoise.
These are important to a man when they make it possible for him to
have a mask made for himself, or to pay for the learning of ritual, or
to entertain the tribal masked gods at the Shalako.² For this last he
must build a new house for the gods to bless at housewarming. All
that year he must feed the cult members who build for him, he must
provide the great beams for the rafters, he must entertain the whole
tribe at the final ceremony. There are endless responsibilities he
must assume. For this purpose he will plan heavily the year before
and increase his herd. He will receive help from his clan group, all
of which he must return in kind. Riches used in this way are of
course indispensable to a man of prestige, but neither he nor anyone
else is concerned with the reckoning of possessions, but with the
ceremonial rôle which he has taken. A "valuable" family, in native
parlance, is always a family which owns permanent fetishes and a
man of importance is one who has undertaken many ceremonial
rôles.

All the traditional arrangements tend to make wealth play as 9
small a part as possible in the performance of ritual prerogatives.
Ceremonial objects, even though they are recognized personal property and attained by the expenditure of money and effort, are free to
the use of anyone who can employ them. There are many sacred
things too dangerous to be handled except by those who have qualified, but the tabus are not property tabus. Hunting fetishes are
owned in the hunters' society, but anyone who is going hunting may
take them for his use. He will have to assume the usual responsibilities for using holy things; he will have to plant prayer-sticks and be
continent and benevolent for four days. But he pays nothing, and
those who possess the fetishes as private property have no monopoly of their supernatural powers. Similarly a man who has no mask
borrows one freely and is not thought of as a beggar or a suppliant.

Besides this unusual discontinuity between vested interests and 10
the ownership of ceremonial objects in Zuñi, other more common
arrangements make wealth of comparative unimportance. Member-

---

² **Shalako** A ritual ceremony honoring the *kachina,* ancestral spirits; often performed during the winter solstice and consisting of communal dances and chants.

ship in a clan with numerous ceremonial prerogatives outweighs wealth, and a poor man may be sought repeatedly for ritual offices because he is of the required lineage. Most ceremonial participation, in addition, is the responsibility of a group of people. An individual acts in assuming ritual posts as he does in all other affairs of life, as a member of a group. He may be a comparatively poor man, but the household or the kiva[3] acting through him provides the ceremonial necessaries. The group gains always from this participation because of the great blessing that accrues to it, and the property owned by a self-respecting individual is not the count on which he is admitted to or denied ceremonial rôles.

The Pueblos are a ceremonious people. But that is not the essen-   11
tial fashion in which they are set off from other peoples of North America and Mexico. It goes much deeper than any difference in degree in the amount of ritual that is current among them. The Aztec civilization of Mexico was as ritualistic as the Pueblo, and even the Plains Indians with their sun dance and their men's societies, their tobacco orders and their war rituals, had a rich ceremonialism.

The basic contrast between the Pueblos and the other cultures   12
of North America is the contrast that is named and described by Nietzsche in his studies of Greek tragedy. He discusses two diametrically opposed ways of arriving at the values of existence. The Dionysian pursues them through "the annihilation of the ordinary bounds and limits of existence"; he seeks to attain in his most valued moments escape from the boundaries imposed upon him by his five senses, to break through into another order of experience. The desire of the Dionysian, in personal experience or in ritual, is to press through it toward a certain psychological state, to achieve excess. The closest analogy to the emotions he seeks is drunkenness, and he values the illuminations of frenzy. With Blake,[4] he believes "the path of excess leads to the palace of wisdom." The Apollonian distrusts all this, and has often little idea of the nature of such experiences. He finds means to outlaw them from his conscious life. He "knows but one law, measure in the Hellenic sense." He keeps the middle of the road, stays within the known map, does not meddle with disruptive psychological states. In Nietzsche's fine phrase, even in the exaltation of the dance, he "remains what he is, and retains his civic name."

The Southwest Pueblos are Apollonian. Not all of Nietzsche's   13
discussion of the contrast between Apollonian and Dionysian applies to the contrast between the Pueblos and the surrounding

---

[3] **kiva** Large one-room dwelling, often underground, usually set aside for religious ceremonies.

[4] **William Blake (1757 – 1827)** English mystic poet who had frequent visions.

peoples. The fragments I have quoted are faithful descriptions, but there were refinements of the types in Greece that do not occur among the Indians of the Southwest, and among these latter, again, there are refinements that did not occur in Greece. It is with no thought of equating the civilization of Greece with that of aboriginal America that I use, in describing the cultural configurations of the latter, terms borrowed from the culture of Greece. I use them because they are categories that bring clearly to the fore the major qualities that differentiate Pueblo culture from those of other American Indians, not because all the attitudes that are found in Greece are found also in aboriginal America.

Apollonian institutions have been carried much further in the   14
pueblos than in Greece. Greece was by no means as single-minded. In particular, Greece did not carry out as the Pueblos have the distrust of individualism that the Apollonian way of life implies, but which in Greece was scanted because of forces with which it came in conflict. Zuñi ideals and institutions on the other hand are rigorous on this point. The known map, the middle of the road, to any Apollonian is embodied in the common tradition of his people. To stay always within it is to commit himself to precedent, to tradition. Therefore those influences that are powerful against tradition are uncongenial and minimized in their institutions, and the greatest of these is individualism. It is disruptive, according to Apollonian philosophy in the Southwest, even when it refines upon and enlarges the tradition itself. That is not to say the Pueblos prevent this. No culture can protect itself from additions and changes. But the process by which these come is suspect and cloaked, and institutions that would give individuals a free hand are outlawed.

It is not possible to understand Pueblo attitudes toward life   15
without some knowledge of the culture from which they have detached themselves: that of the rest of North America. It is by the force of the contrast that we can calculate the strength of their opposite drive and the resistances that have kept out of the Pueblos the most characteristic traits of the American aborigines. For the American Indians as a whole, and including those of Mexico, were passionately Dionysian. They valued all violent experience, all means by which human beings may break through the usual sensory routine, and to all such experiences they attributed the highest value.

The Indians of North America outside the Pueblos have, of   16
course, anything but uniform culture. They contrast violently at almost every point, and there are eight of them that it is convenient to differentiate as separate culture areas. But throughout them all, in one or another guise, there run certain fundamental Dionysian practices. The most conspicuous of these is probably their practice of ob-

taining supernatural power in a dream or vision, of which we have already spoken. On the western plains men sought these visions with hideous tortures. They cut strips from the skin of their arms, they struck off fingers, they swung themselves from tall poles by straps inserted under the muscles of their shoulders. They went without food and water for extreme periods. They sought in every way to achieve an order of experience set apart from daily living. It was grown men, on the plains, who went out after visions. Sometimes they stood motionless, their hands tied behind them, or they staked out a tiny spot from which they could not move till they had received their blessing. Sometimes, in other tribes, they wandered over distant regions, far out into dangerous country. Some tribes chose precipices and places especially associated with danger. At all events a man went alone, or, if he was seeking his vision by torture and someone had to go out with him to tie him to the pole from which he was to swing till he had his supernatural experience, his helper did his part and left him alone for his ordeal.

It was necessary to keep one's mind fixed upon the expected 17 visitation. Concentration was the technique above all others upon which they relied. "Keep thinking it all the time," the old medicine men said always. Sometimes it was necessary to keep the face wet with tears so that the spirits would pity the sufferer and grant him his request. "I am a poor man. Pity me," is a constant prayer. "Have nothing," the medicine men taught, "and the spirits will come to you."

On the western plains they believed that when the vision came 18 it determined their life and the success they might expect. If no vision came, they were doomed to failure. "I was going to be poor, that is why I had no vision." If the experience was of curing, one had curing powers; if of warfare, one had warrior's powers. If one encountered Double Woman, one was a transvestite and took woman's occupations and habits. If one was blessed by the mythical Water Serpent, one had supernatural power for evil and sacrificed the lives of one's wife and children in payment for becoming a sorcerer. Any man who desired general strengthening or success in particular ventures sought visions often. They were necessary for warpaths and for curings and for all kinds of miscellaneous occasions; calling the buffalo, naming children, mourning, revenge, finding lost articles.

When the vision came, it might be visual or auditory hallucina- 19 tion, but it need not be. Most of the accounts tell of the appearance of some animal. When it first appeared it was often in human form, and it talked with the suppliant and gave him a song and a formula for some supernatural practice. As it was leaving, it turned into an animal, and the suppliant knew what animal it was that had blessed him, and what skin or bone or feathers he must get to keep as a memento of the experience and preserve for life as his sacred medicine bundle. On the other hand some experiences were much more casual. There were tribes that valued especially moments of intimacy with nature, occasions when a person alone by the edge of a river or following the trail felt in some otherwise simple event a compelling significance.

It might be from a dream that the supernatural power came to them. Some of the accounts of visions are unmistakable dream experiences, whether they occurred in sleep or under less normal conditions. Some tribes valued the dreams of sleep more highly than any other experiences. Lewis and Clark complained when they crossed the western plains in the early days that no night was fit for sleeping; some old man was always rousing to beat on his drum and ceremonially rehearse the dream he had just had. It was a valuable source of power. 20

In any case the criterion of whether or not the experience had power was necessarily a matter for the individual to decide. It was recognized as subjective, no matter what other social curbs were imposed upon its subsequent practice. Some experiences had power and some had not, and they distinguished by the flash of significance that singled out those that were valuable. If it did not communicate this thrill, an experience they had sought even with torture was counted valueless, and they dared not claim power from it for fear that the animal claimed as guardian spirit would visit death and disgrace upon them. 21

This belief in the power of a vision experience on the western plains is a cultural mechanism which gives a theoretically unlimited freedom to the individual. He might go out and get this supremely coveted power, no matter to what family he belonged. Besides this, he might claim his vision as authority for any innovation, any personal advantage which he might imagine, and this authority he invoked was an experience in solitude which in the nature of the case could not be judged by another person. It was, moreover, probably the experience of greatest instability that he could achieve. It gave individual initiative a scope which is not easily equalled. Practically, of course, the authority of custom remained unchallenged. Even given the freest scope by their institutions, men are never inventive enough to make more than minute changes. From the point of view of an outsider the most radical innovations in any culture amount to no more than a minor revision, and it is a commonplace that prophets have been put to death for the difference between Tweedledum and Tweedledee. In the same way, the cultural license that the vision gave was used to establish, according to the instructions 22 of the vision, a Strawberry Order of the Tobacco Society where before there had been a Snowbird Order, or the power of the skunk in warfare where the usual reliance was upon the buffalo. Other limitations were also inevitable. The emphasis might be placed upon trying out the vision. Only those could claim supernatural power for war who had put their vision to the test and had led a successful war party. In some tribes even the proposition to put the vision to the test had to go before the elders, and the body of elders was guided by no mystic communications.

In cultures other than those of the western plains these limitations upon Dionysian practices were carried much further. Wherever vested rights and privileges were important in any community the conflict occasioned by such a cultural trait as the vision is obvious enough. It is a frankly disruptive cultural mechanism. In tribes where the conflict was strong a number of things might happen. The supernatural experience, to which they still gave lip service, might become an empty shell. If prestige was vested in cult groups and in families, these could not afford to grant individuals free access to the supernatural and teach them that all power came from such contact. There was no reason why they could not still teach the dogma of the free and open vision, and they did. But it was an hypocrisy. No man could exercise power by any authority except that of succession to his father's place in the cult in which he had membership. Among the Omaha, although all power passed down strictly within the family line and was valued for the sorcery that it was, they did not revise their traditional dogma of absolute and sole dependence upon the solitary vision as a sanction for supernatural power. On the Northwest Coast, and among the Aztecs of Mexico, where prestige was also a guarded privilege, different compromises occurred, but they were compromises which did not outlaw the Dionysian values. 23

The Dionysian bent in the North American vision quest, however, did not usually have to make compromise with prestige groups and their privileges. The experience was often sought openly by means of drugs and alcohol. Among the Indian tribes of Mexico the fermented juice of the fruit of the giant cactus was used ceremonially to obtain the blessed state which was to them supremely religious. The great ceremony of the year among the related Pima, by means of which all blessings were obtained, was the brewing of this cactus beer. The priests drank first, and then all the people, "to get religious." Intoxication, in their practice and in their poetry, is the synonym of religion. It has the same mingling of clouded vision and of insight. It gives the whole tribe, together, the exaltation that it associated with religion. 24

Drugs were much commoner means of attaining this experi-   25
ence. The peyote or mescal bean is a cactus button from the highlands of Mexico. The plant is eaten fresh by the Indian tribes within
pilgrimage distance, but the button is traded as far as the Canadian
border. It is always used ceremonially. Its effect is well known. It
gives peculiar sensations of levitation and brilliant colour images,
and is accompanied by very strong affect, either ultimate despair or
release from all inadequacy and insecurity. There is no motor disturbance and no erotic excitation.

The cult of the peyote among the American Indian is still   26
spreading. It is incorporated as the Indian Church in Oklahoma and
among many tribes the older tribal rituals have paled before this
cult. It is associated everywhere with some attitude toward the
whites, either a religious opposition to their influence, or a doctrine
of speedy acceptance of white ways, and it has many Christian elements woven into its fabric. The peyote is passed and eaten in the
manner of the sacrament, first the peyote, then the water, round and
round, with songs and prayers. It is a dignified all-night ceremony,
and the effects prolong themselves during the following day. In
other cases it is eaten for four nights, with four days given up to the
excitation. Peyote, within the cults that espouse it, is identified with
god. A large button of it is placed upon the ground altar and worshipped. All good comes from it. "It is the only holy thing I have
known in my life"; "this medicine alone is holy, and has rid me of all
evil." And it is the Dionysian experience of the peyote trance that
constitutes its appeal and its religious authority.

The datura or the jimson weed is a more drastic poison. It is   27
more local, being used in Mexico and among the tribes of Southern
California. In this latter region it was given to boys at initiation, and
under its influence they received their visions. I have been told of
boys who died as a result of the drink. The boys were comatose, and
some tribes speak of this condition continuing for one day and some
for four. The Mojave, the eastern neighbors of these tribes, used
datura to get luck in gambling and were said to be unconscious for
four days. During this time the dream came which gave them the
luck they sought.

Everywhere among the North American Indians, therefore, ex-   28
cept in the southern Pueblos, we encounter this Dionysian dogma
and practice of the vision-dream from which comes supernatural
power. The Southwest is surrounded by peoples who seek the vision
by fasting, by torture, by drugs and alcohol. But the Pueblos do not
accept disruptive experiences and they do not derive supernatural
power from them. If a Zuñi Indian has by chance a visual or auditory hallucination it is regarded as a sign of death. It is an experience

to avoid, not one to seek by fasting. Supernatural power among the Pueblos comes from cult membership, a membership which has been bought and paid for and which involves the learning of verbatim ritual. There is no occasion when they are expected to overpass the boundaries of sobriety either in preparation for membership, or in initiation, or in the subsequent rise, by payment, to the higher grades, or in the exercise of religious prerogatives. They do not seek or value excess. Nevertheless the elements out of which the widespread vision quest is built up are present: the seeking of dangerous places, the friendship with a bird or animal, fasting, the belief in special blessings from supernatural encounters. But they are no longer integrated as a Dionysian experience. There is complete reinterpretation. Among the Pueblos men go out at night to feared or sacred places and listen for a voice, not that they may break through to communication with the supernatural, but that they may take the omens of good luck and bad. It is regarded as a minor ordeal during which they are badly frightened, and the great tabu connected with it is that they must not look behind on the way home, no matter what seems to be following. The objective performance is much the same as in the vision quest; in each case, they go out during the preparation for a difficult undertaking — in the Southwest, often a foot-race — and make capital of the darkness, the solitariness, the appearance of animals. But the experience which is elsewhere conceived as Dionysian, among the Pueblos is a mechanical taking of omens.

Fasting, the technique upon which the American Indian most 29 depended in attaining a self-induced vision, has received the same sort of reinterpretation. It is no longer utilized to dredge up experiences that normally lie below the level of consciousness; among the Pueblos it is a requirement for ceremonial cleanness. Nothing could be more unexpected to a Pueblo Indian than any theory of a connection between fasting and any sort of exaltation. Fasting is required during all priestly retreats, before participation in a dance, in a race, and on endless ceremonial occasions, but is never followed by power-giving experience; it is never Dionysian.

The fate of the jimson-weed poisoning in the Southwest pueblos 30 is much like that of the technique of fasting. The practice is present, but its teeth are drawn. The one-to-four-day jimson-weed trances of the Indians of Southern California are not for them. The drug is used as it was in ancient Mexico in order to discover a thief. In Zuñi the man who is to take the drug has a small quantity put into his mouth by the officiating priest, who then retires to the next room and listens for the incriminating name from the lips of the man who has taken the jimson weed. He is not supposed to be comatose at any time; he alternately sleeps and walks about the room. In the morning he is said to have no memory of the insight he has received. The chief care is to remove every trace of the drug and two common desacratizing techniques are employed to take away the dangerous sacredness of the plant: first, he is given an emetic, four times, till every vestige of the drug is supposed to be ejected; then his hair is washed in yucca suds. The other Zuñi use of jimson weed is even further from any Dionysian purpose; members of the priestly orders go out at night to plant prayer-sticks on certain occasions "to ask the birds to sing for rain," and at such times a minute quantity of the powdered root is put into the eyes, ears, and mouth of each priest. Here all connections with the physical properties of the drug are lost sight of.

Peyote has had an even more drastic fate. The Pueblos are close   31
to the Mexican plateau where the peyote button is obtained, and the Apache and the tribes of the plains with which they came most in contact were peyote-eaters. But the practice gained no foothold in the pueblos. A small anti-government group in Taos, the most atypical and Plains-like of the Pueblos, has recently taken it up. But elsewhere it has never been accepted. In their strict Apollonian *ethos,* the Pueblos distrust and reject those experiences which take the individual in any way out of bounds and forfeit his sobriety.

This repugnance is so strong that it has even been sufficient to   32
keep American alcohol from becoming an administrative problem. Everywhere else on Indian reservations in the United States alcohol is an inescapable issue. There are no government regulations that can cope with the Indian's passion for whiskey. But in the pueblos the problem has never been important. They did not brew any native intoxicant in the old days, nor do they now. Nor is it a matter of course, as it is for instance with the near-by Apaches, that every trip to town, for old men or young, is a debauch. It is not that the Pueblos have a religious tabu against drinking. It is deeper than that. Drunkenness is repulsive to them. In Zuñi after the early introduction of liquor, the old men voluntarily outlawed it and the rule was congenial enough to be honored.

QUESTIONS FOR CRITICAL READING

1. What is the Zuñi attitude toward individualism? What contradictions seem to be implied in Benedict's description?
2. What do the marriage arrangements Benedict describes imply about relations between the sexes?

3. What is the Zuñi attitude toward material possessions? What does it mean for Zuñi to be wealthy?

4. Explain what a matrilineal family is and how it compares with the family structure of your culture.

5. What is the attitude toward family in Zuñi?

6. Explain the different allegiances for men and women in Zuñi.

SUGGESTIONS FOR WRITING

1. Explain the important distinctions between the respective behaviors of the Apollonian and Dionysian cultures that Benedict describes. What are the most important distinctions, and how do they translate into terms that people in your culture can understand? Is it possible for you to come to a useful understanding of the cultural distinctions Benedict makes?

2. Benedict notes that using the psychological model of the Apollonian and Dionysian has certain inherent risks and problems. Write a brief essay that explores the risks Benedict takes in reducing cultures to psychological models. Decide as you do so whether or not Benedict is successful in her efforts or whether she falls victim to the problems of her approach.

3. Judging from the passage, what seem to be the gender roles appropriate for Zuñi? Do they differ markedly from those of other nearby groups? Are gender roles specific, distinct, and preassigned? Are they rigid and firm, or do they imply flexibility depending on the individual? Can you compare the gender roles among the Zuñi with those in your culture?

4. According to Benedict, "Apollonian institutions have been carried much further in the pueblos than in Greece" (para. 14). What does she mean? Analyze the extent to which the institutions have been carried in the behavior of the Pueblos. What are the key points, and why are they important to our developing an understanding of Zuñi?

5. Benedict describes the vision quest in some detail. Have you had a similar experience to those described? Is the vision quest — perhaps in an altered form — part of the rites or rituals of your culture? Benedict tells us (para. 21) that the individual decides whether a specific vision is truly religious and transforming enough to have a role in shaping his life. Has your culture a similar attitude toward visions? Could it have?

6. **CONNECTIONS** In paragraph 23, Benedict describes the vision quest as "a frankly disruptive cultural mechanism." Her view is a description of the politics of the vision quest. How might Thomas Jefferson have reacted to the issues implied in the vision quest in his efforts to shape a political entity in early America? Is the vision quest included by implication in the Declaration of Independence? Would Jefferson's

Apollonian stance have caused him to ignore such a Dionysian experience?

7. **CONNECTIONS**   What comparisons can be made between the Zuñi, described by Benedict, and the Avavares, whom Álvar Núñez Cabeza de Vaca observed? Write an essay that compares the methods and experiences of Benedict and Cabeza de Vaca. What differences mark their approach to discussing Native Americans' behavior and customs? Which of them draws the most reliable conclusions? Which commentator do you trust more?

8. **CONNECTIONS**   Herodotus and Cabeza de Vaca both speak as travelers who have lived in a community for a while and under different circumstances. Ruth Benedict speaks as a scholar who is removed from the community she discusses. What is the difference in style and substance between the writings of the traveler and the scholar? Which do you find more interesting? Which do you find more convincing?

MARGARET MEAD
Women, Sex, and Sin

MARGARET MEAD (1901–1978), a student of both Franz
Boas and Ruth Benedict, received her Ph.D in anthropology from
Columbia University in 1929. She is renowned for her fieldwork in
the South Pacific and especially for her work on the island of
Manus in the Admiralty Islands northwest of New Guinea. The
fieldwork that she did in 1925 led to her doctoral dissertation and
to the book that established her as one of the most visible and read-
able modern anthropologists: *Coming of Age in Samoa: A Psychological Study of Primitive Youth for Western Civilization* (1928). Her
work in the South Pacific in the 1920s was extensive. She learned
seven indigenous languages and always used the languages of the
people she lived with so that she could think in ways close to the
peoples she studied. Her experiences with the Manus, which she
discusses in this passage, span a period of twenty-five years that included a disastrous world war. She first lived with them in 1928,
when she began the work that led her to write *Growing Up in New
Guinea: A Comparative Study of Primitive Education* (1930).

Her primary interests in research were in the patterns of education of the young and the patterns of socialization of the women
in different communities. She became famous for her views on
women and women's sexuality, particularly on early sexual development. Mead asserted that cultures are relative and that there are
many ways of working out the details of courtship, sex, marriage,
and love. She consistently argued that there is no right way, suggesting rather that there are many ways, all of which are right for
their individual culture.

Like Boas and Benedict, Mead emphasizes the psychological
model of cultures, although the patterns she proposes are not

From *New Lives for Old* (1966).

quite comparable to the patterns of Apollonian, Dionysian, and paranoid that Benedict offers in her study of the American Southwest Pueblo cultures. However, she does make some efforts at typing the culture, such as her attempts in this passage to distinguish between feminine and masculine forms of behavior expected of Manus women. To the dismay of some anthropologists, Mead also emphasizes the social, traditional, and historical aspects of a culture without concerning herself with the biological or genetic. Recent critics of Mead have faulted her for this emphasis and have charged her with ignoring biological determinism in her researches (see Derek Freeman, *Margaret Mead and Samoa* [1983]); some of her critics have opposed her on the grounds that she is subjective — not scientifically detached — in her judgments; but others have opposed her largely because their own basic theories contradict hers.

"Women, Sex, and Sin" is remarkable for its discussion of profound changes in a primitive society. In 1928, the Manus were "a people without history, without any theory of how they came to be, without any belief in a permanent future life," but when Mead returned to the island in 1953 she was greeted by a community that had taken great pains to reinvent itself in the guise of a modern Western culture. She was startled by the astonishing changes they had made in such a short time.

Consequently, what she records in this passage are changes that were made to an entire culture of its own volition. She explains that the Manus "had taken their old culture apart piece by piece and put it together in a new way, in a way which they, who knew it best, thought would make it work to achieve their new goals." The work of changing the culture was essentially the work of one man, Pilau, who had returned to Manus after World War II with a vision of a new way to live. Because of a series of fortunate accidents, he was successful in implanting the "New Way," which is still adhered to by the Manus. The changes in the Manus culture demonstrate one of the ways — perhaps more drastic than usual — in which cultures alter themselves.

MEAD'S RHETORIC

Like Ruth Benedict, Mead writes in a clear, logical style. She entered college as an English major and shifted her interests only after she had studied with Franz Boas. Unlike Benedict, she writes about individuals with whom she lived or whom she remembered from her earlier visit to the Manus. She names them and gives them an identity, so that the reader can understand them and develop a sense of personal concern.

Her major rhetorical technique is to compare the old ways with the new ones. Mead constantly remembers things as they were and contrasts them with the way things are in her second encounter. She records her surprise at the scope of change in the society and marvels that any people could absorb so much change in such a short time. In "Stability of Culture," Boas talks about the fact that cultures change more rapidly when they intersect or interrelate with other cultures; this is what happened to the Manus. Mead explains that the Manus men, who had gone off to work among the Australians and who had seen American films, returned with an entirely new model for relations between the sexes. They instigated change and transformed their society.

However, Mead also points out that the more things change, the more they remain the same. Her comparison gives way to an analysis in which she attempts to demonstrate that beneath the surface — which reflects so much change — are many of the same patterns, the same problems, the same deep cultural traditions. As she remarks at the very end of the essay, "So, in spite of their nominal emancipation, they still live in a world which in repudiating sex also repudiates women, and which in exalting fatherhood leaves less room for motherhood, except as a sort of delegated fatherhood."

Near the end of her life Margaret Mead was the most famous anthropologist in the United States. She wrote a popular column in *Redbook* magazine and frequent articles in other large-circulation magazines. She published more than twenty books and lectured widely to innumerable audiences. Her concerns centered on establishing the relativity of cultures, suggesting, for example, that on the basis of her work in the South Seas the angst of adolescence, which our culture takes as virtually a biological necessity, is tied into cultural expectations. The concept of the "teenager" is by no means universal, any more than the gender roles that our culture or any culture expects its men and women to follow. Mead was popular, but she was also a careful and devoted scientist. Her work on the South Pacific still stands as a major contribution to our knowledge of how different cultures deal with basic social issues.

Women, Sex, and Sin

The Manus didn't know what to do with women twenty-five 1
years ago, and they know almost as little today. The whole ethos is
an essentially masculine one, in which the protective capacities of
the male rather than the specifically maternal capacities of the female are the ones woven into the idea of parenthood. The ideal of
personality is active, assertive, demanding, with great emphasis
upon freedom of movement. There is likewise a very low interest in
biological parenthood, in the breast-feeding tie between mother and
child, or in any softness of feminine sex responsiveness which
would yield too easily to evoke a measure of masculine anger.

Twenty-five years ago, the most valued women in the village 2
were dominating women, even those who dominated their husbands, women who had strong clear minds, and who, as mediums,
controlled a good part of the public affairs of the village. The woman
who was regarded as the most dangerous woman in the village was a
good-natured, easily responsive, slightly stupid widow, who was
said to have been responsible for the deaths of six good men. Young
women who were recalcitrant at marriage could be disciplined into
shape, if necessary, as had been done in the case of one Peri wife
who was finally shaped into compliancy on one of the smaller islands by a weekend of rape in which her husband and a group of his
age mates participated. The pliant, the warm, the responsive were
simply so many danger spots — girls who might be persuaded into
running away or simply yielding to seduction. As daughters, as sisters, as wives, and as widows they were regarded as both dangerous
and essentially unattractive.

In the long years between betrothal as a little girl of eight or ten 3
and marriage, the girl of Old Peri was not being "good" in the sense
that she was expected to be pure in heart and mind and never let
her thoughts wander into areas of lust or even of desire, like the traditional expectation for unmarried Catholic girls in southern Europe. She was, it was true, expected to be circumspect, to obey the
rules and avoidances, expected not to say her future husband's
name, not to let herself get into any situation where property that
had already been expended in her name would be jeopardized. Her
virginity and reputation were rather like a sack of money which she
was left to guard alone in the house, and out of loyalty to her relatives, fear of their anger and of the penalties which their Sir Ghosts[1]
would exact, she guarded them. A theft, or even a slight defection

---

[1] **Sir Ghosts** Powerful ghosts of ancestors.

which turned her head away from the main task for a moment would bring ruin on many people — perhaps death to one of her closest kin. Nor did her kin trust to her conscience; she was watched and chaperoned very severely; the slightest indiscretion brought down torrents of abuse and recrimination.

The young men were in a slightly different position. If one of them had an affair, it would bring about an awful row between the Sir Ghost of their own household and that of the girl's kin; there would be expiations and payments, and perhaps someone would die in the end, but the attitude toward the young men was more that of indulgence toward a successful bandit. Failure to guard in the case of the girl was far more serious than success in breaking in on the part of the boy. Virginity was merely important as it affected the marriage arrangements. If the girl's lapse or the boy's lapse could be glossed over, expiatory payments made, ghosts and Sir Ghosts appeased, the mere technical matter of physical virginity did not matter very much.

To the young girl growing up in the village, the one person on whom her mind could not dwell, the one person about whom she could not daydream, give a sly, quick look or a provocative nudge in a crowd, was her fiancé. Toward him her relatives focused all the feeling they had shown earlier toward any failure of the girl to control her sphincters; his name, his appearance, everything about him was considered shame-evoking. The young girl's mother and all her older female relatives shared in this attitude toward him. Where she had been freer with her father than her mother could be, once betrothed she was again bound in with her mother because her father could no longer take her with him, and because of the taboos which she and her mother shared. Her materials for fantasy were the shame-arousing, unmentionable future marriage relationship, possibilities of seduction and rape which would only bring disaster in their train, and a conscious focus on the outward and visible forms of her present and future position — how many dog's teeth, how much shell money had been and would be given away in her name, how many strings of ornaments, how many money aprons would she wear as a bride, with how many canoe loads of sago[2] would she be fetched back home after the birth of her child.

Thus, all through girlhood the way was paved for married women to shrink from their husbands' advances and still conform to the moral code, avoiding out of sheer fear and not out of any compliancy the anger of their husbands' ghosts as they had avoided the

4

5

6

---

[2] **sago** Edible part of the palm tree.

anger of their own. They ran then, as they do today, the risk of being violently attracted by an extramarital adventure, which presented the contrast between the appeal of danger and the inhibitions of shame. Just as in the men's lives there was an overlay of careful continuous industriousness supported by ghostly sanctions, while underneath there was a far easier, more reckless self-confidence which was given very little scope, so also among the women a heavily sanctioned demand for circumspection and diligence screened a vigorous, reckless wilfulness, which only very, very heavy sanctions could prevent from coming into play. Meanwhile, at no point was there a chance to develop any gentleness associated with sex behavior in marriage itself.

Into this background of active, demanding babyhood and early 7 childhood, inhibited and chaperoned girlhood set against the ever-present possibility of seduction and rape, and finally marriage — which was only made tolerable by emphasis upon the role of the economically successful woman who kept her husband's house and provided beadwork for her brother — came the first teaching of the Mission. Here one of the special aspects of Catholic as compared with Protestant missions came into play. When the Manus saw Catholic women, they saw nuns, not wives. For the little girls who went away to mission schools (there were two such women in Peri), sisters did not present an ideal to which they could ever aspire, but were rather earthly representatives of heavenly powers, intent, like the ghosts of old, upon making the girls quiet, obedient, and well-disciplined. They learned standards of personal neatness, learned to read and write, learned to sing, they had no models of Christian marriage which seriously challenged the models which they had learned in their youth.

Then, in 1946, came the emancipation of women by the New 8 Way, the removal of all taboos, the disappearance of the old name avoidances, the prohibition of child betrothals, the permission of women to consent to their own seductions, the prohibition against fathers or brothers becoming angered by the behavior of daughters or sisters. There was the exhortation to young couples to behave in a way which was a mixture of work boys' memories of the marriages of Australian officials — in which husbands were protective of their wives, helped them on and off with their evening wraps, and hired servants to work for them, talked to them at meals, and kissed them on arrival and departure — and a model derived from American films — in which free choice of a mate and conspicuous, demonstrative public affection was felt to be the key to American marriage.

It was Manus men, and not Manus women, who had been work 9 boys in Australian households, who had seen American films. The emancipation of the women was presented to them by fiat; no more taboos — if you have a husband, speak his name. Explore freely if you are unmarried, and, once married, by choice, of course, publicly demonstrate your affection for your husband, and have as many children as possible so as to make the Manus, now so few, into many. As monarchs in Europe once ordered their people to follow them into baptism and membership in the Christian Church, so Manus men laid down the rules by which women in the New Way were to become emancipated and affectionate. There were to be no more taboos, girls and boys were to go to school together, young people to experiment in the choice of a mate. Having once been ordered to be compliant, to hide behind their avoidance mats and cloaks, to sit quietly and do beadwork, women were now ordered to be spontaneous, responsible, actively loving. And the men, modeling themselves on Australians, who had not expected their wives to care for children and do all the housework, having no servants, took over part of the care of even the very young babies.

The present results of this emancipation of women are both astonishing and depressing. Twenty-five years ago, the most conspicuous thing about Manus women was that they were deprived in those areas of affectionate domesticity which most societies permit to women and driven into continuous public economic participation. Today, the most conspicuous point is the extent to which they have been driven into a public display of a new form of personal relations, with little or no understanding or preparation for the new role. Manus women, twenty-five years ago, were singularly unattractive, angular, assertive, walking without any sense of the appeal of their own femininity, muting and constricting their femininity, emphasizing, with strident voice and sharp, unappealing gestures, that it might be possible to rape them, it might even be possible to seduce them — if enough risk attached — but what love and tenderness they had was already bespoken in formal terms by brothers. Manus women today are almost equally unattractive, but they look and act very differently. Where their contours were once sharp and angular, they are now softer, a little blurred. Where before, if one laid one's hands on a girl's shoulder, the muscles quivered like a taut bowstring, unused to gestures which were not menacing, stylized, and brittle, today they are heavier and slower, their bodies give a little beneath one's hand. The tense restiveness is gone, but no responsiveness has come to take its place. It is easy to see how husbands who once would have beaten them — as opponents in an unresolved contest — now beat them to get any response out of them at all. Whereas twenty-five years ago a husband's main complaints were about acts — a wife gossiped about him with her relatives or

10

his brother's wife, a wife got up at night without her grass skirt when there were strangers sleeping in the house or was careless in feeding the baby — today the overwhelmingly most frequent complaint is that she "fastens her mouth." Some phrase, some slight act, will set her to brooding, and brooding she grows silent until her husband in a rage beats her, a beating which typically ends either in her running away or in a sexual reunion which has the elements of successful rape.

In the past, sex was something to be avoided by women in mar- 11
riage, and in general; for men it was a reckless, brief adventure, usually accompanied by some kind of trouble. Women had grudged their husbands the brief encounters with captured prostituted stranger women, and did their best to spoil their husbands' pleasure by screeching taunts from a distance as they swung on bamboo swings far out over the lagoon, their laughter designed to echo into the men's house and make the men impotent. Today there are constant complaints both of sexual rejection and of wives who insist upon their husbands sleeping with them just to prove they haven't been with other women. "The one time you must have intercourse with your wife," say Peri men, "is if you have already been with another woman. Otherwise she is sure to find out and be angry." Counterpointed to this is the ideal extramarital affair which emphasizes choice — "She paid her half of the fine; she said she had chosen me," "This is really from the desire of both." But, even more important, the wonderful things about lovers is that you don't have to sleep with them. If either man or woman feels tired and disinclined toward love-making, the couple can simply sit and talk, and they need not have sex relations.

So, in spite of the apparent great change from a system in which 12
women were the helpless pawns of complicated marriage exchanges, completely controlled by fathers, brothers, and husbands, to a system of marriage by choice and freedom of consent, the crucial position of sex has not changed very much. Sex is still associated with anger, with rights, with expression of or response to various sorts of resistance, and love is defined as a relationship in which sex can be ignored in favor of affection. As women once screamed their anger and jealousy because a man took a fish from his catch to his sister's house and sat quietly beside her fire, so they now rage over comparable incidents such as a husband bringing home a piece of cloth for his mistress, or his mother cooking him a meal. Quarrels in the village hinge not on the number of actual adulteries, but on the glances, tokens, and hints of adulteries long past, or perhaps never to come. The coincidence of two people who have had an affair turning up in a distant village the same day, even though they

hardly exchange a word there, gives the pair enormous pleasure and is guaranteed, if it is discovered, to throw their offended spouses into a rage.

In fact, there is a correspondence between the present chief re-   13 quirement of a wife, that she should protect her husband's mind-soul from the sin of anger, and the chief enjoyment of illicit love, which is to tease and tantalize one's rivals. This teasing may go so far as, for example, Benedikta taking delight in getting her husband to buy her, with her own money, some conspicuous object, like a knife with a red handle, which she exhibited conspicuously, walking about, certain that her lover's wife would fall into the trap of thinking her lover had given it to her. Or two women whose lovers were friends would put on skirts of the same material, thus emphasizing the relationships and setting echoes going in the heads of the two wives who were their rivals. It is a game played by those who do not in any case expect satisfaction from sex, in whatever form it comes, and who get what satisfaction they can out of playing with dissatisfaction.

Appropriately enough, illicit love affairs and gambling were as-   14 sociated together. Men enjoyed giving women, their own or their friends' mistresses, money to gamble with; women enjoyed borrowing money from their lovers and lovers' friends, and gambling games were watched closely by hawk-eyed spouses alert for trouble. Among the occasional couples where both gambled, the style of the game was upset and inexplicable rows developed, as when Maria had a temper tantrum in "court" because her husband paid back his share of a debt to her with money she had lent a friend of his not knowing that part of it was for her own husband.

So women and sex remain associated with sin; where once they   15 were associated with the punitive anger of ghosts, now they are associated with the jealous anger of men and women. Where once women were unwillingly circumspect and men grudgingly prudent, in order to prevent the ghost from visiting illness and death on them or their relatives because they had violated property rights or upset important economic affairs, today virtue consists in men and women leading quiet lives. Husbands and wives should reject overtures and opportunities so that there will be no anger between them, which might endanger the lives of their children, or anger concealed in the heart of the spouse, or in their own hearts because of the anger of the spouse. The responsiveness of men to resistance, either active or passive, the insistent demand of the jealous woman for sex expression, not for its own sake but as a symbol of her possession of her husband, keep this edge between sex and anger keen and sharp. From Christian teaching the Manus learned that sex was evil — a matter on which they were well convinced already — at least as far as women were concerned, but that sexual sins could be confessed and forgiven. From observation of Australian life, lightly reinforced by American films, they came to the conclusion that somehow Western white men seemed to manage their sex lives better, for there was so much less quarreling, and that this better management came from giving women more consideration, not beating them, helping them with their work, and giving them freedom of choice, and being mildly demonstrative in public. But the type of deeply responsible, tender marriage, which stands as the ideal of Catholic teaching, they never have had a chance to see.

For the woman who is intelligent, ambitious, and active, the New Way, in spite of its nominal emancipation of women, offers no roles comparable to the part that women could play as mediums and entrepreneurs in the old system. The most that the wife of a member of the new bureaucracy is expected to do is to be a model for the rest of the community, keep her house and children in a modern way, and never embarrass her husband by being old-fashioned. This was the role played by the wife of Samol in Bunai; her baby received the most perfect infant care, her clothes were the most carefully chosen. Not until the Manus are introduced to the sort of women's clubs which have grown up around Port Moresby and in modern Samoa will the women have any glimpse of any sort of responsible public role again. 16

Meanwhile, there remains with them in the remembrance of gentleness received from old women, not mothers but grandmothers or aunts, who, freed from the tempestuousness of active sex lives, freed from quarreling with their husbands, were gentle and indulgent to small children. In the memories of the middle-aged men who are still dissatisfied with their marriages, who quarrel with their wives and beat them, the nostalgia for these kind old women can be heard, with its echo that some day their marriages, if they live long enough, will have in them women who are as kind and gentle as Pomat's Tchalolo grandmother or Kilipak's aunt, Isali. Something of the tenderness of these contacts used to survive in the relationship between brother and sister, and appeared again in the marriages of many years' standing, when the shame of speaking together and eating together had worn off. When husband and wife had cooperated in many enterprises, after she had borne him many children, as they came to the point of being grandparents, a gentleness could settle between them. 17

At present when people are still young, public opinion will side strongly with the wife who is asked to do more than her share in supporting the household, but as they grow older, the case of the 18 sickening husband with a wife who neglects him focuses the rage of the community, as it did when Christof, his arm shrunken and help-less, his legs mere sticks, was cut by his wife. When I arrived on this scene a few people were gathered around Christof. His wife, who had done the slashing, was sitting at a distance unconcernedly working on thatch. Suddenly their grown son, a great, husky crea-ture, hurled himself through the room and began kicking his mother violently. People rushed to restrain him, and the councillor pontificated, "Don't add one trouble to another." His mother put on a dramatic, hysterical act to get attention from the bystanders, and even with this she received no sympathy. One of the gentlest of by-standers commented, "I am like that also, Piyap. If my mother didn't give food to my father, I'd fight her." And when I asked, "If your fa-ther would have fought your mother, would you have helped her?" I received an astonished, "Indeed, no!" One of the very young men summed it up: "I heard what it was about. They weren't giving Christof anything to eat. Yesterday he was angry, and he did not eat. Today they all went to the bush, and then they cooked food and gave him none. And he, is he a strong man? His arm and his leg are useless. He's just like a child [a great exaggeration]. Why don't they care for him? Now, Sepa [the daughter] wanted to give food to her father, and her mother was angry and cut her husband with a knife. Tomas heard this and he quarreled with his mother. His mother said, 'All right, beat me if you wish. This food, was it something you produced, so you have a right to talk?' Then Tomas said, 'Every day I bring sago, fish, and other things to you all, and I think you don't give any to my father.' Then Tomas was angry, and he attacked his mother."

The councillor's comment was that if the family decided to bring the matter to "court," Tomas would be in particular trouble because he had broken an important law of the New Way, the law that forbade one to get involved in one's relatives' quarrels. 19

When the case came to "court," the weight of disapproval was directed against the wife. This was a familiar pattern. If the blame could be firmly affixed to a woman, then any failure of the New Way among men need not be faced so directly. Women after all were still uneducated, illiterate, and undependable. For their part, the women felt many of the new procedures as traps. When they gave evidence it was written down and if, on being asked to repeat it, they gave a slightly different version, the whole weight of the "court" would come down upon them. The disapproval of indirect evidence also weighed heavily upon them, for when they would protest that they "knew" something was going on, the men would doggedly confront them with a "Did you see it with your eyes? Did you touch it with 20 your hands?" So, in spite of their nominal emancipation, they still live in a world which in repudiating sex also repudiates women, and which in exalting fatherhood leaves less room for motherhood, except as a sort of delegated fatherhood.

QUESTIONS FOR CRITICAL READING

1. Of the Manus, Mead says their "whole ethos is an essentially masculine one" (para. 1). What does she mean? How does her essay support this statement?
2. What impressed Mead about the women's behavior during her earlier stay with the Manus?
3. What was the preferred behavior of virgins in the earlier period Mead describes? Why did they guard their reputation and virginity?
4. Mead describes the shame associated with the husband's speaking to his wife. What seems to have been the form of communication between husband and wife under the Old Way?
5. What seems to have been the role of fear in the old society?
6. What aspects of equality were women introduced to in 1946? What traditions of the old culture seem especially strange to you?
7. Mead feels that much of Manus culture only *seems* to have changed. What does she mean? Do you agree with her observations?

SUGGESTIONS FOR WRITING

1. Compare the new Manus traditions of courtship and marriage with those of your own culture. What seem to be the new ideals of the Manus regarding appropriate behavior between men and women who have married?
2. Complete detachment is always impossible for an anthropologist, and Mead has sometimes been accused of injecting her personal views and values into her analysis. Find passages in the essay in which Mead's personal opinions show through. How many such passages are there, and to what extent do they qualify or invalidate what Mead tells us about the Manus?
3. What is the attitude of the Manus toward personal property? Is property a major issue? Are women part of the property structure? How might sexuality be an issue related to the property structure?
4. Describe the behavior of women toward husbands who have had affairs. Does their behavior have parallels in your own culture? Draw a careful comparison between both cultures, describing your culture in detail and with some of the same detachment that Mead uses.

5. In your opinion, is Mead's approach and general concern gender-based? Cite examples of how her subject matter is linked to her femaleness or how she approaches the study without gender bias.

6. **CONNECTIONS** What experiences of Herodotus, Álvar Núñez Cabeza de Vaca, or Ruth Benedict help shed light on the cultural details regarding sexuality that interest Margaret Mead? What would Mead have to say about the observations of Herodotus? Is the culture of the Manus so special that their behavior cannot shed light on things that concerned Herodotus and other early writers? Given the observations these writers offer us, to what extent do you think biology and culture are connected?

7. **CONNECTIONS** Mead talks extensively about the ways in which the Manus changed their culture. What indications do you see in Herodotus, Cabeza de Vaca, or Benedict that tend to support the capacity of cultures to change? What promotes such change? What changes in your own culture have you witnessed that parallel changes observed by these writers?

CLIFFORD GEERTZ
"From the Native's Point of View": On the Nature of Anthropological Understanding

CLIFFORD GEERTZ (b. 1926), Harold F. Linder Professor of Social Sciences at the Institute for Advanced Study at Princeton University, has become one of America's most visible anthropologists. Among his books are *The Religion of Java* (1960), *Interpretation of Cultures* (1973), *Kinship in Bali* (1975), *Negara: Theatre-State in Nineteenth-Century Bali* (1980), *Local Knowledge: Further Essays in Interpretive Anthropology* (1983), from which the passage included here comes, *Works and Lives: The Anthropologist as Author* (1988), and *After the Fact: Two Countries, Four Decades, One Anthropologist* (1995). As in the case of "From the Native's Point of View," Geertz is especially effective as an anthropologist when he reflects on the role of the investigator responding to the entire enterprise of studying another culture. In *Works and Lives,* for example, Geertz seems to continue the work he began in "From the Native's Point of View" by examining the methods and results of important anthropologists such as Bronislaw Malinowski, Claude Lévi-Strauss, and Ruth Benedict.

He begins this essay by pointing out that anthropologists are all too human. They have reactions and feelings, and they can run out of patience. In an example from *Works and Lives,* Geertz reveals that Malinowski reported in his diary that once, when he wanted to photograph an important dance, he handed out plenty of tobacco as an incentive to get the natives to dance, only to watch them disappear once their share of tobacco was delivered. There

From *Local Knowledge: Further Essays in Interpretive Anthropology.*

was nothing Malinowski could do, and in his diary he records his frustration and tells himself that at that moment he would have voted to "exterminate the brutes." Geertz's point is that Malinowski's diary calls into question the objectivity of the anthropologist and by implication raises the larger question of whether an anthropologist can ever understand a foreign culture. Everything, after all, is filtered through the anthropologist's own cultural assumptions and therefore distorted.

In the first part of his essay, Geertz explains the extent to which anthropologists are themselves aware of the difficulties of their work. He discusses two polarities of "experience-near" and "experience-distant" approaches (paras. 3–7). In the former, the anthropologist does everything to experience the culture as part of day-to-day life and to bring it as "near" as possible to his or her own culture. In the latter, the distance between the anthropologist's experience and the culture being studied is used to establish an objectivity that makes it possible to observe more dispassionately and, possibly, more accurately. Geertz says flatly, "The ethnographer does not, and, in my opinion, largely cannot, perceive what his informants perceive. What he perceives, and that uncertainly enough, is what they perceive 'with' — or 'by means of,' or 'through' . . . or whatever the word should be" (para. 7). The point is that the ethnographer cannot see beyond the primary culture by using informants because the informants necessarily remain lenses through which the ethnographer must see.

GEERTZ'S RHETORIC

Because he is writing for an audience knowledgeable about contemporary anthropology, Geertz does not pause either to explain who Malinowski is or to say why there should be a stir when Malinowski's diary revealed that he was not without feelings and that he sometimes disliked and distrusted the very people he studied. Yet, assuming a level of knowledge typical of those familiar with the work of Malinowski and others, Geertz writes clearly and with structural care. He begins with an introduction, clarifying his feelings regarding Malinowski's methods and work.

He then presents the conflict between the close and distant methods of studying cultures and states his own position. His aim is not to win over his readers immediately but rather to enable them to draw their own conclusions. Geertz depends on what he considers possible: since he feels the anthropologist can neither be a member of another culture nor depend on an informant who is, he proposes that the ethnographer be content to study the signs of the culture.

Geertz then goes on to describe the results of his own work in three very different cultures: Javanese, Balinese, and Moroccan. His method, as he explains, was not to attempt to be like a native or to live intimately with native culture. Instead, it was to study the "symbolic forms" of the culture. These "words, images, institutions, behaviors" (para. 8) are products of the culture and in many ways define the culture. They are the means by which people in the culture represent themselves to one another and then to the ethnographer. Geertz uses the term *ethnographer* to shift the emphasis from the study of man (a loose translation of the word *anthropology*) to the study of the signs or symbols (*-graphy*) produced by an ethnic group.

His rhetorical strategy is to impose a pattern of three on the experience, a familiar scheme that works well for most readers. The first of his descriptions concerns his work in Java (para. 10), where he set about discovering the defining qualities of an individual and came up with a series of oppositions: "inside/outside" and "refined/vulgar" (paras. 12 – 13). These are complex contrasts, rooted in Javanese religious experience. Geertz spends several pages describing, analyzing, and explaining these contrasts.

Geertz's research in Bali — for which he has become justly famous — centered on an examination of the theater culture. He emphasizes that the people of Bali stylize and ritualize their lives and that in many ways they go through life playing roles almost as if they were performers in a drama of life (paras. 16 – 20). Moroccan culture is so diverse that the language has developed to account for a great many ranges of relationship. Here Geertz explains the *nisba*, or terminology that defines people according to their locale, group, family, and many other details.

Finally, Geertz draws conclusions regarding the three cultures he observed. In the process he distinguishes himself from Malinowski and other anthropologists on either side of the "too close" – "too distant" controversy by defining himself as "a meanings-and-symbols ethnographer" (para. 32). In fact, other anthropologists, especially Malinowski, may be described in the same terms, but Geertz's strategy is not to offer such descriptions himself. Instead he permits the reader to do so. In this sense, the essay reveals itself to be an instrument of self-instruction. It is in the form of a lecture — not the type that fills the mind with knowledge but the type that permits the audience to experience a change in attitude.

"From the Native's Point of View": On the Nature of Anthropological Understanding

Several years ago a minor scandal erupted in anthropology: one of its ancestral figures told the truth in a public place. As benefits an ancestor, he did it posthumously, and through his widow's decision rather than his own, with the result that a number of the sort of right-thinking types who are with us always immediately rose to cry that she, an in-marrier anyway, had betrayed clan secrets, profaned an idol, and let down the side. What will the children think, to say nothing of the layman? But the disturbance was not much lessened by such ceremonial wringing of the hands; the damn thing was, after all, already printed. In much the same fashion as James Watson's *The Double Helix*[1] exposed the way in which biophysics in fact gets done, Bronislaw Malinowski's[2] *A Diary in the Strict Sense of the Term* rendered established accounts of how anthropologists work fairly well implausible. The myth of the chameleon fieldworker, perfectly self-tuned to his exotic surroundings, a walking miracle of empathy, tact, patience, and cosmopolitanism, was demolished by the man who had perhaps done most to create it.

The squabble that arose around the publication of the *Diary* concentrated, naturally, on inessentials and missed, as was only to be expected, the point. Most of the shock seems to have arisen from the mere discovery that Malinowski was not, to put it delicately, an unmitigated nice guy. He had rude things to say about the natives he was living with, and rude words to say it in. He spent a great deal of his time wishing he were elsewhere. And he projected an image of a man about as little complaisant as the world has seen. (He also projected an image of a man consecrated to a strange vocation to the point of self-immolation, but that was less noted.) The discussion was made to come down to Malinowski's moral character or lack of it, and the genuinely profound question his book raised was ignored; namely, if it is not, as we had been taught to believe, through some sort of extraordinary sensibility, an almost preternatural capacity to think, feel, and perceive like a native (a word, I should

---

[1] *The Double Helix* This 1969 book by James Dewey Watson (b. 1928) revealed the infighting and competition among geneticists. Watson and Francis Crick (b. 1916) are credited with mapping the DNA molecule.

[2] **Bronislaw Malinowski (1884 – 1942)** A Polish-American anthropologist noted for his important field studies in the South Pacific.

hurry to say, I use here "in the strict sense of the term"), how is anthropological knowledge of the way natives think, feel, and perceive possible? The issue the *Diary* presents, with a force perhaps only a working ethnographer can fully appreciate, is not moral. (The moral idealization of fieldworkers is a mere sentimentality in the first place, when it is not self-congratulation or a guild pretense.) The issue is epistemological.[3] If we are going to cling — as, in my opinion, we must — to the injunction to see things from the native's point of view, where are we when we can no longer claim some unique form of psychological closeness, a sort of transcultural identification, with our subjects? What happens to *verstehen* when *einfühlen*[4] disappears?

As a matter of fact, this general problem has been exercising   3 methodological discussion in anthropology for the last ten or fifteen years; Malinowski's voice from the grave merely dramatizes it as a human dilemma over and above a professional one. The formulations have been various: "inside" versus "outside," or "first person" versus "third person" descriptions; "phenomenological" versus "objectivist," or "cognitive" versus "behavioral" theories; or, perhaps most commonly "emic" versus "etic" analyses, this last deriving from the distinction in linguistics between phonemics and phonetics, phonemics classifying sounds according to their internal function in language, phonetics classifying them according to their acoustic properties as such. But perhaps the simplest and most directly appreciable way to put the matter is in terms of a distinction formulated, for his own purposes, by the psychoanalyst Heinz Kohut, between what he calls "experience-near" and "experience-distant" concepts.

An experience-near concept is, roughly, one that someone — a   4 patient, a subject, in our case an informant — might himself naturally and effortlessly use to define what he or his fellows see, feel, think, imagine, and so on, and which he would readily understand when similarly applied by others. An experience-distant concept is one that specialists of one sort or another — an analyst, an experimenter, an ethnographer, even a priest or an ideologist — employ to forward their scientific, philosophical, or practical aims. "Love" is an experience-near concept, "object cathexis"[5] is an experience-distant one. "Social stratification" and perhaps for most peoples in the world even "religion" (and certainly "religious system") are experience-

---

[3] **epistemological** Referring to the study of knowledge.

[4] ***verstehen . . . einfühlen*** *Verstehen* is German for "understanding"; *einfühlen* is German for "intuition."

[5] **object cathexis** Transferring emotions to an object.

distant; "caste" and "nirvana" are experience-near, at least for Hindus and Buddhists.

Clearly, the matter is one of degree, not polar opposition — "fear" is experience-nearer than "phobia," and "phobia" experience-nearer than "ego dyssyntonic."[6] And the difference is not, at least so far as anthropology is concerned (the matter is otherwise in poetry and physics), a normative[7] one, in the sense that one sort of concept is to be preferred as such over the other. Confinement to experience-near concepts leaves an ethnographer awash in immediacies, as well as entangled in vernacular.[8] Confinement to experience-distant ones leaves him stranded in abstractions and smothered in jargon. The real question, and the one Malinowski raised by demonstrating that, in the case of "natives," you don't have to be one to know one, is what roles the two sorts of concepts play in anthropological analysis. Or, more exactly, how, in each case, ought one to deploy them so as to produce an interpretation of the way a people lives which is neither imprisoned within their mental horizons, an ethnography of witchcraft as written by a witch, nor systematically deaf to the distinctive tonalities of their existence, an ethnography of witchcraft as written by a geometer.

Putting the matter this way — in terms of how anthropological analysis is to be conducted and its results framed, rather than what psychic constitution anthropologists need to have — reduces the mystery of what "seeing things from the native's point of view" means. But it does not make it any easier, nor does it lessen the demand for perceptiveness on the part of the fieldworker. To grasp concepts that, for another people, are experience-near, and to do so well enough to place them in illuminating connection with experience-distant concepts theorists have fashioned to capture the general features of social life, is clearly a task at least as delicate, if a bit less magical, as putting oneself into someone else's skin. The trick is not to get yourself into some inner correspondence of spirit with your informants. Preferring, like the rest of us, to call their souls their own, they are not going to be altogether keen about such an effort anyhow. The trick is to figure out what the devil they think they are up to.

In one sense, of course, no one knows this better than they do themselves; hence the passion to swim in the stream of their experience, and the illusion afterward that one somehow has. But in another sense, that simple truism is simply not true. People use

---

[6] **dyssyntonic** Ego disorder.

[7] **normative** Judgmental.

[8] **vernacular** The local language.

experience-near concepts spontaneously, unself-consciously, as it were colloquially; they do not, except fleetingly and on occasion, recognize that there are any "concepts" involved at all. That is what experience-near means — that ideas and the realities they inform are naturally and indissolubly bound up together. What else could you call a hippopotamus? Of course the gods are powerful, why else would we fear them? The ethnographer does not, and, in my opinion, largely cannot, perceive what his informants perceive. What he perceives, and that uncertainly enough, is what they perceive "with" — or "by means of," or "through" . . . or whatever the word should be. In the country of the blind, who are not as unobservant as they look, the one-eyed is not king, he is spectator.

Now, to make all this a bit more concrete, I want to turn for a 8 moment to my own work, which, whatever its other faults, has at least the virtue of being mine — in discussions of this sort a distinct advantage. In all three of the societies I have studied intensively, Javanese, Balinese, and Moroccan, I have been concerned, among other things, with attempting to determine how the people who live there define themselves as persons, what goes into the idea they have (but, as I say, only half-realize they have) of what a self, Javanese, Balinese, or Moroccan style, is. And in each case, I have tried to get at this most intimate of notions not by imagining myself someone else, a rice peasant or a tribal sheikh, and then seeing what I thought, but by searching out and analyzing the symbolic forms — words, images, institutions, behaviors — in terms of which, in each place, people actually represented themselves to themselves and to one another.

The concept of person is, in fact, an excellent vehicle by means 9 of which to examine this whole question of how to go about poking into another people's turn of mind. In the first place, some sort of concept of this kind, one feels reasonably safe in saying, exists in recognizable form among all social groups. The notions of what persons are may be, from our point of view, sometimes more than a little odd. They may be conceived to dart about nervously at night shaped like fireflies. Essential elements of their psyches, like hatred, may be thought to be lodged in granular black bodies within their livers, discoverable upon autopsy. They may share their fates with *doppelgänger*[9] beasts, so that when the beast sickens or dies they sicken or die too. But at least some conception of what a human individual is, as opposed to a rock, an animal, a rainstorm, or a god, is, so far as I can see, universal. Yet, at the same time, as these off-

----

[9] *doppelgänger* A double; in this case, an animal who is the person's other self.

hand examples suggest, the actual conceptions involved vary from one group to the next, and often quite sharply. The Western conception of the person as a bounded, unique, more or less integrated motivational and cognitive universe, a dynamic center of awareness, emotion, judgment, and action organized into a distinctive whole and set contrastively both against other such wholes and against its social and natural background, is, however incorrigible it may seem to us, a rather peculiar idea within the context of the world's cultures. Rather than attempting to place the experience of others within the framework of such a conception, which is what the extolled "empathy" in fact usually comes down to, understanding them demands setting that conception aside and seeing their experiences within the framework of their own idea of what selfhood is. And for Java, Bali, and Morocco, at least, that idea differs markedly not only from our own but, no less dramatically and no less instructively, from one to the other.

In Java, where I worked in the fifties, I studied a small, shabby   10
inland county-seat sort of place; two shadeless streets of whitewashed wooden shops and offices, and even less substantial bamboo shacks crammed in helter-skelter behind them, the whole surrounded by a great half-circle of densely packed rice-bowl villages. Land was short, jobs were scarce, politics was unstable, health was poor, prices were rising, and life was altogether far from promising, a kind of agitated stagnancy in which, as I once put it, thinking of the curious mixture of borrowed fragments of modernity and exhausted relics of tradition that characterized the place, the future seemed about as remote as the past. Yet in the midst of this depressing scene there was an absolutely astonishing intellectual vitality, a philosophical passion really, and a popular one besides, to track the riddles of existence right down to the ground. Destitute peasants would discuss questions of freedom of the will, illiterate tradesmen discoursed on the properties of God, common laborers had theories about the relations between reason and passion, the nature of time, or the reliability of the senses. And, perhaps most importantly, the problem of the self — its nature, function, and mode of operation — was pursued with the sort of reflective intensity one could find among ourselves in only the most recherché[10] settings indeed.

The central ideas in terms of which this reflection proceeded,   11
and which thus defined its boundaries and the Javanese sense of what a person is, were arranged into two sets of contrasts, at base re-

---

[10] **recherché** Refined.

ligious, one between "inside" and "outside," and one between "refined" and "vulgar." These glosses are, of course, crude and imprecise; determining exactly what the terms involved signified, sorting out their shades of meaning, was what all the discussion was about. But together they formed a distinctive conception of the self which, far from being merely theoretical, was the one in terms of which Javanese in fact perceived one another and, of course, themselves.

The "inside"/"outside" words, *batin* and *lair* (terms borrowed, as 12 a matter of fact, from the Sufi tradition of Muslim mysticism, but locally reworked) refer on the one hand to the felt realm of human experience and on the other to the observed realm of human behavior. These have, one hastens to say, nothing to do with "soul" and "body" in our sense, for which there are in fact quite other words with quite other implications. *Batin,* the "inside" word, does not refer to a separate seat of encapsulated spirituality detached or detachable from the body, or indeed to a bounded unit at all, but to the emotional life of human beings taken generally. It consists of the fuzzy, shifting flow of subjective feeling perceived directly in all its phenomenological immediacy but considered to be, at its roots at least, identical across all individuals, whose individuality it thus effaces. And similarly, *lair,* the "outside" word, has nothing to do with the body as an object, even an experienced object. Rather, it refers to that part of human life which, in our culture, strict behaviorists limit themselves to studying — external actions, movements, postures, speech — again conceived as in its essence invariant from one individual to the next. These two sets of phenomena — inward feelings and outward actions — are then regarded not as functions of one another but as independent realms of being to be put in proper order independently.

It is in connection with this "proper ordering" that the contrast 13 between *alus,* the word meaning "pure," "refined," "polished," "exquisite," "ethereal," "subtle," "civilized," "smooth," and *kasar,* the word meaning "impolite," "rough," "uncivilized," "coarse," "insensitive," "vulgar," comes into play. The goal is to be *alus* in both the separated realms of the self. In the inner realm this is to be achieved through religious discipline, much but not all of it mystical. In the outer realm, it is to be achieved through etiquette, the rules of which here are not only extraordinarily elaborate but have something of the force of law. Through meditation the civilized man thins out his emotional life to a kind of constant hum; through etiquette, he both shields that life from external disruptions and regularizes his outer behavior in such a way that it appears to others as a predictable, undisturbing, elegant, and rather vacant set of choreographed motions and settled forms of speech.

There is much more to all this, because it connects up to both   14
an ontology[11] and an aesthetic.[12] But so far as our problem is concerned, the result is a bifurcate conception of the self, half unges-
tured feeling and half unfelt gesture. An inner world of stilled emotion and an outer world of shaped behavior confront one another as
sharply distinguished realms unto themselves, any particular person
being but the momentary locus, so to speak, of that confrontation, a
passing expression of their permanent existence, their permanent
separation, and their permanent need to be kept in their own order.
Only when you have seen, as I have, a young man whose wife — a
woman he had in fact raised from childhood and who had been the
center of his life — has suddenly and inexplicably died, greeting
everyone with a set smile and formal apologies for his wife's absence
and trying, by mystical techniques, to flatten out, as he himself put
it, the hills and valleys of his emotion into an even, level plain ("That
is what you have to do," he said to me, "be smooth inside and out")
can you come, in the face of our own notions of the intrinsic honesty of deep feeling and the moral importance of personal sincerity,
to take the possibility of such a conception of selfhood seriously and
appreciate, however inaccessible it is to you, its own sort of force.

Bali, where I worked both in another small provincial town,   15
though one rather less drifting and dispirited, and, later, in an up-
land village of highly skilled musical instruments makers, is of
course in many ways similar to Java, with which it shared a common
culture to the fifteenth century. But at a deeper level, having continued Hindu while Java was, nominally at least, Islamized, it is quite
different. The intricate, obsessive ritual life — Hindu, Buddhist, and
Polynesian in about equal proportions — whose development was
more or less cut off in Java, leaving its Indic spirit to turn reflective
and phenomenological,[13] even quietistic, in the way I have just described, flourished in Bali to reach levels of scale and flamboyance
that have startled the world and made the Balinese a much more
dramaturgical people with a self to match. What is philosophy in
Java is theater in Bali.

As a result, there is in Bali a persistent and systematic attempt to   16
stylize all aspects of personal expression to the point where anything
idiosyncratic, anything characteristic of the individual merely because he is who he is physically, psychologically, or biographically,

---

[11] **ontology** Philosophy of existence or being.
[12] **aesthetic** Philosophy of art.
[13] **phenomenological** Pertaining to a philosophy of consciousness.

is muted in favor of his assigned place in the continuing and, so it is thought, never-changing pageant that is Balinese life. It is *dramatis personae*,[14] not actors, that endure; indeed, it is *dramatis personae*, not actors, that in the proper sense really exist. Physically men come and go, mere incidents in a happenstance history, of no genuine importance even to themselves. But the masks they wear, the stage they occupy, the parts they play, and, most important, the spectacle they mount remain, and comprise not the façade but the substance of things, not least the self. Shakespeare's old-trouper view of the vanity of action in the face of mortality — all the world's a stage and we but poor players, content to strut our hour, and so on — makes no sense here. There is no make-believe; of course players perish, but the play does not, and it is the latter, the performed rather than the performer, that really matters.

Again, all this is realized not in terms of some general mood the   17
anthropologist in his spiritual versatility somehow captures, but through a set of readily observable symbolic forms: an elaborate repertoire of designations and titles. The Balinese have at least a half-dozen major sorts of labels, ascriptive, fixed, and absolute, which one person can apply to another (or, of course, to himself) to place him among his fellows. There are birth-order markers, kinship terms, caste titles, sex indicators, teknonyms,[15] and so on and so forth, each of which consists not of a mere collection of useful tags but a distinct and bounded, internally very complex, terminological system. When one applies one of these designations or titles (or, as is more common, several at once) to someone, one therefore defines him as a determinate point in a fixed pattern, as the temporary occupant of a particular, quite untemporary, cultural locus. To identify someone, yourself or somebody else, in Bali is thus to locate him within the familiar cast of characters — "king," "grandmother," "third-born," "Brahman" — of which the social drama is, like some stock company roadshow piece — *Charley's Aunt* or *Springtime for Henry* — inevitably composed.

The drama is of course not farce, and especially not transvestite   18
farce, though there are such elements in it. It is an enactment of hierarchy, a theater of status. But that, though critical, is unpursuable here. The immediate point is that, in both their structure and their mode of operation, the terminological systems conduce to a view of the human person as an appropriate representative of a generic type, not a unique creature with a private fate. To see how they do this,

---

[14] **dramatis personae** Characters in the play.
[15] **teknonyms** Names associated with one's profession.

how they tend to obscure the mere materialities — biological, psychological, historical — of individual existence in favor of standardized status qualities would involve an extended analysis. But perhaps a single example, the simplest further simplified, will suffice to suggest the pattern.

All Balinese receive what might be called birth-order names. 19 There are four of these, "first-born," "second-born," "third-born," "fourth-born," after which they recycle, so that the fifth-born child is called again "first-born," the sixth "second-born," and so on. Further, these names are bestowed independently of the fates of the children. Dead children, even stillborn ones, count, so that in fact, in this still high-birthrate, high-mortality society, the names do not really tell you anything very reliable about the birth-order relations of concrete individuals. Within a set of living siblings, someone called "first-born" may actually be first, fifth, or ninth-born, or, if somebody is missing, almost anything in between, and someone called "second-born" may in fact be older. The birth-order naming system does not identify individuals as individuals, nor is it intended to; what it does is to suggest that, for all procreating couples, births form a circular succession of "firsts," "seconds," "thirds," and "fourths," an endless four-stage replication of an imperishable form. Physically men appear and disappear as the ephemerae they are, but socially the acting figures remain eternally the same as new "firsts," "seconds," and so on emerge from the timeless world of the gods to replace those who, dying, dissolve once more into it. All the designation and title systems, so I would argue, function in the same way: they represent the most time-saturated aspects of the human condition as but ingredients in an eternal, footlight present.

Nor is this sense the Balinese have of always being on stage a 20 vague and ineffable one either. It is, in fact, exactly summed up in what is surely one of their experience-nearest concepts: *lek*. *Lek* has been variously translated or mistranslated ("shame" is the most common attempt); but what it really means is close to what we call stage fright. Stage fright consists, of course, in the fear that, for want of skill or self-control, or perhaps by mere accident, an aesthetic illusion will not be maintained, that the actor will show through his part. Aesthetic distance collapses, the audience (and the actor) lose sight of Hamlet and gain it, uncomfortably for all concerned, of bumbling John Smith painfully miscast as the Prince of Denmark. In Bali, the case is the same: what is feared is that the public performance to which one's cultural location commits one will be botched and that the personality — as we would call it but the Balinese, of course, not believing in such a thing, would not — of the individual will break through to dissolve his standardized public identity.

When this occurs, as it sometimes does, the immediacy of the moment is felt with excruciating intensity and men become suddenly and unwillingly creatural, locked in mutual embarrassment, as though they had happened upon each other's nakedness. It is the fear of faux pas,[16] rendered only that much more probable by the extraordinary ritualization of daily life, that keeps social intercourse on its deliberately narrowed rails and protects the dramatistical sense of self against the disruptive threat implicit in the immediacy and spontaneity even the most passionate ceremoniousness cannot fully eradicate from face-to-face encounters.

Morocco, Middle Eastern and dry rather than East Asian and   21
wet, extrovert, fluid, activist, masculine, informal to a fault, a Wild West sort of place without the barrooms and the cattle drives, is another kettle of selves altogether. My work there, which began in the mid-sixties, has been centered around a moderately large town or small city in the foothills of the Middle Atlas, about twenty miles south of Fez. It's an old place, probably founded in the tenth century, conceivably even earlier. It has the walls, the gates, the narrow minarets rising to prayer-call platforms of a classical Muslim town, and, from a distance anyway, it is a rather pretty place, an irregular oval of blinding white set in the deep-sea-green of an olive grove oasis, the mountains, bronze and stony here, slanting up immediately behind it. Close up, it is less prepossessing, though more exciting: a labyrinth of passages and alleyways, three quarters of them blind,[17] pressed in by wall-like buildings and curbside shops and filled with a simply astounding variety of very emphatic human beings. Arabs, Berbers, and Jews; tailors, herdsmen, and soldiers; people out of offices, people out of markets, people out of tribes; rich, superrich, poor, superpoor; locals, immigrants, mimic Frenchmen, unbending medievalists, and somewhere, according to the official government census for 1960, an unemployed Jewish airplane pilot — the town houses one of the finest collections of rugged individuals I, at least, have ever come up against. Next to Sefrou (the name of the place), Manhattan seems almost monotonous.

Yet no society consists of anonymous eccentrics bouncing off   22
one another like billiard balls, and Moroccans, too, have symbolic means by which to sort people out from one another and form an idea of what it is to be a person. The main such means — not the only one, but I think the most important and the one I want to talk

---

[16] **faux pas** Mistake.
[17] **blind** Dead end.

about particularly here — is a peculiar linguistic form called in Arabic the *nisba*. The word derives from the triliteral root, *n-s-b,* for "ascription," "attribution," "imputation," "relationship," "affinity," "correlation," "connection," "kinship." *Nsīb* means "in-law"; *nsab* means "to attribute or impute to"; *munāsaba* means "a relation," "an analogy," "a correspondence"; *mansūb* means "belonging to," "pertaining to"; and so on to at least a dozen derivatives, from *nassāb* ("genealogist") to *nīsbīya* ("[physical] relativity").

Nisba itself, then, refers to a combination morphological,[18]   23 grammatical, and semantic process that consists in transforming a noun into what we would call a relative adjective but what for Arabs is just another sort of noun by adding ī (f., *īya*): *Sefrū/ Sefrou—Sfrūwī*/native son of Sefrou; *Sūs*/region of southwestern Morocco — *Sūsī*/man coming from that region; *Beni Yazğa*/a tribe near Sefrou — *Yazğī*/a member of that tribe; *Yahūd*/the Jews as a people, Jewry — *Yahūdī*/a Jew; *'Adlun*/surname of a prominent Sefrou family — *'Adlūnī*/a member of that family. Nor is the procedure confined to this more or less straightforward "ethnicizing" use, but is employed in a wide range of domains to attribute relational properties to persons. For example, occupation (*hrār*/silk — *hrārī*/silk merchant); religious sect (*Darqāwā*/a mystical brotherhood — *Darqāwī*/an adept of that brotherhood or spiritual status), (*'Ali*/The Prophet's son-in-law — *'Alawī*/descendant of the Prophet's son-in-law, and thus of the Prophet).

Now, as once formed, nisbas tend to be incorporated into per-   24 sonal names — Umar Al-Buhadiwi/Umar of the Buhadu Tribe; Muhammed Al-Sussi/Muhammed from the Sus Region — this sort of adjectival attributive classification is quite publicly stamped onto an individual's identity. I was unable to find a single case where an individual was generally known, or known about, but his or her nisba was not. Indeed, Sefrouis are far more likely to be ignorant of how well-off a man is, how long he has been around, what his personal character is, or where exactly he lives, than they are of what his nisba is — Sussi or Sefroui, Buhadiwi or Adluni, Harari or Darqawi. (Of women to whom he is not related that is very likely to be all that he knows — or, more exactly, is permitted to know.) The selves that bump and jostle each other in the alleys of Sefrou gain their definition from associative relations they are imputed to have with the society that surrounds them. They are contextualized persons.

But the situation is even more radical than this; nisbas render   25 men relative to their contexts, but as contexts themselves are rela-

---

[18] **morphological** Referring to form and structure of words.

tive, so too are nisbas, and the whole thing rises, so to speak, to the second power: relativism squared. Thus, at one level, everyone in Sefrou has the same nisba, or at least the potential of it — namely, Sefroui. However, within Sefrou such a nisba, precisely because it does not discriminate, will never be heard as part of an individual designation. It is only outside of Sefrou that the relationship to that particular context becomes identifying. Inside it, he is an Adluni, Alawi, Meghrawi, Ngadi, or whatever. And similarly within these categories: there are, for example, twelve different nisbas (Shakibis, Zuinis, and so forth) by means of which, among themselves, Sefrou Alawis distinguish one another.

The whole matter is far from regular: what level or sort of nisba 26 is used and seems relevant and appropriate (to the users, that is) depends heavily on the situation. A man I knew who lived in Sefrou and worked in Fez but came from the Beni Yazgha tribe settled nearby — and from the Hima lineage of the Taghut subfraction of the Wulad Ben Ydir fraction within it — was known as a Sefroui to his work fellows in Fez, a Yazghi to all of us non-Yazghis in Sefrou, an Ydiri to other Beni Yazghas around, except for those who were themselves of the Wulad Ben Ydir fraction, who called him a Taghuti. As for the few other Taghutis, they called him a Himiwi. That is as far as things went here, but not as far as they can go, in either direction. Should, by chance, our friend journey to Egypt, he would become a Maghrebi, the nisba formed from the Arabic word for North Africa. The social contextualization of persons is pervasive and, in its curiously unmethodical way, systematic. Men do not float as bounded psychic entities, detached from their backgrounds and singularly named. As individualistic, even willful, as the Moroccans in fact are, their identity is an attribute they borrow from their setting.

Now as with the Javanese inside/outside, smooth/rough phe- 27 nomenological sort of reality dividing, and the absolutizing Balinese title systems, the nisba way of looking at persons — as though they were outlines waiting to be filled in — is not an isolated custom, but part of a total pattern of social life. This pattern is, like the others, difficult to characterize succinctly, but surely one of its outstanding features is a promiscuous tumbling in public settings of varieties of men kept carefully segregated in private ones — all-out cosmopolitanism in the streets, strict communalism (of which the famous secluded woman is only the most striking index) in the home. This is, indeed, the so-called mosaic system of social organization so often held to be characteristic of the Middle East generally: differently shaped and colored chips jammed in irregularly together to generate an intricate overall design within which their individual distinctiveness remains nonetheless intact. Nothing if not diverse, Moroccan society does not cope with its diversity by sealing it into castes, isolating it into tribes, dividing it into ethnic groups, or covering it over with some common-denominator concept of nationality, though, fitfully, all have now and then been tried. It copes with it by distinguishing, with elaborate precision, the contexts — marriage, worship, and to an extent diet, law, and education — within which men are separated by their dissimilitudes, and those — work, friendship, politics, trade — where, however warily and however conditionally, they are connected by them.

To such a social pattern, a concept of selfhood which marks 28 public identity contextually and relativistically, but yet does so in terms — tribal, territorial, linguistic, religious, familial — that grow out of the more private and settled arenas of life and have a deep and permanent resonance there, would seem particularly appropriate. Indeed, the social pattern would seem virtually to create this concept of selfhood, for it produces a situation where people interact with one another in terms of categories whose meaning is almost purely positional, location in the general mosaic, leaving the substantive content of the categories, what they mean subjectively as experienced forms of life, aside as something properly concealed in apartments, temples, and tents. Nisba discriminations can be more specific or less, indicate location within the mosaic roughly or finely, and they can be adapted to almost any changes in circumstance. But they cannot carry with them more than the most sketchy, outline implications concerning what men so named as a rule are like. Calling a man a Sefroui is like calling him a San Franciscan: it classifies him, but it does not type him; it places him without portraying him.

It is the nisba system's capacity to do this — to create a frame- 29 work within which persons can be identified in terms of supposedly immanent characteristics (speech, blood, faith, provenance,[19] and the rest) — and yet to minimize the impact of those characteristics in determining the practical relations among such persons in markets, shops, bureaus, fields, cafés, baths, and roadways that makes it so central to the Moroccan idea of the self. Nisba-type categorization leads, paradoxically, to a hyperindividualism in public relationships, because by providing only a vacant sketch, and that shifting, of who the actors are — Yazghis, Adlunis, Buhadiwis, or whatever — it leaves the rest, that is, almost everything, to be filled in by the process of interaction itself. What makes the mosaic work is the confidence that one can be as totally pragmatic, adaptive, oppor-

---

[19] **provenance** Origin.

tunistic, and generally ad hoc[20] in one's relations with others — a fox among foxes, a crocodile among crocodiles — as one wants without any risk of losing one's sense of who one is. Selfhood is never in danger because, outside the immediacies of procreation and prayer, only its coordinates are asserted.

Now, without trying to tie up the dozens of loose ends I have   30 not only left dangling in these rather breathless accounts of the senses of selfhood of nearly ninety million people but have doubtless frazzled even more, let us return to the question of what all this can tell us, or could if it were done adequately, about "the native's point of view" in Java, Bali, and Morocco. Are we, in describing symbol uses, describing perceptions, sentiments, outlooks, experiences? And in what sense? What do we claim when we claim that we understand the semiotic means by which, in this case, persons are defined to one another? That we know words or that we know minds?

In answering this question, it is necessary, I think, first to notice   31 the characteristic intellectual movement, the inward conceptual rhythm, in each of these analyses, and indeed in all similar analyses, including those of Malinowski — namely, a continuous dialectical tacking between the most local of local detail and the most global of global structure in such a way as to bring them into simultaneous view. In seeking to uncover the Javanese, Balinese, or Moroccan sense of self, one oscillates restlessly between the sort of exotic minutiae (lexical antitheses, categorical schemes, morphophonemic[21] transformations) that make even the best ethnographies a trial to read and the sort of sweeping characterizations ("quietism," "dramatism," "contextualism") that make all but the most pedestrian of them somewhat implausible. Hopping back and forth between the whole conceived through the parts that actualize it and the parts conceived through the whole that motivates them, we seek to turn them, by a sort of intellectual perpetual motion, into explications of one another.

All this is, of course, but the now familiar trajectory of what   32 Dilthey called the hermeneutic circle,[22] and my argument here is merely that it is as central to ethnographic interpretation, and thus to the penetration of other people's modes of thought, as it is to lit-

---

[20] **ad hoc** Latin for "to this"; in this case meaning one temporarily behaves toward another as that other would in the same situation.

[21] **morphophonemic** Forms of words.

[22] **hermeneutic circle** Interpretive circle in which interpreting the part contributes to interpreting the whole.

erary, historical, philological, psychoanalytic, or biblical interpretation, or for that matter to the informal annotation of everyday experience we call common sense. In order to follow a baseball game one must understand what a bat, a hit, an inning, a left fielder, a squeeze play, a hanging curve, and a tightened infield are, and what the game in which these "things" are elements is all about. When an *explication de texte*[23] critic like Leo Spitzer attempts to interpret Keats's "Ode on a Grecian Urn," he does so by repetitively asking himself the alternating question "What is the whole poem about?" and "What exactly has Keats seen (or chosen to show us) depicted on the urn he is describing?," emerging at the end of an advancing spiral of general observations and specific remarks with a reading of the poem as an assertion of the triumph of the aesthetic mode of perception over the historical. In the same way, when a meanings-and-symbols ethnographer like myself attempts to find out what some pack of natives conceive a person to be, he moves back and forth between asking himself, "What is the general form of their life?" and "What exactly are the vehicles in which that form is embodied?," emerging in the end of a similar sort of spiral with the notion that they see the self as a composite, a persona, or a point in a pattern. You can no more know what *lek* is if you do not know what Balinese dramatism is than you can know what a catcher's mitt is if you do not know what baseball is. And you can no more know what mosaic social organization is if you do not know what a nisba is than you can know what Keats's Platonism is if you are unable to grasp, to use Spitzer's own formulation, the "intellectual thread of thought" captured in such fragment phrases as "Attic shape," "silent form," "bride of quietness," "cold pastoral," "silence and slow time," "peaceful citadel," or "ditties of no tone."[24]

In short, accounts of other peoples' subjectives can be built up without recourse to pretensions to more-than-normal capacities for ego effacement and fellow feeling. Normal capacities in these respects are, of course, essential, as is their cultivation, if we expect people to tolerate our intrusions into their lives at all and accept us as persons worth talking to. I am certainly not arguing for insensitivity here, and hope I have not demonstrated it. But whatever accurate or half-accurate sense one gets of what one's informants are, as the phrase goes, really like does not come from the experience of that acceptance as such, which is part of one's own biography, not of

33

---

[23] *explication de texte* Critical, close reading of a text.
[24] **"Attic . . . tone"** Quotations are from John Keats's "Ode on a Grecian Urn."

theirs. It comes from the ability to construe their modes of expression, what I would call their symbol systems, which such an acceptance allows one to work toward developing. Understanding the form and pressure of, to use the dangerous word one more time, natives' inner lives is more like grasping a proverb, catching an allusion, seeing a joke — or, as I have suggested, reading a poem — than it is like achieving communion.

QUESTIONS FOR CRITICAL READING

1. Geertz says Malinowski's diary shattered the myth of the chameleon fieldworker adapting to the society being studied. How does Geertz treat the myth? Have you felt its presence in other readings in this section?
2. How important is the distinction between "ethnographer" and "anthropologist"?
3. What are Geertz's views on the relationship between empathy and anthropology?
4. Where do you stand on the question of experience-distant versus experience-close study of cultures (paras. 3 – 5)? Where does Geertz stand?
5. What does it mean to "think, feel, and perceive like a native" (para. 2)?
6. What is Geertz's own method of work in relation to other cultures? How does it differ from the methods he describes?
7. How does the Balinese attitude toward hierarchy and status compare to your own culture (paras. 17 – 20)? How does your culture express status?
8. Geertz spends a great deal of time discussing words specific to the languages of the cultures he describes. Why? What insights into the cultures do his observations offer?

SUGGESTIONS FOR WRITING

1. If you were "a meanings-and-symbols ethnographer" (para. 32), how would you examine your own culture? What symbolic forms would you center on in your examination? Geertz defines symbolic forms as "words, images, institutions, behaviors" (para. 8). What patterns are most characteristic of such symbolic forms? You might want to search for oppositions of the kind Geertz uses in his own studies.
2. Describe how "the Western conception of the person as a bounded, unique, more or less integrated motivational and cognitive universe" (para. 9) reveals itself in the culture you know best. How do people you know well regard their individuality? Create a Geertzian portrait of individualism as you have observed it functioning in your society.

3. Clarify the distinctions between the inside and outside as Geertz uses the terms in describing the Javanese individual. What Western concepts are similar to these? Are you aware of having an inside and an outside to your character, personality, or self? How do such concepts manifest themselves? What contrasting aspects do Westerners have that are similar to the Javanese "refined/vulgar"?

4. In paragraph 14, Geertz talks about a split in personality, referring to "an inner world of stilled emotion and an outer world of shaped behavior." Examine this concept, and explain it in your own words. Then describe instances in which such a description would apply to your own culture. When do people's actions hide their emotions? Under what conditions do their emotions go unexpressed? Are such moments culturally determined? Under what special circumstances in your culture is such a split essential and expected?

5. Geertz describes Moroccans as "anonymous eccentrics bouncing off one another like billiard balls" (para. 22). In what ways are the individuals you know in your immediate environment like the Moroccans? How is it possible for distinct and eccentric people to get along together? What conditions make it work?

6. Which of the three cultures Geertz describes is closest in form to the culture you know best? What qualities does your culture share with them?

7. In paragraph 27, Geertz describes the *nisba* way of looking at people "as though they were outlines waiting to be filled in." What does he mean? To what extent do you find a similar pattern in your own culture? Under what conditions does that approach most often seem to be used? How do institutions use that approach? How do individuals use it?

8. Examine the special symbolic forms of your own culture, with a special emphasis on your music. What are the cultural messages implicit in the music you hear and in the music that is played in homes, in auditoriums, on television, and in public places?

9. **CONNECTIONS** Margaret Mead and Ruth Benedict both observed the cultures they studied from the "experience-near" point of view. Comment on the success or failure of their efforts to transmit to you a clear sense of these cultures. Do they indulge in any of the kinds of excess that Geertz comments on in the opening paragraphs of his essay? Is the method of Herodotus or Alvar Núñez Cabeza de Vaca experience-near or experience-distant? Would they have understood the terms?

PART SEVEN

FAITH

Siddhārtha Gautama, the Buddha
St. Matthew
The Bhagavad Gītā
The Prophet Muhammad
St. Teresa of Avila
Friedrich Nietzsche
Martin Buber

INTRODUCTION

Faith is one of the most compelling and enduring ideas that the world has known. Some of the earliest prehistoric artifacts show evidence of belief in a higher power or powers that shape the course of human events, and archaeological digs have revealed the materials of religious practice and of worship of deities spanning thousands of years. Although much of the history of faith is lost in the eons of prehistory, we know that during the last six or seven thousand years of humanity's development, faith has grown and changed as other human ideas and institutions have grown and changed. The earliest evidence suggests that nature worship was common among people all over the globe, often centering on variations on sun worshiping. Animism, the belief that all things in nature have a spiritual force and must be respected — and in some cases worshiped or deferred to — thrived in ancient times and continues to be practiced to this day. The pantheon of gods that the Egyptians developed and recorded, doubtless from earlier vestiges of their prehistory, are identified by Herodotus as the precursors of some of the Greek gods that are familiar to us through myth. The Greek and Roman myths center on Zeus and Jupiter but pay tribute to a range of gods with specialized responsibilities.

The rise of monotheism is evident in many cultures, but for westerners its earliest development centers most prominently in Judaism. The development of monotheism has been seen as evolutionary, but the term *evolution* is a metaphor in this case: there is no objective means of establishing progress in matters of faith. Herodotus, Plato, and Aristotle were what modern theologians would call pagans and based their faith — insofar as faith can be identified in any of them — on the polytheism of their time. Later thinkers, such as St. Matthew, absorbed the contemporary revolution of monotheistic thought. Identifying human figures with the godhead occurred relatively late in the development of religious faith. The Buddha, Jesus, and Krishna represent important human figures for the religious systems of which they are part. The idea of their humanity is one of their most important contributions to modern religious faith.

The selections that follow are drawn from several different religions and approaches to the concept of faith. However, the idea that faith transforms the individual is constant in these selections. Some emphasize that change comes from within and that individuals must work at becoming worthy of their faith. Discipline is another common theme among these writers, but it takes several forms and is not always clearly related to moral behavior. In fact, morality — or right action in one's relations with others — is not always central to these writers, although we can infer that it is usually present. Their focus is clearly on making the individual worthy and spiritually unencumbered.

The range of behavior in matters of faith is extraordinary in these selections. The Buddha recommends using self-control and meditation to achieve enlightenment. St. Matthew describes the path that Jesus set out for the disciples, emphasizing mercy and charity. The Lord Krishna tells Arjuna in the *Bhagavad Gītā* that only through discipline and a renouncing of the senses will he know the divinity. The Prophet Muhammad holds a dialogue with Allah concerning the fate of believers and non-believers. St. Teresa of Avila, one of the most influential and inspiring of modern mystics, describes visions of rapturous encounters with Jesus and several angels. Friedrich Nietzsche describes aspects of religious faith as practiced by the ancient Greeks and Romans, ranging from cerebral and controlled Apollonian expressions of faith to ecstatic Dionysian effusions. Martin Buber continues the theme of dialogue in *I and Thou* when he holds that God is the ultimate Thou in human relationships.

Siddhārtha Gautama, the Buddha, directs our attention inward to the deepest spiritual resources of the individual. According to the Buddha, meditation is the path to enlightenment, revealing a spiritual life that follows an eightfold path and eventually provides the soul with peace. The Buddha provides instructions in how to control the senses, how to moderate the appetites, and how to control the wandering mind through focus and concentration. Following the eightfold path requires right behavior, which can be achieved only by gaining knowledge of what right behavior is.

St. Matthew's Gospel can be found in the New Testament of the Bible. It tells the story of Jesus' youth and brief ministry. In the Sermon on the Mount, the selection that appears here, Jesus instructs his disciples beginning with the beatitudes, the blessings that the disciples enjoy as a result of their having faith in Jesus. The Sermon on the Mount focuses on interpretation of the laws, including the subjects of adultery, divorce, vengeance, and charity. It ends with the Lord's Prayer, which Jesus says is the only prayer one needs, since it includes all prayers. The core of the selection focuses on the morality of the individual in daily behavior and an understanding of the spirit of the law.

The *Bhagavad Gītā* presents a portrait of the Hindu divinity Lord Krishna, who, in the guise of Arjuna's charioteer, advises Arjuna on matters of faith. He reveals himself to Arjuna and describes his two selves — the natural self, which is the material of all nature, and the spiritual self, which is the ineffable divinity. Like the

Buddha, Lord Krishna emphasizes the role of meditation in seeking enlightenment. For the Hindu, enlightenment involves reaching the end of the indefinite number of incarnations that the individual soul must pass through before reaching nirvana, the point of ultimate oneness with the divine. The path involves self-discipline and a withdrawal from the distractions of the sensory world.

"The Believer," from the Koran, presents a dialogue between Allah and the Prophet Muhammad, a structure similar to that used in the excerpts from St. Matthew and the *Bhagavad Gītā.* The angel Gabriel reveals the word of Allah to Muhammed. In "The Believer" Muhammed compares the fate of those who believe in Allah with that of unbelievers. According to Muhammad, believers will enter into paradise, while unbelievers will be lost. "The Believer" moves from discussing the fate of the unfaithful to a review of biblical history to the story of the Egyptian Pharaoh and others who bring destruction upon themselves by refusing to believe in Allah.

St. Teresa of Avila was a sixteenth-century nun who founded a number of Carmelite convents in an effort to help reform the Carmelite order. She was a woman of action and a manager of daily business affairs, but she was also a powerfully magnetic personality whose faith was unusually passionate and strong. She describes in this selection a series of visions that revealed to her the human nature of God. Her fervor convinced highly skeptical members of the Spanish Inquisition that the visions were genuine and that Teresa's faith existed on a level that few could ever know.

Although Friedrich Nietzsche is famous for saying in 1899 that "God is dead," he was nonetheless deeply interested in faith and religion in their many manifestations. In "Apollonianism and Dionysianism" he describes two polarities in religious behavior as they were understood by both the ancients and his contemporaries. Nietzsche seems to have leaned toward approving the divine "madness" of the Dionysian spirit, but he realized that both paths — the thoughtful, restrained Apollonian and the ecstatic, feverish Dionysian — exist and both serve the purposes of faith.

Martin Buber, among the most important modern Jewish thinkers, was influenced by Nietzsche and is sometimes described as an existentialist. Existentialists emphasize our daily actions — our existence — as a measure for who we are. Buber uses the term *actualize* to describe the process by which the individual realizes the fullness of the life experience. The excerpt included here from *I and Thou,* like St. Matthew's and Muhammad's, focuses on the individual's dialogue with God. For Buber God is the eternal Thou who helps us actualize ourselves. As he tells us, we as individuals realize ourselves in relation to others, and the primary other for everyone is God.

These expressions of faith from seven very different points of view demonstrate only a small portion of the variety of experience encompassed by human faith. Religions are complex structures of belief, demanding a special commitment from their members. Some of the attitudes and expressions of faith in this section may seem arbitrary, extreme, or even unbelievable. Yet they are the basic materials of any inquiry into the relationship between human beings and the divine.

SIDDHĀRTHA GAUTAMA, THE BUDDHA
Meditation:
The Path to Enlightenment

SIDDHĀRTHA GAUTAMA (563? – 483? B.C.), known as the Buddha (Sanskrit for "enlightened one"), was born in Kapilavastu, the chief town of Kapila in what is now Nepal. His family was petty royalty, and he himself a minor prince. One of his names is Sakya-muni, "sage of the Sakya clan." Early texts state that he was pro-tected from knowledge of the outside world so that when he was twenty-nine, after finally witnessing poverty, illness, and death, he renounced his aristocratic position and his wife and family. He left his home and wandered, living the ascetic religious life, until he reached Bodh Gaya, where he spent his time in meditation until he achieved enlightenment.

His purpose in seeking enlightenment was to show the way to people so they could relieve the misery of their own lives. In most versions of Buddhism, the Buddha is regarded as Lord Buddha. In other versions, he is regarded as a man who reached a level of perfection that is possible for ordinary people to achieve. Some branches of Buddhism describe several Buddhas, or bodhisattvas — those who enter different spiritual stages at different times and may be viewed as either great teachers or as heavenly saviors.

In the religion that developed from the Buddha's teachings, the purpose of life is to achieve the enlightenment that will enable the individual to end *samsāra* — the wandering of the soul from one becoming (incarnation) to another — and reach *nirvana,* a peace that lies beyond human understanding. In the selection that fol-lows, nirvana is referred to as the end of being.

Translated by Edward Conze.

Because Buddhists hope to achieve nirvana, they live their lives guided by firm precepts. They believe that the existence they now enjoy was shaped and formed by the soul in a previous existence and that since their present way of life shapes existences to come, they need to make their own *karma. Karma* is a Sanskrit word for "making," translated sometimes as "action." Therefore, Buddhists have established eight principles of behavior for creating their karma called the noble eightfold path:

1. Right views — the avoidance of delusion
2. Right aims — purposive intentions to achieve nirvana
3. Right speech — preferring the truth
4. Right conduct — being honest, true, pure in behavior
5. Right living — avoiding hurting all beings and thus preferring a vegetarian diet
6. Self-control — preferring disciplined behavior
7. Right-mindedness — being aware and alert
8. Right meditation — deep contemplation of life and the process of thought

The ethical implications of Buddhism are evident in the eight admonitions of the Noble Eightfold Path.

The Buddhist scriptures, from which the following passage comes, were not written by the Buddha but gathered from his teachings by disciples such as his personal follower, Ānanda. The scriptures date from the fifth century B.C. and were written down sometime in the seventh century A.D. by monks who were fearful that the teachings, because of intense persecution of Buddhists, might be lost. Buddhism is rare in India today — its adherents are located mainly in Sri Lanka — but it was transplanted to Tibet, China, and Japan, where it remains influential. Although Southeast Asia today is largely Buddhist, Buddhism coexists with many local religions, some of which contain dramatically opposing views.

The volume of Buddhist scriptures — hundreds of thousands of pages — resulted from the contribution of many different schools of Buddhism, each with its own interpretation. In Japan, for example, several schools of Buddhism have been prominent. One is the Rinzai sect, a form of Buddhism that meditates on complex and baffling riddles, such as the question "What is the sound of one hand clapping?" Such a riddle, called a *koan,* is especially difficult for the western mind to comprehend. Another is the Soto sect, which dates from the thirteenth century A.D. and emphasizes quiet sitting — *zazen* — as a means to enlightenment. Both of these sects are still vital in modern Buddhism.

Buddhist meditation, which originated from Zen Buddhism, depends on a willingness to remain quiet and suspend all logical thought, desire, and attachments. It is an extremely difficult discipline but is recognized by all Buddhists as the one true path to enlightenment, demanding the denial of the sensory world, of transitory events and values.

The following passage emphasizes the advantages of meditation as well as the advantages of introversion. The material world is seen as a distraction that incessantly robs people of their peace and their awareness of the truth about existence. Zen meditation is a radical technique for bringing the external world under the control of the spirit. However, it is similar to Greek and Roman advice and fundamental western views concerning spiritual values in modern times.

BUDDHIST RHETORIC

The material in this selection is not only translated from a language and a tradition quite foreign to English but is also derived from several sources. "The Advantages of Meditation" comes from a scripture called *Milindapanha* and is rendered in prose. "The Practice of Introversion," however, originates from another text, Santideva, and is rendered in poetry. The third section, "The Progressive Steps of Meditation," is from the *Asvaghosa,* yet another important Buddhist text. That these texts differ in age and in approach makes the rhetorical situation unusual.

However, certain qualities are present in all the texts. All are "how-to" texts, offering a step-by-step examination of the nature of meditation, its benefits, characteristics, and results. Typical of many Buddhist texts is the technique of enumeration: listing eight noble paths, twenty-eight advantages to meditation, and so on. Such a technique is especially useful for instruction because of its clear, progressive approach.

However, there is a further problem that the translator must resolve. As Edward Conze, the translator of these texts, explains, "For Buddhists the founder of their religion is the 'Lord Buddha,' a godlike being who has transcended the conditions of ordinary life, and his words are not those of a mere man, but a voice issuing from another world. It is therefore quite inconceivable that the Buddha should speak as ordinary people do." Therefore, the text as translated employs an elevated diction in a tone that is formal and distant. We might consider it priestlike. We usually expect and appreciate conversational, direct prose. But in confronting material that is so serious, dignified, and spiritual, it seems more appropriate that the level of diction be high and the tone formal.

Meditation:
The Path to Enlightenment

1. The Advantages of Meditation

Secluded meditation has many virtues. All the Tathagatas[1] have 1
won their all-knowledge in a state of secluded meditation, and, even
after their enlightenment, they have continued to cultivate meditation in the recollection of the benefits it brought to them in the past.
It is just as a man who has received some boon from a king, and
who would, in recollection of the benefits he has had, remain also in
the future in attendance on that king.

There are, in fact, twenty-eight advantages to be gained from se- 2
cluded meditation, and they are the reason why the Tathagatas have
devoted themselves to it. They are as follows: secluded meditation
guards him who meditates, lengthens his life, gives him strength,
and shuts out faults; it removes illfame, and leads to good repute; it
drives out discontent, and makes for contentment; it removes fear,
and gives confidence; it removes sloth and generates vigor; it removes greed, hate, and delusion; it slays pride, breaks up preoccu-
pations, makes thought one-pointed, softens the mind, generates
gladness, makes one venerable, gives rise to much profit, makes one
worthy of homage, brings exuberant joy, causes delight, shows the
own-being of all conditioned things, abolishes rebirth in the world
of becoming, and it bestows all the benefits of an ascetic life. These
are the twenty-eight advantages of meditation which induce the
Tathagatas to practice it.

And it is because the Tathagatas wish to experience the calm 3
and easeful delight of meditational attainments that they practice
meditation with this end in view. Four are the reasons why the
Tathagatas tend meditation: so that they may dwell at ease; on account of the manifoldness of its faultless virtues; because it is the
road to all holy states without exception; and because it has been
praised, lauded, exalted, and commended by all the Buddhas.

2. The Practice of Introversion

With his vigor grown strong, his mind should be placed in   4
    samadhi,[2]

---

[1] **Tathagata** One of the Buddha's titles. It means "he who has thus come."
[2] **samādhi** Trancelike concentration.

For if thought be distracted we lie in the fangs of the passions.

No distractions can touch the man who's alone both in his body and   5
    mind.
Therefore renounce you the world, give up all thinking discursive!

Thirsting for gain, and loving the world, the people fail to renounce   6
    it.
But the wise can discard this love, reflecting as follows:

Through stillness joined to insight true,   7
His passions are annihilated.
Stillness must first of all be found.
That springs from disregarding worldly satisfactions.

Shortlived yourself, how can you think that others, quite as fleeting,   8
    are worthy of your love?
Thousands of births will pass without a sight of him you cherish so.

When unable to see your beloved, discontent disturbs your   9
    samadhi;
When you have seen, your longing, unsated as ever, returns as
    before.

Then you forfeit the truth of the Real; your fallen condition shocks   10
    you no longer;
Burning with grief you yearn for reunion with him whom you
    cherish.

Worries like these consume a brief life — over and over again to no   11
    purpose;
You stray from the Dharma[3] eternal, for the sake of a transient
    friend.

To share in the life of the foolish will lead to the states of woe;   12
You share not, and they will hate you; what good comes from
    contact with fools?

Good friends at one time, of a sudden they dislike you,   13
You try to please them, quite in vain — the worldly are not easily
    contented!

---

[3] **Dharma** Truth, divine law, virtue. This word has numerous meanings, depending on its context.

Advice on their duties stirs anger; your own good deeds they   14
     impede;
When you ignore what they say they are angry, and head for a state
     of woe.

Of his betters he is envious, with his equals there is strife;   15
To inferiors he is haughty, mad for praise and wroth at blame;
Is there ever any goodness in these foolish common men?

Self-applause, belittling others, or encouragement to sin,   16
Some such evil's sure to happen where one fool another meets.

Two evils meet when fools consort together.   17
Alone I'll live, in peace and with unblemished mind.

Far should one flee from fools. When met, they should be won by   18
     kindness,
Not in the hope of intimacy, but so as to preserve an even, holy,
     mind.

Enough for Dharma's work I'll take from him, just as a bee takes   19
     honey from a flower.
Hidden and unknown, like the new moon, I will live my life.

The fools are no one's friends, so have the Buddhas taught us;   20
They cannot love unless their interest in themselves impels them.

Trees do not show disdain, and they demand no toilsome wooing;   21
Fain would I now consort with them as my companions.

Fain would I dwell in a deserted sanctuary, beneath a tree, or in a   22
     cave,
In noble disregard for all, and never looking back on what I left.

Fain would I dwell in spacious regions owned by no one,   23
And there, a homeless wanderer, follow my own mind,

A clay bowl as my only wealth, a robe that does not tempt the   24
     robbers,
Dwelling exempt from fear, and careless of my body.

Alone a man is born, and quite alone he also meets his death;   25

This private anguish no one shares; and friends can only bar true
 welfare.

Those who travel through Becoming should regard each incarnation   26
As no more than a passing station on their journey through
 Samsāra.[4]

So will I ever tend delightful and untroubled solitude,   27
Bestowing bliss, and stilling all distractions.

And from all other care released, the mind set on collecting my own   28
 spirit,
To unify and discipline my spirit I will strive.

3. The Progressive Steps of Meditation

The Restraint of the Senses.   By taking your stand on mindful-   29
ness you must hold back from the sense-objects your senses, unsteady by nature. Fire, snakes, and lightning are less inimical to us
than our own senses, so much more dangerous. For they assail us all
the time. Even the most vicious enemies can attack only some
people at some times, and not at others, but everybody is always
and everywhere weighed down by his senses. And people do not go
to hell because some enemy has knocked them down and cast them
into it; it is because they have been knocked down by their unsteady
senses that they are helplessly dragged there. Those attacked by external enemies may, or may not, suffer injury to their souls; but
those who are weighed down by the senses suffer in body and soul
alike. For the five senses are rather like arrows which have been
smeared with the poison of fancies, have cares for their feathers and
happiness for their points, and fly about in the space provided by
the range of the sense-objects; shot off by Kama, the God of Love,
they hit men in their very hearts as a hunter hits a deer, and if men
do not know how to ward off these arrows they will be their undo-
ing; when they come near us we should stand firm in self-control,
be agile and steadfast, and ward them off with the great armor of
mindfulness. As a man who has subdued his enemies can everywhere live and sleep at ease and free from care, so can he who has
pacified his senses. For the senses constantly ask for more by way of
worldly objects, and normally behave like voracious dogs who can

---

[4] **Samsāra** The cycle of birth, death, and rebirth.

never have enough. This disorderly mob of the senses can never reach satiety, not by any amount of sense-objects; they are rather like the sea, which one can go on indefinitely replenishing with water.

In this world the senses cannot be prevented from being active, 30 each in its own sphere. But they should not be allowed to grasp either the general features of an object, or its particularities. When you have beheld a sight-object with your eyes, you must merely determine the basic element (which it represents, e.g., it is a "sight-object") and should not under any circumstances fancy it as, say, a woman or a man. But if now and then you have inadvertently grasped something as a "woman" or a "man," you should not follow that up by determining the hairs, teeth, etc., as lovely. Nothing should be subtracted from the datum, nothing added to it; it should be seen as it really is, as what it is like in real truth.

If you thus try to look continually for the true reality in that 31 which the senses present to you, covetousness and aversion will soon be left without a foothold. Coveting ruins those living beings who are bent on sensuous enjoyment by means of pleasing forms, like an enemy with a friendly face who speaks loving words, but plans dark deeds. But what is called "aversion" is a kind of anger directed towards certain objects, and anyone who is deluded enough to pursue it is bound to suffer for it either in this or a future life. Afflicted by their likes and dislikes, as by excessive heat or cold, men will never find either happiness or the highest good as long as they put their trust in the unsteady senses.

How the Senses Cause Bondage. A sense-organ, although it 32 may have begun to react to a sense-object, does not get caught up in it unless the mind conceives imaginary ideas about the object. Both fuel and air must be present for a fire to blaze up; so the fire of the passions is born from a combination of a sense-object with imaginations. For people are tied down by a sense-object when they cover it with unreal imaginations; likewise they are liberated from it when they see it as it really is. The sight of one and the same object may attract one person, repel another, and leave a third indifferent; a fourth may be moved to withdraw gently from it. Hence the sense-object itself is not the decisive cause of either bondage or emancipation. It is the presence or absence of imaginations which determines whether attachment takes place or not. Supreme exertions should therefore be made to bring about a restraint of the senses; for unguarded senses lead to suffering and continued becomings. In all circumstances you should therefore watch out for these enemies which cause so much evil, and you should always control them, i.e., your seeing, hearing, smelling, tasting, and touching. Do not be negligent in this matter even for a moment. The onrush of sense-experiences must be shut out with the sluice-gate of mindfulness.

Moderation in Eating.   Moreover you must learn to be moder-   33
ate in eating, and eat only enough to remain healthy, and fit for trance. For excessive food obstructs the flow of the breath as it goes in and out, induces lassitude and sleepiness, and kills all valor. And as too much food has unfortunate consequences, so also starvation does not lead to efficiency. For starvation drains away the body's volume, luster, firmness, performance, and strength. You should take food in accordance with your individual capacity, neither too much, nor, from pride, too little. As somebody with a running sore puts healing ointment on it, so the man who seeks liberation should use food only to remove his hunger. As the axle of a chariot must be lubricated so that it may work properly, so the wise man employs food only to maintain his life. He takes care of his body, and carries it along with him, not because he has any affection for it, but simply because it enables him to cross the flood of suffering. The spiritual man offers food to his body merely to dispel hunger, and not from greed, or from any love for it.

The Avoidance of Sleep.   After he has passed his day in keep-   34
ing his mind collected, the self-possessed man should shake off his sleepiness and spend also the night in the practice of Yoga.[5] When threatened with sleepiness you should constantly mobilize in your mind the factors of exertion and fortitude, of stamina and courage. You should repeat long passages from the Scriptures which you know by heart, expound them to others and reflect on them your-self. In order to keep awake all the time, wet your face with water, look round in all directions and fix your eyes on the stars. With your senses turned inwards, unmoved and well-controlled, with your mind undistracted, you should walk about or sit down at night. Fear, zest, and grief keep sleepiness away; therefore cultivate these three when you feel drowsy. Fear is best fostered by the thought of death coming upon you, zest by thinking of the blessings of the Dharma, grief by dwelling on the boundless ills which result from birth. These, and similar steps, my friend, you should take to keep awake. For what wise man would not regret sleeping away his life uselessly? In fact a wise man, who wants to be saved from the great danger, would not want to go to sleep while ignoring his

---

[5] **Yoga** Disciplined exercise designed to further self-control. A yogi or yogin is one who practices yoga.

faults, which are like vicious snakes that have crept into a house. Who would think of lying down to sleep undisturbed when the whole living world is like a house on fire, blazing with the flames of death, disease, and old age? Therefore you should recognize sleep as a darkening of your mind, and it would be unworthy of you to become absorbed in it while your faults are still with you and threaten you like enemies with their swords. The first three of the nine hours of the night you should spend in strenuous activity; then only should you rest your body, and lie down to sleep, but without relaxing your self-control. With a tranquil mind you should lie on your right side, you should look forward to the time when you will wake up and when the sun will shine again. In the third watch you should get up, and, either walking or sitting, with a pure mind and well-guarded senses, continue your practice of Yoga.

Full Awareness of the Postures, Etc.   You are further asked to   35
apply mindfulness to your sitting, walking, standing, looking, speaking, and so on, and to remain fully conscious in all your activities. The man who has imposed strict mindfulness on all he does, and remains as watchful as a gatekeeper at a city-gate, is safe from injury by the passions, just as a well-guarded town is safe from its foes. No defilement can arise in him whose mindfulness is directed on all that concerns his body. On all occasions he guards his thought, as a nurse guards a child. Without the armor of mindfulness a man is an easy target for the defilements, just as on a battlefield someone who has lost his armor is easily shot by his enemies. A mind which is not protected by mindfulness is as helpless as a sightless man walking over uneven ground without a guide. Loss of mindfulness is the reason why people engage in useless pursuits, do not care for their own true interests, and remain unalarmed in the presence of things which actually menace their welfare. And, as a herdsman runs after his scattered cows, so mindfulness runs after all the virtues, such as morality, etc., wherever they can be found. The Deathless is beyond the reach of those who disperse their attention, but it is within the grasp of those who direct their mindfulness on all that concerns the body. Without mindfulness no one can have the correct holy method; and in the absence of the holy method he has lost the true Path. By losing the true Path he has lost the road to the Deathless; the Deathless being outside his reach, he cannot win freedom from suffering. Therefore you should superintend your walking by thinking "I am walking," your standing by thinking "I am standing," and so on; that is how you are asked to apply mindfulness to all such activities.

The Advantages of Solitary Meditation.   Then, my friend, you 36
should find yourself a living-place which, to be suitable for Yoga,
must be without noise and without people. First the body must be
placed in seclusion; then detachment of the mind is easy to attain.
But those who do not like to live in solitude, because their hearts are
not at peace and because they are full of greed, they will hurt themselves there, like someone who walks on very thorny ground because he cannot find the proper road. It is no easier to deny the
urges of a man who has not seen the real truth, and who finds himself standing in the fairground of the sensory world, fascinated by its
brightness, than it is to deny those of a bull who is eating corn in the
middle of a cornfield. A brightly shining fire, when not stirred by
the wind, is soon appeased; so the unstimulated heart of those who
live in seclusion wins peace without much effort. One who delights
in solitude is content with his own company, eats wherever he may
be, lodges anywhere, and wears just anything. To shun familiarity
with others, as if they were a thorn in the flesh, shows a sound judgment, and helps to accomplish a useful purpose and to know the
taste of a happy tranquillity. In a world which takes pleasure in
worldly conditions and which is made unrestful by the sense-
objects, he dwells in solitude indifferent to worldly conditions, as
one who has attained his object, who is tranquil in his heart. The
solitary man then drinks the nectar of the Deathless, he becomes
content in his heart, and he grieves for the world made wretched by
its attachment to sense-objects. If he is satisfied with living alone for
a long time in an empty place, if he refrains from dallying with the
agents of defilement, regarding them as bitter enemies, and if, content with his own company, he drinks the nectar of spiritual exulta-
tion, then he enjoys a happiness greater than that of paradise.

remain alone — Do not pay mind to crowd.

Concentration, and the Forsaking of Idle Thoughts.   Sitting 37
cross-legged in some solitary spot, hold your body straight, and for a
time keep your attention in front of you, either on the tip of the nose
or the space on your forehead between the eyebrows. Then force
your wandering mind to become wholly occupied with one object.
If that mental fever, the preoccupation with sensuous desires,
should dare to attack you, do not give your consent, but shake it off,
as if it were dust on your clothes. Although, out of wise consideration, you may habitually eschew sense-desires, you can definitely rid
yourself of them only through an antidote which acts on them like
sunshine on darkness. There remains a latent tendency towards
them, like a fire hidden under the ashes; this, like fire by water,
must be put out by systematic meditation. As plants sprout forth

from a seed, so sense-desires continue to come forth from that latent tendency; they will cease only when that seed is destroyed. When you consider what sufferings these sense-pleasures entail, by way of their acquisition, and so on, you will be prepared to cut them off at the root, for they are false friends. Sense-pleasures are impermanent, deceptive, trivial, ruinous, and largely in the power of others; avoid them as if they were poisonous vipers! The search for them involves suffering and they are enjoyed in constant disquiet; their loss leads to much grief, and their gain can never result in lasting satisfaction. A man is lost if he expects contentment from great possessions, the fulfilment of all his wishes from entry into heaven, or happiness from the sense-pleasures. These sense-pleasures are not worth paying any attention to, for they are unstable, unreal, hollow, and uncertain, and the happiness they can give is merely imaginary.

But if ill-will or the desire to hurt others should stir your mind, 38 purify it again with its opposite, which will act on it like a wishing jewel on muddied water. Friendliness and compassionateness are, you should know, their antidotes; for they are forever as opposed to hatred as light is to darkness. A man who, although he has learned to abstain from overt immoral acts, still persists in nursing ill-will, harms himself by throwing dirt over himself, like an elephant after his bath. For a holy man forms a tender estimate of the true condition of mortal beings, and how should he want to inflict further suffering on them when they are already suffering enough from disease, death, old age, and so on? With his malevolent mind a man may cause damage to others, or he may not; in any case his own malevolent mind will be forthwith burned up. Therefore you should strive to think of all that lives with friendliness and compassion, and not with ill-will and a desire to hurt. For whatever a man thinks about continually, to that his mind becomes inclined by the force of habit. Abandoning what is unwholesome, you therefore ought to ponder what is wholesome; for that will bring you advantages in this world and help you to win the highest goal. For unwholesome thoughts will grow when nursed in the heart, and breed misfortunes for yourself and others alike. They not only bring calamities to oneself by obstructing the way to supreme beatitude, but they also ruin the affection of others, because one ceases to be worthy of it.

You must also learn to avoid confusion in your mental actions, 39 and you should, my friend, never think even one single unwholesome thought. All the ideas in your mind which are tainted by greed, hate, and delusion deprive you of virtue and fashion your bondage. Delusion injures others, brings hardship to oneself, soils the mind, and may well lead to hell. It is better for you not to hurt yourself with such unwholesome thoughts! Just as an unintelligent person might burn precious aloe wood as if it were a piece of ordinary timber, so by not observing the correct method which leads to emancipation you would waste the rare opportunities offered by a human birth. To neglect the most excellent Dharma, and instead to think demeritorious thoughts, is like neglecting the jewels on a jewel-island and collecting lumps of earth instead. A person who has won existence as a human being, and who would pursue evil rather than good, is like a traveler to the Himalayas who would feed on deadly rather than on health-giving herbs. Having understood this, try to drive out disturbing thoughts by means of their appropriate antidotes, just as one pushes a wedge out of a cleft in a log with the help of a slender counterwedge.

How to Deal with Thoughts Concerning Family and Homeland. 40 But if you start worrying about the prosperity or difficulties of your relatives, you should investigate the true nature of the world of the living, and these ideas will disappear again. Among beings whom their Karma drags along in the cycle of Samsāra, who is a stranger, who a relation? Delusion alone ties one person to another. For in the past the person who is now one of your own people happened to be a stranger to you; in the future the stranger of today will be one of your own people. Over a number of lives a person is no more firmly associated with his own people than birds who flock together at the close of day, some here, some there. Relatives are no more closely united than travellers who for a while meet at an inn, and then part again, losing sight of each other. This world is by nature split up into disjointed parts; no one really belongs to anyone else; it is held together by cause and effect, as loose sand by a clenched fist. And yet, a mother will cherish her son because she expects that he will support her, and a son loves his mother because she bore him in her womb. As long as relatives agree with each other, they display affection; but disagreements turn them into enemies. We see relatives behave unkindly, while nonrelatives may show us kindness. Men, indeed, make and break affections according to their interests. As an artist becomes enamored of a woman he has himself painted, so the affection, which a person has for another with whom he feels at one, is entirely of his own making. As for him who in another life was bound to you by ties to kinship, and who was so dear to you then, what is he to you now or you to him? Therefore it is unworthy of you to allow your mind to become preoccupied with thoughts of your relatives. In the Samsaric world there is no fixed division between your own people and other people.

And if you should hit on the idea that this or that country is 41 safe, prosperous, or fortunate, give it up, my friend, and do not entertain it in any way; for you ought to know that the world everywhere is ablaze with the fires of some faults or others. There is certain to be some suffering, either from the cycle of the seasons, or from hunger, thirst, or exhaustion, and a wholly fortunate country does not exist anywhere. Whether it be excessive cold or heat, sickness or danger, something always afflicts people everywhere; no safe refuge can thus be found in the world. And in all countries of the world people are greatly afraid of old age, disease, and death, and there is none where these fears do not arise. Wherever this body may go, there suffering must follow; there is no place in the world where it is not accompanied by afflictions. However delightful, prosperous, and safe a country may appear to be, it should be recognized as a bad country if consumed by the defilements. This world is smitten with countless ills, which affect both body and mind, and we cannot go to any country which is safe from them and where we can expect to live at ease.

Suffering is the lot of everyone, everywhere and all the time; 42 therefore, my friend, do not hanker after the glittering objects of this world! And, once this hankering is extinct in you, then you will clearly see that this entire world of the living can be said to be on fire.

How to Be Mindful of Death. But if you should make any 43 plans that do not reckon with the inevitability of death, you must make an effort to lay them down again, as if they were an illness which attacks your own self. Not even for a moment should you rely on life going on, for Time, like a hidden tiger, lies in wait to slay the unsuspecting. There is no point in your feeling too strong or too young to die, for death strikes down people whatever their circumstances, and is no respecter of youthful vitality. The body we drag along with us is a fertile soil for all sorts of mishaps, and no sensible person would entertain any firm expectation of well-being or of life. Who could ever be free from cares as long as he has to bear with this body which, as a receptacle of the four great elements, resembles a pot full of snakes at war with each other? Consider how strange and wonderful it is that this man, on drawing in his breath, can immediately afterwards breathe out again; so little can life be trusted! And this is another strange and wonderful thing that, having slept, he wakes up again, and that, having got up, he goes to sleep again; for many are the adversities of those who have a body. How can we ever feel secure from death, when from the womb onwards it follows us like a murderer with his sword raised to kill us? No man born into this world, however pious or strong he be, ever gets the better of the King of Death, either now, or in the past or the future. For when

Death in all its ferocity has arrived on the scene, no bargaining can ward him off, no gifts, no attempt at sowing dissension, no force of arms and no restraint. Our hold on life is so uncertain that it is not worth relying on. All the time Death constantly carries people away, and does not wait for them to reach the age of seventy! Who, unless he be quite mad, would make plans which do not reckon with death, when he sees the world so unsubstantial and frail, like a water bubble?

The Four Holy Truths.   Investigating the true nature of reality   44
and directing his mind towards the complete destruction of the Out-flows, the Yogin learns to understand correctly the four statements which express the four Truths, i.e., suffering, and the rest. First there is the ubiquitous fact of suffering, which can be defined as op-pression; then the cause of suffering, which is the same as its origi-nation; the extinction of suffering, which consists essentially in the definite escape from it; and finally the path which leads to tranquil-lity, and which has the essential function of saving. And those whose intellect has awakened to these four holy truths, and who have correctly penetrated to their meaning, their meditations shall overcome all the Outflows, they will gain the blessed calm, and no more will they be reborn. It is, on the other hand, through its failure to awaken to these four facts which summarize the essential nature of true reality, and through its inability to penetrate to their mean-ing, that the Samsaric world whirls round and round, that it goes from one becoming to another, and that it cannot win the blessed calm.

You should therefore, to explain it briefly, know with regard to   45
the fact of ill, that birth is the basis of all the other misfortunes, like old age, and so on; for as all plants grow on the earth, so all calami-ties grow on the soil of birth. For the birth of a body endowed with sense-organs leads of necessity to manifold ills, and the production of a person's physical existence automatically implies that of death and sickness. As food, whether good or bad, far from sustaining us becomes merely destructive when mixed with poison, so all birth into this world, whether among animals, or above or below them, tends to ill and not to ease. The numerous afflictions of living be-ings, such as old age and so on, are unavoidably produced wherever there is Worldly Activity; but even the most frightful gales could not possibly shake trees that have never been planted. Where there is a body, there must also be such sufferings as disease, old age, and so on, and likewise hunger, thirst, wetness, heat, cold, etc. And the mind which is dependent on the body involves us in such ills as

grief, discontent, anger, fear, etc. Wherever there is a psycho-physical organism, suffering is bound to take place; but for him who is liberated from it there can be no suffering, either now, or in the past, or the future.

And that suffering which we find bound up with Worldly Activity 46 in this world is caused by the multitude of the defilements, such as craving, and the rest; but it is not due to a Creator, or Primordial Matter, or Time, or the Nature of things, or Fate, or Chance. And for that reason, i.e., because all Worldly Activity is a result of the defilements, we can be sure that the passionate and the dull will die, whereas those who are without passion and dullness will not be born again.

Therefore, once you have seen, my friend, that craving, etc., are 47 the causes of the manifold ills which follow on birth, remove those causes if you want to be free from suffering; for an effect ceases when its cause has been stopped, and so also suffering becomes extinct when its cause has been quite exhausted. You must therefore come face to face with the holy, calm, and fortunate Dharma, which through dispassion has turned away from craving, which is the supreme place of rest, wherein all Worldly Activity is stopped, a shelter which abides eternally and which nothing can ever take away; that secure place which is final and imperishable, and where there is no birth, old age, death, or disease, no conjunction with unpleasant things, no disappointment over one's wishes, nor separation from what is dear. When the flame of a lamp comes to an end, it does not go anywhere down in the earth or up in the sky, nor into any of the directions of space, but because its oil is exhausted it simply ceases to burn. So, when an accomplished saint comes to the end, he does not go anywhere down in the earth or up in the sky, nor into any of the directions of space, but because his defilements have become extinct he simply ceases to be disturbed.

The wise man who wishes to carry out the sacred precepts of 48 tradition should, as a means for the attainment of this Dharma, develop the eightfold Path — three of its steps, i.e., right speech, right bodily action, and right livelihood concern morality; three, i.e., right views, right intentions, and right effort concern wisdom; two again, i.e., right mindfulness and right concentration promote tranquilizing concentration. As a result of morality the defilements no longer proliferate, as seeds no longer germinate after the right season for them has passed; for when a man's morality is pure, the vices attack his mind but halfheartedly, as if they had become ashamed. Concentration, in its turn, blocks the defilements, as a rock blocks the torrent of a mighty river; for the faults are unable to attack a man who is absorbed in trance, as if they were spellbound snakes immobilized by mantras. Wisdom, finally, completely destroys the defilements, as a river, which in the rainy season overflows its banks, sweeps away the trees that grow on them; consumed by wisdom, the faults cease to thrive and grow, like a tree burnt up by the fire which flares up after it has been struck by a thunderbolt. By entering on this eightfold path, which has morality, concentration, and wisdom for its three divisions, and which is holy, incorruptible, and straight, one forsakes those faults which are the causes of suffering, and one attains the state of absolute peace. Ten qualities are required of those who proceed along it: steadfastness, sincerity, self-respect, vigilance, seclusion from the world, contentment with little, simplicity of tastes, nonattachment, aversion to Worldly Activity, and patience. For he who discovers the true nature of ill, its origin and its cessation, can advance on the holy path, in the company of spiritual friends, towards Peace. It is like someone who correctly diagnoses a disease as a disease, and who correctly determines its cause and its cure; when treated by skilful friends he will soon be healthy again. You should therefore regard ill as a disease, the defilements as its cause, their cessation as the state of health, and the path as the remedy. What you must furthermore understand is that suffering is the same as Worldly Activity, and that it is kept going by the defilements; that their stopping is the same as inactivity, and that it is the path which leads to that. As though your turban or your clothes were on fire, so with a sense or urgency should you apply your intellect to the comprehension of the truths. It is because it fails to perceive the guidance given by these truths that the world of the living is being burnt alive. When therefore someone sees that this psychophysical organism is something that ought to be extinguished, then he has the correct vision; in consequence of his correct insight he becomes disgusted with the things of the world; and as he is no longer drawn to them, his greed gradually exhausts itself. Solemnly I assure you that his mind is definitely liberated when passion and the hope of pleasure have become extinct; and that, once his mind is well freed of those two, there is nothing further that he has to do. For I proclaim it as a fact that the effective extinction of all the Outflows lies in seeing and discerning the own-being of the psychophysical personality, its cause and its disappearance.

QUESTIONS FOR CRITICAL READING

1. What does it mean to restrain the senses?
2. According to the selection, how can restraining the senses produce the results that the Buddha desires?

3. In paragraphs 29 to 31, the Buddha complains about the unsteadiness of the senses. What does he mean? In what ways have you experienced the unsteadiness of the senses?

4. What seem to be the primary advantages of meditation? Which advantages are religious, and which are secular?

5. What is the Buddhist attitude toward the body? How does it seem to differ from western culture's current attitudes?

6. The Buddha recommends constant mindfulness. What does this entail?

7. Why should meditation be solitary? Are you convinced that solitariness is essential?

8. What does enlightenment seem to mean for the Buddha? Do you feel that it is possible for you to achieve it? How?

SUGGESTIONS FOR WRITING

1. Follow the directions for meditation as closely as possible. Try to spend at least three days meditating for ten minutes a day or longer. Record your experiences and determine the advantages of meditation for you. Reread paragraph 37 closely before beginning this experiment.

2. In paragraph 37, we find the statement "Sense-pleasures are impermanent, deceptive, trivial, ruinous, and largely in the power of others; avoid them as if they were poisonous vipers!" Obviously, this attitude is not generally shared by westerners. What is your position on the sense-pleasures? Are they as evil as the Buddha suggests? What value do they possess?

3. The Buddha suggests that greed, hate, and delusion lead people into bondage. Refer to specific historical examples or examples from your own experience to explain how this observation is true. How can such ideas potentially damage those who hold them? Does the Buddha recommend ways to avoid holding such ideas? Fashion an essay that examines these questions.

4. In paragraph 44, the Buddha states that suffering is universal. He equates suffering with oppression. Examine his teachings on this question, and relate the question of suffering to modern western society. Do you feel that oppression produces suffering today as it did in the Buddha's time? Is there a sense in which the Buddha's suggestions for the relief of suffering — implied in the techniques of meditation — would alleviate the sufferings of oppressed people in our time?

5. The noble eightfold path is discussed in paragraph 48 as well as in the introduction to this selection. Determine its applicability to your life, and take a stand on how your life would improve if you were to follow this path. Be as specific as possible, referring to definitive actions, either actual or potential, and particular relationships, either actual or potential, that would be altered in your life.

6. **CONNECTIONS** Compare the basic principles of "Meditation: The Path to Enlightenment" with the views of Plato on the trustworthiness

of the senses. How closely does the Buddha seem to agree with Plato? What distinctions make their approaches different?

7. **CONNECTIONS**   Are Francis Bacon's four idols related to the Buddha's eightfold path? Establish the distinctions and the similarities between the two programs, and decide whether they are basically compatible or incompatible. How can the Buddha's path be adapted to questions of secular knowledge? How can Bacon's four idols be applied to questions of spiritual knowledge?

8. **CONNECTIONS**   To what extent are the philosophies of Lao-tzu and the Buddha parallel in their ultimate intentions regarding the happiness of humankind? What important connections identify them as products of eastern thought? How can they be contrasted with western thought?

ST. MATTHEW
The Sermon on the Mount

MATTHEW, believed to be the author of the Gospel of St. Matthew, was also known as Levi, one of the twelve disciples of Jesus. He was a Jewish tax collector working for the Roman governors in Galilee, a region of what was then known as Palestine. His dates are uncertain, but he lived in the period of A.D. 10 to 80, and the best modern sources suggest that his gospel was composed sometime after A.D. 70 and probably written in Greek. Although some early church historians say this gospel was written originally in Hebrew, there is no evidence that a Hebrew text existed. This detail is important only because of the reputation of the Gospel of St. Matthew: it is said to be the most Jewish of the gospels. Even though it originally was addressed not to Jewish Christians but to Gentile Christians, it frequently quotes from and refers to Jewish law and the teachings and text of the Old Testament. Because the Romans repressed the Jews after their uprising in A.D. 66 to 70, few if any Jews were thought to remain in Palestine.

The Gospels of St. Matthew, St. Mark, and St. Luke are called synoptic, because they contain a great deal of the same material: the story of the ministry of Jesus. The Gospel of St. Matthew may not have been written first, as it seems to rely in part on the Gospel of St. Mark. However, it has special authority because Matthew (and not Mark or Luke) was one of Jesus' twelve disciples. Despite his importance to the early church, very little is known about Matthew, and it is uncertain whether he wrote the Gospel that bears his name or whether he was the sole author. The strongest evidence in favor of his authorship is tradition, particularly the attribution of Papias, a second-century bishop of the church.

From the King James version, 1611.

Matthew's plan in the gospel seems to have been to structure his observations in five parts, possibly emulating the Pentateuch (five books) of Moses, who is known as the law giver. Matthew is very knowledgeable about Jewish law and interprets that law through the teachings of Jesus. His focus, on at least one level, is on the details, or letter, of the law. Jesus felt the scribes and Pharisees — two groups of "righteous" citizens — concerned themselves with the details of following legal prescripts and not with the spirit of the law. Thus, it was against the law to work on the Sabbath, so pulling a donkey out of a hole on the Sabbath, thus relieving its misery, was a crime according to the Pharisees — but not to Jesus.

The Gospel of St. Matthew tells of the early life of Jesus, his activity in Galilee, including the Sermon on the Mount, which appears here, his activity in Jerusalem, and his eventual crucifixion. Matthew emphasizes Jesus' powers as a healer and the spiritual value of his message. Part of the Sermon on the Mount includes the Beatitudes (5:1 – 13), nine blessings that Jesus offers the multitude. The Gospel of St. Luke (6:20 – 23) includes four more beatitudes:

> Blessed are you poor, for yours is the kingdom of God.
> Blessed are you that hunger now, for you shall be satisfied.
> Blessed are you that weep now, for you shall laugh.
> Blessed are you when men hate you, and when they exclude you and revile you, and cast out your name as evil, on account of the Son of man! Rejoice in that day, and leap for joy, for behold, your reward is great in heaven; for so their fathers did to the prophets.

These blessings indicate the spiritual comfort that Matthew and the disciples received from the teachings of Jesus.

The Sermon on the Mount goes beyond spiritual comfort, however, by offering a guide for living as a Christian. In it, Jesus discourses on the law itself, the power of anger, adultery, lawsuits, loving one's enemies, charity, prayer, fasting, heaven, and God, as well as many other subjects. Some of this guidance is similar to the guidance that Buddha offers in his efforts to point the way to enlightenment. Thus, the Sermon on the Mount offers the followers of Jesus a pattern for faith and a prescription for moral behavior.

ST. MATTHEW'S RHETORIC

The Gospel of St. Matthew is by far the most quoted of the four gospels. Matthew's style is crisp, sharpened, and pared to a remarkable economy of expression. By fashioning statements to make them memorable, he hopes to make the sayings of Jesus available to a multitude. Expressions such as "an eye for an eye" (5:38), "whosoever shall smite thee on thy right cheek, turn to him the other also" (5:39), "judge not, that ye be not judged" (7:1), "wide *is* the gate, and broad *is* the way, that leadeth to destruction" (7:13), "false prophets . . . in sheep's clothing" (7:15), and many more are found in the selection that is presented here. Even though he borrows or modifies expressions from the Old Testament, Matthew's Gospel shows him to be a gifted literary man as well as spiritual guide.

The structure of the selection presented here is a narration of the story of Jesus' ministry, beginning with Jesus preaching to the multitude in Galilee (4:23 – 25). Chapter 5 contains the Sermon on the Mount ("he went up into a mountain," 5:1) and first examines the blessings — the beatitudes — that Jesus taught to the disciples. The Sermon on the Mount is an oral presentation of important teachings delivered directly to the disciples who have been chosen to carry out Jesus' work. The teachings continue in Chapters 6 and 7, which cover many of the important issues that had concerned people who desired to learn how to live by proper precepts. Interestingly, when Jesus came down from the mount, one of his first acts was to cleanse a leper.

Most of the following selection records what Jesus said more than what he did, and part of Matthew's skill centers on getting Jesus' words, including his tone, "right." One reason for comparing the Gospel of St. Matthew with the Gospels of St. Mark and St. Luke is to see the nuances they each perceived in Jesus' tone and manner.

Partly because Matthew is economical in his recording of Jesus' sayings, later generations have pored over them carefully in an effort to decide exactly what they mean. Matthew is able to freight expressions with a considerable range of significance. An expression such as "an eye for an eye, and a tooth for a tooth" (5:38) needs careful examination, both in the context in which Jesus uses it and in the context of the entire Bible, since it also appears in the Old Testament in Exodus (21:24). The amplification that Jesus offers the expression effectively alters its meaning to help accomplish the reinterpretation of the law that is central to Matthew's understanding of Jesus' mission. Therefore, one of the rewards of reading St. Matthew lies in the invitation to read carefully and in depth.

The Sermon on the Mount

23 And Jesus went about all Galilee, teaching in their synagogues, and preaching the gospel of the kingdom, and healing all manner of sickness and all manner of disease among the people.

24 And his fame went throughout all Syria: and they brought unto him all sick people that were taken with divers diseases and torments, and those which were possessed with devils, and those which were lunatic, and those that had the palsy; and he healed them.

25 And there followed him great multitudes of people from Galilee, and *from* Decapolis, and *from* Jerusalem, and *from* Judea, and *from* beyond Jordan.

5

And seeing the multitudes, he went up into a mountain: and when he was set, his disciples came unto him:

2 And he opened his mouth, and taught them, saying,

3 Blessed *are* the poor in spirit: for theirs is the kingdom of heaven.

4 Blessed *are* they that mourn: for they shall be comforted.

5 Blessed *are* the meek: for they shall inherit the earth.

6 Blessed *are* they which do hunger and thirst after righteousness: for they shall be filled.

7 Blessed *are* the merciful: for they shall obtain mercy.

8 Blessed *are* the pure in heart: for they shall see God.

9 Blessed *are* the peacemakers: for they shall be called the children of God.

10 Blessed *are* they which are persecuted for righteousness' sake: for theirs is the kingdom of heaven.

11 Blessed are ye, when *men* shall revile you, and persecute *you,* and shall say all manner of evil against you falsely, for my sake.

12 Rejoice, and be exceeding glad: for great *is* your reward in heaven: for so persecuted they the prophets which were before you.

13 Ye are the salt of the earth: but if the salt have lost his savor, wherewith shall it be salted? It is thenceforth good for nothing, but to be cast out, and to be trodden under foot of men.

14 Ye are the light of the world. A city that is set on a hill cannot be hid.

15 Neither do men light a candle, and put it under a bushel, but on a candlestick; and it giveth light unto all that are in the house.

16 Let your light so shine before men, that they may see your good works, and glorify your Father which is in heaven.

17 Think not that I am come to destroy the law, or the prophets: I am not come to destroy, but to fulfil.

18 For verily I say unto you, Till heaven and earth pass, one jot or one tittle shall in no wise pass from the law, till all be fulfilled.

19 Whosoever therefore shall break one of these least commandments, and shall teach men so, he shall be called the least in the kingdom of heaven: but whosoever shall do and teach *them,* the same shall be called great in the kingdom of heaven.

20 For I say unto you, That except your righteousness shall exceed *the righteousness* of the scribes and Pharisees, ye shall in no case enter into the kingdom of heaven.

21 Ye have heard that it was said by them of old time, Thou shalt not kill; and whosoever shall kill shall be in danger of the judgment:

22 But I say unto you, That whosoever is angry with his brother without a cause shall be in danger of the judgment: and whosoever shall say to his brother, Raca, shall be in danger of the council: but whosoever shall say, Thou fool, shall be in danger of hell fire.

23 Therefore if thou bring thy gift to the altar, and there rememberest that thy brother hath aught against thee;

24 Leave there thy gift before the altar, and go thy way; first be reconciled to thy brother, and then come and offer thy gift.

25 Agree with thine adversary quickly, while thou art in the way with him; lest at any time the adversary deliver thee to the judge, and the judge deliver thee to the officer, and thou be cast into prison.

26 Verily I say unto thee, Thou shalt by no means come out thence, till thou hast paid the uttermost farthing.

27 Ye have heard that it was said by them of old time, Thou shalt not commit adultery:

28 But I say unto you, That whosoever looketh on a woman to lust after her hath committed adultery with her already in his heart.

29 And if thy right eye offend thee, pluck it out, and cast *it* from thee: for it is profitable for thee that one of thy members should perish, and not *that* thy whole body should be cast into hell.

30 And if thy right hand offend thee, cut it off, and cast *it* from thee: for it is profitable for thee that one of thy members should perish, and not *that* thy whole body should be cast into hell.

31 It hath been said, Whosoever shall put away his wife, let him give her a writing of divorcement:

32 But I say unto you, That whosoever shall put away his wife, saving for the cause of fornication, causeth her to commit adultery: and whosoever shall marry her that is divorced committeth adultery.

33 Again, ye have heard that it hath been said by them of old time, Thou shalt not forswear thyself, but shalt perform unto the Lord thine oaths:

34 But I say unto you, Swear not at all; neither by heaven; for it is God's throne:

35 Nor by the earth; for it is his footstool: neither by Jerusalem; for it is the city of the great King.

36 Neither shalt thou swear by thy head, because thou canst not make one hair white or black.

37 But let your communication be, Yea, yea; Nay, nay: for whatsoever is more than these cometh of evil.

38 Ye have heard that it hath been said, An eye for an eye, and a tooth for a tooth:

39 But I say unto you, That ye resist not evil: but whosoever shall smite thee on thy right cheek, turn to him the other also.

40 And if any man will sue thee at the law, and take away thy coat, let him have *thy* cloak also.

41 And whosoever shall compel thee to go a mile, go with him twain.

42 Give to him that asketh thee, and from him that would borrow of thee turn not thou away.

43 Ye have heard that it hath been said, Thou shalt love thy neighbor, and hate thine enemy.

44 But I say unto you, Love your enemies, bless them that curse you, do good to them that hate you, and pray for them which despitefully use you, and persecute you;

45 That ye may be the children of your Father which is in heaven: for he maketh his sun to rise on the evil and on the good, and sendeth rain on the just and on the unjust.

46 For if ye love them which love you, what reward have ye? do not even the publicans the same?

47 And if ye salute your brethren only, what do ye more *than others*? do not even the publicans so?

48 Be ye therefore perfect, even as your Father which is in heaven is perfect.

6

Take heed that ye do not your alms before men, to be seen of them: otherwise ye have no reward of your Father which is in heaven.

2 Therefore when thou doest *thine* alms, do not sound a trumpet before thee, as the hypocrites do in the synagogues and in the

streets, that they may have glory of men. Verily I say unto you, They have their reward.

3 But when thou doest alms, let not thy left hand know what thy right hand doeth:

4 That thine alms may be in secret: and thy Father which seeth in secret himself shall reward thee openly.

5 And when thou prayest, thou shalt not be as the hypocrites *are:* for they love to pray standing in the synagogues and in the corners of the streets, that they may be seen of men. Verily I say unto you, They have their reward.

6 But thou, when thou prayest, enter into thy closet, and when thou hast shut thy door, pray to thy Father which is in secret; and thy Father which seeth in secret shall reward thee openly.

7 But when ye pray, use not vain repetitions, as the heathen *do:* for they think that they shall be heard for their much speaking.

8 Be not ye therefore like unto them: for your Father knoweth what things ye have need of, before ye ask him.

9 After this manner therefore pray ye: Our father which art in heaven, Hallowed be thy name.

10 Thy kingdom come. Thy will be done in earth, as *it is* in heaven.

11 Give us this day our daily bread.

12 And forgive us our debts, as we forgive our debtors.

13 And lead us not into temptation, but deliver us from evil: For thine is the kingdom, and the power, and the glory, for ever. Amen.

14 For if ye forgive men their trespasses, your heavenly Father will also forgive you:

15 But if ye forgive not men their trespasses, neither will your Father forgive your trespasses.

16 Moreover when ye fast, be not, as the hypocrites, of a sad countenance: for they disfigure their faces, that they may appear unto men to fast. Verily I say unto you, They have their reward.

17 But thou, when thou fastest, anoint thine head, and wash thy face;

18 That thou appear not unto men to fast, but unto thy Father which is in secret: and thy Father which seeth in secret shall reward thee openly.

19 Lay not up for yourselves treasures upon earth, where moth and rust doth corrupt, and where thieves break through and steal:

20 But lay up for yourselves treasures in heaven, where neither moth nor rust doth corrupt, and where thieves do not break through nor steal:

21 For where your treasure is, there will your heart be also.

22 The light of the body is the eye: if therefore thine eye be single, thy whole body shall be full of light.

23 But if thine eye be evil, thy whole body shall be full of darkness. If therefore the light that is in thee be darkness, how great *is* that darkness!

24 No man can serve two masters: for either he will hate the one, and love the other; or else he will hold to the one, and despise the other. Ye cannot serve God and mammon.

25 Therefore I say unto you, Take no thought for your life, what ye shall eat, or what ye shall drink; nor yet for your body, what ye shall put on. Is not the life more than meat, and the body than raiment?

26 Behold the fowls of the air: for they sow not, neither do they reap, nor gather into barns; yet your heavenly Father feedeth them. Are ye not much better than they?

27 Which of you by taking thought can add one cubit unto his stature?

28 And why take ye thought for raiment? Consider the lilies of the field, how they grow; they toil not, neither do they spin:

29 And yet I say unto you, That even Solomon in all his glory was not arrayed like one of these.

30 Wherefore, if God so clothe the grass of the field, which today is, and tomorrow is cast into the oven, *shall he* not much more *clothe* you, O ye of little faith?

31 Therefore take no thought, saying, What shall we eat? or, What shall we drink? or, Wherewithal shall we be clothed?

32 (For after all these things do the Gentiles seek:) for your heavenly Father knoweth that ye have need of all these things.

33 But seek ye first the kingdom of God, and his righteousness; and all these things shall be added unto you.

34 Take therefore no thought for the morrow: for the morrow shall take thought for the things of itself. Sufficient unto the day *is* the evil thereof.

7

Judge not, that ye be not judged.

2 For with what judgment ye judge, ye shall be judged: and with what measure ye mete, it shall be measured to you again.

3 And why beholdest thou the mote that is in thy brother's eye, but considerest not the beam that is in thine own eye?

4 Or how wilt thou say to thy brother, Let me pull out the mote out of thine eye; and, behold, a beam *is* in thine own eye?

5 Thou hypocrite, first cast out the beam out of thine own eye; and then shalt thou see clearly to cast out the mote out of thy brother's eye.

6 Give not that which is holy unto the dogs, neither cast ye your pearls before swine, lest they trample them under their feet, and turn again and rend you.

7 Ask, and it shall be given you; seek, and ye shall find; knock, and it shall be opened unto you:

8 For every one that asketh receiveth; and he that seeketh findeth; and to him that knocketh it shall be opened.

9 Or what man is there of you, whom if his son ask bread, will he give him a stone?

10 Or if he ask a fish, will he give him a serpent?

11 If ye then, being evil, know how to give good gifts unto your children, how much more shall your Father which is in heaven give good things to them that ask him?

12 Therefore all things whatsoever ye would that men should do to you, do ye even so to them: for this is the law and the prophets.

13 Enter ye in at the strait gate: for wide *is* the gate, and broad *is* the way, that leadeth to destruction, and many there be which go in thereat:

14 Beause strait *is* the gate, and narrow *is* the way, which leadeth unto life, and few there be that find it.

15 Beware of false prophets, which come to you in sheep's clothing, but inwardly they are ravening wolves.

16 Ye shall know them by their fruits. Do men gather grapes of thorns, or figs of thistles?

17 Even so every good tree bringeth forth good fruit; but a corrupt tree bringeth forth evil fruit.

18 A good tree cannot bring forth evil fruit, neither *can* a corrupt tree bring forth good fruit.

19 Every tree that bringeth not forth good fruit is hewn down, and cast into the fire.

20 Wherefore by their fruits ye shall know them.

21 Not every one that saith unto me, Lord, Lord, shall enter into the kingdom of heaven; but he that doeth the will of my Father which is in heaven.

22 Many will say to me in that day, Lord, Lord, have we not prophesied in thy name? and in thy name have cast out devils? and in thy name done many wonderful works?

23 And then will I profess unto them, I never knew you: depart from me, ye that work iniquity.

24 Therefore whosoever heareth these sayings of mine, and doeth them, I will liken him unto a wise man, which built his house upon a rock:

25 And the rain descended, and the floods came, and the winds blew, and beat upon that house; and it fell not: for it was founded upon a rock.

26 And every one that heareth these sayings of mine, and doeth them not, shall be likened unto a foolish man, which built his house upon the sand:

27 And the rain descended, and the floods came, and the winds blew, and beat upon that house; and it fell: and great was the fall of it.

28 And it came to pass, when Jesus had ended these sayings, the people were astonished at his doctrine:

29 For he taught them as *one* having authority, and not as the scribes.

QUESTIONS FOR CRITICAL READING

1. What is a beatitude?
2. What is Jesus' attitude toward adultery?
3. What is the connection between "an eye for an eye" (5:38) and turning the other cheek?
4. What is Jesus' teaching on charity?
5. What is of importance in Jesus' references to the "lilies of the field" (6:28)?

SUGGESTIONS FOR WRITING

1. Describe what you feel is the central spiritual message of the selection. What prescription for living does the Sermon on the Mount offer the individual? What basis of faith does Jesus seem to require of his followers? Is faith a moral issue in this selection?
2. Why should a person's faith demand a specific manner of behavior? What is the connection between actions and beliefs as St. Matthew sees it?
3. Which of the teachings of Jesus is most difficult to follow? Why? Does the emphasis that Matthew gives that teaching imply its difficulty? Which of Jesus' teachings seem problematic for Matthew?
4. Apart from the fact that the Lord's Prayer begins with "Our Father," which of Jesus' teachings are patriarchal in implication? Would following his teachings produce a patriarchal society in which women are devalued? What implications for the modern world do you derive from your analysis of this issue?
5. The expression "eye for an eye" (5:38) appears in Exodus (21:23) as well as in the Sermon on the Mount. How does Jesus modify this ex-

pression? Read both versions to make your comparison. Analyze the text carefully in this selection (5:38 – 39) for the significance of the saying.

6. What are Jesus' teachings about lawbreakers? He speaks both of a higher law to which we are to adhere and also of the ordinary laws of the land. What distinctions does he make between those laws? And what are his directives regarding our responsibility to these laws? Which contemporary legal cases reveal important distinctions that would be of interest to St. Matthew or Jesus?

7. **CONNECTIONS** How compatible are the teachings of Jesus with the teachings of the Buddha? Are both equally moral in nature? Is the question of faith more important in one than in the other? How do the ultimate goals of each text differ? How are they similar? In what ways would the path of the disciples also be the path to enlightenment?

8. **CONNECTIONS** Consider the views of those who comment on government. How would this selection be interpreted by Jefferson? By Rousseau? By Machiavelli? Which commentators on government could be considered in general alignment with the teachings of Jesus as imparted by St. Matthew?

THE BHAGAVAD GĪTĀ
Meditation and Knowledge

THE *BHAGAVAD GĪTĀ* — song (gītā) of the Lord (Bhagavat) —
is a religious poem embedded within a vastly larger epic called the
Mahabharata. Its author or authors remain unknown, as do the authors of most early Indian religious and philosophical literature.
Most estimates date the work from the first or second century A.D.
For most Hindus, the *Bhagavad Gītā* serves the same purpose as the
New Testament does for Christians. The poem is essentially a long
dialogue, with most of the speaking done by Lord Krishna to his
disciple Arjuna. (The portrait on the facing page is based on religious depictions of Lord Krishna.)

For modern thinkers concerned with Hindu philosophy and religion, an important aspect of the *Bhagavad Gītā* is its tendency toward monotheism. Although this point is still controversial, some
commentators suggest that the cult of the Bhagavata was specifically monotheistic and promoted a single god with several names:
Vishnu (the old name for the Vedic god found in the Rig Veda, one
of the most ancient of Indian religious documents), Vāsudeva (a
name used in the following text), Krishna, Hari, and Nārāyana. All
these names refer to the same person, although, as in the case of
Lord Krishna, an individual name implies a specific incarnation of
the deity. The important point is that the deity is personal. In the
Bhagavad Gītā the Lord Krishna is a strong personality, and the
monotheistic practice of establishing a personal god is clearly
present.

The Mahabharata is loosely translated as the "Great Epic of the
Bharata Dynasty." It tells of an epic battle between two great families, the Kauravas and the Pandavas. Pandu is the father of the Pan-
dava brothers, and in the *Bhagavad Gītā* one of the five brothers,

---

Translated by Franklin Edgerton, 1944.

Arjuna, is often referred to as "son of Pandu." The sole survivors of the great battle are the Pandova brothers and Krishna, who acts as Arjuna's charioteer. In the epic Krishna overcomes Arjuna's reluctance to fight the Kauravas (he is related to both families) by explaining that those who are slain only seem to be slain, while those who slay only seem to slay. These actions are illusions. By freeing the soul from illusions and imparting the truth, the teachings of the *Bhagavad Gītā* aim to help readers set free their souls.

In his introduction, Franklin Edgerton, the translator and interpreter of the passages selected here, explains some of the basic beliefs of Hinduism in this fashion: "First, *pessimism:* all empiric existence is evil. Second, *transmigration,* with the doctrine of *karma:* all living beings are subject to an indefinite series of reincarnations, and the conditions of each incarnation are determined by the moral quality of acts performed in previous incarnations. Third, *salvation* lies in release from this chain of existences; it is to be gained primarily by knowledge of the supreme truth." The world of the senses — empiric existence — is beguiling and potentially destructive because it generates desires and desires entangle the soul and condemn it to further incarnations. The goal of the individual is to gain the knowledge of the truth necessary to put an end to the soul's transmigration — movement from being to being — and reunite it with the great oversoul, sometimes referred to as the Brahman.

The *Bhagavad Gītā* is divided into eighteen chapters that in some versions and translations are called Yogas. Thus, for the two chapters that appear here, Chapter 6 is sometimes called The Yoga of Meditation, and Chapter 7 is sometimes called The Yoga of Spirit and Nature. Calling each chapter a Yoga identifies the text as a meditation leading to wisdom. Although the materials of meditation offered in specific verses will sometimes appear to introduce contradictions, it is important to keep in mind that the text as we have it is not concerned with a logical consistency and will sometimes appear to move in several directions simultaneously.

Chapter 6 focuses on the "Discipline of Meditation," and the way to knowledge of Krishna through discipline. As Krishna says in verse 46, "The man of discipline is higher than men of austerities, / Also than men of knowledge he is held to be higher; / And the man of discipline is higher than men of ritual action; / Therefore be a man of discipline, Arjuna." In this, Krishna offers advice that parallels both that of the Buddha and that of Jesus in St. Matthew's gospel. The first verse of Chapter 6 recommends action ("action that is required") and the "renunciation and discipline (of action)." Thus, according to Krishna, some action is necessary, but action ultimately must give way to discipline and knowledge of the truth.

The discourse on the self is meaningful especially in relation to the invitation to Arjuna to be disciplined. When Lord Krishna says "the self is the self's only friend, / And the self is the self's only enemy" (6:5 – 6), he reminds Arjuna that the important thing is what happens within him. The disciplined person retires to meditation, fixing the mind on a "single object" as a means to "practise / Discipline unto self-purification" (6:12). Lord Krishna offers some advice about temperate eating habits, temperate behavior, and a path toward freeing one from "all desires" (6:18). These are preliminary to becoming disciplined, which is preliminary to gaining knowledge.

Chapter 7, called "Discipline of Theoretical and Practical Knowledge," continues the message of Krishna. It begins with the invitation to focus on Krishna and to know "Me in very truth" (7:3). He reminds Arjuna that many begin the struggle toward truth but only a few have the endurance to continue the way. Lord Krishna reveals in the early verses that he has two natures, the lower nature being the things of the world that may be perceived, such as the basic natural elements of verse 4, and the higher invisible self (Spirit). Thus, Krishna can say "I am taste in water," "I am light in the moon and sun, / The sacred syllable (*om*) in all the Vedas, / Sound in ether, manliness in men" (verse 8). Krishna says "On Me all this (universe) is strung, / Like heaps of pearls on a string" (verse 7), echoing in a remarkable way the theories of Michio Kaku in Part Five of this book.

The chapter ends with a concern for knowledge. In verse 26 Krishna says, "I know those that are past, / And that are present, Arjuna, / And beings that are yet to be, / But no one knows Me." And in the last verse, after having praised knowledge and "the possessor of knowledge, constantly disciplined" (7:17), Lord Krishna says, "And (who know) Me even at the hour of death, / They (truly) know (Me), with disciplined hearts" (7:30).

THE RHETORIC
OF THE BHAGAVAD GĪTĀ

The *Bhagavad Gītā* is written in very high quality verse within a poem whose own standards of poetic excellence are high. Some English translations render the text in prose, and this translation is essentially prose that is set up to look like poetry and that tries to maintain the poetic nature of the original by supplying some of the prayer-like repetition of the original. As with all texts that are scriptural in nature, the text does not present an argument but rather a system of recommended behavior. Such texts make no effort to convince readers why the proper behavior should be followed but simply tell you what that behavior is.

Although it is found within a long narrative poem, the *Bhagavad Gītā* does not tell a story. The most important and obvious rhetorical device the text uses is the dialogue. In this sense, it shares the same rhetorical structure Plato uses in most of his writings. However, the *Bhagavad Gītā* does not invite response from Arjuna. In Chapter 7, Arjuna does not speak at all. In Chapter 6, when he does speak, he explains how difficult it is for anyone to do the things Krishna demands. When Lord Krishna explains that the mind must be disciplined thoroughly, Arjuna replies, "fickle is the thought-organ, Krishna, / Impetuous, mighty, and hard; / The restraining of it, I conceive, / Is very difficult, as of the wind" (6:34). Lord Krishna is gentle with Arjuna and reassures him that by "practice" (6:35) it is possible to bring the "impetuous" organ under control.

The use of careful comparisons helps illuminate specific teachings of Lord Krishna, as when he compares the disciplined person to "a lamp stationed in a windless place / [that] Flickers not" (6:19). But the text relies on only a few such comparisons, choosing to be more direct and specific. Careful repetition is one strategy of the text, while another is the variety achieved by using different names to address Arjuna. "Son of Kuntī," "son of Kuru," and "son of Parathā" are all used to address Arjuna and remind the reader of Arjuna's ancestors. This is similar to the lists of ancestors sometimes provided in the Bible.

Ultimately, the *Bhagavad Gītā* is a text that is intended to be examined in detail and depth. It is compressed, as we expect of all poetry, and needs expansion. Many modern editions of the *Bhagavad Gītā* offer extensive interpretations between most of the verses, and most of them do not print merely the verses as they appear in this book. For most modern editors the interlineated commentary is as important as the verses themselves. For us, part of the pleasure of the text is meditating on its possible meanings.

Meditation and Knowledge

Chapter 6

The Blessed One said:

Not interested in the fruit of action,   1
    Who does action that is required (by religion),
He is the possessor of both renunciation and discipline (of action);
    Not he who builds no sacred fires and does no (ritual) acts.

What they call renunciation,   2
    Know that that is discipline (of action), son of Paṇḍu.
For not without renouncing purpose
    Does any one become possessed of discipline.

For the sage that desires to mount to discipline   3
    Action is called the means;
For the same man when he has mounted to discipline
    Quiescence is called the means.

For when not to the objects of sense   4
    Nor to actions is he attached,
Renouncing all purpose,
    Then he is said to have mounted to discipline.

One should lift up the self by the self,   5
    And should not let the self down;
For the self is the self's only friend,
    And the self is the self's only enemy.

The self is a friend to that self   6
    By which self the very self is subdued;
But to him that does not possess the self, in enmity
    Will abide his very self, like an enemy.

Of the self-subdued, pacified man,   7
    The supreme self remains concentrated (in absorption),
In cold and heat, pleasure and pain,
    Likewise in honor and disgrace.

His self satiated with theoretical and practical knowledge,   8
    Immovable, with subdued senses,
The possessor of discipline is called (truly) disciplined,
    To whom clods, stones, and gold are all one.

To friend, ally, foe, remote neutral, 9
    Holder of middle ground, object of enmity, and kinsman,
To good and evil men alike,
    Who has the same mental attitude, is superior.

Let the disciplined man ever discipline 10
    Himself, abiding in a secret place,
Solitary, restraining his thoughts and soul,
    Free from aspirations and without possessions.

In a clean place establishing 11
    A steady seat for himself,
That is neither too high nor too low,
    Covered with a cloth, a skin, and kuśa-grass,

There fixing the thought-organ on a single object, 12
    Restraining the activity of his mind and senses,
Sitting on the seat, let him practise
    Discipline unto self-purification.

Even body, head, and neck 13
    Holding motionless, (keeping himself) steady,
Gazing at the tip of his own nose,
    And not looking in any direction,

With tranquil soul, rid of fear, 14
    Abiding in the vow of chastity,
Controlling the mind, his thoughts on Me,
    Let him sit disciplined, absorbed in Me.

Thus ever disciplining himself, 15
    The man of discipline, with controlled mind,
To peace that culminates in nirvāṇa,[1]
    And rests in Me, attains.

But he who eats too much has no discipline, 16
    Nor he who eats not at all;
Neither he who is over-given to sleep,
    Nor yet he who is (ever) wakeful, Arjuna.

Who is disciplined (moderate) in food and recreation, 17
    And has disciplined activity in works,
And is disciplined in both sleep and wakefulness,
    To him belongs discipline that bans misery.

---

[1] **nirvāṇa** Enlightenment; the end of material existence.

When the thought, controlled,   18
  Settles on the self alone,
The man free from longing for all desires
  Is then called disciplined.

As a lamp stationed in a windless place   19
  Flickers not, this image is recorded
Of the disciplined man controlled in thought,
  Practising discipline of the self.

When the thought comes to rest,   20
  Checked by the practice of discipline,
And when, the self by the self
  Contemplating, he finds satisfaction in the self;

That supernal bliss which   21
  Is to be grasped by the consciousness and is beyond the
    senses,
When he knows this, and not in the least
  Swerves from the truth, abiding fixed (in it);

And which having gained, other gain   22
  He counts none higher than it;
In which established, by no misery,
  However grievous, is he moved;

This (state), let him know, — from conjunction with misery   23
  The disjunction, — is known as discipline;
With determination must be practised this
  Discipline, with heart undismayed.

The desires that spring from purposes   24
  Abandoning, all without remainder,
With the thought-organ alone the throng of senses
  Restraining altogether,

Little by little let him come to rest   25
  Thru the consciousness, held with firmness;
Keeping the thought-organ fixed in the self,
  He should think on nothing at all.

Because of whatsoever thing strays   26
  The thought-organ, fickle and unstable,
From every such thing holding it back,
  He shall bring it into control in the self alone.

For to him when his thought-organ is tranquil,   27
  To the disciplined one, supreme bliss
Approaches, his passion stilled,
  Become (one with) Brahman, stainless.

Thus ever disciplining himself,   28
     The disciplined man, free from stain,
Easily to contact with Brahman,
     To endless bliss, attains.

Himself as in all beings,   29
     And all beings in himself,
Sees he whose self is disciplined in discipline,
     Who sees the same in all things.

Who sees Me in all,   30
     And sees all in Me,
For him I am not lost,
     And he is not lost for Me.

Me as abiding in all beings whoso   31
     Reveres, adopting (the belief in) one-ness,
Tho abiding in any possible condition,
     That disciplined man abides in Me.

By comparison with himself, in all (beings)   32
     Whoso sees the same, Arjuna,
Whether it be pleasure or pain,
     He is deemed the supreme disciplined man.

     Arjuna said:

This discipline which by Thee has been explained   33
     As indifference, Slayer of Madhu,
Thereof I do not see
     Any permanent establishment, because of (man's) fickleness.

For fickle is the thought-organ, Kṛṣṇa,   34
     Impetuous, mighty, and hard;
The restraining of it, I conceive,
     Is very difficult, as of the wind.

     The Blessed One said:

Without doubt, great-armed one,   35
     The thought-organ is hard to control, and fickle;
But by practice, son of Kuntī,
     And by ascetic aversion, it may be controlled.

For one not self-controlled, discipline   36
     Is hard to reach, I believe;
But by the self-controlled man who strives
     It may be attained thru the proper method.

     Arjuna said:

An unsuccessful striver who is endowed with faith,   37
     Whose mind falls away from discipline

Without attaining perfection of discipline,
  To what goal does he go, Kṛṣṇa?

Fallen from both, does he not   38
  Perish like a cloven cloud,
Having no (religious) foundation, great-armed one,
  Gone astray on Brahman's path?

This matter, my doubt, O Kṛṣṇa,   39
  Be pleased to cleave without remainder;
Other than Thee, of this doubt
  No cleaver, surely, can be found.

The Blessed One said:

Son of Pṛthā, neither in this world nor in the next   40
  Does any destruction of him occur.
For no doer of the right
  Comes to a bad end, my friend.

Attaining the heavenly worlds of the doers of right,   41
  Dwelling there for endless years,
In the house of pure and illustrious folk
  One that has fallen from discipline is born.

Or else of possessors of discipline, rather,   42
  Enlightened folk, in their family he comes into existence;
For this is yet harder to attain,
  Such a birth as that in the world.

There that association of mentality   43
  He obtains, which was his in his former body;
And he strives from that point onward
  Unto perfection, son of Kuru.

For by that same former practice   44
  He is carried on even without his wish.
Even one who (merely) wishes to know discipline
  Transcends the word-Brahman (the Vedic religion).

But striving zealously,   45
  With sins cleansed, the disciplined man,
Perfected thru many rebirths,
  Then (finally) goes to the highest goal.

The man of discipline is higher than men of austerities,   46
  Also than men of knowledge he is held to be higher;
And the man of discipline is higher than men of ritual action;
  Therefore be a man of discipline, Arjuna.

Of all men of discipline, moreover,   47
  With inner soul gone to Me

Whoso reveres Me with faith,
  Him I hold the most disciplined.

   Here ends the Sixth Chapter, called Discipline of Meditation.

Chapter 7

  The Blessed One said:

With mind attached to Me, son of Pṛthā,   1
  Practising discipline with reliance on Me,
Without doubt Me entirely
  How thou shalt know, that hear!

Theoretical knowledge to thee along with practical   2
  I shall now expound completely;
Having known which, in this world no other further
  Thing to be known is left.

Among thousands of men   3
  Perchance one strives for perfection;
Even of those that strive and are perfected,
  Perchance one knows Me in very truth.

Earth, water, fire, wind,   4
  Ether, thought-organ, and consciousness,
And I-faculty: thus My
  Nature is divided eight-fold.

This is My lower (nature). But other than this,   5
  My higher nature know:
It is the Life (soul), great-armed one,
  By which this world is maintained.

Beings spring from it,   6
  All of them, be assured.
Of the whole world I am
  The origin and the dissolution too.

Than Me no other higher thing   7
  Whatsoever exists, Dhanaṃjaya;[2]
On Me all this (universe) is strung,
  Like heaps of pearls on a string.

I am taste in water, son of Kuntī,   8
  I am light in the moon and sun,

---

[2] **Dhanaṃjaya** Winner of good fortune.

The sacred syllable (*om*) in all the Vedas,
  Sound in ether, manliness in men.

Both the goodly odor in earth,   9
  And brilliance in fire am I,
Life in all beings,
  And austerity in ascetics am I.

The seed of all beings am I,   10
  The eternal, be assured, son of Pṛthā;
I am intelligence of the intelligent,
  Majesty of the majestic am I.

Might of the mighty am I, too,   11
  (Such as is) free from desire and passion;
(So far as it is) not inconsistent with right, in creatures
  I am desire, O best of Bharatas.

Both whatsoever states are of (the Strand) goodness,   12
  And those of (the Strands) passion and darkness too,
Know that they are from Me alone;
  But I am not in them; they are in Me.

By the three states[3] (of being), composed of the Strands,   13
  These (just named), all this world,
Deluded, does not recognize
  Me that am higher than they and eternal.

For this is My divine strand-composed   14
  Trick-of-illusion, hard to get past;
Those who resort to Me alone
  Penetrate beyond this trick-of-illusion.

Not to Me do deluded evil-doers   15
  Resort, base men,
Whom this illusion robs of knowledge,
  Who cleave to demoniac estate.

Fourfold are those that worship Me,   16
  (All) virtuous folk, Arjuna:
The afflicted, the knowledge-seeker, he who seeks personal ends,
  And the possessor of knowledge, bull of Bharatas.

Of these the possessor of knowledge, constantly disciplined,   17
  Of single devotion, is the best;
For extremely dear to the possessor of knowledge
  Am I, and he is dear to Me.

---

[3] **states** Goodness, passion, and darkness. These are known as the gunas (primal qualities) of nature.

All these are noble;   18
   But the man of knowledge is My very self, so I hold.
For he with disciplined soul has resorted
   To Me alone as the highest goal.

At the end of many births   19
   The man of knowledge resorts to Me;
Who thinks 'Vāsudeva (Kṛṣṇa) is all,'
   That noble soul is hard to find.

Deprived of knowledge by this or that desire,   20
   Men resort to other deities,
Taking to this or that (religious) rule,
   Constrained by their own nature.

Whatsoever (divine) form any devotee   21
   With faith seeks to worship,
For every such (devotee), faith unswerving
   I ordain that same to be.

He, disciplined with that faith,   22
   Seeks to propitiate that (divine being),
And obtains therefrom his desires,
   Because I myself ordain them.

But finite fruition for them   23
   That becomes, (since) they are of scant intelligence;
The worshipers of the gods go to the gods,
   My devotees go to Me also.

Unmanifest, as having come into manifestation   24
   Fools conceive Me,
Not knowing the higher essence
   Of Me, which is imperishable, supreme.

I am not revealed to every one,   25
   Being veiled by My magic trick-of-illusion;
'Tis deluded and does not recognize
   Me the unborn, imperishable, — this world.

I know those that are past,   26
   And that are present, Arjuna,
And beings that are yet to be,
   But no one knows Me.

It arises from desire and loathing,   27
   The delusion of the pairs (of opposites), son of Bharata;
Because of it all beings to confusion
   Are subject at their birth, scorcher of the foe.

But those whose sin is ended,   28
   Men of virtuous deeds,
Freed from the delusion of the pairs,
   Revere Me with firm resolve.

Unto freedom from old age and death   29
   Those who strive, relying on Me,
They know that Brahman entire,
   And the over-soul, and action altogether.

Me together with the over-being and the over-divinity,   30
   And with the over-worship, whoso know,
And (who know) Me even at the hour of death,
   They (truly) know (Me), with disciplined hearts.

   Here ends the Seventh Chapter, called Discipline of Theoretical
and Practical Knowledge.

QUESTIONS FOR CRITICAL READING

1. What is the connection between renouncing purpose and discipline
   (see Chapter 6, verses 1 and 2)?
2. How does one renounce purpose? Does it mean renouncing action?
3. What action does the sage use to "mount to discipline" (6:3)?
4. What does Lord Krishna tell us about the senses and their role in coming to know him?
5. What is the "supernal bliss" that Lord Krishna describes (6:21)?
6. Is it possible to tell what kinds of sins a person must be "cleansed" of
   before achieving the "highest goal" (6:45)?
7. What is the knowledge Lord Krishna refers to (7:2)?
8. Explain the role devotion has in the discipline Lord Krishna describes.

SUGGESTIONS FOR WRITING

1. In this selection, Lord Krishna is in the form of Arjuna's charioteer on
   the field of battle and is speaking directly to Arjuna. What constitutes
   the issues of faith in this dialogue? What faith does Lord Krishna demand of Arjuna? Lord Krishna explains his nature in Chapter 7. What
   about his explanation would test the faith of Arjuna? Why is faith important to Lord Krishna? He says, "Whoso reveres Me with faith, / Him
   I hold the most disciplined" (6:47). What, then, is the relationship of
   faith and discipline?

2. Is it true that "the self is the self's only friend, / And the self is the self's only enemy" (6:5)? In what ways is this verse generally true for people? Cite examples that can validate or invalidate the insight of that verse.

3. Beginning with verse 10 in Chapter 6, describe the method the Lord Krishna recommends for achieving discipline. Is such discipline possible? How could you achieve it in today's world? What obstacles would you face? What are your chances of success?

4. Lord Krishna constantly refers to the "disciplined man." Do you feel these chapters are patriarchal in their message? Does Lord Krishna mean to exclude women from his teachings, or does the term "man" include all people? What about the message in these chapters convinces you that it is inclusive of feminist values or perhaps ignores them?

5. In a brief essay, explain the relation that Lord Krishna sees between the body and the soul, between nature and spirit.

6. **CONNECTIONS** Compare the discipline described by Lord Krishna with the disciplines recommended by the Buddha and Jesus in the Gospel of St. Matthew. In what ways are they similar, and in what important ways are they dissimilar? Is it possible to isolate important differences between these three writings?

THE PROPHET MUHAMMAD
From *the Koran*

THE PROPHET MUHAMMAD (A.D. c. 570 – c. 632) was born
in Mecca in what is now Saudi Arabia. Mecca is the holiest city in
Islam in part for that reason. He was born a few months after his father died and became an orphan six years later when his mother
died. For reasons of health he spent part of his early life with nomadic tribes outside Mecca. Families in Mecca belonged to tight
knit clans, some of which held great power. His family, led by an
uncle, Abu Talib, was part of the Hashim, a strong clan involved in
trading with Syria. In around 595, while in his middle twenties and
on a trading journey with his uncle, he managed the merchandise
of a wealthy older woman, Khadijah, who was so impressed with
him that she agreed to marriage. The marriage was successful and
produced a number of children, two boys who died young and four
daughters who survived. When Khadijah died in 619, Muhammad
inherited her fortune and achieved independence.

Muhammad was a deeply religious man in early life. In Mecca
during his youth, religion was marked by idol worship and pagan-
ism centering on a sacred site called the Ka'bah. Some time around
610 Muhammad began having visions and revelations, which he believed were given to him by the Archangel Gabriel. He was much
shaken by these revelations, but his wife Khadijah reassured and
encouraged him to welcome them. Gabriel told him, "You are the
messenger of God." The word *messenger* may also be translated as
"apostle." In Arabic, it is *rasūl,* and he was described as *rasūl Allah*
(messenger of God). As far as is known, because Muhammad was
illiterate, he memorized these revelations, which the angel Gabriel
told him came directly from God, and they were later written down

Translated by N. J. Dawood, 1956.

by others early in the period during which the revelations occurred. They were gathered together in written form around 650.

In 613, Muhammad began preaching in response to his revelations and was early known as the Prophet. He faced derision at
first. Meccans claimed he was possessed by spirits and that he was
a shaman, not a true prophet, or a mere poet — because the Koran
is in rhymed Arabic prose. In response he claimed this as proof
that the Koran was a miracle, which his followers accepted.
Nonetheless, he was generally ridiculed and rejected by people in
his own clan and by others who denied him their business.

He eventually drew followers — about thirty-nine at first but
growing soon to seventy. At the time of Muhammad Mecca had no
powerful central religion. The idols in the Ka'bah and the place itself were important, but most citizens were involved in mercantile
activities and devoted little energy to religion. Muhammad, on the
other hand, was fervent in his beliefs and seems to have represented a threat to the order of Mecca as early as 620, when he took
the famous "night journey" to Jerusalem and envisioned heaven.
Later, in 622 he began the *Hejira*, the emigration from Mecca to
Medina with his followers, sending them off in small groups and
taking a circuitous route to avoid assassination. Muhammad's religion was known as Islam, meaning something close to "surrender
to God's will," and his followers were known as Muslims — those
who have surrendered — and it is from this year, 622, that the
Muslims begin their modern era.

The following years were filled with struggle as the number of
Muslims increased. Raids on trading parties of both Meccans and
Muslims led to battles between relatively large armies. Most of the
struggles were won by Muhammad, but in 625 at the battle of
Uhud the Muslims were defeated. Because Muhammad firmly believed that the will of God determines victory, the experience of defeat shook the faith of his followers. His opponents were unable to
take advantage of their victory, however, and Muhammad soon restored faith in his followers and pressed forward.

In the year 627 Muhammad defeated a large Meccan army that
attacked him at Medina. In the same year he expelled a Jewish clan,
al-Nadīr, from Medina on the grounds that it was conspiring
against him and attacked and dispersed the Jewish clan of the
Qurayzah on the same grounds. Although by 628 Muhammad and
his followers were strong enough to enforce a truce with Mecca, his
men soon were attacked by groups associated with Mecca, and
Muhammad gathered ten thousand men to attack Mecca. When he
arrived in 630, however, the city essentially gave up without a
fight, and Muhammad triumphed. Most Meccans converted to

Islam even though Muhammad did not make that a condition of surrender. He sent his messengers to other parts of the Middle East to encourage other nations to convert to Islam and to recognize the Muslims as a formidable power in the Arab world.

By the time he died, his movement had grown enormously. Islam was destined to spread throughout the entire Arab world and beyond, rapidly becoming one of the world's largest religions.

THE RHETORIC OF THE KORAN

The Koran was composed in prose but with rhymes that were sometimes very close and sometimes rather distant. According to Arab scholars, there is no adequate way to translate the Koran, and therefore the English version that follows, like all non-Arabic versions, must be regarded as a paraphrase rather than a strict translation. The beauty of the original Arabic often depends on the sounds of words and their association with the words' meaning. But it also depends on the subtlety of possible interpretations resulting from careful ambiguities designed to produce a richly significant text. Many of these qualities are lost in English.

On the other hand, the sense that this is a text from a holy book is plain in terms of its resemblance to the Bible. Muhammad was aware of the Jewish Bible and the Christian New Testament. In the Koran he saw that the Muslims now had their own holy book. The Koran consists of 114 surahs, or chapters. The names of the surahs usually relate to a detail in the surah or to the subject of the surah. Examples are "The Ant," surah 27; "Smoke," surah 44; "The Hypocrites," surah 63; "The Soul-Snatchers," surah 79. "The Believer" is surah 40 and is also sometimes called "The Forgiving One." The order of the surahs is not chronological but traditional. The order of composition is uncertain, although surah 93, "Daylight," is sometimes cited as the first.

"The Believer" begins with an untranslatable Arabic letter: *Hā' mīm.* The Koran contains several such expressions that are undefinable. N. J. Dawood, the translator, says that "Traditional commentators dismiss them by saying 'God alone knows what He means by these letters.' " The surah opens by telling us that it is "revealed by God" and then goes on to explain the fate of unbelievers.

God speaks directly to Muhammad, usually speaking as "we" but sometimes shifting to "I" or "he." The shifting point of view may imply the all-inclusive nature of God. The use of dialogue is characteristic of the text, but narrative is also introduced early on. The story of Moses (para. 13 – 32) demonstrates how God sends his messages to the world and how believers will respond to those messages. Noah (para. 3) was a believer who built the ark in response to the word he received from God. The willingness of unbelievers to be violent toward him is an important detail, just as is Pharaoh's willingness to slay infants and children in order to "slay Moses" (para. 15).

For religious purposes, the most important rhetorical quality of the text is its use of declarations such as "He reveals to you His signs" (para. 53), coupled with questions to the listener, such as "Which of God's signs do you deny?" (para. 53). This method involves the listener in an active role, while also imparting the truth. Jewish and Christian wisdom books also used these techniques, particularly interspersing rhetorical questions to keep the listener alert to the need eventually to answer to his God.

"The Believer" is especially important because it contrasts those who believe in Allah with those who believe in idols. It is said that when Muhammad returned triumphantly to Mecca, he entered the Ka'bah, approached each of the more than one hundred idols, and reached from his camel with his stick to knock over each idol as he said: "The truth has come." "The Believer" is about the truth that has come and describes the necessity of faith in a God who supplants all idols and all others.

From *the Koran*

The Believer

In the Name of God, the Compassionate, the Merciful

Hā' mīm. This Book is revealed by God, the Mighty One, the All-knowing, who forgives sin and accepts repentance. 1

His punishment is stern, and His bounty infinite. There is no god but Him. All shall return to Him. 2

None but the unbelievers dispute the revelations of God. Do not be deceived by their prosperous dealings in the land. Long before them the people of Noah denied Our revelations, and so did the factions after them. Every nation strove to slay their apostle, seeking with false arguments to refute the truth; but I smote them, and how stern was My punishment! Thus shall the word of your Lord be fulfilled concerning the unbelievers: they are the heirs of the Fire. 3

Those who bear the Throne and those who stand around it give　4
glory to their Lord and believe in Him. They implore forgiveness for
the faithful, saying: "Lord, you embrace all things with Your mercy
and Your knowledge. Forgive those that repent and follow Your
path. Shield them from the scourge of Hell. Admit them, Lord, to
the gardens of Eden which You have promised them, together with
all the righteous among their fathers, their spouses, and their descendants. You are the Almighty, the Wise One. Deliver them from
all evil. He whom You will deliver from evil on that day will surely
earn Your mercy. That is the supreme triumph."

But to the unbelievers a voice will cry: "God's abhorrence of you　5
is greater than your hatred of yourselves. You were called to the
Faith, but you denied it."

They shall say: "Lord, twice have You made us die, and twice　6
have You given us life. We now confess our sins. Is there no way
out?"

They shall be answered: "This is because when God was in-　7
voked alone, you disbelieved; but when you were bidden to serve
other gods besides Him you believed in them. Today judgement
rests with God, the Most High, the Supreme One."

It is He who reveals His signs to you, and sends down suste-　8
nance from the sky for you. Yet none takes heed except the repen-
tant. Pray, then, to God and worship none but Him, however much
the unbelievers may dislike it.

Exalted and throned on high, He lets the Spirit descend at His　9
behest on those of His servants whom He chooses, that He may
warn them of the day when they shall meet Him; the day when they
shall rise up from their graves with nothing hidden from God. And
who shall reign supreme on that day? God, the One, the Almighty.

On that day every soul shall be paid back according to what it　10
did. On that day none shall be wronged. Swift is God's reckoning.

Forewarn them of the approaching day, when men's hearts will　11
leap up to their throats and choke them; when the wrongdoers will
have neither friend nor intercessor to be heard. He knows the furtive
look and the secret thought. God will judge with fairness, but the
idols to which they pray besides Him can judge nothing. God alone
hears all and observes all.

Have they never journeyed through the land and seen what was　12
the end of those who have gone before them, nations far greater in
prowess and in splendour? God scourged them for their sins, and
from God they had none to protect them. That was because their
apostles had come to them with clear revelations and they denied
them. So God smote them. Mighty is God, and stern His retribution.

We sent forth Moses with Our signs and with clear authority to 13 Pharaoh, Haman, and Korah. But they said: "A sorcerer, a teller of lies."

And when he brought them the Truth from Ourself, they said: 14 "Put to death the sons of those who share his faith, and spare only their daughters." Futile were the schemes of the unbelievers.

Pharaoh said: "Let me slay Moses, and then let him invoke his 15 god! I fear that he will change your religion and spread disorder in the land."

Moses said: "I take refuge in my Lord and in your Lord from 16 every tyrant who denies the Day of Reckoning."

But one of Pharaoh's kinsmen, who in secret was a true believer, 17 said: "Would you slay a man merely because he says: 'My Lord is God'?" He has brought you evident signs from your Lord. If he is lying, may his lie be on his head; but if he is speaking the truth, a part at least of what he threatens will smite you. God does not guide the lying transgressor. Today you are the masters, my people, illustrious throughout the earth. But who will save us from the might of God when it bears down upon us?"

Pharaoh said: "I have told you what I think. I will surely guide 18 you to the right path."

He who was a true believer said: "I warn you, my people, 19 against the fate which overtook the factions: the people of Noah, 'Ād, and Thamūd, and those that came after them. God does not seek to wrong His servants.

"I warn you, my people, against the day when men will cry out to 20 one another, when you will turn and flee, with none to defend you against God. He whom God confounds shall have none to guide him. Long before this, Joseph came to you with veritable signs, but you never ceased to doubt them; and when he died you said: 'After him God will never send another apostle.' Thus God confounds the doubting transgressor. Those who dispute God's revelations, with no authority vouchsafed to them, are held in deep abhorrence by God and by the faithful. Thus God seals up the heart of every scornful tyrant."

Pharaoh said to Haman: "Build me a tower that I may reach the 21 highways — the very highways — of the heavens, and look upon the god of Moses. I am convinced that he is lying."

Thus was Pharaoh seduced by his foul deeds, and he was turned 22 away from the right path. Pharaoh's cunning led to nothing but perdition.

He who was a true believer said: "Follow me, my people, that I 23 may guide you to the right path. My people, the life of this world is a fleeting comfort, but the life to come is an everlasting mansion. Those that do evil shall be rewarded with like evil; but those that have faith and do good works, both men and women, shall enter the gardens of Paradise and therein receive blessings without number.

"My people, how is it that I call you to salvation, while you call 24 me to the Fire? You bid me deny God and serve other gods I know nothing of; while I exhort you to serve the Almighty, the Benignant One. Indeed, the gods to whom you call me can be invoked neither in this world nor in the hereafter. To God we shall return. The transgressors are the heirs of the Fire.

"Bear in mind what I have told you. To God I commend myself. 25 God is cognizant of all His servants."

God delivered him from the evils which they planned, and a 26 grievous scourge encompassed Pharaoh's people. They shall be brought before the Fire morning and evening, and on the day the Hour strikes, a voice will cry: "Mete out to the people of Pharaoh the sternest punishment!"

And when they argue in the Fire, the humble will say to those 27 who deemed themselves mighty: "We have been your followers: will you now ward off from us some of these flames?" But those who deemed themselves mighty will reply: "Here are all of us now. God has judged His servants."

And those in the Fire will say to the keepers of Hell: "Implore 28 your Lord to relieve our torment for one day!"

"But did your apostles not come to you with undoubted signs?" 29 they will ask.

"Yes," they will answer. And their keepers will say: "Then offer 30 your prayers." But vain shall be the prayers of the unbelievers.

We shall help Our apostles and the true believers both in this 31 world and on the day when the witnesses rise to testify. On that day no excuse will avail the guilty. The Curse shall be their lot, and the scourge of the hereafter.

We gave Moses Our guidance and the Israelites the Book to in- 32 herit: a guide and an admonition to men of understanding. Therefore have patience; God's promise is surely true. Implore forgiveness for your sins, and celebrate the praise of your Lord evening and morning.

As for those who dispute the revelations of God, with no au- 33 thority vouchsafed to them, they nurture in their hearts ambitions they shall never attain. Therefore seek refuge in God; it is He that hears all and observes all.

Surely, the creation of the heavens and the earth is greater than 34 the creation of man; yet most men have no knowledge.

The blind and the seeing are not equal, nor are the wicked the 35 equal of those that have faith and do good works. Yet do you seldom give thought.

The Hour of Doom is sure to come: of this there is no doubt;   36
and yet most men do not believe.

Your Lord has said: "Call on me and I will answer you. Those   37
that disdain My service shall enter Hell with all humility."

It was God who made for you the night to rest in and the day to   38
give you light. God is bountiful to men, yet most men do not give
thanks.

Such is God your Lord, the Creator of all things. There is no   39
god but Him. How then can you turn away from Him? Yet even thus
the men who deny God's revelations turn away from Him.

It is God who has made the earth a dwelling-place for you, and   40
the sky a ceiling. He has moulded your bodies into a comely shape
and provided you with good things.

Such is God, your Lord. Blessed be God, Lord of the Universe.   41

He is the Living One; there is no god but Him. Pray to Him,   42
then, and worship none besides Him. Praise be to God, Lord of the
Universe!

Say: "I am forbidden to serve your idols, now that clear proofs   43
have been given me from my Lord. I am commanded to surrender
myself to the Lord of the Universe."

It was He who created you from dust, then from a little germ,   44
and then from a clot of blood. He brings you infants into the world;
you reach manhood, then decline into old age (though some of you
die young), so that you may complete your appointed term and
grow in wisdom.

It is He who ordains life and death. If He decrees a thing, He   45
need only say: "Be," and it is.

Do you not see how those who dispute the revelations of God   46
turn away from the right path? Those who have denied the Book and
the message We sent through Our apostles shall realize the truth hereafter: when, with chains and shackles round their necks, they shall be
dragged through scalding water and burnt in the fire of Hell.

They will be asked: "Where are the gods whom you have served   47
besides God?"

"They have forsaken us," they will reply. "Indeed, they were   48
nothing, those gods to whom we prayed." Thus God confounds the
unbelievers.

And they will be told: "That is because on earth you took de-   49
light in falsehoods, and led a wanton life. Enter the gates of Hell and
stay therein for ever. Evil is the home of the arrogant."

Therefore have patience: God's promise is surely true. Whether   50
We let you[1] glimpse in some measure the scourge We threaten them

---

[1] Muḥammad. [Translator's note]

with, or call you back to Us before We smite them, to Us they shall return.

We sent forth other apostles before your time; of some We have al- 51 ready told you, of others We have not yet told you. None of those apostles could bring a sign except by God's leave. And when God's will was done, justice prevailed and there and then the disbelievers lost.

It is God who has provided you with beasts, that you may ride 52 on some and eat the flesh of others. You put them to many uses; they take you where you wish to go, carrying you by land as ships carry you by sea.

He reveals to you His signs. Which of God's signs do you deny? 53

Have they never journeyed through the land and seen what was 54 the end of those who have gone before them? More numerous were they in the land, and far greater in prowess and in splendour; yet all their labours proved of no avail to them.

When their apostles brought them veritable signs they proudly 55 boasted of their own knowledge; but soon the scourge at which they scoffed encompassed them. And when they beheld Our might they said: "We now believe in God alone. We deny the idols which We served besides Him."

But their new faith was of no use to them, when they beheld 56 Our might: such being the way of God with His creatures; and there and then the unbelievers lost.

QUESTIONS FOR CRITICAL READING

1. What are the characteristics of a believer?
2. To what extent are faith and belief the same? To what extent are they different?
3. What does the believer believe?
4. What does God promise to the believer?
5. How might one describe the tone of God's words in this surah?
6. Why is punishment meted out to people? What behavior deserves punishment?
7. What signs does God reveal to humanity?
8. What is the meaning of "Mighty is God, and stern his retribution" (para. 12)?

SUGGESTIONS FOR WRITING

1. According to this surah, what are the qualities of God? Choose specific passages that help you understand the qualities of God. See especially

paragraphs 8 to 12. What are God's concerns? What are God's views about the world and the history that He describes?

2. What does God expect of men and women? Why does he speak so earnestly to Muhammad? What are God's views of humanity? Find passages that establish these concerns.

3. When Muhammad experienced these revelations, idol worship was common in Mecca. Is idol worship common in modern life? What might be considered our modern idols? Write an essay that clarifies the nature of modern idol worship and that contrasts that kind of worship with the belief that is promoted in this surah.

4. For Muhammad, what is the fate of unbelievers? Does their fate differ widely from the fate of unbelievers in your own religion? If you are not religious, compare the fate of the unbeliever in this surah with the fate of unbelievers in any religion that you know enough about to speak confidently.

5. **CONNECTIONS**   In paragraphs 23 to 25 "He who was a true believer" is described in action. In what ways does this description compare with Matthew's description of Jesus? The Koran refers often to Joseph and Mary as well as to Jesus, who is considered a prophet. Compare the portraits of Matthew's Jesus with the "true believer" in "The Believer."

6. **CONNECTIONS**   In the Bhagavad Gītā Lord Krishna reveals himself to Arjuna, and in "The Believer" Allah reveals himself to Muhammad. How are these portrayals of the Lord similar and different? What are His concerns for humanity? How does He view the nature of men and women?

ST. TERESA OF AVILA
The Raptures of St. Teresa

TERESA DE CEPEDA Y AHUMADA (1515–1582) was born in Avila, Spain, in the central region of Castile. One of ten children in an aristocratic family, she was twelve when her mother, then only thirty-three, died. Her father, with another two children by his first marriage, placed her in a religious boarding school to give her proper training. Despite her father's strong disapproval, Teresa decided that she wanted to join the church and become a nun. While she was at home recovering from an illness, she "eloped" to a Carmelite convent and began the process of taking the veil, and her father relented in his anger soon after. In 1538 Teresa contracted a mysterious illness that left her in a coma for three days, during most of which she was thought to be dead. She recovered but was partially paralyzed for several years after. Much of her life was spent in residual pain.

Teresa lived a life filled with controversy, especially after gaining the approval of the leader of the Carmelites to begin reforming the order and to found new convents throughout Spain. She enlisted St. John of the Cross (1542–1591), a Carmelite friar and great mystical Spanish poet, also born in Castile, to help her by reforming the male Carmelites. Much of this activity brought difficulties with it because many Carmelites resisted changes in the order. Her emphasis was on prayer, and much of her writing concerns the exercise of prayer and meditation. Relying on prayer and on her ability to influence important churchmen, Teresa was able to achieve a great deal during her lifetime and was beatified in 1614 and canonized in 1622 — a remarkably short time after her death. She was a woman of action as well as a woman possessed by intense mystical experiences.

From *The Autobiography of St. Teresa of Avila,* translated by E. Allison Peers, 1960.

Among her many works is *The Book of Her Life,* most of which was written by 1562 and which was finished in 1565. The selection which appears here is Chapter 29 from that book. *The Book of Her Life* was written at the suggestion of her confessors, among them García de Toledo and Domingo Báñez, both of whom were close to her and deeply concerned when she revealed that she had visions of Jesus and of angels.

Writing this book entailed many dangers. While Teresa of Avila was writing, the Inquisition was at its height in Spain. The Inquisition claimed as its purpose rooting out the work of the devil in all its forms, and some of those forms involved diabolic seductions, especially of nuns. A respected nun with influence at court was arrested and imprisoned in 1532 for diabolical possession, and it was clear that one's aristocratic status would not guarantee protection if the Inquisition determined that the devil was at work. Consequently, Teresa's book was gone over very carefully by her confessors, and the manuscripts that still exist show corrections, excisions, and changes in the handwriting of her confessors, who essentially acted as editors. The changes are not great or critical for the modern reader. But only after they were made was it possible for others to read her work.

Teresa was a prolific writer. After writing the *Life,* she went on to write a handbook for Carmelite nuns called *The Way of Perfection* (c. 1565). Her directors encouraged this project, but because it was much more ambitious in scope than they had expected, they directed her to revise it when it was completed. She did so, but enlarged the book to include commentary not only on matters of prayer but on day-to-day life in the convent. Its audience was the sisters of the convent, and it was designed to help make their lives richer. The writing of *The Interior Castle,* one of her most influential books concerning the power of prayer, began in 1577, after Teresa received a vision of the entire book, and continued with interruptions until 1580. Like her other books, it was reviewed carefully by her directors and eventually published despite its sometimes unusual content.

The selection that appears here concerns Teresa's visions of Jesus and the angels. She describes her visions very carefully in this chapter and in other chapters in her *Life,* claiming that at first she was able to see only the hands of Jesus, then later his face, and then eventually his body. She emphasizes that she saw his human form as resurrected and that sometimes Jesus showed her his wounds. Sometimes Jesus appeared with a crown of thorns and sometimes bearing the cross. These visions naturally disturbed her confessors, some of whom were convinced that she was being beguiled by the devil. But other important church authorities listened closely to her and believed that the visions she had were divine and of great significance.

Part of the teaching of the Carmelites insisted on the union of the individual with God. The visions of St. Teresa reinforced this teaching, emphasizing her direct contact with Jesus. But the special qualities of her visions emphasize a personal rapture and ecstasy that seem to surpass normal human feelings. Teresa describes them with great care, reminding her readers that she realizes that no one who has not experienced the visions could ever understand what they are like or understand the significance they have in spiritual life. At the end of this chapter Teresa talks of the ecstatic feelings that accompany one of her most intense experiences with the appearance of an angel. The result is to communicate the expansiveness of the religious experience rather than to restrict herself to discussing the benefits of discipline alone.

ST. TERESA'S RHETORIC

Authorities differ in their assessments of Teresa's style and her rhetorical intentions. One recent translator sees her as a writer with relatively little skill but with an immediacy and simplicity of style, and another sees her as unsophisticated and hasty. Some modern commentators, however, see her as a careful writer who knew her audience and knew how to communicate with both her male confessors and her female convent sisters. Teresa frequently complains that she is unworthy and that her writing skills are poor, but such expressions of humility are common in writing of the period.

Those who knew her and watched her write marveled at the fact that she rarely paused or hesitated in her writing and that she rarely if ever crossed out a word. They compared her with professional scribes. Because her important managerial responsibilities as well as responsibilities for founding convents, took her all over Spain, she often left her writing for long periods of time. She was obligated to break off in the middle of the writing of *The Interior Castle,* and when she returned to it much later, she asks for forgiveness if she repeats herself because she had no time to reread what she had written and had a bad memory to begin with.

Such a confession may well be exactly what it says it is: she may have worked intensely and felt pressured to finish her work. But the result is that the reader feels an immediacy with St. Teresa that is born out of the intimacy that her confession reveals. Her language is colloquial, and her style is relaxed and easy. She avoids formality. She often speaks in generalities and rarely loads a sentence with unwanted details and unneeded information. One feels that she is trying to make the reader feel at ease by noting common experiences and common interests.

In earlier chapters, Teresa discussed the visions she had and the problems that are associated with them — including the fear that the visions might have been sent to her from the devil. She explains that she thought of such a possibility right away but that it is impossible. Later, she explains how her confessors taught her to confront the vision of Jesus, to discover whether it is a devilish fraud. When she reveals her conflicted emotions as she snaps her fingers at Jesus, we understand how she feels even though we have never had her visions. She is able to help us understand even the most unintelligible of human experiences by virtue of her directness and simplicity.

Teresa's simplicity and directness reveal the depth of her faith in the goodness of the visions she has received. She has such intense belief in Jesus that she believes she is in his presence, much the way Arjuna is in the presence of Lord Krishna in the *Bhagavad Gītā*. But her faith is in her union with God, and the raptures that are associated with this faith are clearly communicated in this selection.

The Raptures of St. Teresa

I have strayed far from any intention, for I was trying to give the reasons why this kind of vision cannot be the work of the imagination. How could we picture Christ's Humanity by merely studying the subject or form any impression of His great beauty by means of the imagination? No little time would be necessary if such a reproduction was to be in the least like the original. One can indeed make such a picture with one's imagination, and spend time in regarding it, and considering the form and the brilliance of it; little by little one may even learn to perfect such an image and store it up in the memory. Who can prevent this? Such a picture can undoubtedly be fashioned with the understanding. But with regard to the vision which we are discussing there is no way of doing this: we have to look at it when the Lord is pleased to reveal it to us — to look as He wills and at whatever He wills. And there is no possibility of our subtracting from it or adding to it, or any way in which we can obtain it, whatever we may do, or look at it when we like or refrain from looking at it. If we try to look at any particular part of it, we at once lose Christ.

For two years and a half things went on like this and it was 2 quite usual for God to grant me this favor. It must now be more than three years since He took it from me as a continually recurring favor, by giving me something else of a higher kind, which I shall describe later. Though I saw that He was speaking to me, and though I was looking upon that great beauty of His, and experiencing the sweetness with which He uttered those words — sometimes stern words — with that most lovely and Divine mouth, and though, too, I was extremely desirous of observing the color of His eyes, or His height, so that I should be able to describe it, I have never been sufficiently worthy to see this, nor has it been of any use for me to attempt to do so; if I tried, I lost the vision altogether. Though I sometimes see Him looking at me compassionately, His gaze has such power that my soul cannot endure it and remains in so sublime a rapture that it loses this beauteous vision in order to have the greater fruition of it all. So there is no question here of our wanting or not wanting to see the vision. It is clear that the Lord wants of us only humility and shame, our acceptance of what is given us and our praise of its Giver.

This refers to all visions, none excepted. There is nothing that 3 we can do about them; we cannot see more or less of them at will; and we can neither call them up nor banish them by our own efforts. The Lord's will is that we shall see quite clearly that they are produced, not by us but by His Majesty. Still less can we be proud of them: on the contrary, they make us humble and fearful, when we find that, just as the Lord takes from us the power of seeing what we desire, so He can also take from us these favours and His grace, with the result that we are completely lost. So while we live in this exile let us always walk with fear.

Almost invariably the Lord showed Himself to me in His resur- 4 rection body, and it was thus, too, that I saw Him in the Host. Only occasionally, to strengthen me when I was in tribulation, did He show me His wounds, and then He would appear sometimes as He was on the Cross and sometimes as in the Garden. On a few occasions I saw Him wearing the crown of thorns and sometimes He would also be carrying the Cross — because of my necessities, as I say, and those of others — but always in His glorified flesh. Many are the affronts and trials that I have suffered through telling this and many are the fears and persecutions that it has brought me. So sure were those whom I told of it that I had a devil that some of them wanted to exorcise me. This troubled me very little, but I was

sorry when I found that my confessors were afraid to hear my confessions or when I heard that people were saying things to them
against me. None the less, I could never regret having seen these
heavenly visions and I would not exchange them for all the good
things and delights of this world. I always considered them a great
favor from the Lord, and I think they were the greatest of treasures;
often the Lord Himself would reassure me about them. I found my
love for Him growing exceedingly: I used to go to Him and tell Him
about all these trials and I always came away from prayer comforted
and with new strength. I did not dare to argue with my critics, because I saw that that made things worse, as they thought me lacking
in humility. With my confessor, however, I did discuss these matters; and whenever he saw that I was troubled he would comfort me
greatly.

   As the visions became more numerous, one of those who had   5
previously been in the habit of helping me and who used sometimes
to hear my confessions when the minister was unable to do so,
began to say that it was clear I was being deceived by the devil. So,
as I was quite unable to resist it, they commanded me to make the
sign of the Cross whenever I had a vision, and to snap my fingers at
it so as to convince myself that it came from the devil, whereupon it
would not come again: I was not to be afraid, they said, and God
would protect me and take the vision away. This caused me great
distress: as I could not help believing that my visions came from
God, it was a terrible thing to have to do; and, as I have said, I could
not possibly wish them to be taken from me. However, I did as they
commanded me. I besought God often to set me free from deception; indeed, I was continually doing so and with many tears. I
would also invoke Saint Peter and Saint Paul, for the Lord had told
me (it was on their festival that He had first appeared to me) that
they would prevent me from being deluded; and I used often to see
them very clearly on my left hand, though not in an imaginary vision. These glorious Saints were in a very real sense my lords.

   To be obliged to snap my fingers at a vision in which I saw the   6
Lord caused me the sorest distress. For, when I saw Him before me,
I could not have believed that the vision had come from the devil
even if the alternative were my being cut to pieces. So this was a
kind of penance to me, and a heavy one. In order not to have to be
so continually crossing myself, I would carry a cross in my hand.
This I did almost invariably; but I was not so particular about snap-
ping my fingers at the vision, for it hurt me too much to do that. It
reminded me of the way the Jews had insulted Him, and I would beseech Him to forgive me, since I did it out of obedience to him who
was in His own place, and not to blame me, since he was one of the

ministers whom He had placed in His Church. He told me not to worry about it and said I was quite right to obey, but He would see that my confessor learned the truth. When they made me stop my prayer He seemed to me to have become angry, and He told me to tell them that this was tyranny. He used to show me ways of knowing that the visions were not of the devil; some of these I shall describe later.

Once, when I was holding in my hand the cross of a rosary, He 7 put out His own hand and took it from me, and, when He gave it back to me, it had become four large stones, much more precious than diamonds — incomparably more so, for it is impossible, of course, to make comparisons with what is supernatural, and diamonds seem imperfect counterfeits beside the precious stones which I saw in that vision. On the cross, with exquisite workmanship, were portrayed the five wounds. He told me that henceforward it would always look to me like that, and so it did: I could never see the wood of which it was made, but only these stones. To nobody, however, did it look like this except to myself. As soon as they had begun to order me to test my visions in this way, and to resist them, the favors became more and more numerous. In my efforts to divert my attention from them, I never ceased from prayer; even when asleep I used to seem to be praying, for this made me grow in love. I would address my complaints to the Lord, telling Him I could not bear it. Desire and strive to cease thinking of Him as I would, it was not in my power to do so. In every respect I was as obedient as I could be, but about this I could do little or nothing, and the Lord never gave me leave to disobey. But, though He told me to do as I was bidden. He reassured me in another way, by teaching me what I was to say to my critics; and this He does still. The arguments with which He provided me were so conclusive that they made me feel perfectly secure.

Shortly after this, His Majesty began to give me clearer signs of 8 His presence, as He had promised me to do. There grew within me so strong a love of God that I did not know who was inspiring me with it, for it was entirely supernatural and I had made no efforts to obtain it. I found myself dying with the desire to see God and I knew no way of seeking that life save through death. This love came to me in vehement impulses, which, though less unbearable, and of less worth, than those of which I have spoken previously, took from me all power of action. For nothing afforded me satisfaction and I was incapable of containing myself: it really seemed as though my soul were being torn from me. O sovereign artifice of the Lord, with what subtle diligence dost Thou work upon Thy miserable slave! Thou didst hide Thyself from me, and out of Thy love didst oppress me with a death so delectable that my soul's desire was never to escape from it.

No one who has not experienced these vehement impulses can 9 possibly understand this: it is no question of physical restlessness within the breast, or of uncontrollable devotional feelings which occur frequently and seem to stifle the spirit. That is prayer of a much lower kind, and we should check such quickenings of emotion by endeavoring gently to turn them into inward recollection and to keep the soul hushed and still. Such prayer is like the violent sobbing of children: they seem as if they are going to choke, but if they are given something to drink their superabundant emotion is checked immediately. So it is here: reason must step in and take the reins, for it may be that this is partly accountable for by the temperament. On reflection comes a fear that there is some imperfection, which may in great part be due to the senses. So this child must be hushed with a loving caress which will move it to a gentle kind of love; it must not, as they say, be driven at the point of the fist. Its love must find an outlet in interior recollection and not be allowed to boil right over like a pot to which fuel has been applied indiscriminately. The fire must be controlled at its source and an endeavor must be made to quench the flame with gentle tears, not with tears caused by affliction, for these proceed from the emotions already referred to and do a great deal of harm. I used at first to shed tears of this kind, which left my brain so distracted and my spirit so wearied that for a day or more I was not fit to return to prayer. Great discretion, then, is necessary at first so that everything may proceed gently and the operations of the spirit may express themselves interiorly; great care should be taken to prevent operations of an exterior kind.

These other impulses are very different. It is not we who put on 10 the fuel; it seems rather as if the fire is already kindled and it is we who are suddenly thrown into it to be burned up. The soul does not try to feel the pain of the wound caused by the Lord's absence. Rather an arrow is driven into the very depths of the entrails, and sometimes into the heart, so that the soul does not know either what is the matter with it or what it desires. It knows quite well that it desires God and that the arrow seems to have been dipped in some drug which leads it to hate itself for the love of this Lord so that it would gladly lose its life for Him. No words will suffice to describe the way in which God wounds the soul and the sore distress which He causes it, so that it hardly knows what it is doing. Yet so delectable is this distress that life holds no delight which can give greater satisfaction. As I have said, the soul would gladly be dying of this ill.

This distress and this bliss between them bewildered me so 11 much that I was never able to understand how such a thing could be. Oh, what it is to see a wounded soul — I mean when it understands its condition sufficiently to be able to describe itself as wounded for so excellent a cause! It sees clearly that this love has come to it through no act of its own, but that, from the exceeding great love which the Lord bears it, a spark seems suddenly to have fallen upon it and to have set it wholly on fire. Oh, how often, when in this state, do I remember that verse of David: *Quemadmodum desiderat cervus ad fontes aquarum,*[1] which I seem to see fulfilled literally in myself!

When these impulses are not very strong they appear to calm down a little, or, at any rate, the soul seeks some relief from them because it knows not what to do. It performs certain penances, but is quite unable to feel them, while the shedding of its blood causes it no more distress than if its body were dead. It seeks ways and means whereby it may express something of what it feels for the love of God; but its initial pain is so great that I know of no physical torture which can drown it. There is no relief to be found in these medicines: they are quite inadequate for so sublime an ill. A certain alleviation of the pain is possible, which may cause some of it to pass away, if the soul begs God to grant it relief from its ill, though it sees none save death, by means of which it believes it can have complete fruition of its Good. At other times the impulses are so strong that the soul is unable to do either this or anything else. The entire body contracts and neither arm nor foot can be moved. If the subject is on his feet, he remains as though transported and cannot even breathe: all he does is to moan — not aloud, for that is impossible, but inwardly, out of pain.

It pleased the Lord that I should sometimes see the following vision. I would see beside me, on my left hand, an angel in bodily form — a type of vision which I am not in the habit of seeing, except very rarely. Though I often see representations of angels, my visions of them are of the type which I first mentioned. It pleased the Lord that I should see this angel in the following way. He was not tall, but short, and very beautiful, his face so aflame that he appeared to be one of the highest types of angel who seem to be all afire. They must be those who are called cherubim: they do not tell me their names but I am well aware that there is a great difference between certain angels and others, and between these and others still, of a kind that I could not possibly explain. In his hands I saw a

12

13

---

[1] Psalm xli, 1 [A.V., xlii, 1]: "As the hart panteth after the fountains of water, so my soul panteth after thee, O God." [Translator's note]

long golden spear and at the end of the iron tip I seemed to see a point of fire. With this he seemed to pierce my heart several times so that it penetrated to my entrails. When he drew it out, I thought he was drawing them out with it and he left me completely afire with a great love for God. The pain was so sharp that it made me utter several moans; and so excessive was the sweetness caused me by this intense pain that one can never wish to lose it, nor will one's soul be content with anything less than God. It is not bodily pain, but spiritual, though the body has a share in it — indeed, a great share. So sweet are the colloquies of love which pass between the soul and God that if anyone thinks I am lying I beseech God in His goodness, to give him the same experience.

During the days that this continued, I went about as if in a stupor. I had no wish to see or speak with anyone, but only to hug my pain, which caused me greater bliss than any that can come from the whole of creation. I was like this on several occasions, when the Lord was pleased to send me these raptures, and so deep were they that, even when I was with other people, I could not resist them; so, greatly to my distress, they began to be talked about. Since I have had them, I do not feel this pain so much, but only the pain of which I spoke somewhere before — I do not remember in what chapter. The latter is, in many respects, very different from this, and of greater worth. But, when this pain of which I am now speaking begins, the Lord seems to transport the soul and to send it into an ecstasy, so that it cannot possibly suffer or have any pain because it immediately begins to experience fruition. May He be blessed for ever, Who bestows so many favors on one who so ill requites such great benefits.

QUESTIONS FOR CRITICAL READING

1. Why does Teresa say her visions could not be the work of the imagination? Why do you agree or disagree with her?
2. How does she describe Jesus?
3. How did people react to her visions? What did they propose? Why was she concerned with what they thought?
4. How did Teresa approach the vision to determine whether it was from the devil?
5. What is Teresa's attitude toward her visions?
6. Why do you think Teresa's experiences are possible or impossible?

SUGGESTIONS FOR WRITING

1. Much of the content of Teresa's writing relies on erotic imagery. The teachings of the Carmelites emphasized the fact that Jesus was the spouse to which the church aspired. How do you react to the central vision of the angel piercing Teresa with the arrow? Is this Freudian imagery of sexual repression, or is it the fulfillment of the "marriage" of the church and Jesus?

2. How would you describe the faith that Teresa has in her religious beliefs? What sustains her? How does the Jesus of her visions strengthen her faith?

3. Depending only on this passage from *The Life,* what would you say is the duty of the person who believes as Teresa does? What moral obligations would such a person have? What religious duties would such a person be expected to keep? What role would contemplation or meditation play in the life of such a person?

4. What role do the five senses have in the religious life of St. Teresa? Are they dangerous? Are they essential to the religious life? Which senses seem to dominate in Teresa's descriptions of her experiences?

5. If you have had an experience that few — if any — other people have had, compare your efforts to communicate it with those of Teresa's. Describe your experiences, and explain what problems are involved in communicating them. Teresa, for example, describes her visions with great exactness, including her emotional state and emotional reaction. Yet she says that no one will believe her and no one would possibly understand her who has not gone through the same experience.

6. **CONNECTIONS**   If you have read Nietzsche's "Apollonianism and Dionysianism," decide whether St. Teresa is Apollonian or Dionysian in her approach to religion. What evidence convinces you one way or the other? Give a careful account of your views of Teresa's experiences that supports your argument.

7. **CONNECTIONS**   St. Matthew spent time with Jesus. Compare his description of Jesus with that of Teresa. What is different? How does the emotional content of each author differ? How does it seem similar? What does beauty mean for each of these writers? How does the term apply to Jesus?

8. **CONNECTIONS**   What similarities do you find between Lord Krishna's revealing himself to Arjuna and Jesus' revealing himself to Teresa? Are these both religious experiences of the same kind, or are they completely different? What are the similarities and differences?

FRIEDRICH NIETZSCHE
Apollonianism and Dionysianism

FRIEDRICH NIETZSCHE (1844 – 1900), one of the most influential modern thinkers, was concerned that the rise of science in the modern world and the changes in attitudes toward religion and the nature of God would leave people with a loss of purpose. Like many historians and philosophers of the day, he feared that modern civilization itself was somehow hanging in the balance, and that unless people struggled to reclaim the spiritual energy that brought progress and prosperity, the foundations of society would collapse.

His solution for the malaise that he felt was settling on modern society involved a search for meaning through a form of introspection and self-understanding that might well have been intelligible to Buddha, Plato, or St. Matthew. For Nietzsche, self-mastery was the key to transcending the confusion of modern thought. Realizing that self-domination was not an easy state to achieve, he called the man who succeeded in mastering himself "superman" — a man who could create his own values instead of blindly following conventional or societal standards.

Nietzsche's own personal life was difficult. His minister-father died when he was four, leaving Nietzsche to be raised by a household of women. Some critics have felt that the antifemale tone in certain of his writings is a result of his upbringing, but it also may be related to the syphilis that he may have contracted from a prostitute when he was a young man.

He was a brilliant student, particularly of the classics, and he became a professor at the University of Basel at a young age. His

---

From *The Birth of Tragedy from the Spirit of Music.* Translated by Francis Golffing.

first book, *The Birth of Tragedy from the Spirit of Music* (1872), is the result of his effort to clarify certain aspects of the music of Richard Wagner, the contemporary composer who created a mythology depicting Scandinavian gods for his Ring Cycle of operas. Nietzsche eventually broke with Wagner on philosophical matters, but his regard for Wagner's music remained strong. The insight on which *The Birth of Tragedy* rests, presented in the selection reprinted here, is an attempt to clarify the two basic religious forces in humankind: Apollonian intellectuality and Dionysian passion. The first reflects the thoughtfulness associated with the god Apollo, whose symbols were the bow and the lyre, implying his fierceness as a god of conscience combined with his love of the arts and music. The second reflects the god Dionysus, a deity associated with vegetation, plentifulness, passion, and especially wine. Both were sons of Zeus, and each represented extremes in behavior, whether religious or secular.

Both forces were present in ancient Greek society, which Nietzsche takes as a standard of high civilization, particularly in its Doric phase — a phase of clear, calm, beautiful works of religious expression, such as the Parthenon in Athens. Although Apollonian qualities appear to oppose Dionysian qualities, Nietzsche notes that the Greeks discovered the need for both forces to be present in their culture. Greek tragedy, he says, was the ground on which these forces were able to meet in ancient Greece. In Nietzsche's time — as he points out in a section not included here — they meet in the music of Richard Wagner.

The kinds of personal behavior countenanced by these two gods are quite different, but each god represents an aspect of the larger divinity. The rational qualities of Apollonianism approximate the ideals of Plato and Aristotle, whereas the ecstatic qualities of Dionysianism come closer to the views of some saints, such as Teresa of Avila. The distinction between these two states of mind is considerable, but both are associated with artistic expression and religious practice throughout the world.

Nietzsche relies on art to help him clarify the distinction between each of these Greek gods. Apollo dominates intellectually. He demands clarity, order, reason, and calm. He is also the god of the individual. Dionysus, on the other hand, is the god of ecstasy and passion. Obscurity, disorder, irrational behavior, even hysteria are encouraged by Dionysus. He is the god of throngs and mobs. After reading this excerpt, we can realize that most of us have both capacities within us and that one of life's challenges is learning how to balance them.

NIETZSCHE'S RHETORIC

The most obvious rhetorical device Nietzsche uses is comparison and contrast. The Apollonian contrasts with the Dionysian, the Greek with the barbarian, the dream with the illusion, the god with the human, the individual with the group, the one with the many, even life with death. In this sense, the subject at hand has governed the basic shape of the work.

Nietzsche's task was to explain the polarities, their form of expression, and their effect. Since these terms were quite new to most contemporary readers, he took time to clarify the nature of the Apollonian and the Dionysian. In a sense, the first paragraphs are spent in the task of definition. Once each polarity is defined, Nietzsche goes on to explain its sphere of influence, its nature, and its implications. Insofar as those qualities are present in the rhetoric, this essay is itself Apollonian.

There is a surprise in Nietzsche's use of rhetoric here, however. Through rhetorical techniques, he also illustrates some aspects of the Dionysian nature. There are passages in the selection, such as the discussion of Dionysus in paragraph 5, that can best be described as ecstatic, poetic, and, if not irrational, certainly obscure and difficult to grasp. The Dionysian aspects of the passage are based on feeling. We all know that some poems cannot be broken down into other words — or even explained to others. What we extract from such poems is not an understanding but a complex feeling or impression. The same is true of the passages we confront in this essay. They challenge us because we know that the general character of any essay must be Apollonian. When we are greeted by Dionysian verbal excursions, we are thrown off. Yet that is part of Nietzsche's point: verbal artifacts (such as Greek tragedy) can combine both forces.

Nietzsche's most important point may be that the original religious forces implied by both gods are expressed in the modern world in terms of art. It has become something of a commonplace for contemporary people to assert that the emotion that went into religion in the time of the Greeks or in the great age of the cathedrals in Europe is now expressed in art. The power of Wagnerian music and Wagnerian opera, whose shape borrows some aspects from Greek tragedy, would have been as much a religious experience as an aesthetic experience for many people. Apollo was the god around whom the muses gathered, and therefore he was a caretaker of music, poetry, and dance. Dionysus was the god to whom the citizens of Athens sacrificed when they put on their great tragic competitions. The City Dionysia was the most important of the celebrations involving Greek drama, and its god was Dionysus.

If it can be said that religious faith can be embodied in dramatic art, then it might be said that for the ancients it was present in the work of the Greek tragedians, for the Elizabethans it was present in Shakespeare, and for Nietzsche's contemporaries it was in Wagner's Ring Cycle. The ultimate effect of using the rhetorical device of comparison and contrast is to emphasize the need for these two forces to be unified in the highest cultures. Diversity is everywhere in nature, as Nietzsche implies throughout, but that diversity has one deep longing: to be one with the One. As he says (para. 14), the eternal goal of the original Oneness is its redemption through illusion. Illusion is art, not just dream. Great artists of all ages understood that dream and illusion are the means of art and make accessible the inner nature of humanity.

Apollonianism and Dionysianism

Much will have been gained for esthetics once we have succeeded   1
in apprehending directly — rather than merely *ascertaining* — that art owes its continuous evolution to the Apollonian-Dionysiac duality, even as the propagation of the species depends on the duality of the sexes, their constant conflicts and periodic acts of reconciliation. I have borrowed my adjectives from the Greeks, who developed their mystical doctrines of art through plausible *embodiments,* not through purely conceptual means. It is by those two art-sponsoring deities, Apollo and Dionysos,[1] that we are made to recognize the tremendous split, as regards both origins and objectives, between the plastic, Apollonian arts and the non-visual art of music inspired by Dionysos. The two creative tendencies developed alongside one another, usually in fierce opposition, each by its taunts forcing the other to more energetic production, both perpetuating in a discordant concord that agon[2] which the term *art* but feebly denominates: until at last, by the thaumaturgy[3] of an Hellenic art of will, the pair accepted the yoke of

---

[1] **Apollo and Dionysos (Dionysus)** Apollo is the god of music, healing, and archery, and, as Phoebus Apollo, is also regarded as the god of light. Dionysus is the god of wine and drunkenness.

[2] **agon** A contest or opposition of forces.

[3] **thaumaturgy** A magical change. Nietzsche means that a powerful transformation was needed for Apollo and Dionysus to be able to join together.

marriage and, in this condition, begot Attic tragedy,[4] which exhibits the salient features of both parents.

To reach a closer understanding of both these tendencies, let us begin by viewing them as the separate art realms of *dream* and *intoxication,* two physiological phenomena standing toward one another in much the same relationship as the Apollonian and Dionysiac. It was in a dream, according to Lucretius,[5] that the marvelous gods and goddesses first presented themselves to the minds of men. That great healing sculptor, Phidias,[6] beheld in a dream the entrancing bodies of more-than-human beings, and likewise, if anyone had asked the Greek poets about the mystery of poetic creation, they too would have referred him to dreams and instructed him much as Hans Sachs[7] instructs us in *Die Meistersinger:*

> My friend, it is the poet's work
> Dreams to interpret and to mark.
> Believe me that man's true conceit
> In a dream becomes complete:
> All poetry we ever read
> Is but true dreams interpreted.

The fair illusion of the dream sphere, in the production of which every man proves himself an accomplished artist, is a precondition not only of all plastic art, but even, as we shall see presently, of a wide range of poetry. Here we enjoy an immediate apprehension of form, all shapes speak to us directly, nothing seems indifferent or redundant. Despite the high intensity with which these dream realities exist for us, we still have a residual sensation that they are illusions; at least such has been my experience — and the frequency, not to say normality, of the experience is borne out in many passages of the poets. Men of philosophical disposition are known for their constant premonition that our everyday reality, too, is an illusion, hiding another, totally different kind of reality. It was Schopenhauer[8] who considered the ability to view at certain times

---

[4] **Attic tragedy** Greek tragedy performed in Athens, in the Greek region of Attica, sixth century to fourth century B.C.

[5] **Lucretius (100? – 55 B.C.)** A Roman philosopher whose book on natural science was standard for more than a millennium.

[6] **Phidias (fl. 430 B.C.)** Greek sculptor who carved the figures of the gods and goddesses on the Parthenon.

[7] **Hans Sachs** The legendary singer-hero of Richard Wagner's opera *The Master-Singer;* the lines quoted are from that opera.

[8] **Arthur Schopenhauer (1788 – 1860)** German philosopher who influenced Nietzsche. His books, *The World as Will and Idea* (1819) and *On the Will in Nature* (1836; tr. 1889), emphasized the power of free will as a chief force in the world.

all men and things as mere phantoms or dream images to be the true mark of philosophic talent. The person who is responsive to the stimuli of art behaves toward the reality of dream much the way the philosopher behaves toward the reality of existence: he observes exactly and enjoys his observations, for it is by these images that he interprets life, by these processes that he rehearses it. Nor is it by pleasant images only that such plausible connections are made: the whole divine comedy of life, including its somber aspects, its sudden balkings, impish accidents, anxious expectations, moves past him, not quite like a shadow play — for it is he himself, after all, who lives and suffers through these scenes — yet never without giving a fleeting sense of illusion; and I imagine that many persons have reassured themselves amidst the perils of dream by calling out, "It is a dream! I want it to go on." I have even heard of people spinning out the causality of one and the same dream over three or more successive nights. All these facts clearly bear witness that our innermost being, the common substratum of humanity, experiences dreams with deep delight and a sense of real necessity. This deep and happy sense of the necessity of dream experiences was expressed by the Greeks in the image of Apollo. Apollo is at once the god of all plastic powers and the soothsaying god. He who is etymologically the "lucent" one, the god of light, reigns also over the fair illusions of our inner world of fantasy. The perfection of these conditions in contrast to our imperfectly understood waking reality, as well as our profound awareness of nature's healing powers during the interval of sleep and dream, furnishes a symbolic analogue to the soothsaying faculty and quite generally to the arts, which make life possible and worth living. But the image of Apollo must incorporate that thin line which the dream image may not cross, under penalty of becoming pathological, of imposing itself on us as crass reality: a discreet limitation, a freedom from all extravagant urges, the sapient tranquility of the plastic god. His eye must be sunlike, in keeping with his origin. Even at those moments when he is angry and ill-tempered there lies upon him the consecration of fair illusion. In an eccentric way one might say of Apollo what Schopenhauer says, in the first part of *The World as Will and Idea,* of man caught in the veil of Maya:[9] "Even as on an immense, raging sea, assailed by huge wave crests, a man sits in a little rowboat trusting his frail craft, so, amidst the furious torments of this world, the individual sits tranquilly, supported by

---

[9] **Maya** A Hindu term for the delusion of the senses by the material world. The veil of Maya is the illusion hiding the reality that lies beneath material surfaces.

the *principium individuationis*[10] and relying on it." One might say that the unshakable confidence in that principle has received its most magnificent expression in Apollo, and that Apollo himself may be regarded as the marvelous divine image of the *principium individuationis,* whose looks and gestures radiate the full delight, wisdom, and beauty of "illusion."

In the same context Schopenhauer has described for us the tremendous awe which seizes man when he suddenly begins to doubt the cognitive modes of experience, in other words, when in a given instance the law of causation seems to suspend itself. If we add to this awe the glorious transport which arises in man, even from the very depths of nature, at the shattering of the *principium individuationis,* then we are in a position to apprehend the essence of Dionysiac rapture, whose closest analogy is furnished by physical intoxication. Dionysiac stirrings arise either through the influence of those narcotic potions of which all primitive races speak in their hymns, or through the powerful approach of spring, which penetrates with joy the whole frame of nature. So stirred, the individual forgets himself completely. It is the same Dionysiac power which in medieval Germany drove ever increasing crowds of people singing and dancing from place to place; we recognize in these St. John's and St. Vitus' dancers the bacchic choruses[11] of the Greeks, who had their precursors in Asia Minor and as far back as Babylon and the orgiastic Sacaea.[12] There are people who, either from lack of experience or out of sheer stupidity, turn away from such phenomena, and, strong in the sense of their own sanity, label them either mockingly or pityingly "endemic diseases." These benighted souls have no idea how cadaverous and ghostly their "sanity" appears as the intense throng of Dionysiac revelers sweeps past them.

Not only does the bond between man and man come to be forged once more by the magic of the Dionysiac rite, but nature itself, long alienated or subjugated, rises again to celebrate the reconciliation with her prodigal son, man. The earth offers its gifts voluntarily, and the savage beasts of mountain and desert approach in

---

[10] *principium individuationis* The principle of the individual, as apart from the crowd.

[11] **bacchic choruses** Bacchus was the god of wine and of ecstasy (a variant of Dionysus); thus, this term means ecstatic choruses. The St. John's and St. Vitus's dancers were ecstatic Christian dancers of the Middle Ages. Their dance was a mania that spread to a number of major religious centers.

[12] **Sacaea** A Babylonian summer festival for the god Ishtar. The point is that such religious orgies are ancient.

peace. The chariot of Dionysos is bedecked with flowers and garlands; panthers and tigers stride beneath his yoke. If one were to
convert Beethoven's "Paean to Joy"[13] into a painting and refuse to
curb the imagination when that multitude prostrates itself reverently
in the dust, one might form some apprehension of Dionysiac ritual.
Now the slave emerges as a freeman; all the rigid, hostile walls
which either necessity or despotism has erected between men are
shattered. Now that the gospel or universal harmony is sounded,
each individual becomes not only reconciled to his fellow but actually at one with him — as though the veil of Maya had been torn
apart and there remained only shreds floating before the vision of
mystical Oneness. Man now expresses himself through song and
dance as the member of a higher community; he has forgotten how
to walk, how to speak, and is on the brink of taking wing as he
dances. Each of his gestures betokens enchantment; through him
sounds a supernatural power, the same power which makes the animals speak and the earth render up milk and honey. "He feels himself to be godlike and strides with the same elation and ecstasy as
the gods he has seen in his dreams." No longer the *artist,* he has himself become a *work of art:* the productive power of the whole universe is now manifest in his transport, to the glorious satisfaction of
the primordial One. The finest clay, the most precious marble —
man — is here kneaded and hewn, and the chisel blows of the
Dionysiac world artist are accompanied by the cry of the Eleusinian
mystagogues:[14] "Do you fall on your knees, multitudes, do you divine your creator?"

So far we have examined the Apollonian and Dionysiac states as
the product of formative forces arising directly from nature without
the mediation of the human artist. At this stage artistic urges are satisfied directly, on the one hand through the imagery of dreams,
whose perfection is quite independent of the intellectual rank, the
artistic development of the individual; on the other hand, through
an ecstatic reality which once again takes no account of the individual and may even destroy him, or else redeem him through a mystical experience of the collective. In relation to these immediate creative conditions of nature every artist must appear as "imitator,"
either as the Apollonian dream artist or the Dionysiac ecstatic artist,
or, finally (as in Greek tragedy, for example) as dream and ecstatic

---

[13] **"Paean to Joy"** This is Friedrich von Schiller's (1759 – 1805) poem, *Ode to
Joy,* which Ludwig van Beethoven (1770 – 1827) set to music in the last movement
of his Symphony no. 9 *(Choral).*
 [14] **Eleusinian mystagogues** Those who participate in the ancient Greek Eleusinian secret ceremonies celebrating life after death.

artist in one. We might picture to ourselves how the last of these, in a state of Dionysiac intoxication and mystical self-abrogation,[15] wandering apart from the reveling throng, sinks upon the ground, and how there is then revealed to him his own condition — complete oneness with the essence of the universe — in a dream similitude.

Having set down these general premises and distinctions, we   7 now turn to the Greeks in order to realize to what degree the formative forces of nature were developed in them. Such an inquiry will enable us to assess properly the relation of the Greek artist to his prototypes or, to use Aristotle's expression, his "imitation of nature."[16] Of the dreams the Greeks dreamed it is not possible to speak with any certainty, despite the extant dream literature and the large number of dream anecdotes. But considering the incredible accuracy of their eyes, their keen and unabashed delight in colors, one can hardly be wrong in assuming that their dreams too showed a strict consequence of lines and contours, hues and groupings, a progression of scenes similar to their best bas-reliefs.[17] The perfection of these dream scenes might almost tempt us to consider the dreaming Greek as a Homer and Homer as a dreaming Greek; which would be as though the modern man were to compare himself in his dreaming to Shakespeare.

Yet there is another point about which we do not have to conjec-   8 ture at all: I mean the profound gap separating the Dionysiac Greeks from the Dionysiac barbarians. Throughout the range of ancient civilization (leaving the newer civilizations out of account for the moment) we find evidence of Dionysiac celebrations which stand to the Greek type in much the same relation as the bearded satyr,[18] whose name and attributes are derived from the he-goat, stands to the god Dionysos. The central concern of such celebrations was, almost universally, a complete sexual promiscuity overriding every form of established tribal law; all the savage urges of the mind were unleashed on those occasions until they reached that paroxysm of lust and cruelty which has always struck me as the "witches' cauldron" *par excellence*. It would appear that the Greeks were for a while quite immune

---

[15] **self-abrogation** The reveler "loses" his self, his sense of being an individual apart from the throng.

[16] **"imitation of nature"** A key term in Aristotle's theory of *mimesis*, the doctrine that art imitates nature and that the artist must observe nature carefully. Nietzsche emphasizes dreams as a part of nature and something to be closely observed by the artist.

[17] **bas-reliefs** Sculptures projecting only slightly from a flat surface; they usually tell a story in a series of scenes.

[18] **satyr** Greek god, half man, half goat; a symbol of lechery.

from these feverish excesses which must have reached them by every known land or sea route. What kept Greece safe was the proud, imposing image of Apollo, who in holding up the head of the Gorgon[19] to those brutal and grotesque Dionysiac forces subdued them. Doric art has immortalized Apollo's majestic rejection of all license. But resistance became difficult, even impossible, as soon as similar urges began to break forth from the deep substratum of Hellenism itself. Soon the function of the Delphic god[20] developed into something quite different and much more limited: all he could hope to accomplish now was to wrest the destructive weapon, by a timely gesture of pacification, from his opponent's hand. That act of pacification represents the most important event in the history of Greek ritual, every department of life now shows symptoms of a revolutionary change. The two great antagonists have been reconciled. Each feels obliged henceforth to keep to his bounds, each will honor the other by the bestowal of periodic gifts, while the cleavage remains fundamentally the same. And yet, if we examine what happened to the Dionysiac powers under the pressure of that treaty we notice a great difference: in the place of the Babylonian Sacaea, with their throwback of men to the condition of apes and tigers, we now see entirely new rites celebrated: rites of universal redemption, of glorious transfiguration. Only now has it become possible to speak of nature's celebrating an *esthetic* triumph; only now has the abrogation of the *principium individuationis* become an esthetic event. That terrible witches' brew concocted of lust and cruelty has lost all power under the new conditions. Yet the peculiar blending of emotions in the heart of the Dionysiac reveler — his ambiguity if you will — seems still to hark back (as the medicinal drug harks back to the deadly poison) to the days when the infliction of pain was experienced as joy while a sense of supreme triumph elicited cries of anguish from the heart. For now in every exuberant joy there is heard an undertone of terror, or else a wistful lament over an irrecoverable loss. It is as though in these Greek festivals a sentimental trait of nature were coming to the fore, as though nature were bemoaning the fact of her fragmentation, her decomposition into separate individuals. The chants and gestures of these revelers, so ambigu-

---

[19] **Gorgon** Powerful monster in Greek mythology with serpents for hair. There were three Gorgons, all sisters, but only Medusa was not immortal. With the help of the goddess Athena, Perseus beheaded Medusa, whose very glance was supposed to turn men to stone. Later Perseus vanquished his enemies by exposing the head to them and turning them to stone.

[20] **Delphic god** Apollo. The oracle at the temple to Apollo at Delphi, in Greece, was for more than 1,000 years a source of prophecies of the future. It was among the most sacred places in Greece.

ous in their motivation, represented an absolute *novum*[21] in the world of the Homeric Greeks; their Dionysiac music, in especial, spread abroad terror and a deep shudder. It is true: music had long been familiar to the Greeks as an Apollonian art, as a regular beat like that of waves lapping the shore, a plastic rhythm[22] expressly developed for the portrayal of Apollonian conditions. Apollo's music was a Doric architecture of sound — of barely hinted sounds such as are proper to the cithara.[23] Those very elements which characterize Dionysiac music and, after it, music quite generally: the heart-shaking power of tone, the uniform stream of melody, the incomparable resources of harmony — all those elements had been carefully kept at a distance as being inconsonant with the Apollonian norm. In the Dionysiac dithyramb[24] man is incited to strain his symbolic faculties to the utmost; something quite unheard of is now clamoring to be heard: the desire to tear asunder the veil of Maya, to sink back into the original oneness of nature; the desire to express the very essence of nature symbolically. Thus an entirely new set of symbols springs into being. First, all the symbols pertaining to physical features: mouth, face, the spoken word, the dance movement which coordinates the limbs and bends them to its rhythm. Then suddenly all the rest of the symbolic forces — music and rhythm as such, dynamics, harmony — assert themselves with great energy. In order to comprehend this total emancipation of all the symbolic powers one must have reached the same measure of inner freedom those powers themselves were making manifest; which is to say that the votary of Dionysos[25] could not be understood except by his own kind. It is not difficult to imagine the awed surprise with which the Apollonian Greek must have looked on him. And that surprise would be further increased as the latter realized, with a shudder, that all this was not so alien to him after all, that his Apollonian consciousness was but a thin veil hiding from him the whole Dionysiac realm.

In order to comprehend this we must take down the elaborate edifice of Apollonian culture stone by stone until we discover its foundations. At first the eye is struck by the marvelous shapes of the

---

[21] **an absolute *novum*** A genuine novelty.

[22] **plastic rhythm** Plastic in this sense means capable of being shaped, responsive to slight changes — not rigid.

[23] **cithara** An ancient stringed instrument, similar to the lyre, used to accompany songs and recitations.

[24] **Dionysiac dithyramb** A passionate hymn to Dionysus, usually delivered by a chorus.

[25] **votary of Dionysos** A follower of Dionysus; one devoted to Dionysian ecstasy.

Olympian gods who stand upon its pediments, and whose exploits, in shining bas-relief, adorn its friezes. The fact that among them we find Apollo as one god among many, making no claim to a privileged position, should not mislead us. The same drive that found its most complete representation in Apollo generated the whole Olympian world, and in this sense we may consider Apollo the father of that world. But what was the radical need out of which that illustrious society of Olympian beings sprang?

Whoever approaches the Olympians with a different religion in   10
his heart, seeking moral elevation, sanctity, spirituality, loving-kindness, will presently be forced to turn away from them in ill-humored disappointment. Nothing in these deities reminds us of asceticism, high intellect, or duty: we are confronted by luxuriant, triumphant *existence,* which defies the good and the bad indifferently. And the beholder may find himself dismayed in the presence of such overflowing life and ask himself what potion these heady people must have drunk in order to behold, in whatever direction they looked, Helen[26] laughing back at them, the beguiling image of their own existence. But we shall call out to this beholder, who has already turned his back: Don't go! Listen first to what the Greeks themselves have to say of this life, which spreads itself before you with such puzzling serenity. An old legend has it that King Midas[27] hunted a long time in the woods for the wise Silenus, companion of Dionysos, without being able to catch him. When he had finally caught him the king asked him what he considered man's greatest good. The daemon remained sullen and uncommunicative until finally, forced by the king, he broke into a shrill laugh and spoke: "Ephemeral wretch, begotten by accident and toil, why do you force me to tell you what it would be your greatest boon not to hear? What would be best for you is quite beyond your reach: not to have been born, not to *be,* to be *nothing.* But the second best is to die soon."

What is the relation of the Olympian gods to this popular wis-   11
dom? It is that of the entranced vision of the martyr to his torment.

Now the Olympian magic mountain opens itself before us,   12
showing us its very roots. The Greeks were keenly aware of the ter-

---

[26] **Helen** The runaway wife of Menelaus, immortalized in Homer's *Iliad* as the cause of the ten-year Trojan War. She was not "good" or ascetic, but her intensity of living secured her a permanent place in history and myth.

[27] **King Midas** Midas was a foolish king who kidnapped Silenus, a satyr (half man, half goat) who was a companion of Dionysus. Silenus, a daemon or spirit, granted Midas his wish to have everything he touched turn to gold. Because his food turned to gold, he almost died. Dionysus eventually saved him by bathing him in a sacred river.

rors and horrors of existence; in order to be able to live at all they had to place before them the shining fantasy of the Olympians. Their tremendous distrust of the titanic forces of nature: *Moira*,[28] mercilessly enthroned beyond the knowable world; the vulture which fed upon the great philanthropist Prometheus;[29] the terrible lot drawn by wise Oedipus; the curse on the house of Atreus which brought Orestes to the murder of his mother: that whole Panic philosophy,[30] in short, with its mythic examples, by which the gloomy Etruscans perished, the Greeks conquered — or at least hid from view — again and again by means of this artificial Olympus. In order to live at all the Greeks had to construct these deities. The Apollonian need for beauty had to develop the Olympian hierarchy of joy by slow degrees from the original titanic hierarchy of terror, as roses are seen to break from a thorny thicket. How else could life have been borne by a race so hypersensitive, so emotionally intense, so equipped for suffering? The same drive which called art into being as a completion and consummation of existence, and as a guarantee of further existence, gave rise also to that Olympian realm which acted as a transfiguring mirror to the Hellenic will. The gods justified human life by living it themselves — the only satisfactory theodicy[31] ever invented. To exist in the clear sunlight of such deities was now felt to be the highest good, and the only real grief suffered by Homeric man was inspired by the thought of leaving that sunlight, especially when the departure seemed imminent. Now it became possible to stand the wisdom of Silenus on its head and proclaim that it was the worst evil for man to die soon, and second worst for him to die at all. Such laments as arise now arise over short-lived Achilles,[32] over the generations ephemeral as leaves, the decline of the heroic age. It is not unbecoming to even the greatest hero to yearn for an afterlife, though it be as a day laborer. So impetuously, during the Apollonian phase, does man's will desire to remain on

---

[28] **Moira** Fate personified; the figure who gives each person his fate.

[29] **Prometheus** The god who gave men fire — thus, his generosity is philanthropy, the love of man. He was punished by the gods.

[30] **Panic philosophy** Belief in fate. Oedipus's fate was to murder his father and marry his mother. He tried to escape it but could not. Orestes murdered his mother, Clytemnestra, because she had murdered his father, Agamemnon. All of these were members of the cursed house of Atreus and provide examples of how fate works.

[31] **theodicy** Examination of the question of whether the gods are just. Because the gods shared human life, they ennobled it; they suffered evil as well.

[32] **short-lived Achilles** Achilles' fate was to lead the Greeks to victory at Troy but to die by an arrow shot by Paris, who had taken Helen to Troy. Apollo guided the arrow so that it hit Achilles in the heel, his one vulnerable spot. Achilles, like many heroes, lived a brief but intense life.

earth, so identified does he become with existence, that even his lament turns to a song of praise.

It should have become apparent by now that the harmony with   13 nature which we late-comers regard with such nostalgia, and for which Schiller has coined the cant term *naïve*,[33] is by no means a simple and inevitable condition to be found at the gateway to every culture, a kind of paradise. Such a belief could have been endorsed only by a period for which Rousseau's *Émile* was an artist and Homer just such an artist nurtured in the bosom of nature. Whenever we encounter "naïveté" in art, we are face to face with the ripest fruit of Apollonian culture — which must always triumph first over titans, kill monsters, and overcome the somber contemplation of actuality, the intense susceptibility to suffering, by means of illusions strenuously and zestfully entertained. But how rare are the instances of true naïveté, of that complete identification with the beauty of appearance! It is this achievement which makes Homer so magnificent — Homer, who, as a single individual, stood to Apollonian popular culture in the same relation as the individual dream artist to the oneiric[34] capacity of a race and of nature generally. The naïveté of Homer must be viewed as a complete victory of Apollonian illusion. Nature often uses illusions of this sort in order to accomplish its secret purposes. The true goal is covered over by a phantasm. We stretch out our hands to the latter, while nature, aided by our deception, attains the former. In the case of the Greeks it was the will wishing to behold itself in the work of art, in the transcendence of genius; but in order so to behold itself its creatures had first to view themselves as glorious, to transpose themselves to a higher sphere, without having that sphere of pure contemplation either challenge them or upbraid them with insufficiency. It was in that sphere of beauty that the Greeks saw the Olympians as their mirror images; it was by means of that esthetic mirror that the Greek will opposed suffering and the somber wisdom of suffering which always accompanies artistic talent. As a monument to its victory stands Homer, the naïve artist.

We can learn something about that naïve artist through the   14 analogy of dream. We can imagine the dreamer as he calls out to himself, still caught in the illusion of his dream and without disturbing it, "This is a dream, and I want to go on dreaming," and we can

---

[33] **naïve** Schiller's *On the Naïve and the Sentimental in Poetry* (1795 – 1796) contrasted the classic (naïve) with the romantic (sentimental) in art. It is not the same as Nietzsche's distinction, but it is similar. Nietzsche uses *naïve* to refer to a kind of classical purity and temper.

[34] **oneiric** Pertaining to dreams.

infer, on the one hand, that he takes deep delight in the contemplation of his dream, and, on the other, that he must have forgotten the day, with its horrible importunity, so to enjoy his dream. Apollo, the interpreter of dreams, will furnish the clue to what is happening here. Although of the two halves of life — the waking and the dreaming — the former is generally considered not only the more important but the only one which is truly lived, I would, at the risk of sounding paradoxical, propose the opposite view. The more I have come to realize in nature those omnipotent formative tendencies and, with them, an intense longing for illusion, the more I feel inclined to the hypothesis that the original Oneness, the ground of Being, ever-suffering and contradictory, time and again has need of rapt vision and delightful illusion to redeem itself. Since we ourselves are the very stuff of such illusions, we must view ourselves as the truly non-existent, that is to say, as a perpetual unfolding in time, space, and causality — what we label "empiric reality."[35] But if, for the moment, we abstract from our own reality, viewing our empiric existence, as well as the existence of the world at large, as the *idea* of the original Oneness, produced anew each instant, then our dreams will appear to us as illusions of illusions, hence as a still higher form of satisfaction of the original desire for illusion. It is for this reason that the very core of nature takes such a deep delight in the naïve artist and the naïve work of art, which likewise is merely the illusion of an illusion. Raphael,[36] himself one of those immortal "naïve" artists, in a symbolic canvas has illustrated that reduction of illusion to further illusion which is the original act of the naïve artist and at the same time of all Apollonian culture. In the lower half of his "Transfiguration," through the figures of the possessed boy, the despairing bearers, the helpless, terrified disciples, we see a reflection of original pain, the sole ground of being: "illusion" here is a reflection of eternal contradiction, begetter of all things. From this illusion there rises, like the fragrance of ambrosia, a new illusory world, invisible to those enmeshed in the first: a radiant vision of pure delight, a rapt seeing through wide-open eyes. Here we have, in a great symbol of art, both the fair world of Apollo and its substratum, the terrible wisdom of Silenus, and we can comprehend intuitively how they mutually require one another. But Apollo appears

---

[35] **"empiric reality"** The reality we can test by experience.

[36] **Raphael (1483 – 1520)** A Renaissance artist. Raphael was influenced by classical forms, but his work became progressively more humanistic, in some cases tending to Schiller's "sentimental." *Transfiguration* (1517 – 1520), his last painting, points to the new age of baroque painting: an intense, emotional, ecstatic style.

to us once again as the apotheosis[37] of the *principium individuationis,* in whom the eternal goal of the original Oneness, namely its redemption through illusion, accomplishes itself. With august gesture the god shows us how there is need for a whole world of torment in order for the individual to produce the redemptive vision and to sit quietly in his rocking rowboat in mid-sea, absorbed in contemplation.

If this apotheosis of individuation is to be read in nominative   15
terms, we may infer that there is one norm only: the individual — or, more precisely, the observance of the limits of the individual: *sophrosyne.*[38] As a moral deity Apollo demands self-control from his people and, in order to observe such self-control, a knowledge of self. And so we find that the esthetic necessity of beauty is accompanied by the imperatives, "Know thyself," and "Nothing too much." Conversely, excess and *hubris*[39] come to be regarded as the hostile spirits of the non-Apollonian sphere, hence as properties of the pre-Apollonian era — the age of Titans[40] — and the extra-Apollonian world, that is to say the world of the barbarians. It was because of his Titanic love of man that Prometheus had to be devoured by vultures; it was because of his extravagant wisdom which succeeded in solving the riddle of the Sphinx[41] that Oedipus had to be cast into a whirlpool of crime: in this fashion does the Delphic god interpret the Greek past.

The effects of the Dionysiac spirit struck the Apollonian Greeks   16
as titanic and barbaric; yet they could not disguise from themselves the fact that they were essentially akin to those deposed Titans and heroes. They felt more than that: their whole existence, with its temperate beauty, rested upon a base of suffering and *knowledge* which had been hidden from them until the reinstatement of Dionysos uncovered it once more. And lo and behold! Apollo found it impossible to live without Dionysos. The elements of titanism and bar-

---

[37] **apotheosis** Godlike embodiment. Nietzsche is saying that Apollo is the god in whom the concept of the individual is best expressed.

[38] *sophrosyne* Greek word for wisdom, moderation.

[39] **hubris** Greek word for pride, especially dangerous, defiant pride.

[40] **age of Titans** A reference to the gods who reigned before Zeus; an unenlightened, violent age.

[41] **riddle of the Sphinx** The sphinx, part woman and part beast, waited outside Thebes for years, killing all who tried to pass by but could not solve its riddle. Oedipus (see note 30) answered the riddle: "What walks on four legs in the morning, two legs in the day, and three legs in the evening?" The answer: man, who crawls in infancy, walks upright in his prime, and uses a cane in old age. The solution freed Thebes from its bondage to the Sphinx, but it brought Oedipus closer to his awful fate.

barism turned out to be quite as fundamental as the Apollonian element. And now let us imagine how the ecstatic sounds of the Dionysiac rites penetrated ever more enticingly into that artificially restrained and discreet world of illusion, how this clamor expressed the whole outrageous gamut of nature — delight, grief, knowledge — even to the most piercing cry; and then let us imagine how the Apollonian artist with his thin, monotonous harp music must have sounded beside the demoniac chant of the multitude! The muses presiding over the illusory arts paled before an art which enthusiastically told the truth, and the wisdom of Silenus cried "Woe!" against the serene Olympians. The individual, with his limits and moderations, forgot himself in the Dionysiac vortex and became oblivious to the laws of Apollo. Indiscreet extravagance revealed itself as truth, and contradiction, a delight born of pain, spoke out of the bosom of nature. Wherever the Dionysiac voice was heard, the Apollonian norm seemed suspended or destroyed. Yet it is equally true that, in those places where the first assault was withstood, the prestige and majesty of the Delphic god appeared more rigid and threatening than before. The only way I am able to view Doric art and the Doric[42] state is as a perpetual military encampment of the Apollonian forces. An art so defiantly austere, so ringed about with fortifications — an education so military and exacting — a polity so ruthlessly cruel — could endure only in a continual state of resistance against the titanic and barbaric menace of Dionysos.

Up to this point I have developed at some length a theme which 17 was sounded at the beginning of this essay: how the Dionysiac and Apollonian elements, in a continuous chain of creations, each enhancing the other, dominated the Hellenic mind: how from the Iron Age,[43] with its battles of Titans and its austere popular philosophy, there developed under the aegis of Apollo the Homeric world of beauty; how this "naïve" splendor was then absorbed once more by the Dionysiac torrent, and how, face to face with this new power, the Apollonian code rigidified into the majesty of Doric art and contemplation. If the earlier phase of Greek history may justly be broken down into four major artistic epochs dramatizing the battle between the two hostile principles, then we must inquire further (lest Doric art appear to us as the acme and final goal of all these striving tendencies) what was the true end toward which that evolution moved. And our eyes will come to rest on the sublime and much

---

[42] **Doric** The Doric styles were unadorned, clear, intellectual rather than sensual. They represent purity and uprightness.

[43] **Iron Age** An earlier age, ruled by sterner, less humane gods, the Titans.

lauded achievement of the dramatic dithyramb and Attic tragedy, as the common goal of both urges; whose mysterious marriage, after long discord, ennobled itself with such a child, at once Antigone and Cassandra.[44]

---

[44] **Antigone and Cassandra** Children in Greek tragedies; Antigone, daughter of Oedipus, defied the authorities in *Antigone* by Sophocles (496? – 406 B.C.) and suffered death; Cassandra, daughter of Priam, king of Troy, appears in Homer's *Iliad* and several tragedies by Aeschylus (525 – 456 B.C.) and Euripides (484? – 406 B.C.). She had the gift of prophecy but was doomed never to be believed. She foresaw the destruction of Troy, and after its fall she was taken prisoner by Agamemnon and was killed with him. She and Antigone were both heroic in their suffering.

QUESTIONS FOR CRITICAL READING

1. Define *Apollonianism* and *Dionysianism*. What kind of behavior does each word stand for?
2. What are the important distinctions between the self and the mob? Dream and illusion?
3. In paragraph 6, Nietzsche speaks of the "mystical experience of the collective." What does he mean by this phrase? Is there such a thing?
4. Which paragraphs in the selection are most obscure and difficult to understand? How do they seem to show Dionysian qualities?
5. What contemporary art unifies the Apollonian and the Dionysian? Would Nietzsche have thought a modern film could do so?
6. How do the distinctions Nietzsche makes give you useful insights into religion or faith?
7. What moral issues might the Apollonian person and the Dionysian person interpret differently?
8. For which of these polarities of behavior is self-control more likely a virtue?

SUGGESTIONS FOR WRITING

1. Examine paragraph 6 carefully. How valid are Nietzsche's insights concerning the self and the "reveling throng"? Drawing on personal experience, contrast the behavior of yourself or a friend — first as an individual and then as a member of a large gathering of people. Are you (or your friend) "possessed" when a member of such an assemblage? Be as specific as possible in writing about this contrast.
2. Establish a principle of moral behavior by which you feel the Apollonian can live. Then establish one for the Dionysian. Compare the two personalities to determine their differences and their similarities. How

do the mental states represented by these polarities make their moral systems different? On what would they agree? Is either of these polarities in danger of appearing immoral to people in general?

3. Music is the inspiration for this essay. Choose a piece of music that is important to you. Consider it as an artifact, and describe the qualities it has that you feel are Apollonian and Dionysian, respectively. Is the range of the music — in terms of exciting or sustaining emotional response — narrow or great? Describe your emotional and intellectual reactions to the music, and ask others about their responses to the same music. Is music an appropriate source for finding the conjunction of these two forces?

4. Examine aspects of our culture that reveal whether it is basically Apollonian or basically Dionysian. Be sure to consider matters of religion, literature, music, faith, and art and any aspects of personal life in your immediate environment. In considering these features of our culture, use Nietzsche's technique of comparison and contrast. For instance, you may find the Apollonian and Dionysian sides of, say, the modern film as interesting contrasts, just as you may wish to contrast rock music and Muzak, or any other related pairs.

5. Which of these two polarities of behavior most resembles your own behavior? Are you Apollonian or Dionysian? Define your behavior with reference to Nietzsche. Ask others who have read this selection to comment on your character in terms of the Apollonian-Dionysian distinction. Do you think that you achieve the kind of control that enables you to realize yourself fully in terms of these polarities, or do you feel that control is not an issue? Is inspiration an issue?

6. **CONNECTIONS** How would the Buddha critique Nietzsche's proposals? What ethical issues might he find in Nietzsche's suggestions that the Apollonian and Dionysian extremes are desirable? What fault might Plato have found with Nietzsche's views? Do you find yourself convinced more by Plato and the Buddha or by Nietzsche?

7. **CONNECTIONS** Ruth Benedict relies on this essay by Nietzsche for her distinctions between cultures of Pueblo Indians and their neighbors. Examine "The Pueblos of New Mexico" and decide whether her representation of the distinctions between cultures as Apollonian and Dionysian seems to be an accurate interpretation of Nietzsche. Does she treat Nietzsche's ideas fairly, and does she seem to apply them reasonably?

MARTIN BUBER
From *I and Thou*

M ARTIN BUBER (1878 – 1965), born in Vienna, was three when his mother left his father. As a result, he was sent to his paternal grandparents to be raised. His grandfather, Solomon Buber, was a wealthy man who devoted much of his life to writing and study. Fluent in Hebrew and a student of Greek, he was a thoroughly humanistic scholar and a perfect teacher for Martin, who grew up speaking Hebrew and studying Jewish texts. However, he found himself often preferring nineteenth-century German poetry to the literature of faith. As he grew into adolescence, he found himself moving away from religious practice altogether.

Later, when he took up university studies, at Vienna, Berlin, and elsewhere, he discovered the works of two Christian mystics — Nicholas of Cusa (1401 – 1464) and Jakob Bohme (1575 – 1624) — and made them the subject of his doctoral dissertation in Vienna in 1904. Mysticism, which is the belief in a personal experience with God, much like those reported by Teresa of Avila, remained a central strand of Buber's thought throughout his life. He is largely responsible for a renewed interest in Hasidism, Jewish mystical life and thought. Later in his life he wrote some important works on Hasidism and remained profoundly interested in its nature, although he himself did not become Hasidic.

During the years between the world wars, Buber edited a prominent Jewish newspaper but eventually became a teacher. Hitler began to attack Jews while Buber was on the faculty at the University of Frankfurt, and he was outspoken in his defense of Judaism. He spent much of his time in the 1930s trying to help Jewish teachers who had been removed from their teaching positions because of their religion. Ultimately, it became impossible for him to remain in Germany, and in 1938 he moved to Palestine, where he took a position in the Hebrew University in Jerusalem. By that time, his writing had made him one of the most prominent Jewish thinkers of his time. Maurice Friedman, his biographer, said, "No Jewish thinker has had a greater cultural, intellectual, and religious influence on the last four decades than Martin Buber."[1]

I and Thou, his best-known work, was published in German in 1923. It was translated into English first in 1937 and again by Walter Kaufmann in 1970. In 1957 Buber made some important revisions to the text, which appear in Kaufmann's translation. Buber's work has often been compared to the philosophy of existentialism, of which Kaufmann is a special student. One of the most important philosophical influences on Buber was Friedrich Nietzsche, also regarded as an early existentialist thinker. According to existentialism, individuals are not measured by an "essential nature" (we are not essentially thieves, saints, sinners, or hypocrites) but measured by what they do. In other words, our existence — the way we choose to live — establishes who we are, and one of the purposes of life is to actualize oneself — to achieve our fullest potential through action. Buber puts it in religious perspective when he says "the unification of the soul occurs in lived actuality" (para. 24). Therefore, our decisions are crucial and determine the character and quality of our life.

The principle of faith developed in *I and Thou* is based on establishing relationships. The individual actualizes his or her life in relationship to others, which means the individual must always be in dialogue with others. The relationship Buber focused on was between the I and the Thou. The use of the term *Thou* implies a profound level of reverence. When the relationship and dialogue are healthy, a unique I-Thou relation implies mutual respect and in some cases love. When I (as an individual) attend to the needs of Thou (another person) and make an effort to experience what the Thou experiences, empathy results. However, people, like things, can sometimes become an It, producing an I-It relationship. With people, such a relationship can be problematic because it implies a projected loss of human status as Thou becomes It. It also implies a one-sided dialogue and, in the case of a human being or an animal, a loss of empathy.

Buber points out that even though loved ones sometimes can have an I-It relationship, the relationship with God is always I-Thou. Maurice Friedman puts it clearly: "The fullness of dialogue, however, into which all other dialogue enters, is that between man and God. In contrast to the customary view that monotheism is the

---

[1] Maurice Friedman, "Martin Buber," in *Great Jewish Thinkers of the Twentieth Century* (Washington: B'nai B'rith Books, 1985), p. 183.

major contribution of Judaism to the religions of the world, Buber regards the dialogue with God as the center and significance of Jewish religion."[2] The relationship of the individual with God, which is to say the dialogue the individual has with God, is unlike all others. The segment of *I and Thou* that follows examines that relationship in detail.

Buber begins by noting that most people feel dependence when they think about their relationship with God. He surprises us, however, by expanding this idea beyond the individual's dependence on God to include God's need for the individual. He says, "That you need God more than anything, you know at all times in your heart. But don't you know also that God needs you — in the fullness of his eternity, you?" (para. 5). This is an arresting concept. Since the usual Judeo-Christian view is that God is self-sufficient, this emphasis on the concept of relationship appears to break with at least one aspect of tradition. His view is based on reasoning about why humanity would exist if God did not somehow need humanity: What would be the point?

The traditional view, that only people are dependent in their relationship with God, "means wishing to deactualize one partner of the relationship and thus the relationship itself" (para. 8). Therefore, the relationship from God's perspective must be seen as an I-Thou relationship, not an I-It relationship. Buber examines, as well, the individual's potential loss of self in death, when he or she returns to the oneness of God and becomes, as Plotinus said, "one with the all-in-all." Buber rejects this view because it denies the validity of the I-Thou dialogue, which for him characterizes our relationship with God now and forever. In the process of considering this view, Buber responds to both St. John in the Bible and the Buddha in his teachings. He concludes: "God and man, being consubstantial, are actually and forever Two" (para. 13). Thus he rejects what he calls "the raptures of the ecstasy of 'unification'" (para. 17).

Buber's emphasis throughout is on what he calls "lived actuality" (para. 21). By living in relation to others, we actualize ourselves. "The strongest and deepest actuality is to be found where everything enters into activity — the whole human being, without reserve, and the all-embracing god; the unified I and the boundless You" (para. 23). The lived actuality must take place in the world of experience, and it represents a mission on earth. As he says, "Whoever goes forth in truth to the world, goes forth to God" (para. 38).

---

[2] Friedman, p. 197.

BUBER'S RHETORIC

The selection that appears here is a translation, but it was approved by Buber's son and is the product of a sympathetic and understanding philosopher who acknowledges that Buber's writing requires thought and study. However, this selection becomes more clear once the concept of the dialogue of I and Thou or I and It is understood. Buber speaks directly to his subject and focuses on the primary issues. He does not use metaphoric language or dynamic techniques such as rhetorical questions or repetition.

One of Buber's techniques is to establish principles and move logically to a conclusion. In his opening paragraphs he clarifies the concept of the dialogue when he says "every feeling has its place in a polar tension; it derives its color and meaning not from itself alone but also from its polar opposite; every feeling is conditioned by its opposite" (para. 2). Accepting this view then leads to accepting the I-Thou relationship and then to accepting that the individual exists and changes in dialogue with nature, art, other people, and God.

Buber writes in a tradition of mystical literature that does not attempt absolute clarity of expression. The subject of faith often defies logic. Rational discourse does not necessarily move individuals toward faith. This paradox, which is present in many religious texts, is based on the conjunction of opposites and the failure to resolve the resultant conflict. Buber mentions "paradoxes of intuition" (para. 29) and insists that we learn to tolerate paradox and inform our feelings through faith in God. For this reason, he discusses the teachings of the Buddha, locating Buddha's position in desiring an "annulment of suffering" in the "I" (para. 28). Buber's view, then, is to push onward toward the "you" that he believes to be implicit in Buddha's philosophy.

In both sections in this passage, Buber begins with a proposal that he examines and analyzes. He then considers what people think and feel about the idea, reviews positions that contradict his view, resolves these contradictions, and then ends with a conclusion that he feels is warranted by the discussion. This approach is amply illustrated in his examination of the idea of dependence in the first part of the passage: paragraphs 1 to 8. The remaining part of the passage (paras. 9–39) examines the idea of unification, of oneness or being "stripped of all subjectivity and I-hood" (para. 9), ending with the conclusion that "God embraces but is not the universe; just so, God embraces but is not my self" (para. 39). Such views show him to be an extraordinarily original thinker.

From *I and Thou*

The essential element in our relationship to God has been 1
sought in a feeling that has been called a feeling of dependence or,
more recently, in an attempt to be more precise, creature-feeling.
While the insistence on this element and its definition are right, the
onesided emphasis on this factor leads to a misunderstanding of the
character of the perfect relationship.

What has been said earlier of love is even more clearly true at 2
this point: feelings merely accompany the fact of the relationship
which after all is established not in the soul but between an I and a
You. However essential one considers a feeling, it still remains subject to the dynamics of the soul where one feeling is surpassed, ex-
celled, and replaced by another; feelings, unlike relationships, can
be compared on a scale. Above all, every feeling has its place in a
polar tension; it derives its color and meaning not from itself alone
but also from its polar opposite; every feeling is conditioned by its
opposite. Actually, the absolute relationship includes all relative relationships and is, unlike them, no longer a part but the whole in
which all of them are consummated and become one. But in psychology the absolute relationship is relativized by being derived
from a particular and limited feeling that is emphasized.

If one starts out from the soul, the perfect relationship can only 3
be seen as bipolar, as *coincidentia oppositorum*,[3] as the fusion of opposite feelings. Of course, as one looks back one pole frequently disappears, suppressed by the basic religious orientation of the person,
and it is only in the purest and most open-minded and profound introspection that it can be recalled.

Yes, in the pure relationship you felt altogether dependent, as 4
you could never possibly feel in any other — and yet also altogether
free as never and nowhere else; created — and creative. You no
longer felt the one, limited by the other; you felt both without
bounds, both at once.

That you need God more than anything, you know at all times 5
in your heart. But don't you know also that God needs you — in the
fullness of his eternity, you? How would man exist if God did not
need him, and how would you exist? You need God in order to be,
and God needs you — for that which is the meaning of your life.
Teachings and poems try to say more, and say too much: how
murky and presumptuous is the chatter of "the emerging God" —

---

[3] *coincidentia oppositorum* A coinciding of opposites.

but the emergence of the living God we know unswervingly in our hearts. The world is not divine play, it is divine fate. That there are world, man, the human person, you and I, has divine meaning.

Creation — happens to us, burns into us, changes us, we trem- 6 ble and swoon, we submit. Creation — we participate in it, we encounter the creator, offer ourselves to him, helpers and companions.

Two great servants move through the ages: prayer and sacrifice. 7 In prayer man pours himself out, dependent without reservation, knowing that, incomprehensibly, he acts on God, albeit without exacting anything from God; for when he no longer covets anything for himself, he beholds his effective activity burning in the supreme flame. And those who sacrifice? I cannot despise the honest servants of the remote past who thought that God desired the smell of their burnt sacrifices: they knew in a foolish and vigorous way that one can and should give to God; and that is also known to him who offers his little will to God and encounters him in a great will. "Let your will be done" — is all he says, but truth goes on to say for him: "through me whom you need." What distinguishes sacrifice and prayer from all magic? Magic wants to be effective without entering into any relationship and performs its arts in the void, while sacrifice and prayer step "before the countenance," into the perfection of the sacred basic word that signifies reciprocity. They say You and listen.

Wishing to understand the pure relationship as dependence 8 means wishing to deactualize one partner of the relationship and thus the relationship itself.

The same thing happens if one starts from the opposite side and 9 finds the essential element of the religious act in immersion or a descent into the self — whether the self is to be stripped of all subjectivity and I-hood or whether the self is to be understood as the One that thinks and is. The former view supposes that God will enter the being that has been freed of I-hood or that at that point one merges into God; the other view supposes that one stands immediately in oneself as the divine One. Thus the first holds that in a supreme moment all You-saying ends because there is no longer any duality; the second, that there is no truth in You-saying at all because in truth there is no duality. The first believes in the unification, the second in the identity of the human and the divine. Both insist on what is beyond I and You: for the first this comes to be, perhaps in ecstasy, while for the second it is there all along and reveals itself, perhaps as the thinking subject beholds its self. Both annul relationship — the first, as it were, dynamically, as the I is swallowed by the You, which now ceases to be a You and becomes the only being; the second, as

it were, statically, as the I is freed, becomes a self, and recognizes itself as the only being. The doctrine of dependence considers the
I-supporter of the world-arch of pure relation as so weak and insignificant that his ability to support the arch ceases to be credible,
while the one doctrine of immersion does away altogether with the
arch in its perfection and the other one treats it as a chimera that has
to be overcome.

The doctrines of immersion invoke the great epigrams of identi-   10
fication — one of them above all the Johannine "I and the Father are
one," and the other one the doctrine of Sandilya: "The All-embracing
is my self in the inner heart."[4]

The paths of these two epigrams are diametrically opposed. The   11
former (after a long subterranean course) has its source in the myth-
sized life of a person and then unfolds in a doctrine. The second
emerges in a doctrine and culminates (provisionally) in the myth-
sized life of a person. On these paths the character of each epigram
is changed. The Christ of the Johannine tradition, the Word that has
become flesh but once, takes us to Eckhart's Christ whom God
begets eternally in the human soul. The formula of the coronation of
the self in the Upanishads[5] — "That is the actual, it is the self, and
that you are" takes us far more quickly to the Buddhistic formula of
deposition: "A self and what pertains to the self are not to be found
in truth and actuality."

Beginning and end of both paths have to be considered sepa-   12
rately.

That there is no justification for invoking the "are one" is ob-   13
vious for anyone who reads the Gospel according to John without
skipping and with an open mind. It is really nothing less than the
Gospel of the pure relationship. There are truer things here than the
familiar mystic verse: "I am you, and you are I." The father and
the son, being consubstantial — we may say: God and man, being
consubstantial, are actually and forever Two, the two partners of the
primal relationship that, from God to man, is called mission and
commandment; from man to God, seeing and hearing; between
both, knowledge and love. And in this relationship the son, although the father dwells and works in him, bows before him that is
"greater" and prays to him. All modern attempts to reinterpret this
primal actuality of dialogue and to make of it a relationship of the I

---

[4] **Sandilya** A character in the Upanishads, sacred Hindu writings that date
from 1000 B.C.

[5] **Upanishads** A term derived from a word meaning "sitting at the feet of the
master." The Upanishads are Hindu scriptures in prose and verse that contain sacred
narratives.

to the self or something of that sort, as if it were a process confined
to man's self-sufficient inwardness, are vain and belong to the
abysmal history of deactualization.

— But mysticism? It relates how unity within duality feels.   14
Have we any right to doubt the faithfulness of this testimony?

— I know not only of one but of two kinds of events in which   15
one is no longer aware of any duality. Mysticism sometimes confounds them, as I, too, did at one time.

First, the soul may become one. This event occurs not between   16
man and God but in man. All forces are concentrated into the core,
everything that would distract them is pulled in, and the being
stands alone in itself and jubilates, as Paracelsus[6] put it, in its exaltation. This is a man's decisive moment. Without this he is not fit for
the work of the spirit. With this — it is decided deep down whether
this means preparation or sufficient satisfaction. Concentrated into a
unity, a human being can proceed to his encounter — wholly successful only now — with mystery and perfection. But he can also
savor the bliss of his unity and, without incurring the supreme duty,
return into distraction. Everything along our way is decision —
intentional, dimly sensed, or altogether secret — but this one, deep
down, is the primally secret decision, pregnant with the most powerful destiny.

The other event is that unfathomable kind of relational act itself   17
in which one has the feeling that Two have become One: "one and
one made one, bare shineth in bare." I and You drown; humanity
that but now confronted the deity is absorbed into it; glorification,
deification, universal unity have appeared. But when one returns
into the wretchedness of daily turmoil, transfigured and exhausted,
and with a knowing heart reflects on both, is one not bound to feel
that Being is split, with one part abandoned to hopelessness? What
help is it to my soul that it can be transported again from this world
into that unity, when this world itself has, of necessity, no share
whatever in that unity — what does all "enjoyment of God" profit a
life rent in two? If that extravagantly rich heavenly Moment has
nothing to do with my poor earthly moment — what is it to me as
long as I still have to live on earth — must in all seriousness still live
on earth? That is the way to understand those masters who renounced the raptures of the ecstasy of "unification."

Which was no unification. Those human beings may serve as a   18
metaphor who in the passion of erotic fulfillment are so carried

---

[6] **Paracelsus (1493 – 1541)** Swiss-born physician and alchemist. His given
name was Philippus Aureolus Theophrastus Bombastus von Hohenheim.

away by the miracle of the embrace that all knowledge of I and You drowns in the feeling of a unity that neither exists nor can exist. What the ecstatic calls unification is the rapturous dynamics of the relationship; not a unity that has come into being at this moment in world time, fusing I and You, but the dynamics of the relationship itself which can stand before the two carriers of this relationship, although they confront each other immovably, and cover the eyes of the enraptured. What we find here is a marginal exorbitance of the act of relation: the relationship itself in its vital unity is felt so vehemently that its members pale in the process: its life predominates so much that the I and the You between whom it is established are forgotten. This is one of the phenomena that we find on the margins where actuality becomes blurred. But what is greater for us than all enigmatic webs at the margins of being is the central actuality of an everyday hour on earth, with a streak of sunshine on a maple twig and an intimation of the eternal You.

Against this stands the claim of the other doctrine of immersion 19 that at heart the universe and the self are identical and hence no You-saying can ever grant any ultimate actuality.

This claim is answered by the doctrine itself. One of the Upani- 20 shads relates how Indra, the prince of the gods, comes to Prajapati, the creator spirit, to learn how one can find and recognize the self. He remains a student for a century and is twice sent away with inadequate information, before he finally attains the right information: "When one rests in a deep sleep, without dreams, that is the self, the immortal, the assured, the All-being." Indra goes hence but is soon troubled by a scruple. He returns and asks: "In that state, O sublime one, we do not know of our self, 'That am I'; neither, 'Those are the beings.' We are gone to annihilation. I see no profit here." "That, my lord, is indeed how it is," replies Prajapati.

Insofar as this doctrine contains an assertion about true being, 21 we cannot find out in this life whether the doctrine is true; but however that may be, there is one thing with which this doctrine has nothing in common: lived actuality; and it therefore has to demote this to the level of a merely illusory world. And insofar as this doctrine contains directions for immersion in true being, it does not lead into lived actuality but into "annihilation," in which there is no consciousness, from which no memory survives — and the man who has emerged from it may profess the experience by using the limit-word of non-duality, but without any right to proclaim this as unity.

We, however, are resolved to tend with holy care the holy trea- 22 sure of our actuality that has been given to us for this life and perhaps for no other life that might be closer to the truth.

In lived actuality there is no unity of being. Actuality is to be   23
found only in effective activity; strength and depth of the former
only in that of the latter. "Inner" actuality, too, is only where there is
reciprocal activity. The strongest and deepest actuality is to be found
where everything enters into activity — the whole human being,
without reserve, and the all-embracing god; the unified I and the
boundless You.

The unified I: for (as I have said earlier) the unification of the   24
soul occurs in lived actuality — the concentration of all forces into
the core, the decisive moment of man. But unlike that immersion,
this does not entail ignoring the actual person. Immersion wants to
preserve only what is "pure," essential, and enduring, while strip-
ping away everything else; the concentration of which I speak does
not consider our instincts as too impure, the sensuous as too peripheral, or our emotions as too fleeting — everything must be included
and integrated. What is wanted is not the abstracted self but the
whole, undiminished man. This concentration aims at and is actuality.

The doctrine of immersion demands and promises penetration   25
into the thinking One, "that by which this world is thought," the
pure subject. But in lived actuality no one thinks without something
being thought; rather is that which thinks as dependent on that
which is thought as vice versa. A subject that annuls the object to
rise above it annuls its own actuality. A thinking subject by itself exists — in thought, as the product and object of thought, as a limit-
concept that lacks all imaginable content; also in the anticipatory determination of death for which one may also substitute its metaphor,
that deep sleep which is virtually no less impenetrable; and finally in
the assertions of a doctrine concerning a state of immersion that
resembles such deep sleep and is essentially without consciousness and without memory. These are the supreme excesses of It-
language. One has to respect its sublime power to ignore while at
the same time recognizing it as something that can at most be an object of living experience but that cannot be lived.

Buddha, the "Perfected" and perfecter, asserts not. He refuses to   26
claim that unity exists or does not exist; that he who has passed
through all the trials of immersion will persist in unity after death or
that he will not persist in it. This refusal, this "noble silence," has
been explained in two ways. Theoretically: because perfection is said
to elude the categories of thought and assertion. Practically: because
the unveiling of such truths would not aid salvation. In truth both
explanations belong together: whoever treats being as the object of
an assertion, pulls it down into division, into the antitheses of the It-
world — in which there is no salvation. "When, O monk, the view

prevails that soul and body are identical, there is no salvation; when, O monk, the view prevails that the soul is one and the body another, then also there is no salvation." In the envisaged mystery, even as in lived actuality, neither "thus it is" nor "thus it is not" prevails, neither being nor not-being, but rather thus-and-otherwise, being and not-being, the indissoluble. To confront the undivided mystery undivided, that is the primal condition of salvation. That the Buddha belongs to those who recognized this, is certain. Like all true teachers, he wishes to teach not a view but the way. He contests only one assertion, that of the "fools" who say that there is no acting, no deed, no strength: we *can* go the way. He risks only one assertion, the decisive one: "There is, O monks, what is Unborn, Unbecome, Uncreated, Unformed"; if that were not, there would be no goal; this *is*, the way has a goal.

So far we may follow the Buddha, faithful to the truth of our encounter; going further would involve a betrayal of the actuality of our own life. For according to the truth and actuality that we do not fetch from our own depths but that has been inspired in us and apportioned to us, we know: if this is merely one of the goals, then it cannot be ours; and if it is *the* goal, then it has been misnamed. And: if it is one of the goals, then the path may lead all the way to it; if it is *the* goal, then the path merely leads closer to it.   27

The goal was for the Buddha "the annulment of suffering," which is to say, of becoming and passing away — the salvation from the wheel of rebirth. "Henceforth there is no recurrence" was to be the formula for those who had liberated themselves from the desire for existence and thus from the compulsion to become again ceaselessly. We do not know whether there is a recurrence; the line of this dimension of time in which we live we do not extend beyond this life; and we do not try to uncover what will reveal itself to us in its own time and law. But if we did know that there was recurrence, then we should not seek to escape from it: we should desire not crude existence but the chance to speak in every existence, in its appropriate manner and language, the eternal I of the destructible and the eternal You of the indestructible.   28

Whether the Buddha leads men to the goal of redemption from having to recur, we do not know. Certainly he leads to an intermediate goal that concerns us, too: the unification of the soul. But he leads there not only, as is necessary, away from the "jungle of opinions," but also away from the "deception of forms" — which for us is no deception but (in spite of all the paradoxes of intuition that make for subjectivity but *for us simply belong to it*) the reliable world. His path, too, is a way of ignoring something, and when he bids us become aware of the processes in our body, what he means is almost   29 the opposite of our sense-assured insight into the body. Nor does he lead the unified being further to that supreme You-saying that is open to it. His inmost decision seems to aim at the annulment of the ability to say You.

The Buddha knows saying You to man — that is clear from his greatly superior, but also greatly direct, intercourse with his disciples — but he does not teach it: to this love, which means "boundless inclusion in the heart of all that has become," the simple confrontation of being by being remains alien. In the depths of his silence he certainly knows, too, the You-saying to the primal ground, transcending all the "gods" whom he treats like disciples; it was from a relational process that became substance that his deed came, clearly as an answer to the You; but of this he remains silent. **30**

His following among the nations, however, "the great vehicle," denied him gloriously. They addressed the eternal You of man — using the name of the Buddha. And they expect as the coming Buddha, the last one of his eon, him that shall fulfill love. **31**

All doctrines of immersion are based on the gigantic delusion of a human spirit bent back into itself — the delusion that spirit occurs in man. In truth it occurs from man — between man and what he is not. As the spirit bent back into itself renounces this sense, this sense of relation, he must draw into man that which is not man, he must psychologize world and God. This is the psychical delusion of the spirit. **32**

"I proclaim, friend," says the Buddha, "that in this fathom-sized, feeling-afflicted ascetic's body dwell the world and the origin of the world and the annulment of the world and the path that leads to the annulment of the world." **33**

That is true, but ultimately it is no longer true. **34**

Certainly, the world dwells in me as a notion, just as I dwell in it as a thing. But that does not mean that it is in me, just as I am not in it. The world and I include each other reciprocally. This contradiction for thought, which inheres in the It-relation, is annulled by the You-relation which detaches me from the world in order to relate me to it. **35**

The self-sense, that which cannot be included in the world, I carry in myself. The being-sense, that which cannot be included in any notion, the world carries in itself. But this is not a thinkable "will" but the whole worldliness of the world, just as the former is not a "knowing subject" but the whole I-likeness of the I. No further "reduction" is valid here: whoever does not honor the ultimate unities thwarts the sense that is only comprehensible but not conceptual. **36**

The origin of the world and the annulment of the world are not in me; neither are they outside me; they simply are not — they al- **37** ways occur, and their occurrence is also connected with me, with my life, my decision, my work, my service, and also depends on me, on my life, my decision, my work, and my service. But what it depends on is not whether I "affirm" or "negate" the world in my soul, but how I let the attitude of my soul toward the world come to life, life that affects the world, actual life — and in actual life paths coming from very different attitudes of the soul can cross. But whoever merely has a living "experience" of his attitude and retains it in his soul may be as thoughtful as can be, he is worldless — and all the games, arts, intoxications, enthusiasms, and mysteries that happen within him do not touch the world's skin. As long as one attains redemption only in his self, he cannot do any good or harm to the world; he does not concern it. Only he that believes in the world achieves contact with it; and if he commits himself he also cannot remain godless. Let us love the actual world that never wishes to be annulled, but love it in all its terror, but dare to embrace it with our spirit's arms — and our hands encounter the hands that hold it.

I know nothing of a "world" and of "worldly life" that separate 38 us from God. What is designated that way is life with an alienated It-world, the life of experience and use. Whoever goes forth in truth to the world, goes forth to God. Concentration and going forth, both in truth, the one-and-the-other which is the One, are what is needful.

God embraces but is not the universe; just so, God embraces 39 but is not my self. On account of this which cannot be spoken about, I can say in my language, as all can say in theirs: You. For the sake of this there are I and You, there is dialogue, there is language, and spirit whose primal deed language is, and there is, in eternity, the word.

QUESTIONS FOR CRITICAL READING

1. How does Buber explain the idea of dependence in "our relationship to God" (para. 1)?
2. How does Buber explain God's needing "you" (para. 5)? Do you find his ideas persuasive on this point?
3. How does the idea of dependence affect traditional views of faith as you understand them?
4. Why does Buber call prayer and sacrifice "two great servants" (para. 7)?
5. What does Buber mean by "immersion or a descent into the self" (para. 9)? How does this relate to the idea of "unification" in the same paragraph?

6. What is the significance of Prajapati's response to Indra when he asks how one can "find and recognize the self" (para. 20)?

7. Do you agree that "In lived actuality there is no unity of being" (para. 23)? Explain what Buber means by that statement.

SUGGESTIONS FOR WRITING

1. Establish the nature of the faith that Buber holds. Which of his beliefs seem most important to qualifying his faith? What importance does faith have for Buber? What role does he feel that faith has in the life of human beings?

2. Based on the passage from *I and Thou,* establish what you feel would be important guidelines for living. If what Buber says is true, then how should one conduct a meaningful life? What moral views are most important, and how ought one to behave? Would behavior be as important as faith in determining one's ultimate fate?

3. Examine the second half of the essay, which considers "immersion" and "unification." Do you support or oppose Buber's position regarding the surrender of selfhood to God? What are the most powerful arguments that can be made against his views? What arguments can you make to support them?

4. Consider this phrase: "Actuality is to be found only in effective activity" (para. 23). If the existential view is that we must actualize our own life and that the way we live our life determines who and what we really are — even in the eyes of God — then how should we live? What steps must you take in order to actualize your own life?

5. Establish which of Buber's ideas you find most important, and then establish a dialogue with Buber in which you clarify your own thinking concerning the ideas that interest you most. In what ways is your thinking in line with Buber's, and in what ways do you find yourself moving in a different direction?

6. **CONNECTIONS**   Discuss the idea of dialogue as it is developed in Martin Buber's writing and in the *Bhagavad Gītā.* Would Buber feel that the relationship between Lord Krishna and Arjuna resembles the relationship he envisions between God and humanity? What are the differences between these two relationships, and what are the similarities?

7. **CONNECTIONS**   On what points does Buber agree with the Buddha? Refer to "Meditation: The Path to Enlightenment." How close is the thinking of these two writers? On what major points do they disagree? Explain the nature of their disagreement and the implications of the disagreement for your acceptance of Buber's ideas.

PART EIGHT

POETICS

Aristotle
Alexander Pope
William Wordsworth
Virginia Woolf
Susan Sontag

INTRODUCTION

According to the Greeks, poetics was the art of crafting verses that enhanced men's and women's interpretations of the natural world and their place in it. The poetry of Homer (believed to have lived between 1100 and 800 B.C.) not only entertained willing listeners but immortalized heroes, praised civilizations, and explored the nature of humanity. However, not all Greeks celebrated the art form. Plato denounced poets on the grounds that they stirred the emotions and appealed to the senses and thereby distracted people from moral concerns. Although Aristotle, Plato's student, never openly contradicted his teacher, he did not view poetry as immoral. In fact, he praised art in general for its ability to imitate (or represent) life in a fashion that deepened human understanding. Moreover, Aristotle felt that tragic poetry purged the emotions of pity and fear and thus performed an important service for individuals. To him, this catharsis — or cleansing — of the emotions was an important psychological benefit of the poetic art.

The connection between the poetic and the moral remained controversial even after Aristotle's defense. In the Middle Ages, poetry and its ability to arouse the emotions were regarded with deep suspicion by the church. However, in the late Middle Ages poets such as Dante again defended the ability of poetry to instruct the reader morally. But it was during the romantic era in the nineteenth century when the poetic — the appeal to the emotions through eloquent verse and dramatic imagery — was fully embraced.

The relationship between poetry that excites emotion, as in the lyric, and poetry that praises and glorifies, as in the epic, has long been of interest to both poets and critics. To some thinkers, the formal elements — rhyme, meter, imagery, and grand themes — have been the decisive measures of quality in poetry. For others, the poetic has been more closely connected with what the writer Edgar Allan Poe (1809 – 1849) called "the poetic sentiment" — the emotions associated with the experience of poetry. For these thinkers and poets, the effect of the poem is the most important measure of its quality.

Ideas of the poetic can be expanded to other forms of art as well. The rhythm of language relates to the rhythm of music or even to the parts of a sculpture. The imagery and comparisons in poetry have their counterparts in painting. All art forms struggle, as Aristotle points out, to clarify and deepen human experience.

Aristotle's *Poetics* is a landmark document that continues to influence modern thought. He approaches poetics in this selection through a discussion of poetic drama, especially tragedy. For him, the tragic drama appeals to what is most noble in the audience. The strength of the dramatic action — the plot — was most important for Aristotle. Although he commented on the use of language, characterization, music, and other stage conventions, he felt the audience was most deeply moved by what happened to the characters on stage — the action. By contemplating action that imitates a life in nature, the audience would be cleansed emotionally.

Alexander Pope was a neoclassicist in eighteenth-century England and therefore respected both the Aristotelian and Platonic positions in literature. But he was, like most thinkers of his time, influenced more by Roman rather than Greek thinkers. Roman experts in the poetic were Virgil, Horace, Catullus, and Cicero. Their concerns often centered on moral issues and the obligations of the individual to live an upstanding life and contribute to the body politic. In his *Essay on Criticism* Pope praises poetry that has a strong moral center balanced by temperate qualities and the avoidance of excess. His advice to critics also recommends that they take a holistic view of poetry and not praise or disparage a specific part, such as its language or its metrical patterns. Pope echoes Roman moralists by favoring a middle path and by packaging his central thoughts in concise and memorable phrases: "Be not the first by whom the new are tried / Nor yet the last to lay the old aside" (ll. 135 – 36).

Wordsworth's preface to his and Coleridge's volume of verse *Lyrical Ballads* was a declaration of poetic independence that was in many ways a reaction to Pope's views. Wordsworth felt that Pope's tight couplets and serious message were inappropriate for the new romantic movement. For the romantics, artificiality of language and form gave way to ease and informality. Rhyme was still possible, although by no means a requirement, while the language of Wordsworth's poetry emulated as much as possible the language of the people he heard in daily speech. His emphasis is on lyric poetry and the emotional responses it evokes. He is also unusually democratic in his views, elevating the "humble and rustic" life as appropriate subject matter for poetry. This view contrasted with Aristotle's emphasis on characters of high birth and Pope's emphasis on high thought.

Virginia Woolf gives advice in a letter to a young poet who wrote to her complaining that it was all but impossible to write poetry in 1931. Woolf was famous for her novels and essays and used powerfully poetic language, even though she says she is not qualified to write about poetry. She quotes from some modern poetry and points out to her young correspondent that the poetry is difficult to understand and centers largely on the limited experience of the poet. She argues against writing only about oneself and suggests that he follow the lead of the great poets of the past, such as Shakespeare, who gave us great characters. In one sense, she argues for a poetry that, like her own novels, treats the world of experience rather than the limited experience of the individual. She echoes the views of Aristotle, who valued a poetic experience where characters in action emulate the lives of all of us. Her advice to the young poet is to look outward and to achieve poetry by representing the world of real people.

In "Against Interpretation," Susan Sontag warns against constructing an overly intellectual interpretation of a work of art. Instead, she emphasizes the importance of sensory experience in the individual's encounter with the work, whether it be poetry, prose, or even film. According to Sontag, all these art forms have a poetics of structure and technique, and all impress themselves on the emotions. It is this emotional impact that moves her to encourage us to experience "an erotics of art," by which she means privileging the emotional rather than the intellectual response to a work.

Just as previous writers enlarged the meaning of poetics to include more varieties of poetry and prose, Sontag moves to include film, which she sees as a variety of literature with its own standards. However, it is important to note that she arrives at this conclusion only after having taken into account the work of classical writers such as Homer, psychologists such as Freud, thinkers such as Marx, novelists such as Kafka, and playwrights such as Tennessee Williams. Interestingly, just as she complains of the limitations of interpretation, she also complains of the limitations of the novel — saying most novelists are journalists or sociologists — and of the film, which is often visually sophisticated but pseudointellectual in story and dialogue.

The following essays discuss poetry, but they are also about the poetic in art — the arrangement of parts that affects our emotions. Aristotle begins with drama, Pope continues with ideas, Wordsworth with lyric emotion, Woolf with recommendations that also apply to the modern novel, and Sontag extends her vision beyond the novel to film. Similar views apply to painting, sculpture, and the many arts that appeal to our emotions and that all, in their way, imitate experience. These writers see the interrelationship of the arts and apply the poetic to experience in the largest possible way.

ARISTOTLE
Tragedy and the Emotions
of Pity and Fear

ARISTOTLE (384 – 322 B.C.) is one of a succession of Greeks who changed the world of ideas in ancient times. Socrates was Plato's teacher, and Plato was Aristotle's teacher, who in turn was Alexander the Great's teacher. Aristotle was a brilliant student in Plato's Academy, remaining there for twenty years and earning the nickname of the "Intellect" of the school. He later conducted his own school, called the Lyceum, in a spot sacred to Apollo in Athens. His views differed essentially from Plato's, although as long as Plato lived, Aristotle avoided direct conflict with his teacher.

The *Poetics* is western culture's landmark document regarding dramatic poetry. Its date of composition is unknown. Although it was unavailable during the medieval period, it was rediscovered during the Renaissance by Giorgio Valla, who translated it into Latin in 1498, thus beginning an important movement in literary analysis and discussion. Aristotle focuses on several kinds of poetry but the selection included here focuses on tragedy, the profoundest form of dramatic poetry. His work on this subject is rooted in observation and knowledge of the traditions of the major tragedians. Based on his observations at numerous competitions for tragedy in Athens, he establishes the nature of tragedy and theorizes about its role.

Ancient Greeks held a series of contests between dramatists during the festival of Dionysus. By the time Aristotle began to write about it, many of the greatest Greek dramatists had already done their work, and the occasion was highly organized. Play-

Translated by Gerald F. Else.

wrights were chosen for the competition by experts. Prominent and wealthy citizens were awarded the honor of paying for the costs of the production of the plays, including the actors, the scaena (stage setting), and other equipment. The archons, or judges, sat in a place of honor during performances and awarded prizes. It was an immense honor to be awarded a prize, and all the greatest playwrights — Aeschylus, Sophocles, Euripides, and Aristophanes — won several prizes during their lives.

Tragedy is poetic drama whose heros or heroines are noble. In a tragedy, a noble person's fortune changes because of circumstances that are — or may sometimes seem to be — beyond his or her control. It was essential for main characters in a tragedy to be noble since they must fall from a great height, which makes their fate inherently more moving and dramatic than the fall of an ordinary person. The hero in a tragedy presents a model for all of us: if someone of noble blood can fall from a great height, we can do so as well.

Aristotle also mentions the concept of the tragic flaw, a character flaw made visible through words and actions that leads a great hero to fall. Some obvious flaws in tragic figures are Othello's jealousy in *Othello* and Macbeth's ambition in *Macbeth*. The tragic hero's or heroine's flaw, working in conjunction with fate, brings about the tragic outcome of the play.

Aristotle pointed to the power of poetic tragedy to evoke intense emotions in the audience, particularly terror and pity. The terror results from our realization that the hero's fate might just as easily be ours; the pity results from our human sympathy with a fellow sufferer. Therefore, the fearful and pathetic represent significant emotions crucial to our witnessing of the drama, and poetry must evoke emotion and use it in an artful fashion. For Aristotle, the evocation of these emotions was cleansing — he used the word *katharsis,* meaning purging. Tragedy purges us of these emotions.

In this selection Aristotle talks at length about the specific requirements of tragedy and their relative importance. He cites plot, characters, verbal expression, thought, visual adornment, and songcomposition (in order of importance) and takes each of these in turn to demonstrate its significance. Among the more surprising aspects of his discussion may be the declaration that plot is more important than character (para. 4). He even suggests that tragedy may exist without character but not without plot (para. 5). He also says that beginning dramatists are capable of creating characters but definitely not of creating plot. To us, this is surprising because most modern theories of literature emphasize character. And when we think of great Shakespearian tragedies, we think of the title characters of the plays — *Hamlet, King Lear, Macbeth, Othello, Julius Caesar,* and *Antony and Cleopatra.*

Aristotle's concepts of peripety and recognition are also central to any understanding of tragedy. *Peripety* (para. 22), derived from the Greek word meaning "to walk around," means a sudden change in the fortune of a character or in the direction of events. For example, a character may be heading toward a personal victory only to have his efforts suddenly end in his unexpected defeat. Peripety is essential to tragedy. *Recognition* is the awareness of a significant truth that may, in fact, produce the peripety. As Aristotle says, the best recognition takes place at the same time as the peripety. Usually, the recognition in tragedy is the chief character's awareness of a truth that the character would rather suppress. Oedipus, in Sophocles' *Oedipus Rex,* discovers that the man who has cursed the land and whom he has condemned to exile is himself. Long before, the oracle told him that he was fated to kill his father and marry his mother, and he left home as a result. But he does not know that he was adopted or that when he is challenged at a crossroads by an older man — whom he fights and kills — he has begun to carry out his fate. Only after he marries his mother and takes his father's place does he learn that he is the "criminal" he set out to find. In *Oedipus Rex,* the recognition comes at the moment of the peripety, when Oedipus's fate "turns around."

ARISTOTLE'S RHETORIC

The works Aristotle prepared for publication and by which he gained immense fame and influence were for the most part lost to the world by the end of the first century A.D. At that time, another group of works surfaced that was edited in Rome and produced in a scholarly edition. This group is peculiar for its clipped and notelike style, which has led many modern Aristotle experts to conclude that these works were reconstructed from lectures. The modern world lost these works with the fall of Rome and did not recover them until the Renaissance, when they were rediscovered and printed beginning in the late fifteenth and early sixteenth centuries.

The *Poetics* closely resembles a lecture that might have been given to students of drama. It has a number of the rhetorical hallmarks of the lecture: it is on a single subject, along with related adjuncts, and it relies on a step-by-step procedure that always pauses to review what has already been said. In this selection Aristotle provides adequate definitions for all the key terms he introduces;

he also takes care to refer his audience to elements that have been previously discussed (a number of these are referred to but are not included in this passage).

Another Aristotelian hallmark is his categorical structure. He constantly reminds us that things have a specific number of categories that will be discussed: tragedy has six elements, plot has two kinds, and so on. Aristotle breaks things into parts or categories and then examines each component separately on the assumption that such an examination will yield greater knowledge of the thing under discussion. The *Poetics* is a discussion of several categories of poetic performance, beginning with the comedy and proceeding to the epic and then the tragedy. First, each category is discussed, and then its subcategories are discussed. The chief category is tragedy, and Aristotle devoted considerable thought to what he must have believed to be the most noble, uplifting, serious, and important category of all — poetry.

Today, this essay is an important starting point for all who wish to talk and think seriously about poetics. The principles presented in this essay are relevant to any current discussion of poetry. Aristotle's approach is so thorough that many critics feel no critical statement has since penetrated as deeply into the heart of dramatic poetry.

Tragedy and the Emotions of Pity and Fear

Tragedy and Its Six Constituent Elements

Our discussions of imitative poetry in hexameters,[1] and of comedy, will come later; at present let us deal with tragedy, recovering from what has been said so far the definition of its essential nature, as it was in development. Tragedy, then, is a process of imitating an action which has serious implications, is complete, and possesses magnitude; by means of language which has been made sensuously

1

---

[1] **hexameters** The first known metrical form for classical verse. Each line had six metrical feet, some of which were prescribed in advance. It is the meter used for epic poetry and for poetry designed to teach a lesson. The form has sometimes been used in comparatively modern poetry but rarely with success except in French.

attractive, with each of its varieties found separately in the parts; enacted by the persons themselves and not presented through narrative; through a course of pity and fear completing the purification of tragic acts which have those emotional characteristics. By "language made sensuously attractive" I mean language that has rhythm and melody, and by "its varieties found separately" I mean the fact that certain parts of the play are carried on through spoken verses alone and others the other way around, through song.

Now first of all, since they perform the imitation through action 2 (by acting it), the adornment of their visual appearance will perforce constitute some part of the making of tragedy; and song-composition and verbal expression also, for those are the media in which they perform the imitation. By "verbal expression" I mean the actual composition of the verses, and by "song-composition" something whose meaning is entirely clear.

Next, since it is an imitation of an action and is enacted by cer- 3 tain people who are performing the action, and since those people must necessarily have certain traits both of character and thought (for it is thanks to these two factors that we speak of people's actions also as having a defined character, and it is in accordance with their actions that all either succeed or fail); and since the imitation of the action is the plot, for by "plot" I mean here the structuring of the events, and by the "characters" that in accordance with which we say that the persons who are acting have a defined moral character, and by "thought" all the passages in which they attempt to prove some thesis or set forth an opinion — it follows of necessity, then, that tragedy as a whole has just six constituent elements, in relation to the essence that makes it a distinct species; and they are plot, characters, verbal expression, thought, visual adornment, and song-composition. For the elements by which they imitate are two (i.e., verbal expression and song-composition), the manner in which they imitate is one (visual adornment), the things they imitate are three (plot, characters, thought), and there is nothing more beyond these. These then are the constituent forms they use.

The Relative Importance of the Six Elements

The greatest of these elements is the structuring of the incidents. 4 For tragedy is an imitation not of men but of a life, an action, and they have moral quality in accordance with their characters but are happy or unhappy in accordance with their actions; hence they are not active in order to imitate their characters, but they include the characters along with the actions for the sake of the latter. Thus the structure of events, the plot, is the goal of tragedy, and the goal is the greatest thing of all.

Again: a tragedy cannot exist without a plot, but it can without   5
characters: thus the tragedies of most of our modern poets are devoid of character, and in general many poets are like that; so also with the relationship between Zeuxis and Polygnotus,[2] among the painters: Polygnotus is a good portrayer of character, while Zeuxis' painting has no dimension of character at all.

Again: if one strings end to end speeches that are expressive of   6
character and carefully worked in thought and expression, he still will not achieve the result which we said was the aim of tragedy; the job will be done much better by a tragedy that is more deficient in these other respects but has a plot, a structure of events. It is much the same case as with painting: the most beautiful pigments smeared on at random will not give as much pleasure as a black-and-white outline picture. Besides, the most powerful means tragedy has for swaying our feelings, namely the peripeties and recognitions,[3] are elements of plot.

Again: an indicative sign is that those who are beginning a po-   7
etic career manage to hit the mark in verbal expression and character portrayal sooner than they do in plot construction; and the same is true of practically all the earliest poets.

So plot is the basic principle, the heart and soul, as it were, of   8
tragedy, and the characters come second: . . . it is the imitation of an action and imitates the persons primarily for the sake of their action.

Third in rank is thought. This is the ability to state the issues   9
and appropriate points pertaining to a given topic, an ability which springs from the arts of politics and rhetoric; in fact the earlier poets made their characters talk "politically," the present-day poets rhetorically. But "character" is that kind of utterance which clearly reveals the bent of a man's moral choice (hence there is no character in that class of utterances in which there is nothing at all that the speaker is

---

[2] **Zeuxis (fl. 420 – 390 B.C.) and Polygnotus (c. 470 – 440 B.C.)** Zeuxis developed a method of painting in which the figures were rounded and apparently three-dimensional. Thus, he was an illusionistic painter, imitating life in a realistic style. Polygnotus was famous as a painter, and his works were on the Acropolis as well as at Delphi. His draftsmanship was especially praised.

[3] **peripeties and recognitions** The turning-about of fortune and the recognition on the part of the tragic hero of the truth. This is, for Aristotle, a critical moment in the drama, especially if both events happen simultaneously, as they do in *Oedipus Rex*. It is quite possible for these moments to happen apart from one another.

choosing or rejecting), while "thought" is the passages in which they try to prove that something is so or not so, or state some general principle.

Fourth is the verbal expression of the speeches. I mean by this   10 the same thing that was said earlier, that the "verbal expression" is the conveyance of thought through language: a statement which has the same meaning whether one says "verses" or "speeches."

The song-composition of the remaining parts is the greatest of   11 the sensuous attractions, and the visual adornment of the dramatic persons can have a strong emotional effect but is the least artistic element, the least connected with the poetic art; in fact the force of tragedy can be felt even without benefit of public performance and actors, while for the production of the visual effect the property man's art is even more decisive than that of the poets.

General Principles of the Tragic Plot

With these distinctions out of the way, let us next discuss what   12 the structuring of the events should be like, since this is both the basic and the most important element in the tragic art. We have established, then, that tragedy is an imitation of an action which is complete and whole and has some magnitude (for there is also such a thing as a whole that has no magnitude). "Whole" is that which has beginning, middle, and end. "Beginning" is that which does not necessarily follow on something else, but after it something else naturally is or happens; "end," the other way around, is that which naturally follows on something else, either necessarily or for the most part, but nothing else after it; and "middle" that which naturally follows on something else and something else on it. So, then, well constructed plots should neither begin nor end at any chance point but follow the guidelines just laid down.

Furthermore, since the beautiful, whether a living creature or   13 anything that is composed of parts, should not only have these in a fixed order to one another but also possess a definite size which does not depend on chance — for beauty depends on size and order; hence neither can a very tiny creature turn out to be beautiful (since our perception of it grows blurred as it approaches the period of imperceptibility) nor an excessively huge one (for then it cannot all be perceived at once and so its unity and wholeness are lost), if for example there were a creature a thousand miles long — so, just as in the case of living creatures they must have some size, but one that can be taken in a single view, so with plots: they should have length, but such that they are easy to remember. As to a limit of the

length, the one is determined by the tragic competitions and the ordinary span of attention. (If they had to compete with a hundred
tragedies they would compete by the water clock, as they say used
to be done [?].) But the limit fixed by the very nature of the case is:
the longer the plot, up to the point of still being perspicuous as a
whole, the finer it is so far as size is concerned; or to put it in general
terms, the length in which, with things happening in unbroken sequence, a shift takes place either probably or necessarily from bad to
good fortune or from good to bad — that is an acceptable norm of
length.

But a plot is not unified, as some people think, simply because   14
it has to do with a single person. A large, indeed an indefinite number of things can happen to a given individual, some of which go to
constitute no unified event; and in the same way there can be many
acts of a given individual from which no single action emerges.
Hence it seems clear that those poets are wrong who have composed
Heracleïds, Theseïds, and the like. They think that since Heracles was
a single person it follows that the plot will be single too. But Homer,
superior as he is in all other respects, appears to have grasped this
point well also, thanks either to art or nature, for in composing an
Odyssey he did not incorporate into it everything that happened to
the hero, for example how he was wounded on Mt. Parnassus[4] or
how he feigned madness at the muster, neither of which events, by
happening, made it at all necessary or probable that the other
should happen. Instead, he composed the *Odyssey* — and the *Iliad*
similarly — around a unified action of the kind we have been talking
about.

A poetic imitation, then, ought to be unified in the same way as   15
a single imitation in any other mimetic field, by having a single object: since the plot is an imitation of an action, the latter ought to be
both unified and complete, and the component events ought to be
so firmly compacted that if any one of them is shifted to another
place, or removed, the whole is loosened up and dislocated; for an
element whose addition or subtraction makes no perceptible extra
difference is not really a part of the whole.

From what has been said it is also clear that the poet's job is not to   16
report what has happened but what is likely to happen: that is, what is
capable of happening according to the rule of probability or necessity.

---

[4] **Mt. Parnassus** A mountain in central Greece traditionally sacred to Apollo.
In legend, Odysseus was wounded there, but the point Aristotle is making is that the
writer of epics need not include every detail of his hero's life in a given work.
Homer, in writing the *Odyssey,* was working with a hero, Odysseus, whose story had
been legendary long before he began writing.

Thus the difference between the historian and the poet is not in their utterances being in verse or prose (it would be quite possible for Herodotus' work to be translated into verse, and it would not be any the less a history with verse than it is without it); the difference lies in the fact that the historian speaks of what has happened, the poet of the kind of thing that *can* happen. Hence also poetry is a more philosophical and serious business than history; for poetry speaks more of universals, history of particulars. "Universal" in this case is what kind of person is likely to do or say certain kinds of things, according to probability or necessity; that is what poetry aims at, although it gives its persons particular names afterward; while the "particular" is what Alcibiades did or what happened to him.

In the field of comedy this point has been grasped: our comic poets construct their plots on the basis of general probabilities and then assign names to the persons quite arbitrarily, instead of dealing with individuals as the old iambic poets[5] did. But in tragedy they still cling to the historically given names. The reason is that what is possible is persuasive; so what has not happened we are not yet ready to believe is possible, while what has happened is, we feel, obviously possible: for it would not have happened if it were impossible. Nevertheless, it is a fact that even in our tragedies, in some cases only one or two of the names are traditional, the rest being invented, and in some others none at all. It is so, for example, in Agathon's *Antheus* — the names in it are as fictional as the events — and it gives no less pleasure because of that. Hence the poets ought not to cling at all costs to the traditional plots, around which our tragedies are constructed. And in fact it is absurd to go searching for this kind of authentication, since even the familiar names are familiar to only a few in the audience and yet give the same kind of pleasure to all.

So from these considerations it is evident that the poet should be a maker of his plots more than of his verses, insofar as he is a poet by virtue of his imitations and what he imitates is actions. Hence even if it happens that he puts something that has actually taken place into poetry, he is none the less a poet; for there is nothing to prevent some of the things that have happened from being the kind of things that can happen, and that is the sense in which he is their maker.

17

18

---

[5] **old iambic poets** Aristotle may be referring to Archilochus (fl. 650 B.C.) and the iambic style he developed. The iambic is a metrical foot of two syllables, a short and a long stress, and was the most popular metrical style before the time of Aristotle. "Dealing with individuals" implies using figures already known to the audience rather than figures whose names can be arbitrarily assigned because no one knows who they are.

Simple and Complex Plots

Among simple plots and actions the episodic are the worst. By 19
"episodic" plot I mean one in which there is no probability or necessity for the order in which the episodes follow one another. Such structures are composed by the bad poets because they are bad poets, but by the good poets because of the actors: in composing contest pieces for them, and stretching out the plot beyond its capacity, they are forced frequently to dislocate the sequence.

Furthermore, since the tragic imitation is not only of a complete 20
action but also of events that are fearful and pathetic,[6] and these come about best when they come about contrary to one's expectation yet logically, one following from the other; that way they will be more productive of wonder than if they happen merely at random, by chance — because even among chance occurrences the ones people consider most marvelous are those that seem to have come about as if on purpose: for example the way the statue of Mitys at Argos killed the man who had been the cause of Mitys' death, by falling on him while he was attending the festival; it stands to reason, people think, that such things don't happen by chance — so plots of that sort cannot fail to be artistically superior.

Some plots are simple, others are complex; indeed the actions of 21
which the plots are imitations already fall into these two categories. By "*simple*" action I mean one the development of which being continuous and unified in the manner stated above, the reversal comes without peripety or recognition, and by "complex" action one in which the reversal is continuous but with recognition or peripety or both. And these developments must grow out of the very structure of the plot itself, in such a way that on the basis of what has happened previously this particular outcome follows either by necessity or in accordance with probability; for there is a great difference in whether these events happen because of those or merely after them.

"Peripety" is a shift of what is being undertaken to the opposite 22
in the way previously stated, and that in accordance with probability or necessity as we have just been saying; as for example in the *Oedipus* the man who has come, thinking that he will reassure Oedipus,

---

[6] **fearful and pathetic** Aristotle said that tragedy should evoke two emotions: terror and pity. The terror results from our realizing that what is happening to the hero might just as easily happen to us; the pity results from our human sympathy with a fellow sufferer. Therefore, the fearful and pathetic represent significant emotions appropriate to our witnessing drama.

that is, relieve him of his fear with respect to his mother, by revealing who he once was, brings about the opposite; and in the *Lynceus,* as he (Lynceus) is being led away with every prospect of being executed, and Danaus pursuing him with every prospect of doing the executing, it comes about as a result of the other things that have happened in the play that *he* is executed and Lynceus is saved. And "recognition" is, as indeed the name indicates, a shift from ignorance to awareness, pointing to the direction either of close blood ties or of hostility, of people who have previously been in a clearly marked state of happiness or unhappiness.

The finest recognition is one that happens at the same time as a   23
peripety, as is the case with the one in the *Oedipus*. Naturally, there are also other kinds of recognition: it is possible for one to take place in the prescribed manner in relation to inanimate objects and chance occurrences, and it is possible to recognize whether a person has acted or not acted. But the form that is most integrally a part of the plot, the action, is the one aforesaid; for that kind of recognition combined with peripety will excite either pity or fear (and these are the kinds of action of which tragedy is an imitation according to our definition), because both good and bad fortune will also be most likely to follow that kind of event. Since, further, the recognition is a recognition of persons, some are of one person by the other one only (when it is already known who the "other one" is), but sometimes it is necessary for both persons to go through a recognition, as for example Iphigenia is recognized by her brother through the sending of the letter, but of him by Iphigenia another recognition is required.

These then are two elements of plot: peripety and recognition;   24
third is the *pathos*. Of these, peripety and recognition have been discussed; a *pathos* is a destructive or painful act, such as deaths on stage, paroxysms of pain, woundings, and all that sort of thing.

The Tragic Side of Tragedy: Pity and Fear and the Patterns of the Complex Plot

The "parts" of tragedy which should be used as constituent ele-   25
ments were mentioned earlier; (. . .) but what one should aim at and what one should avoid in composing one's plots, and whence the effect of tragedy is to come, remains to be discussed now, following immediately upon what has just been said.

Since, then, the construction of the finest tragedy should be not   26
simple but complex, and at the same time imitative of fearful and pitiable happenings (that being the special character of this kind of

poetry), it is clear first of all that (1) neither should virtuous men appear undergoing a change from good to bad fortune, for that is not fearful, nor pitiable either, but morally repugnant; nor (2) the wicked from bad fortune to good — that is the most untragic form of all, it has none of the qualities that one wants: it is productive neither of ordinary sympathy nor of pity nor of fear — nor again (3) the really wicked man changing from good fortune to bad, for that kind of structure will excite sympathy but neither pity nor fear, since the one (pity) is directed towards the man who does not deserve his misfortune and the other (fear) towards the one who is like the rest of mankind — what is left is the man who falls between these extremes. Such is a man who is neither a paragon of virtue and justice nor undergoes the change to misfortune through any real badness or wickedness but because of some mistake; one of those who stand in great repute and prosperity, like Oedipus and Thyestes: conspicuous men from families of that kind.

So, then, the artistically made plot must necessarily be single rather 27
that double, as some maintain, and involve a change not from bad fortune to good fortune but the other way round, from good fortune to bad, and not thanks to wickedness but because of some mistake of great weight and consequence, by a man such as we have described or else on the good rather than the bad side. An indication comes from what has been happening in tragedy: at the beginning the poets used to "tick off" whatever plots came their way, but nowadays the finest tragedies are composed about a few houses: they deal with Alcmeon, Oedipus, Orestes, Meleager, Thyestes, Telephus,[7] and whichever others have had the misfortune to do or undergo fearful things.

Thus the technically finest tragedy is based on this structure. 28
Hence those who bring charges against Euripides[8] for doing this in his tragedies are making the same mistake. His practice is correct in the way that has been shown. There is a very significant indication: on our stages and in the competitions, plays of this structure are accepted as the most tragic, *if* they are handled successfully, and Euripides, though he may not make his other arrangements effectively, still is felt by the audience to be the most tragic, at least, of the poets.

Second comes the kind which is rated first by certain people, 29
having its structure double like the *Odyssey*[9] and with opposite end-

---

[7] **Alcmeon . . . Telephus** Mythical characters who have been the heroes of Greek tragedies.

[8] **Euripides (480? – ?406 B.C.)** Tragic playwright, author of *Alcestis, Medea, Elektra,* and *The Bacchae.*

[9] **Odyssey** Greek epic poem by Homer (c.750 B.C.), many of whose characters, including Odysseus, appear in Greek tragedies.

ings for the good and bad. Its being put first is due to the weakness of the audiences; for the poets follow along, catering to their wishes. But this particular pleasure is not the one that springs from tragedy but is more characteristic of comedy.

Pity and Fear and the Tragic Act

Now it is possible for the fearful or pathetic effect to come from   30
the actors' appearance, but it is also possible for it to arise from the very structure of the events, and this is closer to the mark and characteristic of a better poet. Namely, the plot must be so structured, even without benefit of any visual effect, that the one who is hearing the events unroll shudders with fear and feels pity at what happens: which is what one would experience on hearing the plot of the *Oedipus*. To set out to achieve this by means of the masks and costumes is less artistic, and requires technical support in the staging. As for those who do not set out to achieve the fearful through the masks and costumes, but only the monstrous, they have nothing to do with tragedy at all; for one should not seek any and every pleasure from tragedy, but the one that is appropriate to it.

Since it is the pleasure derived from pity and fear by means of   31
imitation that the poet should seek to produce, it is clear that these qualities must be built into the constituent events. Let us determine, then, which kinds of happening are felt by the spectator to be fearful, and which pitiable. Now such acts are necessarily the work of persons who are near and dear (close blood kin) to one another, or enemies, or neither. But when an enemy attacks an enemy there is nothing pathetic about either the intention or the deed, except in the actual pain suffered by the victim; nor when the act is done by "neutrals"; but when the tragic acts come within the limits of close blood relationship, as when brother kills or intends to kill brother or do something else of that kind to him, or son to father or mother to son or son to mother — those are the situations one should look for.

Now although it is not admissible to break up the transmitted   32
stories — I mean for instance that Clytemnestra was killed by Orestes, or Eriphyle by Alcmeon — one should be artistic both in inventing stories and in managing the ones that have been handed down. But what we mean by "artistic" requires some explanation.

It is possible, then (1) for the act to be performed as the older   33
poets presented it, knowingly and wittingly; Euripides did it that way also, in Medea's murder of her children. It is possible (2) to refrain from performing the deed, with knowledge. Or it is possible (3) to perform the fearful act, but unwittingly, then recognize the

blood relationship later, as Sophocles' Oedipus does; in that case the
act is outside the play, but it can be in the tragedy itself, as with
Astydamas'[10] Alcmeon, or Telegonus in the *Wounding of Odysseus*.[11]
A further mode, in addition to these, is (4) while intending because
of ignorance to perform some black crime, to discover the relationship before one does it. And there is no other mode besides these;
for one must necessarily either do the deed or not, and with or without knowledge of what it is.

Of these modes, to know what one is doing but hold off and not   34
perform the act (no. 2) is worst: it has the morally repulsive character
and at the same time is not tragic; for there is no tragic act. Hence nobody composes that way, or only rarely, as, for example, Haemon
threatens Creon in the *Antigone*.[12] Performing the act (with knowledge) (no. 1) is second (poorest). Better is to perform it in ignorance
and recognize what one has done afterward (no. 3); for the repulsive
quality does not attach to the act, and the recognition has a shattering
emotional effect. But the best is the last (no. 4): I mean a case like the
one in the *Cresphontes* where Merope is about to kill her son but does
not do so because she recognizes him first; or in *Iphigenia in Tauris* the
same happens with sister and brother; or in the *Helle*[13] the son recognizes his mother just as he is about to hand her over to the enemy.

The reason for what was mentioned a while ago, namely that our   35
tragedies have to do with only a few families, is this: It was because the
poets, when they discovered how to produce this kind of effect in
their plots, were conducting their search on the basis of chance, not
art; hence they have been forced to focus upon those families which
happen to have suffered tragic happenings of this kind.

Enough, then, concerning the structure of events and what   36
traits the tragic plots should have.

---

[10] **Astydamas** Greek poet of the fourth century B.C.

[11] **the *Wounding of Odysseus*** A play about the hero of *The Odyssey* that has
not survived.

[12] ***Antigone*** A play by Sophocles (c. 496? – ?406 B.C.).

[13] ***Cresphontes . . . Iphigenia in Tauris . . . Helle*** Tragedies by Euripides; the
Cresphontes is lost.

QUESTIONS FOR CRITICAL READING

1. What are some possible reasons that Aristotle emphasized plot
   more than character in tragedy?

2. Do we still feel the emotions of terror and pity in tragic poetry? What modern equivalents have we substituted for them?

3. How would you rank the six constituent elements of tragedy in order of importance?

4. Aristotle discusses the demands of unity. What are they? What is unity in a poetic composition? See paragraph 12 and thereafter.

5. In this discussion how important is probability for Aristotle?

6. What does the poet imitate (see para. 18)? What is imitation?

SUGGESTIONS FOR WRITING

1. Aristotle (para. 16) suggests that tragedy is more important than history because tragic poetry "is more philosophical and serious business" and deals with what might be rather than simply with what has been. He goes so far as to say that even if history, such as Herodotus's work, were written in verse, tragedy would still be more important. Argue the case either to agree with Aristotle or to disagree with him.

2. What emotional effects do you perceive in tragic drama? Are those effects magnified by the use of poetic language, as in, for example, the tragedies of Shakespeare, such as *Romeo and Juliet, Hamlet,* or *Othello*? How does the powerful use of language in those plays contribute to your emotional response?

3. Analyze a recent film that you feel is serious enough in content to be a reasonable candidate for tragedy. How does it treat the six constituent elements of tragedy? Is there a reversal of fortune? Is there a clear moment of recognition? To what extent do you feel the film follows Aristotle's suggestions?

4. Imitation of an action is part of the poet's work. This idea has been central to Aristotelian criticism for generations and has been interpreted widely. Judging from your experience in either reading or seeing tragedies, what does imitation imply? What does it mean for a poet to imitate an action? How can a poet do so? If you wish to research this idea, look up *imitation* or *mimesis* in a dictionary of literary terms or examine Erich Auerbach's book, *Mimesis.*

5. In paragraph 24 Aristotle mentions a third element of plot to accompany peripety and recognition — pathos. *Pathos* ordinarily means "feeling" or "emotion." However, for Aristotle a pathos is "a destructive or painful act, such as deaths on stage." The usual rule in Greek tragedy is for death to happen off stage, but Aristotle considers the possibility of such actions occurring onstage. Is it possible that the current trend toward more and more graphic gore and violence in popular drama is an extension of Aristotle's pathos? What is the effect of such pathos in contemporary drama? What is its relationship to poetry?

6. **CONNECTIONS** Aristotle's concept of the imitation of an action has been taken to include the concept of the work of art staying true to life — which is another way of saying that it should imitate life. Does

the advice of William Wordsworth seem to support Aristotle's views? Would Wordsworth say that poetry ought to imitate life? In what ways does Wordsworth agree with Aristotle and in what ways does he differ in regard to the role of imitation? Aristotle emphasizes plot when he discusses imitation; what might the lyric poet aim to imitate in place of plot or action?

7. **CONNECTIONS**   Referring back to the personal accounts of Herodotus and Alvar Nuñez Cabeza de Vaca, would you say that they were careful to make their works truthful representations of their experiences? What qualities do those narratives have that would make them satisfying works of literature? Comment on the use of plot, character, language, and thought. Would Aristotle have found these works important and moving?

ALEXANDER POPE
From *An Essay on Criticism*

ALEXANDER POPE (1688 – 1744) was one of London's great
literary figures during the first half of the eighteenth century, a
contemporary of Jonathan Swift (1667 – 1745), Joseph Addison
(1672 – 1719), Sir Richard Steele (1672 – 1729), and Samuel Johnson (1709 – 1784). Pope lived during one of the great periods of
English life and culture: the age was rich in art, drama, music, and
literary achievement in part because the early 1700s was essentially a time of peace and expansion for England.

Pope — four feet six inches tall, with a twisted spine and a delicate constitution — was a very popular figure in London society
because of his gentleness and keen mind. Although he was not
born into a prominent family, he was at ease with aristocrats as
well as ordinary people. When he visited the homes of wealthy
friends, his health made him the center of attention, and he required a maid in constant attendance through the day and into the
night. In his later years he could not dress himself and was often in
pain from headaches and other ailments. He was such a lively and
interesting conversationalist, however, that no one, including the
maids who waited on him, complained about entertaining him.

Pope was a Catholic in England at a time when no Catholic
could receive a university degree, vote, or hold office. His father
was a wealthy linens dealer who provided Pope with a good but
somewhat limited education. In an age in which most educated
men (no women were permitted in the universities) read Latin and
Greek literature in the original languages, Pope's education was
sufficient in Latin but not in Greek. Moreover, during this period
most successful writers had patrons who supported them in return
for occasional poems on the subject of their families. Being
Catholic, he had no patron and thus had to earn money with his
pen. Ironically, one of his most successful ventures was his translation of Homer's *Iliad*, followed a few years later by his translation

of *The Odyssey.* To create his translation, he worked from translations provided by hack poets who worked for him, but the result was extraordinary poetry and a financial return that gave him independence.

The eighteenth century is usually known as the neoclassical period in English poetry because it was an age strongly affected by the theories of Aristotle in the *Poetics* and by the poetic practices of the Roman poets Virgil and Horace. Some of the principles of neoclassical poetry are spelled out by Pope in this selection from his *Essay on Criticism* (1711). The selection contained here is all but the last stanza of Book II (there are four books of this length in the essay).

The poem is serious and somewhat didactic in its purpose, which is to impart good manners to critics and suggest useful strategies for poets. The form of the poem — rhymed couplets with each line possessing five metrical feet and ten syllables — is called *rhymed iambic pentameter.* This was the form chosen by most poets of the age whenever they felt they had important ideas to discuss. Pope's purpose is to improve criticism, but because he also aims to improve poetry, he tries to make the poem do what he feels good poetry should do. He speaks directly, without a great deal of ornamentation, and makes his rhymes work sensibly and without strain. At their best, they are intelligent and sensible rhymes that reinforce the meaning of the lines, and often they are witty and amusing. Some are among the most memorable lines in English poetry, such as "A *little learning* is a dangerous thing; / Drink deep, or taste not the Pierian spring" (lines 15 – 16); "Be not the first by whom the new are tried, / Nor yet the last to lay the old aside" (lines 135 – 36); and "Good nature and good sense must ever join; / To err is human, to forgive, divine" (lines 324 – 25).

POPE'S RHETORIC

Children in the eighteenth century were trained carefully in rhetoric both in the grammar schools and in the universities, and Pope's solid education in rhetoric is reflected in this poem. Book II is devoted to a single subject — the causes of bad criticism of poetry — and its structure makes its segments clearly evident to the reader. The causes of poor judgment are

Pride (stanza 1, lines 1 – 14),

Lack of learning (stanza 2, lines 15 – 32),

Judging only parts of the poem rather than the whole (stanzas 3 to 6, lines 33 – 88),

Judging only wit, language, or versification (stanzas 7 to 9, lines 89 – 183),

Being too easy or too hard to please (stanza 10, lines 184 – 93),

Being partial to groups the critic favors (stanza 11, lines 194 – 207),

Being influenced by others (stanza 12, lines 208 – 23),

Being too easy to sway (stanza 13, lines 224 – 51),

Being prejudiced toward one's own party (stanza 14, lines 252 – 73), and

Being envious and not developing a good spirit (stanzas 15 to 17, lines 274 – 325).

With this structure, Pope provides signposts that help us to understand each section and to anticipate his message. Most of what he says about critics — whether of poetry, drama, or the arts — is still pertinent. In virtually any major newspaper one can find examples of critics who dissect a detail in a work of art and forget to evaluate the work as a whole. Some critics sacrifice their objectivity by favoring their friends or members of their own group. Other critics overwhelm their readers with evidence of their specialized learning, while still others say what everyone else is saying. In literary criticism, many things have not changed.

Because Pope writes his *Essay* in verse, certain opportunities offer themselves rhetorically. One has already been mentioned: the use of rhyme, which can make an important idea memorable and weighty. When Pope says, "Avoid Extremes; and shun the fault of such, / Who still are pleased too little or too much" (lines 184 – 85), we give his thought serious consideration. Although his idea is not original — Lao-tzu, the Buddha, Aristotle, and other ancient thinkers have advised men and women to be temperate in all things — the rhymed couplet gives extra weight to the idea.

Pope talks about wit in these lines as imagination used to find a novel and surprising way to say things and not as comedy or sarcasm. When he talks about the critics who judge "by numbers a Poet's song" (line 137), he is referring to critics who evaluate the underlying metrical pattern of the lines. In the eighteenth century iambic pentameter (a line of ten syllables with accents generally falling on every other syllable) ruled. All poets varied this pattern but generally followed the rule. Some poets managed the iambic pentameter better than others, and Pope complains that some poets have trouble filling out their lines: "And ten low words oft creep in one dull line" (line 147). He complains about it in a line that has ten ordinary words — thus offering an example of his own wit through clever imitation.

He uses irony when he talks about learning:

> Drink deep, or taste not the Pierian spring:
> There shallow draughts intoxicate the brain,
> And drinking largely sobers us again. (lines 16 – 18)

Ordinarily, people who drink too much become drunk, but ironically, the more they drink from the spring that is the fountain of knowledge, the more sober they become. Pope uses rhetorical devices such as irony sparingly.

Other devices he uses sparingly are imagery and any associated metaphors, which suggests that his poetic strategies are meant to appeal more to our intellect than our feelings. Among the few metaphors he uses is a consistent pattern of heights, beginning with Mount Parnassus, on which the Greeks and Romans believed the muses, patron goddesses of the arts, live. In one extended passage he talks about the "heights of Arts" (line 20) and continues to discuss the "Alps" (lines 25 – 32) that rise above us as in our youth we try to attain those heights: "Th' increasing prospect tires our wandering eyes, / Hills peep o'er hills, and Alps on Alps arise!" (lines 31 – 32).

While addressing the problems that inadequate criticism produces, Pope offers some trenchant thoughts about poetry. In the process, he gave advice that many in his age regarded as wise and sound.

From *An Essay on Criticism*

Of all the Causes which conspire to blind
Man's erring judgment, and misguide the mind,
What the weak head with strongest bias rules,
Is *Pride,* the never-failing vice of fools.
Whatever Nature has in worth denied,   5
She gives in large recruits of needful Pride:
For as in bodies, thus in souls, we find
What wants in blood and spirits, swelled with wind:
Pride, where Wit fails, steps in to our defence,
And fills up all the mighty Void of sense.   10

If once right reason drives that cloud away,
Truth breaks upon us with resistless day.
Trust not yourself; but your defects to know,
Make use of every friend — and every foe.
    A *little learning* is a dangerous thing;   15
Drink deep, or taste not the Pierian spring:[1]
There shallow draughts intoxicate the brain,
And drinking largely sobers us again.
Fired at first sight with what the Muse imparts,
In fearless youth we tempt the heights of Arts,   20
While from the bounded level of our mind,
Short views we take, nor see the lengths behind;
But more advanced, behold with strange surprise
New distant scenes of endless science rise!
So pleased at first the towering Alps we try,   25
Mount o'er the vales, and seem to tread the sky,
Th' eternal snows appear already past,
And the first clouds and mountains seem the last:
But, those attained, we tremble to survey
The growing labours of the lengthened way,   30
Th' increasing prospect tires our wandering eyes,
Hills peep o'er hills, and Alps on Alps arise!
    A perfect Judge will read each work of Wit
With the same spirit that its author writ:
Survey the WHOLE, nor seek slight faults to find   35
Where nature moves, and rapture warms the mind;
Nor lose, for that malignant dull delight,
The generous pleasure to be charmed with wit.
But in such lays as neither ebb, nor flow,
Correctly cold, and regularly low,   40
That shunning faults, one quiet tenour keep;
We cannot blame indeed ———— but we may sleep.
In Wit, as Nature, what affects our hearts
Is not th' exactness of peculiar parts;
'Tis not a lip, or eye, we beauty call,   45
But the joint force and full result of all.
Thus when we view some well-proportioned dome,
(The world's just wonder, and even thine, O Rome!)
No single parts unequally surprise,
All comes united to th' admiring eyes;   50
No monstrous height, or breadth, or length appear;

---

[1] **Pierian spring** The spring on Mt. Olympus, sacred to the muses.

The Whole at once is bold, and regular.
  Whoever thinks a faultless piece to see,
Thinks what ne'er was, nor is, nor e'er shall be.
In every work regard the writer's End,   55
Since none can compass more than they intend;
And if the means be just, the conduct true,
Applause, in spite of trivial faults, is due.
As men of breeding, sometimes men of wit,
T' avoid great errors, must the less commit: 60
Neglect the rules each verbal Critic lays,
For not to know some trifles, is a praise.
Most Critics, fond of some subservient art,
Still make the Whole depend upon a Part:
They talk of principles, but notions prize,   65
And all to one loved Folly sacrifice.
  Once on a time, La Mancha's Knight, they say,[2]
A certain Bard encountering on the way,
Discoursed in terms as just, with looks as sage,
As e'er could Dennis[3] of the Grecian stage;   70
Concluding all were desperate sots and fools,
Who durst depart from Aristotle's rules.[4]
Our Author, happy in a judge so nice,
Produced his Play, and begged the Knight's advice;
Made him observe the subject, and the plot,   75
The manners, passions, unities; what not?
All which, exact to rule, were brought about,
Were but a Combat in the lists left out.
"What! leave the Combat out?" exclaims the Knight;
Yes, or we must renounce the Stagirite.[5]   80
"Not so by Heaven" (he answers in a rage)
"Knights, squires, and steeds, must enter on the stage."
So vast a throng the stage can ne'er contain.
"Then build a new, or act it in a plain."
  Thus Critics, of less judgment than caprice,   85
Curious not knowing, not exact but nice,
Form short Ideas; and offend in arts
(As most in manners) by a love to parts.

---

[2] **La Mancha's Knight . . .** This is from Don Alonzo Fernandez de Avellaneda's false continuation of *Don Quixote*.

[3] **Dennis** John Dennis (1657 – 1734), a well-known critic of poetry.

[4] **Aristotle's rules** Codification of Aristotle's suggestion in the *Poetics* that a drama have one plot, have unity of character, and cover only the span of time it takes to act.

[5] **Stagirite** Aristotle, who was from Stagira, in Macedon.

Some to *Conceit*[6] alone their taste confine,
And glittering thoughts struck out at every line;   90
Pleased with a work where nothing's just or fit;
One glaring Chaos and wild heap of wit.
Poets like painters, thus, unskilled to trace
The naked nature and the living grace,
With gold and jewels cover every part,   95
And hide with ornaments their want of art.
True Wit is Nature to advantage dressed,
What oft was thought, but ne'er so well expressed;
Something, whose truth convinced at sight we find,
That gives us back the image of our mind.   100
As shades more sweetly recommend the light,
So modest plainness sets off sprightly wit.
For works may have more wit than does 'em good,
As bodies perish through excess of blood.
  Others for *Language* all their care express,   105
And value books, as women men, for Dress:
Their praise is still, — the Style is excellent:
The Sense, they humbly take upon content.
Words are like leaves; and where they most abound,
Much fruit of sense beneath is rarely found.   110
False Eloquence, like the prismatic glass,
Its gaudy colours spreads on every place;
The face of Nature we no more survey,
All glares alike, without distinction gay:
But true Expression, like th' unchanging Sun,   115
Clears, and improves whate'er it shines upon,
It gilds all objects, but it alters none.
Expression is the dress of thought, and still
Appears more decent, as more suitable;
A vile conceit in pompous words expressed,   120
Is like a clown in regal purple dressed:
For different styles with different subjects sort,
As several garbs with country, town, and court.
Some by old words to fame have made pretence,
Ancients in phrase, mere moderns in their sense;   125
Such laboured nothings, in so strange a style,
Amaze th' unlearned, and make the learnèd smile.
Unlucky, as Fungoso in the Play,[7]

---

[6] ***Conceit*** Complex use of wit, as in an unlikely simile.
[7] **Fungoso in the Play** Character in Ben Jonson's *Every Man Out of His Humour*.

These sparks with awkward vanity display
What the fine gentleman wore yesterday;   130
And but so mimic ancient wits at best,
As apes our grandsires, in their doublets drest.
In words, as fashions, the same rule will hold;
Alike fantastic, if too new, or old:
Be not the first by whom the new are tried,   135
Nor yet the last to lay the old aside.
    But most by Numbers judge a Poet's song;
And smooth or rough, with them is right or wrong:
In the bright Muse though thousand charms conspire,
Her Voice is all these tuneful fools admire;   140
Who haunt Parnassus[8] but to please their ear,
Not mend their minds; as some to Church repair,
Not for the doctrine, but the music there.
These equal syllables alone require,
Though oft the ear the open vowels tire;   145
While expletives their feeble aid do join;
And ten low words oft creep in one dull line:
While they ring round the same unvaried chimes,
With sure returns of still expected rhymes;
Where'er you find "the cooling western breeze,"   150
In the next line, it "whispers through the trees:"
If crystal streams "with pleasing murmurs creep,"
The reader's threatened (not in vain) with "sleep:"
Then, at the last and only couplet fraught
With some unmeaning thing they call a thought,   155
A needless Alexandrine[9] ends the song,
That, like a wounded snake, drags its slow length along.
Leave such to tune their own dull rhymes, and know
What's roundly smooth, or languishingly slow;
And praise the easy vigour of a line,   160
Where Denham's strength, and Waller's[10] sweetness join.
True ease in writing comes from art, not chance,
As those move easiest who have learned to dance.
'Tis not enough no harshness gives offence,
The sound must seem an Echo to the sense: 165
Soft is the strain when Zephyr[11] gently blows,

---

    [8] **Parnassus** A mountain in Greece on which the muses were believed to dwell.
    [9] **Alexandrine** A line with six metrical feet (Pope's lines have five metrical feet with ten syllables). Line 157 is an Alexandrine.
    [10] **Sir John Denham (1615–1668) and Edmund Waller (1605–1687)** Poets who helped develop the line that Pope uses in this poem, the closed pentameter couplet.
    [11] **Zephyr** The west wind.

And the smooth stream in smoother numbers flows;
But when loud surges lash the sounding shore,
The hoarse, rough verse should like the torrent roar:
When Ajax strives some rock's vast weight to throw,   170
The line too labours, and the words move slow;
Not so, when swift Camilla[12] scours the plain,
Flies o'er th' unbending corn, and skims along the main.
Hear how Timotheus' varied lays surprise,[13]
And bid alternate passions fall and rise!   175
While, at each change, the son of Libyan Jove
Now burns with glory, and then melts with love;
Now his fierce eyes with sparkling fury glow,
Now sighs steal out, and tears begin to flow:
Persians and Greeks like turns of nature found,   180
And the World's victor stood subdued by Sound!
The power of Music all our hearts allow,
And what Timotheus was, is DRYDEN now.
    Avoid Extremes; and shun the fault of such,
Who still are pleased too little or too much.   185
At every trifle scorn to take offence,
That always shows great pride, or little sense;
Those heads, as stomachs, are not sure the best,
Which nauseate all, and nothing can digest.
Yet let not each gay Turn thy rapture move;   190
For fools admire, but men of sense approve:
As things seem large which we through mists descry,
Dulness is ever apt to magnify.
    Some foreign writers, some our own despise;
The Ancients only, or the Moderns prize.   195
Thus Wit, like Faith, by each man is applied
To one small sect, and all are damned beside.
Meanly they seek the blessing to confine,
And force that sun but on a part to shine,
Which not alone the southern wit sublimes,   200
But ripens spirits in cold northern climes;
Which from the first has shone on ages past,
Enlights the present, and shall warm the last;
Though each may feel increases and decays,
And see now clearer and now darker days.   205

---

[12] **Camilla** An Amazon in Virgil's *Aeneid*.
[13] **Timotheus** Alexander the Great's master court musician in "Alexander's Feast," a poem by John Dryden (1673 – 1700).

Regard not then if Wit be old or new,
But blame the false, and value still the true.
    Some ne'er advance a Judgment of their own,
But catch the spreading notion of the Town;
They reason and conclude by precedent,   210
And own stale nonsense which they ne'er invent.
Some judge of authors' names, not works, and then
Nor praise nor blame the writings, but the men.
Of all this servile herd, the worse is he
That in proud dulness joins with Quality.   215
A constant Critic at the great man's board,
To fetch and carry nonsense for my Lord.
What woeful stuff this madrigal would be,
In some starved hackney sonneteer, or me?
But let a Lord once own the happy lines,   220
How the wit brightens! How the style refines!
Before his sacred name flies every fault,
And each exalted stanza teems with thought!
    The Vulgar thus through Imitation err;
As oft the Learned by being singular;   225
So much they scorn the crowd, that if the throng
By chance go right, they purposely go wrong:
So Schismatics the plain believers quit,
And are but damned for having too much wit.
Some praise at morning what they blame at night;   230
But always think the last opinion right.
A Muse by these is like a mistress used,
This hour she's idolized, the next abused;
While their weak heads like towns unfortified,
Twixt sense and nonsense daily change their side.   235
Ask them the cause; they're wiser still, they say;
And still tomorrow's wiser than today.
We think our fathers fools, so wise we grow;
Our wiser sons, no doubt, will think us so.
Once School divines this zealous isle o'erspread;   240
Who knew most Sentences, was deepest read;
Faith, Gospel, all, seemed made to be disputed,
And none had sense enough to be confuted:
Scotists and Thomists,[14] now, in peace remain,
Amidst their kindred cobwebs in Duck Lane.[15]   245

---

[14] **Scotists and Thomists** Followers of Dun Scotus (c. 1266 – 1308) and
Thomas Aquinas (c. 1224 – 1274) who wrangled over religious philosophy.
   [15] **Duck Lane** A street in London where remaindered books were sold.

If Faith itself has different dresses worn,
What wonder modes in Wit should take their turn?
Oft, leaving what is natural and fit,
The current folly proves the ready wit;
And authors think their reputation safe,   250
Which lives as long as fools are pleased to laugh.
    Some valuing those of their own side or mind,
Still make themselves the measure of mankind:
Fondly we think we honour merit then,
When we but praise ourselves in other men.   255
Parties in Wit attend on those of State,
And public faction doubles private hate.
Pride, Malice, Folly, against Dryden rose,
In various shapes of Parsons, Critics, Beaus;
But sense survived, when merry jests were past;   260
For rising merit will buoy up at last.
Might he return, and bless once more our eyes,
New Blackmores and new Milbourns[16] must arise:
Nay should great Homer lift his awful head,
Zoilus[17] again would start up from the dead.   265
Envy will merit, as its shade, pursue;
But like a shadow, proves the substance true;
For envied Wit, like Sol eclipsed, makes known
Th' opposing body's grossness, not its own.
When first that sun too powerful beams displays,   270
It draws up vapours which obscure its rays;
But even those clouds at last adorn its way,
Reflect new glories, and augment the day.
    Be thou the first true merit to befriend;
His praise is lost, who stays till all commend.   275
Short is the date, alas, of modern rhymes,
And 'tis but just to let them live betimes.
No longer now that golden age appears,
When Patriarch wits survived a thousand years:
Now length of Fame (our second life) is lost,   280
And bare threescore is all even that can boast;
Our sons their fathers' failing language see,
And such as Chaucer is, shall Dryden be.
So when the faithful pencil has designed

---

    [16] **Blackmores and new Milbourns** Sir Richard Blackmore (1654–1729), a physician and poet, had criticized Dryden for the immorality of his plays; Reverend Luke Milbourn had criticized Dryden's translation of Virgil.
    [17] **Zoilus** A fourth-century B.C. critic of Homer.

Some bright Idea of the master's mind,   285
Where a new world leaps out at his command,
And ready Nature waits upon his hand;
When the ripe colours soften and unite,
And sweetly melt into just shade and light;
When mellowing years their full perfection give,   290
And each bold figure just begins to live,
The treacherous colours the fair art betray,
And all the bright creation fades away!
    Unhappy Wit, like most mistaken things,
Atones not for that envy which it brings.   295
In youth alone its empty praise we boast,
But soon the short-lived vanity is lost:
Like some fair flower the early spring supplies,
That gaily blooms, but even in blooming dies.
What is this Wit, which must our cares employ?   300
The owner's wife, that other men enjoy;
Then most our trouble still when most admired,
And still the more we give, the more required;
Whose fame with pains we guard, but lose with ease,
Sure some to vex, but never all to please;   305
'Tis what the vicious fear, the virtuous shun,
By fools 'tis hated, and by knaves undone!
    If Wit so much from Ignorance undergo,
Ah let not Learning too commence its foe!
Of old, those met rewards who could excel,   310
And such were praised who but endeavoured well:
Though triumphs were to generals only due,
Crowns were reserved to grace the soldiers too.
Now, they who reach Parnassus' lofty crown,
Employ their pains to spurn some others down;   315
And while self-love each jealous writer rules,
Contending wits become the sport of fools:
But still the worst with most regret commend,
For each ill Author is as bad a Friend.
To what base ends, and by what abject ways,   320
Are mortals urged through sacred lust of praise!
Ah ne'er so dire a thirst of glory boast,
Nor in the Critic let the Man be lost.
Good nature and good sense must ever join;
To err is human, to forgive, divine.   325

QUESTIONS FOR CRITICAL READING

1. What does Pope mean when he says that "a *little learning* is a danger-ous thing" (line 15)? Do you agree with him? How does your personal experience support or refute his point?
2. What importance does poetry seem to have in Pope's life? What im-portance does it have in your life?
3. How effective is Pope's use of rhyme? Why do you feel that rhyming in poetry either is or is not important?
4. What are Pope's views on finding fault with details in a poem? What faults can you find with this poem's details?
5. What is the point of the story Pope tells about "La Mancha's Knight" (67 – 85)?
6. What is the pervasive late twentieth-century attitude toward the ex-pression "Avoid Extremes" (184)? What is your attitude?

SUGGESTIONS FOR WRITING

1. Pope says, "Whoever thinks a faultless piece to see, / Thinks what ne'er was, nor is, nor e'er shall be" (53 – 54). Apply this truism in your daily life as a critic of poetry, art, or music. How is this idea reflected in your daily life? How is it reflected in the lives of people you know?
2. Offer a critical interpretation of this poem that avoids focusing on only conceit (use of wit and metaphor), language, and numbers (the under-lying rhythms and metrics) and discusses all of these in an effort to un-derstand the whole poem. Consider the effectiveness of commenting on poetry in verse. Why should verse be any more convincing than prose?
3. How true is Pope's observation about the potential longevity of a poet's fame? He says, "No longer now that golden age appears, / When Patri-arch wits survived a thousand years: / Now length of Fame (our second life) is lost, / And bare threescore is all even that can boast" (278 – 81) Does it seem to be true that after the poet dies, the most he can expect of fame is sixty years or so? What poets are important to you? What poets have survived in the popular imagination longer than Pope ex-pected?
4. In one interesting passage, Pope concerns himself with the potential changes in the English language: "Our sons their fathers' failing lan-guage see, / And such as Chaucer is, shall Dryden be" (282 – 83). Only three hundred years passed between Chaucer and Dryden, and in that time the English language changed immensely. Pope speculates that in another three hundred years Dryden's language would be as difficult as Chaucer's to understand. Pope was only a little younger than Dryden. How difficult is his language for the modern reader to understand? What changes do you expect in English in the next century that might make Pope as difficult to understand as Chaucer?

5. **CONNECTIONS** Judging from what you have read of Aristotle and Pope, what do you feel the purposes of poetry should be? If you were to write a poem, what subject would you choose? What poetic techniques would you find most comfortable and useful? What do Aristotle and Pope seem to agree on concerning the value of poetry to the community? What are your views of the value of poetry to your society?

6. **CONNECTIONS** Alexander Pope is considered a neoclassical poet, which means that he follows the precepts set by classical writers. No classical writer was more respected than Aristotle, even though Pope discusses Roman writers more often than Greek writers. Using Aristotle as your touchstone for classical values in poetics, decide just how closely Pope follows those values. In what ways does he seem to be in agreement with Aristotle and in what ways is it clear that he veers away? What views does Pope support that would put him in the same intellectual camp as Aristotle?

WILLIAM WORDSWORTH
From the preface to *Lyrical Ballads*

WILLIAM WORDSWORTH (1770–1850) was prominent among the English Romantic poets, who succeeded the neoclassic poets of Alexander Pope's time. He was born in comfortable circumstances, but by age thirteen he was an orphan. His sister Dorothy (1771 – 1855) was taken in by family on her mother's side, and later she and Wordsworth joined forces and took a house together in 1795. Dorothy devoted most of her life to looking after Wordsworth, inspiring him as a poet and writing important works of her own describing their life together.

In the summer of 1790, while still enrolled at Cambridge, Wordsworth visited France during the French Revolution. The political excitement led him to return to France in 1791, when a brief love affair with Annette Vallon produced a baby girl named Caroline. Because war broke out between France and England, it was nine years before he saw his daughter. In 1802, after receiving some notice as a poet, Wordsworth married Mary Hutchinson, a childhood friend.

The preface to *Lyrical Ballads* first appeared in the second edition (1800) of the book, which was a collection of his and Samuel Taylor Coleridge's (1772 – 1834) poetry originally published by a minor regional press in 1798. The collaboration resulted from a visit Coleridge made to praise one of Wordsworth's earliest poems. The two decided to produce a volume of poetry that would combine inspiration from natural and supernatural sources. Coleridge contributed the supernatural poem, "The Rime of the Ancient Mariner," while Wordsworth contributed a number of important early poems, such as "Lines Composed a Few Miles Above Tintern Abbey." The first edition was not received well, which led to Wordsworth's defense of the volume in his preface to the second edition. The poems were novel and used language that did not seem especially poetic to the critics, which made them difficult to praise. This volume is sometimes regarded as the beginning of the English Romantic movement, which had been brewing in the work of a number of minor poets in the later part of the eighteenth century.

The preface emphasizes several points that help clarify the nature of romantic poetry in general. The poetry generally avoids the couplet style of Pope and opts for a lyric verse with alternate rhyme or, in the case of "Tintern Abbey," with no rhyme. The poetry treats simple subjects — the meditations on a walking tour, the observations of country people about their lives, or reflections on the poet's emotions. The language of the poems is simple, direct, and, as Wordsworth tells us in the preface, as natural and close to ordinary speech as he could make it. The metrical pattern beneath the lines did not disturb the impression that the speech was what one would expect to hear from someone in a reflective mood, as the first two stanzas of "Lines Written in Early Spring," help demonstrate:

> I heard a thousand blended notes,
> While in a grove I sate reclined,
> In that sweet mood when pleasant thoughts
> Bring sad thoughts to the mind.
>
> To her fair works did Nature link
> The human soul that through me ran;
> And much it grieved my heart to think
> What man has made of man.

In these lines the romantic note of attachment to nature is sounded, as it is in many of the poems in *Lyrical Ballads*. If you compare these lines with those Wordsworth quotes from Thomas Gray or with Pope's *Essay on Criticism,* you may see why the relaxed language and tone of "Lines Written in Early Spring" might not have seemed poetic to critics in the late 1790s. On the other hand, they seem natural and lyrical to most modern ears.

A number of things Wordsworth says in the preface have had lasting importance for understanding romantic poetry. His emphasis on imagination and emotion is apparent from the first paragraph, when he talks about the association of ideas when we are in a state of excitement. He aims, he tells us, for an understanding of "the primary laws of our nature" (para. 1) governing the connection of emotion and ideas and observation. He sees these laws as supporting his view that "humble and rustic life" (para. 1) should be the subject matter of most of the poems of *Lyrical Ballads*. Throughout the preface, he reminds us that choosing the humble and rustic does not imply choosing the trivial. He sees deep spiritual and emotional issues at work in the lives of ordinary country people.

One of his extensive discussions concerns language (para. 8). He discusses at length the difference between the language of poetry and the language of prose, using examples from the poetry of Gray. His view is that there is no essential difference between the language of poetry and prose, but he also goes on to discuss the power of metrical language and its effect on the reader. Nonetheless, he maintains that the poetry in *Lyrical Ballads* uses a "selection of the language really spoken by men" (para. 9). This statement represents an important break with poetic tradition in his time.

He also goes on to discuss the question of metaphor (para. 9), the role of the passions (para. 12), the "delusion" that poets slip into as they write (para. 13), and the ultimate question: "What is a Poet?" (para. 11). In paragraph 15, Wordsworth treats one of the most enduring of his concerns in poetry: emotion. As he says, "Poetry is the spontaneous overflow of powerful feelings: it takes its origin from emotion recollected in tranquility." These words have been examined in detail by critics over the years because they are key to understanding Wordsworth's own poetic practice. He intends us to understand that poetry comes not from the intellect alone but from a powerful emotional life. However, he writes poetry not while he is in possession of "powerful feelings" (para. 15) but while he is reflecting on the experience.

WORDSWORTH'S RHETORIC

The preface to *Lyrical Ballads* was written in response to unfavorable responses to the volume of verse that Wordsworth and Coleridge published. For that reason, it is carefully constructed to guide the reader to an understanding of the purpose of the book. Wordsworth discusses purpose carefully (para. 2) to ensure that his readers understand him. Indeed, he carefully defines his terms and says things in a way that avoids confusing his audience. He seems to have felt that critics and readers were confounded by the poems because they did not understand them in relation to the poetry of the day. At one point Wordsworth permits himself a bit of spontaneous overflow of feeling when he attacks the generally insipid literature that he thought people of his day were reading: especially "stupid German Tragedies" (para. 4).

Wordsworth sometimes communicates the feeling that popular taste is degraded to such an extent that it cannot recognize genuine poetry. He complains of his time's desire for "gross and violent stimulants" in literature and suggests that *Lyrical Ballads* will counter this trend. He realizes that "a multitude of causes, unknown to former times, are now acting with a combined force to blunt the discriminating powers of the mind" (para. 4). Chief among the astounding incidents of his own time were the French Revolution and its bloody excesses as well as England's war with France, then at a very difficult point, with the French having landed in Ireland to stimulate rebellion in 1798. Poetry written under such thrilling and frightening circumstances was by no means certain to catch the attention of the reading public.

However, Wordsworth had high expectations. He wrote a direct unadorned prose, but he also made demands on his reader's attention. His preface paragraphs are very long — especially for our modern taste. But their length was warranted by the fact that Wordsworth developed his ideas thoroughly and carefully. His language is simple and uncomplicated, much as he recommends in his own poetry. He also speaks directly to the reader (para. 4) as if soliciting the reader's patience. The reference to the reader as a man is common to the period and does not necessarily imply an antifeminist view. His most cherished reader was always Dorothy, and one of the achievements of the Romantics was to begin developing a modern feminist attitude.

From the preface to *Lyrical Ballads*

The principal object, then, proposed in these Poems, was to 1 choose incidents and situations from common life, and to relate or describe them throughout, as far as was possible, in a selection of language really used by men, and, at the same time, to throw over them a certain colouring of imagination, whereby ordinary things should be presented to the mind in an unusual aspect; and further, and above all, to make these incidents and situations interesting by tracing in them, truly though not ostentatiously, the primary laws of our nature: chiefly, as far as regards the manner in which we associate ideas in a state of excitement. Humble and rustic life was generally chosen, because in that condition the essential passions of the heart find a better soil in which they can attain their maturity, are less under restraint, and speak a plainer and more emphatic language; because in that condition of life our elementary feelings coexist in a state of greater simplicity, and, consequently, may be more accurately contemplated, and more forcibly communicated; because the manners of rural life germinate from those elementary feelings, and, from the necessary character of rural occupations, are more easily comprehended, and are more durable; and, lastly, because in that condition the passions of men are incorporated with the beautiful and permanent forms of nature. The language, too, of these men has been adopted (purified indeed from what appear to be its real defects, from all lasting and rational causes of dislike or disgust), because such men hourly communicate with the best objects from which the best part of language is originally derived; and because, from their rank in society and the sameness and narrow circle of their intercourse, being less under the influence of social vanity, they convey their feelings and notions in simple and unelaborated expressions. Accordingly, such a language, arising out of repeated experience and regular feelings, is a more permanent, and a far more philosophical language, than that which is frequently substituted for it by Poets, who think that they are conferring honour upon themselves and their art in proportion as they separate themselves from the sympathies of men, and indulge in arbitrary and capricious habits of expression, in order to furnish food for fickle tastes and fickle appetites of their own creation.[1]

I cannot, however, be insensible to the present outcry against   2 the triviality and meanness, both of thought and language, which some of my contemporaries have occasionally introduced into their metrical compositions; and I acknowledge that this defect, where it exists, is more dishonourable to the Writer's own character than false refinement or arbitrary innovation, though I should contend at the same time that it is far less pernicious in the sum of its consequences. From such verses the Poems in these volumes will be found distinguished at least by one mark of difference, that each of them has a worthy *purpose*. Not that I always began to write with a distinct purpose formally conceived, but habits of meditation have, I trust, so prompted and regulated my feelings, that my descriptions of such objects as strongly excite those feelings will be found to carry along with them a *purpose*. If this opinion be erroneous, I can have little right to the name of a Poet. For all good poetry is the spontaneous overflow of powerful feelings: and though this be true, Poems to which any value can be attached were never produced on any variety of subjects but by a man who, being possessed of more

---

[1] It is worth while here to observe that the affecting parts of Chaucer are almost always expressed in language pure and universally intelligible even to this day. [Wordsworth's note]

than usual organic sensibility, had also thought long and deeply. For our continued influxes of feeling are modified and directed by our thoughts, which are indeed the representatives of all our past feelings; and as, by contemplating the relation of these general representatives to each other, we discover what is really important to men, so, by the repetition and continuance of this act, our feelings will be connected with important subjects, till at length, if we be originally possessed of much sensibility, such habits of mind will be produced that, by obeying blindly and mechanically the impulses of those habits, we shall describe objects, and utter sentiments, of such a nature, and in such connection with each other, that the understanding of the Reader must necessarily be in some degree enlightened, and his affection strengthened and purified.

It has been said that each of these Poems has a purpose. Another circumstance must be mentioned which distinguishes these Poems from the popular Poetry of the day; it is this, that the feeling therein developed gives importance to the action and situation, and not the action and situation to the feeling. 3

A sense of false modesty shall not prevent me from asserting that the Reader's attention is pointed to this mark of distinction, far less for the sake of these particular Poems than from the general importance of the subject. The subject is indeed important! For the human mind is capable of being excited without the application of gross and violent stimulants; and he must have a very faint perception of its beauty and dignity who does not know this, and who does not further know, that one being is elevated above another in proportion as he possesses this capability. It has therefore appeared to me, that to endeavour to produce or enlarge this capability is one of the best services in which, at any period, a Writer can be engaged; but this service, excellent at all times, is especially so at the present day. For a multitude of causes, unknown to former times, are now acting with a combined force to blunt the discriminating powers of the mind, and, unfitting it for all voluntary exertion, to reduce it to a state of almost savage torpor. The most effective of these causes are the great national events which are daily taking place, and the increasing accumulation of men in cities, where the uniformity of their occupations produces a craving for extraordinary incident which the rapid communication of intelligence hourly gratifies. To this tendency of life and manners the literature and theatrical exhibitions of the country have conformed themselves. The invaluable works of our elder writers, I had almost said the works of Shakespeare and Milton, are driven into neglect by frantic novels, sickly and stupid German Tragedies, and deluges of idle and extravagant stories in verse. — When I think upon this degrading thirst after outrageous 4

stimulation, I am almost ashamed to have spoken of the feeble endeavour made in these volumes to counteract it; and, reflecting
upon the magnitude of the general evil, I should be oppressed with
no dishonourable melancholy, had I not a deep impression of certain inherent and indestructible qualities of the human mind, and
likewise of certain powers in the great and permanent objects that
act upon it, which are equally inherent and indestructible; and were
there not added to this impression a belief that the time is approaching when the evil will be systematically opposed by men of greater
powers, and with far more distinguished success.

Having dwelt thus long on the subjects and aim of these Poems,   5
I shall request the Reader's permission to apprise him of a few circumstances relating to their *style,* in order, among other reasons,
that he may not censure me for not having performed what I never
attempted. The Reader will find that personifications of abstract
ideas rarely occur in these volumes, and are utterly rejected as an ordinary device to elevate the style and raise it above prose. My purpose was to imitate, and, as far as is possible, to adopt the very language of men; and assuredly such personifications do not make any
natural or regular part of that language. They are, indeed, a figure of
speech occasionally prompted by passion, and I have made use of
them as such; but have endeavoured utterly to reject them as a mechanical devise of style, or as a family language which Writers in
metre seem to lay claim to by prescription. I have wished to keep
the Reader in the company of flesh and blood, persuaded that by so
doing I shall interest him. Others who pursue a different track will
interest him likewise; I do not interfere with their claim, but wish to
prefer a claim of my own. There will also be found in these volumes
little of what is usually called poetic diction; as much pains have been
taken to avoid it as is ordinarily taken to produce it; this have been
done for the reason already alleged, to bring my language near to the
language of men; and further, because the pleasure which I have
proposed to myself to impart is of a kind very different from that
which is supposed by many persons to be the proper object of poetry. Without being culpably particular, I do not know how to give
my Reader a more exact notion of the style in which it was my wish
and intention to write, than by informing him that I have at all times
endeavoured to look steadily at my subject; consequently there is, I
hope, in these Poems little falsehood of description, and my ideas
are expressed in language fitted to their respective importance.
Something must have been gained by this practice, as it is friendly to
one property of all good poetry, namely, good sense: but it has necessarily cut me off from a large portion of phrases and figures of
speech which from father to son have long been regarded as the

common inheritance of Poets. I have also thought it expedient to restrict myself still further, having abstained from the use of many expressions, in themselves proper and beautiful, but which have been
foolishly repeated by bad Poets, till such feelings of disgust are connected with them as it is scarcely possible by any art of association
to overpower.

If in a poem there should be found a series of lines, or even a   6
single line, in which the language, though naturally arranged, and
according to the strict laws of metre, does not differ from that of
prose, there is a numerous class of critics, who, when they stumble
upon these prosaisms, as they call them, imagine that they have
made a notable discovery, and exult over the Poet as over a man ignorant of his own profession. Now these men would establish a
canon of criticism which the Reader will conclude he must utterly
reject, if he wishes to be pleased with these volumes. And it would
be a most easy task to prove to him that not only the language of a
large portion of every good poem, even of the most elevated character, must necessarily, except with reference to the metre, in no respect differ from that of good prose, but likewise that some of the
most interesting parts of the best poems will be found to be strictly
the language of prose when prose is well written. The truth of this
assertion might be demonstrated by innumerable passages from almost all the poetical writings, even of Milton himself. To illustrate
the subject in a general manner, I will here adduce a short composition of Gray,[2] who was at the head of those who, by their reason-
ings, have attempted to widen the space of separation betwixt Prose
and Metrical composition, and was more than any other man curiously elaborate in the structure of his own poetic diction.

> "In vain to me the smiling mornings shine,
> And reddening Phœbus[3] lifts his golden fire;
> The birds in vain their amorous descant[4] join,
> Or cheerful fields resume their green attire.
> These ears, alas! for other notes repine;
> *A different object do these eyes require;*
> *My lonely anguish melts no heart but mine;*
> *And in my breast the imperfect joys expire;*
> Yet morning smiles the busy race to cheer,
> And new-born pleasure brings to happier men;
> The fields to all their wonted tribute bear;

---

[2] **Thomas Gray (1716–1771)** Author of "An Elegy Written in a Country
Churchyard." He was an influential lyric poet in the generation before Wordsworth.
[3] **Phœbus** The sun.
[4] **descant** Song.

To warm their little loves the birds complain.
I fruitless mourn to him that cannot hear,
And weep the more because I weep in vain."

It will easily be perceived, that the only part of this Sonnet   7
which is of any value is the lines printed in Italics; it is equally obvious that, except in the rhyme and in the use of the single word
"fruitless" for fruitlessly, which is so far a defect, the language of
these lines does in no respect differ from that of prose.

By the foregoing quotation it has been shown that the language   8
of Prose may yet be well adapted to Poetry; and it was previously asserted that a large portion of the language of every good poem can in
no respect differ from that of good Prose. We will go further. It may
be safely affirmed that there neither is, nor can be, any *essential* difference between the language of prose and metrical composition.
We are fond of tracing the resemblance between Poetry and Painting, and, accordingly, we call them Sisters: but where shall we find
bonds of connection sufficiently strict to typify the affinity betwixt
metrical and prose composition? They both speak by and to the
same organs; the bodies in which both of them are clothed may be
said to be of the same substance, their affections are kindred, and almost identical, not necessarily differing even in degree; Poetry[5]
sheds no tears "such as Angels weep," but natural and human tears;
she can boast of no celestial ichor that distinguishes her vital juices
from those of Prose; the same human blood circulates through the
veins of them both.

If it be affirmed that rhyme and metrical arrangement of them-   9
selves constitute a distinction which overturns what has just been
said on the strict affinity of metrical language with that of Prose, and
paves the way for other artificial distinctions which the mind voluntarily admits, I answer that the language of such Poetry as is here
recommended is, as far as is possible, a selection of the language
really spoken by men; that this selection, wherever it is made with
true taste and feeling, will of itself form a distinction far greater than
would at first be imagined, and will entirely separate the composition from the vulgarity and meanness of ordinary life; and, if metre
be superadded thereto, I believe that a dissimilitude will be pro-

---

[5] I here use the word "Poetry" (though against my own judgment) as opposed
to the word Prose, and synonymous with metrical composition. But much confusion
has been introduced into criticism by this contradistinction of Poetry and Prose, instead of the more philosophical one of Poetry and Matter of Fact, or Science. The
only strict antithesis to Prose is Metre; nor is this, in truth, a *strict* antithesis, because
lines and passages of metre so naturally occur in writing prose, that it would be
scarcely possible to avoid them, even were it desirable. [Wordsworth's note]

duced altogether sufficient for the gratification of a rational mind. What other distinction would we have? Whence is it to come? And where is it to exist? Not, surely, where the Poet speaks through the mouths of his characters: it cannot be necessary here, either for elevation of style, or any of its supposed ornaments; for, if the Poet's subject be judiciously chosen, it will naturally, and upon fit occasion, lead him to passions, the language of which, if selected truly and judiciously, must necessarily be dignified and variegated, and alive with metaphors and figures. I forbear to speak of an incongruity which would shock the intelligent Reader, should the Poet interweave any foreign splendour of his own with that which the passion naturally suggests: it is sufficient to say that such addition is unnecessary. And, surely, it is more probable that those passages, which with propriety abound with metaphors and figures, will have their due effect if, upon other occasions where the passions are of a milder character, the style also be subdued and temperate.

But, as the pleasure which I hope to give by the Poems now pre- 10 sented to the Reader must depend entirely on just notions upon this subject, and as it is in itself of high importance to our taste and moral feelings, I cannot content myself with these detached remarks. And if, in what I am about to say, it shall appear to some that my labour is unnecessary, and that I am like a man fighting a battle without enemies, such persons may be reminded that, whatever be the language outwardly holden by men, a practical faith in the opinions which I am wishing to establish is almost unknown. If my conclusions are admitted, and carried as far as they must be carried if admitted at all, our judgments concerning the works of the greatest Poets, both ancient and modern, will be far different from what they are at present, both when we praise and when we censure: and our moral feelings influencing and influenced by these judgments will, I believe, be corrected and purified.

Taking up the subject, then, upon general grounds, let me ask, 11 what is meant by the word Poet? What is a Poet? To whom does he address himself? And what language is to be expected from him? — He is a man speaking to men: a man, it is true, endowed with more lively sensibility, more enthusiasm and tenderness, who has a greater knowledge of human nature, and a more comprehensive soul, than are supposed to be common among mankind; a man pleased with his own passions, and volitions, and who rejoices more than other men in the spirit of life that is in him; delighting to contemplate similar volitions and passions as manifested in the goings-on of the Universe, and habitually impelled to create them where he does not find them. To these qualities he has added a disposition to be affected more than any other men by absent things as if they were present; an ability of conjuring up in himself passions, which are indeed far from being the same as those produced by real events, yet (especially in those parts of the general sympathy which are pleasing and delightful) do more nearly resemble the passions produced by real events than anything which, from the motions of their own minds merely, other men are accustomed to feel in themselves: — whence, and from practice, he has acquired a greater readiness and power in expressing what he thinks and feels, and especially those thoughts and feelings which, by his own choice, or from the structure of his own mind, arise in him without the immediate external excitement.

But whatever portion of this faculty we may suppose even the greatest Poet to possess, there cannot be a doubt that the language which it will suggest to him must often, in liveliness and truth, fall short of that which is uttered by men in real life under the actual pressure of those passions, certain shadows of which the Poet thus produces, or feels to be produced, in himself.   12

However exalted a notion we would wish to cherish of the character of a Poet, it is obvious that, while he describes and imitates passions, his employment is in some degree mechanical compared with the freedom and power of real and substantial action and suffering. So that it will be the wish of the Poet to bring his feelings near to those of the persons whose feelings he describes, nay, for short spaces of time, perhaps, to let himself slip into an entire delusion, and even confound and identify his own feelings with theirs; modifying only the language which is thus suggested to him by a consideration that he describes for a particular purpose, that of giving pleasure. Here, then, he will apply the principle of selection which has been already insisted upon. He will depend upon this for removing what would otherwise be painful or disgusting in the passion; he will feel that there is no necessity to trick out or to elevate nature: and the more industriously he applies this principle the deeper will be his faith that no words, which *his* fancy or imagination can suggest, will be to be compared with those which are the emanations of reality and truth.   13

But it may be said by those who do not object to the general spirit of these remarks, that, as it is impossible for the Poet to produce upon all occasions language as exquisitely fitted for the passion as that which the real passion itself suggests, it is proper that he should consider himself as in the situation of a translator, who does not scruple to substitute excellences of another kind for those which are unattainable by him; and endeavours occasionally to surpass his original, in order to make some amends for the general inferiority to which he feels he must submit. But this would be to encourage idleness and unmanly despair. Further, it is the language of men who   14 speak of what they do not understand; who talk of Poetry, as of a matter of amusement and idle pleasure; who will converse with us as gravely about a *taste* for Poetry, as they express it, as if it were a thing as indifferent as a taste for rope-dancing, or Frontiniac or Sherry. Aristotle, I have been told, has said, that Poetry is the most philosophic of all writing: it is so: its object is truth, not individual and local, but general and operative; not standing upon external testimony, but carried alive into the heart by passion; truth which is its own testimony, which gives competence and confidence to the tribunal to which it appeals, and receives them from the same tribunal. Poetry is the image of man and nature. The obstacles which stand in the way of the fidelity of the Biographer and Historian, and of their consequent utility, are incalculably greater than those which are to be encountered by the Poet who comprehends the dignity of his art. The Poet writes under one restriction only, namely, the necessity of giving immediate pleasure to a human Being possessed of that information which may be expected from him, not as a lawyer, a physician, a mariner, an astronomer, or a natural philosopher, but as a Man. Except this one restriction, there is no object standing between the Poet and the image of things; between this, and the Biographer and Historian, there are a thousand.

●　●　●

I have said that poetry is the spontaneous overflow of powerful 15 feelings: it takes its origin from emotion recollected in tranquillity; the emotion is contemplated till, by a species of re-action, the tranquillity gradually disappears, and an emotion, kindred to that which was before the subject of contemplation, is gradually produced, and does itself actually exist in the mind. In this mood successful composition generally begins, and in a mood similar to this it is carried on; but the emotion, of whatever kind, and in whatever degree, from various causes, is qualified by various pleasures, so that in describing any passions whatsoever, which are voluntarily described, the mind will, upon the whole, be in a state of enjoyment. If Nature be thus cautious to preserve in a state of enjoyment a being so employed, the Poet ought to profit by the lesson held forth to him, and ought especially to take care that, whatever passions he communicates to his Reader, those passions, if his Reader's mind be sound and vigorous, should always be accompanied with an over-balance of pleasure. Now the music of harmonious metrical language, the sense of difficulty overcome, and the blind association of pleasure which has been previously received from works of rhyme or metre of the same or similar construction, an indistinct perception perpetually renewed of language closely resembling that of real life, and yet, in the circumstance of metre, differing from it so widely — all these imperceptibly make up a complex feeling of delight, which is of the most important use in tempering the painful feeling always found intermingled with powerful descriptions of the deeper passions. This effect is always produced in pathetic and impassioned poetry; while, in lighter compositions, the ease and gracefulness with which the Poet manages his numbers are themselves confessedly a principal source of the gratification of the Reader. All that it is *necessary* to say, however, upon this subject, may be effected by affirming, what few persons will deny, that of two descriptions, either of passions, manners, or characters, each of them equally well executed, the one in prose and the other in verse, the verse will be read a hundred times where the prose is read once.

QUESTIONS FOR CRITICAL READING

1. What pleasures does Wordsworth expect his readers to derive from poetry? What pleasures do you derive from it?
2. According to Wordsworth, what are some purposes for writing poetry? What is a worthy purpose for a poem?
3. How would you qualify the statement that "all good poetry is the spontaneous overflow of powerful feelings" (para. 2)?
4. What are the most important things Wordsworth says about the style of the poems in *Lyrical Ballads*? See paragraph 5 for his most explicit comments.
5. What do you think of Wordsworth's assertion that there is no basic difference between the language of poetry and prose? Does Wordsworth's sample discussion of Gray's poem prove his point?
6. In paragraph 11 Wordsworth asks, "What is a Poet?" How does he answer that question (paras. 11–13)?

SUGGESTIONS FOR WRITING

1. Offer your own answer to the question "What is a poet?" Examine some of the issues that Wordsworth considers to be important, and then offer your own additions. You may refer to the work of specific poets if you like. You may also wish to expand the field and include contemporary songwriters.
2. Wordsworth says that he chose "humble and rustic life . . . because in that condition the passions of men are incorporated with the beautiful and permanent forms of nature" (para. 1). How is what Wordsworth said still true? Consider your own experience in rustic life, and decide

whether your emotions respond positively to the "forms of nature." How might good poetry arise from modern rustic life?

3. Given Wordsworth's concern that the tastes of his age were degraded by "frantic novels, sickly and stupid German Tragedies, and deluges of idle and extravagant stories in verse" (para. 4), how do you think he would respond to the popular literature of today?

4. Consider the opening lines of "Tintern Abbey," from *Lyrical Ballads*. Do these lines conform with Wordsworth's description of what he was trying to do in his poetry?

> Five years have passed; five summers, with the length
> Of five long winters! And again I hear
> These waters, rolling from their mountain-springs
> With a soft inland murmur. Once again
> Do I behold these steep and lofty cliffs,
> That on a wild secluded scene impress
> Thoughts of a more deep seclusion; and connect
> The landscape with the quiet of the sky.

If you have access to the entire poem, you may use it in writing about the nature of these lines and Wordsworth's explanation of his purpose and style.

5. Examine what Wordsworth says about the artist who lets "himself slip into an entire delusion" (para. 13) when writing poetry. What do you feel Wordsworth means by such a statement, and how reasonable do you find it? Which of your own experiences might validate Wordsworth's theory? Who do you know who might agree with Wordsworth's description of what a poet sometimes experiences?

6. **CONNECTIONS** In many ways, Wordsworth's preface is a response to the critics' comments on the first edition of *Lyrical Ballads*. He wrote in reaction to what he felt were misunderstandings and faulty criticism. Compare the preface with Pope's description of inappropriate criticism in his "Essay on Criticism." To what extent does Wordsworth appear to be responding to criticism of the type Pope condemns? What, ideally, would Wordsworth expect from a competent critic?

7. **CONNECTIONS** Wordsworth was familiar with Aristotle's *Poetics* and understood the implications of imitating an action in terms of the importance of a poem's imitating life. How significant is the imitation of an action for Wordsworth's conception of poetry as he explains it in his preface? Is imitation of life important? What steps does he take to insure that his poetry imitates life so as to produce a "realistic" vision of the world as it is?

VIRGINIA WOOLF
A Letter to a Young Poet

VIRGINIA WOOLF (1882 – 1941) was one of the most gifted of the modernist writers. She was a prolific essayist and novelist in what came to be known as the Bloomsbury group, named after a section of London near the British Museum. Most members of the group were writers, such as Lytton Strachey and the critic Clive Bell, and some were artists, such as Duncan Grant and Virginia Woolf's sister, Vanessa Bell. The eminent economist John Maynard Keynes was part of the group as well, along with a variety of other accomplished intellectuals.

Virginia Woolf published some of the era's most important works, such as the novels *Jacob's Room* (1922), *Mrs. Dalloway* (1925), *To the Lighthouse* (1927), *Orlando* (1928), and *The Waves* (1931). Among her best-known nonfiction is *A Room of One's Own* (1929), in which she examines the opportunities for women in writing and, in discussing Shakespeare's (imaginary) sister, compares the opportunities available for women writers in the Renaissance.

Her "Letter to a Young Poet" (1932) is probably not directed at a specific recipient but is rather an essay written in the form of a letter. An individual may have requested her thoughts on poetry, but she intended to have these comments read by a larger audience. The pretense of writing a letter permits her a special kind of intimacy in talking about the circumstances of modern poetry as she understands them.

In paragraph 2 of the letter, Woolf confesses to inadequacies and prejudices — chief among them that she is a novelist and prose writer and not a poet. The irony of this confession would have been apparent to any knowledgeable reader at the time because her work is among the most poetic of the important English writers of her generation. She may not have written volumes of verse or technically be a poet, but she knew as much about writing poetry as any-

one in England. Another irony concerns her reasons for excusing
herself from taking an authoritative stance about poetry. Although
she says that "The lack of a sound university training has always
made it impossible for me to distinguish between an iambic and a
dactyl" (para. 2) (most of the Bloomsbury group came from Oxford
or Cambridge), she received a rigorous schooling at home in the extensive and remarkable library of her father Sir Leslie Stephen.
His tutelage certainly included some of the technical details of pros-
ody (what Pope refers to as "numbers" — the rhythm and meter of
poetry).

   Woolf begins with a brief discussion of rhyme in the abstract,
explaining that prose writers are instinctively opposed to rhyme
because it is "not only childish, but dishonest" (para. 2). In 1931
rhyme had been replaced by free verse, especially in the work of
T. S. Eliot and Ezra Pound, as the dominant mode for contemporary poets. One of the interesting realities of poetry in 1931 was
that far more readers were available to the poet than had been
available to Shakespeare and other great early poets. Most people
were now readers and expected to be served. She tells the young
poet that "You have a touch of Chaucer in you" (para. 3) as well as
"something of" the great poets of the past and thus must speak to
readers in a language that will give them satisfaction.

   The young poet apparently thinks that it has never been more
difficult to write poetry than "in this particular autumn of 1931"
(para. 3). She reviews the case and imagines him sitting down to
write a poem, only to end with his "page crumbled in a ball" (para.
4). Part of the problem is that he cannot write a poem about "Mrs.
Gape" or "Miss Curtis" or anyone else who has told him a story. In
ages past, the poet — such as Shakespeare — could do so, but "in
the autumn of 1931" those poems are left for the novelist to write.
Long narratives about the actions of others are now the province of
the novel writer and no longer that of the poet. As Woolf imagines
the poet in his room resuming the act of writing, she sees him solving the problem of what to write about: "I hazard a guess that you
are thinking now, not about things in general, but about yourself in
particular" (para. 7). At this point, she randomly quotes from three
poems and finds "three different poets writing about nothing, if not
about the poet himself" (para. 8).

   Woolf recognizes "the extreme difficulty" (para. 8) of these
poems: "I have to confess that it would floor me completely to say
from one reading or even from two or three what these poems
mean" (para. 8). Because the poet refers to a world that only the
poet knows, the more careful and "sincere" he is in representing

that world, "the more he puzzles us." Woolf finally admits that if the poet cannot represent the world outside and must "contemplate landscapes and emotions within" (para. 9), then things are indeed difficult for the modern poet.

The solution, Woolf tells her friend, is for poetry to reclaim some of its former glories: to "open its eyes, look out of the window and write about other people" (para. 10). The poet, she tells him, produced Hamlet, Cleopatra, Falstaff, and dozens of other interesting characters and can do so again. She asks this young poet to attempt something of that sort, even though she knows this is not a simple solution. "But how are you going to get out, into the world of other people?" (para. 11), she asks. She ruminates on this question and makes a suggestion: "All you need now is to stand at the window and let your rhythmical sense open and shut, open and shut, boldly and freely, until one thing melts in another, until the taxis are dancing with the daffodils." Such a statement is curiously whimsical (and poetical) for a modern novelist, but when she tells him that his job is "to find the relation between things that seem incompatible yet have a mysterious affinity," she is telling him that his job as a poet is quite similar to her job as a novelist.

Ultimately, she encourages the young poet to write — to be expansive and join the poets who write about the world. She complains that modern poets create a poetry that is devoid of sights and sounds, as if they were insensitive to the world around them: "How can you learn to write," she asks, "if you write only about one single person?" (para. 13). And yet she suggests that the young poet publish nothing before he is thirty — to experiment and "give the rein to every impulse" (para. 14) before "thinking what people will say." Woolf ends her letter by noting that poetry lives as long as young poets are inspired to write.

WOOLF'S RHETORIC

The most important rhetorical device used in the essay is its form: it is a letter written to an acquaintance. This letter, however, was written to be published, and as a letter, it is a fiction. The young poet may indeed have existed and may even be the future poet laureate, John Betjeman, who was twenty-five in 1931 and had not yet published his first volume of poems. Woolf's letter is literary, much as Martin Luther King, Jr.'s letter is part of a tradition of open letters. Woolf mentions that many letters are written for publication, but that "true" (para. 1) letters are filled with the scraps and details of real life and therefore are burned. She knows this letter will not be burned, but she alludes to omitted scraps of gossip as if the letter were adapted from a genuine posted work. By building this sense of intimacy into the letter, she allows readers to feel that they are participating in a direct, personal correspondence. Readers who would be poets attend all the more closely to what she says.

As a novelist, Woolf includes a number of narrative infusions in her letter. The invention of the "old gentleman" — Mr. Peabody? — who is in love with the dead past is a novelist's twist. He is "necrophilous" and dies at the end of the letter choking on a piece of toast — again, a touch of novelistic irony. Another novelistic device is the imaginary scenario where her young poet sits down to write, finds writing difficult, throws out his first draft, rethinks his subject matter, and then finally continues with the poem (para. 4). In the process of sketching this imaginary scene, Woolf develops her thinking on what the poet ought to be writing about and how the poet ought to avoid limiting himself to writing about "one single person" (para. 13).

Woolf naturally follows her own advice. She excuses herself as no expert in the opening paragraphs (itself the venerable rhetorical device of invoking the gods of humility), but she knows that as a ranking storyteller she participates in the world of poetry. As a novelist, she does now what Chaucer, Shakespeare, and Milton did in years gone by, but in her essay she avoids writing about herself. Instead, she urges her young poet to write the stories of many people and let those characters teach him to write.

A Letter to a Young Poet

My dear John,

Did you ever meet, or was he before your day, that old gentleman — I forget his name — who used to enliven conversation, especially at breakfast when the post came in, by saying that the art of letter-writing is dead? The penny post, the old gentleman used to say, has killed the art of letter-writing. Nobody, he continued, examining an envelope through his eyeglasses, has the time even to cross their t's. We rush, he went on, spreading his toast with marmalade, to the telephone. We commit our half-formed thoughts in ungrammatical phrases to the post card. Gray is dead, he continued; Horace Walpole is dead; Madame de Sévigné[1] — she is dead too, I suppose he was about to add, but a fit of choking cut him short, and he had to leave the room before he had time to condemn all the arts, as his pleasure was, to the cemetery. But when the post came in this morning and I opened your letter stuffed with little blue sheets written all over in a cramped but not illegible hand — I regret to say, however, that several *t*'s were uncrossed and the grammar of one sentence seems to be dubious — I replied after all these years to that elderly necrophilist[2] — Nonsense. The art of letter-writing has only just come into existence. It is the child of the penny post. And there is some truth in that remark, I think. Naturally when a letter cost half a crown to send, it had to prove itself a document of some importance; it was read aloud; it was tied up with green silk; after a certain number of years it was published for the infinite delectation of posterity. But your letter, on the contrary, will have to be burnt. It only cost three-halfpence to send. Therefore you could afford to be intimate, irreticent, indiscreet in the extreme. What you tell me about poor dear C. and his adventure on the Channel boat is deadly private; your ribald jests at the expense of M. would certainly ruin your friendship if they got about; I doubt, too, that posterity, unless it is much quicker in the wit than I expect, could follow the line of your thought from the roof which leaks ("splash, splash, splash into the soap dish") past Mrs. Gape, the charwoman, whose retort to the green-grocer gives me the keenest pleasure, via Miss Curtis and her odd confidence on the steps of the omnibus; to Siamese cats ("Wrap their noses in an old stocking my Aunt says if they howl"); so to the value of criticism to a writer; so to Donne; so to Gerard Hopkins;[3] so to tombstones; so to goldfish; and so with a sudden alarming swoop to "Do write and tell me where poetry's going, or if it's dead?" No, your letter, because it is a true letter — one that can neither be read aloud now, nor printed in time to come — will have to

---

[1] **Thomas Gray (1716 – 1771), Horace Walpole (1717 – 1797), Madame de Sévigné (1626 – 1696)** Thomas Gray is famous for his "Elegy in a Country Churchyard" (1751) and is an important preromantic poet. Walpole, an intimate of Gray's at Eton, wrote *The Castle of Otranto* (1764), one of the first romantic novels. Like Gray and Walpole, Madame de Sévigné was well known for her vibrant letters and was part of one of the most dazzling intellectual circles in the history of France. She was a brilliant writer and a dashing woman.

[2] **necrophilist** One who loves the dead (because the elderly gentleman believed that the arts were dead).

[3] **John Donne (1572 – 1631), Gerard Manley Hopkins (1844 – 1889)** Poets noted both for their intellectuality and for the complex wit of their poems. Both were clergymen: Donne was dean of St. Paul's, an Anglican cathedral; Hopkins was a Jesuit priest.

be burnt. Posterity must live upon Walpole and Madame de Sévigné. The great age of letter-writing, which is, of course, the present, will leave no letters behind it. And in making my reply there is only one question that I can answer or attempt to answer in public; about poetry and its death.

But before I begin, I must own up to those defects, both natural   2 and acquired, which, as you will find, distort and invalidate all that I have to say about poetry. The lack of a sound university training has always made it impossible for me to distinguish between an iambic and a dactyl,[4] and if this were not enough to condemn one for ever, the practice of prose has bred in me, as in most prose writers, a foolish jealousy, a righteous indignation—anyhow, an emotion which the critic should be without. For how, we despised prose writers ask when we get together, could one say what one meant and observe the rules of poetry? Conceive dragging in "blade" because one had mentioned "maid"; and pairing "sorrow" with "borrow"? Rhyme is not only childish, but dishonest, we prose writers say. Then we go on to say, And look at their rules! How easy to be a poet! How strait the path is for them, and how strict! This you must do; this you must not. I would rather be a child and walk in a crocodile down a suburban path than write poetry, I have heard prose writers say. It must be like taking the veil and entering a religious order — observing the rites and rigors of meter. That explains why they repeat the same thing over and over again. Whereas we prose writers (I am only telling you the sort of nonsense prose writers talk when they are alone) are masters of language, not its slaves; nobody can teach us; nobody can coerce us; we say what we mean; we have the whole of life for our province. We are the creators, we are the explorers. . . . So we run on — nonsensically enough, I must admit.

Now that I have made a clean breast of these deficiencies, let us   3 proceed. From certain phrases in your letter I gather that you think that poetry is in a parlous way, and that your case as a poet in this particular autumn of 1931 is a great deal harder than Shakespeare's, Dryden's, Pope's or Tennyson's.[5] In fact it is the hardest case that has ever been known. Here you give me an opening, which I am prompt to seize, for a little lecture. Never think yourself singular, never think

---

[4] **an iambic and a dactyl** Metrical feet: the iamb has an unaccented syllable followed by an accented syllable; the dactyl has an accented syllable followed by two unaccented syllables.

[5] **William Shakespeare (1564 – 1616), John Dryden (1631 – 1700), Alexander Pope (1688 – 1744), Alfred, Lord Tennyson (1809 – 1892)** Each of these poets was a giant in his own time. Shakespeare was the greatest Elizabethan poet, Dryden the most visible Restoration poet, Pope the most influential neoclassical poet, and Tennyson one of the greatest Victorian poets.

your own case much harder than other people's. I admit that the age we live in makes this difficult. For the first time in history there are readers — a large body of people, occupied in business, in sport, in nursing their grandfathers, in tying up parcels behind counters — they all read now; and they want to be told how to read and what to read; and their teachers — the reviewers, the lecturers, the broadcasters — must in all humanity make reading easy for them; assure them that literature is violent and exciting, full of heroes and villains; of hostile forces perpetually in conflict; of fields strewn with bones; of solitary victors riding off on white horses wrapped in black cloaks to meet their death at the turn of the road. A pistol shot rings out. "The age of romance was over. The age of realism had begun" — you know the sort of thing. Now of course writers themselves know very well that there is not a word of truth in all this — there are no battles, and no murders and no defeats and no victories. But as it is of the utmost importance that readers should be amused, writers acquiesce. They dress themselves up. They act their parts. One leads; the other follows. One is romantic, the other realist. One is advanced, the other out of date. There is no harm in it, so long as you take it as a joke, but once you believe in it, once you begin to take yourself seriously as a leader or as a follower, as a modern or as a conservative, then you become a self-conscious, biting, and scratching little animal whose work is not of the slightest value or importance to anybody. Think of yourself rather as something much humbler and less spectacular, but to my mind far more interesting — a poet in whom live all the poets of the past, from whom all poets in time to come will spring. You have a touch of Chaucer[6] in you, and something of Shakespeare; Dryden, Pope, Tennyson — to mention only the respectable among your ancestors — stir in your blood and sometimes move your pen a little to the right or to the left. In short you are an immensely ancient, complex, and continuous character, for which reason please treat yourself with respect and think twice before you dress up as Guy Fawkes[7] and spring out upon timid old ladies at street corners, threatening death and demanding twopence-halfpenny.

However, as you say that you are in a fix ("it has never been so hard to write poetry as it is today") and that poetry may be, you   4

---

[6] **Geoffrey Chaucer (1342 – 1400)** The most important English poet of the Middle Ages. He is best known for *The Canterbury Tales* (c. 1387 – 1400).

[7] **Guy Fawkes (1570 – 1606)** A would-be revolutionary English Catholic who plotted to blow up the assembled gathering of the king, his court, the law justices, and the House of Commons during King James I's coronation. He was discovered; the plot was revealed; and Fawkes and his fellow conspirators were tried, convicted, and executed.

think, at its last gasp in England ("the novelists are doing all the interesting things now"), let me while away the time before the post
goes in imagining your state and in hazarding one or two guesses
which, since this is a letter, need not be taken too seriously or
pressed too far. Let me try to put myself in your place; let me try to
imagine, with your letter to help me, what it feels like to be a young
poet in the autumn of 1931. (And taking my own advice, I shall
treat you not as one poet in particular, but as several poets in one.)
On the floor of your mind, then — is it not this that makes you a
poet? — rhythm keeps up its perpetual beat. Sometimes it seems to
die down to nothing; it lets you eat, sleep, talk like other people.
Then again it swells and rises and attempts to sweep all the contents
of your mind into one dominant dance. Tonight is such an occasion.
Although you are alone, and have taken one boot off and are about
to undo the other, you cannot go on with the process of undressing,
but must instantly write at the bidding of the dance. You snatch pen
and paper; you hardly trouble to hold the one or to straighten the
other. And while you write, while the first stanzas of the dance are
being fastened down, I will withdraw a little and look out of the
window. A woman passes, then a man; a car glides to a stop and
then — but there is no need to say what I see out of the window, nor
indeed is there time, for I am suddenly recalled from my observations by a cry of rage or despair. Your page is crumpled in a ball;
your pen sticks upright by the nib in the carpet. If there were a cat
to swing or a wife to murder now would be the time. So at least I
infer from the ferocity of your expression. You are rasped, jarred,
thoroughly out of temper. And if I am to guess the reason, it is, I
should say, that the rhythm which was opening and shutting with a
force that sent shocks of excitement from your head to your heels
has encountered some hard and hostile object upon which it has
smashed itself to pieces. Something has worked in which cannot be
made into poetry; some foreign body, angular, sharp-edged, gritty,
has refused to join in the dance. Obviously, suspicion attaches to
Mrs. Gape; she has asked you to make a poem of her; then to Miss
Curtis and her confidences on the omnibus; then to C., who has in-
fected you with a wish to tell his story — and a very amusing one it
was — in verse. But for some reason you cannot do their bidding.
Chaucer could; Shakespeare could; so could Crabbe, Byron, and
perhaps Robert Browning.[8] But it is October 1931, and for a long

---

[8]**George Crabbe (1754–1832), George Gordon, Lord Byron (1788–
1824), Robert Browning (1812–1889)** Crabbe and Byron were prominent
Romantic poets; Browning was one of the dominant poets of the later nineteenth
century.

time now poetry has shirked contact with — what shall we call it? — Shall we shortly and no doubt inaccurately call it life? And will you come to my help by guessing what I mean? Well then, it has left all that to the novelist. Here you see how easy it would be for me to write two or three volumes in honor of prose and in mockery of verse; to say how wide and ample is the domain of the one, how starved and stunted the little grove of the other. But it would be simpler and perhaps fairer to check these theories by opening one of the thin books of modern verse that lie on your table. I open and I find myself instantly confused. Here are the common objects of daily prose — the bicycle and the omnibus. Obviously the poet is making his muse face facts. Listen:

> Which of you waking early and watching daybreak
> Will not hasten in heart, handsome, aware of wonder
> At light unleashed, advancing, a leader of movement,
> Breaking like surf on turf on road and roof,
> Or chasing shadow on downs like whippet racing,
> The stilled stone, halting at eyelash barrier,
> Enforcing in face a profile, marks of misuse,
> Beating impatient and importunate on boudoir shutters
> Where the old life is not up yet, with rays
> Exploring through rotting floor a dismantled mill —
> The old life never to be born again?

Yes, but how will he get through with it? I read on and find: 5

> Whistling as he shuts
> His door behind him, travelling to work by tube
> Or walking to the park to it to *ease the bowels,*

and read on and find again:

> As a boy lately come up from country to town
> Returns for the day to his village in *expensive shoes —*

and so on again to:

> Seeking a heaven on earth he chases his shadow,
> Loses his capital and his nerve in pursuing
> What yachtsmen, explorers, climbers and *buggers are after.*

These lines and the words I have emphasized are enough to   6 confirm me in part of my guess at least. The poet is trying to include Mrs. Gape. He is honestly of opinion that she can be brought into poetry and will do very well there. Poetry, he feels, will be improved by the actual, the colloquial. But though I honor him for the attempt, I doubt that it is wholly successful. I feel a jar. I feel a shock.

I feel as if I had stubbed my toe on the corner of the wardrobe.[9] Am I then, I go on to ask, shocked, prudishly and conventionally, by the words themselves? I think not. The shock is literally a shock. The poet as I guess has strained himself to include an emotion that is not domesticated and acclimatized to poetry; the effort has thrown him off his balance; he rights himself, as I am sure I shall find if I turn the page, by a violent recourse to the poetical — he invokes the moon or the nightingale. Anyhow, the transition is sharp. The poem is cracked in the middle. Look, it comes apart in my hands: here is reality on one side, here is beauty on the other; and instead of acquiring a whole object rounded and entire, I am left with broken parts in my hands which, since my reason has been roused and my imagination has not been allowed to take entire possession of me, I contemplate coldly, critically, and with distaste.

Such at least is the hasty analysis I make of my own sensations as a reader; but again I am interrupted. I see that you have overcome your difficulty, whatever it was; the pen is once more in action, and having torn up the first poem you are at work upon another. Now then if I want to understand your state of mind I must invent another explanation to account for this return of fluency. You have dismissed, as I suppose, all sorts of things that would come naturally to your pen if you had been writing prose — the charwoman, the omnibus, the incident on the Channel boat. Your range is restricted — I judge from your expression — concentrated and intensified. I hazard a guess that you are thinking now, not about things in general, but about yourself in particular. There is a fixity, a gloom, yet an inner glow that seem to hint that you are looking within and not without. But in order to consolidate these flimsy guesses about the meaning of an expression on a face, let me open another of the books on your table and check it by what I find there. Again I open at random and read this:

> To penetrate that room is my desire,
> The extreme attic of the mind, that lies
> Just beyond the last bend in the corridor.
> Writing I do it. Phrases, poems are keys.
> Loving's another way (but not so sure).
> A fire's in there, I think, there's truth at last
> Deep in a lumber chest. Sometimes I'm near
> But draughts puff out the matches, and I'm lost.
> Sometimes I'm lucky, find a key to turn,
> Open an inch or two — but always then

----

[9] **wardrobe**   A freestanding piece of bedroom furniture used for storing clothes.

> A bell rings, someone calls, or cries of "fire"
> Arrest my hand when nothing's known or seen,
> And running down the stairs again I mourn.

And then this:

> There is a dark room,
> The locked and shuttered womb,
> Where negative's made positive.
> Another dark room,
> The blind and bolted tomb,
> Where positives change to negative.
> We may not undo that or escape this, who
> Have birth and death coiled in our bones,
> Nothing we can do
> Will sweeten the real rue,
> That we begin, and end, with groans.

And then this:

> Never being, but always at the edge of Being
> My head, like Death mask, is brought into the Sun.
> The shadow pointing finger across cheek,
> I move lips for tasting, I move hands for touching,
> But never am nearer than touching,
> Though the spirit leans outward for seeing.
> Observing rose, gold, eyes, an admired landscape,
> My senses record the act of wishing
> Wishing to be
> Rose, gold, landscape or another —
> Claiming fulfilment in the act of loving.

Since these quotations are chosen at random and I have yet 8 found three different poets writing about nothing, if not about the poet himself, I hold that the chances are that you too are engaged in the same occupation. I conclude that self offers no impediment; self joins in the dance; self lends itself to the rhythm; it is apparently easier to write a poem about oneself than about any other subject. But what does one mean by "oneself"? Not the self that Wordsworth, Keats, and Shelley[10] have described — not the self that loves a woman, or that hates a tyrant, or that broods over the mystery of the world. No, the self that you are engaged in describing is shut out from all that. It is a self that sits alone in the room at night with the blinds drawn. In other words the poet is much less interested in

---

[10] **William Wordsworth (1770 – 1850), John Keats (1795 – 1821), Percy Bysshe Shelley (1792 – 1822)** All three are among the most important of the Romantic poets.

what we have in common than in what he has apart. Hence I suppose the extreme difficulty of these poems — and I have to confess that it would floor me completely to say from one reading or even from two or three what these poems mean. The poet is trying honestly and exactly to describe a world that has perhaps no existence except for one particular person at one particular moment. And the more sincere he is in keeping to the precise outline of the roses and cabbages of his private universe, the more he puzzles us who have agreed in a lazy spirit of compromise to see roses and cabbages as they are seen, more or less, by the twenty-six passengers on the outside of an omnibus. He strains to describe; we strain to see; he flickers his torch; we catch a flying gleam. It is exciting; it is stimulating; but is that a tree, we ask, or is it perhaps an old woman tying up her shoe in the gutter?

Well, then, if there is any truth in what I am saying — if that is   9
you cannot write about the actual, the colloquial, Mrs. Gape or the Channel boat or Miss Curtis on the omnibus, without straining the machine of poetry, if, therefore, you are driven to contemplate landscapes and emotions within and must render visible to the world at large what you alone can see, then indeed yours is a hard case, and poetry, though still breathing — witness these little books — is drawing her breath in short, sharp gasps. Still, consider the symptoms. They are not the symptoms of death in the least. Death in literature, and I need not tell you how often literature has died in this country or in that, comes gracefully, smoothly, quietly. Lines slip easily down the accustomed grooves. The old designs are copied so glibly that we are half inclined to think them original, save for that very glibness. But here the very opposite is happening: here in my first quotation the poet breaks his machine because he will clog it with raw fact. In my second, he is unintelligible because of his desperate determination to tell the truth about himself. Thus I cannot help thinking that though you may be right in talking of the difficulty of the time, you are wrong to despair.

Is there not, alas, good reason to hope? I say "alas" because then   10
I must give my reasons, which are bound to be foolish and certain also to cause pain to the large and highly respectable society of necrophiles — Mr. Peabody, and his like — who much prefer death to life and are even now intoning the sacred and comfortable words, Keats is dead, Shelley is dead, Byron is dead. But it is late: necrophily induces slumber; the old gentlemen have fallen asleep over their classics, and if what I am about to say takes a sanguine tone — and for my part I do not believe in poets dying; Keats, Shelley, Byron are alive here in this room in you and you and you — I can take comfort from the thought that my hoping will not disturb

their snoring. So to continue — why should not poetry, now that it has so honestly scraped itself free from certain falsities, the wreckage of the great Victorian age,[11] now that it has so sincerely gone down into the mind of the poet and verified its outlines — a work of renovation that has to be done from time to time and was certainly needed, for bad poetry is almost always the result of forgetting oneself — all becomes distorted and impure if you lose sight of that central reality — now, I say, that poetry has done all this, why should it not once more open its eyes, look out of the window and write about other people? Two or three hundred years ago you were always writing about other people. Your pages were crammed with characters of the most opposite and various kinds — Hamlet, Cleopatra, Falstaff.[12] Not only did we go to you for drama, and for the subtleties of human character, but we also went to you, incredible though this now seems, for laughter. You made us roar with laughter. Then later, not more than a hundred years ago, you were lashing our follies, trouncing our hypocrisies, and dashing off the most brilliant of satires. You were Byron, remember; you wrote *Don Juan*.[13] You were Crabbe also; you took the most sordid details of the lives of peasants for your theme. Clearly therefore you have it in you to deal with a vast variety of subjects; it is only a temporary necessity that has shut you up in one room, alone, by yourself.

But how are you going to get out, into the world of other people? That is your problem now, if I may hazard a guess — to find the right relationship, now that you know yourself, between the self that you know and the world outside. It is a difficult problem. No living poet has, I think, altogether solved it. And there are a thousand voices prophesying despair. Science, they say, has made poetry impossible; there is no poetry in motor cars and wireless. And we have no religion. All is tumultuous and transitional. Therefore, so people say, there can be no relation between the poet and the present age. But surely that is nonsense. These accidents are superficial; they do not go nearly deep enough to destroy the most profound and primitive of instincts, the instinct of rhythm. All you need now

---

[11] **great Victorian age** A historical era, dating essentially from 1837, the accession of Queen Victoria to the throne of England, to 1901, the year of her death. It was an age of great industrial expansion, colonialization, and imperial design. It also was marked by a straitlaced social surface influenced by the manners of Victoria that produced "certain falsities" we now refer to as hypocrisies.

[12] **Hamlet, Cleopatra, Falstaff** Characters in plays of Shakespeare. Falstaff appears in several plays, most notably *Henry IV, Part I* (1598), and *The Merry Wives of Windsor* (1602).

[13] **Don Juan** A long poem by Lord Byron centering on the romantic escapades of the legendary lover.

is to stand at the window and let your rhythmical sense open and shut, open and shut, boldly and freely, until one thing melts in another, until the taxis are dancing with the daffodils, until a whole has been made from all these separate fragments. I am talking nonsense, I know. What I mean is, summon all your courage, exert all your vigilance, invoke all the gifts that Nature has been induced to bestow. Then let your rhythmical sense wind itself in and out among men and women, omnibuses, sparrows — whatever comes along the street — until it has strung them together in one harmonious whole. That perhaps is your task — to find the relation between things that seem incompatible yet have a mysterious affinity, to absorb every experience that comes your way fearlessly and saturate it completely so that your poem is a whole, not a fragment; to rethink human life into poetry and so give us tragedy again and comedy by means of characters not spun out at length in the novelist's way, but condensed and synthesized in the poet's way — that is what we look to you to do now. But as I do not know what I mean by rhythm nor what I mean by life, and as most certainly I cannot tell you which objects can properly be combined together in a poem — that is entirely your affair — and as I cannot tell a dactyl from an iambic, and am therefore unable to say how you must modify and expand the rites and ceremonies of your ancient and mysterious art — I will move on to safer ground and turn again to these little books themselves.

When, then, I return to them I am, as I have admitted, filled,   12
not with forebodings of death, but with hopes for the future. But one does not always want to be thinking of the future, if, as sometimes happens, one is living in the present. When I read these poems, now, at the present moment, I find myself — reading, you know, is rather like opening the door to a horde of rebels who swarm out attacking one in twenty places at once — hit, roused, scraped, bared, swung through the air, so that life seems to flash by; then again blinded, knocked on the head — all of which are agreeable sensations for a reader (since nothing is more dismal than to open the door and get no response), and all I believe certain proof that this poet is alive and kicking. And yet mingling with these cries of delight, of jubilation, I record also, as I read, the repetition in the bass of one word intoned over and over again by some malcontent. At last then, silencing the others, I say to this malcontent, "Well, and what do *you* want?" Whereupon he bursts out, rather to my discomfort, "Beauty." Let me repeat, I take no responsibility for what my senses say when I read; I merely record the fact that there is a malcontent in me who complains that it seems to him odd, considering that English is a mixed language, a rich language; a language un-

matched for its sound and color, for its power of imagery and suggestion — it seems to him odd that these modern poets should write
as if they had neither ears nor eyes, neither soles to their feet nor
palms to their hands, but only honest enterprising book-fed brains,
unisexual bodies and — but here I interrupted him. For when it
comes to saying that a poet should be bisexual, and that I think is
what he was about to say, even I, who have had no scientific training
whatsoever, draw the line and tell that voice to be silent.

But how far, if we discount these obvious absurdities, do you   13
think there is truth in this complaint? For my own part now that I
have stopped reading, and can see the poems more or less as a whole,
I think it is true that the eye and ear are starved of their rights. There is
no sense of riches held in reserve behind the admirable exactitude of
the lines I have quoted, as there is, for example, behind the exactitude
of Mr. Yeats.[14] The poet clings to his one word, his only word, as a
drowning man to a spar. And if this is so, I am ready to hazard a reason for it all the more readily because I think it bears out what I have
just been saying. The art of writing, and that is perhaps what my malcontent means by "beauty," the art of having at one's beck and call
every word in the language, of knowing their weights, colors, sounds,
associations, and thus making them, as is so necessary in English, suggest more than they can state, can be learnt of course to some extent
by reading — it is impossible to read too much; but much more drastically and effectively by imagining that one is not oneself but somebody different. How can you learn to write if you write only about one
single person? To take the obvious example. Can you doubt that the
reason why Shakespeare knew every sound and syllable in the language and could do precisely what he liked with grammar and syntax,
was that Hamlet, Falstaff and Cleopatra rushed him into this knowledge; that the lords, officers, dependents, murderers and common
soldiers of the plays insisted that he should say exactly what they felt
in the words expressing their feelings? It was they who taught him to
write, not the begetter of the Sonnets. So that if you want to satisfy all
those senses that rise in a swarm whenever we drop a poem among
them — the reason, the imagination, the eyes, the ears, the palms of
the hands and the soles of the feet, not to mention a million more that
the psychologists have yet to name, you will do well to embark upon
a long poem in which people as unlike yourself as possible talk at the
tops of their voices. And for heaven's sake, publish nothing before you
are thirty.

---

[14] **William Butler Yeats (1865 – 1939)** Yeats called himself the last Romantic.
He is considered one of the most influential modern poets writing in English.

That, I am sure, is of very great importance. Most of the faults in   14
the poems I have been reading can be explained, I think, by the fact
that they have been exposed to the fierce light of publicity while
they were still too young to stand the strain. It has shriveled them
into a skeleton austerity, both emotional and verbal, which should
not be characteristic of youth. The poet writes very well; he writes
for the eye of a severe and intelligent public; but how much better
he would have written if for ten years he had written for no eye but
his own! After all, the years from twenty to thirty are years (let me
refer to your letter again) of emotional excitement. The rain drip-
ping, a wing flashing, someone passing — the commonest sounds
and sights have power to fling one, as I seem to remember, from the
heights of rapture to the depths of despair. And if the actual life is
thus extreme, the visionary life should be free to follow. Write then,
now that you are young, nonsense by the ream. Be silly, be sentimental, imitate Shelley, imitate Samuel Smiles;[15] give the rein to
every impulse; commit every fault of style, grammar, taste, and syntax; pour out; tumble over; loose anger, love, satire, in whatever
words you can catch, coerce or create, in whatever meter, prose, poetry, or gibberish that comes to hand. Thus you will learn to write.
But if you publish, your freedom will be checked; you will be thinking what people will say; you will write for others when you ought
only to be writing for yourself. And what point can there be in curb-
ing the wild torrent of spontaneous nonsense which is now, for a
few years only, your divine gift in order to publish prim little books
of experimental verses? To make money? That, we both know, is out
of the question. To get criticism? But your friends will pepper your
manuscripts with far more serious and searching criticism than any
you will get from the reviewers. As for fame, look I implore you at
famous people; see how the waters of dullness spread around them
as they enter; observe their pomposity, their prophetic airs; reflect
that the greatest poets were anonymous; think how Shakespeare
cared nothing for fame; how Donne tossed his poems into the
wastepaper basket; write an essay giving a single instance of any
modern English writer who has survived the disciples and the ad-
mirers, the autograph hunters and the interviewers, the dinners and
the luncheons, the celebrations and the commemorations with
which English society so effectively stops the mouths of its singers
and silences their songs.

----

[15] **Samuel Smiles (1812 – 1904)** A Scots author and journalist, best known
for numerous volumes of popular biography. He also wrote a widely read book titled
Self-Help.

But enough. I, at any rate, refuse to be necrophilous. So long as   15
you and you and you, venerable and ancient representatives of Sappho,[16] Shakespeare, and Shelley, are aged precisely twenty-three and
propose — O enviable lot! — to spend the next fifty years of your
lives in writing poetry, I refuse to think that the art is dead. And if
ever the temptation to necrophilize comes over you, be warned by
the fate of that old gentleman whose name I forget, but I think that
it was Peabody. In the very act of consigning all the arts to the grave
he choked over a large piece of hot buttered toast and the consolation then offered him that he was about to join the elder Pliny in the
shades gave him, I am told, no sort of satisfaction whatsoever.

And now for the intimate, the indiscreet, and indeed, the only   16
really interesting parts of this letter. . . .

---

[16] **Sappho (fl. c. 610 – 580 B.C.)** A Greek lyric poet of the island of Lesbos.
Her work exists only in fragments, but she had a great reputation among the
ancients.

QUESTIONS FOR CRITICAL READING

1. Do you think this was a real letter sent to a real poet and then adapted
   for publication? What examples from the text might support your answer?
2. Why does the young poet think it is difficult to write poetry "in this
   particular autumn of 1931" (para. 3)?
3. What do the excerpts from poems quoted in this essay tell you about
   the condition of poetry when Woolf was writing? Do you find the samples good poetry? What are their strengths, and what are their weaknesses?
4. Do you agree that the novelist is doing today what the poet did in
   Shakespeare's or in Aristotle's time? What are your reasons for supposing that this is or is not the case?
5. How effective for you are the literary devices of Mr. Peabody and Mrs.
   Gape? In what ways do they help communicate Woolf's message, and
   in what ways do they act as unnecessary intrusions?
6. In what ways is Woolf herself poetic in writing this letter?

SUGGESTIONS FOR WRITING

1. How would you evaluate Woolf's advice to "embark upon a long poem
   in which people as unlike yourself as possible talk at the tops of their
   voices" (para. 13)? What would be the benefits of writing such a poem,

and why would a writer make this suggestion, particularly to a young poet? What are the advantages and disadvantages of this advice today? If you were interested in writing poetry, would you take this advice? Why?

2. Early in her essay, Woolf comments on the art of letter writing. She links the letter with the cost of sending it, referring at one point to the penny post. What is your assessment of the current state of the art of letter writing? Woolf says that her era is the great age of letter writing. Do you think she would say that today? Examine a variety of letters in the course of constructing your essay, including letters you have written and letters written to you (both personal and business). Then turn to the pages of the *New York Times,* your local or regional newspaper, a campus publication, *Time* magazine, the *Christian Science Monitor, TV Guide, Ebony,* and at least three other published sources. What is the state of the art of letter writing today?

3. Write a letter in response to Woolf's letter. Imagine yourself to be the person she addresses (though you need not think of yourself as "John"), and respond with your own thoughts regarding her observations on poetry. Concern yourself with her main points and her attitudes toward the writing of poetry. Do not hesitate to take issue with her evaluations or her advice. Ask her questions that might elicit a further letter from her.

4. In paragraph 8, Woolf says, "it is apparently easier to write a poem about oneself than about any other subject." Determine whether this is true by writing a poem about yourself and by commenting on the ease or difficulty of the task. Give some thought to whether you felt it would be easy or difficult before you began, whether your expectations were fulfilled, and whether you think that other poets would be likely to have similar experiences.

5. In paragraph 11, Woolf gives the poet very detailed advice on what to do about his work. She urges him to listen to rhythms in language and to respond by observing life closely:

> What I mean is, summon all your courage, exert all your vigilance, invoke all the gifts that Nature has been induced to bestow. Then let your rhythmical sense wind itself in and out among men and women, omnibuses, sparrows — whatever comes along the street — until it has strung them together in one harmonious whole. That perhaps is your task — to find the relation between things that seem incompatible yet have a mysterious affinity, to absorb every experience that comes your way fearlessly and saturate it completely so that your poem is a whole, not a fragment; to rethink human life into poetry and so give us tragedy again and comedy by means of characters not spun out at length in the novelist's way, but condensed and synthesized in the poet's way — that is what we look to you to do now.

Try to take her advice by observing life around you. Write a poem that includes the speech patterns of people you know and of people you hear from any source at all (including radio and television), and create characters who make demands on you. Capture their speech and their attitudes toward life. Make your poem reflect the living experience that is yours each day.

6. **CONNECTIONS** How does Woolf's advice about poetry compare with the advice of Aristotle, Pope, or Wordsworth? What type of modern poetry would Wordsworth's followers create? How might the lyric impulse point directly to the poet and the poet's experience and make it difficult for the poet to write about other people? Is it possible that the kind of poetry Woolf recommends can be written only in the dramatic forms discussed by Aristotle? Why?

SUSAN SONTAG
Against Interpretation

SUSAN SONTAG (b. 1933) is a probing critic whose commentaries on art, high and low, have earned her a place as a sharp, perceptive interpreter of aesthetic experience. But she is not an observer of art to the exclusion of other human concerns. Her political sensibilities, like those of many of her generation, were aroused by the upheavals of the 1960s brought on by the Vietnam War and by civil disturbances at home. Much of her work has been published in intellectual journals aimed at a politically aware audience.

Sontag holds degrees from the University of Chicago and Harvard University and has been a faculty member at a number of universities in the fields of both English and philosophy. She has been involved in film criticism and filmmaking since the late 1960s and has published screenplays as well as discussions of film. Her novels and creative writing have been a steady part of her work, among them *The Benefactor* (1963, then revised in 1978), *Death Kit* (1967), *Duet for Cannibals* (1970), *I, etcetera* (1978), and *The Volcano Lover* (1992).

Against Interpretation and Other Essays (1966) established her as one of the most provocative and surprising contemporary commentators on literature and art. "Against Interpretation" appears in a book of criticism yet seems to argue against the very process of criticism. Her book *Styles of Radical Will* (1969) continued the discussion of the modern sensibility and explored the issue of how we approach unusual and unexpected modern art forms.

Three of Sontag's books, *On Photography* (1977), *Illness as Metaphor* (1978), and *AIDS and Its Metaphors* (1988), have had much impact. Sontag's experience with cancer served as the impetus for *Illness as Metaphor*, which explores the ways in which society reacts to illness and the ways in which individuals sometimes exploit an illness. It is a book remarkable for its refusal to submit to the temptation to exploit the metaphor of illness in an autobiographical way.

"Against Interpretation," in many ways, is a reaction to an age in which all literature must submit to commentary and interpretation. In the essay, Sontag makes an effort to assess exactly what interpretation is: "The task of interpretation is virtually one of translation. The interpreter says, Look, don't you see that X is really — or, really means — A? That Y is really B? That Z is really C?" (para. 11). She believes that interpretation is not only an intermediary for literature and film but that it substitutes for them and tames them. As she says, "one tames the work of art. Interpretation makes art manageable, comfortable" (para. 18). She is quick to admit that during some ages interpretation is a positive force, but she believes that in other ages — such as the present one — it is not.

Early in the essay Sontag distinguishes between form and content. She focuses on literature and film, though she is obviously referring to all mimetic art. As Aristotle tells us in the *Poetics,* drama is the imitation of an action and is therefore mimetic. Although the word "mimetic" does not appear in the translation from the *Poetics* included in this book, in the rest of the *Poetics* it is a key term that links drama with life. Sontag explains that if art is mimetic it therefore has a content that relates it to life and that is interpretable. Her complaint is not just that commentators separate the form of a work of art from its content but that the act of interpretation concentrates on content to the exclusion of form — or virtually so.

Content is meaning, and interpretation aims to explain the meaning of a work of art. As a result of an overemphasis on content, interpretation has helped to distort art: "Most American novelists and playwrights are really either journalists or gentlemen sociologists and psychologists. They are writing the literary equivalent of program music" (para. 30). The only art forms that escape this fate are those that are not mimetic: abstract and decorative arts. To these categories, she adds Pop Art, which is, like Andy Warhol's Campbell soup cans, uninterpretable as art because it is not only mimetic of life but also replicates life.

Ultimately, Sontag urges us to discontinue our emphasis on content and to restore attention to form. She believes that film is the most vital current art, and she reminds us that modern films — and she is thinking of those by artistic filmmakers, not those by commercial entertainers — are interesting largely by virtue of their visual form, by those elements that transcend content. In essence, she is conceiving a poetics of film based on attention to its formal cinematic qualities.

She ends her essay by making an appeal for a critical approach that does not interpret but that examines and reports back on the facts, the perceptual elements of the work of art. She calls this "an erotics of art" because it emphasizes a growing awareness of sensory experience. She feels that sensory experience is important because the act of interpretation emphasizes intellectualization at the expense of experience. Thus, she says, "We must learn to see more, to hear more, to feel more" (para. 40).

SONTAG'S RHETORIC

Because this essay is an argument, Sontag depends on definition and on logical presentation. Ordinarily, she might have relied on sample interpretations or on concrete examples of works of art, but doing so is not possible in a general essay of this kind. Therefore, she establishes her definition of interpretation, comments on how it affects works of art and their audiences, and then makes a recommendation based on her understanding, expecting that we will share her understanding by the end of the essay.

Prominent in her rhetorical approach is a reliance on the historical survey. Since part of her argument is that interpretation can be good in some ages and not so good in other ages — and especially not good in this age — the historical survey takes on significance. She begins with Plato and Aristotle, reminding us of Plato's view that everything we see on earth is an imitation of the ideal, which is in "heaven." As a result of that view, art is of little interest to Plato, since it can be only an imitation of an imitation. Aristotle developed the more acceptable view of art as mimetic — imitating life in order to reveal it more fully to us — and was, therefore, able to comment incisively on Greek drama in his *Poetics*.

Sontag goes on to discuss those who interpreted the Bible in the first centuries after Christ. She points out that the tradition of biblical hermeneutics — examining the Bible for its hidden meaning — derives from an era in which the text itself was unacceptable. She uses as an example the Song of Solomon, which is an explicit, elaborate love song. The Song of Solomon was interpreted to be a model of the wooing of the church by God — and therefore it was retained among the books of the Bible.

In more recent times, the doctrines of Karl Marx and Sigmund Freud demand that we look behind art to an economic or psychological significance. Freud postulated that the dreams of his patients had a manifest content (what the dream seemed to be saying) and a more important latent content (what the dream was really saying). Psychoanalysis had among its tasks the job of determining the latent content and meaning of dreams, but it was not long before modern interpreters adopted the method and assumed that all literature also had subtexts, hidden meanings that needed to be revealed through the process of interpretation.

Finally, in commenting on contemporary circumstances, Sontag reminds us that generations of commentary have begun to substitute for the literature itself. If we accept this argument we should agree with her that it is time to put interpretation aside so that we can approach the arts with a new sensory freshness.

Against Interpretation

Content is a glimpse of something, an encounter like a flash. It's very tiny — very tiny, content.

— WILLEM DE KOONING,
in an interview

It is only shallow people who do not judge by appearances. The mystery of the world is the visible, not the invisible.

— OSCAR WILDE,
in a letter

The earliest experience of art must have been that it was incantatory, magical; art was an instrument of ritual. (Cf. the paintings in the caves at Lascaux, Altamira, Niaux, La Pasiega,[1] etc.) The earliest *theory* of art, that of the Greek philosophers, proposed that art was mimesis, imitation of reality.[2]   1

It is at this point that the peculiar question of the value of art arose. For the mimetic theory, by its very terms, challenges art to justify itself.   2

Plato,[3] who proposed the theory, seems to have done so in order to rule that the value of art is dubious. Since he considered or-   3

---

[1] **Lascaux, Altamira, Niaux, La Pasiega** Limestone caves in France and Spain on the walls of which are magnificent prehistoric paintings dating possibly to 15,000 B.C. The subjects of the paintings are animals, and the paintings are thought to have been part of magic rituals designed to gain control over the animals.

[2] **mimesis, imitation of reality** In his *Poetics*, Aristotle suggests that art, whether painting or drama, imitates life because art imitates an action.

[3] **Plato (c. 428 – 348 B.C.)** In "The Allegory of the Cave" (see Part Four), he demonstrates that reality is in "heaven" and that what we see on earth is only an imitation of the divine ideal.

dinary material things as themselves mimetic objects, imitations of transcendent forms or structures, even the best painting of a bed would be only an "imitation of an imitation." For Plato, art is neither particularly useful (the painting of a bed is no good to sleep on) nor, in the strict sense, true. And Aristotle's arguments in defense of art do not really challenge Plato's view that all art is an elaborate *trompe l'oeil,*[4] and therefore a lie. But he does dispute Plato's idea that art is useless. Lie or no, art has a certain value according to Aristotle because it is a form of therapy. Art is useful, after all, Aristotle counters, medicinally useful in that it arouses and purges dangerous emotions.

In Plato and Aristotle, the mimetic theory of art goes hand in　4 hand with the assumption that art is always figurative. But advocates of the mimetic theory need not close their eyes to decorative and abstract art. The fallacy that art is necessarily a "realism" can be modified or scrapped without ever moving outside the problems delimited by the mimetic theory.

The fact is, all Western consciousness of and reflection upon art　5 have remained within the confines staked out by the Greek theory of art as mimesis or representation. It is through this theory that art as such — above and beyond given works of art — becomes problematic, in need of defense. And it is the defense of art which gives birth to the odd vision by which something we have learned to call "form" is separated off from something we have learned to call "content," and to the well-intentioned move which makes content essential and form accessory.

Even in modern times, when most artists and critics have dis-　6 carded the theory of art as representation of an outer reality in favor of the theory of art as subjective expression, the main feature of the mimetic theory persists. Whether we conceive of the work of art on the model of a picture (art as a picture of reality) or on the model of a statement (art as the statement of the artist), content still comes first. The content may have changed. It may now be less figurative, less lucidly realistic. But it is still assumed that a work of art *is* its content. Or, as it's usually put today, that a work of art by definition says something. ("What X is saying is . . ." "What X is trying to say is . . ." "What X said is . . ." etc., etc.)

None of us can ever retrieve that innocence before all theory　7 when art knew no need to justify itself, when one did not ask of a

---

[4] *trompe l'oeil* French, "fool the eye"; an optical illusion; a style of painting that gives the illusion of actual objects or a photograph.

work of art what it said because one knew (or thought one knew) what it did. From now to the end of consciousness, we are stuck with the task of defending art. We can only quarrel with one or another means of defense. Indeed, we have an obligation to overthrow any means of defending and justifying art which becomes particularly obtuse or onerous or insensitive to contemporary needs and practice.

This is the case, today, with the very idea of content itself.   8 Whatever it may have been in the past, the idea of content is today mainly a hindrance, a nuisance, a subtle or not so subtle philistinism.[5]

Though the actual developments in many arts may seem to be   9 leading us away from the idea that a work of art is primarily its content, the idea still exerts an extraordinary hegemony. I want to suggest that this is because the idea is now perpetuated in the guise of a certain way of encountering works of art thoroughly ingrained among most people who take any of the arts seriously. What the overemphasis on the idea of content entails is the perennial, never-consummated project of *interpretation*. And, conversely, it is the habit of approaching works of art in order to *interpret* them that sustains the fancy that there really is such a thing as the content of a work of art.

Of course, I don't mean interpretation in the broadest sense, the   10 sense in which Nietzsche[6] (rightly) says, "There are no facts, only interpretations." By interpretation, I mean here a conscious act of the mind which illustrates a certain code, certain "rules" of interpretation.

Directed to art, interpretation means plucking a set of elements   11 (the X, the Y, the Z, and so forth) from the whole work. The task of interpretation is virtually one of translation. The interpreter says, Look, don't you see that X is really — or, really means — A? That Y is really B? That Z is really C?

What situation could prompt this curious project for transform-   12 ing a text? History gives us the materials for an answer. Interpretation first appears in the culture of late classical antiquity, when the power and credibility of myth had been broken by the "realistic" view of the world introduced by scientific enlightenment. Once the question that

---

[5] **philistinism** A smugly uncultured or anticultural position.
[6] **Friedrich Nietzsche (1844–1900)** One of the most important nineteenth-century German philosophers. His theory of the superman asserts that certain individuals are above conventional wisdom and should be permitted to live and act as they wish.

haunts post-mythic consciousness — that of the *seemliness* of religious symbols — had been asked, the ancient texts were, in their pristine form, no longer acceptable. Then interpretation was summoned, to reconcile the ancient texts to "modern" demands. Thus, the Stoics,[7] to accord with their view that the gods had to be moral, allegorized away the rude features of Zeus and his boisterous clan in Homer's epics. What Homer really designated by the adultery of Zeus with Leto, they explained, was the union between power and wisdom. In the same vein, Philo of Alexandria[8] interpreted the literal historical narratives of the Hebrew Bible as spiritual paradigms. The story of the exodus from Egypt, the wandering in the desert for forty years, and the entry into the promised land, said Philo, was really an allegory of the individual soul's emancipation, tribulations, and final deliverance. Interpretation thus presupposes a discrepancy between the clear meaning of the text and the demands of (later) readers. It seeks to resolve that discrepancy. The situation is that for some reason a text has become unacceptable; yet it cannot be discarded. Interpretation is a radical strategy for conserving an old text, which is thought too precious to repudiate, by revamping it. The interpreter, without actually erasing or rewriting the text, *is* altering it. But he can't admit to doing this. He claims to be only making it intelligible, by disclosing its true meaning. However far the interpreters alter the text (another notorious example is the rabbinic and Christian "spiritual" interpretations of the clearly erotic Song of Songs[9]), they must claim to be reading off a sense that is already there.

Interpretation in our own time, however, is even more complex. 13 For the contemporary zeal for the project of interpretation is often prompted not by piety toward the troublesome text (which may conceal an aggression) but by an open aggressiveness, an overt contempt for appearances. The old style of interpretation was insistent,

---

[7] **the Stoics . . . Homer's epics** The Stoic philosophers in ancient Greece interpreted the Greek myths in accordance with their views of a morality of self-sacrifice and public welfare. Homer (9th – 8th centuries B.C.), who preceded the Stoics, could retell the adulterous myths of Zeus without having to interpret them to fit a "higher" public morality.

[8] **Philo of Alexandria (30 B.C. – A.D. 45)** A Jewish philosopher of importance to our knowledge of Jewish thought in the first century A.D. His theories were closely aligned with Stoicism (see note 7). His most important work is a commentary on Genesis in which he sees all the characters as allegorical representations of states of the soul.

[9] **Song of Songs** This is the Song of Solomon in the Bible, referred to in the headnote. The inclusion of the Song of Solomon in the Bible was marked by much dispute because it is an erotic, though beautiful, piece of literature. The dispute was settled when agreement was reached in its interpretation: it was seen as a metaphor of the love of God for his creation.

but respectful; it erected another meaning on top of the literal one. The modern style of interpretation excavates, and as it excavates, destroys; it digs "behind" the text, to find a sub-text which is the true one. The most celebrated and influential modern doctrines, those of Marx and Freud,[10] actually amount to elaborate systems of hermeneutics,[11] aggressive and impious theories of interpretation. All observable phenomena are bracketed, in Freud's phrase, as *manifest content*. This manifest content must be probed and pushed aside to find the true meaning — the *latent content* — beneath. For Marx, social events like revolutions and wars; for Freud, the events of individual lives (like neurotic symptoms and slips of the tongue) as well as texts (like a dream or a work of art) — all are treated as occasions for interpretation. According to Marx and Freud, these events only *seem* to be intelligible. Actually, they have no meaning without interpretation. To understand *is* to interpret. And to interpret is to restate the phenomenon, in effect to find an equivalent for it.

Thus, interpretation is not (as most people assume) an absolute   14
value, a gesture of mind situated in some timeless realm of capabilities. Interpretation must itself be evaluated, within a historical view of human consciousness. In some cultural contexts, interpretation is a liberating act. It is a means of revising, of transvaluing[12] of escaping the dead past. In other cultural contexts, it is reactionary, impertinent, cowardly, stifling.

Today is such a time, when the project of interpretation is   15
largely reactionary, stifling. Like the fumes of the automobile and of heavy industry which befoul the urban atmosphere, the effusion of interpretations of art today poisons our sensibilities. In a culture whose already classical dilemma is the hypertrophy[13] of the intellect at the expense of energy and sensual capability, interpretation is the revenge of the intellect upon art.

Even more. It is the revenge of the intellect upon the world. To   16
interpret is to impoverish, to deplete the world — in order to set up a shadow world of "meanings." It is to turn *the* world into *this* world. ("This world"! As if there were any other.)

The world, our world, is depleted, impoverished enough. Away   17
with all duplicates of it, until we again experience more immediately what we have.

---

[10] **Marx and Freud** See the introductions for each of these authors in Parts Three and Four, respectively.

[11] **hermeneutics** A system of critical analysis that examines texts for their deeper meanings.

[12] **transvaluing** The act of evaluating by a new principle, such as interpreting a sonnet of Shakespeare by means of Freudian principles.

[13] **hypertrophy** Overdevelopment.

In most modern instances, interpretation amounts to the philis-   18
tine refusal to leave the work of art alone. Real art has the capacity to
make us nervous. By reducing the work of art to its content and
then interpreting *that,* one tames the work of art. Interpretation
makes art manageable, conformable.

This philistinism of interpretation is more rife in literature than   19
in any other art. For decades now, literary critics have understood it
to be their task to translate the elements of the poem or play or
novel or story into something else. Sometimes a writer will be so un-
easy before the naked power of his art that he will install within the
work itself — albeit with a little shyness, a touch of the good taste of
irony — the clear and explicit interpretation of it. Thomas Mann[14] is
an example of such an overcooperative author. In the case of more
stubborn authors, the critic is only too happy to perform the job.

The work of Kafka,[15] for example, has been subjected to a mass   20
ravishment by no less than three armies of interpreters. Those who
read Kafka as a social allegory see case studies of the frustrations and
insanity of modern bureaucracy and its ultimate issuance in the totalitarian state. Those who read Kafka as a psychoanalytic allegory
see desperate revelations of Kafka's fear of his father, his castration
anxieties, his sense of his own impotence, his thralldom to his
dreams. Those who read Kafka as a religious allegory explain that K.
in *The Castle* is trying to gain access to heaven, that Joseph K. in *The
Trial* is being judged by the inexorable and mysterious justice of
God. . . . Another body of work that has attracted interpreters like
leeches is that of Samuel Beckett,[16] Beckett's delicate dramas of the
withdrawn consciousness — pared down to essentials, cut off, often
represented as physically immobilized — are read as a statement
about modern man's alienation from meaning or from God, or as an
allegory of psychopathology.

Proust, Joyce, Faulkner, Rilke, Lawrence, Gide[17] . . . one could   21
go on citing author after author; the list is endless of those around
whom thick encrustations of interpretation have taken hold. But it

---

[14] **Thomas Mann (1875 – 1955)** A major modern German novelist. Sontag
may be referring to his most important novel, *The Magic Mountain* (1924).

[15] **Franz Kafka (1883 – 1924)** A largely surrealist writer whose dreamworlds
are often close to the nightmare. The novels referred to, *The Castle* (1926) and *The
Trial* (1925), concentrate on the struggles of the individual against institutions
whose nature is baffling and intimidating.

[16] **Samuel Beckett (1906 – 1989)** Irish writer whose work is enigmatic. He is
best known for his play *Waiting for Godot* (1956).

[17] **Marcel Proust (1871 – 1922), James Joyce (1882 – 1941), William Faulkner (1897 – 1962), Rainer Maria Rilke (1875 – 1926), D. H. Lawrence (1885 –
1930), André Gide (1869 – 1951)** Important modern writers whose work has attracted considerable interpretive attention.

should be noted that interpretation is not simply the compliment that mediocrity pays to genius. It is, indeed, the modern way of understanding something, and is applied to works of every quality. Thus, in the notes that Elia Kazan[18] published on his production of *A Streetcar Named Desire,* it becomes clear that, in order to direct the play, Kazan had to discover that Stanley Kowalski represented the sensual and vengeful barbarism that was engulfing our culture, while Blanche DuBois was Western civilization, poetry, delicate apparel, dim lighting, refined feelings and all, though a little the worse for wear, to be sure. Tennessee Williams's forceful psychological melodrama now became intelligible: it was about something, about the decline of Western civilization. Apparently, were it to go on being a play about a handsome brute named Stanley Kowalski and a faded mangy belle named Blanche DuBois, it would not be manageable.

It doesn't matter whether artists intend, or don't intend, for   22
their works to be interpreted. Perhaps Tennessee Williams thinks *Streetcar* is about what Kazan thinks it to be about. It may be that Cocteau[19] in *The Blood of a Poet* and in *Orpheus* wanted the elaborate readings which have been given these films, in terms of Freudian symbolism and social critique. But the merit of these works certainly lies elsewhere than in their "meanings." Indeed, it is precisely to the extent that Williams's plays and Cocteau's films do suggest these portentous meanings[20] that they are defective, false, contrived, lacking in conviction.

From interviews, it appears that Resnais and Robbe-Grillet[21]   23
consciously designed *Last Year at Marienbad* to accommodate a multiplicity of equally plausible interpretations. But the temptation to interpret *Marienbad* should be resisted. What matters in *Marienbad* is the pure, untranslatable, sensuous immediacy of some of its images, and its rigorous if narrow solutions to certain problems of cinematic form.

---

[18] **Elia Kazan (b. 1909)** American theatrical director who championed the early productions of Tennessee Williams (1914 – 1984), particularly *A Streetcar Named Desire* (1947).

[19] **Jean Cocteau (1889 – 1963)** French writer, painter, filmmaker. His *Orpheus* (1924) reinterpreted the Greek myth for modern times.

[20] **portentous meanings** Meanings that imply great significance or seriousness and that may imply ominous developments. Sontag implies that the meanings suggested for the works are overblown and unlikely.

[21] **Alain Resnais (b. 1922) and Alain Robbe-Grillet (b. 1922)** The filmmaker and screenwriter, respectively, for an experimental film, *Last Year at Marienbad* (1961).

Again, Ingmar Bergman[22] may have meant the tank rumbling   24
down the empty night street in *The Silence* as a phallic symbol. But if
he did, it was a foolish thought. ("Never trust the teller, trust the
tale," said Lawrence.) Taken as a brute object, as an immediate sensory equivalent for the mysterious abrupt armored happenings
going on inside the hotel, that sequence with the tank is the most
striking moment in the film. Those who reach for a Freudian interpretation of the tank are only expressing their lack of response to
what is there on the screen.

It is always the case that interpretation of this type indicates a   25
dissatisfaction (conscious or unconscious) with the work, a wish to
replace it by something else.

Interpretation, based on the highly dubious theory that a work   26
of art is composed of items of content, violates art. It makes art into
an article for use, for arrangement into a mental scheme of categories.

Interpretation does not, of course, always prevail. In fact, a great   27
deal of today's art may be understood as motivated by a flight from
interpretation. To avoid interpretation, art may become parody. Or
it may become abstract. Or it may become ("merely") decorative. Or
it may become non-art.

The flight from interpretation seems particularly a feature of   28
modern painting. Abstract painting is the attempt to have, in the ordinary sense, no content; since there is no content, there can be no
interpretation. Pop Art[23] works by the opposite means to the same
result; using a content so blatant, so "what it is," it, too, ends by
being uninterpretable.

A great deal of modern poetry as well, starting from the great   29
experiments of French poetry (including the movement that is mis-
leadingly called Symbolism)[24] to put silence into poems and to reinstate the *magic* of the word, has escaped from the rough grip of interpretation. The most recent revolution in contemporary taste in

---

[22] **Ingmar Bergman (b. 1918)** Swedish film director, one of the most influential of modern filmmakers.

[23] **Pop Art** A form of art that in the late 1950s and in the 1960s reacted against
the high seriousness of abstract expressionism and other movements of the 1940s
and 1950s. Instead of stressing deep content, it stressed no content; instead of profound meaning, no meaning other than what was observable.

[24] **Symbolism** A movement in poetry begun in France in the late nineteenth
century and popularized in England by Arthur Symons. It sought expression
through the symbol rather than through discursive language. By silencing the discourse, the symbolists hoped to put magic back into poetry — the magic representing what was inexpressible in words but could be felt in symbol.

poetry — the revolution that has deposed Eliot and elevated Pound[25] — represents a turning away from content in poetry in the old sense, an impatience with what made modern poetry prey to the zeal of interpreters.

I am speaking mainly of the situation in America, of course. Interpretation runs rampant here in those arts with a feeble and negligible avant-garde:[26] fiction and the drama. Most American novelists and playwrights are really either journalists or gentlemen sociologists and psychologists. They are writing the literary equivalent of program music. And so rudimentary, uninspired, and stagnant has been the sense of what might be done with form in fiction and drama that even when the content isn't simply information, news, it is still peculiarly visible, handier, more exposed. To the extent that novels and plays (in America), unlike poetry and painting and music, don't reflect any interesting concern with changes in their form, these arts remain prone to assault by interpretation.

But programmatic avant-gardism — which has meant, mostly, experiments with form at the expense of content — is not the only defense against the infestation of art by interpretations. At least, I hope not. For this would be to commit art to being perpetually on the run. (It also perpetuates the very distinction between form and content which is, ultimately, an illusion.) Ideally, it is possible to elude the interpreters in another way, by making works of art whose surface is so unified and clean, whose momentum is so rapid, whose address is so direct that the work can be . . . just what it is. Is this possible now? It does happen in films, I believe. This is why cinema is the most alive, the most exciting, the most important of all art forms right now. Perhaps the way one tells how alive a particular art form is is by the latitude it gives for making mistakes in it and still being good. For example, a few of the films of Bergman — though crammed with lame messages about the modern spirit, thereby inviting interpretations — still triumph over the pretentious intentions of their director. In *Winter Light* and *The Silence,* the beauty and visual sophistication of the images subvert before our eyes the callow pseudo-intellectuality of the story and some of the dialogue. (The most remarkable instance of this sort of discrepancy is the work of D. W. Griffith).[27] In good films, there is always a directness that entirely frees us from the itch to interpret. Many old Hollywood

---

[25] **T. S. Eliot (1888–1965) and Ezra Pound (1885–1972)** Two of America's most important modern poets.

[26] **avante-garde** Art that is ahead of its time; literally, in the advance guard of a movement forward.

[27] **D. W. Griffith (1875–1948)** The first major American film director.

films, like those of Cukor, Walsh, Hawks,[28] and countless other directors, have this liberating antisymbolic quality, no less than the
best work of the new European directors, like Truffaut's *Shoot the
Piano Player* and *Jules and Jim,* Godard's *Breathless* and *Vivre sa Vie,*
Antonioni's *L'Avventura,* and Olmi's *The Fiancés.*[29]

The fact that films have not been overrun by interpreters is in   32
part due simply to the newness of cinema as an art. It also owes to
the happy accident that films for such a long time were just movies;
in other words, that they were understood to be part of mass, as opposed to high, culture, and were left alone by most people with
minds. Then, too, there is always something other than content in
the cinema to grab hold of, for those who want to analyze. For the
cinema, unlike the novel, possesses a vocabulary of forms — the explicit, complex, and discussable technology of camera movements,
cutting, and composition of the frame that goes into the making of a
film.

What kind of criticism, of commentary on the arts, is desirable   33
today? For I am not saying that works of art are ineffable, that they
cannot be described or paraphrased. They can be. The question is
how. What would criticism look like that would serve the work of
art, not usurp its place?

                                                                    34
What is needed, first, is more attention to form in art. If excessive stress on *content* provokes the arrogance of interpretation, more
extended and more thorough descriptions of *form* would silence.
What is needed is a vocabulary — a descriptive, rather than prescriptive, vocabulary[30] — for forms.[31] The best criticism, and it is

---

[28] **George Cukor (1899 – 1983), Raoul Walsh (1887 – 1980), Howard
Hawks (1896 – 1977)** American filmmakers who were important before 1950.

[29] **François Truffaut (1932 – 1984), Jean-Luc Godard (b. 1930), Michelan-
gelo Antonioni (b. 1912), Ermanno Olmi (b. 1931)** Important modern influences
in filmmaking.

[30] **descriptive, rather than prescriptive, vocabulary** A prescriptive vocabulary in criticism aims to establish what a work of art ought to be; a descriptive vocabulary concentrates on what is. Sontag encourages a criticism that tells us what has
happened, not one that tells us what ought to happen.

[31] One of the difficulties is that our idea of form is spatial (the Greek metaphors
for form are all derived from notions of space). This is why we have a more ready
vocabulary of forms for the spatial than for the temporal arts. The exception among
the temporal arts, of course, is the drama; perhaps this is because the drama is a narrative (i.e., temporal) form that extends itself visually and pictorially, upon a stage.
What we don't have yet is a poetics of the novel, any clear notion of the forms of
narration. Perhaps film criticism will be the occasion of a breakthrough here, since
films are primarily a visual form yet they are also a subdivision of literature. [Son-
tag's note]

uncommon, is of this sort that dissolves considerations of content into those of form. On film, drama, and painting respectively, I can think of Erwin Panofsky's essay "Style and Medium in the Motion Pictures," Northrop Frye's essay "A Conspectus of Dramatic Genres," Pierre Francastel's essay "The Destruction of a Plastic Space." Roland Barthes's book *On Racine* and his two essays on Robbe-Grillet are examples of formal analysis applied to the work of a single author. (The best essays in Erich Auerbach's *Mimesis,* like "The Scar of Odysseus," are also of this type.) An example of formal analysis applied simultaneously to genre and author is Walter Benjamin's essay "The Storyteller: Reflections on the Works of Nicolai Leskov."[32]

Equally valuable would be acts of criticism which would supply a really accurate, sharp, loving description of the appearance of a work of art. This seems even harder to do than formal analysis. Some of Manny Farber's film criticism, Dorothy Van Ghent's essay "The Dickens World: A View from Todgers'," Randall Jarrell's essay on Walt Whitman are among the rare examples of what I mean.[33] These are essays which reveal the sensuous surface of art without mucking about in it.

Transparence is the highest, most liberating value in art — and in criticism — today. Transparence means experiencing the luminousness of the thing in itself, of things being what they are. This is the greatness of, for example, the films of Bresson and Ozu and Renoir's[34] *The Rules of the Game.*

Once upon a time (say, for Dante),[35] it must have been a revolutionary and creative move to design works of art so that they might be experienced on several levels. Now it is not. It reinforces the principle of redundancy that is the principal affliction of modern life.

Once upon a time (a time when high art was scarce), it must have been a revolutionary and creative move to interpret works of art. Now it is not. What we decidedly do not need now is further to assimilate Art into Thought, or (worse yet) Art into Culture.

Interpretation takes the sensory experience of the work of art for granted, and proceeds from there. This cannot be taken for granted

35

36

37

38

39

---

[32] **On film . . . Leskov** These are all works by modern critics; they are the kind that Sontag feels will help to reinstate formal analysis.

[33] **Some of . . . I mean** These are examples of critics whose purpose is to describe accurately the surfaces of works of art.

[34] **Robert Bresson (b. 1907), Yasujiro Ozu (1903 – 1963), Alain Renoir (1894 – 1979)** Directors who are or were significant influences on contemporary filmmakers.

[35] **Dante Alighieri (1265 – 1321)** Italian poet and scholar. His most important work was *The Divine Comedy.*

now. Think of the sheer multiplication of works of art available to every one of us, super-added to the conflicting tastes and odors and sights of the urban environment that bombard our senses. Ours is a culture based on excess, on overproduction; the result is a steady loss of sharpness in our sensory experience. All the conditions of modern life — its material plenitude, its sheer crowdedness — conjoin to dull our sensory faculties. And it is in the light of the condition of our senses, our capacities (rather than those of another age), that the task of the critic must be assessed.

What is important now is to recover our senses. We must learn   40
to *see* more, to *hear* more, to *feel* more.

Our task is not to find the maximum amount of content in a   41
work of art, much less to squeeze more content out of the work than is already there. Our task is to cut back content so that we can see the thing at all.

The aim of all commentary on art now should be to make works   42
of art — and, by analogy, our own experience — more, rather than less, real to us. The function of criticism should be to show *how it is what it is,* even *that it is what it is,* rather than to show *what it means.*

In place of a hermeneutics we need an erotics of art.   43

QUESTIONS FOR CRITICAL READING

1. What is Sontag's definition of interpretation? What are its strengths and weaknesses? How does her definition affect the nature of her argument?

2. How would you define interpretation?

3. How does the concept of mimesis relate to works of literature? What does it mean for a work of literature to be true to life? Is that the same as describing it as mimetic?

4. Sontag cites Freud's claim that dreams have a manifest content and a latent content. Why does Sontag feel that Freud's theory of dreams is relevant to acts of interpretation? Why do you agree or disagree with her?

5. Sontag refers to the term "hermeneutics" in paragraph 13 as a form of interpretation. What does she mean by the term and what is her attitude toward it?

6. Explain why Sontag tells us that in relation to a work of literature or art our job ought to be to show what it is rather than what it means. Do you agree with her? Why or why not?

7. What does Sontag mean by an "erotics of art"? Do you feel it would be possible for critics to practice an erotics of art? Would it be a good thing or not?

SUGGESTIONS FOR WRITING

1. Sontag explains that works of art have a content and a form. She also explains that the terminology for formal elements in literary works is not as fully developed as it is for visual works. Therefore, it is difficult to talk about the form of a work of literature. If you were to comment on a work of literary art — of poetry, drama, or fiction — what formal elements would you have to discuss? Can you discuss them without performing an act of interpretation? Choose a specific work for your commentary. Ground your discussion in an examination of one work.

2. Do you agree with Sontag about the artistic vitality of contemporary film? Using examples from films you have seen recently (whether on television or in a theater), defend or attack her judgment regarding the preeminence of the film among contemporary arts.

3. To what extent does Sontag's commentary on "subjective expression" (para. 6) suggest an emotional content in works of art? What kinds of emotions would she admit into art? Which emotions would she wish to omit from art or from discussions of art?

4. Sontag says that "most artists and critics have discarded the theory of art as representation of an outer reality in favor of the theory of art as subjective expression" and that "it is still assumed that a work of art *is* its content" (para. 6). To what extent do you think these statements are true? Refer to your experience in reading, in viewing paintings, or in experiencing other works of art. What special problems might arise in examining the form of a work of art if we assume that art is subjective expression — in other words, the expression of the artist's feelings or of his or her understanding of things? Would subjective expression be more likely to affect the content or the form of a work of art?

5. Take Sontag's advice and approach a favorite poem by doing as she recommends: create an erotics of art instead of a hermeneutics. In other words, heed her final words of advice: "The aim of all commentary on art now should be to make the works of art — and, by analogy, our own experience — more, rather than less, real to us. The function of criticism should be to show *how it is what it is,* even *that it is what it is,* rather than to show *what it means*" (para. 42).

6. Offer a counterargument to Sontag's views. Write an essay called "In Defense of Interpretation," and try to establish clearly what interpretation is, how it functions, and why it is defensible. Why is it good? Why is it desirable? In the process, you may comment on any of Sontag's arguments and counter them in turn. Decide whether her distinction between form and content is acceptable and whether it is necessary to your argument. Use specific examples of your interpretation (or the interpretations of others) of works of art to defend your position.

7. **CONNECTIONS** In the first paragraph of the *Poetics,* Aristotle discusses "language made sensuously attractive." How would Aristotle's view fit in with Sontag's attitude toward literature in general? What does it mean for language to be sensuously attractive? Cite examples

within both pieces and in your own experience that clarify that idea for you.

8. **CONNECTIONS** Alexander Pope complains about critics and their limitations, while Sontag complains about interpreters and their limitations. In what areas do Pope and Sontag seem to agree on the critic's or interpreter's role of commenting on a text? In what areas do they seem to differ? Is it reasonable to say that both Pope and Sontag defend a view supporting a holistic attitude toward literature?

WRITING ABOUT IDEAS
An Introduction to Rhetoric

Writing about ideas has several functions. First, it helps make our thinking available to others for examination. The writers whose works are presented in this book benefited from their first readers' examinations and at times revised their work considerably as a result of such criticism. Writing about ideas also helps us to refine what we think — even without criticism from others — because writing is a self-instructional experience. We learn by writing in part because writing clarifies our thinking. When we think silently, we construct phrases and then reflect on them; when we speak, we both utter these phrases and sort them out in order to give our audience a tidier version of our thoughts. But spoken thought is difficult to sustain because we cannot review or revise what we said an hour earlier. Writing has the advantage of permitting us to expand our ideas, to work them through completely, and possibly to revise in the light of later discoveries. It is by writing that we truly gain control over our ideas.

GENERATING TOPICS FOR WRITING

Filled with sophisticated discussions of important ideas, the selections in this volume endlessly stimulate our responses and our writing. Reading the works of great thinkers can also be chastening to the point of making us feel sometimes that they have said it all and there is no room for our own thoughts. However, the suggestions that follow will assist you in writing your response to the ideas of an important thinker.

Thinking Critically: Asking a Question. One of the most reliable ways to start writing is to ask a question and then to answer it. In many ways, that is what the writers in this book have done again and again. Karen Horney asked whether what Freud said about female psychology was true. Adam Smith asked what the principles of the commercial or mercantile system really were and proceeded to examine the economic system of his time in such detail that his views are still valued. He is associated with the capitalist system as firmly as Marx is with the communist system. John Kenneth Galbraith asked questions about why poverty existed in a prosperous nation such as the United States. Maimonides inquired into the limits of our intellect, trying to see exactly what we cannot know. Michio Kaku's question, "The Theory of the Universe?" asks whether the theory he expounds really explains the way the universe is structured. Such questioning is at the center of all critical thinking.

As a writer stimulated by other thinkers, you can use the same technique. For example, turn back to the Machiavelli excerpt annotated in "Evaluating Ideas: An Introduction to Critical Reading" (pp. 5 – 7). All the annotations can easily be turned into questions. Any of the following questions, based on the annotations and our brief summary of the passage, could be the basis of an essay:

> Should a leader be armed?
>
> Is it true that an unarmed leader is despised?
>
> Will those leaders who are always good come to ruin among those who are not good?
>
> To remain in power, must a leader learn how not to be good?

One technique is to structure an essay around the answer to such a question. Another is to develop a series of questions and to answer each of them in various parts of an essay. Yet another technique is to use the question indirectly — by answering it, but not obviously. In "Why the Rich Are Getting Richer and the Poor, Poorer," for example, Robert Reich answers a question we may not have asked. In the process he examines the nature of our current economy to see what it promises for different sectors of the population. His answer to the question concerns the shift in labor from manufacturing to information, revealing that what he calls "symbolic analysts" have the best opportunities in the future to amass wealth.

Many kinds of questions can be asked of a passage even as brief as the sample from Machiavelli. For one thing, we can limit ourselves to our annotations and go no further. But we also can reflect on larger issues and ask a series of questions that constitute a fuller inquiry. Out of that inquiry we can generate ideas for our own writing.

Two important ideas were isolated in our annotations. The first was that the prince must devote himself to war. In modern times, this implies that a president or other national leader must put matters of defense first — that a leader's knowledge, training, and concerns must revolve around warfare. Taking that idea in general, we can develop other questions that, stimulated by Machiavelli's selection, can be used to generate essays:

> Which modern leaders would Machiavelli support?
>
> Would Machiavelli approve of our current president?
>
> Do military personnel make the best leaders?
>
> Should our president have a military background?
>
> Could a modern state survive with no army or military weapons?
>
> What kind of a nation would we have if we did not stockpile nuclear weapons?

These questions derive from "The prince's profession should be war," the first idea that we isolated in the annotations. The next group of questions comes from the second idea, the issue of whether a leader can afford to be moral:

> Can virtues cause a leader to lose power?
>
> Is Machiavelli being cynical about morality, or is he being realistic (as he claims he is)? (We might also ask if Machiavelli uses the word *realistic* as a synonym for *cynical*.)
>
> Do most American leaders behave morally?
>
> Do most leaders believe that they should behave morally?
>
> Should our leaders be moral all the time?
>
> Which vices can we permit our leaders to have?
>
> Are there any vices we want our leaders to have?
>
> Which world leaders behave most morally? Are they the ones we most respect?
>
> Could a modern government govern well or at all if it were to behave morally in the face of immoral adversaries?

One reason for reading Machiavelli is to help us confront large and serious questions. One reason for writing about these ideas is to help clarify our own positions on such important issues.

Using Suggestions for Writing. Every selection in this book is followed by a number of questions and a number of writing assignments. The questions are designed to help clarify the most important issues raised in the piece. Unlike the questions derived from annotation, their purpose is to stimulate a classroom discussion so that you can benefit from hearing others' thoughts on these issues. Naturally, subjects for essays can arise from such discussion, but the discussion is most important for refining and focusing your ideas. The writing assignments, on the other hand, are explicitly meant to provide a useful starting point for producing an essay of 700 to 1,000 words.

A sample suggestion for writing about Machiavelli follows:

> Machiavelli advises the prince to study history and reflect on the actions of great men. Do you support such advice? Machiavelli mentions a number of great leaders in his essay. Which leaders would you recommend a prince should study? How do you think Machiavelli would agree or disagree with your recommendations?

Like most of the suggestions for writing, this one can be approached in several ways. It can be broken down into three parts. The first question is whether it is useful to study, as Machiavelli does, the performance of past leaders. If you agree, then the second question asks you to name some leaders whose behavior you would recommend studying. If you do not agree, you can point to the performance of some past leaders and explain why their study would be pointless today. Finally, the third question asks how you think Machiavelli would agree or disagree with your choices.

To deal successfully with this suggestion for writing, you could begin by giving your reasons for recommending that a political leader study "the actions of great men." George Santayana once said, "Those who cannot remember the past are condemned to repeat it." That is, we study history in order not to have to live it over again. If you believe that a study of the past is important, the first part of an essay can answer the question of why such study could make a politician more successful.

The second part of the suggestion focuses on examples. In the sample from Machiavelli above, we omitted the examples, but in the complete essay they are very important for bringing Machiavelli's point home. Few things can convince as completely as examples, so the first thing to do is to choose several leaders to work with. If you have studied a world leader, such as Indira Gandhi, Winston Churchill, Franklin Delano Roosevelt, or Margaret Thatcher, you could use that figure as one of your examples. If you have not done so, then use the research library's sections on history and politics to find books or articles on one or two leaders and read them with an eye to establishing their usefulness for your argument. The central question you would seek to answer is how a specific world leader could benefit from studying the behavior and conduct of a modern leader.

The third part of the suggestion for writing — how Machiavelli would agree or disagree with you — is highly speculative. It invites you to look through the selection to find quotes or comments that indicate probable agreement or disagreement on Machiavelli's part. You can base your argument only on what Machiavelli says or implies, and this means that you will have to reread his essay to find evidence that will support your view.

In a sense, this part of the suggestion establishes a procedure for working with the writing assignments. Once you clarify the parts of the assignment and have some useful questions to guide you, and once you determine what research, if any, is necessary, the next step is to reread the selection to find the most appropriate information to help you write your own essay. One of the most important activities in learning how to write from these selections is to reread while paying close attention to the annotations that you've made in the margins of the essays. It is one way in which reading about significant ideas differs from reading for entertainment. Important ideas demand reflection and reconsideration. Rereading provides both.

DEVELOPING IDEAS IN WRITING

Every selection in this book — whether by Francis Bacon or Simone de Beauvoir, Frederick Douglass or Karl Marx — employs specific rhetorical techniques that help the author communicate important ideas. Each introduction identifies the special rhetorical techniques used by the writer, partly to introduce you to the way in which such techniques are used. For example, Clifford Geertz provides an example of enumeration — the numbering of important sections of an essay — in his answer to the following rhetorical question: is it possible to see cultures from the native's point of view? In the course of answering this question, he enumerates three different cultures that he knows well: Javanese, Balinese, and Moroccan. Such techniques are invaluable for every writer. And they are not difficult to apply to your own writing. Some of the suggestions for writing that follow the passages encourage you to use the techniques by isolating and analyzing them.

Rhetoric is a general term used to discuss effective writing techniques. For example, an interesting rhetorical technique that Machiavelli uses is illustration by example, usually to prove his points. Francis Bacon uses the technique of enumeration by partitioning his essay into four sections. Enumeration is especially useful when the writer wishes to be very clear or to cover a subject point by point, using each point to accumulate more authority in the discussion. Martin Luther King, Jr., uses the technique of allusion, reminding the religious leaders who were his readers that St. Paul wrote similar letters to help early Christians better understand the nature of their faith. By alluding to the Bible and St. Paul, King effectively reminded his audience that they all were serving God.

A great many more rhetorical techniques may be found in these readings. Some of the techniques are familiar because many of us already use them, but we study them to understand their value and to use them more effectively. After all, rhetorical techniques make it possible for us to communicate the significance of important ideas. Many of the authors in this book would surely admit that the effect of their ideas actually depends on the way they are expressed, which is a way of saying that they depend on the rhetorical methods used to express them.

Methods of Development

Most of the rhetorical methods used in these essays are discussed in the introductions to the individual selections. Several represent exceptionally useful general techniques. These are methods of development and represent approaches to developing ideas that contribute to the fullness and completeness of an essay. You may think of them as techniques that can be applied to any idea in almost any situation. They can enlarge on the idea, clarify it, express it, and demonstrate its truth or effectiveness. Sometimes a technique may be direct; sometimes, indirect. Sometimes it calls attention to itself; sometimes it works behind the scenes. Sometimes it is used alone; sometimes, in conjunction with other methods. The most important techniques are explained and then illustrated with examples from the selections in the book.

Development by Definition.   Definition is essential for two purposes: to make certain that you have a clear grasp of your concepts and that you communicate a clear understanding to your reader. Definition goes far beyond the use of the dictionary in the manner of "According to Webster's, ..." Such an approach is facile because complex ideas are not easily reduced to dictionary definitions. A more useful strategy is to offer an explanation followed by an example. Since some of the suggestions for writing that follow the selections ask you to use definition as a means of writing about ideas, the following tips should be kept in mind:

- Definition can be used to develop a paragraph, a section, or an entire essay.
- It considers questions of function, purpose, circumstance, origin, and implications for different groups.
- Explanations and examples make all definitions more complete and effective.

Many of the selections are devoted almost entirely to the act of definition. For example, in "The Position of Poverty," John Kenneth Galbraith begins by defining the two kinds of poverty that he feels characterize the economic situation of the poor — case poverty and insular poverty. He defines case poverty in this paragraph:

> Case poverty is commonly and properly related to some characteristic of the individuals so afflicted. Nearly everyone else has mastered his environment; this proves that it is not intractable. But some quality peculiar to the individual or family involved — mental deficiency, bad health, inability to adapt to the discipline of industrial life, uncontrollable procreation, alcohol, discrimination involving a very limited minority, some educational handicap unrelated to community shortcoming, or perhaps a combination of several of these handicaps — has kept these individuals from participating in the general well-being. (para. 9)

When he begins defining insular poverty, however, he is unable to produce a neat single-paragraph definition. He first establishes that insular poverty describes a group of people alienated from the majority for any of many reasons. Next, he spends five paragraphs discussing what can produce such poverty — migration, racial prejudice, and lack of education. When working at the level of seriousness that characterizes his work, Galbraith shows us that definition works best when it employs full description and complex, detailed discussion.

An essay on the annotated selection from Machiavelli might define a number of key ideas. For example, to argue that Machiavelli is cynical in suggesting that his prince would not retain power if he acted morally, we would need to define what it means to be cynical and what moral behavior means in political terms. When we argue any point, it is important to spend time defining key ideas.

Martin Luther King, Jr., in "Letter from Birmingham Jail," takes time to establish some key definitions so that he can speak forcefully to his audience:

> Let us consider a more concrete example of just and unjust laws. An unjust law is a code that a numerical or power majority group compels a minority group to obey but does not make binding on itself. This is a *difference* made legal. By the same token, a

> just law is a code that a majority compels a minority to follow and
> that it is willing to follow itself. This is *sameness* made legal. (para.
> 17)

This is an adequate definition as far as it goes, but most serious ideas
need more extensive definition than this passage gives us. And King
does go further, providing what Machiavelli does in his essay: examples
and explanations. Every full definition will profit from the extension of
understanding that an explanation and example will provide. Consider
this paragraph from King:

> Let me give another explanation. A law is unjust if it is inflicted
> on a minority that, as a result of being denied the right to vote,
> had no part in enacting or devising the law. Who can say that the
> legislature of Alabama which set up that state's segregation laws
> was democratically elected? Throughout Alabama all sorts of devi-
> ous methods are used to prevent Negroes from becoming regis-
> tered voters, and there are some counties in which, even though
> Negroes constitute a majority of the population, not a single
> Negro is registered. Can any law enacted under such circum-
> stances be considered democratically structured? (para. 18)

King makes us aware of the fact that definition is complex and
capable of great subtlety. It is an approach that can be used to develop a paragraph or an essay.

Development by Comparison.   Comparison is a natural operation of the mind. We rarely talk for long about any topic without
comparing it with something else. We are fascinated with comparisons between ourselves and others and come to know ourselves
better as a result of such comparisons. Machiavelli, for example,
compares the armed with the unarmed prince and shows us, by
means of examples, the results of being unarmed.

Comparison usually includes the following:

- A definition of two or more elements to be compared (by exam-
  ple, explanation, description, or any combination of these),
- Discussion of shared qualities,
- Discussion of unique qualities,
- A clear reason for making the comparison.

Ruth Benedict's comparison of the Apollonian Pueblo Indians
with other western tribes she regards as Dionysian begins with a
comparison of the Pueblo Zuñi with the Greeks, who devised the
Apollonian concept that Benedict borrows. Her comparison permits
her to define her terms and make useful distinctions:

Apollonian institutions have been carried much further in the Pueblos than in Greece. Greece was by no means as single-minded. In particular, Greece did not carry out as the Pueblos have the distrust of individualism that the Apollonian way of life implies, but which in Greece was scanted because of forces with which it came in conflict. Zuñi ideals and institutions on the other hand are rigorous on this point. The known map, the middle of the road, to any Apollonian is embodied in the common tradition of his people. To stay always within it is to commit himself to precedent, to tradition. Therefore those influences that are powerful against tradition are uncongenial and minimized in their institutions, and the greatest of these is individualism. It is disruptive, according to Apollonian philosophy in the Southwest, even when it refines upon and enlarges the tradition itself. That is not to say that the Pueblos prevent this. No culture can protect itself from additions and changes. But the process by which these come is suspect and cloaked, and institutions that would give individuals a free hand are outlawed. (para. 14)

Benedict defines Apollonianism in terms of its rejection of individualism. In other words, the Apollonian distrusts individualistic behavior and prefers behavior that reinforces tradition, the ways of the people. Even the Greeks, Apollonian though they sometimes were, did not go as far as the Zuñi in this matter. Benedict thus shows that Greek and Zuñi cultures differ in an important area.

Benedict's general strategy in the essay is comparison. She distinguishes between the Apollonian and Dionysian much as Friedrich Nietzsche does, although she focuses explicitly on the behavior of cultures rather than of individual people. In the process, she reveals a great deal about the Zuñi and their neighbors. As with all comparisons, this one helps us sharpen our understanding and awareness of each component of the discussion. That is one function of good comparison.

Development by Example. Examples make abstract ideas concrete. When Clifford Geertz finishes his generalizations about the study of culture through an examination of the "symbolic structures" of "words, images, institutions, behaviors," he turns to examples "to make this all a bit more concrete." He then chooses specific instances from three cultures — Javanese, Balinese, and Moroccan — that help make his theory explicit. These examples are the most convincing part of his discussion. When Machiavelli talks about looking at history to learn political lessons, he cites specific cases and brings them to the attention of his audience, the prince. Every selection in this book offers examples either to convince us of the truth of a proposition or to deepen our understanding of a statement.

Examples need to be chosen carefully because the burden of proof and of explanation and clarity often depends on them. When the sample suggestion given earlier for writing on Machiavelli's essay asks who among world leaders Machiavelli might have approved, it is asking for carefully chosen examples. When doing research for an essay, it is important to be sure that your example or examples really suit your purposes.

Examples can be used in several ways. One is to do as Darwin does and present a large number of examples that force readers to a given conclusion. This indirect method is sometimes time-consuming, but the weight of numerous examples can be effective. A second method, such as Machiavelli's, also can be effective. By making a statement that is controversial or questionable and that can be tested by example, you can lead your audience to draw a reasonable conclusion.

When using examples, keep these points in mind:

- Choose a few strong examples that support your point.
- Be concrete and specific — naming names, citing events, and giving details where necessary.
- Develop each example as fully as possible, and point out its relevance to your position.

In some selections, such as Charles Darwin's discussion of natural selection, the argument hinges entirely on examples, and Darwin cites one example after another. Stephen Jay Gould shows how a particular example, that of the parasitical ichneumon fly, causes certain philosophical difficulties for theologians studying biology and therefore for anyone who looks closely at nature. The ichneumon, which people find ugly, attacks caterpillars, which people find sympathetic. As he tells us, we tend to dislike the parasite and sympathize with its victim. But there is another side to this, a second theme:

> The second theme, ruthless efficiency of the parasites, leads to the opposite conclusion — grudging admiration for the victors. We learn of their skills in capturing dangerous hosts often many times larger than themselves. Caterpillars may be easy game, but the psammocharid wasps prefer spiders. They must insert their ovipositors in a safe and precise spot. Some leave a paralyzed spider in its own burrow. *Planiceps hirsutus,* for example, parasitizes a California trapdoor spider. It searches for spider tubes on sand dunes, then digs into nearby sand to disturb the spider's home

and drive it out. When the spider emerges, the wasp attacks, paralyzes its victim, drags it back into its own tube, shuts and fastens the trapdoor, and deposits a single egg upon the spider's abdomen. Other psammocharids will drag a heavy spider back to a previously prepared cluster of clay or mud cells. Some amputate a spider's legs to make the passage easier. Others fly back over water, skimming a buoyant spider along the surface. (para. 13)

Gould's example demonstrates that there are two ways of thinking about the effectiveness of the parasitic psammocharid. The wasp does not always make its life easier by attacking defenseless prey; instead, it goes after big game spiders. Gould's description technique, emphasizing the wasp's risk of danger, forces readers to respect the daring and ingenuity of the parasite even if at first we would not think to do so.

Development by Analysis of Cause and Effect.

People are interested in causes. We often ask what causes something, as if understanding the cause will somehow help us accept the result. Yet cause and effect can be subtle. With definition, comparison, and example, we can feel that the connections between a specific topic and our main points are reasonable. With cause and effect, however, we need to reason out the cause. Be warned that development by analysis of cause and effect requires you to pay close attention to the terms and situations you write about. Because it is easy to be wrong about causes and effects, their relationship must be examined thoughtfully. After an event has occurred, only a hypothesis about its cause may be possible. In the same sense, if no effect has been observed, only speculation about outcomes with various plans of action may be possible. In both cases, reasoning and imagination must be employed to establish a relationship between cause and effect.

The power of the rhetorical method of development through cause and effect is such that you will find it in every section of this book, in the work of virtually every author. Keep in mind these suggestions for using it to develop your own thinking:

- Clearly establish in your own mind the cause and the effect you wish to discuss.

- Develop a good line of reasoning that demonstrates the relationship between the cause and the effect.

- Be sure that the cause-effect relationship is real and not merely apparent.

In studying nature, scientists often examine effects in an effort to discover causes. Darwin, for instance, sees the comparable structure of the skeletons of many animals of different species and makes every effort to find the cause of such similarity. His answer is a theory: evolution. Another theorist, Michio Kaku, tries to explain the complexities involved in examining an effect and then postulating an appropriate cause in physics:

> Imagine, for the moment, dropping a heavy shotput on a large bed spread. The shotput will, of course, sink deeply into the bedspread. Now imagine shooting a small marble across the bed. Since the bed is warped, the marble will execute a curved path. However, for a person viewing the marble from a great distance, it will appear that the shotput is exerting an invisible "force" on the marble, forcing it to move in a curved path. In other words, we can now replace the clumsy concept of a "force" with the more elegant concept of a bending of space itself. We now have an entirely new definition of this "force." It is nothing but the byproduct of the warping of space. (para. 28)
>
> In the same way that a marble moves on a curved bedspread, the Earth moves around the Sun in a curved path, because space-time itself is curved. In this new picture, gravity is not a "force" but a byproduct of the warping of space-time. In some sense, gravity does not exist; what moves the planets and stars is the distortion of space and time. (para. 29)

Kaku is asking us to examine an effect — gravity — and to imagine a complex cause. His example of the shotput on the bed is easy to grasp, but thinking that space and time are warped and therefore cause gravity is challenging for anyone. It is similar to the problem that early astronomers faced in explaining that the apparently firm earth was spinning and that the apparently moving sun was, relatively speaking, standing still.

Everywhere in this collection authors rely on cause and effect to develop their thoughts. Thomas Jefferson establishes the relationship between abuses by the British and America's need to sever its colonial ties. Karl Marx establishes the capitalist economic system as the cause of the oppression of the workers who produce the wealth enjoyed by the rich. The Buddha regards spiritual fulfillment as the result of the practice of meditation. John Kenneth Galbraith is concerned with the causes of poverty, which he feels is an anomaly in modern society. Henry David Thoreau establishes the causes that demand civil disobedience as an effect.

Development by Analysis of Circumstances.　　Everything we discuss exists as certain circumstances. Traditionally, the discussion of circumstances has had two parts. The first examines what is possible or impossible in a given situation. Whenever you try to convince your audience to take a specific course of action, it is helpful to show that, given the circumstances, no other action is possible. If you disagree with a course of action that people may intend to follow because none other seems possible, however, you may have to demonstrate that another is indeed possible.

The second part of this method of development analyzes what has been done in the past: if something was done in the past, then it may be possible to do it again in the future. A historical survey of a situation often examines circumstances.

When using the method of examination of circumstances to develop an idea, keep in mind the following tips:

- Clarify the question of possibility and impossibility.
- Review past circumstances so that future ones can be determined.
- Suggest a course of action based on an analysis of possibility and past circumstances.
- Establish the present circumstances, listing them if necessary. Be detailed, and concentrate on facts.

Martin Luther King, Jr., examines the circumstances that led to his imprisonment and the writing of "Letter from Birmingham Jail." He explains that "racial injustice engulfs this community" and reviews the "hard brutal facts of the case." His course of action is clearly stated and reviewed. He explains why some demonstrations were postponed and why his organization and others have been moderate in demands and actions. But he also examines the possibility of using nonviolent action to help change the inequitable social circumstances that existed in Birmingham. His examination of past action goes back to the Bible and the actions of the Apostle Paul. His examination of contemporary action is based on the facts of the situation, which he carefully enumerates. He concludes his letter by inviting the religious leaders to whom he addresses himself to join him in a righteous movement for social change.

Machiavelli is also interested in the question of possibility, since he is trying to encourage his ideal prince to follow a prescribed pattern of behavior. As he constantly reminds us, if the prince does not do so, it is possible that he will be deposed or killed. Taken as a whole, "The Qualities of the Prince" is a recitation of the circumstances that are necessary for success in politics. Machiavelli establishes this in a single paragraph:

> Therefore, it is not necessary for a prince to have all of the above-mentioned qualities, but it is very necessary for him to appear to have them. Furthermore, I shall be so bold as to assert this: that having them and practicing them at all times is harmful;

and appearing to have them is useful; for instance, to seem merciful, faithful, humane, forthright, religious, and to be so; but his mind should be disposed in such a way that should it become necessary not to be so, he will be able and know how to change to the contrary. And it is essential to understand this: that a prince, and especially a new prince, cannot observe all those things by which men are considered good, for in order to maintain the state he is often obliged to act against his promise, against charity, against humanity, and against religion. And therefore, it is necessary that he have a mind ready to turn itself according to the way the winds of Fortune and the changeability of affairs require him; and, as I said above, as long as it is possible, he should not stray from the good, but he should know how to enter into evil when necessity commands. (para. 23)

This is the essential Machiavelli, the Machiavelli who is often thought of as a cynic. He advises his prince to be virtuous but says that it is not always possible to be so. Therefore, the prince must learn how not to be good when "necessity commands." The circumstances, he tells us, always determine whether it is possible to be virtuous. A charitable reading of this passage must conclude that his advice is at best amoral.

Many of the essays in this collection rely on an analysis of circumstances. Frederick Douglass examines the circumstances of slavery and freedom. When Karl Marx reviews the changes in economic history in *The Communist Manifesto,* he examines the circumstances under which labor functions:

> The feudal system of industry, under which industrial production was monopolized by closed guilds, now no longer sufficed for the growing wants of the new market. The manufacturing system took its place. The guild-masters were pushed on one side by the manufacturing middle-class: division of labor between the different corporate guilds vanished in the face of division of labor in each single workshop. (para. 14)

Robert Reich examines the circumstances of our contemporary economy. He determines, among other things, that the wages of in-person servers — bank tellers, retail salespeople, restaurant employees, and others — will continue to be low despite the great demand for such workers. Not only are these workers easily replaced, but automation has led to the elimination of jobs — including bank teller jobs made redundant by automatic tellers and by banking with personal computers and routine factory jobs replaced by automation. Under current circumstances, these workers will lose out to the "symbolic analysts" who know how to make their specialized knowledge work for them and who cannot be easily replaced.

Development by Analysis of Quotations. Not all the essays in this collection rely on quotations from other writers, but many do. "Letter from Birmingham Jail," for example, relies on quotations from the Bible. In that piece, Martin Luther King, Jr., implies his analysis of the quotations because the religious leaders to whom he writes know the quotations well. By invoking the quotations, King gently chides the clergy, who ought to be aware of their relevance. In a variant on using quotations, Robert Reich relies on information taken from various government reports. He includes the information in his text and supplies numerous footnotes indicating the sources, which are usually authoritative and convincing.

When you use quotations, remember these pointers:

- Quote accurately, and avoid distorting the original context.
- Unless the quotation is absolutely self-evident, offer your own clarifying comments.
- To help your audience understand why you have chosen a specific quotation, establish its function in your essay.

Virginia Woolf quotes from modern poets to cast light on the conditions of modern poetry. In the course of her letter she alludes to dozens of important writers — all of whom she presumes her poet would have known and read. But when she quotes a few lines of modern poetry, she pauses to comment on them (para. 6). Instead of analyzing the lines themselves, she analyzes her reactions and compares them to what she suspects the poet imagined they would be:

> I feel a jar. I feel a shock. I feel as if I had stubbed my toe on the corner of the wardrobe. Am I then, I go on to ask, shocked, prudishly and conventionally, by the words themselves? I think not. The shock is literally a shock. The poet as I guess has strained himself to include an emotion that is not domesticated and acclimatized to poetry; the effort has thrown him off his balance; he rights himself, as I am sure I shall find if I turn the page, by a violent recourse to the poetical — he invokes the moon or the nightingale.

Woolf is being somewhat playful here, particularly in her description of what the "poetical" might be. But she is also interested in her own feelings and why she has had them in response to the poetry.

In his examination of our tendency to anthropomorphize nature, Stephen Jay Gould uses quotations to show that there is a considerable literature on his subject. He quotes from J. H. Fabre, a French entomologist, to show how Fabre "humanized" caterpillars and demonstrated sympathy for the paralyzed victims of the parasitic wasps that fed off them. On the other hand, Gould points out that an equally interesting group of thinkers was impressed by the wasps' capacity to provide for their offspring. To support the viewpoint that admires the wasp, Gould quotes extensively from the writing of the Reverend William Kirby and other scientists, including Darwin (see paras. 19–29). Although Gould interprets these paragraphs, they speak clearly for themselves and fit into his argument perfectly. He ends his essay with a quotation from Darwin about the relation of religion and evolution: "I feel most deeply that the whole subject is too profound for the human intellect. A dog might as well speculate on the mind of Newton. Let each man hope and believe what he can."

In your own writing you will find plenty of opportunity to cite passages from an author whose ideas have engaged your attention. In writing an essay in response to Machiavelli, Carl Jung, Ruth Benedict, or any other author in the book, you may find yourself quoting and commenting in some detail on specific lines or passages. This is especially true if you find yourself disagreeing with a point. Your first job, then, is to establish what you disagree with — and usually it helps to quote, which is essentially a way of producing evidence.

Finally, it must be noted that only a few aspects of the rhetorical methods used by the authors in this book have been discussed here. Rhetoric is a complex art that needs fuller study. But the points raised above are important because they are illustrated in many of the texts you will read, and by watching them at work you can begin to learn to use them yourself. By using them you will be able to achieve in your writing the fullness and purposiveness that mark mature prose.

A SAMPLE ESSAY

The following sample essay is based on the first several paragraphs of Machiavelli's "The Qualities of the Prince" that were annotated in "Evaluating Ideas: An Introduction to Critical Reading" (pp. 5–7). The essay is based on the annotations and the questions that were developed from them:

Should a leader be armed?

Is it true that an unarmed leader is despised?

Will those leaders who are always good come to ruin among those who are not good?

To remain in power, must a leader learn how not to be good?

Not all these questions are addressed in the essay, but they serve as a starting point and a focus for writing. The methods of development that are discussed above form the primary rhetorical techniques of the essay, and each method that is used is labeled in the margin. The sample essay does two things simultaneously: it attempts to clarify the meaning of Machiavelli's advice, and then it attempts to apply that advice to a contemporary circumstance. Naturally, the essay could have chosen to discuss only the Renaissance situation that Machiavelli described, but to do so would have required specialized knowledge of that period. In this sample essay the questions prompted by the annotations serve as the basis of the discussion.

The Qualities of the President

Introduction   Machiavelli's essay, "The Qualities of the Prince," has a number of very worrisome points. The ones that worry me most have to do with the question of whether it is reasonable to expect a leader to behave virtuously. I think this is connected to the question of whether the leader should be armed. Machiavelli emphasizes that the prince must be armed or else face the possibility that someone will take over the government. When I think about how that advice applies to modern times, particularly in terms of how our president should behave, I find Machiavelli's position very different from my own.

Circumstance   First, I want to discuss the question of being armed. That is where Machiavelli starts, and it is an important concern. In Machiavelli's time, the late fifteenth and early sixteenth centuries, it was common for men to walk in the streets of Florence wearing a rapier for protection. The possibility of robbery or even attack by rival political groups was great in those days. Even if he had a bodyguard, it was still important for a prince to know how to fight and to be able to defend himself. Machiavelli seems to be talking only about self-defense when he recommends that the prince be armed. In our time, sadly, it too is important to think about protecting the president and other leaders.

Examples   In recent years there have been many assassination attempts on world leaders, and our president, John F. Kennedy, was killed in Dallas in 1963. His brother Robert was killed when he was campaigning for the presidency in 1968. Also in 1968 Martin Luther King, Jr., was killed in Memphis because of his beliefs in racial equality. In the 1980s Pope John Paul II was shot by a would-be assassin, as was President Ronald Reagan. They both lived, but Indira Gandhi, the leader of India, was shot and killed in 1984. This is a frightening record. Probably even Machiavelli would have been appalled. But would his solution--being armed--have helped? I do not think so.

Cause/Effect   For one thing, I cannot believe that if the pope had a gun he would have shot his would-be assassin, Ali Acga. The thought of it is almost silly. Martin Luther King, Jr., who constantly preached the value of nonviolence, logically could not have shot at an assailant. How could John F. Kennedy have returned fire at a sniper? Robert Kennedy had bodyguards, and both President Reagan and Indira Gandhi were protected by armed guards. The presence of arms obviously does not produce the desired effect: security. The only thing that can produce that is to reduce the visibility of a leader. The president could speak on television or, when he must appear in public, use a bulletproof screen. The opportunities for would-be assassins can be reduced. But the thought of an American president carrying arms is unacceptable.

Comparison   The question of whether a president should be armed is to some extent symbolic. Our president stands for America, and if he were to appear in press conferences or state meetings wearing a gun, he would give a symbolic message to the world: look out, we're dangerous. Cuba's Fidel Castro usually appears in a military uniform with a gun, and when

he spoke at the United Nations, he was the first,
and I think the only, world leader to wear a pistol
there. I have seen pictures of Benito Mussolini
and Adolf Hitler appearing in public in military
uniform, but never in a business suit. The same is
true of Libyan leader Muammar al-Qaddafi and Iraq's
Saddam Hussein. Today when a president or a head of
state is armed there is often reason to worry. The
current leaders of Russia usually wear suits, but
Joseph Stalin always wore a military uniform. His
rule in Russia was marked by the extermination of
whole groups of people and the imprisonment of many
more. We do not want an armed president.

Use of   Yet Machiavelli plainly says, "among the other
quotations bad effects it causes, being disarmed makes you
despised . . . for between an armed and an unarmed
also man there is no comparison whatsoever" (para. 2).
The problem with this statement is that it is
Comparison more relevant to the sixteenth century than the
twentieth. In our time the threat of assassination
is so great that being armed would be no sure
protection, as we have seen in the case of the
assassination of President Sadat of Egypt, winner of
the Nobel Peace Prize. On the other hand, the pope,
like Martin Luther King, Jr., would never have
appeared with a weapon, and yet it can hardly be
said they were despised. If anything, the world's
respect for them is enormous. President Clinton also
commands the world's respect, as does Tony Blair,
prime minister of Great Britain. Yet neither would
ever think of being armed. If what Machiavelli said
was true in the early 1500s, it is pretty clear that
it is not true today.

Definition   All this basically translates into a question of
whether a leader should be virtuous. I suppose the
definition of <u>virtuous</u> would differ with different
people, but I think of it as holding a moral
philosophy that you try to live by. No one is ever

completely virtuous, but I think a president ought
to try to be so. That means the president ought to
tell the truth, since that is one of the basic
virtues. The cardinal virtues--which were the same
in Machiavelli's time as in ours--are justice,
prudence, fortitude, and temperance. In a president,
the virtue of justice is absolutely a must, or else
what America stands for is lost. We definitely want
our president to be prudent, to use good judgment,
particularly in this nuclear age, when acts of
imprudence could get us blown up. Fortitude, the
ability to stand up for what is right, is a must for
our president. Temperance is also important; we do
not want a drunk for a president, nor do we want
anyone with excessive bad habits.

Conclusion   It seems to me that a president who was armed
or who emphasized arms in the way Machiavelli
appears to mean would be threatening injustice
(the way Stalin did) and implying intemperance,
like many armed world leaders. When I consider
this issue, I cannot think of any vice that our
president ought to possess at any time. Injustice,
imprudence, cowardice, and intemperance are, for me,
unacceptable. Maybe Machiavelli was thinking of
deception and lying as necessary evils, but they are
a form of injustice, and no competent president--no
president who was truly virtuous--would need them.
Prudence and fortitude are the two virtues most
essential for diplomacy. The president who has those
virtues will govern well and uphold our basic values.

The range of this essay is controlled and expresses a viewpoint
that is focused and coherent. This essay of about 1,000 words illustrates each method of development discussed in the text and uses
each to further the argument. The writer disagrees with one of
Machiavelli's positions and presents an argument based on personal
opinion that is bolstered by example and by analysis of current political conditions as they compare with those of Machiavelli's time. A
longer essay could have gone more deeply into issues raised in any

single paragraph and could have studied more closely the views of a specific president, such as Ronald Reagan, who opposed stricter gun control laws even after he had been shot.

The range of the selections in this volume is great, constituting a significant introduction to important ideas in many areas. They are especially useful for stimulating our own thoughts and ideas. There is an infinite number of ways to approach a subject, but observing how writers apply rhetorical methods in their work is one way to begin our own development as writers. Careful analysis of each selection can guide our exploration of these writers, who encourage our learning and reward our study.

Acknowledgments (continued from page iv)

Martin Buber, from *I and Thou*. Reprinted with the permission of Scribner, a Division of Simon and Schuster, from *I and Thou* by Martin Buber, translated by Walter Kaufmann. Translation copyright © 1970 by Charles Scribner's Sons.

Richard Dawkins, "All Africa and Her Progenies" from *River Out of Eden*. Copyright © 1995 by Richard Dawkins. Reprinted by permission of BasicBooks, a division of HarperCollins Publishers, Inc.

Sigmund Freud, from *The Interpretation of Dreams*. Reprinted by permission of HarperCollins Publishers Ltd.

John Kenneth Galbraith, "The Position of Poverty." Excerpt from *The Affluent Society*, 4/e. Copyright © 1958, 1969, 1976, 1984 by John Kenneth Galbraith. Reprinted by permission of Houghton Mifflin Co. All rights reserved.

Howard Gardner, "A Rounded Version" (excerpt) from *Multiple Intelligences*. Copyright © 1993 by Howard Gardner. Reprinted by permission of BasicBooks, a division of HarperCollins Publishers, Inc.

Clifford Geertz, "'From the Native's Point of View': On the Nature of Anthropological Understanding." Copyright © 1957 by the Antioch Review, Inc. First appeared in the *Antioch Review*, Vol. 17, No. 4 (Winter 1957/58). Reprinted by permission of the Editors.

Stephen Jay Gould, "Nonmoral Nature." With permission from *Natural History*, February 1982. Copyright © 1982 by the American Museum of Natural History.

Herodotus, "Observations on Egypt" from *The History*, translated by David Greene, 1987. Reprinted by permission of the University of Chicago Press.

Karen Horney, "The Distrust between the Sexes." Speech read before the Berlin–Brandenburg Branch of the German Women's Medical Association on November 20, 1930, as "Das Misstrauen zwischen den Geschlechtern." *Die Artzin*, VII (1931), pp. 5–12. Reprinted in translation with the permission of the Karen Horney Estate.

Carl Jung, "The Personal and the Collective Unconscious" from *The Basic Writings of C. G. Jung*, edited by Violet deLaszlo. Copyright © 1990 Princeton University Press. Reprinted by permission.

Michio Kaku, "The Theory of the Universe?" by Michio Kaku. From *Mysteries of Life and the Universe*, edited by William H. Shore, copyright © 1992 by Share Our Strength, Inc., reprinted by permission of Harcourt Brace & Company.

Martin Luther King, Jr., "Letter from Birmingham Jail." Reprinted by arrangement with The Heirs to the Estate of Martin Luther King, Jr., c/o Writers House, Inc. as agent for the proprietor. Copyright © 1963 by Martin Luther King, Jr., copyright renewed 1991 by Coretta Scott King.

Lao-tzu, from the *Tao-te Ching*. Excerpts as submitted from *Tao Te Ching* by Lao-tzu, A New English Version, with Foreword and Notes by Stephen Mitchell. Translation copyright © 1988 by Stephen Mitchell. Reprinted by permission of HarperCollins Publishers, Inc.

Niccolo Machiavelli, excerpts from "The Prince." From *Portable Machiavelli* by Peter Bondanella and Mark Musa. Copyright © 1979 by Viking Penguin, Inc. Used by permission of Viking Penguin, a division of Penguin Books USA, Inc.

Margaret Mead, "Women, Sex, and Sin" from *New Lives for Old* by Margaret Mead. Copyright © 1956, 1966 by Margaret Mead. Reprinted by permission of William Morrow & Company, Inc.

The Prophet Muhammad, "The Believer," from the Koran, translated by N. J. Dawood (Penguin Classics 1956, Fifth revised edition 1990), copyright © N. J. Dawood, 1956, 1959, 1966, 1968, 1974, 1990. Reproduced by permission of Penguin Books Ltd.

Friedrich Nietzsche, "Apollonianism and Dionysianism." From *The Birth of Tragedy and the Geneology of Morals* by Friedrich Nietzsche, translated by Francis Golffing. Copyright © 1956 by Doubleday, a division of Bantam Doubleday Dell Publishing Group, Inc.

Robert Reich, "Why the Rich Are Getting Richer and the Poor, Poorer." From *The Work of Nations* by Robert Reich. Copyright © 1991 by Robert B. Reich. Reprinted by permission of Alfred A. Knopf, Inc.

Jean-Jacques Rousseau, "The Origin of Civil Society." From *Social Contract: Essays by Locke, Hume, and Rousseau*, edited by Sir Ernest Baker, translated by Gerald Hopkins (1947). Reprinted by permission of Oxford University Press.

Siddhārtha Gautama, the Buddha, "Meditation: Path to Enlightenment." Excerpted from *Buddhist Scriptures*, translated by Edward Conze (Penguin Classics, 1959). Reprinted by the permission of Viking Penguin Ltd., London. Copyright © 1959 by Edward Conze.

Susan Sontag, "Against Interpretation." From *Against Interpretation* by Susan Sontag. Copyright © 1961, 1962, 1963, 1964, 1965, 1966 by Susan Sontag. Reprinted with permission of Farrar, Straus & Giroux, Inc.

INDEX OF
RHETORICAL TERMS